BOOKS BY EDMUND WILSON

THE SIXTIES

Photograph © by Jill Krementz
Edmund Wilson in his final years

EDMUND WILSON

The Sixties

The Last Journal, 1960–1972

Edited with an Introduction by
Lewis M. Dabney

FARRAR STRAUS GIROUX

NEW YORK

Library of Congress Cataloging-in-Publication Data
Wilson, Edmund, 1895–1972.
    The sixties: the last journal, 1960–1972 / Edmund Wilson; edited
with an introduction by Lewis M. Dabney. — 1st ed.
        p.   cm.
    Includes index.
    1. Wilson, Edmund, 1895–1972—Diaries.   2. Wilson, Edmund,
1895–1972—Notebooks, sketchbooks, etc.   3. Authors, American—
20th   century—Diaries.   4.   Critics—United   States—Diaries.
I. Dabney, Lewis.   II. Title.
PS3545.I6245Z475   1993   92-16642   CIP
818'.5203—dc20
[B]

CONTENTS

ILLUSTRATIONS

EDITOR'S FOREWORD

As the end of his life approached, Edmund Wilson was intent on recording his experience, just as he had been when he wrote of his formative years in the twenties. People and situations gained "meaning and point" for him upon the page. He knew that a frank account of his acquaintances could not be published for some years, and he did not live to see *The Sixties* in typescript, yet he indicated where letters to his wife Elena would complement the journal. Generally a few weeks afterward and sometimes at longer intervals, he set down what had piqued his interest in one of the old-fashioned ledgers now in the Beinecke Library at Yale. Those of his late years were evidently sent to New Haven and microfilmed as they were completed. Most are 150 pages, but the series for *The Sixties* contains a 300-page notebook and two that are very short. He wrote with a fountain pen, usually on both sides of the page, and the margins are crowded with additions, like the remark of Elena about Stravinsky's likeness to a musical note that is reproduced facing page 14. Wilson's script reminds one of his remark in *A Piece of My Mind* that his father had invented a calligraphy to please himself. It is distinctive, with a certain force and elegance.

He asked that for publication his journals be made "as readable as possible." He wrote them without formal divisions except between the individual scenes, separating these by a line, for which a blank space has been substituted. I have divided *The Sixties* into short chapters with titles that trace the shifting focus of his mind as well as his movements from place to place. There are footnotes and biographical notes, which do not intrude between Wilson's narrative and the reader. The footnotes are not scholarly references; they supply context and make situations more accessible. The biographical notes at the back include most of the people whose identities are not made clear within the text.

For readability, I have often made paragraph divisions and sometimes reordered sentences within a passage. When Wilson reread what he had written he added material in the margins and reshuffled the topics, numbering them for an eventual typist—usually 1 to 3 or 4, though once as many as 14. He let this reorganization lapse as he physically declined, and I have moved passages that seemed out of place. Repetitions have been cleared up and known misstatements of fact corrected. On the other hand, very little has been excised simply because it is potentially embarrassing or offensive. In this book Wilson speaks his mind with little or no regard for people's sensibilities. Several decades have passed since he wrote, and almost without exception his friends have graciously accepted being subjects of his scrutiny.

He wanted an editor to correct and "clean up" his text, not reproducing "contractions and ampersands, misspellings and faulty punctuations" as variant readings, in the pedantic style of the editions of American writers then being published by the Modern Language Association, which Wilson satirized. I retain a few abbreviations to convey the flavor of the journal, such as the familiarity of E. for Elena and T'ville for Talcottville. Arabic numbers have been kept for age and time but written out for other purposes, though Wilson's own practice was inconsistent. Some of his spelling, including elaborate transliteration of Russian words, has been regularized. Whiskey is spelled with the American—originally Irish—"e" when whiskey sours are in question, but without the "e" when the reference is to Scotch.

He drew on the journal in his travel reporting, including *Europe Without Baedecker* (1966) and the account of Israel and Jordan just before the Six-Day War in *The Dead Sea Scrolls* (1969). In a last creative act near the end of his life, he adapted the notebook accounts of his summers at Talcottville for *Upstate*, omitting personal details and adding background. The reader can follow this process, for I have enclosed within < >'s everything about northern New York that was thus reused, whether or not Wilson revised the phrasing. Square brackets indicate words I have added to clarify the text of *The Sixties*, while those apparently omitted in the press of writing are supplied without such identification. At the end pages of the ledgers are miscellaneous notations and what he called "draughts" of verse. In previous volumes these have been incorporated wherever they may fall in the text. In *The Sixties*, except for two short lists of his father's characteristic expressions, such materials are either set in contexts that they illuminate or omitted if marginal. Appendix A contains his letters to Elena in the fall of 1963, Appendix B the "Rat Letters" exchanged at Wesleyan by the critic and his friends.

The aging Wilson was addicted to foreign languages. French is used throughout; there is intermittent Russian and in the first half of the decade a good deal of Hungarian.

I depart from previous volumes of the journal by translating, in parentheses, most of the foreign words and phrases. Friends have been generous with their help. István Deák of the East European Institute at Columbia translated the Hungarian, Paul Flescher of Northwestern University much of the Hebrew, and John Seletti checked my Italian. Among my colleagues at the University of Wyoming, Lewis Bagby translated the Russian, Klaus Hanson the German, Philip Holt the Greek and Latin; Clifford Marks helped with the Hebrew, and Marguerite Van Doorslaer improved upon my French. It seemed unnecessary to translate such a well-known expression as *gemütlich* for the dinner after which Elena's brother Brat Mumm apparently killed himself. Nor are French phrases translated when they are familiar or very close to English.

I am grateful to Leon Edel, editor of Wilson's journals from *The Twenties* through *The Fifties*, for having the manuscript of *The Sixties* transcribed and for sharing his impressions of the critic in the sixties. A number of those who were acquainted with Wilson gave information useful in editing this volume: Daniel Aaron, Austin Briggs, Margaret Briggs, Barry Callaghan, Clelia Carroll Carey, Philip Carroll, Ruth Cheshin, Gilles Couture, Joan Didion, Monroe Engel, Barbara Epstein, Jason Epstein, Penelope Gilliatt, Celia Paget Goodman, Irving Howe, Charlayne Hunter-Gault, Cecil Lang, Alison Lurie, Mary McCarthy, Mary Meigs, Thomas Mendenhall, Dr. Edgar Miller, Malcolm Montgomery, Edward Newhouse, Mike Nichols, Lewis Nkosi, Edith Oliver, Eleanor Perényi, Richard Pipes, Victor and Dorothy Pritchett, Arthur Schlesinger, Helen Sootin Smith, Stephen and Natasha Spender, Roger Straus, Frances Swisher, Eva Thoby-Marcelin, John Wain, Adelaide Walker, Dan Walker, Christopher Walling, Aileen Ward, Reuel Wilson, Sovka Winkelhorn, and Dr. Louis Zetzel. Others who did not know him could clarify particular situations: Virginius Dabney, Valerie Harms, Michael Sheldon, Theodore Sorensen, and Helen Wright. Particular thanks are due to Isaiah Berlin, John Clendenning, Charlotte Kretzoi, Harry and Elena Levin, Anne Miller, Helen Muchnic, and Helen Wilson.

Support was provided by the National Endowment for the Humanities and by Derek Hodgson and the Office of Research of the University of Wyoming. Kathleen Ely helped with the research and Natalie Dykstra with the editing, and Kathryn Flitner in both respects. Phyllida Burlingame, my editor, has been patient, energetic, and perceptive.

A special debt is owed to Roger Straus, Wilson's friend and publisher, and to Neale Reinitz of Colorado College, who made suggestions about the editing and carefully read the typescript. Sarah Dabney's encouragement and wit have helped me to see the project through.

Edmund Wilson
and *The Sixties*

An aged man is but a paltry thing,
A tattered coat upon a stick, unless
Soul clap its hands and sing, and louder sing
For every tatter in its mortal dress . . .

—YEATS, "Sailing to Byzantium"

In August 1961, Edmund Wilson returned to his journal
after a lapse of almost a year and a half. He had been
finishing *Patriotic Gore*. "I got bored dealing with political
and literary history, bored with the limitations of the resources of my own vocabulary in dealing with this sort of
thing, at which I don't think I am really at my best," he
explains a few pages into *The Sixties*, and was glad "to get
back to this journal." He had begun it as an undergraduate
almost fifty years before, at Meredith's house in the greenery of Surrey, looking up the hill at the tiny chalet "where
half a dozen great novels were written." There had been
an earlier diary of a trip to Europe with his family in 1908,
when he was thirteen. This was somewhat perfunctory
and broke off at Paris, where the children were bored, but
it contained a vivid catalogue of the torture instruments
at Nuremberg and their functions. At Princeton he ex-
perimented with an open form that incorporated dialogue,

character, and scene. He was modeling his prose on that of European men of letters. He practiced the stylistic discipline of Flaubert and the Goncourts, and admired Macaulay's "scrupulous thoroughness" in expository narrative, Boswell's "fascination with the glamour and charm of life and rigid conscience in telling the strict truth about it."

By the twenties the journals were a collage of observations, discrete events and reflections, an effort to achieve intimacy with life upon the page. Leon Edel sees Wilson reaching out to the world from an oppressive, even traumatic childhood. At any rate, he needed to impose the order of the mind upon experience. In a generation of brilliant novelists and poets, he wanted to use these materials in fiction. Yet *The Twenties* is much better than *I Thought of Daisy*. Romantic experience is sugary and forced in the novel, while the journal chronicles a coming of age tenderly and with a naturalistic realism not found in *Lady Chatterley's Lover*, written at almost the same time. *The Thirties* ranges from the love affairs on which he later sought perspective in *Memoirs of Hecate County* to the strikes and suicides of *The American Earthquake*. Wilson becomes more personal, including disappointments and moments of pettiness as well as memories and dreams. Always the critic, he brings each episode into the focus of his curiosity, appetite for detail, and will to understand a person or situation in words.

At the same time he was creating an art of portraiture in the tradition of Dr. Johnson, Taine, and Sainte-Beuve. As he realized his gift for narrative and drama in *To the Finland Station*, *The Triple Thinkers*, and *The Wound and the Bow*, he no longer wanted to turn the journals into novels. *The Forties* is skimpy, detouring around his marriage to Mary McCarthy, but the renewed self-confidence of *The Fifties* appears in expansive periodic sentences that (as John Dos Passos once said of Wilson's prose) "fill the room in great coils." In *The Sixties* the pace quickens. Entries are briefer; people are moved in and out rapidly, with shifts that may seem as arbitrary as those of a television viewer switching channels. Wilson is running out of time. He recalls the past as he describes the world around him. This is the most wide-ranging of the journals, capturing the talk and sometimes quirkish behavior of everyone from neighborhood acquaintances to the heroes of high culture. The characterizations are both intense and amusing. He notes Stravinsky's vital personality and diminutive size, how the composer sticks his tongue out for a piece of cheese before agreeing to take some and put it on his plate. When Wilson leaves for his ballet, in an immemorial gesture Stravinsky is seen "first making the motion of clapping, then throwing out his hands." The scene "is very dense yet lively, what Henry James would have called 'bristling,'" Stephen Spender observes of this episode of *The Sixties*, where Auden too is introduced. "These people and the diarist Edmund all seem to be in the next room."

As a youth he had lived in furnished rooms or in his friends' apartments when they were out of town, with no home except his mother's in New Jersey, where he was served breakfast in bed and could ask for a handout from his father's estate. Now he had two country houses. He had bought a frame house off Route 6 on Cape Cod to live in with Mary McCarthy, and Elena Thornton redid the place when they married in 1946, scraping floors and walls, painting and making curtains. "Elena has really effected a tremendous change in Edmund's way of living," Louise Bogan wrote enthusiastically to May Sarton. In *The Sixties* they work their way through *Faust* in German, as they had read the Russians a decade before. Society was a bottle of whisky and talk with friends. He sometimes wearied of the old bohemians of the Cape in flight from a respectable bourgeois life; he missed Dos Passos, who had moved to Virginia. But he and Elena each had a close friend nearby: Charley Walker, who had shared the literary and political experience of the twenties and thirties, and Nina Chavchavadze, a Russian exile Elena had known in Paris. They enjoyed their neighbors Mary Meigs and Barbara Deming, and asked New Yorkers up to visit, like Jason and Barbara Epstein and Edmund's old pal Dawn Powell.

In summer he retreated from the heat of the Cape and the cars pushing past his door to the stone house in northern New York built at the end of the eighteenth century. Big and drafty, with primitive facilities, unlivable in the harsh winters, it was elegant in proportion and line, a reassuring continuity with his family and his father, who had escaped the pressures of the gilded age in the rural community of Talcottville. An only child from Red Bank, New Jersey, Wilson had been exhilarated by "the widening pastures, the great boulders, the black and white cattle, the rivers, stony and thin, the lone elms like feather-dusters, the high air which sharpens all outlines, makes all colors so breathtakingly vivid"; his cousins and he "swam and fished in the rivers, had all sorts of excursions and games." When he restored the house in the fifties, he persuaded Dorothy and Malcolm Sharp, a favorite cousin and her law professor husband, to spend summers down the road, and enjoyed chatting with the elderly Loomis sisters, distant relatives. On occasion he was known to ride a bicycle in his pajamas. Among the unpretentious small-town folk, he could think of himself as something of a country squire.

Elena did not enjoy pioneering in an old house with primitive facilities and, she thought, ancestral ghosts, in a farm community that was deteriorating and far from the

blue water and soft air of the Cape. She loved to swim in
the sea, disliked shallow ponds and rivers where she had
to wade. A dedicated mother, when their daughter, Helen,
born in 1949, and Reuel Wilson, Edmund's son by Mary
McCarthy, were young, she spent summers in Talcottville.
Afterward she stopped trying to adapt to Wilson's upstate
scene. He would go to the stone house late in the spring,
reading and writing for the first few weeks, taking breaks
for visitors later on. She stayed at the Cape except for two
weeks in August. Sometimes he met her in Manhattan for
several days or shuttled back and forth to Wellfleet by plane
or with a driver, since he never learned to drive; or they
would meet halfway between the two houses, at Helen
Muchnic's home in western Massachusetts. When possible
during her Talcottville stay they had a big party for their
local friends, including the Haitian poet Philippe Thoby-
Marcelin, with such guests as Morley Callaghan from Canada. But Elena counted the hours till she could leave.
Talcottville came to embody for her the difficult aspects of
their marriage.

Each enjoyed New York City, staying at the Algonquin
or the Princeton Club. For anywhere between two or three
days and several weeks, Edmund moves from one engagement to the next, from literary lunches to dinners, plays,
movies, and the opera, having friends in or going out for
drinks, talking with one person after another and with his
wife about those whom they both know. Elena is sure in
her knowledge of the world, and her judgments appear in
his journal. He sees veterans of the literary world of his
youth: Janet Flanner at *The New Yorker*, Gerald and Sara
Murphy, Anita Loos. By mid-decade he is aware of a "cultural establishment" in which Robert Lowell, Lillian Hellman, and Mike Nichols figure, with Jackie Kennedy
"somehow on the fringes." His publisher, Roger Straus,
is now a friend. Auden, still living in the unheated loft in

the East Village sketched in *The Fifties*, regularly appears
in the journal, and Wilson records his table talk. Isaiah
Berlin, Stephen Spender, and their wives are encountered
in New York as well as at Harvard and Oxford, in London
and Vienna. They know Stravinsky and Nicholas Nabokov,
and, like the New Yorkers, live in the world of the arts.

The Wilsons spent several winters in Cambridge, beginning in 1959, when he was the Lowell professor at
Harvard. He disliked lecturing but needed money for what
he admitted was a "bad case of tax delinquency." Taxes
had been withheld from his *New Yorker* salary, yet he had
paid nothing on earnings from *The Dead Sea Scrolls* or from
Hecate County a decade before. He was eventually fined
$7,500 and ordered to pay over $70,000 including penalties
and interest. Harry Levin, who arranged the Harvard appointment, had years before seen the nervous critic momentarily retreat from the podium behind a screen that
happened to be transparent, permitting the audience to
observe him take a swig of whisky. Now he read from
Patriotic Gore, in a lecture room, turning the typescript
around to follow emendations in the margins, sometimes
writing in a phrase. He gave a seminar on poetic language
and another on Civil War literature. Never comfortable
in academe, he considered Harvard a "cramped, claustrophobic place," though "the best of the faculty [were] brilliant." Elena thought that many in the English department
treated Edmund shabbily, even snubbed him. Meeting students outside class was not easy, for his reputation was
intimidating and he was not adept at small talk. There was
a jar of sourballs on the desk which he would offer before
interrogating the visitor or launching into an interest of
his own.

The family stayed at 12 Hilliard Street till early 1963.
Helen would remember the house as gloomy, their lives as
shadowed by tax worries. He had bronchitis as well as

asthma and emphysema, and gout, for which he took sulfa drugs that were disorienting when he drank. The journal includes an apparent heart attack in April 1962, later diagnosed as angina, that was brought on by drunken rage. According to Cambridge rumor, Wilson stood behind his desk clutching his chest, shaking his fist as he cursed the gods for trying to strike him down with so much left to do. Yet these years had rewards: he could work in the Harvard library, Helen liked her school, Elena and he enjoyed the people passing through, from Isaac Bashevis Singer to dissident Eastern European writers and intellectuals. The young Nadine Gordimer and an African friend came for dinner and talked of Haitian poetry; George Kennan and Wilson speculated whether Stalin had had Gorky murdered. He resumed a friendship with Arthur Schlesinger, who was about to become an assistant to President Kennedy in Washington.

At the mid-point of *The Sixties* is his account of the Center for Advanced Studies at Wesleyan. Paul Horgan, the director, flattered Wilson by telling him that Stravinsky spoke of *Patriotic Gore* as a masterpiece. Horgan offered a salary that put him back on his feet, along with housing, a secretary, a glass-walled office overlooking the lawn. There from 9:00 to 5:00 he expanded on his early journals. After hours he discussed the classics with Moses Hadas of Columbia, drank and gossiped with the novelist Jean Stafford, talked politics with John Bartlow Martin, a journalist who had just been ambassador to the Dominican Republic. Skeptical as he was of Catholicism, he came to count on the intellectual companionship of the Jesuit Father Martin D'Arcy. At Monday evening get-togethers in a restored Greek Revival home, they were waited on by undergraduates in bright red waistcoats and bow ties, then heard a talk. Yet it was a lonely year: again he met few faculty or students, and the first post-modernist fashions put him off—a lecturer promoting "metacriticism" at the expense of literature, John Cage composing music as a party game. Nostalgic for the literary world of his youth, he called the regular Monday evenings "the revels" and the Greek restaurant where he met people for drinks the Ritz Bar. Elena had little to do in Middletown and they went to New York when they could.

Restlessly the journal moves from Wellfleet to Talcottville to New York City and back, sometimes via Cambridge or Boston. There are side trips in various directions. A working vacation in Toronto and Montreal led to Wilson's account of the two cultures of Canada through their literature. He met writers and recalled his past Canadian associations and Elena's. *O Canada* involved less legwork for the aging critic than had his study of the Iroquois of New York State, and the two-thirds of this book that might have been called *O Quebec* retain their value. He surveyed politics and the intellectual scene as well as fiction and poetry, helping to establish the reputation of the novelist Marie-Claire Blais, who is sometimes seen and often talked about in *The Sixties*. Meanwhile, he was learning Hungarian, for two of his plays had been translated into the language. Guided by politically cautious professors, the elderly tourist in Budapest in the spring of 1964 met none of the dissident writers and intellectuals who, like György Lukács, would have been eager to meet him, nor did he encounter the art of the underground avant-garde. Yet he sensed that the Soviets' hold was weak: "Their imposition on Hungary of their alien and mechanical system is detestable and frankly detested by all Hungarians except those—not many—who have to pretend to go along with it," he wrote to Dos Passos afterward. "They yearn constantly toward the West and especially toward the United States, which they—disturbingly to me—idealize." He ended, "Hungary was the most interesting country I visited. Yet everywhere in the West is getting more and more alike. The people in the Budapest streets do not really seem so very different from the people in Paris and Boston." Wilson believed that the Hungarians would get rid of the Russians as the French Canadians would establish their cultural and social freedom, though he largely ignored the economic dimension of these struggles.

Between Canada and Hungary, he records winter in France when Helen was beginning school in Switzerland. Elena and he drove through Lorraine, revisiting the countryside where he had bicycled as an off-duty hospital orderly during World War I. In Paris they enjoyed her Russian relatives as well as his literary acquaintances. He went to England while she was in Germany. In *The Fifties*, Wilson's memories of London over four decades form a sequence "of which the earlier ones are somehow so far in the past that I cannot hold them up, cannot any more include them in my present functioning consciousness, and they seem to topple over at the end of the curve of the lengthened span of my life, even to be lost as actual." In *The Sixties* he is nostalgic for the Edwardian city of his youth. A sense—sharpened by the assassination of Kennedy—of the deterioration of American life makes him a less boisterous patriot, no longer quite so condescending to the British establishment, where his friends occupy honored places.

Wilson's instincts as a reporter accented the need to be on the move. On his last working trip, in 1967, he returned to the Middle East at *The New Yorker*'s expense, leaving Jerusalem the morning before the Six-Day War began. When Elena and he went to Jamaica two years later, he took vivid notes but had become almost as dependent upon her as he would be during his final, crippled winter in Naples, Florida.

Alfred Kazin has portrayed Wilson on the beach at Well-fleet in the early sixties, wearing a stained old Panama hat, a large white dress shirt hanging down over his paunch, and brown Bermuda shorts, the gold-topped cane that had been his father's planted in the sand. He would hold forth in his "improbably high" and "painfully distinct" voice about current preoccupations or what he had read, talking, Kazin says, "as if reluctant to talk but too stubborn to stop," to the "television producers, government and U.N. 'advisors,' social scientists, professors by the dozen" who might be gathered around the "lonely proud face," the eccentric bulky man. His was a familiar voice in *The New Yorker*, alternately celebrating "the will of the Iroquois people, their vitality, their force to persist" and the survival of the Russian literary and spiritual heritage in Pasternak's *Doctor Zhivago*. He had created an interior history of Civil War America in *Patriotic Gore* (1962), and his antiwar preface was notorious. For the younger intellectuals on the beach he represented the heroic age of modern American culture. With Scott Fitzgerald after college, he had trained for the role of his generation's artistic and intellectual guide. He reviewed *Ulysses* and *The Waste Land*, but was a more eclectic critic than Eliot. In an issue of *The New Republic* in mid-decade he might be writing of Henry James and a finale at the Follies, of the Sacco-Vanzetti case and Proust's use of symbols. *Axel's Castle* and the articles of *The Shores of Light* are dialectical: acknowledging the artistic heritage and the imagination's need for refuge in the modern world, Wilson insists that writers deal with contemporary reality and keep society moving forward.

In *The Sixties* he calls himself a "man of the twenties," still expecting "something exciting: drinks, animated conversation, gaiety, an uninhibited exchange of ideas." Sometimes his mind is inundated with memories that are noted only in passing. He recalls his first sexual experience, with

Edna St. Vincent Millay, who spoke of love's capricious-
ness. He mentions Mary Blair, "the O'Neill actress" whom
he married in 1923. She was often away from him and
their child, Rosalind, yet her career faded as their marriage
did. He thinks of Frances—the Anna of "The Princess
with the Golden Hair"—a dark, petite woman whom he
met in a dance hall on Fourteenth Street and who was his
mistress on and off for seven years. A Ukrainian from
Brooklyn, she made real to him the life of the urban poor.
He remembers Margaret Canby, whom he married in 1930,
a free spirit with, she liked to say, "champagne tastes."
Liquor aggravated the conflicts between them, as did his
involvement in the miseries of working people after the
economic crash. Margaret died when she fell down a set
of stone steps in Santa Barbara in 1932, at a time when
they were living on opposite coasts.

In "those desperate days when nothing worked," the
democratic instinct that was one of Wilson's strengths led
him to investigate the Detroit assembly line—where a sudden silence meant that someone had lost a finger—radical
unions, rural poverty, the dehumanizing skyscrapers and
canyons of New York, "the jumping-off place" in the
Southern California dreamland. He went into the coal
fields of back-country Kentucky with a group of New York
writers to help a left-wing union. His friend Waldo Frank
(whose funeral is described in *The Sixties*) was beaten by
a deputy sheriff, substantiating Wilson's impression of the
class war. Though he put aside "liquorary quiddicism" (as
he had called it, echoing Joyce), he did not subordinate
literature to politics; rather he equated the moral leadership of Lenin in Russia with the inspiration of reading
Proust. His account of the revolutionary intellectual tradition in *To the Finland Station* absorbed the disillusion-
ment of the Moscow Trials. The portrait of Marx, the
largest of Wilson's studies on the theme of the wound and

the bow, sees the father of Communism imposing on himself and others a suffering which distorted his vision, even as it deepened and gave authority to Marx's account of "the wholesale mutilation of humanity, the grim collisions, the uncomprehended convulsions, to which that age of great profits was doomed."

Wilson's own writing incorporated the pain of his private life. In *The Sixties* he recalls bitter quarrels with Mary McCarthy, whom he married in 1938. Having confused her intellectual attraction with a sexual one and become the wife of the critic whom she sought as her mentor, Mary awoke the junior partner of a heavy-handed older man. He treated her like a dependent and she often behaved like one, alternately exploding in a hysteria that owed something to his drinking and much to having been beaten as a child by her Aunt Margaret and Uncle Myers. Their marriage lasted until 1945. He persuaded her of her talent for fiction, and she responded to his desire to be "a seeker after truth, no matter where it led or whom it hurt." Their friend Adelaide Walker liked to think that they would have been happy together if they could have retired at night to separate houses. Neither was ever quite able to understand the darkness of these years. In *The Sixties* Mary tells him, "I was too young," and he replies that he had been "too old."

Memoirs of Hecate County reflects his point of view in the early forties, darkened as well by World War II. By temperament he was resilient, and at *The New Yorker* in 1943 he began addressing a much larger, more heterogeneous audience than at *The New Republic*, in a forum that afforded space and latitude. He was hired as book reviewer, and when not recommending Jane Austen or Evelyn Waugh, he turned his wit loose on detective stories ("the awful whimsical patter of Lord Peter") and American bestsellers. By the fifties he was writing long essays on Turgenev, the Marquis de Sade, *Doctor Zhivago*. The portrait of Michelet in *To the Finland Station* defines Wilson's scholarly ideal: the Frenchman seemed to have "read all the books, been to look at all the monuments and pictures, interviewed personally all the authorities, and explored all the libraries and archives of Europe; and he has it all under his hat. He is simply a man going to the sources and trying to get down on record what can be learned from them; and this role, which claims for itself, on the one hand, no academic sanctions, involves, on the other hand, a more direct responsibility to the reader." Such a criticism freed Wilson's readers to make, as he does, their aesthetic judgments, to connect art and politics, modernism and the standards of the past. As a travel reporter he explored minority cultures whose languages and histories could resist mass society and the imperialism of the Cold War. His book on the Dead Sea scrolls was designed to uncover an ancient religious community, lost somewhere between Judaism and Christianity. In his later years the secular Wilson was interested in the moral discipline religion could supply, though he himself achieved this through writing.

The Sixties lacks the familiar images of the decade—the civil rights movement, student radicals at Berkeley and Columbia, the Watts riots, chaos in the streets at the Democratic convention in Chicago, the Woodstock nation. Yet Wilson's instincts anticipated those of the protesters. A few pages into the journal he is seen at an Iroquois banquet, enjoying their gravity and simplicity after "the deafening cocktail parties of Cambridge." He wonders whether people at such parties are trying "to forget the Bomb? to rival the Bomb?" He notes acquaintances who have the "nuclear age jitters." In New York City in 1962 he describes Barbara Deming's trial for trespassing during a peace demonstration. She was an ally of A. J. Muste, whom he had known as a radical labor organizer in the thirties. The next year he watches as demonstrators led by the old man are arrested at the Rome, New York, air base from which bombers regularly take off toward Russia armed with nuclear weapons. In *The Cold War and the Income Tax* (1963) Wilson denounces the destruction of cities and the use of atomic weapons in World War II, nuclear testing and the promotion of fallout shelters, the devastating new chemical and biological weapons, which have already, he writes, been tried out in Vietnam. The pamphlet ends with the "strategy of tax refusal" promoted by Muste's Fellowship of Reconciliation. Soon after meeting Muste at the air base, in the journal he records a trip to New York, where he arranged with Roger Straus to turn over any profits to the cause.

At the center of his politics of the sixties is *Patriotic Gore*. A critic's tour of neglected works, re-creating personalities from memoirs, letters, polemics, postwar fiction and poetry, it is also something of a national epic. Robert Lowell called the book "our American Plutarch," on account of the major portraits: Grant the democrat and Holmes the skeptical aristocrat, Sherman, Alexander Stephens, Harriet Beecher Stowe and her husband, Calvin. Wilson's Lincoln is a partial portrait, stressing the intelligence, imagination, and command of language that created a mythology for the nation whose future Lincoln could not control. The book draws on Wilson's personal experience and family history. He had been raised with an obligation to the republic of Lincoln and with reservations about the industrialized, capitalist America that emerged after the Civil War. His father, who served a term as Attorney General of New Jersey, had also imposed the Calvinist intellectual drive. When the boy's marks were less than A's, he was warned against "weltering around in a Dead Sea of mediocrity," one of his father's phrases recalled in *The Sixties*. In college (as Wilson later ironically put it) he believed culture to be "the property of the best people and one of the reasons for their superiority," but service as a private in the hospital corps made him resent rank and privilege. He contrasted his America to new friends who were "Irishmen, Swedes, Danes, Swiss, Belgians, and cockneys." There were harrowing months when their unit was overwhelmed by wounded. Wilson laid out the dead in the basement with an elderly undertaker who "knew just how to handle dead bodies," and wrote bitter epitaphs at their graves, one inverting Lincoln's rhetoric at Gettysburg:

> Go, countryman of theirs: they bought you pride;
> Look to it the Republic leave not vain
> The deaths of those who knew not why they died.

The polemical introduction to *Patriotic Gore* ridicules the righteous rhetoric of American expansion. "Whenever we engage in a war or move in on some other country, it is always to liberate somebody." We talk, Wilson says, about the "big bad Russia" and ignore the "United States of Hiroshima." The crushing of the Hungarian revolution by Soviet tanks, the dispossession of the Iroquois by the New York State Power Authority, were for him related symptoms of the faceless despotism of the age. He compares Lincoln's consolidation of the Union through the Civil War to Lenin's historic work of "binding Russia, with its innumerable ethnic groups scattered through immense spaces, in a tight bureaucratic net." Such analogies offended both progressives and middle America (*Life* angrily editorialized, "Lincoln, Lenin, and Bismarck?"). Invoking a Darwinian image of warfare he called nations "sea slugs" impelled to devour one another on the ocean floor. After the failed Cuban invasion, he feared that the country would soon be drawn into another conflict, and his introduction eerily anticipates the helicopters descending into Vietnam:

> The unanimity of men at war is like that of a school of fish, which will swerve, simultaneously and apparently without leadership, when the shadow of an enemy appears, or like a sky-darkening flight of grasshoppers, which, also all compelled by one impulse, will descend to consume the crops.

At the White House dinner in *The Sixties*, when President Kennedy asks for his conclusions about the Civil War and American power, Wilson refers him to this preface. "I don't believe that it is possible to be President and not be willing to lead the country into war," he had written to Barbara Deming before going to Washington. Yet when the President repeated his question as the guests were leaving, he again suggested reading the introduction. Back in New York, writers were pleased that he had not dissipated his protest in polite conversation. As Robert Lowell said in a letter:

> Except for you, everyone there seemed addled with adulation at having been invited. It was all good fun but next morning you read that the President has sent the 7th fleet to Laos, or he might have invaded Cuba again—not that he will, but I feel we intellectuals play a very pompous and frivolous role—we should be windows, not window-dressing . . . I thought of all the big names there, only you acted like yourself.

Perhaps Kennedy was similarly impressed. The following summer in Talcottville, Arthur Schlesinger—who says that Kennedy kept up with Wilson's writing in *The New*

Yorker—called to report that the President had added his name to the list for the new Medal of Freedom. Wilson was then battling over his tax debt with the IRS. They investigated his past radical activities and, he was told, submitted a sixteen-page memorandum against the award. Kennedy responded, "This is not an award for good conduct but for literary merit."

The public world is here only a backdrop for Wilson's account of his own experience. The assassination of Kennedy receives a single biting paragraph. Wilson supports Johnson till the escalation of the Vietnam War, which occasions an argument with a summer friend in Talcottville that—characteristic of the times—almost comes to blows. He is pleased, in 1966, when Robert Kennedy is reported to be reading one of his books while waiting at the polls in New York. The next year Lowell tells him of the protest march on the Pentagon, but by now his energies are given to the expanded *Dead Sea Scrolls*. He notes a fraying in the American social fabric, from upstate to the changing appearance of New York City. In 1968, however, the journal leaves unmentioned Johnson's decision not to run for reelection, the assassinations of Robert Kennedy and Martin Luther King, Jr., the uproar at the Democratic convention.

His horizon shrinks as he ages. He has a tendency to flee from occasions—the parties are too noisy, the dinners too late, he doesn't quite feel among friends, and will stand up and insist upon leaving, later to be lightly rebuked by Elena or to recall the abrupt departure with regret. So he escapes Wellfleet, the *"plage des intellectuels,"* for the freedom and balance he feels in Talcottville.

There is a moment when he sees in his face the features of ancestors on both sides, and he looks for traces of these in Helen, Reuel, and Rosalind. His first two marriages had been hard on the children. Rosalind, born when he was twenty-eight, was abandoned by Mary Blair and raised by his mother in Red Bank, spending summers at Cape Cod with Wilson, at first with a nurse as well. She grew up resenting most of the women in her father's life, and resenting him, among other things, for having in her youth tried to rein her in. "She is closer to me than either of my other children," Wilson writes in *The Sixties*. He was also most critical of her, impatient with her weak ambition and discipline, her vivid fantasy life. When fantasy collided with reality in the fall of 1963, the journal documents her emotional collapse. In *Near the Magician*, Rosalind remembers her father's kindness in these weeks, but his letters to Elena in Europe suggest that the recovery was difficult. When Talcottville becomes home to her in the late sixties, father and daughter are often together. She is witty and good company, but each is moody and drinks too much, and she now physically resembles him. He worries over her, wanting to understand and believe in her, exaggerating her faults and regretting his own bullying ways.

Reuel had been brought up by Mary and Bowden Broadwater, who referred to his father by the pet name "Monstro." His relations with Wilson, who tried to guide him intellectually, were never easy, but Elena had tried to be a second mother to him, and with her help, his father and he had achieved a certain equilibrium. He is in graduate school at the beginning of the decade, and in 1963 returns to his adolescent haunts on the Cape in a marriage that will not last. Wilson visits him in 1968 at the University of Chicago, where Reuel is teaching. The pride in his son that was difficult to express in person was confided to friends whom he told that Reuel was the apple of his eye.

Helen was his only child to grow up living with both parents. Enthusiastic about her youthful talents, he includes her writing in the journal. Elena seems sometimes to stand between them, making her daughter an ally. They send a birthday telegram inviting him to judge a beauty contest among Magyar women, an allusion to his several attractive teachers of Hungarian. Elena's constant support, however, made it easier for Helen to achieve independence of her "Pa" than for Rosalind and Reuel. When last seen in the journal she is a college girl studying Russian. Her interest in art would lead her to a career like her father's.

The men of Wilson's journal are not as physically vivid as the women. He always discriminates about women's bodies and their changing appearances, and can also be seduced by their minds. When he writes of Frances, Margaret Canby, or the passionate "K." of *The Twenties* and *The Thirties*, his understanding of love is not separable from lovemaking. Yet there were literary women—Elinor Wylie, Louise Bogan, Dawn Powell, Helen Muchnic— with whom he had comfortable and witty relationships, a mutual loyalty that did not keep them from putting him in his place and was uncomplicated by getting into bed. Neither of his first two marriages met the need for intellectual compatibility, and when this was achieved with Mary McCarthy, the results were otherwise disastrous. With Elena Thornton he was able to integrate the intellectual and physical, the emotional and social, as once he had wanted to do with Millay. He records their attraction in *The Forties*—"she would wind herself around me like an eel, telling me how much she enjoyed it." Her European background may have made it easier for her to be the wife of such a man. "She has always that beauty that shines like a light—the intelligence you can't get a grip on or wrestle with in an exchange of wisecracks, love that is tempered by intelligence and knows where to place itself," Wilson writes when they are getting married.

She was born Helen-Marthe von Mumm, of the German champagne family and the Russian émigré aristocracy in

Paris. She lived in Montreal in the early years of her marriage to Jimmy Thornton, son of Sir James Thornton, president of the Canadian Northern Railway, but was assistant to the editor of *Town and Country* in New York when Wilson and she fell in love. In *The Sixties* he is still writing of Elena's body and of longing to make love to her, though his heart condition makes him anxious and his vitality is waning. He tells her their lovemaking has been the best thing in his life. She also tackled the income tax mess, as the journal does not quite make clear. She was a sounding board on many subjects of his writing, and after his death devotedly edited Wilson's correspondence. In conversation, McCarthy dismissed Elena as a "Cosima Wagner," willing to live through her husband's work. Her self-image derived from the Punch and Judy show that he liked to put on with Helen: since he saw himself as the raucous, rebellious Punch, she cast herself as his Judy, loving him and keeping him in line.

The latter was difficult. His first two wives had been heavy drinkers, and his drinking was hard on both Mary McCarthy and Elena, for he could also lose his temper. Elena tolerated his romantic flirtations. He had a fantasy of running away with Mary Meigs. Aware of Meigs's lesbianism, Elena said, "Let us see who will do what with whom." She teased him that he was captivated by Clelia Carroll's "M-O-N-E-Y." This too was a platonic affair— Carroll recalled that when she let Wilson hold her hand in a taxi all the way downtown to the Algonquin, he asked, "Do you believe in God?" and, when she replied that she didn't think so, said "Isn't that wonderful? I don't either." Wilson's relationship with Mary Pcolar was more irritating to his wife. In Elena's absence, Mary drove for him and kept him company when he was in upstate New York. She was from an immigrant community that interested him, like the Frances of *The Twenties* and *The Thirties*. She tutored him in Hungarian, and he talked with her of literature and history, and paid her tuition at Utica College. He followed the drama of her life like a soap opera. Elena called Mary the "Madame Bovary of Boonville."

She was not his mistress, at any rate until he was no longer able to make love to Elena—and at that point "what difference did it make," Elena said. In a letter from Jerusalem in 1967, Edmund tells his wife that every morning when he first wakes up he wonders "why, when I still had it, I didn't make love to you every day." During the last years his relationships with other women changed. There is a tender intimate scene with Mary Pcolar. "When I told her that I wanted to see the rest of her body, she said, with conscious humor, 'I'm perfectly beautiful, but no.' " The image of the old man with his head in a younger woman's lap recalls that of mother and child. "I kissed her as long as it seemed rewarding, and in my pauses she sometimes gave me little kisses on the cheek. She would murmur little remarks so softly that, in my deafness, I could not understand and would have to put my ear to her mouth and ask her to repeat it."

The initial "O" disguises his "conquest" of a friend at the Princeton Club in November 1970, when he was seventy-five. It is a romantic escapade—they are at ease and frankly sensual. After his heart attack in New York in that year he becomes close to Anne Miller, the wife of his dentist in Lowville. Restless in their small community, husband and wife responded to the aging critic's loneliness. Ned Miller would remember him rising from four hours in the dental chair to ask where they could get the best champagne in town. Direct and warm, Anne admired Wilson's mind as well as his manners and his knowledge of books and the world. This friendship was the Pygmalion exchange that he could never quite create with Mary Pcolar, though she aspired to transcend her own background.

The wonderfully evocative account of the landscape on their walk at Sugar River shows how Anne renewed his enthusiasm for the world.

I spent four days at Talcottville in the summer of 1963. The drive west through the Berkshires recalled the trek of Wilson's ministerial ancestor and his Mather bride when they left the "narrow coops" of colonial Massachusetts for the upstate countryside, becoming "part of the new America, now forever for a century on the move." The old stone house with its carved fireplaces and branching columns evoked the making of a civilization in the wilderness. When Wilson showed me around, I admired the poems he had had his friends cut with a diamond stylus into the windows of the house or in some cases into panes of glass that he brought back after visiting them. Greek and Hebrew faced each other in the large arched windows of the third-story room he still sometimes used as a study. On the door to the balcony, in the old Russian, was Nabokov's

бывают ночи только лягу
в Россию поплывет кровать....

[There are nights I will just lie down/Into Russia the bed will sail away . . .]. Louise Bogan's "The Landscape Where I Lie" was in Helen's room, and in mine Auden's "Make the night loveable moon/And with eye single,/Looking down from above there," set so that I saw the moon through the verses. The picture of "great still spaces,/White hills, glittering deeps," the dark concluding prayer lest any "Wake alone in a bed/ . . . /Wishing his friend were dead," showed why Wilson judged Auden a great poet.

He was working on his journals and *A Prelude*. He spoke of his boyhood, of the sense of America his father had given him, the vigor of his doctor uncle at work, and his escapes on drunken binges. Oppressed by the evangelical piety of Hill School, at Princeton, Wilson recalled, "I had a very pleasant time except when my reforming zeal would rise to the surface." James's essay "The Art of Fiction" had impressed him. When I cited the famous directive "Try to be one of the people on whom nothing is lost," Wilson said he had not forgotten that line, and it is echoed in a flattering couplet about his friend Ed O'Connor in *The Sixties*. We talked of the twenties, of the Hemingways and Dos Passos, who had been friends of my mother in Paris. Troubled by Dos Passos's fading reputation, he said that Dos was a farmer now and only had between six and nine o'clock in the morning to write. When I mentioned Robert Frost and the Kennedys, Wilson asked why Frost was given to comparing John Kennedy to Augustus Caesar. With a hearty laugh and slapping his thigh, he answered his own question, "Because it makes him Virgil!" We drank white wine and talked into the morning. When we drove around the countryside with Elena he showed me the collapsing buildings of the abandoned town of Highmarket, which at the end of *The Sixties* convey his consciousness of physical decay.

Late one night I asked a question about his relationship to his father for the dissertation I had begun on his early years. With a darkly glaring look Wilson said, "You know too much about me," adding, "You should be writing your own essays and stories instead of annotating mine." The next day there was a knock at my door and he stood there with one of the journals open in his hands. "When did I write this?" he queried. Unsure whether he didn't know or was testing me, I recognized a detail in the corner of the page and produced a date which satisfied him. Before we said goodbye, he offered two observations about his work. He hadn't written well till 1925—which I believe too much discounts the lightness and wit, the flair of his *Vanity Fair* period. Now, he said, he was doing his best work in the journal. Handing me a glass of orange juice as we stood at the dining table at breakfast, he swigged his down with the Hebrew words *Hazak, Hazak, Venit-hazayk,* explaining that it meant to be strong enough to begin reading the Torah all over again. When I asked what the phrase did for him, he replied, "It helps me jack up my waning powers."

The contest of life against death in *The Sixties* begins on the first page, where the octogenarian son of William James, now getting married again, is told by the clerks in the office that he'd better hurry up. Wilson, feeling his age, counterposes moments of fatigue with "spells of expanding ambition." A few pages later he states that his books are "marching through me: they live, I am ceasing to live." In mid-decade his commentary on *Faust* stresses the hero's self-absorption and questions whether Faust's famous "striving" was enough to save him. For Elena he composes anniversary verse: "Surprised to find myself now old and slow/The man who loved you twenty years ago." Dawn Powell's death makes him feel "that some part of his own life was gone," and the "lecherous eye" of the Wellfleet undertaker at Waldo Frank's funeral deepens his sadness at his friend's artistic failure. A social week in New York now ensures Wilson's own collapse, while his routine at the Cape is dull. The lover of life protests its ebbing:

> Cities I'll never visit, books that I'll never read,
> Magic I'll never master. In a cage,
> I stalk from room to room, lose heat and speed,
> Now entering the dark defile of age.

He lives hard and doggedly even as old age takes him over, travels despite the discomfort and the hardly mentioned cane, reads the inscriptions when he cannot climb the stairs at Bomarzo. "A definite point has now been passed in my life," he concludes in 1968, feeling detached from his past by the maladies that cripple him. Six months later, as he is about to undergo dental surgery, he has finished with the scrolls and feels "a kind of regeneration—inspiration for writing on Svetlana, new introduction to *Finland Station*, Barham review, T'ville memoir and memoirs of the twenties, all more or less bound up with one another." He keeps studying and making judgments, almost boyishly inquisitive about people and situations.

In May 1971, drinking with Penelope Gilliatt in his room at the Princeton Club, Wilson broke one of his vertebrae when he sat down and missed the bed. He had outlived his ability to enjoy life, and the journal shrinks away as its tone grows somber, for he does not want to describe that which he cannot affirm. He continued to do his work, completing the Russian essays, the new *Finland Station*, and *Upstate*, which he lived to see selling a thousand copies a week. As always, he kept up his correspondence with old friends and new, ranging from Angus Wilson to Joan Didion, whose *Play It As It Lays* he recommended and who drew inspiration from Wilson's reportage for her own. He defied the doctors, refusing a pacemaker. In his final weeks he summoned himself to support McGovern against Nixon. The last notes, "T'ville, May 31–June 5," were written on Sunday, June 11, 1972, after four months with no journal entries. Wilson died, at seventy-seven, the following morning, attached to an oxygen machine but managing to get to the chair by his desk, just as Karl Marx was found dead "at his worktable."

In the medley of the last page are the unexplained words "Tennyson and Musset." It is a contrast that had moved Wilson as a young man in Greenwich Village, when E. E. Cummings called him "the man in the iron necktie" and Dos Passos was delighted to come on him doing a handstand in front of the elevators at *Vanity Fair*. At the

end of the *History of English Literature*, Taine sets off the
British poet on the lawns of the Isle of Wight and the
Frenchman in his Paris garret, writing of Musset, "He
suffered, but he invented. He fainted, but he produced.
He tore from his vitals the idea which he had conceived
and held it up to the multitude, bloody but alive." This
is the rhetoric of *The Wound and the Bow*, the difficult
psychic origin of art and ideas. Yet what follows his
"Tennyson and Musset" is a tribute, apparently from
the period of Walter Pater, to "the wonderful breadth
of beauty and the perfect force of truth in a single verse"
of Tennyson's "Elaine." Wilson had always been a stylist,
with a demanding concentration on the page that was
remote from the life, the drinking, and the volatile
temper.

In a letter to Louise Bogan in 1931 he had said that "the
only thing that we can really make is our work. And de-
liberate work of the mind, imagination, and hand, done,
as Nietzsche said, 'notwithstanding,' in the long run re-
makes the world." *The Sixties*, while not the great poem
or novel he might have wished to leave, is an achievement
of similar power. As Wilson wrote in 1965 of Francis
Parkman's multivolume history of early Canada, his "genius is shown not only in his well-controlled and steadily
advancing prose but in his avoidance of generalizations,
his economizing of abstract analysis, his sticking to concrete events. Each incident, each episode is different, each
is particularized, each is presented, when possible, in
sharply realistic detail, no matter how absurd or how
homely." Probing in its observation, uncomfortably familiar, *The Sixties* makes us all players on the stage of our
daily lives, elevating the isolated individual struggle to the
heroic. The book continues a tradition going back through
Yeats's lyrics to the *Iliad*—to Helen and Paris, on whom,
in Richmond Lattimore's translation, "Zeus set a vile des-

tiny, so that hereafter we shall be made into things of song for the men of the future."

A simple description of flowers near Wilson's home, written near the end of his life, balances life and death in a prose that, resonating with sexuality, invites the reader to join him imaginatively, to see what he sees: "The yellow lilies are out in the back garden, and the Showy Lady Slippers in front of the house. I go out to look at them from time to time: the roundish streakish bright pink lip, speckled inside, with its three white streamers, and the pink-dotted yellow patch hooded away above it. They are thriving and have multiplied here, but the plant in the back garden seems to have died. They give me much pleasure."

CHRONOLOGY

The Sixties

1960   Lowell Professor of English at Harvard, reading from chapters of his Civil War book. In July IRS notifies him he will be prosecuted for tax delinquency. In November fined $7,500 and assessed back taxes of nearly $70,000. Quarterly income from his mother's estate seized by the government. Sells papers to Yale. *Apologies to the Iroquois.*

1961   Angina in the winter. Death of Hemingway. IRS cuts off income from publishers. Writing Introduction to *Patriotic Gore. Night Thoughts.*

1962   Dinner at the White House. *The New Yorker* funds trip to Canada. *Patriotic Gore: Studies in the Literature of the American Civil War.*

1963   President Kennedy adds name to list for Presidential Medal of Freedom. IRS in Washington finally approves tax settlement negotiated in Syracuse. EW mortgages future work for $30,000, as well as the old stone house. Interviews himself for first issue of *The New York Review of Books*. Ten days in Canada. Goes to Europe, and hears news of Kennedy assassination. Revisits the Vosges, where he was a hospital orderly in 1917–18. *The Cold War and the Income Tax.*

1964   Spring in Paris, Rome, and Budapest. In fall starts year's residence as a Fellow at Wesleyan Center for Advanced Studies.

1965   At Wesleyan till May; seventieth birthday May 8. Begins his battle with Nabokov over translation of *Evgeni Onegin. O Canada: An American's Notes on Canadian Culture.*

1966   Celebrates twentieth anniversary of marriage to Elena. Receives award from the American Academy of Arts and Sciences and the National Medal for Literature. *The Bit Between My Teeth: A Literary Chronicle of 1950–1965. Europe Without Baedeker* reissued, together with *Notes from a European Diary, 1963–1964.*

1967   Travels to Israel and Jordan to bring *Dead Sea Scrolls* up to date; leaves Jerusalem on eve of Six-Day War. *A Prelude: Characters and Conversations from the Early Years of My Life. I Thought of Daisy* reissued together with *Galahad.*

1968   Charlottesville and Chicago trips. Aspen Award of $30,000 in New York. Satirizes pedantry in "The Fruits of the M.L.A.," starting a literary controversy. Working on "my academic play" and on the Dead Sea scrolls.

1969 Stalin's daughter visits the Cape. A month in Jamaica. Begins *Upstate: Records and Recollections of Northern New York*. His work slows as illness overtakes him. *The Dead Sea Scrolls, 1947–1969. The Duke of Palermo and Other Plays.*

1970 Has coronary in New York in March, checks into Hyannis hospital for three days. Slight stroke around Christmas. Writing articles for *A Window on Russia*.

1971 Falls off his bed in Princeton Club and fractures vertebra. Writes new Introduction to *To the Finland Station* and assembles essays for *The Devils and Canon Barham*. Hospitalized in Boston, where he refuses a pacemaker. *Upstate.*

1972 Spends two months in Naples, Florida. Has another stroke in May. Dies in Talcottville, June 12, at seventy-seven; is buried at Wellfleet, June 15. *A Window on Russia* and new edition of *To the Finland Station* published posthumously.

1973–1992

> *The Devils and Canon Barham* (1973)
> *The Twenties* (1975)
> *Letters on Literature and Politics* (1977)
> *The Thirties* (1980)
> *The Forties* (1983)
> *The Portable Edmund Wilson* (1983)
> *The Fifties* (1986)
> *The Sixties* (1993)

THE SIXTIES

A NEW DECADE BEGINS

Harvard 1960

Jan. 1, 1960. At my age, I find that I alternate between spells of fatigue and indifference when I am almost ready to give up the struggle, and spells of expanding ambition, when I feel that I can do more than ever before.

Sometime early in December we went to dinner at old *Billy James's*. We had already heard from Rosalind [Wilson] that he had just been married to the mother of a friend of hers, and this was the first time they had entertained. She was a Mrs. Pierce, a daughter of the painter George de Forest Brush. Rosalind thought that she had been rather destructive in her relations with her children. A son had committed suicide; a daughter, Rosalind's friend, was in McLean's.* Rosalind had just been to see her, and she had said, "Mother did it so quickly that I think Mother must have been pregnant." The girl, while at McLean's, had had an admirer who suffered from a no doubt neurotic condition of the stomach. The mother, who is a food faddist, had taken him away from the daughter by curing him

---

* McLean's is a psychiatric institution in Belmont, Massachusetts, near Boston.

by a different diet. She seems partly to have taken the step of marrying Billy because she couldn't bear the idea of his living alone on Irving St. and eating nothing but frankfurters and marinated herring.

He had a very funny account of their difficulties in getting married. It had taken four or five days. In the first place, in order to get a license, they had to pass a Wassermann test. Then, since neither had been baptized, that required some special dispensation. He got someone to intervene with a judge whom he knew; the friend applied to him while court was in session and the judge signed a waiver for them. Then it turned out to be difficult to get a clergyman to marry them, and Billy finally resorted to another friend, a retired dean of the Divinity School, 90 years old. At one office they told him he "better hurry up," and when he left the building the girls waved at him from the windows. His wife said there were moments when she had to pretend that she didn't have anything to do with him. He was obviously very much pleased. He had several drinks and sometimes, in telling us stories, his memory would fail him. Someone told me that he could not always remember the former married name of his wife. Both Leon Edel and I noticed that Mrs. Pierce had something of a Southern accent, but she said that she had always lived in Europe and New York. When I looked up G. de F. Brush, I found that he had been born in Tennessee. She and Billy had evidently known one another from long back in Cornish, N.H.

Gossip in Cambridge: Elena met Elena Levin on the street, who said, "I hear you have a new fur coat." Our disastrous dinner at the Lowells', before he went into McLean's a few years ago, seemed immediately known to everyone in Boston and Cambridge. When I went to New York, I was at first surprised that Katharine White should know about it, then remembered that she came from Boston. I found, during the last semester, that Robert knew what was going on in my seminar. Mrs. [McGeorge] Bundy, whom I met on the street, knew that I had been very busy. Last Tuesday, the 29th, the Levins and Marian Schlesinger came to dinner and Isaiah Berlin, on his way to New York from an historians' conference in Chicago, appeared at about half past ten. We thought that the evening had been very successful and that the Levins had been very good-humored, but when I afterwards talked with Isaiah on the phone, he assured me that Harry, on his way back home, had been most disagreeable about "everybody."

This is the Oxford-cliquish side of *Isaiah*. (Just before he went, he got started on the C.P. Snows, whom he wanted to denigrate and discredit, and was worrying like a terrier with a rat.) Harry [Levin] is no doubt a little jealous of Isaiah, on account of his understanding with Elena [Levin]—on the basis of their common Russian background—as well as of his greater freedom as a Jew in academic life; but it is also true that Isaiah's indistinct way of talking makes it difficult for Harry, with his deafness, to understand what he is saying and so puts him under a strain. Isaiah is behaving more and more like royalty. He first called me up from New York to try to persuade me to come to New York; then, failing that, to meet him halfway in New Haven. Then I got a series of telegrams first announcing then cancelling a visit to Cambridge, then announcing his arrival on the night of the 29th. He had told me over the telephone that he couldn't possibly come to Cambridge because there would be "forty people" who would expect to see him; that Mrs. Whitehead and we were the only ones he had to see. His visit was to be strictly incognito. But he had told the Schlesingers the same thing—having seen Arthur in New York—and Marian had asked us, when we called on her, whether we were expecting "a mysterious guest." Later on, after his visit, Elena met Stuart Hughes on the street, and he said that he had just seen Isaiah at the historians' congress in Chicago and that he had said he was paying us "a secret visit." We sent him off in a cab to call on Mrs. Whitehead— which he afterwards told me he had failed to do. Mrs. Whitehead is over 90, and it was after 12 at night.

Elena Levin said that Max Hayward was a kind of Raskolnikov, and Isaiah said that he was like Genet—with which my Elena agreed and said the name had just come into her mind. She had seen him, as I had not done, overstaying his welcome at the Chavchavadzes', putting through long-distance telephone calls at their expense, drinking a lot and "letting himself go." He had told them that he never had more than one suit and one pair of shoes at a time; he wore them till they were worn out.

The night of Jan. 1. I read Nancy Hale's new novel *Dear Beast*—amusing about Virginia but fundamentally a woman's magazine production (with a title, I should say, aimed at the movies). Went to sleep late and not long before waking had, for the first time in I don't know how long, *another dream about Margaret* [Canby].* I thought that I had quarrelled in an apartment with some woman—I thought she was begging off from going to bed with me at the time I wanted her (this evidently inspired by an incident in the novel)—and an unexpected visit by Ted Para-

---

* EW had dreamed about his second wife, Margaret Canby, since her death in 1932. In these dreams, recorded in previous volumes of the journal, she is not dead and they are together again, but in the dream he always loses her. Ted Paramore, his fun-loving apartment mate of the early twenties, had been engaged to Margaret before Edmund knew her and was jealous of their marriage. Ted had seen something of her during her last summer in Santa Barbara, as had Henry Eichheim, the composer, and his wife.

more gave me an excuse to reject her altogether, to let her go away. Then I went out with him to some kind of bar, taking, however, a bottle of bourbon from my own room (this from the novel, too). I brought up again my old idea that Margaret was still on the Coast, that she had merely cut off communications with me. He refused to tell me where she was, how I could find her again. I said, But you know that I can find out in other ways where she is. He said yes but he wouldn't tell me. He told me, however, that at first she had been glad when she had been told that I cared about her, that I wanted to find her again (an echo of what the Eichheims or somebody had told me: that when she had had a letter from me at the end of the summer, she had said something like "It's nice to feel you're wanted"). I kept after him, and we kept drinking bourbon. I couldn't believe that he would keep on refusing, then realized that I should presently have to change the subject, return to our joking conversation and gossip about Santa Barbara. But I would find her now, nevertheless—even after so long a separation.

Charley Curtis's death just before Christmas. He had been looking at television or listening to radio with his wife when the next room caught fire from the fireplace. She got out the window but he went back to his study to save a manuscript. There was also photographing apparatus there, and the film—I suppose—blazed up. He was blinded and stifled and fell on the floor. The firemen rescued him and he was taken to the hospital, where he died. Though I did not see him often, I miss him—I knew that he read what I wrote, and he occasionally sent me notes about it. When I instinctively say to myself, Charley Curtis will appreciate this, I have to remember that he is no longer there. —Rosalind thinks that he was rather unhappy. When he divorced his wife and married again, his new wife im-

mediately developed some more or less neurotic disease—
what I take to have been an hysterical paralysis that made
it impossible to move from her chair. She had to be carried
and three nurses looked after her. Charley himself was in
constant attendance. He had partially given up his law
business and seemed more and more to occupy himself
with writing. I always had the impression that it was
harder for him than most people to resign himself to the
position of political subordination that the Irish Catholic
dominance had imposed on Boston. I think he compensated
for this by such dissidences as taking the unpopular side
in his book on the Oppenheimer case.* Then the scandal
of his divorce cost him his overseership at Harvard. When
Bostonians of this old upper stratum do not become set in
the conventional mold, they are likely to become formidably
the other way:

> Their humor and charm
> Become cause for alarm—
> I am thinking of Cummings and Curtis.

I had a *dream* in which I thought that at last I was going
to write a wonderful poem. I composed two magnificent
lines, then realized that in order to complete it I should
have to have something to drink. Yes: Elena *had* left something in the icebox: scarcely more than a drop of a decanter
of sweet white wine, but the better part of another decanter
of white wine, which turned out to be almost intolerably
sour. However, I started in on it. I found that the first
two lines had partly melted away in my head, but I did my
best to recover them, then woke up and mustered the
strength of mind to go into my study and write them down:

---

* In *The Trial of a Security System*, Curtis attacked the government's
revocation, in 1953, of Oppenheimer's security clearance because of
his radical connections.

You in that lovely splendor have endured,
Beside that vague and honey-vapored deep.

I think that this last is an echo of a line of Yeats's:
Beneath that . . . and vapor-turbanned steep (?).*

Stravinsky in New York

We were invited by a Mr. Graf to attend a reception in
New York (January 10) to meet Stravinsky. I had never
met him so wanted to go. Elena had known his wife,
formerly married to the painter Sudeikin, who had played
the non-dancing bride in the first production of *Les Noces*,
and her mother had known Stravinsky from almost his first
days in Paris. Elena and Olili [Mumm] had known every
note of his scores, and he had several times visited Johannisberg. I called up Sylvia Marlowe to ask her who Mr.
Graf was, and she said that she knew nothing about him
except that he was a man who gave parties for Stravinsky.
She and Leonid [Berman] were giving a party Saturday
afternoon, and she would give us two seats in her box at
the concert Sunday afternoon at which a new work of
Stravinsky's was to be played. We went and had such a
spree as we have not been able to afford in a long time.
The party was a get-together of the artistic and literary
worlds on a scale, I think, unequalled in my experience:
Wystan Auden and Chester Kallman; Eleanor Perényi and
her dreadful mother, who reminded me who she was and
talked to me without ever mentioning that Eleanor was
there, so that when Eleanor presented herself I did not at
first recognize her—when I inquired what had happened
to Perényi, Mrs. Stone [Eleanor's mother] had said that

* The line from Yeats's "The Man Who Dreamed of Faeryland" is "Under
that cold and vapour-turbanned steep."

it was too long a story to tell: he was now "rather pathetic,"
a schoolmaster, I think, in Switzerland; there was also that
bearded semi-pansy whose initials are L.L., who teaches
somewhere, lives with his mother and entertains celebrities: I had met him first at the Stores; Louis and Emmy
Kronenberger, the latter looking very pretty; Virgil Thomson, whom I had not seen since Paris and who, Sylvia said,
sulked on the couch because he did not like opera singers
and there was an important woman opera singer there;
Victoria Ocampo, that splendid old girl, who had just seen
Waldo Frank; he had a new grievance about something
that made him feel he was no longer appreciated in South
America; Margaret de Silver, who surprised us by having
become as slim as a sylph—"I had to die to do it," she had
had an operation; Norman Podhoretz, Jason Epstein and
a young man named Marcus, who is interested in Dickens:
Podhoretz has just been made editor of *Commentary*, which
he says he is going to revolutionize—I reminded of his
remark about אתה האיש [Thou art the man]; Tony West
was standing near the entrance to the front room: I told
him that he was all wrong, in his article about me in the
London *Sunday Times*, in implying that I had no more than
a smattering of Russian—he said this was just "a tease"
—and that I hated Eliot; Red Warren and Eleanor
Clark—I had no conversation with her, but took him into
the back room to talk about the Civil War: he displayed
his usual intelligence on this subject, said that people like
Jefferson Davis were "schizophrenic," did really want the
South to win—it is his coming from Kentucky that makes
him so detached; Kenneth Tynan, but I economized time
by not talking to him since we were having him to lunch
the next day; Helen Carter—Elliott was in Europe—he
had written a new quartet; some Jewish friend of Leonid's,
who *po-russki puccku* [spoke no Russian]; Robert Craft, who
seems to have become to some extent Stravinsky's impre-

sario and mentor; Mme Stravinsky, with whom Elena sat down and had a long conversation—she is still pretty, amiable, comfortable, the *baba* [grandmotherly] type of Russian woman, now somewhat expanding, in this respect the opposite of Stravinsky. We had difficulty in making our departure—people kept arriving and it was hard to get out the door—in order to be at the Algonquin at 8, where Henry and Daphne [Thornton], the Lehoviches and the Winkelhorns were going to meet us for dinner.

At the concert—5:30 the next afternoon—Sylvia, *sans ambages* [without much ado] explained to us the circumstances of the composition of Stravinsky's new piece. Sylvia, some time ago, had offered him $5,000 to write a piece to which, for two years' time, she would have the exclusive rights of performance. He had refused but had later on accepted $25,000 to do a piece—a 12-tone 10 minutes—for the daughter of a rich Swiss. Sylvia, as she confessed, was being catty about the young Swiss pianist: she had done so badly at rehearsal the day before that they were afraid she'd go up at the performance: those 12-tone pieces were hard to remember. Actually it went off all right; but the girl was rather clumsy on the stage and, when the usual enormous bouquet tied with a huge pink bow was handed up from the house, didn't know how to come forward and receive it. Stravinsky attempted to guide her, to make her receive the bouquet and to get her on and off the stage for encores; Sylvia said, "Go on and take it—go on, you dope!" I couldn't follow the piece properly, but it had his usual terseness, variety, clear calligraphy, incisiveness. Leonid's reactions seemed mainly visual: the women in the chorus for the other numbers all had thin waists, legs and ankles; Stravinsky, hunching over to conduct, looked "ugly" making those jerky motions.

At the reception were Craft, Wystan and Chester and other people that we did not know. The host and hostess were fairly young, evidently fairly well off, had collected some not absolutely first-rate modern pictures. The pianist and her father and I think other members of her family were there. Elena thought the Grafs were in some way Swiss—Mrs. Graf talked French with a very American accent. Mme Stravinsky had told them that Str. would have something to eat immediately after the concert. They had said they weren't sure that they had enough plates: "Give him chicken à la king on an ashtray, but he has to have something to eat." The result was ham, crab meat salad, brownies and bread and cheese. As I was filling my plate, Wystan appeared and said in a hushed voice which was perhaps not quite hushed enough, "That ham's too salt. The only excuse for rich people is that they do things like that right." His face is now crisscrossed with creases; it looks squarer than when I saw him last and like some kind of technical map. He went early, leaving Chester, with whom, for the first time without Wystan, I had a longish talk. He is gentle, not unintelligent, has to surmount a not obstructive stammer.

The Russians made their own little nuclear group, in which we came to be included. I found out from the hostess later that it was the Stravinskys who had wanted us invited. Str. began by saying to me, "I read your lines" . . . I didn't understand this at first, and he explained *"vashi stroky,"* making lines in the air with his finger. I tried to tell him how much his music had meant to me—difficult in conversation: I said that it had been to me "an inspiration" when what I really meant was that, besides my enjoying it so much, it had helped to keep up my artistic morale. *"C'est réciproque, c'est réciproque,"* he said. He was jolly, amusing, even bubbling—quite frank and accessible, I thought, as we find with delight that such masters may be. I had not quite realized what a little wisp of a man he was—in France they used to call him "the insect." Even I seemed to have to bend over him, and I felt that his tiny stature, his in themselves unimpressive features, must in certain ways have made him shy, at the mercy of the world around him—I remembered *Petrushka* and *L'Histoire du Soldat*. Elena says he looks like a musical note: his legs and feet dwindle to tininess. But his opinions in conversation, like his music, are fearless and firm. Isaiah Berlin and some other friend had persuaded him to read *Doctor Zhivago*, which he had got through between rehearsals, but he had not liked it at all: he thought it a second-rate novel (comparing it, I imagine, with Turgenev, Tolstoy, etc.)—it was simply a collection of fragments, would have no lasting value—he had not even liked the poems, had never read any of Pasternak's poetry written before these. He adored—what seemed rather surprising— the writings of Harold Nicolson, thought they were very well written. His spoken English is not very good—his French a good deal better. With Elena he spoke mainly Russian.

He gave me to understand that he hoped that the Dead Sea scrolls had turned out not to be authentic: I remembered that he was very pious and said his prayers every day, so did not pursue the subject. He spoke of Schoenberg with less respect than he had seemed to in his published conversations: he was a man of considerable talent but *"désagréable"* and too romantic for him. I said that Schoenberg came out of Wagner. "Mahler—and Wagner, yes." It was Anton Webern that he really admired. I said that the English critics had been writing rave notices of *Moses und Aron* after the recent performance in Berlin. "The English critics are not very certain," he said, meaning not sure of what was what. He was depressing to Elena about Nicholas Nabokov—I had asked him about Nicholas's opera on Rasputin, which Virgil Thomson had told me was quite good. In the first place, the subject had shocked him: it was too early to write an opera about Rasputin. Then Nicholas was so unsatisfactory—half professional and half amateur. He said that Nicholas would bring him a piece and offer to dedicate it to him if he liked it; would play it and then Stravinsky would say nothing. He told us that if we ever came out to the Coast, we must visit him. He had his wife write their address and number and handed it to me, saying, "That's everything about Stravinsky!"

A hanger-on would bring him cheese and brownies. When offered a piece of cheese, he would lean forward and stick his tongue out. She called his attention to a plate at his side and induced him to put the cheese on it, rather than take it on his tongue. All this time, Elena tells me, the Russian ladies—Mme Str. and a woman whom E. already knew, a hanger-on of the musical world, of Stravinsky and the American ballet—were saying all kinds of "horrors" about the Swiss guests: "What *poshlost'* [crassness]! *Bogaty* [They're wealthy]." At last Mme Str. advised her husband, "You must congratulate *vashu shveitsarku* [your Swiss lady]," so he went to her with hands outstretched. "Who are all these people that we don't know?" said one of the ladies to the other. "*Esche shveitsary* [More Swiss]," with a shrug. When we left, we went down in the elevator with the Russians. "Now let's have a drink," said Str., with the mischievous smile of a small boy. I said that we wanted to go to his ballet—an all-Stravinsky evening, which would be only half over. As he was getting into his car, he faced us and said, "*Apploud!*" first making the motion of clapping, then throwing out his hands.

We took Dawn Powell and the Tynans to luncheon at the Plaza the next day. Tynan was very funny about the rival "literary molls" in London: Barbara Skelton and somebody else. One would say to the other, "*I* had Peter Quen-

Elena says, he looks like a musical note: his lips and face deviate to Vivien.

wanted us invited. He began by saying to me: "I read your lines"... I did not understand this at first, & he explained "Bawu cтроки" making lines in the air with his finger. I tried to tell him how much his music had meant to me — difficult in conversation: I said that it had been done "an inspiration" when that I really meant was that, beside my enjoying it so much, it had helped to keep up my artistic morale. "C'est réciproque, c'est réciproque," he said. He was jolly, amusing, even bubbling — quite frank & accessible. I thought, as one finds with Diliska that each meeting may be. I had not quite realized what a little wisp of a man he was — in France they used to call him "the insect." Even I wanted to bend to bend over him, & I felt that his tiny stature, his in themselves uninpressive features, made her in certain ways her unto him shy, at the mercy of the world around him — I remembered Petrushka & Histoire du Soldat. But his opinions in conversation, like his music, are fearless & firm. Isaiah Berlin & some other friends had persuaded him to read Doktor Zhivago, which he had got through between me & herself, but he had not liked it at all: he thought it a laccurtrate word (comparing it, I imagine, with Turgeney, Tolstoy, etc.) — it was simply a collection of fragments of no real or lasting value — he had not even liked the poems, had never read any of Pasternak's poetry written before these. He added — what seemed rather surprising — the rest

nell when you were 2 years old."* "You've never had a
dramatist, though."—"Yes: Graham Greene writes plays!"
Also, about the Reader's Subscription Book Club TV feature, with Lionel Trilling, Jacques Barzun and Auden, of
which I heard, also, other accounts. Wystan had been
"sloshed," was holding what was ostensibly a cup of tea,
but actually pure gin, which he would from time to time
send out for replenishment. In the middle of what was
supposed to be a discussion of Robert Frost, he said,
"How old are you, Lionel?"—"52."—"How old are you,
Jacques?"—"51." (Not sure that I have these ages
right.)—"Well, I'm two years up on one of you and three
years up on the other." —While the camera was fixed on
an interchange between Barzun and Trilling, "a slithering
crash" was heard, and you knew that Wystan had slipped
off his chair; but presently the camera was turned on him,
and you saw him sitting there smiling and holding his cup
in his hand. Edith Oliver told me that it had made her so
nervous she couldn't watch it. Wystan, though somewhat
piped, was trying to say what he thought, while the other
two were sparring for the public.

Night of Jan. 16–17 (early morning). I had another dream
about running away with Mary Meigs. There seemed to
be nothing to prevent it, and she was taking everything
coolly, almost as a matter of course. It was one of my
railroad dreams but less troubled by anxiety than usual. I
had my briefcase on the station platform and was looking
for something in it, making sure that I had it. I realized,
on awaking, that it was the gimmick that makes the cards
rise, which, along with the diamond-point pencil, I like to

* Peter Quennell (1905–   ) was the biographer of Byron. In *The Fifties*
EW relates that once when Quennell kept Barbara Skelton waiting in
the street, "she had rapped him on the head with the heel of her shoe
and made him completely groggy."

have with me wherever I am living. But then Mary came
to meet me, and I started to go to the train, leaving the
briefcase on the bench. Then I remembered and went back
to get it. We were not, however, crowded for time. We
had to make a connection, but it would be hours before
we had to get the other train and only several blocks to
walk from the station. I had no idea where we were
going—simply somewhere a little farther on. Everything
seemed quite natural with Mary, complete absence of
strain.

Norman Podhoretz: I was telling him about Pasternak's
postscript to the letter of the writers to Stalin on the occasion of the death of his wife. Podhoretz interjected: "He
said, אתה האיש. * I then told him about the man who had
written me that the scene between Nathan and David,
when the former told the story of the ewe lamb, was not
a denunciatory one—"Thou art the man!," pointing the
finger—but something much quieter: Nathan simply
touched the King's sleeve and said, "The story is about
you." "Why, that's anti-Semitic!" cried Podhoretz. I afterwards wondered why. It was suggested to me by Doc
Lowell that this way of saying it was equivalent to "You
pulled off something there," but Irving Howe thought that
it simply made Nathan appear more insidious and sly. In
any case, it would have deprived him of his accusatory
prophetic role.

Esther [Kimball] came to see us in Cambridge with *Bob
Hartshorne* and his wife and children—a baby who had to
be put away upstairs. I thought that she had become more

---

* The Russian poet and novelist had refused to sign a fawning public
letter by his colleagues, adding a postscript that he had been thinking,
as an artist, of Stalin and was shaken by Alliluyeva's suicide. Podhoretz
assumed that he was blaming Stalin for her death ("Thou art the
man!"). In Pasternak's statement Wilson saw the empathetic wisdom
that, with his courage, enabled him to survive the dictator's reign.

agreeable and comfortable—we talked about our trip abroad and her grandmother's house at Seabright. She had only come to Talcottville once. She told me that when somebody had once brought Aunt Lin [Rosalind Baker] a fourleaf clover, she had said, rather inappropriately, "Its fragrance permeates my whole being!"

<Talcottville: a *pied à terre* in stability.>*

Cambridge Parties

Feb. 27. Auden read in Sanders Theater under the auspices of the *Advocate*. He was evidently a little tight but articulated perfectly distinctly and now puts on a much better performance than he used to. But he had brought the whole galleys of his forthcoming book [*Homage to Clio*] and did not seem to have picked out beforehand the poems that he wanted to read. The proofs would slip out of his grasp and fall on the floor as he fumbled with them, and then he would have to plunge down after them. It was a little like one of those comic paperhanger acts. At one point, when there seemed to be an intermission, we came down from the top tier in order to get better seats and found that in the meantime he had started again and was sitting at the table with his hat on. This also gave a comic effect, and I thought he had put it on in order to indicate a change of mood—something informal, a little droll. But he explained to us, when he came to lunch here next day, that the poem had two alternating elements, one of which he printed in italics, and that for the passages that were italicized he put on his hat and took it off for the non-italicized

* Materials reworked in *Upstate* are set off in < >.

passages. We had missed this explanation as we came downstairs.

Deafening party for him afterwards at the *Advocate* office, deafening cocktail party for the Tates at the Lowells', deafening dinner at the Cunliffes' the night before. These noisy occasions wear me out, and there are likely to be people with whom you would enjoy talking if you only did not have to shout and to ask people to repeat what they have said. Something ought to be done about this: things do not get so loud in England unless at a very large party where there are too many people for the size of the room. Elena says that at a dinner like the Cunliffes', the hostess at a given point ought to ask everybody to drop his voice. I used to think that this uproar was entirely caused by too many people in a room till I found at the Chavchavadzes' one summer they made just as much noise clustering around the back terrace with the whole lawn around them available. Wystan says that there is always a point at which the addition of one or two more persons makes a normal conversation become deafening. Mary [Meigs] and Barbara [Deming] came with us to the Lowells' and the *Advocate* party and were evidently quite overwhelmed.

A cocktail party at the blind Indian's at Eliot House was so deafening that it almost crushed us both; the next day we were invited to another at the Gilmores'; but in the afternoon he [Ved Mehta] came to my study in Widener and suggested that we might like to skip the cocktail party proper and come about 7 for supper with a few other people to meet George Kennan. Though we arrived at the tail end, when most of the guests had gone, those that were left were still shouting. We have decided to avoid these cocktail parties. —At the Walkers', on my visit to New Haven, there were only eight people to dinner, but the

conversation seemed almost as loud as it had at the Cunliffes' dinner—this, of course, was partly due to the Walkers themselves. —Ed O'Connor suggests that the shouting
is competitive; I believe that people want to assert themselves without listening to the other person. Are they trying
to forget the Bomb? to rival the Bomb?

I should have noted above, in connection with the Cunliffes' dinner party, Elena's conversation with Kenneth
Murdock. He rather astonished and horrified her by saying
that in order to teach young people properly what good
literature was, you ought to begin by having them read
bad. A characteristic New England idea: you must first
impress people with Sin before they can aspire to virtue.

Two parties for the visiting Russian writers: Leonid Leonov
and two other writers of about his age: a popular poet with
whom neither Elena nor I talked—tall and thin with white
hair, shedding a smug Russian *poshlost'* [mediocrity]—
whom I sized up as a well-established Soviet hack, and a
man from Kazakhstan (if that is right), who Elena said
was interesting; the fourth was a young Ukrainian, likable
and, I think, innocent, who held some sort of official position. The first affair was at Ted Weeks's; the second,
the next afternoon, at the Schlesingers'. When the delegation was introduced, they were accompanied by several
interpreters and a blond and blank-faced young man, who
stepped forward and said simply, "State Department." One
of the interpreters had been brought with them from the
Soviet Union, an old Russian-Jewish witch. She had been
fastened on Arthur Schlesinger on his visit to Russia, and
he found in making a journey that he was supposed to
share an apartment with her at night; when it came time
to go to bed and he realized the situation, he registered
sufficient surprise so that she sought accommodations elsewhere. She became a nuisance in my conversations with

Gonchar, the young Ukrainian, kept getting between us and urging me to speak English when I could express myself more directly and forcibly in bad Russian. I finally asked him whether it wasn't possible for him to meet people here "without interpreters and without State Department *chinovniki* [petty bureaucrats]." He said that without an interpreter it would be difficult for him to communicate with people. I told him that when I had been in Russia in 1935, it had been impossible for me to buy the volumes I needed of the Marx-Engels *Gesammtausgabe*, that I had finally had to get them in New York—he said it had been merely accidental. I went on to say that it was surprising that people should think in Russia that Marx couldn't be read over here, that I had found that the volumes of Marx and Engels had been among those that had been most read in the New York Public Library. Evidently this embarrassed him, and he turned away to put out his cigarette. I felt that I was a little engaged in the same kind of wagging and baiting that I objected to on the part of others. I finally got to the point of saying that the Soviet Union was not a real Communist society nor the U.S. a real capitalist society: they were both just countries run by the army, the engineers and the *chinovniki*. This ended the conversation. The Russians evaporated. A little later the young government man came up to me—I didn't know that he had overheard the conversation—and said, "I am the State Department *chinovnik*."

Arthur Schlesinger began with Leonov in his relentlessly publicity-minded way by asking what had surprised him most in America. Leonov replied that it had been like his experience in flying over the Himalayas. To another question he answered: "If you and I had spent an evening together and had been talking for four hours, I might answer that question at the end of the evening." Arthur had met him in Moscow and had asked him whether he

really felt that writers needed guidance from the government, we didn't have it over here, etc. Leonov now took
this up and said, "If [you] had had your wife with you in
Moscow, and I had asked you whether you had seen any
women in Russia that you thought were particularly attractive, what kind of an answer could I have expected?"
It seemed that Surkov had been present, the former head
of the Writers' Union, who had made all the row about
Pasternak and who hated every writer of talent. I inquired
about the Alymovs. He told me that Sergei was dead—
which I knew—and that Maria Fedorovna had married a
critic—"I don't meet them." I told him that Elena admired
Vor [*The Thief*] and asked if it was included in his collected
works. He said there was a new collected works, in which
Vor was included. I also understood him to say that it had
been published separately and had sold very well. He was
evidently proud of this. But I have since been told by
Roman Grynberg that it now appears in a revised text.

With Elena at our second session, they had a long, she
says, relaxed conversation, with no interpreter present. It
came out that Pyotr Struve was her cousin, and he said
that Struve was a remarkable man. She told him about
her cousin Kyril, the priest, who had made a trip to
Russia, and he said that to understand Russia, you
ought to read Monomakh.* They talked about their
grandchildren, and Leonov said that the most important
things were probably one's personal relations. He had
been married to his wife for many years. He said he
had survived all those terrible years—"*Ya ochen'
khitry* [I am very clever]," he added. When they shook
hands goodbye, he said "*Bog s vami* [God be with you]."
This surprised me, but I was afterwards told that Khru-

* Vladimir Vsewolodovich Monomakh (1053–1125) was a prince whose
crown became part of the coronation ceremony of the Russian tsars;
his name evokes the aristocracy.

shchev had said this to everybody. Elena Levin [had] asked them if they had read Nabokov. Leonov said, "*Nyet—khorosho?* [No—is that okay?]." The young Ukrainian said that he hadn't known he had written in Russian.

Both parties were very well handled: not too many people, and most of them could speak Russian. These four Russian writers were a cultural exchange for the four that had gone to Russia when Arthur Schlesinger went—the others were Alfred Kazin, Paddy Chayefsky and Ted Weeks. Ted Weeks had wanted to ingratiate himself and taken a non-official line—he had much surprised Arthur by announcing to the Russians that he was "the Red Brahmin of Beacon Hill."

The mud, the nude monotony of March.

I now have in my bedroom four framed prints of the little Audubon animals, and they have made it a good deal more cheerful. I suppose it is a return of my delight in my childhood in rabbits and guinea pigs. Looking out the window from my bed one morning, I saw that the gray bristling trees in the gray air outside were exactly balanced by the winter woods in the background of the meadow mouse print on the bureau.

New Haven, Yaddo, and the Iroquois

Trip to New Haven to get the rest of the De Forest volumes, March 24–26. Stayed with Walkers: Charley is a good deal better, has been working on the technological effects on the personnel of Raytheon electronics plants; Adelaide more frantic than ever, rushing around doing all kinds of things at once and talking at the top of her voice. I complain about Elena's mumbling but, much as I like Adelaide, I would rather live with it than with Adelaide's shouting. The Haights and the Troxells to dinner, and an attractive Beatrice Schabert, half-German and half-American, who turned out to have known Elena and her family from childhood. The gossip of New Haven amuses me. Gilbert Troxell told me of his eventual and consummate revenge on Alfred Bellinger, who, at the time they were undergraduates, had tried to keep him out of the Elizabethan Club. Gilbert is now a big shot there, and Alfred has been recently on the board of governors, or whatever it is called. He attempted, according to Gilbert, to do several highhanded things which Gilbert was able to point out to him would violate the constitution—a kind of consideration that Alfred could not dismiss. After dinner Norman Pearson and his wife. Pearson is a hunchback and cripple but a bright little man, very much on his toes. He cannot, I gather, be interested in doing anything about Phelps Putnam's poems and papers. It would take too long to go through the manuscripts; would a book of the poems alone be well enough received to make it worthwhile, etc. I think that his own fragility, his difficulty in getting around must have made him abnormally cautious. I didn't think of the obvious rejoinder that if so much could be done about De Forest—of whom someone there is doing a biography— why couldn't they afford to do Phelps?

I had a dream there that I was forcing myself to do morning sitting-up exercises in order to reduce my abdomen, then woke up to find that all the effort was only a dream. I think I must have been disturbed by the idea that Charley, in spite of his ailments, had managed to keep his figure.

I said to Adelaide that I had the illusion that everybody else was getting older whereas I was more or less the same age, and she told me that she had been in the Yale Club and sat just across the room from a woman who seemed

familiar without Adelaide's being able to place her. She
had gray hair and was playing "the New York grande
dame." She said to the man with her, "And when the
doctor came in, he said, '*Il y en a deux.*' " It took Adelaide
half an hour to realize it was Margaret Bishop. She left
without speaking to her because she couldn't remember
her present married name and had sat there so long without
recognizing her. She knew that Margaret had had an illness
and thought her face had been changed somewhat by a
stroke. How she aged, Adelaide had thought as [she] left;
then realized that she herself had not been recognized by
Margaret.

Yale today after Cambridge—though in my youth it
seemed so dynamic from Princeton—seems positively provincial, bucolic.

*Brief trip Rosalind and I took in April to Yaddo, Utica and
Talcottville:* Only three inmates at *Yaddo*, the off season:
Dawn Powell, Pati Hill and another girl who was writing
a novel but hadn't published anything yet. We brought
them a bottle of Old Grand-dad. The "mansion" is closed
at this time of the year, and the place, with its big gates
and dark trees, seemed like something between a girls'
school and a mental sanitarium like McLean's. When we
had entered and were following the curves of the drive,
Rosalind said, "I wonder whether they'll let us out again."
Dawn said, in the course of the conversation, "I *don't* think
I'm any crazier than you people." When we were leaving,
Rosalind said, "My doctor doesn't want me to go out yet."
—I asked them all about *dreams of flying.* Rosalind said
she had never had any; but the other three all had. Pati
Hill is supported by something that she says is like wa-
terwings. She feels that she is able to do it, or ought to be
able to do it without support, but never has quite enough
self-confidence. Dawn goes along just above the ground,

restrains herself from bounding too high because she doesn't want to attract attention; the Green girl from Cincinnati plunges down a flight of stairs and at the bottom there appears a gigantic man's face.

Dawn said that *John Lardner*, who just died, told her that his father had Indian blood (he certainly looked it, and his deadpan humor was very much in the Indian manner). She also had Indian blood—of which her sisters were ashamed but which she amused herself by talking about. Lardner would say, "Oh, you Ohio Indians are just poor red trash."

My trip to Onondaga for the Peter Doctor Banquet (*April 23*): Olive Fenton drove me. The dinner took place in the Good Shepherd Mission, and was attended by Christianized Indians—"salad-eating" Indians as distinguished from "corn-soup-eating Indians." Olive said there ought to be a substantive for them, They Eat Salad, on the analogy of Mohawk, They Eat Men, and Adirondack, They Eat Bark. I had not seen much of these Christians before. The only people present I knew were the Crouses and Cornelius Seneca.* Everybody spoke English, though the man who presided was not completely fluent. There were prayers, and a speech by a pastor who told them that nothing they did was worthwhile unless they had Christ in it. Citations and replicas of the organization's charter to all the original founders. If they were dead or couldn't come, others came forward to receive and acknowledge. Musical selections: a woman who sang, a barbershop quartet—one of whom, after a sentimental song was followed by a comic song, remarked, "From the sublime to the ridiculous"—a very

---

* The Onondaga reservation, near Syracuse, was the capital of the Six Nations where EW had attended the council in 1957. The Crouses were a local Indian family; Cornelius Seneca had been president of the Seneca Republic.

old lady who advanced to the piano and played a very brief selection, a mother and daughter with guitars who sang hillbilly songs. After all this, a few speeches, treasurer's report, etc. All well-dressed in completely non-Indian clothes; one man whose mother, I was told, was Indian but looked entirely white—like any successful young Syracuse businessman. So far as I could see, no chiefs; Cattaraugus and Allegheny of course have none. When I said to Mrs. Crouse that I hoped she didn't mind my having described her family in my book, she answered, "Not at all"; and when I was going, she said that she hoped I would come to their house again. I realized that Olive Fenton had come partly to see her. They had gone to school together and were now clan sisters. Though she was formal in talking to me, Olive said that she was immensely funny in telling about and mimicking her neighbors. Olive wished she could see her more often—she has evidently few friends in Albany: Myrtle would not only amuse her but help her out with her housekeeping. Maxine, in the short time since I had seen her, was already becoming quite bulky in the manner of Seneca women. She not only taught school in Kennedy but also advised Indians in the high schools—it was hard for them to make up their minds what they wanted to do.

After the deafening cocktail parties of Cambridge, this occasion was very pleasantly quiet and decorous. If it had been a church supper in western New York, I am sure that there would have been shrieking cackling women and loudly guffawing men, but though they lingered to talk after dinner, nobody raised his voice. During the program, the applause was moderate and the laughter never extravagant. The Indians are more likely to smile than laugh.

After dinner a Tuscarora woman introduced herself to me. Her skin was nearly white but she otherwise ran true to Tuscarora type, round-faced and broad-bodied. She was the widow of one of the founders, who had only just died, and had had tears in her eyes when she acknowledged the tribute to her husband. She explained that she was one of the people dispossessed by the power project reservoir and showed me a photograph of the transmission lines running above her house. She was going to move back into the reservation instead of going outside. She said that one of the families had been given a day and half to move.

The object of the association is to raise money for Indian education. They have only about $3,000. There were favors in the shape of black academic caps, filled with little candies.

I have sometimes lately had the impression that my appearance and personality have almost entirely disappeared, and that there is little but my books marching through me: the Indian book, the Civil War. They live, I am ceasing to live. —But this is partly due to too much drinking, reading and thinking at night, then plunging into work at the library. At Wellfleet I found that Paul Chavchavadze lays off drink twice a year for ten days or two weeks. He thus loses, he says, about 7 pounds and reduces that bloated look. Inspired by this noble example, I have adopted the same course—beginning on my 65th birthday—and feel much the better for it. My contacts with life have become more normal, and I find that I will have to make a new hole in my belt.

NEW YORK AND UPSTATE,
1961–1962

Retrospect from Talcottville

Talcottville, August 2, 1961. I have not written in this book since the early spring of 1960. The last entries were made in Cambridge. I wanted to record the birthday celebration in Cambridge for A. J. Muste. I was very much affected by it. I had never heard Muste speak in public before: he reaches a pitch of eloquence and intensity which explains his influence on his followers. Dr. McCrackin, the Middle Western minister, who went to Leavenworth for six months so as not to pay taxes for atomic weapons, also spoke. He was not what I expected but a hard-hitting resolute man. He said that nothing could be done to stop nuclear warfare till there were so many people protesting that the jails would no longer hold them. He said that the policy was, he had found, to make it tough for such protesters as himself.

1960 from the spring on was, on the whole, a very bad year for us. First, the crisis over Frances Swisher, about whom, thinking I had designs on her, Elena became perfectly hysterical. She said that Frances was rude to her when I was not there, but if this is true, it might not have happened if I hadn't been rather silly in talking so much about her. For my part, I had been very glad to have a young person working for me who was so quick and effective and eager. I left Wellfleet earlier than I had meant to in order to get Frances and myself away. —Elena afterwards had a kind of collapse and refused to come to T'ville at all. This estranged Rosalind, who was worried by Elena's condition and would not come to T'ville or Wellfleet either. It is more than a year since we have seen her.

<Summer in T'ville (1960) was uncomfortable and very strained. Barbara and Mary came to see me just when there was an income tax crisis. Most of my other guests arrived in August: Bill Fenton (I think then), Stephen Spender, Sam Behrman, [Thoby-]Marcelin. Without Elena to entertain them, I found this rather a trial. I saw, I think, Spender at his best; he likes to be encouraged and reassured. He inscribed one of his poems on the hall window at the top of the stairs and wrote one especially for me, which I have put in a front window of the big downstairs room. We had a pleasant picnic at Independence River, with sandwiches and a bottle of wine: closed gentians and cardinal flowers, little boys diving and swimming, with a dog that was worried and barked when he had difficulty in following them across the stones and the water. Stephen thought it very Huckleberry Finn.> Sam Behrman carried even up here his exaggerated luxury tastes. When I came down to breakfast, I found that he had actually called a taxi and he went over to the Parquet, leaving me to breakfast alone when Mrs. Hutchins arrived. It was the nearest thing he could find to the Ritz. He was evidently afraid that the food here would not be up to standard, thought I might be going to cook it myself. Striking contrast with Stephen, who arrived with a few things in a rucksack. I gave Sam my Hebrew routine, by which

he is always impressed, and played the Nichols and May record, which delighted him—he did not know about them. He was also much impressed and delighted by Malcolm Sharp, who gave him the Rosenberg case. By the time the Marcelins arrived, I was not able to do them justice and even forgot to show Phito his verses on the third-floor window.

<*Beverly* [Yelton] had been married on the 25th of June, just before I arrived. She still went on working at the Park Market.> She brought her husband around to see me. He was very shy, and she treated him like a child, petting him and prodding him not to be so tongue-tied.

<The winter of 1960–61 was overshadowed by worry about the income tax. I came on to Utica sometime in November and was fined $7,500 by Judge Brennan, about whom I had written in *Apologies to the Iroquois*—he evidently, however, behaved honorably. He knocked off the same day several similar cases. I borrowed the money from Roman Grynberg and Barbara Deming, then paid it back by selling my papers to Yale.> I had to see three different library buyers, going up to Wellfleet from Cambridge for the last two. I could have had $75,000 by selling to the University of Texas, but I didn't like Lew Feldman, who was buying for them, and didn't want my stuff so far off. I finally sold to Yale, where I knew that the people were decent and where I could always stop off to look anything up. I ended by pretty well clearing out the correspondence and old magazines in my attic—am rather relieved to have them in safe hands. They have sorted out the letters and filed them. <—I was gouty and began to realize that I had something wrong with my heart, went to Niles on the Cape and he told me that I had a touch of angina,> gave me pills which proved to be helpful and said that I ought to lose weight. Elena worried much about Olili, who is apparently dying of cancer. Dorothy Paget when she died

left no will, so her sister got everything and Olili got nothing. She lived alone in lodgings in some English town till Brat [Mumm] had her come to Johannisberg. Elena began to bleed during Xmas vacation and had a curettage after Xmas. They said then that there was nothing wrong with her but her gynecologist in Boston afterwards found a small cyst. I think that her anxiety about this was partly a self-identification with Olili. —Since I no longer had a job at Harvard, we saw far fewer people than the year before: mostly the Hugheses, the Levins and the Engels across the street. The new Loeb Theater on the corner of the street provided some pleasant diversion. Philippe Radley and Frances Swisher were married—they had met in my seminar. I suffered during both of these last winters in Cambridge from a nose and throat infection like hay fever— especially at night and in the morning in bed. I often could not taste my breakfast. At last I went to Dr. Lurie in Boston. He asked me what I had been writing. When I told him about my Civil War book, he asked if I had been reading old books. I had: old yellowed works that were falling apart and volumes of bound periodicals that gave out clouds of dust. It seems that there is a dust allergy; that one of the librarians at Lamont had to resign on account of it, and Bill Fenton told me that his secretary, who does some of his research for him, has to put on a gauze mask to go into the stacks.

Just before waking Feb. 14, 1961. Morning April persisted after the war in countries where it had not been produced. The manufacture of bras followed suit. History was sound, if uncertain, and presently expelled the rest.*

---

* EW had just sent to Morton Zabel a Christmas card containing "Joycean" attempts "to write down when awake the prose that I compose in my dreams."

T'ville fragments, '60–'61

This cold and lonely countryside of May,
So blank at first before I fill it in—
A comfort and a challenge—
The beauty of the skies and far blue mountains
Abandoned by my race

—And those old ragged dying elms

—And burned an orange moon through the great elm trees.

> That pale and lovely maid,
> Who then went glimmering down the glade
> (This was noted at the Princeton Club—I can't
> imagine what inspired it.)

—I burned my boats before I came, so now where am I please?

—The flood of golden morning light,
  The low-mountain air

<*Zoölogist who was studying the small mammals of Tug Hill in the summer of 1960:* An enthusiastic and able young man, excited at having found water shrews with fringed hind feet, the only animal known which can skate on the surface of the water like water bugs. He had had one that had been maimed but not killed by the trap and which was able to "skitter around" on the surface of a pan of water. Not much has been known about them, but they exist on Tug Hill in abundance. He had a laboratory in a little old schoolhouse that had been turned into a camp, and an assistant who, though he knew his business in dissecting the animals, was so illiterate that I didn't recognize the word *placenta* when he used it. The little pelts were all mounted, and some of the little organs preserved in jars. He explained to me the various species of mice, the shrews and the flying squirrel. It made rather a pathetic impres-

sion: among the fresh specimens, one of the females was pregnant, and the pale tiny penises of the males stuck out. From there, we went to visit the traps. I had never been in that wild part of Tug Hill before: unfamiliar birds, animals, flowers; yellow-beaked cuckoos and a huge blue crane (heron?); cardinal flower and closed gentian along a stream; (bright reddish pink flower in a marsh that I had never seen before and now can't identify in the flower book) and pitcher plant with its rosette: like red flowers and red-veined green pitchers. These last in a sphagnum swamp where they gave an uncomfortable impression of being animal-like and voracious. As one walked on the sphagnum it gave like a hammock. The small-mammals man did his trapping with mousetraps and rat traps mostly not far from the road. Beyond is a forest, and a wilderness, in which there are wildcats and bears and in which it is easy to get lost. Many water shrews and mice in the traps. It gave one satisfaction to go into the woods with someone who could tell you about not only every animal but every bird, every tree, every plant. He knew what each of his little animals ate and where it would be likely to live. I had mixed feelings and admiration for the techniques of zoö-logical science and of sympathy with the poor little beasts. They have sometimes, however, little mercy on one an-other: a shrew, it seems, will eat its own kind if he finds it caught in a trap. On the way back, he confessed he felt badly about killing the little creatures. He took me to his house for a drink. He and his little wife and their children seemed rather like little mammals themselves.

Albert Grubel: House in Boonville—woman shot her hus-band last fall—he had bet on the World Series and lost—came home and got rough with his wife, kicked her in stomach when she was pregnant—threatened to shoot children—she shot him with a double-barrelled shotgun while he laid right in bed—she appeared in court at Utica, was let out on bail and had her child. (There have, I think, been two other cases lately of women who shot their husbands and went scot-free.)

Boy who got lost—some people think something kind of funny about it—wasn't quite right, family did something to him—they drained the lakes.

This year, '61, Albert was much gratified by the highest 4th of July death rate yet.

He is getting rather feeble but still drives me to Boonville.

I spent all last winter in Cambridge finishing the Civil War book, did not even write in this journal. I got bored with dealing with political and literary history, bored with the limitations of the resources of my own vocabulary in dealing with this sort of thing, at which I don't think I am really at my best. It is a relief to get back to this journal. >

Mike Nichols and Elaine May

Nichols and May. The summer before last, I think it was, Rosalind brought me their first record when she came to Talcottville. I was delighted with it and would play it for guests. I found that even when they didn't, as some don't, like the John Betjeman record, they enjoyed the Nichols and May. The effect of this on people is to make them sound immediately afterwards as if they were having N. and M. conversations—as in the case of Mary Meigs and me last summer. Then I got their second record and made a point of going to see them when I was in New York. I saw their show four times. Even after I had ceased to laugh very much, I was fascinated by their ability to take the stage and hold it and to create a dramatic tension in every

one of their sketches. The "Pirandello" playlet is not really
Pirandello, but something that Nichols has invented himself. He strikes me as being something of a writer. He has
read a good deal and enjoys the virtuosity of the improvisation act at the end, in which he gets first and last lines
from the audience and an author in whose manner the act
must be done. They have had at various times to take on
Plato, Aristotle, Beowulf and Chaucer. He is now expecting someone to ask them to do the new English Bible
and has been boning up on this. He swears that it has a
rendering: "If your eye gives you trouble, take it out and
throw it away." He likes to play a game of making people
guess the first and last lines of books and plays. Elaine is
perhaps something of a genius. She transforms herself so
completely in her various roles that until I saw her off the
stage I had no real idea how she looked. She is extremely
handsome, with powerful black eyes—probably passionate
and strongwilled. Rosalind told me that they quarrelled
terribly when they were together. Yet in certain ways she
defers to him. Twice when, after a performance, she came
into his dressing room, she apologized for mistakes she had
made. She is emotional, imaginative, rather somber. Her
somber and bitter Jewish side gives pathos or edge to her
sketches. Teenagers, PTA and the father going to prison
on the record have moments when they are almost heartbreaking. Their relationship is very curious. Their understanding is, as Elena says, almost telepathic; but they
are evidently trying to keep their relations on a more or
less professional basis. When I was in N.Y. alone and met
them, after the show, at the Plaza, Michael and his new
girl were there before Elaine arrived. The new girl is
Joanna Brown, a niece of my old friend the painter Katy
Schmidt, who has been married to Harold Brodkey, a writer
of short stories in *The New Yorker*. She is very goodlooking,

Nichols and May in their cabaret act: a program found in Wilson's journal

but it is perhaps not a good sign that she gets herself up like Elaine.

Elaine then arrived, looking beautiful in a plain black dress with shoulder straps, and from the moment of her appearance all attention was concentrated on her. I had to make an effort at one point to transfer my attention to Joanna. Elaine told about an incident that had happened that afternoon when she went to the Bronx. In some very public place, she had seen a woman lying in the street moaning, with a small child standing beside her. Nobody was paying any attention to her—she had evidently been knocked down. Elaine tried to find out what was the matter with her, made her wiggle her fingers and toes. "It's easy," she said, "to take command in a situation like that. Nobody knows what to do, and I didn't really know myself." But she got the police and an ambulance, and the woman was taken to I forgot what hospital—"where they'll probably kill her," said Elaine, "the way they did with me when I was there with my arm." They have no stage personality off the stage, nothing that I could see of the actors' vanity. One can see from her way of talking off the stage that she grew up in a Yiddish-speaking household; but this rarely comes out in her performances—perhaps most in the Pirandello playlet when the parents are quarrelling.

When the Oak Room closed, we went to Michael's apartment, where he played the Peter Sellers records and gave me one. I had talked to them about Ruth Draper, whom neither had ever seen, and since I had seen them last he had given her the Italian Lesson record, and she now gave her very positive opinion that it was excellent, and that in "Three Generations in the Juvenile Court" (on the other side) the Jewish accents were all right but that the drama was essentially "phoney." When we first came into the apartment, Elaine went into the bedroom with Joanna, and Michael, evidently dismayed and impatient, said, "Oh,

Elaine, go on in there, too!" When they came out, he
rebuked her, telling her she had no business to go in Joanna's room—to which she made no reply. She was evidently
so much in the habit of making herself at home wherever
he lived that she did not think of being tactful. In the taxi,
Joanna—I think it was—had said that someone had said
that Elaine and she might be twins, which made me a
little nervous, and in general it seemed to me that this
situation was all a little precarious. Michael, when Elaine
was there, was afraid that Joanna would say something
banal, something that sounded like Nichols and May conversation, and once rather rudely squelched her. I took
Elaine home in a taxi and on the way told her how much
I admired them. She said, "We've read some of your
books." It is a good thing I am too old to fall in love with
her. I've always been such easy game for beautiful, gifted
women and she is the most so I've seen since Mary
McCarthy in the thirties. I imagine that she, too, would
be rough going.

The next time I came to New York, Elena and I went
out to Stamford in the afternoon to see Michael and
Joanna—for lunch and also stayed to supper. She had her
little girl by Brodkey. House that he had rented for the
summer had a partly sloping wood ceiling. This reminded
me of Trees, where I used to do the trick of nailing a card
to the roof. Elaine presently entered with *her* little girl.
She was wearing old slacks and perhaps tennis shoes; she
looked sallow and her hair seemed rather stringy. It didn't
occur to me at the time that—as Elena afterwards suggested—she had got herself up like this on purpose in order
not to eclipse Joanna. It was the first time she had been
to see them there, and she was this time discreet and quiet.
She had her older girl with her—Elena thought she had
a good relation with her—and her boyfriend, a Jewish
writer of lyrics for musical shows. I talked with Joanna

about Katy Schmidt and her present husband, Irving Shubert, and the Spencers and all that circle of painters. I sat next to Elaine and since the first and last line game had been revived I reminded her that she had never told us what novel "Hurrah for Karamazov!"—with which Michael had teased her the last time I had seen them before (she is supposed to be a great admirer of Dostoevsky)—was the last line of. She said, "Let me see—*The Last Hurrah.*"

After lunch, I talked to Michael separately and was rather surprised when he showed that he worried about being Jewish. In the New York literary and theatrical world this would seem to be unnecessary; but since his father had gone to Germany from Russia, and then come here to escape the Nazis, there was, I suppose, some justification. He said that I might have noticed that they occasionally inserted a Jewish joke. Elaine had done this when she was in difficulties with the Chaucer improvisation—in order to help herself out by raising a laugh with the Jews in the audience who would understand a Yiddish word she used in her character of a Chaucerian nun who had said she was a Jewish girl and could not marry a Chinaman. It may be, too, that the fiction of being not only Christian but a nun had made her a little self-conscious. I told Michael that 80% of the audience did not know or care whether they were Jewish or not. If the matter comes up again, I shall tell him that Jewish jokes are irrelevant to work of the quality they are doing: after all, they are not Jewish comedians. I also had a little talk with her—by that time a number of other people were there—she had said that she was going to send her 11-year-old daughter to summer camp and spend the summer writing a play, and I asked her if she would have dinner with me sometime in the summer when I came to New York. She replied that she would be glad to. They are serious-minded young people and ambitious in a curious way. She was complaining, when I saw them at the Plaza, that her daughter, at the Walden School, was not learning any "facts." Michael said that he had hated all his schools but had hated Walden the most. He has conscientious scruples about what they are doing—says that "irreverence now has a commercial value." When I said, after one performance, that their audiences seemed to have got to the point at which their responses seemed automatic, that they would detonate at what they thought were gags, as with Shaw or Gilbert and Sullivan, he answered, "It's rather frightening—we feel as if *they* are directing us." With extreme sensitivity he combines what Elena calls "a vicious streak." He behaves rather badly with Joanna when Elaine is around, calling her "an idiot," etc.

Before I went to New York in July, I called up Michael to get Elaine's telephone number. I asked him how they were getting along with the play that they were rumored to be writing together. He said that he had not done anything about it. I explained that I wanted to try to see her in New York. "Well, she's right there," he said. "Say hello to her when you call her—I haven't talked to her for a week." I wondered what this meant, but found out when I tried to call her. I was brushed off by the colored maid, who said that Miss May was not there but she would take a message for her. I gathered from the *New Yorker* profile that she would sometimes hold off Michael for days.

He is evidently still in love with her, but her boyfriend, who seems gentle and unpretentious, is no doubt the kind of man most comfortable for her. Michael told me that he had recently met Dorothy Parker and had been overwhelmed, didn't know how to cope with her. I said that she was a little like Elaine, and he said that that was what he had thought. Elaine had been so sharp—at Chicago he and she had been "the terrors of the campus, and that was

what had brought them together," but she was somewhat
less prickly now. As we were having this conversation, our
tone about Elaine was mounting; both were making as-
sertions about her and in the way that one does when some
magnetic and particularly interesting person is under discussion. In the midst of this, dramatically, Elaine entered.
I regretted not hearing him talk more about her, but was
just as glad, at my age, not to show too much interest
myself, as if it had been Edna Millay. I feel that the warmth
and tenderness that she sometimes puts on in her performances, though it is always ironically used, does represent
something in her nature. They are both being analyzed,
which rather depressed me when they told me—especially
in view of their very funny psychoanalytic skit—as it did
in the case of Stuart and Suzanne Hughes; but their relationship is so peculiar, both alienated and incredibly
close, that it must make their relationships with other
people precarious; this is perhaps not surprising.

In the middle of the afternoon, I got Elena to drive me
once to *Trees*. I had so much forgotten the locality that we
had to drive into Stamford and inquire the way from there.
I didn't even remember the name of the Westover Road.
We found the rather vulgar doctor, who bought it from
Harry de Silver, having a meal in the patio with his family
and friends. He had made a kind of lawn in front, with
none too attractive garden ornaments. I found that it meant
nothing to me—places in which I have lived never do
unless I still have some relation to them: Talcottville,
Charlottesville, Princeton.

"A Man of the Twenties"

One night when, after the performance, I went up to see Michael Nichols in his dressing room, I met *Don Stewart* on the stairs with his son who works at *The New Yorker*. Nichols had met him last summer in London and said that he was the only person there he had liked. I had not seen Don since the (middle, I think) twenties. He dropped in on me next day at the *New Yorker* office. It is curious and amusing to see how seriously he still takes himself: Skull and Bones and the romantic egoism of the twenties. He is writing his autobiography and talked about his early days in New York. The last time we had seen one another was at a party [1926] at Elinor Wylie's. I remembered it very well and better than I let him know, and was surprised at how well he remembered it. He was just back from Europe and was tight: he kept saying, "Scott is finished! Dos is finished! Ernest is finished!" I felt that the only person who was possibly finished was Don. I don't think I can have said this, but he told me that I had been "mean" to him, but that he thought he had been "obnoxious." We both apologized for the past. He reviewed the writing he had done at that time and seemed to think he might have been a great satirist if America had accepted satire. I mentioned Sinclair Lewis and Mencken.* He then told me of his Hollywood adventures. He was dropped as the result of his Communist involvement and told that he could only get back by "straightening out his record." This meant

* Mencken and Lewis were national figures when EW "set up shop" as a critic after World War I. Though never warming to Lewis's fiction, he appreciated its satire on American mores, and his own criticism profited by the wit and rollicking enthusiasm of Mencken, his absorption in the culture he reviled. Pleasant as it was to see Donald Ogden Stewart again, Stewart's pretensions still put Wilson off.

informing on his former associates, which he honorably refused to do. He wanted to leave the country but had great difficulty getting a passport and had to spend, I think, $9,000. His lawyer tried to get some official statement of what the charges were against him, but this was always left vague. He now lives in London with Ella Winters, his ex-Communist wife. (Mike Nichols says he likes her, but I never heard of anyone else who did.) Somebody else told me that he lives by working on English movie scripts. He had just been to his Yale reunion, and he and his old roommate Charley Walker had had a very good time together. Don was evidently pleased that their friendship had not been chilled by political considerations. I very much enjoyed seeing him: it always reassures me a little to talk to old friends of the twenties.

In Cambridge, I spent an evening at the Albert Guerards' with *Lillian Hellman* and a young man from Brown University [Jay Martin], who was doing a book on *Nathanael West*. Lillian and I gave the young man a good show talking to one another about him and the Perelmans. It seems to me a little strange that, good though West was, so much should be made of him now. She told me an amusing story about West. When he was running the Sutton Hotel and she was living there, she used to help him steam open the letters of the guests by means of a kettle which he kept in his rooms. He said that he was a novelist and that he had to find out about people.* The letters were, however, so dull that Lillian was unable to read them, and I believe that he eventually became discouraged. When some rela-

---

* West's 1933 novel, *Miss Lonelyhearts*, about a columnist for the lovelorn, reflected this practice. Wilson had admired the book and recommended the author to Maxwell Perkins at Scribners. "I liked him personally as well as admiring his work," he recalled in 1952.

tive sent them a check, he knew that he was going to get paid.

Oliver Austin and [his wife] Sliver revisited Wellfleet early this summer. We met them at Edie Shay's after dinner, by which time Oliver was very tight. He showed with great pride the color plates for the popular volume on birds that he had designed for Golden Books. Later I produced one by one such scraps of zoölogical information as I had recently acquired. He does not confine himself to ornithology, but knows about all the fields of zoölogy, and I always find him interesting on these subjects. I told about the young state zoölogist who was working on Tug Hill last summer and said that it was very curious that he should have been sent to Long Island from here in order to try to find out whether the recent encephalitis down there was caused by any of the small mammals at the same time that the federal government, in its department of bacteriological warfare, was preparing to give the enemy anthrax and a cattle disease. He said, "You're not supposed to know that!" I replied that I nonetheless did know it. "Anthrax," he said, "is the least of the things that they're going to be able to give them!" He knew about all this because he had been employed by the government to work on what he called a "very hush-hush" project to destroy the enemy's wheat crop by infecting it with wheat rust, which was to be conveyed on the wings of larks. Larks, it seems, by preference nest in wheat. I asked him whether he approved of this. He retorted, "You probably voted for Kennedy!" I said I had, and he added, "I voted for Nixon because I thought there ought to be one man in Florida who voted for the Republicans." I asked him again whether he really approved of what "biological warfare" was doing. He said, "Well, I don't want the Russians bothering us. I want to go to Lake

Baikal and study the birdlife there." I asked him what was to prevent his going: and he said that even if the Russians would let him, an expedition needed too much money.

1961. The Stone House now seems to me so completely mine that I think much less about the family. This, however, when I have no one with me and the Sharps are not here, has made me feel lonelier this summer. I have seen little of the Loomises to talk to about the family, so I quite enjoyed a dinner with Otis and Fern [Munn] in which we discussed family subjects. Otis has always been rather hurt that his grandmother's house was not left to him, and he spoke for the first time of his pain when he was young that his father and mother were outlawed by the rest of the family.

Last year, alone here all summer, I felt, when I had an erection, what a pity it was that so splendid a thing should not have a chance to enjoy itself. This summer I have fewer erections and do not have such vivid feelings about them. I think that I have aged in the last year, but I hope that this does not mean that an abrupt drop has taken place.

I find that I get more than for many years *le béguin* [a yen] for attractive women I know: Mary Meigs, Suzanne Hughes, Elaine May, Clelia Carroll, Mary Pcolar, but I am too sexually fond of Elena to try to start a new love affair; and I am also, I suppose, too old: I could not be attractive to younger women and should only make myself ridiculous.

<I sometimes feel nowadays as I did in the Soviet Union when I first got out of that hospital. I have to recite poetry or reread something I have written in order to assert my

identity against the income tax people and Robert Moses and all the rest of it.

Death of Hemingway. This upset me very much. Absurd and insufferable though he often was, he was one of the foundation stones of my generation, and to have him commit suicide is to have a prop knocked out. I have now been told that his mind had been going and that he had had shock treatments in Rochester; I hear reports that he was quite demoralized and could sometimes hardly talk intelligently. But at the time I was depressed by the notion that, after encouraging writers "to last and get their work done," he should have died in such a panicky and undignified way as by blowing his head off with a shotgun. The desperation in his stories had always been real: his most convincing characters are always just a few jumps ahead of death. It is a wonder that this was not more noticed. Instead, the press and the public mainly took their cue for their conception of him from his show of full-blooded vitality. He was vain enough to fall in with this and to play up to the popular press. This phoney public *persona* begins to get into his work in the interludes of *Death in the Afternoon*, and it became after this quite rampant—though mostly in magazine and newspaper articles which he afterwards did not reprint—and one gets the impression that the serious artist had actually to struggle against it. The thing about the two bullfighters, parts of which came out in *Life*, looked to me perfectly awful; it was the only thing of his that I felt I could not read. *Life* was exploiting him for all he was worth, and he was collaborating. There was a picture of H. on every page: H. towering over the bullfighters. H. dining with Spanish friends who adored him, even the bull seemed to have his face. Something he said about this work in an interview or a statement printed by the editors made me think that he realized its badness and did not want to have it published as a book in that form. In any case, it did not appear.*

It is a sign of Mary Pcolar's real sensibility that when I gave her two of Hemingway's books, she should have noted with special appreciation the moment in *Big Two-Hearted River* in which the boy, having just caught a magnificent trout, delays before cleaning and cooking to savor his high satisfaction.

As a character in one of Chekhov's plays says he's "a man of the eighties," so I find that I am a man of the twenties. I still expect something exciting: drinks, animated conversation, gaiety: an uninhibited exchange of ideas. Scott Fitzgerald's idea that somewhere things were "glimmering." I am managing to discipline myself now so that I shan't be silly in this way: diet and non-drinking, non-expectation of sprees. I believe that I am more or less succeeding in becoming a sedate old gentleman.

Aug. 17, '61. Helen and I went to the *Lowville Fair* with Mary Pcolar and her two little girls—a more enjoyable day at this fair than usual. Helen also very much enjoyed it. There was a better sideshow entertainment than usual—which included a magician and a sword-swallower, and an errant fake, a supposed baby with a dog face. The magician got Helen up on the platform and—somewhat to my surprise—she seemed to be enjoying her own performance. He had also a really pretty and young assistant. Later I met the magician on the fairground and told him that he

---

* EW was proud that his reviews of *In Our Time* and *The Sun Also Rises* had helped Hemingway to establish himself as an artist. Surveying his fiction to 1940, in *The Wound and the Bow* (1941) Wilson identified the work in which Hemingway's emotional insecurities and his ego subverted artistic control.

had done well with the coins and that I was an amateur magician myself. He said, "I can see you're a carnival man." I was carrying a hooked cane and wearing my old shapeless panama with one side of the brim torn. He showed me how he could palm a quarter on his wrist, catching it between two folds of skin, and said, I taught Indian Jim that. It was all very quiet and pleasant. Helen inspected the horses; the poultry exhibition, which I always enjoy, was more varied and interesting than ever: all kinds of fowls and pigeons, pheasant, even "bob whites"; guinea pigs and rabbits, Siamese kittens. Helen took the two little girls on the Ferris wheel and merry-go-round and bought them candied apples with nuts stuck in them, which turned out to be rather green. The Pcolar children are so well trained that they never ask for things or interrupt. The younger gray-eyed blonde—a little more assertive than her shy brunette sister—did, however, at one point say: "I don't feel like seeing that exhibition." Mary ran into her former art teacher, a young man named Burt Green, now studying at Syracuse; and she found that she and a co-worker had won second prize— $8—for the booth that they had arranged for their Home Demonstration Unit, of which Mary is president. This is an agency for improving the domestic arts which has been organized from Cornell. Mary's exhibit dealt with the problem of removing spots not by cleaning fluids but by starch and other household staples. The various kinds of stains were illustrated by a cake of wax, some artificial apples, a bowl of grass (she was tremendously proud of this), etc. The whole occasion was comfortable and local. >

John Betjeman has for years been telling people that he possesses *Henry James's underwear*, which he somehow acquired from Oxford. Actually, I was told by Billy James, it is not the novelist's underwear but that of his nephew Henry, Billy's brother, who had for some reason left it at Oxford. I asked Billy if he had explained this to Betjeman, and he said that he not been able to bring himself to do so, because it would so much disappoint Betjeman: a regular Henry James story. The next step is for me to wonder whether I should be mischievous enough to tell Betjeman. When I asked Mary Meigs if she thought I should, she said immediately and firmly, "Yes." I don't believe I shall, but after all I have told Angus Wilson when he was over here last winter, so it will doubtless get back to Betjeman.

<My trip to New York in summer of '61: I saw three old friends who seemed to me all to have a kind of nuclear age jitters: Thurber, Janet Flanner and Morton Zabel. Morton gave me a travelogue on his five months in Europe which sounded less like his usual conversation than like one of his interminable compulsive letters. Janet had in some strange way severely injured her hand—as far as I could make out, by picking some kind of sharp-leaved plant. But I couldn't understand her at first, her utterances had become so rushed and blurred. She was going to Italy. Why? For no better reason, apparently, than that there were certain things she wanted to see. But she more or less cleared up and became as amusing as ever. I ran into Thurber's wife in the lobby of the Algonquin. I asked her if Jim was there. Yes—he's in very bad shape. I asked whether he was ill or drunk or both. Yes, she said,—Don't tell him that I said he was in bad shape. I had a drink with them in the dining room, where as usual he was throwing his weight around. I saw him again the day that I was having drinks with Janet. He was with some other woman, middle-aged and not particularly attractive. He's treating her terribly, said Janet, meaning Helen. He's

drinking himself to death.* That evening or the next I was
having dinner with Mike Nichols and Joanna and ran into
the Thurbers again in the lobby. We sat down with them.
Jim said he had been having "vastations." He said, Janet's
in very bad shape. I think it was hurting her hand. I left
them for a moment when I went to cash a check at the
desk; then took Mike and Joanna in to dinner. Why, asked
Mike, does Mr. Thurber feel that he has to tell us about
the people who came backstage to see him (when he had
recently been acting in the show made out of his own
writings)? I answered that, depressing though it might
seem to him, getting older, for a writer, did not necessarily
give you self-confidence so that you felt you could disregard
the evidence of your importance. I told him that I sometimes got up at four o'clock in the morning to read old
reviews of my books. He asked what "vastations" were. I
explained that Jim Thurber had got the word from Leon
Edel's biography of Henry James. The elder Henry James
had used this word for a kind of blackout that he sometimes
had and when his mind had simply gone blank, he hadn't
known where he was. Mike said: I'm in that state a good
deal of the time. He told me about the play that Elaine
had been writing for them and which they hoped to have
open in February: it was about a Jewish family. He was
to be the husband and the main action seemed to hinge
on the wife's unsuccessful attempts to get him to get out
of bed. I said that I hoped she got him up at the end. She
was rewriting the end, he explained, and he didn't know
yet what was going to happen. He was supposed to go

* Wilson was fond of Thurber and, in a conversation about *New Yorker*
personalities several years later, lamented his last phase. "Blindness
had brought on drinking, and the drinking brought on barrages of insults
that made the humorist unrecognizable to anyone who knew him in
better days." This is Costa's paraphrase of EW in *Edmund Wilson: Our
Neighbor from Talcottville.*

around to see her after dinner; but he evidently stayed longer and drank more than he had expected to, because he finally declared that he didn't feel able to cope with Elaine just then and that he would go home and go to bed.

I felt that my contemporary friends were demoralized by the insecurity in which we are living at present—as I, of course, was myself; by a feeling of the ultimate futility of the work they had been doing all their lives, even the prospect of its possible annihilation. Mike Nichols, who had to face this at a much earlier age, said that he was reconciled to it in the sense that, in any case, one had to be reconciled to the prospect of one's own eventual death, whether or not this occurred as an item in a more general destruction of humanity.> This is perhaps a Jewish point of view.

<*Jim Thurber's death:* it depressed me and he was just my age. The "vastations" of which he spoke when I saw him in the Algonquin were evidently real. They must have been real blackouts caused by his cerebral tumor.>

Studying Hungarian

<*Trip to Utica and Talcottville, Nov. 30–Dec. 3.* Usual gloom and strain of tax business with Penberthy and tax people (only talked with them on the telephone this time). Spent Thursday night at Fort Schuyler Club; comfort at least of good breakfast in a well-served old-fashioned club. Mary Pcolar met me there for lunch and drove me to T'ville. She came in through the front door instead of the ladies' entrance. From the moment she talked to the manager at the desk inside the door, she recognized him as a Hungarian and established an understanding with him. When I came out and called her, he was sneaking her

through the ladies' dining room. On the way to Boonville, she told me at length about the situation at Raymond Kramer's pharmacy. She had left the bakery and gone back there—had really been on strike, she said; but was getting only $1.25 an hour (at the bakery only $1). Out of $36 a week, $8.50 is taken for taxes. She had felt before that it was Kramer's wife who opposed her getting a raise and made him let her go; but now the wife wanted her back —she was working in the pharmacy herself (she is trained as a pharmacist): and the balance of the situation was now changed. Mrs. K., it seems, has money—she has bought a $1,000 car and is contemplating buying a rug that costs $750. Some relation had a pharmacy in Rome, and when this went out of business, she made Raymond take on a fat brother-in-law who had been working in that pharmacy. It now appeared that she wanted Mary to gang up with her against Raymond, and this Mary didn't want to do. She didn't like the way that Mrs. K. treated her husband. One day he had hurt himself, shut his finger in the door or something, and Mrs. K. had laughed very hard and said, "It couldn't have happened to a nicer guy!" Mary didn't approve of this. I stopped in at the Park Market and found Beverly looking somewhat stouter. I asked her how was married life, and she answered, "Good. You're only supposed to be married once." —Everybody in Boonville said the same thing to me: that I had lost weight and that I must be surprised at there not being any snow. It was warm for that time of year, and the Stone House was perfectly comfortable. Mrs. Hutchins had closed off the third floor and all the second floor except the little room. But it was gray and rather sad up there. I felt that the people were lonely—it would even have been more cheerful, I thought, to have the ground covered with snow. The bears had been moving in on them, because for some reason the beechnuts had given out. In B'ville a bear had got into a garage, and in T'ville one had been seen on the bridge that goes over to the "island." The Hutchinses' old dog had barked so that they thought a bear must be near the barn. A cub had been seen in a tree. Walter Edmonds afterwards told me that before he left in early November, he had encountered a young bear on his place, and that his retriever had made off barking, evidently in the direction of the mother.

I told Mary about my weekly *Hungarian sessions with Zoltán Harasjti.** They were invariably so tumultuous that Elena called them "Hungarian rhapsodies." He and I would do Hungarian from five to about seven; then Elena would join us, and we would all have dinner together, alternating in Boston and at our house. All such Hungarians have been in their youth deeply "committed" patriots, and to ask them questions about Hungary is to bring forth a torrent of information, to mention the poetry of Ady is to stimulate a spate of quotation. I had had this experience with Sándor Radó when he came to see us in Wellfleet. Zoltán would go on so long about Hungarian politics or literature if I asked him some questions while we were reading a poem that I would have to make an effort to get him back to the text, and he would talk so much at dinner that he forgot to eat or drink. I suppose that people rarely encourage

* Hungarian translations of two of EW's plays, *This Room and This Gin and These Sandwiches* and *Beppo and Beth*, reached him in the summer of 1960, along with the flattering explanation "that they know nothing of my other work in Hungary, but that I am obviously a first-rate dramatist." He asked Mary Pcolar, who worked in the drugstore in Boonville, to teach him the language, but she was initially reluctant. Zoltán Harasjti, a friend who was rare books librarian at the Boston Public Library, began his instruction and Mary took over a year later when she was out of a job. She had wanted to be a teacher and Wilson considered her gifted—though his émigré friend Agatha Fassett thought that she taught him "peasant Hungarian."

them to talk about the Hungarian past. Zoltán was always afraid that I was not getting the point of what we read. With Móricz's story, *Hét krajcár* ["Seven Pennies"], he was continually afraid, in the early part—and I myself had been—that the joking and excessive laughter of the boy and his mother were silly: but, "I think," he said, "that it is hysterical"; and when we came to the end of the part I had read, he said, "Let us go on to the end: my honor as a Hungarian is involved!" When it ended with the mother coughing blood, he triumphantly expounded this climax. With Petőfi's poem *Befordultam a konyhara* . . . ["I Went into the Kitchen . . ."]—the point of which couldn't be clearer—he impressed it upon me, violently gesticulating: "Do you see?! His pipe goes out, but at that moment his heart, his sleeping heart, awakens!" I asked why *megláttam* instead of simply *láttam* when he sees the beautiful girl in the kitchen: "*megláttam!* It is something almost physical—it is sensual—as if he touches her with his eye!"

I told Mary about this in T'ville. "What does *megláttam* really mean?" I asked. "There's nothing like that in my dictionary. It simply says *to glimpse*." "It means what he told you," she answered. "It's something very personal." I asked her to give me an example of how she would use *megláttam*. She answered touchingly and tactfully: "If I were to go to New York and come back and tell my mother about it, I'd say that I saw this or that—*láttam*—but if I'd come upon you, I'd say, '*Megláttam Mr. Wilsont.*' " I purposely had her read Ady's wonderful winter poem, so full of terror and mystery, *Az eltévedt lovas* ["The Lost Rider"], which reminded me a little of upstate New York, which has not, however, except for the Indians, the ancient folklore and the obscure bloody past of which Ady speaks in the poem. I did not mention this, but when we afterwards drove to Glenfield to see Mihályi, she was struck by it and spoke of it herself in the bleak and misty landscape beneath a completely ashen sky, as we approached the Adirondacks. "*Köd-gubában jár a november*," "November wears a fog-cocoon"—or so I read it on the authority of my dictionary. Zoltán told me, however, that *Gubá* here was a peasant overcoat—the same, perhaps, as Russian *Shuba*. Then,

> S a köd—bozótból kirohan
> Ordas, bölény s nagymérgü medve.
>
> [As from the fog-bound thicket break
> The aurochs, wolf and angry bear.]

was also peculiarly appropriate in view of the emergence of our local bears. I thought, too, of the gigantic and frightening bears that figure in the Iroquois folk tales.

Zoltán had told me that, long though he had lived in this country, he could not talk English to another Hungarian without his compatriot not only immediately recognizing him as Hungarian but knowing what part of Hungary he came from. He had said that he thought he could tell by my accent when I read Hungarian what part of Hungary Mary came from and asked me to inquire about it. She had written me that her parents came from near Vasmegye and Ungmegye. It appeared that she had her father's accent, one that had a strong Slavic tinge, which Zoltán said she had communicated to me—she had told me that she had adored her father and liked to walk with him around the farm. When I told Mihályi what Zoltán had said about accents, he said that he had run into a Hungarian over here who had at once told him what town he came from. How did you know that? I came from there, too. I brought *Mihályi* the coin collection that I inherited by way of Minor from Uncle John. They are mostly American pennies collected from the graveyard of his father's Shrewsbury [N.J.] church—the sexton had found them in digging new graves: they had been used to close the eyes of the dead. Mihályi expertly sorted out all these coins, scrutinizing them through a magnifying glass. He said he had a nearly complete collection of American pennies, but could use the better ones for trading and offered me $35. I did not want to sell them, though I don't know what to do with them: they have been getting in very bad shape. There are also a lot of Civil War tokens which I did not know about. I left the box in the T'ville house—before we examined the coins. I asked M. about the Transylvania situation and "*Nem, nem, soha!* [No, no, never!],"* the only words of Hungarian that most Hungarian-Americans know. As in the cases of Sándor and Zoltán, he overwhelmed me with information. He is an able tough short chunky man, evidently the king of the Hungarian community and the biggest real estate operator over something like 200 square miles of the Adirondacks. Mary tells me that it was he who brought the Poles and the Hungarians in: selling them their little farms. Her parents had bought their farm from him.

We had to leave rather soon, since Mary was going to drive me to Prospect and had to get back for her Saturday-night bowling at 7—she is a champion and very keen on it. She was anxious and I was nervous. We several times lost our way. > She is so capable in many ways that I always think she knows her way, though she is actually rather dreamy and likely to lose it. The *Gauses*, with whom I was going to dinner, have extended and rearranged their home, and I envied them a little in the quiet of Prospect. Their home seemed so attractive and comfortable. He has just

* "*Nem, nem, soha!*" was the cry of Hungarian nationalists, declaring they would never give up the territory of the fatherland.

retired from Harvard, so he has not had to go back for the school year and is simply staying on at his ease, with an occasional trip to Montreal or Washington.

I get the impression that *Ady* has played a somewhat similar role in Hungary to that of Yeats in Ireland. Radó said that Ady had become "a conception." Like many Hungarian poets, he was a part of the nationalist movement—more so, I suppose, than Yeats, though both seem to have felt that they were intimately attached to the gentry of the native countryside. The final introductory piece of Ady's collected poems—*Góg és Magóg fia vagyok én* [I'm the son of Gog and Magog]*—has much in common with similar poems of Yeats: allusions to national mythology, references to landmarks and localities that have been given intense meaning for the native but have to be explained to the foreigner, and the destiny and personality of the poet in relation to all this.

The Social Round: New York, Wellfleet, New York

I met Elena at the Algonquin in New York. She had much enjoyed her visit at Henry and Daphne's. The little girls are very observant and talkative, and she is delighted with them. We had to come back Tuesday but had a very good time at the Algonquin. Had dinner in the Edwardian Room of the Plaza—a relief after the drabness of Cambridge and for me after my ghastly trip down from Utica when I had had to ride backwards all the way, which does not usually make me sick but did then. I was, besides, on the other side of the train from the Hudson and took account for

---

* Gog and Magog are mythical ancestral figures. The phrase implies "I'm deeply rooted in my race."

the first time of how ugly and sordid the east bank is: steep lumpy and unpleasant brown rocks, horrible dumps and decayed and deserted inns. On Monday the Looking Glass Library people at our usual corner of the Algonquin: Clelia Carroll, Ted Gorey, the Epsteins, and a very pretty girl, married to one of the Canfields, who has joined the staff, Sovka [Winkelhorn] and Elena, and later Wystan Auden and Henry. Wystan and the Epsteins stayed late, and we drank several bottles of Beaujolais. Altogether very pleasant—it was wonderful to be with Elena away from home.

Sometime in 1961, I had another of those dreams about Margaret: she was still out there in California—she could not be still so angry with me, surely she would let me see her, perhaps come back to me. In a dream I had had some time before that, I had gone out there to look for her, waked up without finding her—fountains and gardens, but not her. In this dream, I think, I was surely going to call up some friend of hers and try to find out where she was.

I stayed in *Wellfleet* at the end of Helen's Christmas vacation when Elena and Helen went to New York.

While *Mary Meigs* and I sat drinking in the kitchen, our smaller cat, Lulu, got wind of the remains of the Virginia ham in a pasteboard box on top of the frigidaire: for a moment she calculated the height, then made a straight standing jump from the floor to the top of the icebox. One couldn't help applauding this feat.

I had dinner Thursday night at Mary's, Friday night again with her at a strange "period" restaurant in Orleans with an "Edwardian Room" and an Englishman with a period mustache who did duty as both cook and waiter. The next night I was going to the Givens'. I tried to shift it because Mary was leaving on Sunday, but they thought they might have to be away on Saturday. Mary, however, came in in the afternoon, and we had a long talk. I had never seen her alone for so long. Barbara was in Lebanon waging peace with Muste and stayed on to go to see Martin Buber in Jerusalem.

Sunday night I got the Wallings to invite me for dinner. They told me all the gossip of the woods. Story about Jack Phillips when he was married to Dasya Chalyapin: she wanted him to make love to her all the time and Jack had finally said there are other things to do besides making love. She had asked him what they were. Why, you can go fishing or take a walk. Hayden went on, when I had laughed at this uproariously: just to show you how cozy we are out here: Libby and her present husband (she had formerly been married to Jack) moved into Jack's house with him last summer, and my former wife was living with them, too.

After New Year's, '62. I went back to getting *my journals* in order and typed the pages about Margaret's death. This depressed me horribly: it made me realize that I had been repeating with Elena the same "pattern" of my behavior with Margaret, and I tried to be very nice with her. It is upsetting to have to retrace one's life of thirty years ago —things one had wanted to forget. It was also sad to be copying my old notes about Louise Connor when she is now quite insane and writing me crazy letters, and my account of [her twin sister] Henrietta in the hospital just after she had had the baby, sadder in view of what happened afterwards: the little boy died, partly, I think, as a result of his parents' break-up.

Trip to New York late in March: I was away for about three weeks. Elena joined me for about a week. We stayed at the Algonquin. I finished my Swinburne and the "Interview" in the *New Yorker* office.

Before Elena came, I had dinner with *Mike Nichols* and his new girlfriend. I had heard that he and Joanna were married and written him a note of congratulations; but not at all: he has another girl, who also resembles Elaine— brunette who wears her hair in the same way, very pretty, has read at least a little. He had just read Tolstoy's *Death of Ivan Ilyich*, which had made a great impression on him. I do not care for this story as much as many people do: I don't believe that a man like Ivan Ilyich could ever look back on his life and find it so empty and futile; I don't believe that Tolstoy, in the period when he was writing his great novels, would ever have invented such a character. Mike said that that was just the way he felt about his own life. I expressed surprise at this. When I had last seen him, he had said he was gratified at what he had achieved. He had money after having been poor, and pointing to Joanna—"I have her." He and Elaine are going out in the summer to do their show at the Seattle World's Fair. Her play is to be done in the fall. She wants to direct it, so doesn't want to act in it, because she says that if she does, she can't direct properly. I think that is a great mistake. Her one-acter that was done in an Off-Broadway bill was taken off just before I arrived. People said that one problem was that she had directed it and not acted in it. Sylvia Marlowe says that teams like Nichols and May are likely to get into a professional relationship in which it is impossible for them either to marry one another or seriously to marry anyone else: Comden and Green,* a similar team, and a team of pianists to whose recital she told me that some time ago she took me. Elaine was preparing to get married to the writer of musical show lyrics with whom we had seen her at Stamford; but I felt that Mike was rather skeptical. I told him to tell Elaine that I

* Betty Comden and Adolph Green are Broadway songwriters and actors, who composed and played in *On the Town* and *Singin' in the Rain*.

was sorry not to be young enough to fall in love with her
and ruin my life. He said, "I'll tell her exactly what you
say."

Elena and I had dinner at the Algonquin with *Gerald
and Sara Murphy* and Dawn Powell. I had met Sara a
number of times, without talking to her very much or
getting much impression of her. I was surprised at how
youthful and pretty her face was. She asked me whether
I thought she had changed and evidently hoped I would
say she had not. Him I had met only once, behind the
scenes of the Swedish Ballet, for which I was acting as
press agent when they came to New York in the twenties
and for which he had designed a set (for a ballet by Cole
Porter). I think that it is perfectly true, as Dos [Passos]
says, that all the masculine traits seem to be concentrated
in Esther [Murphy] and the feminine ones in Gerald. I
felt that I was talking to a woman who wanted very much
to charm me. I was astonished when he told me that he
was ten years older than Esther: he actually looks younger.

He began by saying, "How much longer are we going to
be dragged at Scott's chariot?" This was apropos of Andrew
Turnbull's book about him, by which they were rather
annoyed. They resented his having said that they put the
children up to throwing sand at people who intruded on
their beach at Antibes. They would have punished them,
said Sara, if they had known of their doing anything of
the kind. And Gerald objected to his saying that he had
ever had a gold-headed cane: he had had a number of canes
but they were always the hooked kind. It was curious how
ignorant they seemed of things I should have thought they
would have known. Esther had told me that her Boston
family was related to Ben Butler; but Gerald did not know
about this and did not know who Butler was. He remembered, however, that for his mother some prestige had
attached to the Butler name and that she had wanted to

perpetuate it. Sara knew nothing about Benjamin Smith, Katy Dos Passos's father. One felt the limitations of their perfect life. I think there is something in Gerald's theory, which he had communicated to Dawn, that Dos had been keeping us for years from knowing one another. He has always been notorious for trying to keep his friends in separate compartments, like the characters in his novels, who never or hardly impinge on one another's lives. He likes to feel that he sees the whole picture, which the other people do not see; in his novels, that they are his puppets, to whom he is always superior; in real life, that he can, at will, take them out, put them through their paces, then put them away till next time, deriving satisfaction from feeling that they don't know what he knows, since they don't know one another, and that he never has to become involved with them. At the same time, I may have been put off by the idea of the Murphys' perfect life, which seemed to exclude so much and to be so artificially maintained. They seemed to have cast a spell over both the Fitzgeralds and the Dos Passoses.

Elena and I were both very tired—she had been out to see her Thornton grandchildren—and she didn't enjoy the evening. She sat by Gerald, separated from Dawn, with whom she likes to talk, and complained that he had bored her extremely, two hours of him was too much, she had finally been reduced to talking about cookbooks with him —he is apparently a very good cook. But it was fun for me to talk about the old friends we had in common. It was characteristic of them that, in inviting us to Sneden's Landing, Gerald should have made a point that the way —only half an hour—led through large and attractive estates, none of the ugliness of the city's outskirts. By the end of the evening, Gerald was singing old commercials of the twenties—one about the St. George Hotel. I responded with *The platform I stand on/Is Moët and Chandon.*

After Elena went back to Cambridge, I took *Dawn* to The Little Players. When I had had dinner with her before, I had told her that Elena had said that she (Dawn) was one of my only real friends. She said, "The reason for that is that there's never been anything between us." I agreed; but I later realized that the death of Joe since I had last seen her had somehow upset the equilibrium of our relationship. As long as we were both married, this equilibrium was perfectly maintained; but at the time Mary [McCarthy] and I had separated, we became somewhat warmer and closer. She would get me dinner in her apartment, which she had never done before, and conceived a dislike of Mary, which she had never felt before. Now, the evening I took her to The Little Players, I talked about my impression of the Murphys, and she became furious with me, said disagreeable things about Rosalind and even Helen. The next morning I got a telegram: "Darling what happened to us was it my money or your music was it just the club where did we go wrong dear. Aurore." I replied on an Algonquin postcard with something like: "Dear Aurore: It might perhaps be better for us not to see one another for a while. Our relationship under the circumstances is becoming too much of a strain. I am leaving for Boston today. *Mille baisers*. Raoul."*

She has had the state income tax people after her. They froze her bank account, which amounted to three hundred sixty some dollars. She says that she thinks that this really

---

* "For years Dawn Powell and I carried on a correspondence in which she was supposed to be Mrs. Humphrey Ward and I a seedy literary man named Ernest Wigmore. Later on, we were a sophisticated French pair: Raoul and Aurore." This note in EW's handwriting was attached to Dawn Powell's letters and is transcribed in *Letters on Literature and Politics* beside a comic sketch of Wigmore the book reviewer, which Wilson pretends has been "drawn by John Sargent for the *New York Herald Tribune*."

killed Joe. I suppose she has been getting along under the largesse of Margaret de Silver.

After Elena left, I had evenings with the *Lehoviches* and the *Winkelhorns*—thoroughly enjoyed myself and gave them vivacious performances. But I can only do this nowadays at the price of pretty heavy drinking, with terrible depressions the next day. Too much of this during my three weeks in New York—with the result that I slighted the Swinburne and the "Interview," and have had drastically to redo them now that I am back in Cambridge.

Had dinner with *Wystan Auden* before Elena arrived. He was pleased at having what he described as an honor on the part of the Establishment. He has been made an honorary fellow (I think that is the phrase) of Christ Church. I gather that he can retire and live there for nothing. As usual, we got through three bottles of red wine—though I always try to swear to myself beforehand that I am not going to do this: the trouble is that he refuses whisky before dinner, only drinks a "gimlet" (which I feel he enjoys ordering, because he likes the name), whereas I drink both whisky and the wine. He thinks that *Down There on a Visit* is [Christopher] Isherwood's best book—I was just in the middle of reading it. He says the disintegrating homo on his horrible island in Greece was a real person whom he knew and the only person he knew who would drink the spirits out of lamps when there was nothing else to be had. He thought that "Paul" was the best of the stories. I agreed with him when I came to read it; but the whole book is rather disgusting. I am getting sick of this subject. The attitude in these books toward homosexuality involves of course a revolt against society. See the diatribe of the man on the island about putting the heterosexuals in ghettos. Paul is made by Isherwood into a hero. But *Genet* is the best of these writers. He is the most in revolt, the most genuinely an outlaw. (A little pansy photographer, an expatriate New Yorker, who came to take pictures of me in the *New Yorker* office, had just photographed Genet. He is living, he says, in the Dolomites; Genet says that he can't stand Paris on account of Malraux, who has authorized a censorship.)

Barbara Deming on Trial; Isaac Bashevis Singer

Barbara Deming was arrested at one of the peace demonstrations. She would not offer bail and spent a night in prison; but her organization bailed her out. She was quite shaken by the experience. They had stripped her and searched her everywhere.* I had dinner with her and Mary Meigs at the Algonquin the day she was released; we had a bottle of champagne and afterwards went to *L'Année Dernière à Marienbad*; but the combination of things left with me a nightmarish impression. All the puzzling about this film and saying it is "enigmatic" seems to me rather silly. It turns out to be simply the old French triangle played as an interminable teaser. It bored me and annoyed me in the same way as *Hiroshima, Mon Amour*, made by the same man (which Elena, however, adored—she saw it three or four times). In the middle of it, Mary said, "Think what Nichols and May could do with this!" It was perhaps not a bad thing to have taken Barbara to that film, because, with its monotonous voices and its languuorous

---

* Deming recalls this experience of being strip-searched at the beginning of her *Prison Notes* (1966), which details her twenty-seven days in the Albany, Georgia, jail, from January 27 to February 22, 1964. EW wrote to William Shawn that her book "is not a mere piece of agitation but a notably well-written document that throws more light than anything else I have read on the meaning of their non-violent protests for the more serious of these demonstrators."

pace, it simply put her to sleep. On Thursday, when Barbara's case came up, Elena and I spent the morning in
court on Centre St. The magistrate was a bull-necked
Irishman. The main business was disposing of petty crim-
inals, and one got a horrible picture of the dregs of life in
New York: nasty-looking narcotics offenders, two Negroes
accused of rape, two men accused of felonious assault,
with heads and faces plastered and bandaged, a miserable
Puerto Rican boy who had been caught with heroin and a
needle either on or just off the school grounds—it was not
clear whether he had been peddling it or simply taking it
himself—he had dropped it all in an ashcan when he saw
that the cops were after him; a man who was supposed to
have forged a check had his wife or his girlfriend with
him, and when he was arraigned, she fell to the floor
howling; one couldn't tell if this was an act or a real display
of emotion; the judge recessed the court. One of the magistrate's principal problems was to communicate with the
defendants. In the case of the Puerto Ricans he sometimes
had to have an interpreter. He would sometimes say to the
lawyer, "Does he know what it's all about?" They had been
dragged out of their underworld like mud turtles or sala-
manders and hardly knew where they were. He would ask
them first whether they had a lawyer and often get no
response. If he elicited the fact that they did not, he would
ask them how much they made. If what they made seemed
sufficiently substantial, he would tell them to hire a lawyer.
Otherwise, they were defended by the Legal Aid lawyer
who sat to his right at a long table. He undoubtedly has
hundreds of such petty cases and has cultivated a routine
patience. The court interpreter told me that, in the Legal
Aid defenses, the lawyers, with their thankless job, undoubtedly meagerly remunerated, had more or less abandoned the principle that anybody should be presumed to
be innocent until he is proved guilty and would persuade

them to plead guilty, in which case the magistrate could sentence them at once—in order to polish them off expeditiously.

But the demonstrators for peace must have presented the magistrate with an unfamiliar problem. The demonstrators came up incongruously in the midst of all this squalor and petty crime. Barbara detached her case from the others by refusing to plead guilty, so a group of, I think, five, all pleading guilty, appeared before the judge before her case was allowed to come up. They were young people mostly, all men except one girl of 16. The magistrate interrogated them one by one. He bullied them for all he was worth. His line was that they had a right to their opinion but that they must not violate the law. They had done this by obstructing traffic. They were not Americans then: Americans did not violate the law. He tried to make each one promise that they would never do anything of this kind again, and all of them refused to promise. In the case of one young man who had apparently been born in Poland or some other foreign country, he gave him the old blast which has been in use ever since the deportation of the Reds at the end of World War I: "If you won't obey the laws, get out of the country! We don't want you here! You're not an American!" The young man said, "I consider myself an American." He gave them all thirty days in the workhouse "to think it over"—with the exception of the girl, who was underage, to whom he gave five days in jail and a suspended sentence. Their Jewish lawyer was allowed to make a statement that they had done what they did on principle; but the judge did his best to forestall and to cut short such statements. Then the string of petty crimes was resumed.

I imagine that Barbara's case was purposely put off till almost one so that the contrast between her testament and that of the other accused would not appear too striking.

One had supposed that the others would be dismissed and
Barbara get some kind of sentence, so that after the others
were sentenced, she and her family and friends became
very tense: Mary wept. But it turned out the other way.
When Elena had been in Wellfleet before she joined me
in New York, she had sat up one night with Barbara, who
was trying to make up her mind whether or not to plead
guilty. Elena had urged her not to. When Helen at the
Weston School had been hit in the head with a hockey
stick and Elena had been rushing to her, she had been
stopped by a cop for speeding but when she explained the
emergency was allowed to go on. Elena told Barbara that
her argument should be that this was an emergency for
the human race. Barbara's pleading not guilty turned out
to have a good result for reasons quite other than the
magistrate's susceptibility to persuasion by this argument.
I don't know whether any preliminary consultation had
taken place between him and Barbara's lawyer (not the
same who had defended the others) and the policeman who
had picked Barbara up and removed her from the sidewalk;
but while Barbara stood like Joan of Arc, a pale slender
figure alone before the judge, he never addressed her or
looked at her and her lawyer gave her no chance to speak,
but they both interrogated the policeman, who was, as
Mary said, a goodlooking fellow and who obviously did not
want to make trouble for her. The whole situation was
made to hinge on the exact position of Barbara's legs: were
they inside or outside the barrier. The lawyer finally re-
quested that the case should be dismissed, since it could
not be established that Barbara was actually obstructing
the traffic. The judge granted this, dismissed the case,
since "a doubt" existed. Outside in the corridor, Barbara
said to me, "I don't understand. I'm very displeased. I was
going to make this statement"—and she handed me a type-
written sheet. She had been all ready to go to jail. The

truth was, I think, that the judge had sized her up as a well-to-do woman of superior social position. She had been sitting in the front row with her mother and brother. I dare say that her brothers, one of them a lawyer, had managed to influence the proceedings. Carey McWilliams, whom I saw that night at Betty Huling's, told me that he knew, from his experience as a lawyer, that those judges have "antennae" and adapt their decisions to the quality of the accused.

In order to hear better, I had gone up on the platform of the court, thinking I could press a claim to be reporting for *The New Yorker* in order to get a place at the press table; but what I had thought was the press table was for Legal Aid. I stayed there, however, and I got into a conversation with the woman interpreter for Italian, French and Spanish. She was well educated and rather handsome, and I learned later that she had been an opera singer. She had been born in Puerto Rico. She asked me what I thought about the demonstrators. I said that I was sympathetic— "So am I: I don't see how anything can be done in any other way—so as not to live in this uncertainty!" I told her that I had come to court because a friend of mine was one of the demonstrators. "Is that your friend?" she presently said, looking at Barbara in the front row. "I was impressed by her when she was arraigned. She reminded me of Greta Garbo. Not that she is like her physically; but she is spiritually like her. There is something about the way she walks."

April 19, '62. The income tax (my "offer in compromise" has just been rejected), my ailments—heart, teeth and gout—and having endured another winter in Cambridge have lately been getting me down. I drink too much to get me out of my depression, then *relapse into something like despair*. The other night, after an active and serious day,

I had a paroxysm of exasperation with Elena combined
with an acute heart attack and smashed her filing cabinet,
her typewriter and something else made of glass. She was
frightened and called Monroe Engel, who got me a doctor.
He checked my pulse and my heart and gave me a shot in
the arm to put me to sleep.* Now I have pulled myself
together, got myself on my feet again—have been writing
in this journal and concentrating more intensively on Hungarian, having sessions with Agatha Fassett. We have been
having great fun with Molnár's comedy, *Uri Divat.*

Elena and I have had two good evenings: one with *Isaac
[Bashevis] Singer*—dinner at the Hillel House, at which
we sat on either side of him, and afterwards a reading at
the Divinity School—he is learned, witty and wise, very
resourceful and serious in answering questions. —I had
been moved by his *Magician of Lublin*, a remarkable religious novel. He made it clear, in the autobiographical chapter he read, that he had polarized with his socialist-realist
brother, who wrote *The Brothers Ashkenazy*. Isaac is ma-
terialistic, mystic (they are the sons of a rabbi), steeped
in the Talmud, the Kabbala and all the rest, as much a
Hassid as Agnon. He admires Agnon but doesn't think
much of Kafka or Buber. Kafka he finds a bore; and Buber
he regards as a popularizer of the Hasidic literature, which
Singer knows at first hand and thinks that Buber somewhat
distorts—as, he added to his audience, with characteristic
modesty and justice, he himself was somewhat distorting
the Kabbala in trying to explain it in English. We discussed
at dinner, with a Jewish sinologist Schwartz, who was
sitting on my other side, the various philosophical conceptions of "Nature." Singer said that what was meant by

* Engel tells of the evening in a memoir in the *Yale Review*, Spring 1987.
The physician was Louis Zetzel, who attended Wilson for the next ten
years. When Dr. Zetzel saw him two weeks later, he diagnosed the
attack as angina.

Nature was likely to be simply a blank, but "Nature is supernatural." He believes in some sort of survival after death. I said that I didn't want to survive. "If survival has been arranged," he answered, "you will have no choice in the matter." Our other evening, agreeable but not so inspiring, was a recital by Elisabeth Schwarzkopf last night. Elena, who has heard Lotte Lehmann, objected to her "hamming" some of her songs; but Schwarzkopf, after all, exults in Johann Strauss and Lehár as well as Mozart and Richard Strauss. The Soviet movie of Prokofiev's *Cinderella* was very disappointing—settings and costumes and everything else in terrible taste—as had been also true of *Pikovaya Dama* [*The Queen of Spades*].

May '62. Our Trip to Glen Head, Washington and New York: I decided to go with Elena to spend two nights with Henry and Daphne. It was a rest and very pleasant. They both seem flourishing and the twins are old enough to be interesting. One of them, Elena, seems more like Henry, not aggressive; but Sandra seems more like Daphne, makes personal remarks about people. They have polarized. Henry and Daphne have shaken down to what is evidently a good relationship and from their point of view an enjoyable life. They have acquired their attractive place and wrestled with furnishing and painting it—much improved since I was there before. Secluded, not suburban, with its blossoming forsythia and dogwood; big back lawn for the children to play in and a playhouse for them. It brought back to me New Jersey and my visits to Long Island. I am more at home here than in Massachusetts. It was relaxing: sitting out in the sunporch with a highball and the smooth green grass. Pleasant to be in a house that is not on the main road. Elena was alarmed at one time for fear Daphne was influencing Henry to be more socially stuffy and commonplace; but now it seems to be somewhat the other way around. She had surprised me when I saw her at the

Algonquin in New York by having more to say for herself,
expressing strong opinions. She is to some extent losing
her provincial snobberies. Elena had apparently done something to modify her anti-Semitism, and Henry has succeeded in interesting her in things that she can previously
have known nothing about. I was surprised when Daphne
told me that she had once flown a plane on her own. She
had been daring in those days, had once (in camp?) defended the other children with a revolver against a pack
of wolves (I may not have this quite right).

I talked to her about the Kennedys and Jackie. Jackie
she has known all her life, and the Kennedy children later.
With the exception of Teddy, who was about her own age,
she evidently did not like them at all. She explained that
she had been brought up to think that Democrats were
practically beneath contempt, had apparently had something like the same point of view about them that a white
Southerner has about Negroes; and that she should even
be conscious that this may not be right already shows an
advance. I think that there is something, too, in Elena's
idea that, being partly Irish herself, she drew back from
their raucous Irishness. Not long after she had married
Henry, she felt somebody at a party rubbing his hands up
and down her sides: it turned out to be Jack Kennedy. He
was famous for this kind of thing. When he was about to
run for President, somebody asked him, "What will become
of your favorite pastime?" "I'll have to be more careful."
Daphne said that she thought he and Jackie went their
separate ways without really being much involved with one
another; Jackie liked to see herself in the role of a little
queen.

We had come straight from Boston to Idlewild by plane
and went from Idlewild straight by plane to Washington.
The trips were short, smooth, and restful, so much less
effort than other ways of travelling.

WASHINGTON AND THE KENNEDYS

A White House Dinner

May 11, 1962. At Washington, Arthur Schlesinger had made reservations for us at the Sheraton. Pleasant courtesy and amiability of the servants and taxi drivers. Elena had bought a peach-colored dress and white gloves for the dinner at the White House. Arthur had asked me on the phone whether I would come to a dinner for Malraux [whom I had known since 1935, when, on my way back from Russia, I had had dinner with him and his first wife in Paris].* I had at first expected a small affair, but then found that we were in for a big cultural blowout with 168 guests. In the reception room—huge portrait of Washington and glass chandeliers—we found the Tates, the Lowells, the Warrens, Thornton Wilder and Saul Bellow and his wife at one end of the room—a Frenchwoman who taught French at Smith, I don't know why she was there. Allen Tate [a very family-conscious Southerner] told Elena that it was

---

* Bracketed material here and in the next chapter, unlike that elsewhere supplied by the editor within brackets, was added by EW when he had these pages separately typed in 1968, sending copies to one or two friends.

the first time "a man of my blood" had been in the White House since Buchanan. He said also that the White House had been built by somebody "of my blood." We queued up alphabetically to be received by the Malraux and Kennedys. This put us just behind Tennessee Williams, for whom Elena feels such physical repulsion that she says she cannot stand to be near him. She said something of this kind to me in Russian. He turned: "What language is that?" "Russian." "Fine." Behind us was the painter Andrew Wyeth, who has become the approved official American painter [I found in Hungary that he seemed to be the only contemporary American painter they had heard about—*Christina's World* was much admired]. The occasion brought out in Elena as it were atavistic reactions, which I had never seen her manifest to that degree. The women of her mother's family were ladies in waiting at the Tsarina's court, and her grandfather was the Tsar's ambassador in Tokyo, The Hague and Washington. I had never before been with her anywhere remotely resembling a court, and wasn't prepared for her stiffening attitude. The first sign of this was her "squeamishness," as she calls it—this is a Russian groping for *brezglivost*—for which, since it also means *fastidiousness*, they always say there is no English equivalent—in the presence of Tennessee Williams—after all he had been in our house in Wellfleet. Then the sight of a waiter wiping up a spilt drink from the floor made a disagreeable impression on her. Afterwards, she commented unfavorably on the way the guests behaved and wore their clothes. I realized that she felt that many of them should not have been asked to the White House at all. When somebody asked her in New York whether she thought that such parties were a good thing, she said, "Yes, I suppose they are: they made those people take a bath for the first time."

The dinner was in two large rooms, at tables of about ten people. Elena was at a table presided over by one of Kennedy's sisters and sat between "Chip" Bohlen and the director of the Metropolitan Museum. I found myself at Kennedy's table between Agnes de Mille and Geraldine Page. Kennedy had Mme Malraux, looking very beautiful, on his right, Mme Alphand on the other side, the wife of the French ambassador, a much less attractive lady. I didn't know then who Geraldine Page was, but she took it very well. She is handsome and seems intelligent; is not at all like an actress, has no public personality for off the stage. She told me that she had appeared in Tennessee Williams's *Summer and Smoke* and *Sweet Bird of Youth*. Agnes de Mille explained to me that she was a granddaughter of Henry George, and we talked about *Progress and Poverty*. She is apparently still a loyal Taxer.*

Kennedy told me he had seen a review of *Patriotic Gore* and asked why I had called it that. He asked what conclusions I had come to about the Civil War. I answered that I couldn't very well tell him then and there and referred him to the Introduction. He said something about its being unusual for an author not to want to talk about his book. Later I asked him whether he ever saw Pat Jackson [Gardner Jackson, an old friend of mine, a well-to-do near-radical, who lived in Washington, served in the New Deal and once occupied Kennedy's apartment]. "Not for a year," he said. "He used to come and give me advice. He wanted me to help him get a plaque put up in Boston for Sacco and Vanzetti. I told him it wasn't time yet." I mentioned the monument in Boston to the Quaker who was executed by the Puritans. "That took them three

---

* In *Progress and Poverty* (1879), which sold millions of copies worldwide, George proposed to bring about the good society through a single tax on land ownership. Agnes de Mille had published a study of her grandfather in 1950.

hundred years," he said. "Those Puritans were brutal."*

Irwin Shaw was on Mme Malraux's other side, talking vigorously to her in French. He has been living in Switzerland to avoid taxes, and had flown over especially for the dinner. The *New Yorker* people, who don't much like him, expressed surprise at his being there; but I found out from Alfred Kazin the probable reason: Kennedy has a friend who wants to make a play out of one of Shaw's stories, and he must have been asked at the President's instance. I said to Kennedy that he had certainly done a thorough job of entertaining the literary world: "Maybe they ought to entertain *me*." I told Mme Malraux that I had been surprised, as Camus said he had been, that Camus rather than Malraux should have been given the Nobel Prize. I said that I supposed that his past politics had had nothing to do with this. She said no, but I couldn't hear her explanation well enough to understand it. I had had, perhaps wrongly, the impression that Camus seemed to them safer than Malraux.

The President, who had had paper and pencil brought him and who had either been writing a message or making notes, now got up and introduced Malraux. He said, as he had at a previous such dinner, that there were more brains assembled that evening in the dining room of the White House than any time since Thomas Jefferson dined alone. He said that this was one occasion in celebration of Franco-American amity at which mention of Lafayette was not going to be one of the main features. "Of course we all know that, after Washington, Lafayette was the greatest American of his time." He gave a brief description of Mal-

---

* Gardner Jackson (1896–1965) was chairman of the Sacco-Vanzetti Defense Committee in 1927, when the immigrant anarchists were executed for murder, after fruitless demonstrations in which Wilson's friends Dos Passos and Millay took part. Kennedy's remark about the Puritans may reflect Irish Catholic resentment of the old Boston aristocracy.

raux as soldier, flier, explorer, writer and Minister of Culture under de Gaulle. Malraux replied by saying that he had been glad to come here and see our *"chef d'oeuvres"*— I couldn't imagine at first what masterpieces he meant, then realized that he was referring to the pictures in the National Gallery. [He had told me once in Paris that the Metropolitan was *"un musée de province,"* but that the National Gallery in Washington was a really important one.] He said that the United States was unlike the Roman Empire, unlike the Byzantine Empire, unlike any empire of the past. I cannot remember his words, so quote from a report of the speech that he made later on in New York, in which he said the same kind of thing: "The United States is the first nation to become the most powerful in the world without having sought to be so. Its exceptional energy and organization have never been oriented toward conquest." I said to Mme Malraux, as I certainly should not have done: *"Dites à Malraux que je n'en crois rien."* I didn't know that Kennedy understood French [I have learned since that he had been taking lessons] and was surprised when he took me up: "You don't tell us what you think." Malraux also in one of these speeches spoke of our having the most powerful weapon in the world and yet not wanting to use it. I was astonished at his going so far in diplomatic absurdities. After all, we had used it.

On the wall opposite me was a rather queer portrait of Lincoln, which must have been a modern production: it made him look as if he were anxiously thinking in a concentrated neurotic way. When the party broke up, I spoke to Sam Behrman, who had been sitting at a nearby table. I told him that I had achieved my ambition—of which I had spoken to him in the country two summers ago—to read Molnár in the original, and that he was really very good. (We used to call Sam the Worcester Molnár.) He said that he always saw me at such grand places: the White House and Talcottville.

After dinner, there was a concert: Schubert's Trio in B Flat Major. The violinist was Isaac Stern. I had never heard it before—it was lovely, but I did not feel much like listening to music. Malraux, it seems, went to sleep. Marian Schlesinger said afterwards that he had had a little too much to drink; but I don't think this was necessarily true. He had been taking Jackie through the National Gallery and had had a long conference with Kennedy. He had evidently come over to try to iron out Kennedy's difficulties with de Gaulle. After the concert, Isaac Stern went to play the violin with a jazz orchestra. Elena had a talk with Balanchine, who, she said, seemed very depressed. He was going to Russia and didn't want to go. [He hated it when he got there and interrupted his stay by a trip back to New York.]

The food at dinner was delicious: soup with *double crème* in the middle and on top of that a dab of caviar. Since it was Friday with a Catholic President in the White House, this was followed by lobster and fish. There were French wines in honor of Malraux, which Elena said were wonderful. Henry and Daphne had kidded her about her obvious eagerness to go to this affair—they said she had been sniffing the breeze, and pawing the ground. She enjoyed it extremely and said afterwards, "I'd like to dine at the White House every night!" With me she doesn't have much opportunity to dress well and *faire valoir* her beauty, and I felt that she had been socially starved. Before dinner, she had talked a little to Adlai Stevenson. She complained that Chip Bohlen didn't have the right reaction to Russia. I wondered whether perhaps she wasn't associating herself with her grandfather, who had spent so many years in Washington—she may have felt she was representing Russia.

When we said goodbye to the Kennedys, he said something again about my not wanting to tell him about my book: "I suppose I'll have to buy it." "I'm afraid so." I thought that it was better to say this than to tell him that Oxford had sent him a copy. Jackie Kennedy is really pretty—much better looking than her photographs—which always make her eyes seem too far apart.

Arthur's hand was everywhere visible, and these parties in Washington are really vast expansions of the parties they gave in Cambridge. The Biddles had invited us for after the party, but it was late, after midnight, when we got to their house, and Francis had gone to bed. Poor Katherine had on her hands the exhilarated Lowells, Tates, Warrens and Wilsons. Allen and Red Warren paid me many compliments on *Patriotic Gore* which I waved away but much enjoyed—especially since they are both Southerners. At last we saw that Katherine was suffering. Taxis were summoned to take us home.

André Malraux

May 12. Luncheon for Malraux. That curious impresario Richman had arranged this with the State Department. I had had him invite Phito Marcelin, the remarkable Haitian poet and novelist, who was then living in Washington and, with Phito standing by, I had a long conversation with Malraux, or rather, he talked to me at some length in his rapid-fire way. His method is to make a point, say *"Bon!,"* then press on to another point without giving the other person a chance to discuss the previous one. I told him, apropos of his speech at the dinner the night before, that I thought he had illusions about the role of the United States: *"Mon discours d'hier soir—c'était de la courtoisie. Mme Kennedy a été très gentille—elle s'intéresse à l'art. Le*

président Kennedy a des problèmes très difficiles." I thanked
him for sending me the first volume of *La Metamorphose
des Dieux*, and asked him about the second. He said that
he had finished it all but two chapters, but that he didn't
have time now to write them. He then expounded the
difference between being an intellectual and being *un
homme politique*. He had thought once that society would
run all right if Marxists could be in control (I doubt
whether he had really thought this); but to be actually in
practical politics was something completely different, the
problems and the means of dealing with them were something altogether different. The intellectuals sometimes did
a lot of harm through not understanding this. He then,
evidently referring to his own case, began speaking of writers and painters who ceased to paint or write simply because *ils n'avaient plus envie d'écrire ou de peindre comme*
[they did not wish to write or paint like] *Goya et Alfred de
Vigny* and, we understood him to say, Titian, though I
don't know his evidence for this. Victor Hugo was an exception. It is actually the exceptional writer who at some
point ceases to write because he no longer wants to. I said
that I hoped this was not true of him, I had hoped that
he might eventually write a novel about French politics.
He assured us that, on the contrary, being not in a position
to write gave him *une grande envie d'écrire*.

I said that I did not like the National Gallery for reasons
I didn't quite know (Elena thinks the lighting is perfect
and that the pictures are very well shown). *"Le bâtiment,"*
he said, *"c'est quelque chose à épater le bourgeois. Ces grandes
colonnes. C'est très pompier."* I told him about Alice [Roo-
sevelt] Longworth showing somebody through and saying,
"There's a very fine Kress. There's a beautiful Mellon."
But those millionaires, said Malraux, had performed a real
service.

At lunch, I sat on Malraux's right. Alexis Léger [Saint-

John Perse, the poet] sat opposite. I told Malraux that life in America was now *une espèce d'enfer*, that there was little to choose between us and the Soviet Union and that I thought of going to live in France or Switzerland. He said merely, *"C'est intéressant."* I am not a good person for such official occasions. Trying gently to sound him out, I said that if it was a question of censorship in France, couldn't something be done about Anouilh's plays, which were becoming an international menace. He replied, but in many more words, *"Il n'y a pas de censure en France; et quant à Anouilh, c'est le nouveau boulevard."**

When I had been telling Malraux *des horreurs* about the United States, I turned to the man on my other side to see how he had been taking it. He was a State Department representative, who had just spent two and a half years in Russia. On the other side of the table near me was a young Jewish man who was bilingual in French and English, and so had understood all that I had been saying to Malraux. He was evidently State Department, too. Everything we said would undoubtedly be reported. When I complained of this to Arthur Schlesinger, he replied, with his usual naïveté, that Malraux was such an important person that the State Department would naturally want to catch any hint of his opinions on French policy. I told the man at my side about my disquieting experience with the State Department men at the Boston and Cambridge parties for the visiting Soviet writers, and he said, "There are ways of doing things, but we're supposed to declare ourselves as soon as possible." [Apropos of a man at one of these parties who, after everybody else had been introduced, had stepped

* By *"le nouveau boulevard"* Malraux means a commercialized melodrama fashionable in nineteenth-century Paris. When first discussing Anouilh with Malraux in 1953, Wilson believed that *L'Alouette* was "more or less of a plagiarism from *Saint Joan*." Not long after their 1962 luncheon, he wrote that Anouilh's plays had a "fraudulent cleverness" new to French literature (*The Bit Between My Teeth*).

forward and announced, "State Department."] At the end of lunch, he said he had been glad to meet me: "We thought you had two heads." I don't quite know what he meant by this. In the meantime, Malraux had been talking to Léger. Léger himself is no mean talker and likes to dominate the conversation, but Malraux really had him on the ropes. He looked overcome, quite pathetic, as I have never known him to do before.

After lunch, we sat around in a circle—about thirty— and obvious questions were asked of Malraux. He would answer any question at once. He is always on the spot with a formulation. He made a greater pretension of seriousness than he had at the dinner the night before, but Phito agreed with me afterwards that *il débitait* statements which sounded impressive without making much real sense. He has, in fact, become a master of double-talk. What did he think of the role of the state in controlling the field of culture? This brought forth a long sequence—into the middle of which Robert Frost suddenly threw his weight. He seems now to have taken up his residence in Washington and is all over the place, full of faking and self-satisfaction. Malraux had been talking about *les poètes maudits* [Verlaine's phrase for Rimbaud, Tristan Corbière, etc.], saying—what I suppose is true—that there are no more *poètes maudits*, that there is nobody now for them to shock, the unconventional can no longer be an issue: "*Moi, j'étais un romancier maudit et maintenant je suis reçu à la Maison Blanche* [I was an accursed novelist and now I am received at the White House]." Frost, hearing the word *poets* when this was being translated, took this cue to go into his act, which for some time held up the proceedings. I recognized it as his regular act from quotations I had seen of his monologues. His drawling accent is Western rather than New Englander. "Poets—well, a poet when he first starts out doesn't have anybody to encourage him

—nobody wants him to be a poet. If he wants to be a poet, he has to do it all himself. Then someday a few people read him, and he makes them feel what he's been feeling." And so forth: he took us at length through the steps of the public recognition of the poet. "And the last thing that discovers him is the government. The government takes him up, and it makes capital out of him." He wanted us to know that he was a shrewd old boy—though obviously eating up the honors being paid him by the President— aware that he was being made use of. "The government discovers the poet—it's like Virgil and Augustus" (he got this, I learned later, from an article by Alfred Kazin). "Virgil was a country boy who wanted to be a poet. Nobody encouraged Virgil. He had to do it for himself. Then Augustus took him up," etc.*

When I was leaving with Phito, I ran into Frost in the hall, shook hands with him and introduced Phito as a novelist and poet from Haiti. "A poet?" said Frost. "Where do you say he comes from?" "Haiti." "Well, it's very important where a poet comes from." But I sidestepped the impending monologue.

Seeing Malraux in his official role, I felt strongly the truth of what I had always been told: that he habitually practices deception. Deception is necessary to him, compulsive. Janet Flanner discovered, when she was working on her *New Yorker* profile, that he misrepresented his age, that he had probably never been in Shanghai, and—what nobody before had known—that he had actually never studied in Paris at l'École des Langues Orientales. She found that he had never been registered, and she astonished the director by telling him this. He had believed that

---

* This account of Frost, then eighty-eight, reflects EW's awareness of the danger of being flattered and coopted by the government. Wilson, however, had underestimated Frost's poetry since the twenties, when he was expounding Eliot and Joyce.

André Malraux was one of their most distinguished products. When she casually tried to confront Malraux with one of these embarrassing discoveries, he would quickly brush them aside with "*Ça n'a pas d'importance*" or "*Ça ne m'intéresse pas.*" When I was coming back from Russia in '35, I asked him what he knew about the Russian Trials. "I don't know any more than you," he replied, "but I am sure that what the government says, *ce sont des mensonges* [they are lies]." He told me that I ought to go to see Trotsky, then living in France, and said that he now had *"un côté King Lear."** Later on, in the Spanish War, he allied himself with the Stalinists, and when he came to America raising funds, he engaged in a polemic with Trotsky: "Trotsky lies and knows he lies." Now he has to justify de Gaulle. Henry Brandon told me that when he had asked Malraux about the suppression of the press, he had answered that when one had been fighting Hitler, one had to be as unscrupulous and merciless as Hitler, and that it was the same situation with the OAS [Organisation de l'Armée Secrète], so that it was perfectly in order to suppress their papers. But I think that Malraux quite enjoys all this. He has always his own judgment of people and things, and he consciously plays a role while attempting to get certain things done. He talked to me at the lunch, before the State Department people were listening, as one old ex-Marxist to another, and quite differently, without doubt, from the way in which he talks to the Kennedys and the way he had talked at the dinner. He told me that he was going to

---

* Wilson had first recalled this conversation with Malraux after their Paris meeting in *The Fifties*: "He described to me *le côté Lear de Trotsky*, told me how he had walked with the old man, who had been acting the tragic grandeur of his rejection by his own people and his isolation in exile. He told me also of Trotsky's attitude toward a working-class man who had come to see him—dealt with his business and dismissed him and went back to his conversation with Malraux, as if from an inferior to an equal."

give them something a little more serious in New York. He believes he is a man of action using realistic means to accomplish desirable ends; but I think there is an element of fantasy in everything he undertakes. I think that he can't help somewhat missing connections with the practical world in which he performs, and that his exploits produce better novels than actual political results. He is a great man nevertheless.

After the luncheon, we went to *Phito's apartment*. Eva is away on some mission to Costa Rica. We drank some whisky, and I had a good conversation with him. He confessed that, like the people of whom Malraux had been speaking, *il n'avait plus envie d'écrire*. It is being so far away from Pierre and his Haitian material. He has given up his job at the Pan-American Union, and he seems to see very few people. He does not like to go to places in Washington on account of his colored blood. He does not even like to pass in restaurants as a South American. He told me that the man sitting next to him at lunch had *des préjugés de couleur*. I must ask him about this. When I left, he had had enough to drink so that he did not want to drive the car. Then he decided that he *could* drive it, but he only got as far as a larger street where I was able to get a taxi.

At Scottie Fitzgerald's

That night I was tired and dulled by the drinks and could not do justice to the Schlesingers' dinner. John Hersey and his wife, whom I had not met; Robert Lowell and Elizabeth had gone back to New York. Sam Behrman, who I was told kept the table in a roar, Henry Brandon and Scottie Fitzgerald [Lenihan], who touched me by kissing me. Paddy Chayefsky, whom I don't like: he is cheap, conceited, and corny, had told me at dinner the night before that he wanted to talk to me about the Russian Revolution—I could see what he was going to do with it: he had some stupid conception of Lenin that he thought would make him a dramatic character, and it was evident that Stalin was going to be rather a noble fellow, too. There were people at that White House dinner—Chayefsky, for example—who would certainly never have been there if they hadn't been friends of Arthur's. Robert Lowell, late in the evening, I understand, began insulting Chayefsky, who told him he was the rudest man he had ever met. I am told that he does this but have never seen him do it. Chayefsky does provide a temptation. I left the table after dinner before the men had done talking and got Elena to leave. She complains that whenever she gets in a conversation that is interesting, I always make her go home early.

May 13. I went to the Schlesingers' late in the morning to talk to Arthur about my income tax difficulties.* He was still in bed, and I was sorry to get him up. The Herseys were staying with them, and I found them very likable.

We went out to Scottie's for lunch. She lives in what is apparently one of the "wealthiest" residential sections. Henry Brandon was there but not her husband, who had not been at the Schlesingers' either, though he had been to dinner at the White House. Elena and I had both the same thought, and afterwards debated the significance of Brandon's having kissed her goodbye when we left. Elena thought it meant no, I thought not necessarily. I remember that when Brandon had come up here (to Talcottville) to interview me, he had talked about Scottie, and that Scottie, in some telephone conversation, had asked me what I

---

* Schlesinger recalls he was unable to help his friend, though he mentioned Wilson's situation to Mortimer Caplin, Commissioner of the IRS. Elena believed that her phone calls to Schlesinger and the White House pressure brought about the final settlement.

thought about him—"many people don't like him." I had heard that Scottie had had at some time some kind of marital trouble, but that it had somehow been got over.

The two girls are very pretty, especially the older one, who has that attractive combination: black eyes and red hair. The other has black eyes, too, and both have very fair skin. The boy, who, when we last visited them, seemed so much like Scott, full of romantic fantasies and leading questions, was this time completely quiet during the few moments we saw him. They all seemed to resemble their extremely dark father. Scottie's nose has become more beaklike—she gets this from her mother. She is a good deal more mature now, but has still a touch of her mother's irresponsibility, her inconsecutive way and offhandedness. She had told us she would come for us at the Sheraton, then called to say that there was something wrong with the car. Before and during lunch she kept telling us that she would take us for a "tour of the house," and finally brought us into a big room with portraits of her Sayre grandparents (the grandmother very beautiful), one or two amusing pictures and relics of Scott and Scott's books in a glass-doored bookcase; then said that was about all there was to it, and we went into another room and sat down. At lunch she said she was terribly sorry but there wasn't any dessert.

Before lunch, we had Bloody Marys. There was a woman from *American Heritage*. In the course of the conversation, I spoke of Dan Aaron's article on *Patriotic Gore*, which— as I told him would be the case—they had decided not to run. Bruce Catton is one of the editors, and Dan gave me to understand that if they printed it, they would be taking the bread out of their own mouths. She corroborated this.

Henry Brandon had been interviewing the President the afternoon before the dinner. The interview had been interrupted, and Kennedy had had to give his attention to a number of different matters. Brandon had been impressed by his quickness in shifting his attention and the force of his application to anything with which he was dealing. He would then shift back to the interview, continuing it where he had left it. It seemed to Brandon astonishing that he could go on to the big dinner and see all those mostly unknown people and say appropriate things to them. At dinner, I had been able to see how alert and intent he was. If you asked him a question, he crouched forward just as he does at his press conferences and pounces upon it with his answer the moment it has been asked. —Brandon had attended a Press Club dinner at which Kennedy was present and which was an immense success. They had brought down from New York an actor who impersonates Kennedy. This Kennedy had much enjoyed, but he had then proceeded to top this impersonator by doing an imitation of himself talking to the steel people. The tickets for admission of outsiders to the press conferences had been raised by the Press Association from $15 to $17.50, and Kennedy put it to them that if the press women's association followed suit, and certain organizations did the same, the whole thing would go spiralling, and the national economy be ruined.* He invited the actor to the White House the next day.

Brandon told me that Malraux had told him that his publishers in France had not really taken his art books seriously till he had shown them my *New Yorker* article in which I treated *Les Voix du Silence* as very important, comparing it to Gibbon, *Das Kapital* and *War and Peace*.

Scottie has no more family left in Montgomery, except

* JFK had convinced the magnates of the steel industry to roll back a price rise that would have led to further wage increases and to more inflation. His manner was anything but gentle.

the aunt who always hated Scott and whom she never sees. Nor does she ever see Scott's sister, married to the naval officer, who lives in California.

Strange to see her and the family pictures. I kept feeling pangs from far back. I remember how Scott, before he married Zelda, was telling me about her in New York— how he said, "I wouldn't mind if she died, but I couldn't stand to have her marry somebody else." When he finally brought her up and John Bishop and I went to meet her, she was wearing a wide summer hat and a white dress, I think rather frilly, and she lay on a couch or chaise longue in the hotel. We celebrated by drinking Orange Blossoms. I mentioned this to her once, telling how pretty she had looked, and I found that the memory embarrassed her. She had said that her mother, in her Southern provincialism, had not known how to dress her for New York. *

We went back to the hotel, where *Phito* was meeting us for drinks. He turned up with Sheba Strunsky and her husband, whose name I forget, and another, German, woman. Sheba suggested coming to their house in Georgetown—a very good idea, for I had forgot that in Washington no drinks are served on Sunday. I had a good talk with Phito. He did not mumble so much or drink so much, and I managed better than usual in French. It was perhaps the only clear conversation of any length that I had ever had with him. He talked about Haiti and said that the only solution for it would be for the UN to take it over. Something was said about his being international, and he replied that he was by no means unique, that there were many Haitians like him scattered around the world.

* Throughout *The Sixties*, EW recalls Scott and Zelda's conversation, though he resists the role of interpreter of the Fitzgerald legend. He had established a relationship with Scottie when editing *The Crack-up* and *The Last Tycoon.*

I felt that the Malraux lunch and our visit had somewhat stimulated him. After all, his father was a diplomat: that kind of thing was natural for him. I wish some use could be found for him by the government. I asked Arthur about him that morning, and he said that they were at that moment particularly interested in Haiti. They wanted to get rid of the current president, with his unopposed reign of terror. Phito thought that I had been *"très sévère pour mon pays"* in *Patriotic Gore*.

Elena talked German to the Austrian woman, who had been through all sorts of horrors with the Nazis. She was not Jewish but had been married to a Jew, who had been killed in a concentration camp. She had been goodlooking but had a look of old distress and shaken self-confidence.

CITY, COUNTRY, AND CAPE:
SUMMER 1962

Return to New York

We had brought our bags with us and went straight from there to the airport, and flew to New York. Henry and Daphne came to dinner; Henry left us to go to his class in accounting but then came back to the Algonquin. Mike Nichols and the Epsteins also dined with us. Jason is extremely sour: he won't admit any more that anything is good. He seems to have nagged Ted Gorey out of Looking Glass books, and said he couldn't stand to look through his new sequence in *Holiday*. Barbara says that Ted, at Bobbs Merrill, is for the first time having to enter the adult world and is having a trying experience. Looking Glass, I suppose, is about to fold up, and I gather that Jason is oppressed by Bennett Cerf. He has bought a $30,000 boat, in which he plans to cruise up and down the Hudson and which he then will take to Wellfleet for the summer. I told him it was suicidal. He is taking a course in boating in order to learn how to run it. Lillian Hellman said to him, "You're just a Jewish boy with a cocktail boat." I can see it docked at Wellfleet with all his old pals on board drinking martinis.

Nichols and May had been asked to perform for the Kennedy birthday rally in Madison Square Garden, and to give something specially prepared for the occasion. They were in doubt as to what they should do: the things they wanted to satirize, such as nuclear testing, seemed in bad taste for a birthday celebration, and they had about decided to do something about these cultural blowouts.

After dinner, we went to the Epsteins', where the Little Player puppeteers joined us, Frank Peschka and Bill Murdock.* The Thorntons enjoyed the evening, talked little but listened attentively and stayed as late as we did. I felt that this was a sign that Daphne was getting interested in things which she had before considered uninteresting or undesirable.

May 14 (Monday). Elena had to go back to Wellfleet, because Joan Colebrook couldn't stay any longer with Helen. I spent the day at *The New Yorker*, then went up to see Clelia [Delafield Carroll] at her apartment. Her husband was down with his mother in Maryland. She was staying with the children. The little girl by her former marriage apparently gets neurotic when the mother goes away. The doctor came to see her while I was there. It was the first I had seen Clelia since before she had had her baby. She looked lovely, after her pregnancy, very slim in a pale yellow dress with white pumps. There is something that charms me so about her. Her voice—"Oh, Edmund!"—and her sophisticated-shy smile. She talked about Ted Gorey and the Epsteins, and we discussed the income tax. Her father, 86, a banker, knows all about it and how the big ones get away with paying nothing.

---

* EW's life-long love of puppetry, including Punch and Judy, drew him to The Little Players. They specialized in "glove puppets—that is, not marionettes but the kind of puppets you put your hands in"—he explains in *The Bit Between My Teeth*, adding that everything was done "by one man," who managed the movements and gestures and impersonated voices and accents. Peschka was the performer, Murdock stage manager.

I then went over and had dinner with Marion Amen. She talks to me nowadays more freely about herself than she has ever done before. She said that she had felt it would be so mean not to be nice to John's mistress. She and Opal are now very close friends. I had wanted to go to *Sweet Bird of Youth*, which was just around the corner in Sutton Place, out of curiosity about Geraldine Page, who Mike Nichols had told me he thought was now the best actress in America; but we got to talking and drinking and never went. Curious to see Marion just after Clelia. She is one of the women of my generation that Clelia a little reminds me of (Margaret [Canby], too); but Marion is now an old lady, as I always find it hard for me to recognize.

May 15. The New Yorker the next day: Swinburne article and my "Interview." Ved Mehta came in in the late afternoon, and we talked about the English historians, about whom he is doing articles for *The New Yorker*. He has just come back from England, which he had found rather empty and disappointing. *The Observer* may not survive.

We went to the Algonquin for a drink and there found Alfred Kazin and Paolo Milano and another friend of Alfred's. It ended by our all having dinner at the Kazins'. Ann turned out an excellent little buffet supper. I regaled them with stories about Washington. Paolo, with his easy Roman cynicism, said, "You know how unreliable Malraux is. Do you know what is the difference between Lumumba and Malraux? *Lumumba est un congolais et Malraux est un con* [fool] *Gaulliste*"* —I took Alfred back to a couch and talked to him about his review of *Patriotic Gore*. He showed a certain indignation over my Introduction: I and my people

* A leader of the Pan-African movement, Patrice Lumumba became the first Prime Minister of the Republic of the Congo (later Zaire). Soon afterward he was imprisoned and killed in Katanga.

"had it made" and didn't sympathize with the Negroes and people like him, the son of immigrants, who had found in the United States freedom and opportunity. He is still full of a romantic faith in American ideals and promises, and it is hard for him to see what we are really doing.

I had to take Ved Mehta home, so was late for meeting Sheilah Graham, with whom I had arranged she should come to the Algonquin after the theater. I see her at such long intervals and her appearance changes so much in the meantime that I can hardly recognize her. She has now grown a good deal broader. As usual, I liked her and got a good impression of her. She lives now in New York all the time: she says that she is closer to the movies here than she is in Hollywood. Mike Nichols had told me that when she had interviewed him and Elaine, she had been stupid about their show. This may well be, but she has admirable British qualities. She had been much hurt by some of the reviews of her book, which had treated her as if she were "a prostitute." I assured her that everybody who knew Scott well knew what the situation had been respecting her; Scottie was very fond of her. She said that she did not feel, however, that she had been very good with Scottie. She had been jealous of her as she had been of Zelda, and had dreaded her vacations because whenever she arrived, Scott would go on a binge. And he had really been horrible to Scottie sometimes—once he had ripped off her dress. I saw she liked to talk about Scott with somebody who had known him. To have been part of his life, she said, "made her feel fascinating." She has been married a number of times, never with any success. She has sent her son to a good prep school, I can't remember which. I told her that the Murphys had been touched by her coming to see them in New York just after Scott's funeral, which it hadn't been thought proper for her to attend. She said that, not having been there, she just wanted to see friends of Scott's and be able to talk about him. Like Scottie and me, she was deluged with letters after her book came out, and a madman has been pursuing her so menacingly for years that she finally alerted the police. She regrets that her ghost Gerald Frank somewhat distorted her story for the sake of dramatic effect. At the home she was sent to, for example, though it was true that they did shave their heads, she had actually become a leader among the girls and a more or less privileged character; but Frank didn't want to put this in because it lessened the pathos of the story. A trace of cockney accent still lingers. In spite of her early masquerade, one of her most striking qualities is honesty. She has never been a very exciting gossip columnist on account of her honesty and her freedom from malice.

Upstaters

<*May 16*. I flew up to *Utica* the next afternoon, spent the night in the Schuyler Club and had dinner there with Cecil Lang. When we were sitting around after dinner, an elderly man, very tight, came and joined us and bored us. He was an old Utican, who knew the Harts. He said that Merwin was 80 and in bad health and that he lived in New York, but made visits to Utica. He thought that Merwin's ideas were fine and wished they could have been made to prevail. He, our friend, had sat for forty years on the election committee of the club and in all that time they had never admitted a new member. He then—what delighted Lang—complained that the club was doing badly, was in fact struggling to survive. I asked Penberthy about it afterwards, and he said that this man was a member of one of the rich old Utica families who had owned the

knitting mills. He had never done a stroke of work in his life. It was possible that those original families had kept everybody else out, that at least there had been no admissions from any other families. But there were plenty of new members. (Nevertheless, I have always been struck by the predominance of elderly men.) He said that the club was not badly in debt—as a matter of fact, it was doing quite well.>

May 17. Talcottville. Mary Pcolar drove me up. On the way, she talked all the time, in the non-stop Hungarian fashion, about her difficult relations with the Kramers. She had quit again a month ago. I imagined that what first happened was that Ray Kramer took such an interest in her that Mrs. Kramer became jealous; and that then, as Mary told me, Mrs. Kramer tried to make an alliance with Mary against Ray, which also made Mary uncomfortable. Glyn Morris and somebody else have interested themselves in getting her a social job, but she has to have some kind of degree and wants to get one at Utica College. She is looking more middle-aged.

<Albert Grubel can't drive me any more. He is too old and has a bad back.

Beverly is about to have a baby. I called on her at her house—they live in a somewhat squalid way, but she is next door to her sister and has an attractive long stretch of back lawn. The husband, who works in a Boonville garage, came home from work while I was there. He is very shy with me, turns away; but when I do catch his eye, there is something not unresponsive and not unattractive about his not-so-simple green-shielded coruscation.

Huldah Loomis has been miserable, she says—in the Utica hospital with flu and the bad eye from which the cataract was removed.

Fern has a political job in Lowville. She appeared very smartly dressed, with patent leather shoes and lilac gloves. >

The Talcottville house now is completely clean and comfortable. Mrs. Hutchins and I have both noticed that the dusty smell is no longer perceptible anywhere. The new heating may have something to do with this; but the heating has been turned off most of the winter, and Mrs. Hutchins thinks that the cutting down last fall of the big elm trees, by letting more sun into the house, has kept it from getting so damp.

<Coming back here, I don't any more think much about the past, though it is always there. I am so completely now living a new chapter. The income tax business, the Indians, what I see of the life of the Munns and getting to know the Hungarians has brought me into contemporary New York State—also Glyn Morris's problems. > I see it now from the point of view of the present inhabitants rather than that of the old life here and Walter Edmonds and the Oneida Community. *

<Whisky in the morning:

The mist that lies before my Eastern door
And morning's golden kingdom of the light. >

---

* The Oneida Community was a nineteenth-century experiment in common ownership and eugenics, the product of perfectionism—the belief that Christ had already come again, eliminating sin. To produce a better human breed, a central committee led by John Humphrey Noyes, the founder, regulated sex within the group. When EW visited the place with Van Wyck Brooks in the fifties, the two critics amused themselves by speculating that the transoms over the bedroom doors were large enough for people to get out and "plan a different parenthood." Wilson describes this social experiment in *To the Finland Station* and *Upstate*.

I saw in New York a few sequences of *Sweet Bird of Youth* in order to get some idea of Geraldine Page as an actress. Then, finding it at the Boonville movie theater, I took the Loomises to it. It affected me rather the way Elena says that T.W. [Tennessee Williams] in person affects her. The sex scenes imagined by a homosexual in which the man is denying or tormenting the woman! When it came to the part I had seen, I closed my eyes and went to sleep and, when I came to, found myself in a complete blackout. I didn't know whether I was in Washington or New York or where and had to ask Huldah who she was.

<I had a complete collapse—got some kind of flu that has been going around: Mary and one of her little girls have had it. I ran up a fairly high temperature and on top of that had a terrible attack of gout, while it lasted one of the worst. Instead of finding relief in lying down, I was writhing all one afternoon, and couldn't even get to the bathroom to take my gout medicine. I had told Elena that noon on the phone that she didn't need to come over, but in the evening got Mabel Hutchins to call her and tell her to come. She flew over and arrived early Sunday afternoon. I moved out of the front room into the big back room, which is quieter and more spacious. This improved my morale—I relaxed. It is my favorite room that I sleep in. It is large and seems higher than the others, perhaps on account of the big old wardrobe. It has the big bed from Minnie Collins's that my mother and father used to sleep in when we stayed there, and for which I have bought a new spring mattress. I began reading Diderot's *Les Bijoux Indiscrets*, which amused me and took my mind off my troubles. Elena stayed for two days, then had to go back on account of Helen; but by that time I was on my feet again.> It was a good thing she came for other reasons. We went to the mat with Penberthy and got him to submit

another offer, and I made him take me to Syracuse to talk to the people in the tax office there, who were decent and I thought quite intelligent. The Utica people are mere underlings, who put on a show of severity. It is the others who make the decisions.

<Driving me back from Utica, Mary talked at length about current methods in the schools. They give them ridiculous courses in such subjects as sex education and don't teach them to cook or sew. The young people get married and don't know how to do anything, and the bride's parents keep buying her gadgets: cars, washing machines, etc. I asked her why she thought it was necessary for Americans to have all these courses and books and doctors' advice about sex, and she told me a story told her by some friend about another girl, a homemaking teacher, who was about to get married and who was studying a book to prepare herself. She learned all about a thing called a "basal thermometer," which showed when ovulation was taking place. When a friend had asked whether she was sure that it would not coincide with her period—"just woman-talk," said Mary—it turned out that the girl was quite ignorant about this: she thought that the period always occurred on the first of the calendar month and had not made any serious calculations. "Yes!" the friend had said, taunting her. "You'll be lookin' in that little book and your husband will be waitin' and wonderin' what's the matter."

When I came out of my collapse, I felt better than I ever had all winter in Cambridge. Dr. Smith's gout-preventive medicine worked—I am now taking three different kinds—and I was able to get around, also felt a good deal more cheerful. I have greatly enjoyed the last few days here: the weather has been beautiful, and I have been writing up this journal. On Saturday I got Mary Pcolar to take me to look for the Showy Orchid. A state botanical report of '31 indicates that it was to be found then in the "dry rocky wood southwest of Orwell" and at Bennet Bridge, which is at the further end of the Salmon River reservoir. We started too late and got lost and never arrived at Bennett Bridge; but I saw for the first time the Pcolar family at home. I got a very pleasant impression of them. When we arrived, we found George and the children doing I don't know exactly what but amusing themselves somehow out of doors, with, in the background, the old Hungarian mother, the ginger cat Ripple that we gave them and a beloved two-year-old beagle bitch who is about to have puppies. The mother lives in a little home detached from the main building. It is an old feed house which Mary has fitted up, and everything inside is as neat as a pin: little bed with old-fashioned white coverlet, colored picture above it of the Mother of God, English Bible and Hungarian prayerbook. She came over when she was fifteen but still speaks with a strong accent. I was taken in to see her as if she were, as she is, the head of the family. I told her that Mary was an exceptionally bright girl. "Do you think so?"—looking at me intently and shrewdly. "She wants something more"—she said later—"but she can't reach it." I asked why her parents had come to America, and she was about to tell me when Mary came in and we thought that we ought to start. I am going to talk with her further. On the way back from our drive, Mary pointed out a little cemetery with a towering white crucifix in the middle. She told me that her mother had had it put up. I was impressed and said that it must have cost quite a lot. $400, made of imitation marble.

The mother had had a shock when Mary's grandfather, eight years ago, had died in her presence of a heart attack, and she had suffered for years from rheumatism and a heart condition of her own. She had prayed all the time, and at last quite recently she had begun to have visions. She was looking one day at the window, which was covered with a "frost formation," and at first she thought she saw the face of a man looking in at the window. She was frightened, but then the window began to take on colors, and she saw it was a stained-glass window that made the room holy. She had other visions, too, and her health became much better—she stopped taking pills.

They are fond of one another, this family, and have a good time together. It is really something very old world. Agatha [Fassett] had told me how self-contained and self-sustaining the Hungarian communities had to be—did everything for themselves, made their own music and cultivated rhyming joking conversations. It has something in common with life here in the early days. The Pcolars are a separate unit and Mary does not have really close friends, and she sharply disapproves of many features of the way others live. They have, I think, 160-some acres, and they know about all of the things that go on there: birds, animals, plants and trees. Her father used to trap mink, weasels, rabbits, etc. She takes responsibility for everything and has settled down to her husband, with whom I thought her relations were good. They amiably kid one another, and she told me on Saturday that they were going out to make a night of it, going to dinner at a good restaurant and maybe not getting back till 2 in the morning. With the children, it seems to me, she is wonderful. She keeps them under firm discipline, will not let them see much television, has them all learning musical instruments, reads to them, and wants to see they get a good education. The result is that they are better brought up than so many of the children of our Wellfleet and Cambridge friends. And they always seem to be having an awfully good time —it is cheerful to see the girls scampering somewhere in their little red pants.

I called Mary up on Sunday, and she said she had gone home after dinner, so that she was perfectly energetic and would willingly go on an expedition to look for the orchid again. George, her husband, and the two girls went along. This time I brought a road map, and we succeeded in finding Bennett Bridge. There were the dry rocky woods all right but no Showy Orchids. George and I spent the rest of the afternoon fishing in the waters at that end of the reservoir. He caught a perch and a small brown trout; I caught a small catfish. The attractions of Mary won her a present from one of the other fishermen: a rock bass and a rainbow trout. I thoroughly enjoyed the afternoon. It was so long since I had done anything out of doors. I had never been much in that part of the world—we were not far from Pulaski on Lake Ontario—where it is wild and there are few people living but a scattering of summer camps in the wood, and it was almost like being in a foreign country—so fresh and unmodernized, so far from the filing cabinets and overhead lighting of the tax and lawyers' offices. I was tired when I got back in a healthy physical way and sleepy during dinner with the Munns.

Fern, in her new office as Commissioner of Elections, had been recently in the even wilder country north of Osceola—Montague and Pinkney—and she says that the people there are still on the level of the early settlers. The older men have long beards and mackinaws. She went to a town meeting consisting of six men, at which the supervisor was reading a comic book all through the proceedings while other people were talking: he was occasionally interrupted when other people spoke to him. Another man was lying on his back on a bench with a jug of liquor beside him from which he would take long swigs. He occasionally offered drinks to other people but still remained on his back. Fern has to check the voting machines after the elections—she says that there is no possibility of fraud unless everybody, including the sheriff, should engage in such a complete conspiracy as these people are incapable of organizing.

The Pcolars told me that the woods around Osceola are swarming with wildcats. They find deer that have been killed by the cats, which leap upon them and bite through their jugular veins and then seem to leave them uneaten. Of course, a wildcat can't eat much of a deer. They may leave them as provision for later on or perhaps merely kill them out of a passion for hunting, as human beings kill so many animals. People shoot wildcats for the bounty.>

The visit up here has included some of the worst, some of the best of my Talcottville days.

<Mary's language: Her vocabulary is sometimes a little unexpected. The children had "spied" the package in which I had sent a book, so she couldn't keep it till Christmas. I asked her if she read a paper regularly, and she said that they took the *Rome Sentinel*, and she at least "scanned" the front page every day.

When I see her with her family (George), she is self-conscious and rather coarse; when she is talking to me about the Kramers, it is all "she said" and "he said" and "I said," on the level of the Boonville store people; when she talks to me about current social problems, she is quite different, talks like a serious and fairly well-educated person>—active in PTA and home decoration movement.

"La Plage des Intellectuels"

Helen went to visit her friend Nina Green at Marblehead and came back saying that her family were stuffed shirts, wanted to be social but hadn't really made it. Mrs. Green wouldn't let her wear the black bathing suit that, without Elena's knowing it, she had cut very low behind. Mrs. Green had said, "We mustn't be too gorgeous!" and had also objected to her slacks and made her wear something looser. Helen said that the wider kind were "a badge of chastity."

In the course of the last winter at Cambridge, she has made close friends and had boy admirers. She disposed of one of the latter by saying to him, "I think I'd better not see any more of you until I'm nineteen." She would have interminable teenage conversations on the telephone, take the phone into the coat closet and crouch there in the darkness. —I found when I looked up Scottie Fitzgerald in the Washington telephone book that she had listed a separate number for "Children."

Helen matured last fall and it has made her more self-confident and cheerful—she is amiable and likes to charm.

Wellfleet, summer, '62. La plage des intellectuels, as Stuart Hughes calls it. After not having been here at this time of year for years, I find that the elite now all congregate, away from the Newcomb's Hollow crowds, on the beach below the little summerhouses that perch on the top of the cliff: the Kazins, the Schlesingers, the Hofstadters, the Aarons, Ed O'Connor and his fiancée, sometimes the Walkers and the Jenckses. The Walkers keep a distance from the rest but also come to that beach. Then there is Mary Grant. The Hugheses go to a beach of their own nearer to their place on Long Pond. Stuart, who is running for Senator from Massachusetts on a pro-peace indepen-dent ticket, does not much want to see Arthur, now a member of the official family. I enjoyed it for a while but have now had a surfeit of it. I thought last autumn that the congregating and drinking were just a feature of the end of the season; but I see now that it goes on all summer.

Elena and I either went out to dinner or had people here almost without interruption: Schlesingers here one night, Kazins another, Hugheses and Hofstadters the night after that; dinner at the Hugheses' with the Hofstadters, dinner at the Francis Biddles' with the Schlesingers, dinner at the Kazins' with the Schlesingers, the Aarons and a man named Goodwin from the State Department, who is visiting the Schlesingers with his wife, dinner at the Jenckses' with the Newmans, Arthur Berger, two other young musicians and the wife of the Richman in Washington who manipulated the Malraux luncheon, with her nine-year-old daughter, a Lolita, who had a pack of cards and was going to play solitaire as I used to do, in childhood, at parties and for whom I did a few card tricks, finding her an interested audience—earlier, dinner at the Chavchavadzes' with the George Biddles, and dinner at our house or their house with Barbara and Mary and others, etc., etc.

Since Barbara and Mary have gone to Maine, the heavy business of the summer has begun, and it makes a striking contrast with the old Jig Cook Provincetown or the Dos Passos–Waugh Provincetown. They were all writers and painters who were working and freely exchanging ideas; but these people are mostly attached to the government or some university, or they at least do part-time teaching. Jim Newman is the editor of *Scientific American*. They are accountable to some institution, and you are likely—especially with the Schlesingers—to run into some subject as to which they have to be dumb, so that you feel it is tactless to talk about it. I did, however, when Arthur was here to dinner, get him into the study alone and talk about the income tax with him. He touched me by saying at the end of it, "I've never been interested in money."

I have become timid, perhaps too timid, on account of my heart, about going into the cold water or struggling with the surf, and it bores me and irritates me to go to the

Elena Wilson in her garden at Wellfleet

ocean without being able to swim, and now that the Sharps are there, I am beginning to get nostalgic for Talcottville.

In the midst of a party at the Kazins', Dick Goodwin, the man from the State Department who was visiting Arthur Schlesinger, talked about the Charles Van Doren case, in which he had been, I think, the investigator.* We talked about the Van Dorens, and he or someone else about Jean [Gorman] Van Doren's suicide. Carl had come back home and found that she had hanged herself. It gave me a shock. I knew that she had committed suicide, but don't think I had known how. I had been thinking of the present as a sinister era, but when I press upon the past in memory, it often seems horrible.†

I stayed in Wellfleet longer than I otherwise should have on account of Reuel's coming on, and I found it rather demoralizing. I thought that, except for Reuel, I should be better off in Talcottville, now that the Sharps were there.

Talcottville in August: Quarrelling with Elena

Talcottville. Reuel drove me over on August 1. We stopped off for the night with Helen [Muchnic] and Dorothy

---

* While an instructor at Columbia, Charles Van Doren was the most celebrated winner on *The $64,000 Question*, a quiz show that turned out to be rigged.

† Jean was a friend from the twenties. First married to the journalist and critic Herbert Gorman, she was a drinking companion of Margaret Canby's and Ted Paramore's, and after Margaret's death pursued Wilson, who is said to have slapped her in the face when they were drunk. In one version of this story—told by Matthew Josephson—he was riding away on his bicycle and she, wanting to stop him, had a car bump into him.

[Walsh]. They had the Linscotts and the Grynbergs to dinner—the latter came up from the Tanglewood Festival. Newton Arvin was there, too. He has passed from being suicidal, as he had been thought to be in the first days of his scandal. It is as if being made to come out in the open has made him more self-confident, less shy. He has finished his book on Longfellow, and told Dan Aaron that he would like to dedicate it "To the Trustees of Smith College," who had fired him and given him leisure to write.

<I found the Sharps very miserable. Dorothy is learning to walk again, and if she makes any special effort, she seems invariably to sprain a wrist or throw a toe out of joint, and a few days ago went into a serious decline. She is now recovering, and yesterday Rosalind and I went in to see her. After talking about her ailments, in which Rosalind was perfect in showing sympathetic interest, she pulled herself together and talked about books and other things. But she does dwell on these ailments a good deal. I have, on account of my gout, some idea of how she feels. To be crippled and uncomfortable all the time does make one morose and irritable. She says that her breaking her hip and all the confinement that followed have had on her a psychological effect. She dislikes almost everything that is going on (but I and so many of my generation feel the same way). She is annoyed by a radio and a barking dog that are now in the house next door. It is plain that she is losing the will to live. Malcolm is always attentive and patient—almost never leaves her alone in the house. They have been over here together only twice, and he very rarely comes alone and never for very long. He will not even take a drink, because, I suppose, he feels he ought always to be equal to an emergency, and his drinking has always made her rather nervous. So I haven't been seeing as much of them as usual. It is impossible for them to do things

with me, and I feel that I mustn't stay long with them because it tires Dorothy out and wears on her nerves.

It is sad for me up here this summer. > Huldah Loomis is also not well, in the early spring came down so badly with the flu that she had to go to the Utica hospital; but she doesn't like to talk about it. Gertrude, as Dorothy says, "doesn't click."

<Mariska Pcolar has partly deserted me, because she now has a job in Rome in a new drugstore in which she runs the cosmetics department and is, she says, "on the crest of the wave." She is resolved to go to Utica College, a newly organized branch of Syracuse University, and get some kind of degree, and this, too, has bucked her up. She came here this morning (Saturday) and is coming tomorrow afternoon to type my letters and do Hungarian with me. I miss having her come almost every afternoon as she did last summer. > Even though I don't make love to her, I like to have her body around, <so extremely well-grown and capable, naturally and beautifully developed to do things. I had her take me to the Boonville greenhouse to get petunias and geraniums for the stone receptacles on the porch, and she said suddenly, Why should you buy petunias when I can give you some. She then brought me ageratum and huge petunias. I said to Rosalind, "Those are Hungarian petunias." Rosalind said, "They'll make trouble!" She brought me vasefuls of her magnificent gladiolas—purple, yellow, blue, scarlet, pink. She also brought me a great glass jar of excellent Hungarian stew. > This all has something to do with the self-dependence and strength of character of the old-life women up here. It came out in the course of the little party that I gave for the Marcelins that, as I got it secondhand from Malcolm, she "had been delivered by her father" (I don't know whether it was one of her children or Mariska herself),

and that she had delivered some friend. This is part of the complete self-dependence that is characteristic, Agatha says, of the country people in Hungary.

<Beverly, who had come to see her Aunt Mabel [Hutchins], brought her baby over for me to see. She was touching and sweet, looked quite pretty after her pregnancy, is crazy about the baby. She said that Elena had told her that what she needed was a baby to occupy her, and she now thinks that Elena was right. She had a hard time giving birth, and still has to wear some kind of brace for her back.>

The Marcelins came for two nights on their usual summer visit to Eva's family in Canastota. I had, as I had had in Washington with Phito, more interesting conversations with them than usual. I asked him who the man had been that he sat beside at the Malraux luncheon and who, he had told me, had *"des préjugés de couleur."* It turned out to be Hervé Alphand, the French ambassador, whose wife had raised a fuss about the Negro family on her block and otherwise, in this connection, made herself disagreeable. Phito is uncomfortable in Washington and wants to get away. I told him of my experiences with the State Department agents at that lunch and at the Russian parties in Boston, and he told me that he was always, at official functions— at the Haitian ambassador's, etc.—afraid to express his true opinion about Latin American affairs, because he never knew to whom he was talking, and as a onetime leftist, he did not want to get in trouble for criticizing our foreign policy, to be called a Communist sympathizer. If he should be sent back to Haiti, the present thug regime would murder him. He said that it was wonderful for him to occasionally get together with a Haitian and be able to speak fluently and freely. When I told Malcolm about this conversation, he remarked very characteristically—slip-

ping past difficult problems with a half-flippant, half-
serious wit—that it ought soon to be possible to talk freely
about Latin American policy, since we had now succeeded
in offending there every possible shade of political opinion.

<*Rosalind* has just been here from Wednesday to Saturday (August 15–18). The only time I really get to talk
to my children is when they drive me around. I had her
drive me up on *Tug Hill* along the road where I went with
that state zoölogist.> All the region seems to belong to the
Gould Paper Co. of Lyons Falls, though I am told that one
of the hunting clubs has bought from them a tract of land
and enclosed it so that they can be sure of the game being
there. They are doing some logging there now and building
a dam to make a swimming pool in Whetstone Gulf, so
that at one place the road has been raised. This makes
rather uncomfortable driving because to go over the side
would be disastrous. Beyond, the road is full of deep holes,
which just now are full of water, and Rosalind was afraid
that the brakes would get wet. We stopped by the gate
that keeps cars out of the domain of the Constableville
Rainey Club and the Fairchild Club, and then walked some
distance farther along the road, but never got to the sphagnum swamp. I did, however, find the strange flowers in
the pond on the left side of the road—the amphibious
knotweed (*Polygonum*) that grows in the water like waterlilies and sticks up its blossoms in pink spikes that are
almost phallic. I pulled in two or three with my cane, but
rather meager specimens. There are water birds that I
cannot identify that one doesn't see elsewhere. Some little
animal crossed the road that Rosalind didn't recognize.
<She was bored at first by the monotony of the thick-
bushed narrow road, but then, when we got into the wilder
part, declared that it was quite beautiful: the fireweed,
past its prime but making a curious screen of pink—the

last blossoms and the pinkish stems—in the background of high goldenrod, joe-pye weed, low yellow St. Johns-wort. A few pink roadside mallows were rearing themselves in their glory as they don't do near our civilization—though they are beginning to dominate everything in my neglected garden, even the hollyhocks (though the balance two summers ago was better held); like all jungles, I suppose, they begin to terrorize a little. One felt that the plant-life were masters there, that they didn't have to bother about us, that the flowers even could overtop us. >

I have found out that a John Constable of Watertown —I didn't know that there were any Constables left around here—controls the admission through the gate, and he has allowed me to borrow a key.

<*Elena and Helen* arrived Friday the 24th.> As usual, she had tried to put it off: the Winkelhorns were coming, the car had to be fixed, then she finally called up to say that Henry and his family were coming to Newport and she wanted to stop off and see them, but they wouldn't be there till Saturday. Penberthy was here at the moment to talk about the income tax appeal, and I told her to come right away. She stopped off for the night at Cummington with Helen Muchnic and Dorothy Walsh, and then drove here through Vermont and the Adirondacks, wanting to avoid the trucks, or so she said. She hadn't made this plan clear, and by the time she arrived at 7 p.m. I was getting worried and had called Helen Muchnic up. This, I'm sure, was really a part of her sabotaging Talcottville.

I hadn't had anything to drink after doing too much drinking the day before, and the delay and this made me nervous. I walked back and forth in the room asking her to tell me all the news. She kept saying, "So-and-so sends you lots of love." I got so annoyed with this—she is always sending people "lots and lots of love"—that when she said it about the fifth time, I said, "Oh, don't." She made a little scene of bursting into tears—à la Auntie Maroussia—and said, "They're your old friends. Don't you want to hear about anybody but these *govna* [shits] up here—except the Sharps?"*

I had been longing so to have her here and make love to her, had been thinking of her in her deep rose bathing suit and her beautiful tanned legs, but of course she was always too tired or her stomach was upset or she had to begin getting dinner.

<The Players Guild at Collinsville did *Blithe Spirit* this summer. Jane Klosner was the first wife's ghost. She has been their main attraction for years but hadn't been in the other two of their performances I had seen, and I was astonished by her: so different from the heaviness of the rest of the cast—lively, amusing, pretty, full of *espiéglerie* [mischief] and charm. I found out afterwards that she is Scotch-Irish, her maiden name was Galbraith. I went behind after the show and invited her and her husband to my little party for the Marcelins.>

She came again when Elena was here. I had invited the Morrises, too, but Glyn's mother was ill and he had to go to Pennsylvania. <Jane called up to say that her husband wasn't well, but could she come alone? It turned out, when she got here, that she was so conventional in terms of her milieu that she thought it wasn't proper for a wife to go anywhere without her husband—but, she said, "I thought if Jackie Kennedy can, I can!"> Being alone with us, she poured out her heart—to Elena rather than to me. She had had three miscarriages and two years ago adopted a little girl, then a baby, through the Catholic Charities. The baby was pure Irish, and she had named her Kathleen.

---

* Elena excludes from this characterization the Sharps, whom she liked.

She didn't know who the parents were, the mother "unwed," but she knew they were a fine class of people, college graduates, and she was proud to think the little girl—I don't know how it would be perceptible at that age—was speaking good English. Her own English is not always perfect, and she combines the local accent with a way of talking that reminds me of Jenny Corbett and her family. She is touching and very likable. <Elena had had her usual stiffening at my making her meet any woman that I had admiringly talked about—she had said, "When is your Sarah Bernhardt coming?"—but she liked her, too, and said, "She's straight."> Jane was worried about the little girl, who was beginning to ask questions about her parents. She wondered whether it wouldn't be better to adopt another child. Elena advised her not to.

Jane Klosner: I asked about the strip-bowling scandal, and she said that she had been "implicated." It had all been an invented story. First, I gathered, the man who had built the new bowling alley had been selling hard liquor when he only had a license for beer; then when he got his hard liquor license, he began to take all the trade away from the Hulburt House and the other bars. The proprietors of these set out to get him by circulating this scandal. She says that she was supposed to have stripped and that another of the ladies accused was a married woman six months pregnant.

Crisis on Elena's birthday (Aug. 27): I had been so angry over her trying to postpone coming to Talcottville that I had forgotten to tell her to bring the little Sidney Nolan painting that she had admired at the Durlacher Gallery and which was still unpacked in my study at Wellfleet. When I spoke of it, she would always say—on account of our reduced resources—"Send it back to the dealers" or

"Sell it back." Not a word of pleasure or thanks. When I bought for dinner the best Garbarino's had in the way of French champagne, she said, "It's not Cordon Rouge," and though it was dry, she assumed that it was "that sweet champagne that they used to make to sell to Russians." When I had to call Penberthy about our appeal, she grew tense and disagreeable. When I told her I wanted to have the Bests to dinner, all she said was, "I don't want to talk about Penberthy!" When I had asked her to write Marion Amen and invite her to come up, she said, "John Amen is a very sore point."* She had announced bitterly the day before her birthday that she was going to do the laundry to celebrate—though Mrs. Hutchins has been doing it all along.

The Sharps came to dinner, which was pleasant enough. After dinner, Malcolm and I drove to his house to get a bottle of red wine which his brother had brought him. He told me he had it on his mind that he was not being good to Dorothy. This surprised me because he seemed to be a model of patience, and I thought he meant he was sometimes impatient; but when I mentioned it afterwards, he said that that was not it, that he was "too serious, didn't give her enough diversion." The wine was horribly sour. I don't think that the brother and his wife had shown very much consideration. The brother, an anthropologist at Cornell, had called me and asked me to tell Malcolm that he wanted them to join him at The Beeches, that big restaurant outside Rome. I had said they wouldn't be able to make it, Dorothy was in rather bad shape. So the others had come to Talcottville and Dorothy seemed somewhat hurt that they had "only stayed fifteen minutes."

After the Sharps left, I drank another glass of the horrible wine, and though I hadn't had much to drink, I set

---

* Amen, who had managed the Wilsons' legal business, had at one point neglected to file their tax return.

off a quarrel with Elena, telling her that she hadn't been
to bed with me for weeks—which led to her ungraciousness
about birthday gifts, etc. She hadn't shown me much affection or sympathy since she had come to Talcottville,
had told me to "snap out of it" and not "pity myself" when
I had told her how depressed I was, and, when I said that
I needed sympathy, had said, "Everybody needs sympathy."
She thought Helen was at the store but then it turned out
she was in her room and had, I suppose, been hearing it
all through the radiator pipe in the living-room ceiling.
This made the situation worse. The next thing I remember, I was sitting in my chair in the big downstairs room
and threw at her an old copy of *Scrutiny*,* which hit the
wall just to the right of the doorway, outside of which she
was standing. She went upstairs, but then came down
again and said sadly and propitiatingly, "Good night." I
should have met her on this, gone and kissed her; but I
threw at her another magazine, a larger and thinner one,
which flapped and fell on the floor. Upstairs she spat at
me about Mary Pcolar and told me that she didn't like my
"spongy body"—which may well be true.

The next morning, when I came out, she had packed
all their things and left with Helen and Button [the dog].
"This is the abyss," she said, accenting it on the first
syllable.

<That night (Wednesday) *Mary* came to do my letters.
I had had most of a pint of Scotch by the time she arrived.
I had asked her whether it wouldn't be possible for them,
on Saturday or Sunday, to drive me over Tug Hill along
that road; but she didn't seem to think so. I told her how
terrible the driving was, dramatizing it, and she said,
"You're building this up." Then I told her about the sphag-

* This was the journal edited by the moralistic British critic F. R. Leavis
  and his wife, Queenie D. Leavis.

num swamp, and that it might perhaps be safer to go in there with a rope. (The mayor of Constableville, who had given me the key, had warned me that there were "some pretty bad holes in those swamps.") Then she began to talk about the swamp in a way which I thought—though it must have been the whisky—was making it a metaphor for a possible relationship in which we should find ourselves in a "mess." "Have you got a rope?" she said. > When she was going, I wanted to turn on the light on the porch but turned off the light in the hall. I kissed her on the neck in the dark and felt how hard and solid she was. It is somehow reassuring to find a woman so well-formed and feminine who is also as strong as an ox.

When Malcolm came to talk to me the day Elena left, he said that Dorothy was again somewhat "confused," as she had been before. Jane Gaus has suggested to me that she may have had a slight stroke when she fell and broke her hip.

<A telegram from *Elena* in Wellfleet arrived August 30: "Arrived last night very sorry have written love."

Last night, the 30th, I had dinner with the Crostens (the attractive children are away and one misses them). Jessie Howland was there and had arranged to take us to see *Mappa Hall* at Barnevald. The Gauses met us there. It is an old stone house somewhat bigger than this, and it has a stone extension at the back. I had wondered about it as I passed it. It had been bought by a retired dentist and his wife, who has interested him madly in American antiques. They put on an extraordinary performance, at which we had to refrain from smiling. He took us from room to room, explaining in a loud voice how rare and precious everything was: lustre pitchers and highboys, like my mother's, candelabra, bas-relief hunting pictures with dried grass for the foliage (I had never seen these), embroidered Biblical pictures with painted paper faces such as Uncle Charley Corlies' mother used to make. He had collected all this himself. There was almost nothing left from the original family. Mappa was a Dutchman who had a grant from the Holland Land Company. The house was built in 1802. It is not unlike ours but rather grander and fancier—fireplaces all carved differently like ours, but with classical Georgian designs. They said that, in passing our house, they always drove slowly to look at it. He is a big, bulky, redfaced, oafish and amorphous upstater; she a small, wiry, white-haired, nasal-voiced housewife. The house was like a museum and arranged without very much taste. As they took one around the fourposter beds, the pianos, desks and grandfather clocks, one wondered how and where they lived. Jessie hesitated over an ashtray when we were waiting for drinks in a living room and asked me, "Is this supposed to be used?" It made me feel superior, and it seemed to me very curious that this man who had evidently never before possessed or lived with such things could now have such a passion for them, such a nostalgia for something he had never known. How far we have come from the era when houses were furnished in this way is shown by the prestige and value now attached to the household objects, most of which in the period to which they belonged were common enough conveniences of modest enough elegance. >

Elena said that flamingos in front of a house—such as the Hutchinses have—were "a status symbol"—you didn't have to plant them or do anything to the soil or water them.

CANADA

"On the Margin of It All"

Trip to Canada: I left Talcottville Wednesday, Sept. 5.
Everett Hutchins drove me to Toronto. I stayed at the
Royal York. Had dinner with the Callaghans the first night:
a highly convivial occasion, but Loretto came down afterwards with a recurrence of her *tic douloureux* [painful
twitch], which she thought had been brought on by unaccustomed drinking. We talked about Hemingway and
Scott and others. Morley, much attacked by Canadian
reviewers—he says partly as a result of my article*—is in
the very curious position of identifying himself with the
Hemingway and Fitzgerald literary world of New York and
Paris of the twenties, of being, as he says, "too American"
for the Canadians and looking down on Canadian literature, and at the same time continuing to live here. Though
I had only actually known him from a few years back, I
felt, on account of friends in common, that I was having
a reunion with an old friend. He is, however, 59 where I
am 67—he says he was "the baby of the group."

---

* In 1960 in *The New Yorker* EW characterized the psychological realism
  of two of Callaghan's novels, calling him "perhaps the most unjustly
  neglected novelist in the English-speaking world."

The old house, probably built in the eighties, with a large central hall into which everything else opens, is furnished without taste, but comfortable, and the atmosphere of the family is affectionate. The two sons are goodlooking, intelligent and able. One of them, Barry, lives at home. He teaches English at the university and constantly frequents a nightclub in pursuit of a Hungarian beauty. His regular girl, however, is a big blond Ukrainian-Russian beauty. The other son, Michael, is in the advertising business and a young man about town. His girlfriend is one of his brother's bright students. They all rally around the parents on Sundays, Michael's girlfriend bringing her friendly dachshund, who constantly sits up to have his stomach scratched. Morley sits at the head of the table, reminding me a little of Gauss, with his high balding dome, his Western accent, his tone in talking to his sons—with an intimate respect for equals—and his seriousness in raising in any conversation the fundamental questions of human life. We would sit on at the table talking, with coffee, liqueurs, wine and whisky, till long after dinner was finished. This was greatly enjoyed by Morley, who calls these occasions "Athenian Evenings." He lives in a modest house, but the garden has a lawn and a fountain at the back; and he obviously made a point of having himself embedded, for security and solidarity, in the residential part of Toronto, where the English old families live. He drove me around this section and seemed to know who lived in every house.

I have been constantly reminded of Margaret [Canby], whose mother came from Toronto and who had even the Toronto accent to the extent of saying *abote* for *about*. I thought about her in the hotel dining room, where they were playing the tunes of old musical comedies—they did not in New York or perhaps in the States at all play these old dreamy tunes for dancing in exactly this old way: I could see her dancing back in the nineteen-tens; and then, with distress and chagrin, when Morley was driving me around, and I saw the old gray fortress-like houses, each shut off from the rest of the world, even, one felt, from its neighbors, in which her relatives must have lived. (I had got their news lately from Camilla [Austin], but didn't have the heart or the nerve to look them up.) She had such a kind of horror of her Scotch Presbyterian origins, and I was reminded of her again when I found the word *worthy* in Hugh MacLennan's *Two Solitudes*, used in the sense in which she used to say protestingly that members of her family were "so *worthy*." Where was the hotel where the "bounder" that she liked had jumped or fallen through the glass ceiling of the ballroom or dining room?

Last night (the 12th), Barry took us to his *nightclub* to meet the Hungarian girl—I having told him that at present I was particularly interested in Hungarians. I hadn't seen anything of the kind since I went to Colosimo's in Chicago years ago, and I had never seen such a dance of bumps and grinds as one of the girls put on: vibrating, revolving, quivering, her hips a little bulging above the low skirt— and a very pretty woman. Coarse energetic stout comic— Jewish or French Canadian or both—who belted out dirty but quite funny jokes, did comic dances and fell on his face, and constantly snatched drinks from the customers' tables till he must have been pretty drunk. Barry said that the place had formerly been a hangout for hoods. Two rival gangs would sit on either side of the house and glare at one another. But the management had put an end to this, and they now had a more respectable clientele of out-of-towners from the big hotels—as the result of which the place was only making about $800 a week. Before that the gangsters had been paying higher prices "for being treated as gentlemen." On the other side of the dance-floor–stage were two ladies with enormous "teased" coiffures and their hair had, I think, been dyed blue—that reminded me of great edifices of hair of the women in Fuseli's drawings. The young Hungarian woman, with whom we sat at a back table between the shows, turned out not to be a "strip-teaser," as Barry had youthfully boasted, but the daughter of the ballet master in Budapest, who had come to the United States after the 1956 rebellion. Very Magyar-type pretty brunette, some of whose mannerisms reminded me of Mariska. I didn't think—as Ted Paramore once said to me about Magda Johann, after seeing us together—that Barry was necessarily "getting away with anything." She was married and had two children, whom her mother, during her present engagement, was looking after in Montreal, where she lived and to which she was about to return. Her husband, according to Barry, had been a big landowner in Hungary but was now a taxi driver in Montreal. She was fond of him but didn't really love him. It all brought back to me the days of Magda. She was merely one of four girls who did a little dancing between the big stomach-dance numbers. Though full of Hungarian charms and wiles, I thought that she was quite a correct young woman who knew perfectly how to handle herself. They hadn't liked paying tribute to Stalin. Budapest was a beautiful city, but she thoroughly enjoyed America. Hungary now seemed so small.

I got back to the hotel between one and two, and sat in the armchair, thoroughly enjoying myself and reading an interview with Ezra Pound in *The Paris Review*. He still seems to make more sense than I should have supposed he did; talked without bogus Americanese and with a surprising absence of egoism about the events of his life. Went to sleep but woke up early and ran through the English weeklies which I had bought at the "Book Cellar" on Bay St., which Morley Callaghan had shown me and to which he told me he and Hemingway had walked when, working on the *Toronto Star*, they had first made one another's acquaintance. Then I went to sleep again and had one of those too vivid dreams that come in the latish morning when you are sleeping later than you need and the mind has begun working. I thought that, having finished our letters, etc., I had taken Mariska from T'ville to a tavern somewhere farther up the road. There she left me sitting at a table, apparently to dance with a young man. I assumed that she went with him willingly, though, perhaps somewhat drunk, he seemed to be pulling her by the arm and she to be resisting his violence. Then they disappeared altogether, and I never saw them again. At this point I began to shit my pants but stopped it. A woman who had driven there now had to go home; but I stayed and waited for Mariska. At last I gave her up and tried to get a ride with somebody who was going in the direction of Boonville, but nobody wanted to take me (this was evidently derived from my difficulty last night in getting a taxi on Bay St.). I wondered whether I could drive with somebody without their noticing my smell. One car was full of children; in another, a married couple, though there was room for an extra person, murmured disagreeably that they had had enough of hitchhiking people and had decided not to do it any more. I went back into the tavern and asked if anybody was going to Boonville. One of the men who ran it said, yes, he would take me. He was playing what I took to be poker but put a pile of chips which he was holding in a kind of long case. Then, while people were obstructing the doorway between him and me—I had started to leave the tavern, thinking he was with me—he called up someone who was evidently a woman and humorously sang her some lines from a song. I still hoped to get away from there, then I woke up. I had to make sure that my pajama pants were clean. It was one of my abandonment dreams. On

account of Elena's real defection, I had substituted
Mariska—conjured up, I suppose, by Barry's Hungarian
friend—who, in spite of our chaste relations, is all I have
to depend on in the way of a woman when Elena is not
there. I had been thinking, when we were sitting at the
nightclub, how old and unattractive I must seem to that
beauty from Budapest.

The people in Toronto, though no Greek statues, seem
healthier and better set up than those in New York and
Boston. Not so driven, not so cramped between big buildings and in narrow streets—more good-natured; they probably enjoy themselves more.

In Canada, after coming from the States, one is to
some extent able to relax. One is off on the margin of it
all. They are not under the same pressure, do not have
the same responsibility. In certain ways, their semi-
dependence on England has been an advantage to them:
they have not had to save the republic, to justify the democratic experiment. They have not been through our crises
and panics. They have been able to remain à l'abri, to
watch the United States from the sidelines. But they are
now having something of a crisis of their own. The recent
inroads of the U.S., which now apparently owns much of
Canadian industry, have stimulated an "anti-American"
nationalism, at the same time that they cannot see how
they can avoid a kind of union with the United States.
Just now, at the conference in London about the Common
Market, Diefenbaker, their Conservative Prime Minister,
is opposing Canada's acceptance of it for the reason that
it would put an end to the preferential treatment that
Canada has had from England; but sensible people with
whom I talked seemed to think this resistance was doomed.

At the same time, the resistance of the French Canadians to British Canadian domination has been stiffened to the point that, in its extreme form, it has produced a separatist movement, demanding complete independence, a parliament of their own. It is the same as the segregating South, as Israel and Iroquoia. I cannot make out at this time whether all these resistances are doomed or whether they will eventually result in some looser organization of national units that will not be accountable to the same extent as the Russians and we are to the exactions and absurdities of the tyrannous bureaucracies of the centralized state.

A certain sound residue of the English tradition: better service in hotels and at airports. Our panicky state of mind is seen in administrative inconsistencies and operational messes. People here are more polite.

Even in Toronto, the air is cleaner than in New York and Boston.

But the driving in Toronto is terrible. As Morley explained to me, they like to play "chicken"—see which of the two drivers can stop the car first when they seem on the point of colliding. There was one such incident when I was driving with Morley. Once when I was riding in a taxi driven by a young Chinese man, the cars in front suddenly stopped, and he had to put on the brakes not to crash into the one ahead of us. This threw me violently forward, but I was not hurt except slightly in the fingers of one hand, which I had thrust forward to prevent myself from being thrown against the seat ahead. But if I had been in the seat ahead, I might have been thrown against the windshield. Everybody got out of all the cars, but no damage had been done.

In shops and public places, they have not developed the instinct, as they have in big American cities, to keep out of people's way, to move and let people pass. They plant themselves squarely. They do not seem to feel that they have to dodge one another.

Elena has let me down three times when I needed her support most. After Mother's death, when she left me alone at Red Bank, with Jenny [Corbett] in the hospital, whom I could not leave; when we first came to Hilliard St., and I had to get my lectures on the Civil War and my seminar in comparative literature under way at the same time that I was trying to finish my Indian book—so that I should have had someone to stand by me, to see that I got out of the house with the books I had to have, etc.; and this summer when the tax situation was getting me down. In the first case, I suppose, she felt that she had been conscientious about attending to the things in the house and that she could not stand it any longer—but I resented her going up to Wellfleet with that Russian couple who turned out to be impossible. In the second case, I suppose that, though she had been so reluctant to leave Wellfleet, she couldn't resist the liberation of being in Cambridge and being able to go more places and see more people on her own. This summer she was worn out with the income tax and as little as usual disposed to face Talcottville. She was indifferent, even sour toward me.

Nevertheless, I have missed her. Her letters have done something to make up for it. I was rather surprised, with the Callaghans, to become aware how often I was quoting her: on MacLennan's *Two Solitudes*, Morley's own work, [Buell's] *The Pyx*, Teilhard de Chardin, Updike, the Murphys—her saying that she could understand Scott's smashing their precious wineglasses.

In Toronto I met three Britishers, an Englishman from Cambridge (the town), a man who I was told was more or less Welsh and a Scotchman who had come to Canada at the age of fifteen. They seem characteristic of Canada: you wouldn't find them in the U.S. The point is that, as I suppose, they or their parents have all come over here with the intention of getting away from the old society, and have failed to have distinguished or successful careers commensurate with their intelligence. The first made a "bad marriage," as Malcolm Montgomery told me, and his wife has gone back to England; he has knocked around a good deal, went to South America for some oil company; now he is editor of a shipping paper. The second started out in philosophy, spent a year at Harvard but did not take the Ph.D.; now he conducts personnel psychological tests—a subject which Morley Callaghan says he never discusses with him. Barry Callaghan says that he thinks the explanation of his accepting this ignoble work is simply that he is "a huge cynic." The third, the most interesting, talks like a brilliant don, a little like Isaiah Berlin. He knows everything about Canada, has facts, quotations, jokes at his fingers' ends. But his job is editing a financial journal—he says that he knows nothing about finance.

Strange to hear them still talking about Wolfe and Montcalm as they do in the South about the Civil War.

Montreal and Elena

I arrived in *Montreal* Friday the 14th. Excitement of coming to a new city. I hadn't been in Montreal since one of our trips from Talcottville in my childhood, when Father took us to Canada. I remember it as crass and ugly, but it now seems quite smart and interesting: French restaurants, theaters and bookstores, high buildings but not too many. The Ritz is old-fashioned and comfortable. I bought Marie-Claire Blais's new book, *Le Jour Est Noir; Le Devoir*,

the more or less liberal paper; and the Hungarian paper
Magyar Hirlap, which I was delighted to find I could read
in spots.

I found an announcement in the paper of what I thought
was the opening of Le Rideau Vert with a play called *Les
Portes Claquent* and went to the Stella theater. On the way,
I noticed the houses with their outside steps that went up
to the second floor. They were houses built by the French.
The taxi driver told me that it had been made illegal a few
years ago to build any more such steps: they were dangerous
in winter, when covered with snow and ice—a woman had
been killed by a fall. It turned out, when I got to the
theater, that the performance was a preview *"pour les jour-
nalistes."* I said that I was a journalist, and they asked my
name and let me in. The play—though well done—was
mediocre: a comedy, French not French Canadian, of bourgeois family life, children in revolt against an old-fashioned
heavy father, but everything is all right at the end when
everybody, including Grandma, has been threatening to
leave home. The whole family settle down at the dinner
table, where they had been seen at the beginning of Act
I, and everything seems to be all right. I was glad to see
that *Le Devoir* said the play was of no importance and
unworthy of Le Rideau Vert.

I thought about Elena during the two years she spent
in Montreal. She had told me that, except on official occasions, she had never met the French-speaking inhabitants. The proportion of French to English is about two
to one. Elena was not able to explain to me about Canadian
titles, and I learned about them in full detail from the Scot
I have mentioned above. They have been something of an
issue here. Since 1935, they have been abolished, and an
attempt was made to have the old titles extinguished. Of
course, Elena was here during the long "Liberal" reign of

Mackenzie King, when I suppose nothing much was happening: but it must have been also the lack of interest of Jimmy [Thornton] that made her experience of life here so limited. The only friends she has kept are the Stewarts, Hilda Hodgson and a lady named Mather whom I haven't met. As she has told me and Marg Stewart reminded me, she and Jimmy had to live, after Sir Henry lost his money, in very reduced circumstances on a street which, Marg seemed to make plain by the way in which she referred to it, was not a street on which to live. All the right kind of families are rich, and this is evidently very important. The Scot in Toronto told me that, among "the elite," not a word of French was ever allowed to be spoken. I found a certain drying up on the part of the dentist and his wife who drove me out to dinner at the Stewarts'. They had apparently never heard of the reforms of Cardinal Léger, which have created so much excitement in the Catholic world. But this is not at all the case with the Stewarts: they had a book about Proust in the living room, had heard about but not read Marie-Claire Blais, and their daughter Pam had just come back from a summer in Paris. Their house at L'Abord-à-Plouffe was not at all what I expected. Instead of being opulent in the Westmount style, it is an old-fashioned country place, comfortable and rather homely. But it is only ten years old. They built it that way, using old beams. Lots of horses and dogs. In the living room, the chairs and couches were partly occupied by friendly beagles—they had had at one time nineteen of them—and they told me I had better take a vacant chair before it was preempted by a dog. Wild duck for dinner, to which I couldn't do justice on account of my teeth.

Sad to think of Elena coming to America with eagerness, on account, as she says, of the Marx Brothers and of the idealization of the country, on the part of the smart people in Paris, as the home of *le jazz hot* and the vertiginous *gratte-ciels* [skyscrapers], and being landed in Montreal at its stuffiest.

They seem always to call it Muntreal here as in Toronto.

The typical figure in the novels of John Buell and Mlle Blais is a lowly and desolate young man or woman. Paul and Marius Tallend in Hugh MacLennan's *Two Solitudes* are very much the same kind of thing. I have just read several of these books one after the other, and I find that I easily confuse Paul Tallend, [Blais's] Tête Blanche and the boy in [Buell's] *Four Days*. One is struck by the efforts these writers make—sometimes to the point of implausibility—not to let their characters escape. Even MacLennan's hero is not allowed a conventional happy ending: he is obliged to leave his wife and go off to the Second World War, she has to stay with her conventional and socially ambitious mother who has so virulently opposed her marriage.

Morley Callaghan, John Buell and Mlle Blais are all products of Catholic education, and it may be that this has been important in their having become good writers who are interesting to readers outside Canada. They are not occupied with local problems—the Catholic Church has given them a wide historical and moral scope. They are able to live intellectually in a less provincial world.

In Toronto, I had to change my room to get away from the television and the conversation going on in the room next to mine, from which I was separated by only a door. I discovered that there were only two rooms on each floor of the huge Royal York Hotel which did not have this inconvenience. I did not expect to find it at the Ritz, but my room here is the same way, though the door seems somewhat thicker, and as I write this I hear the TV in the adjoining room. Walking along the corridor in the Royal York, I could hear a TV program in every room.

I have the impression that the two cultures, the two languages, here tend to neutralize one another, and to make it impossible for any one city to develop a literary center. There are Toronto and McGill Universities as intellectual centers, and Louis Dudek and Hugh MacLennan are at McGill, but there are also Laval and Loyola, the Catholic colleges, to the latter of which Buell is attached. The writers seem to be more scattered than they are even in the United States, and to know less about one another.

They have the habit, I found in Canada, of calling you by your first name the moment they meet you. They do not seem to go in for the British habit of using, as between equals, the last name without "Mr." (In French Canada, it seems always to be "Monsieur." I did not know, in Quebec, if it was safe to call Lemelin "Lemelin," since he always called me "Mr. Wilson.")

Richard II at the Théâtre du Nouveau Monde—very well staged and acted. I thought there was some slant of propaganda: the supreme power drops from the nerveless hands of the English King; Bolingbroke is perhaps imagined as a determined, decisive French nationalist; the big prelate (L'Abbé de Westminster or L'Éveque de Carlisle?) attempts to convince Bolingbroke that the two factions must get along together and is told at the end by Bolingbroke to get out and behave himself. Says the producer, who plays Richard in the program, "*Sans vouloir prendre de libertés avec l'auteur, nous nous sommes sentis libre vis-à-vis de lui. Pour cela, nous avons dû le bousculer souvent pour le forcer à nous dévoiler le fond de sa pensée.* [Without wishing to take liberties with the author, we feel free with respect to him. We have often been obliged to shake him in order to make him reveal the depth of his thought]. In the lobby in the intermission, Elena heard a man say: "*Shakespeare est admirable—surtout en français.*"

Elena's life in Montreal: She has told me more about it, so I see it more clearly. She had no idea, when she first arrived, what she was getting into. They lived in Sir Henry Thornton's big old house on Pine St., and the young marrieds all came to see them. She didn't know what to make of this, thought they were all very bourgeois. Sir Henry was not stuffy, but Jimmy was morbidly conventional and afraid of not doing the right thing. According to one of Duncan Stewart's undoubtedly partly invented stories, Jimmy in New York had said to him, with nervous apprehension, "My wife has been walking on Park Ave., with nothing on but a fur coat!" He had been educated at the military college and never got over it. He was embarrassed if he went to an art gallery or read a serious book. Elena told me this when I told her about something that John Buell had said. I had asked him why everybody was so down on Morley Callaghan, and he said that I ought to realize that in Canada to be an artist was regarded as a form of sin, and that to be a good artist made it worse— no other explanation was necessary.

Excellent French restaurants, so much better and cheaper than in New York—Café Martin, Tour Eiffel. The clean tablecloths and white napkins set up on the plates, bright bottles behind the bar, appetizing dishes well served. The Café Martin is an old private house just around the corner from Sherbrooke St., with carved mahogany mirrors and other mahogany things. Elena and I felt quite "civilized" when we went out to dine in the evenings, after eating in Cambridge at those cramped dreary restaurants where the food is so slapdash and bad. The same kind of thing in Quebec—La Chaumière, Le Bacchus. They are quiet, people talk in low voices, do not get in one another's way. Elena said they hadn't existed when she lived here thirty years ago—nor had any French theater, so far as she knew. All that had come since the Second War. Our good relations have been restored. Suzanne Hughes, in talking with Elena about her marital difficulties, said that, in spite of disagreements, she felt that Elena and I had really loved one another and were still bound by love— which is true, it is a love affair that has gone on now for more than fifteen years. Up here, it makes Elena feel better that she is able to help me with the French end of things.

Dinner with Hugh MacLennan: Rather distinguished, as Elena says, with his Oxford-Princeton education and the summer he spent teaching in Russia, his detailed and comprehensive knowledge of Canada. He comes from Cape Breton, and his ancestors, he says, spoke Gaelic—he has something of a Gaelic accent, refers to himself as a "Celt." He said that it had been frustrating for Canada to have offered a loyalty to Britain which Britain did not want. And French Canada feels, I find, that it has been abandoned by France. Although more French Canadian books are now being published in Paris, I gather that a French Canadian is no more warmly received in France than a British one is in England.

Louis Dudek took us out for a drive and lunch among the Laurentian hills. He is the child of Polish parents, knows Polish and is learning Russian, speaks and reads French. Very opinionated and fixated ineradicably on Williams and Ezra Pound. When I was [unsuccessfully advancing] the "mainstream" theory about poetry, that the

age of the great poet who did not come out of the mainstream or contribute to it was perhaps coming to an end—
Dudek declared in opposition that poetry would consist in
the future of a number of less notable poets working on a
fairly high level. I felt that this was special pleading for
the only middling level hitherto unsurmounted in English
by any Canadian poet. He also seemed rather indignant at
my speaking of Auden as a great poet—though both he
and Irving Layton have been influenced by him—and at
my praising the lyrics of Betjeman. Elena said afterwards—I had not thought of this—that she believed it was
an anti-English instinct on the part of a Polish Canadian.
He feels closer to contemporary Americans. I find this
situation described, in *Masks of Poetry*, in an essay by
W. P. Wilgar. Apart from the Polish angle, the British
orientation of English-speaking Canada has, for men of
Louis Dudek's generation, largely ceased to exist. The
tradition is still there, but they naturally turn toward the
United States.

The Buells: They are both half-French. He is 35—a
graduate of Loyola and now teaches there. *The Pyx* has
been translated into Dutch and German, and he hopes that
it will be translated into French, because he thinks that
it is really a French book. It seems that it is very rare for
a Catholic to write books in English. He knows nothing
about Marie-Claire Blais, and she knows nothing about
him. The only people I saw in Canada who had read him
were Morley Callaghan, who had learned about him from
me, and Hugh MacLennan, who had read *The Pyx* but not
Four Days. They live in a little house near Loyola. They
have three children, whom they evidently adore. When
they took me upstairs, they showed them to me, all sleeping
in the same room, two in a double-decker bed. Before Elena
came, I took them to dinner at the Berkeley, then went

to their house, and Elena and I had dinner there, with an Irish-Jesuit priest, who had befriended and helped John. The brother said that John was one of the only, I think, four of his students who had shown real literary talent. John, when I saw him before, had complained about the Catholic "squares" who had disapproved of his books.

Francis Parkman is not very much read here. I was surprised to find that young Gzowsky of *Maclean's* [magazine], otherwise well read and informed, had never heard of Parkman. This neglect, MacLennan told me, was due to a ban of the Catholic Church, which did not want to have Parkman's objective account of the conflicts between the religious orders, the career of Laval, etc., circulated among their congregations. Falardeau in Quebec confirmed this, and explained that it was also, in French Canada, a matter of emotional pride not to take their history in English from an American. He was under the impression that Parkman's history had never been translated into French.

Quebec City after Half a Century

On Saturday the 22nd, Marg Stewart drove us to Quebec. We stopped off for lunch at Pierreville, at a little French hotel; then in the afternoon at the old French *seigneury* of Lobinière, and met an old lady with urbane and grand manners who had married a Lobinière and who had a retainer show us the documents that recorded the original grant; and another old lady, visiting her, a Taschereau, who, Elena told me, was one of the rare offspring of an English-French intermarriage among these primeval Quebecois. What seemed improbable, she was reading *The Shores of Light*, read it every night in bed and said she was excited at meeting me. I had been thinking how in Mme Lobinière the type had persisted of the great French lady: she was tall, quite pink-cheeked, Roman-nosed and a model of courtesy and dignity. But it turned out that she came from Asheville, North Carolina. It reminded me of the Nabokovs' party in Cambridge, when I had mistaken the English faculty of Wellesley for entomologists who resembled the insects they studied.

Marg is well informed, quite intelligent, quite amusing and very likable. Her family made their money out of Dawes's beer. The only thing I don't quite like about her is her "Mmm'ing" in the presence of food. If she likes the look of your French pastry when she has ordered something else, she will put on a whole little act about it. The moment she goes into a restaurant, she exclaims at how good it smells. When I remarked upon this to Elena, she said that Marg's sense of smell was unusually acute, and reminded me that, in passing through Trois-Rivières, she had complained of the smell of the factories, of which I had been unaware. Elena said that she was very sensual and, when she was younger, had behaved about goodlooking men just as she does now about food.

Duncan Stewart joined us at the Château Frontenac— he had been snipe shooting somewhere along the St. Lawrence between here and Montreal. He is more sensitive and varied in his interests than you might at first suspect; but something of a professional Irishman who fatigues you, like Ed O'Connor, with his funny stories. He talks endlessly, hopping from one subject to another, with anecdotes which are usually intended to put him in a favorable light. He says that his grandfather came to Canada after having been steward on some big Irish estate, and he loves being a big country squire and master of the local hunt and going to Ireland for the hunting. Stories about how they promise to do things in Ireland and then make no pretense of doing them; of the man who had him drink poteen in order to "lower the fences"; about the hunt dinner where a mouse was seen and they chased it through, I think, Lismore Castle with hounds and blowing the horn; about the hunt dinner he had offered to pay for, since no one else had very much money, and Lord Somebody had announced at the end of the evening that someone there had been "vulgar enough" to offer to pay for everything: they would accept but only on condition that he would drink a tall glass of straight whisky—he did this and passed out.

Stewart's desire to pay for everything and arrange everything for you got very much on my nerves—and he is always ordering taxis and tables ahead and showing off his intimacy with the servants and the management. I finally in Quebec began snubbing him—signing for drinks and paying for dinner myself and preventing him from ordering a taxi from the restaurant La Chaumière. This overdone hospitality is to some extent a device for getting people to listen to and like him—something which he evidently has to have. Elena says that he was always bringing home every Tom, Dick and Harry with whom he did business (Lloyd's Insurance) or who had, for any reason, come from somewhere to Montreal. He is also a bore about his army experience—he was in Europe six years in the Second War—a member of the Black Watch and saw active service, one of his great heroes is "Monty." A good deal of observation, quite realistic and spontaneous Irish wit; he would be likable if he left you alone. Elena has always been grateful to him for standing by her when Sir Henry had lost his money and when her brother Kiki killed himself up here. Just now, in Montreal, he tried to make her feel better about Kiki by telling her that a little sympathetic understanding such as, he said—I don't know why, she's

always so vague—was not available then, would have
straightened him out and saved him.*

I availed myself of Duncan's resources, however, in letting him get us a room up here and a room tomorrow at
the Ritz, when I go back, Sept. 27, to Montreal. His
influence seems irresistible. Both cities are packed with
conventions, and they tell you that they are all booked up.
Jean Something, the manager of the Ritz, Duncan says,
will always do anything for him because it flatters him to
ride Duncan's horses when he doesn't know how to ride.

It is strange to be back in Quebec for the first time since
1906, when I was here with my mother and father, and
Sandy and probably Esther [Kimball]. We were riding in
those open horse-drawn hacks and running around the
hotel, and now I am 67 and, on account of my "heart
condition," have a hard time getting around on the steeply
sloping streets, have to stop with my mouth open and, in
case of special effort, take a nitroglycerine pill. I remembered the Golden Dog, and I find that it is no longer over
the tavern where I saw it fifty-five years ago but is now
set in the façade of the post office. I remembered the
entrance to the Château Frontenac, surmounted by arches
and another building so that it seems enclosed in a court-

* Kiki (Kyril von Mumm), then a handsome twenty-three, still living in
the family establishment in Johannisberg, was framed by the Nazis
after his father had publicly spoken out against the expulsion of the
Jews from his club in Frankfurt. A beautiful woman who began flirting
with him at a dance asked him to hold her compact, then disappeared.
When he took it home in his pocket, he was arrested and jailed, with
a big story in the tabloid about the disgrace to the Mumm family. When
released he was sent to Montreal, where he killed himself the next
spring. By that time Elena had moved to New York and was unable to
console her brother or relieve his shame. By "a little sympathetic understanding," Duncan Stewart meant that counselling could have given
him perspective.

yard; but other things I don't recognize: there was something rather Renaissance about going into the dining room.
The dining room is now on the second floor, and the hotel
has been much enlarged and rearranged. I remember it as
quite romantic—I think I must have imagined it was really
old. I find now that it was built in 1893. Coming to Canada
now, I suppose, is another of my attempts—as Angus Wilson rightly assumed they were—to go back and examine
things that had meant something to me in my childhood
and find out what they actually were: Dickens, Kipling,
upstate New York. It was the thing then to visit Canada
—it was a part of the Antaeus American tradition of getting
away to, of challenging, the wild. McGeachie in Toronto
told me this was still true: people arrive in summer with
skis, take planes to unfrequented lakes in the north.

My father had bought with a couple of friends an island
in one of the Canadian rivers, where he went to hunt and
fish—he never could get me to go with him—and he usually took us to Canada at some point in our summers at
Talcottville. We went to Yarmouth in Nova Scotia, to
Halifax, to Quebec and Montreal. He liked, also, to go to
Ottawa to see how Canada was getting along with its government, but he never took me there. From his trips that
he made without us, he would bring me books published
in England—an abridgment of *The Faerie Queene* and a
morocco-bound India-paper volume of Dickens's less well
known Christmas stories. The little silver spoon with the
maple leaf enamelled on the handle must have been brought
me in my infancy (we still have it in Wellfleet)—I see that
they are still selling them here. He took my mother and
me to the West Coast in the summer of 1915, and we
stopped off at Winnipeg, Calgary, Lake Louise (there are
entries about this trip in the early part of my journal).* I

* EW refers to the "Princeton, 1912–1916" section of *A Prelude*.

still feel close to Father, though it bored me so to travel
with him alone. But Sandy's presence made it great fun.
He was actually very indulgent, and Sandy, with his will-
ingness to play up to him, got on better with him than I
did.

My family are always with me, parents, grandparents,
cousins, and uncles and aunts. I have thought of them all
my life, see them in me, see myself as a product of them:
Kimballs, Wilsons, Bakers and Millers. I have developed
the Wilson eyebrows—which I never noticed till lately,
but I see that they are like Carolyn Link's—and now have
the stocky, short-legged Kimball build with its tendency,
on the part of the men, to develop a paunch in later life,
with my grandfather Kimball's large squarish head set solid
on a short neck, broad Kimball shoulders; father's forward-
slung jawbones; something of Thomas Baker's mailbox
mouth. And I try to think from which of my forebears I
have inherited my mental traits. The curiosity that makes
me travel has something in common with my father's—
the same thing that brought me up here. What would be
the equivalent of the way I study or the way in which my
imagination works on the part of my Wilson and Kimball
grandfathers? There are moments when a superior little
frozen smile reminds me of Susan Wilson, and we must
have got it from the family. I wonder how many people
have associated themselves in this way with their relations.
It is partly, I suppose, that till I went away to school, my
immediate family and my relatives were the only people I
really knew well.

At The Château Elena and I had a splendid corner room
very high up: with the green-roofed turrets below it, looking out from two sides on the St. Lawrence, which seems
as wide here as the Great Lakes, with the Île d'Orléans
on the opposite side, the barges going up and down and

the ferryboat steamers back and forth. Elena, who has
never been here before, thoroughly enjoyed the whole
thing—French restaurants, ride on the ramparts in one
of those open "carrioles," as she calls them—felt that
we had come to a foreign country. So long since we have
had such a holiday. The queer but beautiful city: gray
seventeenth-century buildings, huge convents and priests
in black gowns, high statues of Champlain and the rest,
the now heroic figures who founded and defended the city,
the old church and other fine buildings and Laval University, with, in front of it in the square, the towering
figure of Laval in his robes with his miter and staff, stooping
forward in a way that seems sinister—it may be that Parkman's account of him has given me this idea—like Ivan
Groznyi [Ivan the Terrible] in Eisenstein's film*; the beautifully kept green expanse of the Plains of Abraham, with
its gardens, that overlooks the river; the steep streets and
the gray buildings with their signs in French that look
exactly like the signs and buildings in a French provincial
town.

The first night, after dinner with the Stewarts, we went
to the apartment of the Falardeaux—he is head of the
Conseil des Artes—where we met Jeanne Lapointe, who
teaches a course in the novel at Laval University, Roger
Lemelin, the novelist, and another couple, the husband
some sort of official in the cultural field. The next day the
Falardeaux took us for a tour of the Île d'Orléans, stopping
at their summer cottage, where we sat and had a drink in
the back yard, looking out from the high cliff over the wide

---

* In the film "he is seen, in a remarkable shot, lurking within an arch-
way—suspicious, malignant, sinister—while a procession with banner
and icons comes winding through the snow to recall him" (*The American
Earthquake*).

flat dramatic St. Lawrence vista—so immense as to seem overpowering, and it would not, I should think, be stimulating to artistic activity. Elena said to the Falardeaux—over whom, as she said, she worked hard—that, with such a view, one did not need painting. How can one get a hold on such country? see it in terms of human significance? I have called it dramatic above, but astounding is rather the word, annulling to human assertion, which is lost in the vast continuum of unpeopled water and land. No bathers along the beaches: the water is rather dangerous, and there are, they say, no proper beaches; there are houses along the opposite bank, which is punctuated by one sharp church steeple. These steeples that point the shore—more frequently at Quebec—give the land its human meaning.

Lunch with Roger Lemelin at the Garrison Club: He is obviously proud of belonging to this, one of the oldest clubs, he says, in North America. It was a place of meeting originally for the English garrison after the English had taken Quebec, and the membership had long been exclusively confined to resident British officers—old colonels, he said, who had been on safaris. But they had recently been letting the French in, and now the French were in a majority, and they mixed on equal terms with the English. The English now had a much better time, the club was a good deal larger. The rooms were ample and comfortable, but still very plain and British—though I think that Lemelin rather enjoyed their being so. He took evident satisfaction in the photographs of mustachioed English officers in the corridor that leads to the dining room. He is evidently popular there; he is greeted by the other members and exchanges with them genial remarks. I noted that he was wearing an army ulster with officer's insignia on the shoulders, and asked him whether the membership was

confined to officers. No: anybody who occupied a distinguished position.

Falardeau and Jeanne Lapointe—we had gone to her
apartment for "apéritifs" after our expedition Sunday
afternoon—had talked humorously about Lemelin: he first
told about his adventures, then afterwards lived them. I
said that he had complained to me, the night before, that
he had been "a prisoner—a prisoner!" to television for the
last five years—he had exploited the family of his novel
Les Plouffe for an endless kind of soap opera. Falardeau
said that if Lemelin was a prisoner, it was a remarkable
case of "self-captivity." Now he had his *revanche* on what
he knew that the others must have been telling me about
him. They were way behind the times, he said, might be
living in the early nineteen hundreds. He couldn't stand
the sterility and desolation of the old French Canadian
fiction. He enjoyed life, took an active part in it, was a
businessman (lumber) not merely a writer. If he had been
away somewhere, they would ask him what book he had
been working on. He might not have been working on any
book, but sleeping with Spanish girls perhaps—he had
bought a place on one of the West Indian islands to get
away from the Quebec winters—or he might have been
organizing a chain of stores.

He had recently been getting away from the monotony
of the *Plouffe* soap opera by writing instead scripts for little
plays that had nothing to do with the Plouffes, but he
would never go back again to the kind of novels he had
written. He wanted to appeal to a larger audience. Jeanne
Lapointe had been annoyed with him because she thought
he had caricatured her as a character in one of his television
plays. I said, "You probably had." "It's possible." He had
not learned English till he was 25, and then it was in order
to be able to write for *Time*. He did the Canadian news,
and he said he was successful because he invented it. He

once went to a huge banquet in New York. They had a
lot to drink before and during the banquet, and heavy rye
whiskey afterwards, and while Henry Luce was making
a speech, he went to sleep and snored. They told him
that this would ruin him and made a point of explaining that Lemelin was the one who had snored.
Luce asked him why he had gone to sleep, and he answered that in his youth he had had to go constantly to
church and a sermon always sent him to sleep. According to Lemelin, Luce had exclaimed something like
"That's my man!" and had given him a raise. Lemelin has
humor and charm, and MacLennan says he is perfectly
straight.

All the hotels I have stayed at have been crammed with
businessmen's conventions. The Frontenac was full of
realtors, who were extremely noisy on our floor at night.
As we were going back to our room, a man rushed out from
one of the opposite rooms, exclaiming, "That looks like a
good party!" and hurried to another room, from whose open
door sounds were coming. At night, the noise ebbed and
flowed, would subside for a few minutes, then become loud
again, and at the climax a woman would laugh or shriek.
The next night when I went to my room, the men were
wearing straw sombreros, and I heard one of them say,
"It's been flagging—we needed this fun night." A woman
with whom I rode up in the elevator told me she came
from Winnipeg, and that the city now had half a million
people. The men wear labels telling their names and where
they live. I rode in the bus to the airport with some of
them. There was a joke about Winnipeg and Calgary,
apropos of some item in the paper. Calgary has now about
270,000. There are several thousand French in Winnipeg,
a man from there told me, but they are not like those in
Quebec. He evidently felt that you could not trust them.

He had been surprised by the cordiality of the French he had met in Quebec.

Elena was struck by the way in which the French in Quebec had remained unchanged. Transplanted, they were still the same. I had noticed that Mme Falardeau, who is small and pretty and vocal and who runs to do things like a little girl, has the same coquettish mannerisms as Suzanne Hughes: a modest dropping of the eyelids which is actually provocative. (I noticed similar mannerisms in common between Mariska Pcolar and Barry Callaghan's Hungarian girl.) She had a somewhat vulgar but not unattractive laugh on three notes each louder than the last. She has an expression, *"Je vous gage un champs* [I'll wager you a field]," which must be old rural French.

Elena and I made love when she first came to Montreal, which completely healed our estrangement—and again the night before she left Quebec. But by that night my heart had got more strained, and making love to her excites me so that I had to stop and let it relax. She caressed me, and I started again, but by that time Elena was exhausted, and afterwards I had to lie down and moan and take one of the pills for my heart. It is awful to be in such bad shape and must be so depressing for her and make her anxious and nervous. I can't bear having this spoiled—she is so divine.

She now has for the first time a perfectly shapeless nightgown that reminds me of what used to be called a Mother Hubbard. It conceals her lovely figure and is covered with red roses, so that we say she looks like an old couch upon which it is comfortable to lie. It is wonderful to take it off and uncover her beautiful body. Her wearing it is, I suppose, a part of her self-mortification, self-depreciation.

Elena had to go back on Tuesday, because Hedwig could

only stay with Helen a week. She really had a good time, had never been in Quebec before—because, as she thought, it had not been on the Canadian Northern Railroad that Jimmy's father ran, and so had no CNR hotel. We had had no such holiday for years.

More on Writers

Visit to Père Lévesque (pronounced Levêque) of the Maison Montmorency: He had a schedule for days ahead, but Falardeau had persuaded him to get me in for a few minutes. He was most cordial, regretted that our conversation had to be so brief—a short pink-faced round-faced Dominican in spectacles, with a spotless white robe. Energetic, bustling, very intelligent, he had made La Maison Montmorency an intellectual and cultural center—not merely a place for retreats, as he said, though people could come there for retreats, but a place where groups could quietly meet—many of them Protestants, he pointed out—and where artists and writers could come to work. Literature was not his field—his field was sociology; but he was interested in literature. I did not feel it was true, as Lemelin had told me, that he knew nothing about literature. He said that Marie-Claire Blais had not known what to do with *La Belle Bête*, when she had written it and was only eighteen, so she had brought it to him for advice. He had got the Institut de Québec to publish it, and had got her a scholarship for a year in France. People had expressed horror and said, "How can you, a Dominican monk, sponsor such a book?"—but he had known that she had real talent, and he respected talent so much that he thought one ought to do what one could for it.

I asked him why in all her books she reiterated the same situations: wives and husbands abandoning one another, parents abandoning their children. He said that these were all fantasies, things created by her own imagination. Her family had stayed together, there was nothing singular about it. Then he added, "That's not quite true," and told me the story about her sister, something of which I had already heard. The sister was a case of arrested development, and I had got the impression—though not from him—that Marie-Claire had been devoted to her before she found out that something was wrong, and that finding this out had been traumatic. Lévesque told me that the ignorant parents had not put her in an institution, not realizing the bad effect she would have on the other children. I asked if she was now in an institution, and he first said yes, then, "Or she may have died." The horrific nature of Blais's subjects came, he thought, from her having been given by friends the books of what he called "the black literature: Rimbaud, Lautréamont." He said this without any moral condemnation; and when I said that there was no religion in her books, he simply answered, "No." He expressed no disapproval, but said he had not seen her for the last two years. He had done what he could to help her, and then, with a dismissive movement of his arms, he said, "I let them go their way and make room for others." I said that I did not think that the translations of her books had attracted very much attention. "No," he said with a smile at the expense of the English-speaking public; they had been scandalized by *La Belle Bête*.

I was much impressed by Lévesque—he seemed the freest Catholic priest I had ever met, and the happiest in what he was doing. He sat there smiling and smoking a cigarette, quickly responsive and with perfect composure. He gave me a pamphlet which contained the text of an address—"*Le Chevauchement des Cultures*"—that he had delivered in 1955 at a Conférence de l'Institut Canadien des Affaires Publiques. There was nothing about the

Church or religion: it was all about the importance of culture, how a culture had to be *"ouverte,"* how the French and English cultures in Canada ought to learn from one another. He had been, up to five or six years ago, the dean of the Faculty of Social Sciences, which he had founded, at Laval University, then his superiors, on account of his liberal views, had put him out—"tried to break him," MacLennan said. He had gone on to the Maison Montmorency, and had up to last winter been the awarder of the Canada Council grants.

I came on to Montreal on Thursday and in the afternoon, in the lounge here, had farewell drinks with the *Stewarts* —Pam was also present. I noted, in talking with Marg about the French Canadian nationalists in Quebec, that even a woman so little provincial as she adopts toward them the same quietly depreciative and derisory tone that the English always adopt toward "the natives." (MacLennan afterwards corroborated this, and asked, "How did you know that?") Duncan came in later and was very agreeable and amusing. It is surprising how many things he knows about. We discussed the history of *Punch*, and he was improvising old-fashioned jokes of the type in which the little girl asks Mummy something and the beginnings of the standard type of story in which the colonel from India tells a story about a tiger at his club. I told him Paul Manship's story about Rockefeller sitting for his bust.* I think that Duncan and I are both entertainers who like to

---

* Paul Manship, the monumental sculptor of Rockefeller Center—who at seventy-five made the medal for the Kennedy Inaugural—had done a bust of John D. Rockefeller in 1918. EW liked to repeat Manship's story of making conversation with the tycoon during a sitting. When Rockefeller mentioned a rival with whom he had had business dealings, Manship asked what had become of him, and the otherwise low-keyed, taciturn old man became quite animated, responding gleefully, "He didn't last long, you know."

hold our audiences, and there is always likely to be some competition when two such people get together.

Strange how different *T'ville* looks from here: another country, dark and special; the Stone House seems quite a different thing from the Canadian stone houses, which are tighter, blanker, narrower-windowed, with no front porches, with for me no real physiognomies. It is almost as if down there they were having a different autumn. The people with their limited lives but enclosed in a different countryside, with different orientation—and even under more constricting pressures from which the Canadians seem so far free. There is all the difference between a place in which one feels the fibers of family and a place in which one is totally unaware of other people's fibers of family.

This (almost) month in Canada has done me good—relieved me for a while from myself and the damned American problems.

Dinner with Hugh MacLennan (Friday): He took me to the Café Martin, where Elena and I had been one night; and we drank quantities of white wine, three bottles at least. He has a special kind of cosmopolitanism that seems to make him unique in Canada—Oxford, Princeton, a summer of teaching in Russia—and with this a comprehensive knowledge of Canada, east and west, French and English, and all through its history. He is especially conscious of being a Nova Scotian, and explained to me that the Nova Scotians, since Acadia had originally covered part of Maine, were in some ways closer to New England than they were to the rest of Canada, and referred to "Canada"—Morley says "Upper Canada"—as if they lived in a different country. Behind this was his patriotism as a Highlander. When I told him that the Wilsons had come from Londonderry, he asked rather grimly whether I was aware that Grant and several of our Presidents and other famous "Americans" had been Ulstermen. He said—it was of course a joke, but he had evidently cherished in his mind the conflict between the Highlander and the Lowlander—"I recognize the enemy when I see him!" His father had been a doctor—with better opportunities, Hugh thought, he might have been a brain surgeon, and he had read Latin and Greek to the end of his life.

Hugh had studied classics and had evidently set out to get a Ph.D. in them (I suppose) and teach. He had spent three years in the Princeton graduate school. I said that this must have been an ordeal, and he assured me that it had been—about his only relief had been to talk and drink with Ronald Bottrell at some tavern near the golf links. In the end he had been frustrated by Kelly Prentice, who had, I gathered, refused him a degree, on the ground that he was a Canadian. I explained to him that Kelly was a famous snob—of a special kind, the Albany snob, who snubbed faculty and students alike. I told him how he had been in the habit, in the course in the *Iliad* I had with him (a very good one, however: a serious upperclass course, in which we studied the attempts to date the various parts of the poem), of insulting the stupider students. Uninteresting though they were, and quite uninterested in the classics as literature (those to me unaccountable young men who found that with steady diligence they could translate Greek and Latin as they might have discovered that they could do mathematics), they should have been treated with decent courtesy. He said that this experience with Kelly Prentice had really been traumatic—had perhaps cast him back on his Canadian identity. Kelly had, I think, when Hugh interviewed him, been lying on his back on a couch and had behaved with his usual disdainful coolness. Since this story came at the end of the evening, when we were both rather excited by the wine, it has remained with me as something slightly nightmarish. Kelly Prentice had had a certain brilliance and a distinction that was real. His unpleasantness had been at college merely a "part of the act"; and it seemed excessive and gruesome that it should have been possible for him to blight another man's career. We started more interesting subjects than we were able to discuss satisfactorily: Calvinism, Princeton, Canada.

Marie-Claire Blais: I had assumed that she was in Quebec and only the last day I was in Montreal (my first stay) learned from Falardeau that she had been in Montreal all the time, was spending the winter there. I called her up at once and invited her to the hotel. We had a dinner engagement so I had her come in at four, and we sat in the lounge. She could not have been more different from what the photographs had led me to expect: a big tall rather coarse-featured country girl with ill-kept coarse hair. She is actually an attractive little woman, with well-developed breasts but tiny hands and feet, a sharp nose, a very small mouth and deep-thinking, gray-green eyes, with the good quiet manners and the very pure French that I suppose she learned from the nuns. She was twelve years in the convent as a pensionnaire (is now only 22) and had evidently not been very happy. But from the age of 14 she had borrowed surreptitiously from "older friends" all the forbidden books of French literature. She had read Flaubert, but told me that she particularly liked Balzac and Proust. When I asked her by whom she had been influenced, she astonished me by naming Lautréamont, André Breton's *Nadja* and Jean Cocteau's *Thomas l'Imposteur*. I shouldn't have thought that what she wrote had anything in common with any of them—her poetry a little perhaps with the *Chants de Maldoror*. She was interested in Carson McCullers (*The Heart Is a Lonely Hunter*), Lillian

Smith and *L'Attrape-Coeur* [*The Catcher in the Rye*] of
J. D. Salinger.

She is perfectly self-possessed and has an unusual simplicity and directness that are the signs of a remarkable
person. One might have expected a trying intensity or some
dramatization of herself: but she has nothing at all of these.
Hugh MacLennan could not have been more wrong in
conjecturing—from *La Belle Bête*—that she might be close
to paranoia. She told me that her novels were not autobiographical (I am here combining this with the conversation that Elena and I had with her last Saturday when
I took her out to dinner). When I asked her why, in *Tête
Blanche*, Émilie had not written to Tête Blanche and why
he had made no effort to find her again, she replied, "*C'était
fini*," and when I pressed her about this further the second
time I saw her, she explained, as I understood her, that
their separation was forced by circumstances, that it was
not "*intérieur*." When I asked her why Jessy, after his wife
had had a baby, had hanged himself in the winter forest,
she said that he had been reduced to despair by his love
affairs having always failed. I decided that it was really no
use to ask her such questions about her books; but I said
later that she sometimes laughed—why did her characters
never laugh? She replied that she was writing a book that
was quite unlike her former ones. I told her about Morley
Callaghan and explained the title of *The Loved and the
Lost*. "Doesn't he believe in love?" she asked. I asked her
whether she didn't believe in love: Yes, she did. She had
talked to Elena about Simone Weil and Teilhard de Chardin. Elena picked up in Montreal a volume of Simone Weil
and read it after she left. When I talked to her on the
phone, she told me that the influence of Weil—her cult
of suffering—was evident in the work of "*la petite Blais*,"
and that I should tell her that she ought to read Chardin
rather than Weil.

I told Blais that I had met Lévesque and thought him *un homme extraordinaire*. She answered, *"Il est très géné-reux,"* and she repeated this later when I said something more about him. That was her only comment. She is starting to read English books, is interested in Emily Dickinson. (Strange that those professors in Quebec should have supposed that in the United States there had not been many women writers.) I told her that there were good passages in the poems she had given me but that they lacked concentration. "Concentration?" she said. "I haven't thought about that." She had always lived in Quebec, not in the country. In connection with something she told me, I said, "Your youth was sad?" She said yes, with no pose or self-pity. I can't be sure that she didn't say, *"Oui, peut-être."* That was in any case the impression conveyed by her tone. She had said in an interview in *Chatelaine* that yes, she had had to adapt herself to France and that it was hardly worth the trouble. She surprised me by saying with dissatisfaction, when I asked her about Paris, that it was "old." "But it's a beautiful city!" "The design is beautiful but everything is so old!" I said that Quebec was fine and *"très sévère."* She answered, *"Peut-être trop."* Her parents, who had not been able to understand her wanting to be a writer—and who, I gather, had violently objected—had now accepted the fact. She had not been happy in the convent.

After dinner, I took her to the Buells'. Mrs. Buell explained that her French was not as good as John's. She had one French parent, too, but they had not spoken French in the household whereas in John's they had. With her effort and my lack of fluency, the conversation was at first a little clumsy, but then John and Marie-Claire *s'emballaient* [ran off with it] and left the other two of us far behind. He turned into a complete Frenchman, with all the French gestures of his eyebrows and hands. When we left, he gave her copies of his two books.

Three Canadians made a point of telling me about the shortcomings of the American Army in the last war. McGeachie spoke of their sloppiness compared to the Canadians and British; Duncan said that American soldiers are brave enough but they haven't, like the English and Canadians, got the endurance to slog it out—if there is nothing going on and a prospect of indefinite waiting, they simply take things into their own hands and leave—very independent, don't have the unquestioning obedience that keeps the British troops at their posts. Ken Johnston brought to our *Press Club dinner* a man who had flown a plane for the UN in the Korean War especially to tell me stories about the mess we had made of things there, wasting the lives of our pilots, not having planned their movements clearly. Johnston had already told me some of these stories—"stories that have never been published!" One of the others had said, "That sounds rather anti-American." When I left the dinner at 9:30, fatigued with the funny stories, he said, "That's just like an American!" I wonder whether they feel the Americans are getting too much credit for their part in the war.

I flew to Toronto from Montreal at noon, Sept. 30. It was good to see the Callaghans again. It was Sunday night, and the boys were rallying round. Morley was disappointed when Nina said she couldn't stay for dinner, and evidently irritated when Michael didn't show up in time. There is rivalry and certain antagonism between Toronto and Montreal. The Montrealers will tell you that Toronto is not typical of Canada—a Western industrial city; and Morley, before I went there, said he feared I was under a misapprehension as to Montreal's being the intellectual center:

"This is the center here"—most of the publishing was done in Toronto, and the University of Toronto was one of the best in the country, far better than McGill. Barry amused me by telling me that Toronto now had every kind of nightlife, "places for every kind of vice"—and at the same time avant-garde theaters that put on Ionesco and Beckett.

Poor Loretto is still miserable with her *tic douloureux*. They don't know what to do about it. One doctor gives her pills and another, a surgeon, wants to operate, but it would be a more serious operation than the one she had before. The pills make her dopey, and when the nerve constricts her, she can hardly talk. But she is always retiring and quiet, always with good manners, with none of the heartiness or aggressiveness of many Canadian women. Morley explained this to me when I was telling him of Marie-Claire's good manners. It was the convent training, he said—Loretto, like Morley, is Irish: if the girls weren't going to be nuns, they were taught the modest social graces which would make them good wives. Loretto is still a devout Catholic; but Morley, though loyal to the Catholic Church as against the Protestant churches, does not subscribe to all its doctrines. He feels strongly that the Fall is a pernicious idea, and he says that his next novel will deal with it. I asked whether his boys were devout, and he said that he didn't know, had never asked them about it.

I feel that in his case as well as in those of Buell and Marie-Claire, the Catholic Church has given them—however much they may criticize it or even turn their backs on it (has Marie-Claire done this? I imagine not entirely)—their contact with a moral world, an international institution, that saves them from preoccupation with the more provincial problems of Canada. I have a very good time with Morley, who is always thinking about fundamental questions: we can't know the meaning of or the reason for life: most people have no ideologies—they go on living and attending to their immediate interests without worrying about ideas. Yet it is wrong to run down the human race—what we have done is very remarkable.

"A NEW LEASE ON LIFE":
THE END OF 1962

The Country and Cambridge;
Isaiah Berlin

<*Return to Talcottville (Oct. 2):* A perfectly marvelous day. Everett Hutchins picked me up at the airport in Buffalo. We came in through the Boonville Gorge, which was all rose and yellow and orange and crimson. I like to see this country here at different times of the year and to think that it must have looked so to my relations when they were living—pathos of feeling this. The next day was also beautiful. The tree in front of the house was all rose madder and gold, with a little light green still left on its underside, and in the lot across the road by which it stands, the young sprouts of trees looked like goldenrod and the milkweed was wearing white puffs.

It seemed a pity to have to leave; but the next day (Thursday) was clouded, and today there is nothing but dreary rain. The colors of trees are rusted, and the leaves are falling away. In the old days, I suppose, they were kept so busy that a merely rainy day could not have depressed them much.

Dinner with the Morrises last night, and our usual animated conversation. Their friend [Barbara Erwin] was there, the nice and somewhat unconventional school-teacher, who, I take it, is one of their only local kinspirits. Glyn, at one point after dinner, began questioning me— "It may be very impertinent to ask you this"—I didn't know why it should be—as to whether I didn't feel that there was something behind our lives that would make things come out all right. He approached the subject so discreetly that I did not at first understand that he was talking about God as a purpose and power in the universe. He has mainly dropped his Protestant theology, but he still feels under the necessity of keeping hold of the belief in some divine intention. Since I have never had to think in these terms, I did not grasp at first what he was getting at, and so my answers must have been unsatisfactory.

I don't believe I have noted his excellent remark that a language is really "a way of life." He was born in Wales and used to speak Welsh, and Welsh conceptions with the words that represent them still to some extent figure in his thought. *Hwyl*, for example, which means the gift of tongues that descends on the Welsh orator and sometimes carries him beyond his own comprehension. > *Stuart Hughes* has something of this—he and Glyn were discussing it when he came to see me summer before last—as I noted when I heard him speak in public in his senatorial campaign. He did not let himself go in an inspirational way, but became more incisive and shining than in either his writing or his conversation, answering questions instantly with conviction and point. When he spoke on Boston Common, I was told, he was picketed and heckled by anti-Soviet elements, including exiled Hungarians, who marched around the platform and demanded that we go to war with Russia. He is said to have handled this extremely well, never losing his temper but joking, and finally making his speech.

<I saw *Mariska* only once after I got back from Canada. She now goes two nights a week to Utica College, driving there from her job in Rome, which is not so very far, but then having, after her class, to make the hour's trip back to West Leyden. Her husband wants her to bowl every Saturday night, so on Sunday she is, she says, "in pieces." She did letters for me Saturday afternoon. In order to get some kind of certificate, she has to have 30 credits, which would apparently take her three years, but has already so convinced them of her competence that they are going to let her skip English I and II. She stayed for a drink when we had finished the letters, and we had a longish talk; then the Loomises came in, then Glyn Morris to take me to dinner. I enjoy these rather rare occasions when I am able to summon some local social life. In the middle of it, George called Mariska and said that the bowling was off for the night. She was delighted and said that she could now relax. Glyn invited her to dinner. She was tempted, but did not waver more than a second, said that she must go home and get her husband dinner.

She spoke of having delivered a neighbor's baby. I asked whether it had been her that her father had delivered or one of her babies—she said that it had been her. They were caught on their farm by a snowstorm and were not able to get anyone in. In the night class, they had to make little speeches on the subject of snowstorms, and she had talked four and a half minutes, longer than the stipulated allowance, and they had kidded her about it afterwards. I told her, truly, that it was the Hungarian in her: they are never at a loss to express themselves.

The Hutchinses drove me to Cummington. The forests on the Mohawk hills are wonderful. It is not true, as Loren Crosten seemed to think, that the people who live in that country are not appreciative of the landscape. Mabel had brought along her sister, Mrs. Yelton, Beverly's mother, to "visit with," and they are all so accustomed to me now that among themselves their conversation is quite uninhibited. They were in ecstasies about the colors all along the way. > The rest of the time they talked mostly about things to eat: new recipes, delicious dishes. Mrs. Yelton, whom I had thought rather tragic—and she complained in a lower voice about her husband's not having sent her money—did a good deal of jovial laughing in a rich raucous fat woman's voice.

<Elena met me at Cummington. > We spent the night with Helen, had a very agreeable lunch the next day with Newton Arvin in Northampton and then drove on to *Cambridge*.

It was enough to get back to Cambridge for us both to become ill again and collapse. Elena only averted with penicillin one of her serious attacks of the flu, and then when she was able to be up, I came down with one of my worst attacks of gout—which Dr. Zetzel says, as I suspected, is now something rather beyond gout: "rheumatoid" arthritis. I had it in both hands and both legs, so that I could not even get to the bathroom—the worst since last May in Talcottville; but the medicine he gave me has now quelled it.

Isaiah Berlin came to dinner just when Elena was about to give way—she went to bed right after dinner. I said that we had been counting on him to brace up our lapsing morale, and he said that he himself had lost his *joie de vivre*. He did indeed look rather haggard and seemed relatively subdued.

He told us a very funny story about Spender and Evelyn Waugh. They had met at dinner somewhere, and Waugh had talked to Stephen about an old watch of his which he was unable to get repaired. Stephen said that he had once understood mending watches, and would be glad to see what he could do. Waugh had said that was very kind. (It was unwise, as Elena said, to give Stephen a watch to repair.) But that evening Stephen had a visitation from Francis Bacon with a band of beatniks, who overran him and when they left got away with the watch and some other things. Stephen the next day called up Bacon and asked him to return the watch—which he did, but the hands were gone and it was otherwise the worse for wear. Stephen wrote Waugh his regrets, addressing him as "Dear Evelyn." He answered that to Stephen he was "Mr. Waugh," and went around telling people that that Jew Spender consorted with "petty thieves" and was a disreputable character who had ruined his watch.

With Isaiah, I am less at home with his Oxford aspect than with his international personality. He is so sunk in his cozy Oxford circle—David Cecil, Maurice Bowra, Stuart Hampshire—with their prejudices, favorites and accepted canons, that it limits the free range of his mind. Thumbs down on Snow, a certain respect for Leavis, etc. Even in those non-English fields of which he has the freedom in his international character, he fences himself off from his Oxford colleagues: Cecil Roth, A.J.P. Taylor, Max Hayward (of whom he used to speak contemptuously on account of his humble origins but whom he now treats with more respect). He is much more *accueillant* [receptive] in the United States—Sam Behrman, the Backers, Morton White, old and sometimes dubious friends from Washington days; and it may be that he likes to escape from Oxford from time to time and that that is why he likes to come to America. His present visit seems more or less gratuitous. He has a grant from one of the foundations to do research on two books he is working on: does not give any lectures or teach at all, simply reads in the Widener Library.

Isaiah Berlin in a quiet moment at All Souls College

Morley Callaghan, like his novels, seems at first rather commonplace on the surface; but like them is deeply sensitive and understanding. I find that I sometimes miss the Callaghans.

I seem to be taking something of *a new lease on life*, after my period of ailments and depression—frustration over the income tax and nuclear war and the difficulty of writing on the subject. I had one bad evening here (Tuesday) when I got started drinking after dinner and ended with spasms of heart pressure when I was rolling around howling in bed. But the next morning I had subsided and have been quite calm and happy ever since. General relief of tension between Elena and me. I read to her the other evening Mark Twain's nightmare story "The Great Dark," which I have been curious about for years and which has now only just been published. I had already been under pressure from an hour-and-a-half session (on Tuesday) with Filman about the income tax, and, at once dulled and stimulated by whisky, reading the Mark Twain story to Elena really taxed and excited me more: the blind voyage in a drop of water, attacked by blind monster-bacteria; the husband and the wife who have been living in different dreams and have difficulty in agreeing on any common experiences— is the life that the husband remembers something real that they have had together or has the aimless menaced voyage with their children been the only reality all along? The story was never finished: they were to be left with the dead children floating into the cold.

The next day Brett-Smith of Oxford Press came to lunch. He told me, to my surprise, that *Patriotic Gore* and my other books had made $8,677.85 in the last six months. When advances, etc., were deducted, this left me a little over $5,000; then something over $4,000 would be due me from the book club to which they have sold it. This has made me feel somewhat better, though I don't see what is to be done to prevent the Internal Revenue people from collecting the $5,000 instead of me.

Have gone back to reading Parkman—am now in *A Half-Century of Conflict*—which has upon me—in spite of the treacheries and massacres and incredible pioneering ordeals—a quieting and reassuring effect. What sustained imagination and sureness of craftsman competence it shows to be able, after skipping ahead to finish *Wolfe and Montcalm* in case he should die, to go back and to fill in the gap, to keep gradually intensifying the conflict at an earlier and less acute stage in recounting such minor episodes as the Deerfield massacre, the Lovewell fight and the siege of the French by the Ontagamies.

We are going up to Wellfleet tomorrow morning to stay through into Monday, while Helen spends the weekend with Martha Chase. I am looking forward to it. Elena will get a rest and a space to recover from her illness. I'll clean up my correspondence and my dictionary and grammar articles.

Isaiah came in for tea in the afternoon before we left for Wellfleet. His way of saying Yes, or Certainly, just after he has made you agree to or accept something he has said is a part of his need to tuck himself in, make himself comfortable with you. But he has had a cheering effect on us. He ranges so much more freely than most men in an academic community; his "coverage" is so extraordinary: in that single conversation, the numerical significance of Hebrew words and letters and a discussion of the legend about פרדם [paradise]*; the dropping of A.J.P. Taylor from

---

* The "legend about paradise," from the Babylonian Talmud, is the story of four important rabbis who entered into the heavenly courts, or paradise, and what happened to them. One died, one went crazy, and one turned from his beliefs. Only Akiba escaped unharmed, which proved his holiness.

his lectureship and his controversy with Trevor-Roper,
which involved an anecdote about Lytton Strachey's voting
for Edgar Wallace*; Taylor's relation to [Sir Lewis] Namier; a biography of Namier, with anecdotes—"That's Namier"; Harry Levin and what to do about him—I suggested
that, when he becomes insulting, one ought to say, "Stop
it, stop it! Down, Pongo, down!"; Isaiah's recent visit to
Washington—Kennedy like Napoleon with his marshals,
certain of them "physically in love with him," he enjoyed
holding court, liked to have "panache"; dinner at the Alsops', with the Kennedys present, Mrs. Kennedy had put
Isaiah at ease, but the presence of royalty was always rather
freezing; Pipes working on Pyotr Struve, whom I thought
overrated, but whose writings he knew well and ran
through; Gerschonken, who led to Khlebnikov.

Aunt Addie's Bed, and a
Talk with James Baldwin

In Wellfleet, *Carolyn Wilson* [Link] came to see us with
the curious bald man who is apparently now her boyfriend.
His family are Swedish, he says, and he does look like a
fairy-tale troll. He had made a huge collection of book-
plates, which he has given to the Yale Library, and he
spends part of his time there as a curator of the collection.
He has known my ex-Stilwell cousins for years—Helen,
Dorothy and Adelaide—and was rather gruesome about
them, said they were "fiends," had never known people
who hated one another so. But he seems to have had a

---

* Lytton Strachey (1880–1932), the biographer, had influenced the young
Wilson. Edgar Wallace (1875–1932) was a journalist and mystery
writer. Isaiah Berlin explains that when Wallace was a candidate for
Parliament, Strachey—though he neither admired the work nor liked
the man, considering him in every way unremarkable—said he would
vote for him "because he is right."

good effect on Carolyn. They had come first the day before, when I hadn't seen them, and Elena had reported that she was better dressed, more elegant, than she had ever seen her, had cut her hair. I found that this was true, and Carolyn confided to me, in a moment when we were alone, that somebody—her brother Andrew, I think—had said that she had changed for the better.

I am very glad that Carolyn at last has been able to get away from the curse of Henry Link; but it always upsets me to see her, and I invariably take to drink. The revival of the Stilwells made it even more trying—though I was glad to hear something about them. Under the influence of bourbon, I insisted, for a second night, on sleeping in *Aunt Addie's old fourposter bed*, which she left me, so that Elena slept in Helen's room, and it partly spoiled the weekend for her. That bed has an emotional pull on me. It is the past and somehow gives me a sense of position. The traditional master's bed. Elena doesn't, I think, understand this. She always says the next morning, "Even a dog has a place to sleep." When I am sober, I can say to myself, "The least I can do for her, after all, is to let her sleep in that bed."

Thoughts about death such as, now that it is closer, I have never had before. Relative feebleness and futility of human lives: all the facts and ideas and experiences of our life, after a very few years, fading out. A foretaste of it in our memory letting go, infirmities that limit one's energy, sexual desire declining.

Nevertheless, since my trip to Canada, I have been more composed and calm, have perhaps adapted myself to a lower key of living, sleep better, don't drink so much, feel more consistently affectionate towards Elena, more bound to her, I like less to be separated from her.

———

Echoes from the past: Edna Millay's saying, when I had made love to her for the first time in my life to anyone, "I know just how you feel: it was here, and it was beautiful, and now it's gone!"

When Elena said, "There's that policeman I hate—he's always so disagreeable!" I remembered Paul Rosenfeld's story about his saying to Sherwood Anderson that he couldn't feel with a policeman any human solidarity. Sherwood had said that a policeman was a man just like anyone else. "Tell me something about a policeman that would make me feel that he was a human being." "Well, the first thing he does when he gets home at night is he takes off his shoes."

James Baldwin was on here twice. We heard him give a lecture at Brandeis. He was able to handle it admirably—sat at a table and talked quietly.* His subject was "Evil in Fiction," and I suppose it was something of an apologia for the obscenities of *Another Country*. He spoke of the refusal to live fully, which Henry James advises against in *The Ambassadors*. Baldwin's point was that evil was the fear of taking chances, which amounted to choosing death. Everything worthwhile in life was dangerous—marriage, birth, etc. When, after the lecture, he answered questions, some boy said, "Well, Allen Ginsberg has slept with his mother and sister, been homosexual, and done other things I forget, and still he's not happy."† In answering this,

---

* Not long before, EW had called Baldwin "not only one of the best Negro writers that we have in this country" but "one of the best writers that we have" (*The Bit Between My Teeth*).

† Ginsberg summed up his experiences slightly differently in a yearning letter to Wilson. He had tried "every way out" including "poetry, haranguing, taking off my clothes, Signs and Symbols public and private, but all I met and all I finally wound up with was indifference misconception or hatred and paranoia my own as well as outside me." Now, however, he had found the loving gospel of Vishnu and Father Zossima. He urged the critic (whom he called "dear old heart") to "put [his] direct feelings into practice" by embracing his postman.

Baldwin gave one of his rare broad-toothed grins. He seems to have taken over something of Kennedy's manner at his press conferences, leaning forward, listening intently and seriously, answering right away and without hesitation, only at such times and in such a way as to be sure he has the sympathy of his listener.

He came here for a drink and stayed to dinner after making a recording for Steve Fassett, and had with him a bearded stalwart, half Jewish and half Irish, who had formerly been a labor organizer in the South and was now teaching sociology at Brandeis—he had been looking after Baldwin and steering him around. —I asked Baldwin why he thought that Strether had turned Mme Vionnet down when she practically offered herself to him. He said that he knew men of his own generation who did the same kind of thing—they drew back from any serious relationship with a woman. Henry James of course is making his hero behave as he does from New England inhibitions, where the men Baldwin knows are near beatniks who simply don't want responsibility. —I talked to him about embittered Negro nationalism, of which I had first seen the signs when I took Louise Bogan to the Savoy in Harlem not long after the race riots there and instead of being cordially received was in various ways made to feel that whites weren't wanted, so that eventually we left, and of which I was made to feel the full force at the time when Phil Hamburger and I in Rome were lunching and dining with Roi Ottley. I asked Baldwin whether he had known Roi Ottley. "I met him once. He was a hero of mine." I told him about the occasion when we had made a date with Ottley, and at one of the official new handouts of information which none of us took seriously we ran into the other Harlem correspondents, who ate together as a group and with whom Roi did not seem to have close relations. He had to agree to come dine with them when they asked him, treating us with a certain rudeness.* Baldwin said that he had been running into this himself, had recently brought a white friend to Harlem and had not been well received. "And Ottley had a white wife," I added. "And that didn't help," he said.

At dinner he became excited—furiously indignant—in arguing with his friend about Cuba. He said that we were responsible for what had happened—if the U.S. invaded Cuba, the Negroes would identify themselves with Castro. I agreed with him about our being to blame but succeeded in turning down the heat. When Elena left the table to go into the kitchen, he turned on his adjectival "fucking"— like the people in his novel—and the Brandeis man answered him in kind. I had been wondering whether ordinary people really talked to one another that way now. I reflected, after seeing later in New York Albee's play *Who's Afraid of Virginia Woolf?*, whether most of the dirty language in fiction and on stage didn't occur in the work of homosexuals: Albee, Tennessee Williams, Isherwood, Baldwin, Genet, and the beatniks Ginsberg and Burroughs. When I suggested this to Elena, she said that if this was true, it was probably because these writers were always thinking in terms of male companions. It is, I suppose, true that though these writers do often deal intensely with women, they have no awareness of the presence of ladies they want to please—and if I say "ladies," it is because most women one wants to please have to be treated as ladies. Henry Miller is perhaps an exception, but he, too, is putting himself in the company of male companions,

* EW and the essayist Philip Hamburger were both on assignment for *The New Yorker* in Italy at the end of World War II. Roi Ottley was a correspondent for the New York daily *PM*. Ottley also told them how other black correspondents reported on events and social situations in accord with the racial attitudes of their readers in African-American newspapers (*The Forties*).

and, in *The Tropic of Cancer* at least, is dealing almost exclusively with whores.

After doing Hungarian one afternoon with Mrs. Benedek, I arranged to meet Elena in the bar of one of the nearby hotels (The Commander). It had suddenly turned cold, and though it was only a few blocks, my angina began to squeeze me and I found that I could hardly make it to the Continental across the street in order to get a taxi to carry me a block or two farther. A couple of Scotches fortified me while I talked animatedly and relievedly about the idiosyncrasies of Hungarian grammar, polite forms, etc. Then Elena drove me home. I was uncomfortable sitting around downstairs, then thought that if I went to bed, I should be able to relax and relieve it, as I had been able to do that night in Quebec. But it seemed to get worse and worse, and I finally had Elena call Zetzel. He came and gave me a shot, so the ache calmed down and I finally got to sleep. He sent a heart specialist the next day to take a cardiogram, and this doctor had a specimen of my blood tested. They established that I had not had a coronary and that the condition of my heart was no worse than it had been two summers ago when Dr. Hicks took a cardiogram in New York; but they made me stay in bed and move around as little as possible. It is both a relaxation and an embarrassment to have other people go up and down the stairs and run errands for me.

When you realize that it won't be so long before you fade out of life, the activities of so short-lived human beings begin to seem rather futile and the beings themselves flimsy. Does it really matter that much? And all that energy and worry expended on merely getting themselves reproduced!

Nevertheless, up to the moment when I had that attack, I had been having ideas and writing them quite fluently and enjoyably again.

The new Canadian poetry: Louis Dudek and Irving Layton and the rest—I have just been going through Dudek's magazine *Delta*—have done something for Canadian poetry in making it less provincial: Dudek's parents are Polish, and he is trilingual in Polish, French and English, and Layton is Jewish and born in Romania. But they can't seem to get away from Pound and Williams. They are monotonous in their imitations of Pound's epigrams, and instead of being sharp, they are pulpy. As for the content, a good deal of it consists in establishing that they have sex in Canada, too, and are no longer afraid to admit it.

Auden, Mike Nichols, and Flying in New York

Trip to New York (I left Cambridge on Tuesday, Nov. 26, returned on Thursday, Dec. 4): I couldn't rush around as much as I usually do, had continually to put on the brakes: two evenings with the Lowells, two with Mike Nichols, two with the Epsteins, two evenings at The Little Players and Peschka and Murdock afterwards; the Jonathan Millers at the Epsteins' and The Little Players, Auden, Carol Radowitz, Sovka [Winkelhorn], Clelia [Carroll] and her husband, Muriel Spark and Ved Mehta, luncheon with William Shawn, luncheon with Dawn [Powell], Renata [Adler], Brett-Smith, Roger Straus, Leon Edel (some of these overlapping—I made them come to the Algonquin, when possible); I would creep into my office on the 18th floor and quietly write and answer letters there, did not visit other offices, since I could not go up and down stairs, and it was so much trouble to take the elevator to go from one floor to another.

Wystan, with all his feeling for landscape and geological formations, his metrics and generalizations, does not have much understanding of people. I remonstrated with him about Falstaff (essay in *The Dyer's Hand*): it is not true that he never fornicates—scene in the second act, when he is waiting offstage for Doll Tearsheet to come to him —and the nasty things he does that Wystan objects to— stabbing the dying soldiers, etc.—are perfectly in character. Wystan doesn't want him to be realistic, wants to make him a figure of fairyland. He is reviewing the Oscar Wilde letters for *The New Yorker*: he does not want to admit that Wilde had syphilis or that he was capable of caring for a woman—his interest in Douglas was "not sexual"—Douglas and Wilde were both bad poets, thinks *The Importance of Being Earnest* a masterpiece—I don't agree: except for one or two scenes, I still feel about it as I did when I read it at college and as Bernard Shaw says he did: that it is rather silly and thin and written under the influence of Gilbert.

He said that he had never in his boyhood known anything about America—it was all just a blur over there, and he still knew nothing after Oxford. I asked how he had come to know such American songs as "Frankie and Johnny" and "Casey Jones," and he said they had been to him just folk songs. How had he discovered America? In coming through the States, on his way back from China. What he liked about it was that it was not class-ridden like England. That was why he had become an American. When he had last been in England, it had been during the Cuban crisis. Someone had come to get him to sign a protest, and he had taken great satisfaction in saying, "I'm an American!" and throwing him out.

———

Mike Nichols has taken a beating on the play that Elaine wrote for him and that they found that they couldn't go on with when they had tried it out for two weeks in Philadelphia. I had felt when he first told me about it that she was going to make him ridiculous, to express toward him some kind of contempt. Now he told me that the character he was supposed to play was actually based on her conception of him, and that she had made him a moral monster whom the audience couldn't like. When he would ask her what her idea was about this character, she would say that she could not explain. They mustn't ask her: her ideas would come to her in the middle of the night. They imposed themselves upon her, and she would get up and write. She didn't understand them herself. And she had no sense of form—I had noticed this—but would go on and on in their dialogues. It was he who made the steps from point to point. The director had wanted changes, and Mike himself was deeply dissatisfied with it. She had treated him abominably, he said, and her insistence on directing him instead of acting with him had dislocated and ruined their relationship. I said that they were still in love. Not on her side, he said. She was sleeping now with her analyst— the man she had recently married had only lasted two months—and Mike and Elaine were hardly on speaking terms. They had commitments for TV and records, but were now on such bad terms with one another that it was hard to see how they could fulfill them.

I told him that women like that were likely to end up marrying rather well-to-do middle-aged men who were not remarkably clever, and afterwards I reflected that Mary McCarthy and Edna had perhaps, having both lost their fathers very early, provided themselves with father substitutes. (I didn't do in this role for Mary: I was cast as the horrid false father, her uncle, and the things that, in her hysteria, she would accuse me of were usually his crimes and not mine.) The same may well be true in the case of Elaine. She lost her father, Mike tells me, when she was seven, and she hasn't found a substitute yet. I suppose that lyric writer she married served the same purpose for her that Bowden [Broadwater] did for Mary.

He insisted on taking us to *Virginia Woolf*—he was glad to see it again—partly I think because it has something in common with their Pirandello piece. It also seems to owe something to O'Neill.

He looked thin and rather shrunken, less sure of himself than in the winter of their great success. Elena felt very sorry for him. He has been asked by Lillian Hellman to be in her new play, a dramatic adaptation of *How Much*, but has not been able to decide because he has not seen all the script. I said that he and Elaine would probably do another show together. It would take some time, he said.

Dreams of flying: Philip Carroll (Clelia's husband) said he often flew. How high? A foot or two above the ground. Oh, I said, I flew to the ceiling.* It was a delicious sensation, he just glided along. Did he have an audience, as I always did? No; but yes, he did occasionally. He would slip through the traffic on the street. He would also rise above a business conference and float around in the air— he thought it indicated a feeling of superiority to the people he had sometimes to work with. It turned out that he had the same kind of dreams, in connection with his Maryland "Mansion" or "Manse," as I have about Talcottville. People who don't belong there come in, and he has to get them out. But he on certain occasions, as I do not do, keeps them out with a gun, as if they were Indians. He had just,

---

* Philip Carroll remembered that Wilson was wearing a rather worn, ratty linen suit, an "ice cream suit," such as had been out of fashion for decades. He extended his arms and went swooping around the tables at the Algonquin, saying, "This is how I fly."

with a certain embarrassment and boredom, been trying to write advertising copy for the family dairy business.

He had arrived, when Clelia was there (in the Algonquin lobby) as well as Elena and Sovka, announcing himself as "the jealous husband." This was nonsense and I find him sympathetic, yet I suppose I do like to see Clelia by herself. I feel that I should have loved her and had a delightful time with her if we had met at the right age, and I always look forward to seeing her, though it is always so briefly in New York. One thing that charms me is that, in spite of her worldliness, she blushes, and I don't always know why; and I love her frank direct way of talking. She has something very feminine, shy, accessible, combined with a sharp sense of money and other practical matters.

After Sovka had left and Elena had gone upstairs, Clelia told me that, before I came, Elena had told them that I had "a Hungarian mistress" in every place that I lived. When I taxed Elena with this afterwards, she said that she had meant "schoolmistress," that she thought you could use mistress in this way.

My present fear of making love on account of starting up my angina nags me and irritates me. The morning before I left New York I made love to Elena for the first time in weeks. It was a very mild performance—I didn't want to repeat my experience in Quebec. It irks me to see her body when in a hotel she dresses and undresses, and to realize that I can't do it justice.

Hungarians and French Novels

Hungarian and Hungary: Agatha said that the vocabulary of Hungarian was limited, but that it was like the Hungarian cuisine: out of a few elements, they could produce a wonderful dinner. Out of their limited vocabulary they could produce such marvelous poetry. Was it she or Mrs. Benedek who said that the language was clumsy but that the poets could turn it to silk?

Eleanor Perényi said to me the same thing that I had been saying to other people: that Hungarian was almost Japanese in its use of honorifics. I have been much amused by the results of asking Hungarians how they say *you*. It seems to be possible to place them by what they tell you about this. Mrs. Benedek says she doesn't like to call people either *maga* or *ön*, the latter for equals, the former for inferiors, because it is invidious to the *magas* and apparently because *maga* in itself is an ugly word (the plural *magak* is worse): "Just put the verb in the third person." Eleanor says that *ön* is "non-U," self-consciously refined, like saying *serviette* in England. She and her husband called one another *maga*; he only said *te* to his men friends. Agatha could not quite accept either *maga* or *ön*, and after a little thought suggested my trying *kegyed*, which she said was the real old Hungarian (she is all for the language of the countryside), but which turned out, when I looked it up, to be "archaic, obsolete," and which Mrs. Benedek seemed to think rather a joke. Sándor Radó had a very strong aversion to *ön*: it was something that was supposed to be polite, but the effect of which was really degrading. Mariska was hardly aware of *ön*: her family never used it. Agatha finally showed me a contemporary novel she was reading in which everybody seemed to be calling everybody else *maga*, and Eleanor said that they were doing this as a consequence of the Communist regime.

I asked Eleanor as a joke whether they had been much troubled with vampires when she lived in the Perényi castle. Yes, they had, as a matter of fact. The peasants would come in and tell them that a vampire was sucking the blood of the cows. They had also had ghosts in the castle. In a corner of the house with guest rooms, the guests had been disturbed by tappings and the sound of footsteps—Mamaine [Koestler] and Celia [Goodman] had heard them. Then they took a partition down and found two human skeletons. The family records showed that two priests had been walled up by some early baron. They were buried, and the noises ceased.

She apparently got fed up with the barbarous feudal life, just as, Elena says, Charley Curtis's sister-in-law the baroness Palfi did, and Louise de Vilmorin when she was married to Palfi: stag killings and such reckless amusements as shooting the Sèvres china. The Perényis seem to have been in the wildest Carpathians.

Finished *Parkman* Dec. 12. One gets a little tired of it toward the end: one has to read about so many sieges; but each one of these episodes is different, each is so particularized. This is one of the things I most admire: the avoidance of generalization, the description of the events always in concrete detail. The larger tendencies are shown by a chronicle of individualized persons and actions. It is what I try to do myself. The objectivity of Parkman is wonderful: he will not allow himself bias against the French, whose bravery is always honored; and he even praises Vaudreuil, after making him something of a villain. But of course it was the colonists and the English who won, and he ends on a note of patriotism and celebration of English institutions.

The same night I started Balzac's *La Cousine Bette*, because I want to use a reference to Baron Hulot in my article on dictionaries and grammars. It is amusing me more than I expected. I have never had an appetite for Balzac. I have never wanted to read about *La Vie de Province* or César Birotteau's bankruptcy. I didn't care much for *Le Père Goriot*, but I may like the Paris section better.

He seems to be an author either that you can't read or that
you read from beginning to end: Henry James of course
devoured him. Proust got interested after at first rejecting
him. Thornton Wilder has read him through, and so has
even Volodya Nabokov, who, after telling me how terrible
he was, tried to surprise me, in his characteristic way, by
announcing: "I've read all of Balzac!"

Cartier-Bresson, who was here a few nights ago, says he
has been in my situation: approves of Balzac "on principle"
but does not really enjoy reading him. Cartier-Bresson is
an old friend of Elena's and used to visit them in Johannisberg. I liked him: he is so little provincial that one would
not take him for a modern Frenchman. He has been in
Russia and China, speaks English very well, spent three
years in prison in Germany, during which time he learned
German; escaped and swam the Rhine and rejoined his
wife at their country house, where he had told her to go
and wait for him. She had been there for weeks all alone.
She is a Javanese—I met her when they called on us at
Wellfleet—with a caste mark (or beauty spot) on her forehead. He told Elena that they were *"un petit peu séparés."*
We talked about French Canadians, and he said that he
was self-conscious, uncomfortable with them.

Some evenings, when I go out to the Loeb Theater on
the corner or the Brattle around the corner, I feel like that
old dope-addict doctor in Red Bank, who used to be taken
by his daughter to all the shows at Frick's Lyceum and sit
in the front row. He was absolutely pale and flabby, and
going out occasionally to the theater was apparently his
only social activity. The only time the town ever saw him.

Finished *La Cousine Bette.* The only entertaining Balzac
I have read—must read more of the Parisian novels—*La*

Vie de Province bores me. The audacious and unscrupulous badness of Valérie Marneffe and *la cousine* Bette seems to derive from [Laclos's] *Les Liaisons Dangereuses*, to which Balzac occasionally refers, at one point calling Valérie Madame Meursault. And everybody looks back toward Napoleon. I had never really understood why Stendhal should have said that Julien Sorel was based on Napoleon till I read the last volumes of Michelet's history in which Napoleon is shown as a brazen and cynical little adventurer who puts himself over through audacity and brutality. This kind of unscrupulous careerist is of course a specialty of Balzac's. It was something which undoubtedly existed in his time. It is allied to the Balzacian monomania, but I cannot quite believe in this: *la cousine* Bette, for example. Such people are too much all of a piece: they are not allowed complexities or waverings.

I had not taken account till I read this book of the extent to which both Zola and Proust were influenced by Balzac: Nana and the relentless old mother in *La Terre*; the hardness and the cruelty of the people in Proust. The trouble is that the later novelists—especially Zola—are so likely to push so far the outrageous heartlessness and greed of their characters that the effect becomes comic instead of frightening. Balzac, along with his realism, is capable of worse absurdities than even Dickens. At the rate that he has launched Valérie Marneffe on her destructive and irresistible career of crime, you don't see how he can get her punished or ever get rid of the character at all. What he hits upon is to have her Brazilian lover—the only one who is capable of retaliating—arrange with his black servant to have both of them infected with a mysterious deadly tropical disease, which they will manage to communicate to Valérie while they have themselves cured (I do not understand the steps of this). The result is that Valérie and her husband suddenly begin to putrefy and expire as little more than heaps of slime (this, too, is no doubt a reminiscence of Laclos).

Afterwards, I read for the first time Taine's excellent essay on Balzac, which renewed my admiration for him. Elsewhere—in *L'Histoire de la Littérature Anglaise*, it must be—he compares Valérie Marneffe with Becky Sharp, saying that the difference between them is that Valérie is hot whereas Becky is cold. But you don't really know much about Valérie in bed: you are told that she had "*beaucoup d'invention*" or something of the kind, and she is supposed to have been able to convince all three of her lovers that she was crazy about them; but two of them, as well as her homosexual husband, could not have been much to her taste. Taine also says, I think, that Balzac, in contradistinction to Thackeray, "*aime sa Valérie*"; but does he any more than Thackeray more or less admires Becky Sharp? It is rather that Balzac is fascinated by this kind of inordinate personality, wickedness that stops at nothing. There is a line that extends from Sade through Laclos—by way of the career of Napoleon—to Stendhal and Balzac and after.

The department of magic called "Silks": I had never done anything with this, but as my amateur magic nowadays, with my fingers, seems to me less skillful, I ignobly fall back on "gimmicks" and have been going in for these. Some of the effects are quite pretty: the large plastic "rainbow" goblet that fills suddenly with different-colored silks, the four silks that come out of a little box—also, the black silk that turns into a walking stick. I am not yet very good at manipulating them: they have to be folded in a certain way, etc.

Lou Tannen's magic supply shop on West 42nd St. has been a delightful discovery. Tannen himself is a first-rate magician and loves to show off his tricks—from childish gimmicks for boy amateurs to difficult sleight-of-hand that is the admiration of other magicians. I love these superior toy stores, with their red and white bells and bouquets of flowers made of gaily dyed feathers and "Jumbo" playing cards in glass "roulettes" and little tables and imitation rabbits and card stars and goldfish bowls and silk-production boxes and linking rings and posters and photographs of magicians and magic shows and ventrilo-quial figures. The magicians enjoy so much having every-thing bright-colored and shiny. Amateur magic, like Punch and Judy, has been a childish recreation that I have carried all through my life. My enjoyment of magic shops dates from my first visit to Martinkas, when my mother con-sented to take me but became rather nervous about it when she found that it was, I think, on Seventh Ave., in what seemed to her a rather dubious neighborhood. I was fascinated and a little frightened by the devils and mys-terious objects of which I did not then know the secrets. My first year at Hill I wrote a story about a couple who kept a magic store which was the first thing the *Record* printed. Right now I am writing with Ed O'Connor—we are doing alternate chapters—a burlesque novel about a magician.

Every Hungarian knows all about every other Hungarian. When I was working on "My Fifty Years with Dictionaries and Grammars," I got Mariska to send me that old grammar in Hungarian intended for immigrants to the U.S. which her parents had long ago used. I discovered that it con-tained most elaborate conjugations—with pluperfects, fu-ture perfects, a passive voice, etc.—which I had never seen before. When I showed them to Agatha, she identified *vala* as an old form from the verb *to be* which occurred in the old ballads and occasionally in modern poems, but said that she had never seen the rest of it in her life. Zoltán,

however, stuck his nose in it and came up with the following explanation: The grammar had been prepared by a
dishonest provincial notary who had to leave Hungary in
consequence of something he had done. I was impressed
by this feat of Sherlock Holmes detection. His reasoning
was as follows: The old language of the educated classes
was Latin, and the legal documents were in Latin. The
author of this part of the grammar was trying to supply in
Hungarian the whole apparatus of Latin conjugations. He
was therefore a man of little learning who did, however,
know Latin, had been drawing up documents for petty
legal transactions. He would not have come to the U.S.,
where his special law and Latin would be of no use, unless
there was something wrong. Zoltán said he had known
several such people. The man would have needed work
and would have undertaken the grammar as a job. The
colloquial part, however, was quite correct and had presumably been prepared by someone who knew the ropes
over here. I added the last conjecture myself and, though
the title page was missing, had discovered that the volume
must have been published not long after 1913, since in its
listing of the American Presidents that was the last date
given, and the printing and inserted advertisements could
not have been much later.

I finished *Úri Divat* [*Clothes for the Quality*] with Agatha.
She—though, like most Hungarians, not really thinking
much of Molnár—felt, as I did, that it created its own
peculiar atmosphere. The clothing store with its goods and
its customers of different ranks and its anxious and ob-
sequious shopkeepers, with their own acute personal problems concealed behind their tradesmen's exteriors. You
could positively smell the fabrics. Agatha—as in Zoltán's
case, at once seeing the man behind the work—said that
Molnár undoubtedly frequented a shop where he got to

know the people and was able to imagine their lives. He was already a well-known writer, and they would have given him credit.

"The Flimsiness of Human Life": Arthur Nock

Arthur Nock called us to explain that he had to go to the hospital and so could not have the party in his rooms at Eliot House to which he had invited us. (He had invited us to bring Button. He had always seemed delighted when he had met Elena at Sage's grocery store: "When I saw Button, I knew you must be here!" She had said that she thought dogs were not allowed, but he had told her that he could do anything.) Elena invited him to come to see us. "Well, I don't know why I shouldn't. I don't know why I shouldn't!"

The Hugheses and Monroe Engel came. Nock was jolly and, as usual, full of stories but had, I noticed, shaved off his small mustache and did look depressed when his face was not animated. He had something in his esophagus which prevented him from swallowing. I told him about the thing that had been taken off my vocal cord and how painless and easy it had been. The conversation was lively, we talked about a variety of things. I told about my article on dictionaries and grammars and read them Hardy's poem about Liddell and Scott, which Arthur did not know. I asked him what ἀάατος was, and he was able to tell me at once that it meant *cursed* and occurred once in Aeschylus.* He had been at the Sorbonne and said that at the

---

* *Aaatos* appears in Hardy's "Liddell and Scott: On the Completion of Their Lexicon," which is quoted by EW in "My Fifty Years with Dictionaries and Grammars," reprinted in *The Bit Between My Teeth*. Nock perhaps mistook this epic word meaning "not to be injured, inviolable" for *aratos* or *araios*, which mean cursed—the latter occurring in Aeschylus.

time he studied French grammar he had encountered certain rules that he didn't believe were ever observed in
practice (apropos of my story about Zoltán above). He and
Suzanne [Hughes] discussed this, and he recited a little
French verse which included all the tenses of the verb,
and he reminded me of the story of the Academician who,
on his deathbed, had said, *"Je m'en vais—ou, je m'en vas."**
We somehow got to discussing Colette. I said that I didn't
very much care for her, and Arthur said that he didn't
either. Suzanne said that she had taken in Colette, as it
were, with her mother's milk—along with Debussy and
Ravel, whom her mother also admired—and didn't really
know how to judge her. I told them that, having previously
been bored with Balzac, I found *Cousine Bette* amusing.
"That's a good one to begin with it, is it?" said Arthur.
He didn't know Balzac at all, but would take this to read
in Bermuda. I offered to lend him my copy, but he said
no, he wouldn't borrow it now.

He stayed after Monroe and the Hugheses left; said he
wanted to take me to a dinner of the Odd Volumes Club
—the only condition was that storytelling for its own sake
was not allowed. He and Elena talked about hating the
cold—it was the worst thing of anything. He said that one
of the worst places in the world for cold was the library
of St. Mark's in Venice in winter. He liked reading biographies of scholars. We had talked about Jowett when the
others were there. I told him the story, which much
pleased him, of Jowett's saying to Tennyson, after the latter
had read a poem after dinner, "Mr. Tennyson, if I were
you, I shouldn't publish that poem," and Tennyson's re-
plying, "If it comes to that, that port you've just given us
is the worst I've ever tasted!" I said that it was amusing
to read about Porson, but he answered, "It was sad—he

* Ironically, the last words of the dying Academician are incorrect
French.

drank." I did not know then that Nock himself had become of late years rather a heavy drinker, and sometimes when he came back to Eliot House had to be put to bed. I talked, apropos of Isaiah and his friends, of the cliquishness and malice of English university life. I began with some light apology, forgetting that Arthur was at Cambridge whereas the others were at Oxford; and he took me up eagerly, saying that Oxford was a hotbed of gossip and scandal. We agreed that we did not like Bowra. Arthur said that some people at Oxford were merely malicious on the surface, but that the malice of Bowra was deep and real. I told him the story, which he had not heard, about Cocteau's being taken to see Bowra at the time he got his honorary degree. Bowra recounted to Cocteau his going to Paris to receive, as I remember, a Légion d'Honneur decoration and ended, *"Et à la fin j'ai été baisé par le Président de la République."* The French professor who, with several French ladies, had accompanied Cocteau to see Bowra had added in telling this story to Sylvester Gates: *"Et devant toutes ces dames françaises!"** I had to explain to Nock what *baiser* as a verb had meant since the eighteenth century [to fuck]. He said that it might have been better if Cecil Rhodes had been to Cambridge: the Rhodes Scholars might have got on better at Cambridge than at Oxford. He asked me whether I didn't think that Isaiah was more agreeable since his marriage. I had never found him disagreeable, and said I didn't notice any difference in his attitude toward people he disliked. Isaiah, when I next saw him, before Arthur's death, talked about Arthur's snobbery—"grotesque"—and said

---

* Bowra, like the Prioress in the *Canterbury Tales*, spoke the French not of Paris but of Stratford atte Bowe. EW—whose own French was uneven—was delighted by the spectacle of a homosexual English don unwittingly boasting of being *baisé* "in front of all those French ladies." A few years later, however, he wrote to Celia Goodman, "Have been reading Maurice Bowra's memoirs and am surprised at what a good impression he makes."

that his attitude toward him (Isaiah) had changed for the better since he was knighted. It is true that I had noticed that Arthur did a certain amount of title-dropping—liked to talk about dining with a princess or to tell Elena that the Vogüés were one of the oldest noble families in Europe. Isaiah thought that Arthur came from humble origins, that when he came to Harvard he had worked up an act as a Cambridge don intended to impress the Americans, but that when any new Englishman appeared at Harvard, he always kept out of the way. Harry Levin afterwards told me that he pretended to be older than he was, and that once when at forty he had gone to a doctor, the latter said that Arthur was in very good condition for a man of fifty.

Nock said to me, as he had once before, that he had nearly become a convert to Roman Catholicism. I didn't know at that time about his book on *Conversion*, nor about his other books, nor even, I think, that at Harvard he taught a course in religious history. All I knew was that he and a French scholar had edited Hermes Trismegistos.*
I had been rather put off when I first used to meet him by his rather non-upper-class exterior—white socks, etc. —and what Harry called his "common-room jokes"; and it had only been gradually with the years that I had got to know him a little and like him. By this time he had got to a point where we had great fun together, and I looked forward to seeing more of him. He had been interested in my article about Swinburne, whom he seemed very much to admire, and I told him that I would give him a copy of the volume of Swinburne's novels, and got a copy to send him in the hospital. We talked about Browning apropos of the hateful aspects of the relations of academic life, which led him to a reference to the *Soliloquy in a Spanish Cloister*, and we agreed that he was now underrated. He recited

---

* Hermes Trismegistos is the putative author of mystical treatises from late antiquity. Nock's collaborator in the edition was A. J. Festugière.

some lines from "The Bishop Orders His Tomb," and asked
me if I had ever visited St. Praxed's, which, he said, was
disappointing after the poem. I mentioned "The Statue
and the Bust," the last stanzas of which I like so much,
and, apropos of *The Ring and the Book*, the last lines—
which have also been favorites with me—of the villain's
second monologue: ". . . Abbate, Christ, Maria, God! /
Pompilia, will you let them murder me?"

"I don't have any morbid idea," he said, "but I have
been cleaning out my papers, putting some codicils to my
will." There were a few kinds of things that he kept: letters
of recommendation—I asked why. "You may need them
again later." And letters that former students had written
him, telling him that he had helped them. He kept them
to reread when he was feeling depressed. As he left, he
said he followed the Russian style and showed me his
Russian fur cap—as well as his fur-lined coat, which he
said had lasted him, I think, thirty years. Elena drove him
home, and when she came back said she was afraid he was
dying. He had told her that though he had known us so
short a time, he felt that he knew us well.

When I called up the hospital later that week, he was
still under observation; when I called up again on Friday
(January 11, 1963), the nurse said, "Mr. Nock expired at
two." I learned later that his operation had lasted seven
hours and they had taken out one of his lungs. It saddened
me and made me feel frustrated. I had never before had
the experience of having had a lively, learned and amusing
conversation with someone I hoped to know better and
then have him go out of existence.

We went Tuesday afternoon to the service in Memorial
Chapel: simply the Episcopal service—he had told us he
was a staunch Episcopalian—without any eulogistic sermon. I believe that there was afterwards a meeting of the
Fellows at which they talked about him. John Finley and

Mark Howe were ushers and pallbearers and looked very gray. I felt that this unexpected sudden death—in the middle of a gray Cambridge winter—was sobering and saddening to everybody. His learning of the old-fashioned British classical sort and his common-room geniality, his celibacy and eccentricity, had made him a kind of pillar in a way that, while he was still alive, I don't think his colleagues had quite realized. When he was at our house, we had been joking about the stories told about him—"All of these untrue!" he exclaimed. When some naval officers had arrived at his rooms—the house during the last war having been taken over by the navy—they are supposed to have found him sitting on the floor in a state of partial undress studying a classical manuscript. One of the officers said, "Jesus Christ!" and Nock is supposed to have corrected him: "Arthur Darby Nock." He told us that this was really "a Copeland story"—they had moved the Copeland stories up to him. But it was, I believe, true that he had refused to get out for the navy—refused to budge from his rooms, like Bartleby the Scrivener in Melville. His quarters had been specially assigned to him when Eliot House was built. There was a terrible pathos in the ceremony in the chapel—in which not a word about his career was said. By this very simplicity one was made to feel his dignity and his devotion.

It intensified the impression, which so haunts me nowadays, of the flimsiness of human life: human relationships—our culture and history—a fabric of imaginary cobwebs hung about the habitable parts of the earth. The subjects we study with such care seem of transitory unreal interest; the analysis of our passions and affections a great expenditure on the parental and reproductive instincts. Is it worth it to impose the order—bound to be superficial and specious—of literature and scientific theory on the mess of our human exploits? Arthur Nock held in his mind all that history and literature and intelligence, and now it was no longer there. Yet his death did brace me up a little. Though I am seven years older than he was—he was only 60—and though I suffer from various ailments, I am not yet so badly off as he was and may yet accomplish something.

A MAN IN MOTION: 1963

Russian Writers and a Faulkner-Frost Story

When it was a question of our meeting *the latest delegation of Russian writers*—Kataev, Rozov and Lourie—I told the Harvard people who were handling it that I'd be glad to see them here at the house but would refuse to have interpreters or State Department agents. But then it turned out that Mme Lourie (Lur'e) was the inevitable escorting Communist Party member. We liked her, however. They came to lunch, and we had a very good time with them. When I asked Kataev whether he had known Alymov, he said that they had been close friends. He had been killed in a motor accident. Maria Fedorovna had married again —a critic; I understood him to say she was 80, which surprised me. Talking about the Alymovs put our relations on a friendly, even quite jolly basis, and took me back to my days in Moscow. He was one of that old generation who had been loyal to the Revolution and had then, as Elena said, undoubtedly suffered a good deal and, in spite of his dignity and forthrightness and his extremely *krupnyi* [strong] physique, showed signs of a severe ordeal, the weariness and almost-sadness of having been subjected to heavy pressures. He was a brother of Petrov of the Golden

Calf,* had been a Party member, an editor of *Krokodil*, but then, more creatively and interestingly, the editor of *Iunost'* [*Youth*], in which he prided himself on having brought out the first works of important writers.

After lunch, I gave him my line about the U.S. and U.S.S.R. being not really capitalist and Communist societies, but being run by bureaucrats and the armed services, and how this had been received by the Russian visitors before. They took it without protest, and he said, "Perhaps." I even went so far as to say that he and I belonged to a period when it had been possible for us to believe that the evils of modern society could be reformed by socialism, but that now we were confronted by a bureaucratic world quite different from what we had imagined. He and she took this perfectly calmly. We liked her—she was far the best of the official woman watchdogs we had met—Jewish, about 40, married, English very good though she had learned it entirely in Russia, and she was a specialist in American literature—told me with pride that they were now translating Faulkner. It had been arranged by their management for them to go to see Robert Frost in the hospital, and I told them emphatically that I considered him *samyi skuchnyi pisatel' v Amerike* [the most boring writer in America]. This made him laugh, and he said, "This is a real conversation. You sound just like Alymov!" At lunch when I was telling of my evenings with Alymov, I had said to her, "You're too young to remember that." She answered that that was a period she unfortunately hadn't known—there had been a good many people from outside then, hadn't there? One saw that the atmosphere was now much relaxed. When the students were

* Under the pseudonym Yevgeni Petrov, Yevgeny Petrovich Kataev wrote the Soviet satire *The Little Golden Calf* (1931) with his collaborator Ilf Ilya.

questioning Kataev at Lowell House and someone asked him what the attitude of the Soviet Union was about something or other, he replied: "Let's have this understood: I am I, and the Soviet Union is the Soviet Union," and he spoke with strong approval of *Ivan Denisovich*, which he said dealt with the "earthshaking" (interpreter's version of the concentration camps). It was a miracle, he said, that they should be having at the same time two such great poets as Voznesensky and Yevtushenko. Voznesensky was a lyric poet, but Yevtushenko was a *grazhdanskii poet* [civic poet]—adding, however, presently that he was none the worse for that.

They were taken to see Robert Frost. He hardly knew who they were—it was only a few days before his death; and they were unnecessarily accompanied by a State Department agent and Elena Levin, who tells me that Tovarishch Lur'e [Comrade Lourie], who is proud of the competence of her English, became rather irritated at all this supervision and intervention. Another Soviet poet, a Nekrasov, has announced publicly that he liked America but found the State Department supervision a nuisance. He had found that his guardians were much upset if he wanted to go to some other museum than the one that they had planned to take him to. He was officially rebuked by them.

Lately I have found it a *nocturnal refuge to read books of the early and middle nineteenth century:* Skeats's edition of Chatterton, Dickens's *Life of Grimaldi*, Collins and Cruikshank's Punch and Judy, Dyce's edition of Beaumont and Fletcher. They take me back to the days when I bought at the old bookshops on 42nd St. the Ettrick Shepherd's Tales, the Roxburghe Ballads and the Mermaid volume of Marlowe, and they are also associated in my mind with

Charles Lamb, Percy's *Reliques* and *The Ingoldsby Legends*.
I like the atmosphere of English antiquities, the Gothic
churches and the slang of old London, the clotted and
cobwebbed prose, the elaborate introductions that are so
close to the original sources, the local gossip and informal
memoirs, and the footnotes that do not care how much
they may impede the main narrative and that may fill up
the bottoms of several pages. When not many years ago I
started to read *The Heart of Midlothian*, I found that I was
impatient with the interminable preface, a perfect example
of this atmosphere and method; but I find a certain solace
in the murkiness and tangledness of texts that leave so
much of the past mysterious. They give me shelter from
the income tax problem, with which I must very soon deal.

Feb 22, '63. My heart is now much better, due to my
having given it a rest. The last time I made love to Elena,
it pinched me so hard that I couldn't finish. That was
weeks ago. It is frustrating and depressing to feel that you
can't make love if you want to—it reminded me of the days
when I had gonorrhea. Yesterday I made love again without
any bad effects at all—afterwards, went out and walked
to the Square in the very cold day. When she came and
lay on my bed, Elena said, "I've forgotten what it's about."
It gave me the delightful intoxication that lasts for a little
while afterwards—so different from the bad reaction after
going to bed with a woman you don't really like. My reaction with Elena has nothing of *omne animale post coitum
triste est*, still less of Shakespeare's "Expense of spirit in a
waste of shame."

Mrs. Benedek (I wonder whether her name may not originally have been Baruch) is charming but opinionated and
obstinate, and sometimes a little difficult in the course of

our Hungarian lessons. I write letters in Hungarian, which she corrects, and she sometimes tries to dictate the content as well as correct the errors. I had the hardest time explaining to her that what I wanted to ask Sándor Radó was whether he had said the autumn before last that a translation of a paper by William James was the first scientific paper or simply the first paper on psychology that had ever been written in Hungarian. (And then there was the difficulty of explaining that by "paper" I did not mean scientific journal.) When she found out that I could have thought for a moment that the first scientific paper in Hungarian had been written in the early nineteen hundreds, she protested and did not want me to write this. At the end, I had written *"Remélem hogy egészséges és boldog* [I hope you are healthy and happy]," and she crossed out *"és boldog,"* saying, "Who is happy?" She asked me to lend her *Úri Divat,* of which I had spoken highly, and when I came the next time I asked her whether she had liked it, and she answered firmly, *"Nem—nem* [No—no]." I said that Juhász úr [Mr.] was a very funny character. "No: he is not funny." People so good as that, that were so soft that they always gave in and let everybody impose on them "ought to be exterminated." Such people were destructive.

She has her brother here and her circle of Hungarian friends, and she says she almost never talks English, though she likes to read English books. She says that nowadays she can't read Hungarian books: they write with too many adjectives.

On one occasion, she was telling me that she hadn't, when she first came here, understood about what I thought was "the baroque" in this country—the baroque in Dawn Powell and Hemingway. I couldn't imagine where she found all this *baroque.* It turned out to be the *bars* that she hadn't understood—*bárok* being the Hungarian plural for *bár*.

March 12. Morton Zabel came to dinner: has been away for six months in Europe, is now full of Ibsen, whose complete works he has read in the original, having studied Old Norse long ago in the line of his scholarly work, and he visited the Scandinavian countries. His travelogue of gossip conversations seems to have become more compulsive than ever. He seizes your arm and starts up some story just as you are going in to dinner or at some other inappropriate time. Coming home from dinner at the Sweeneys', he told us of his experiences in England—it is always a mélange of theaters, concerts and places with literary associations and people whom he has seen. One of his climaxes, which, as Elena said, sounded like the end of a chapter in a picaresque novel—"And then I moved in on the viscountess—I'll come to that later."

We covered all our old common friends: New York and Chicago. He remembers about everybody's activities and connections, all the names and dates. He admits to keeping a diary, which I hope is more interesting than his letters. —He had one very good story about a literary congress he attended in Brazil, just outside Rio de Janeiro. Robert Frost and Faulkner had been invited, and Faulkner, who got there first, drank something that Morton described as "300% Pisco," then—since nobody had warned the welcomers—was regaled with further drinks. As was usual with him on such occasions, he became completely unconscious and was carried to his hotel, where he remained all through the conference. All he had done, apparently, was to read his speech on the occasion of receiving the Nobel Prize. In the meantime, Frost, still in Rio, had learned for the first time that Faulkner was there; his egoism could not face this, and he wired that he could not leave Rio. Thus Morton was the only person there to represent American letters.* He says that Carl Sandburg is now just as bad.

A Political Argument in New York

March 15, Friday. Léonie Adams: Morton had told me that she was still at the Chelsea, so I called her up and asked her to dinner. She had lost her looks so that it shocked me. I felt that she had become brutalized by living with that lowgrade Irishman! But later she told me that she had just had "a virus," so she was probably not looking her best. She seemed to me, when we were first talking, to be just like a middle-aged English teacher—which is what she is at Columbia. She has lost her shyness or conceals it by putting up a barrage of anecdote. She takes very seriously her literary position, founded on her poetry, and has been writing again lately: had been translating Valéry's *Narcisse.* And she is full of the gossip and politics of the contemporary poets' world. It surprised me that anyone so distinguished should be so preoccupied by it. The Library of Congress poets' conference partly financed by the Bol-

* The conference took place in August 1954. Faulkner had stopped off for a day in Lima, where he drank a great deal before a late dinner and was presented with two bottles of the finest Pisco brandy, a Peruvian specialty, as he got on the plane for Brazil the next morning. In São Paulo, Zabel, who had gone to meet him with the embassy people, saw him given "two beautiful decanters" of Brazilian brandy. After dining on vodka, he had an alcoholic collapse of several days. He pulled himself together and at a press conference read the Nobel Prize speech, a copy of which was found for him at the British Embassy. A day later, he was able to resume a demanding schedule (Blotner, *Faulkner*). Meanwhile, Frost attended functions in São Paulo as well as Rio while trying to stay out of the novelist's way. He decided to return to the United States via Lima, where he remained for several days as guest of the American ambassador (Thompson and Winnick, *Frost: The Later Years*).

lingen Foundation had given them a good deal to talk about. I heard from her and Morton and Louise [Bogan] all the ins and outs of this, and she told me that the younger poets had something like a concerted project of "killing off" the older ones. Randall Jarrell, in a speech at Washington, had dealt slightingly, she thought, with Allen Tate, and she had heard that Robert Lowell had also "ditched" Allen, but she couldn't believe that was possible.

We went uptown to see Louise. "I have no whisky," she said on the telephone, so I brought her a fifth of Johnnie Walker, most of which we got through. Impassioned debate about Frost, I taking the negative side. We talked about all our old friends, and it was almost like being back in the late twenties.* I had forgotten how amusing Léonie could be and how much fun I used to have with her; but I felt that I had made no mistake in detaching myself from her: I had found that underneath her shyness there was a strongly demanding ego, all the more difficult for being suppressed.

March 16, Saturday. I had invited *Léonie* to have dinner with me again and to go to The Little Players the next evening; but she called me up to say that with the drinking the night before and the lingering virus she did not feel up to going. Perhaps seeing both Louise and me again had been something of a strain on her. She and Louise had talked at one another so animatedly, as if renewing their old relation, that there were passages of conversation when I might almost as well have gone to sleep.

I took *Evgenia Lehovich* instead. We had dinner at the Café des Artistes. She said that the American ballet hadn't

* EW had promoted the work of both Léonie Adams and Louise Bogan. Adams and he had a brief but complicated affair. Bogan—a confidante of each—was his friend and companion through the next decade.

been able to bear it in Russia. Balanchine at one point had
come back and then had gone over again. He said that the
culture of Russia had been put back to before Peter the
Great, had now as little contact with the West.

Frank Peschka and Bill Murdock entertained us in their
apartment afterwards. I asked Frank to tell me again what
he had said about the superiority of glove puppets to marionettes. It was due, he said, to the fact that everything
was part of your body—figures and voices both—whereas
the operators of marionettes were at a far remove from
their figures, there had to be several people and the voices
were done by others still.

March 17, Sunday. Dinner at East Side Sardi's with
Sheilah Graham and her children, Robert and Wendy: Robert
is 17 and at Putney, Wendy is a junior at Bryn Mawr,
both goodlooking, especially the boy, tall and dark. I have
read his little book about Russia: an Anglo-American teenager with Russian teenagers—quite cute and interesting.
He had learned some Russian but has written down phrases
as he heard them and got them all wrong. Sheilah is now
almost perfect, an occasional relapse into cockney inton-
ation, and she talks about her ex-husbands a little too much
in the presence of her children. She said she found marriage "stifling." She has been pursued for years by the
same man who has been pursuing Scottie. I said he must
be insane; "No, just obsessed by the idea of Scott." The
father of these children is an Englishman.

March 18, Monday. Dinner with *Sándor Radó*. I wanted
him to talk about Hungary and to tell me much Hungarian
science had actually been written in Hungarian. He had
been ill and looked rather old. His face is very kindly,
almost something of Gauss. I have always found him interesting to talk to. I said that I found it depressing that

so many young people should go to analysts and that they
sometimes kept going for years, and told him about a family
with both parents and both children in the hands of analysts. He didn't answer directly, but said that the desirability of the patient's being dependent on the analyst—
complete and continued dependence—was an error which
he had been trying to discourage. The analyst should try
to make the patient find something in himself to depend
on, to get him out of this infantile dependence on the
analyst. (Not, however, that his relationship was something created by the analyst: if a patient of this type
didn't have the analyst to depend on, he would be dependent on someone else.) Once this relationship was
established, a good many of the, he implied, less
bright analysts didn't really understand what was wrong
and would let it go on indefinitely. He said that the
attachment to the "father figure" was natural to the
old Austro-Hungarian Empire or it derived from the attachment to Franz Josef, and that Freud's ideas were partly
a product of this. The Hungarians had had this filial relationship, too. (I had happened that afternoon to have
read Sam Behrman's profile of Molnár, which confirms
this: he admired Franz Josef, so he approved of monarchy.)
He said that all the doctrine of Freud had now hardened
into dogma.

I talked to him about the overpowering bureaucracy that
we have now in the United States. "It doesn't affect
you, I suppose," I ended.—"But I see its effects on my
patients." The U.S. was an entirely different country
from what it had been when he first came here about
thirty years ago. He said that he had spent nine years
"in the Germany of Kaiser Wilhelm." That had been
a bureaucracy but an efficient reliable one; our American one was not efficient. We speculated about what
would happen after another war. I said that there would

be no Marxism to take over and impose a system. He agreed. What then? Military leaders in different parts of the world.

March 19, Tuesday. Elena arrived, and I took her to dinner at the *new Princeton Club*—a horror, just like a hotel and full of tacky-looking people. One of the boys had brought a rather disreputable-looking blonde. Accommodations for couples, women all over the place, the ladies' dining room is now the main dining room. Only the bar is apparently forbidden, and at the entrance there is a marble tablet inlaid in the floor, with a vulgar inscription about getting away from women. The library has a librarian and an exhibit of books and manuscripts by Princeton authors, but the shelves are almost entirely empty, odds and ends from the old library, eked out with a half-shelf of paperbacks. In the lounge on the floor below, *Barron's Weekly* and the more commonplace periodicals. I didn't see anywhere any of the comfortable old leather club chairs in which it was easy to fall asleep. Rooms for businessmen's meetings. The whole place badly decorated and rather bleak—as Elena said, it looks like a ship. We had dinner in the huge shiplike dining room, and were waited on by a little Frenchwoman who was desperately rushing and carrying great laden trays. She said that she came from Brittany. I said that that was why she had red hair. "*C'est pas naturel,*" she replied. I said that she was working hard: "*Il faut travailler pour vivre.*" She thought we must be English. On the stairs between the first and second floors is a ridiculous mural of some college building, and crouching on the grass in the foreground a large tadpole-like tiger, with a huge head and petering-out body. The old bad portraits of the presidents, whose badness in the old place was not so visible, hung higher in the dark rooms. I doubt whether I'll go there again. I am going to try to join the

Century Club, for which several people have offered to put
me up.

March 20, Wednesday. I made love to Elena in the afternoon. It was delightful. I did not feel any pressure on my
heart and did not even have to slow up.

In the evening dinner at the *Strauses'*: Dwight Macdonald, a handsome girl from California [Susan Sontag] who
is one of Roger's new writers. Vincent Sheean, people
named Messer (director of the Guggenheim Museum) and
Adolph Berle and his wife. I hadn't seen Berle since the
night [in 1933] that S. K. Ratcliffe introduced me to him
at the Metropolitan when Bernard Shaw spoke, and I didn't
know who he was, and I don't believe he knew who I was.
His wife did, however. I talked to her before dinner and
thought she was a very boring woman. She had been under
the impression that Michelet had been superseded by Gui-
zot, but had picked up a volume and found it very lively.
After dinner, Berle came to talk to me. He had heard I
was writing about Canada and had very strong opinions on
the subject. What did they want? Did they want us to
defend their border and not do anything about it themselves? Why were they so anti-American? I spoke of the
French nationalist movement, and he said, "Why shouldn't
they" be more independent? But he always referred to the
French Canadians as "the Canucks" or "the Canuck." He
had spoken on the CBC. I asked him who he was and what
he did, and this must have riled him extremely. He has
recently been let out from the State Department. He told
me that he had been assistant secretary of state and now
was teaching at Columbia. This still meant nothing to me.
Talking about Canada led quickly to my strictures on the
United States, and he began peremptorily questioning me:
Why? What? etc. The Russians were after Alaska. How
would I feel if they took over Canada? He agreed that the

Soviet Union had abandoned international revolution but
the old tsarist imperialism was back. When I spoke of our
expansionism, "Name one country we have ever con-
quered! Name one, just one—don't be vague, just name
one!" He went on in this way so long that I felt he was
behaving as the Communists used to—that he was simply
attempting to intimidate me and did not really want me to
answer. When I got a chance to speak, I reviewed our
succession of aggressions, as in the introduction to *Patriotic
Gore*. He never denied my facts or made much show of
countering my statements, but would say, "Continental
expansion!" or "The income tax!" in a sharp and contemptuous tone, as if these were not serious matters. He
became more and more indignant and finally became insulting. I said, "Let's not get insulting," but he continued
to repeat again and again, after I told him that I thought
of going to live in Switzerland, "You're running away but
I'm staying here to serve my country." I said that I had
already served my country. I told him that I was 67 and
felt that I had had it in the United States. He said, "I'm
69!" and I said, "Well, you're one up on me there." But
this proved to be a lie. He had been born, his wife told
me afterwards, in the same year as I, '95. I reminded him
that, after all, Voltaire and Gibbon had gone to live in
Switzerland. He retorted that Gibbon had written about
the past and he suspected that Voltaire was a phoney.
Reverberations were heard and it was felt that we ought
to be broken apart, but when we got up from the couch,
we continued the argument standing in the middle of the
room. When at last I began talking to somebody else, he
sat down on the couch beside Elena and went on with the
angry railing. He was "most disagreeable," she said. Said
that I was running away, that Switzerland was quiet and
boring, that I should be "sitting in the eye"—did Elena
know what that meant? "Yes, the eye of the hurricane"—

that I'd be safe while they were burning. Echoing Thomas
Mann, she told him that there'd be America anywhere
where I was. But why didn't I do something for my country?
She said I'd already done it. Elena thought he was "very
pessimistic." She learned that he was half-German and
said that he was exactly like "a little Prussian functionary."
I felt that he was frustrated and frightened, perhaps full
of guilt. He may have been so indignant about the kind of
things I was saying because he is appalled by them himself
and is so much still an official that he has to put up a
front. I would say to him, "You seem to take these matters
even more seriously than I do"—which I now see must
have annoyed him as one who for years had been working
on relations with Latin America and official organizations
supposed to be dedicated to peace. I remarked when I said
goodbye to him that he had misrepresented his age. I afterwards remembered his having made a humorless remark, after the Bernard Shaw lecture, reducing it to an
abstractly stated position.

Roger and Brendan Gill told me later that he did that
kind of thing quite frequently. He and Mrs. Berle both
had attacked Brendan Gill, when they had met him for
the first time, in a way that made him feel they really
wanted to get him down. Mrs. Berle had called up Dorothea Straus and asked to see the list of guests—that was
when she had looked into my books. Roger says that if
Nelson Rockefeller had been President, Berle would undoubtedly have been Secretary of State. He was one of the
backers of the Cuban invasion.

I told Roger later on that I thought Dorothea would have
been justified, when Mrs. Berle asked for the guest list,
in saying, "I'm sorry, you can't come." But Dorothea, he
said, had been in a weak position: she had accepted a Berle
invitation, forgetting that she had already made an engagement, and had had to get out of it.

March 21, Thursday. Dinner with the Epsteins. I persuaded them to go see *Too True to Be Good,* a play that I very much like on account of the first act and the final speech, all about Shaw himself. I kept telling the Epsteins that we ought to get there on time on account of the death of the bacillus; then discovered, when we got there, that the microbe and the doctor had been cut out, as well as a good deal of the rest, including the Dean Inge character. The whole thing was rattled off at top speed, and unless you had seen it or read it, you couldn't know what it was about. People laughed at the epigrams and jokes in a perfectly mechanical way. There is now an automatic Shaw audience as there is a Gilbert and Sullivan audience. Albert Marre directed it, who directed my *Little Blue Light.* He has fallen low indeed to put on such a nonsensical mutilation, depending, I suppose, on the presence in the cast of Cedric Hardwicke and Gillian Gill, both too old and infirm to do much more than appear in person, and on the interest in *Lawrence of Arabia* recently excited by the film.

Elena talked a little to the Epsteins about her theory that the *Jews are bitterly jealous of the attention that Baldwin and others are directing toward the Negroes.* I did not take this seriously at first, but I now think there's something in it: Podhoretz's article in *Commentary* about his having been persecuted in his childhood by the Negroes, Lillian Hellman's play with its white boy who champions the Negroes, then is robbed by the Negro to whom he has been making an impassioned speech. Elena's conversation at Thalia Howe's with the young Jewish Greek teacher from Brandeis—when Elena asked this young man if he had heard Baldwin's lecture at Brandeis, he had answered certainly not: he had been to school with Baldwin. The Negroes were inferior, they had never produced anything. Why associate with them or bother about them? They were now making capital out of their sufferings, but the Jews had suffered much more. One does get the impression that the Jews regard themselves as having a monopoly on suffering, and do not want the Negroes to muscle in.

A Lunch with the Murphys; Sandy at the State Hospital

March 22, Friday. We went out to Sneden's Landing for *lunch with the Murphys*, with Dawn Powell. Gerald drove us out. Very queer and rather sad. Gerald is now 76, and Sara 78. They both seem to be deaf, and Sara does not always make sense, does not understand what people are saying. They still make a determined effort to keep up their famous tradition of "gracious living." What did we want to drink? He mentioned an invention of his own which someone had named the "Old Lady"—orange juice, lemon juice, gin and "I'm afraid, just a dash of 7-Up." These turned out to be delicious, and we drank them with some sort of pâté in crisp little biscuit shells. Gerald fussed around in an apron between the guests and the kitchen. On the drive out, Gerald had told us a fairly long story about a young man from one of the first families of Sneden's Landing, who had intended to go to Harvard but had never done well at school and had eventually become a professional chef, much to the embarrassment of his father. He appeared in his white apron-dress and his high white French chef's hat, and produced a most marvelous lunch, which lasted a long time and about which you had to do a great deal of talking. There were menus in French, which began with *rouget américain* (red snapper) with *sauce mousseline*, then strips of lamb served rather rare, with *pommes paillasse* and *purée de petits pois*, Liederkranz cheese (which appeared on the menu, however, as Brie), and a

brioche over which was poured a kirsch-flavored strawberry sauce, which had had, on Sara's account, to be
strained of all its seeds, and on that a curlicue of cream,
which gave, as was merrily noted, the effect of a Pollock
painting. White and red wine, Montrachet and Beaujolais.
Gerald said that he did not really care for the great French
wines, and quoted Thurber's joke about "This little wine
may amuse you, and I hope you'll pardon its presumption."
I had just lost again the gold bridge from my lower jaw
and had almost no teeth there to chew with, so I could
not eat the lamb at all, thus adding another macabre note
to the almost ghostly revival of the gaiety and good living
of the twenties. Another note had unintentionally been
added by Gerald. He had told us a story of some party in
New York, at which late-arriving guests had been surprised, on arriving at the living room after leaving their
coats and hats, to find everybody sitting in silence. Esther
[Murphy] was standing in the middle of the room going
through all the motions of holding forth, but with no au-
dible sound. She had completely lost her voice, yet com-
manded the attention of her audience. But Gerald told it
in such a way that it seemed to be something that had
taken place after Esther's death, and Dawn and I were
somewhat chilled at imagining it was Esther's ghost.

After lunch, the young chef joined us with his wife, and
he drove us back to New York. He is an odd and special
case. I found him very amusing, and as everyone said about
him, it's much better for him to earn a living at something
in which he can excel than to become a professional beatnik
or a vocationless son of a good family. He is very American
and funny in English but has also a French alter ego, which
possesses him, and then he talks voluble French. He described his adventures with French chefs, their seriousness about their work—but they sometimes go off on a
tangent, begin, for example, serving everything *en croûte*.

His great hero is a chef called Pierre, who seems to have taken him on a tour of the provincial restaurants. I asked him about escargots, and he evidently found this subject repellent. He didn't want to describe the process of preparing them, but I insisted on his doing so. "It's grim," he said. They put them in a big glass jar, and they come crawling up the sides. Then they put a lot of salt on them, "and that makes the snails quite sick, and they void their excrement." Then they stick out their heads, and they hook them out of their shells, and put them in hot water. Then they wash them and wash them, and clip off "the little piece of nonsense" (I suppose the protruding eyes) —though one chef he knew insisted that this ought not be done. You boil them and boil them till the muscle is softened, and the shells are washed out with potassium, and then the potassium washed out. They make a sauce of garlic and other things. I had only eaten one once—at the Lafayette, I think—and had had no impression at all of it. I asked how they were supposed to taste, and he could not report on this. They belonged to the class of *amuse-gueule* [cocktail snack]. They served them with all that equipment, which was not at all necessary. It was easier to take them in your fingers. He always wanted to pinch the waitress's behind with those tongs. I wondered how they had come to eat them. Sara said it was probably simple poverty. They picked them off the vines. I asked why we did not eat dandelion greens. He said that he was going to introduce some. He thought that *pissenlit* [dandelion] salad only had come in, in the First World War, as a result of the food shortage; but when I used to get it in Vittel, it seemed already well established. I had never got much out of truffles. They were decorative, he said, because they were black. But what was their flavor? Like mushrooms—the white Italian truffle had a very strong flavor. The French ate everything—tripe, intestines: *an-*

douillettes were apparently intestines stuffed with chopped intestines. They had shops where the non-meat parts of animals were sold. Chicken croquettes and other things were made out of leftovers—but also some things that were excellent. I had remarked at lunch that the only thing the menu lacked was the article before every dish. Elena told me that it was only in restaurants that the dishes were thus announced; they did not do it in private houses. The young man now said that yes, putting the definite article before everything made you feel that there was only one and that you had had it. The French were crazy—he loved them.

We had had coffee in the living room, with an exquisite choice of liqueurs. Gerald suggested a cognac and Cointreau, which was delicious—when he got me a second one, he said, "I'll make this one a little sharper." Gerald and I talked about Dos. We agreed that he was just as unreliable in his extreme rightist phase as he had been in his extreme leftist. He lacks judgment, as Gerald says. He says Dos has to shirk certain subjects. He is rabid about the Roosevelts, won't hear a good word spoken for any of the people he has decided to hate. Dawn thinks that all his life nowadays is based on his solicitude for his wife and Lucy, as well as his stepson and the Spence's Point place. He has to make money for them all.

Gerald's stories are in some ways like Esther's, except that they do not go on forever. He tells you that he is going to tell two stories, tells them, then says, "End of story." He is also evidently accurate. Antiquities of Sneden's Landing. It was rescued by some Hudson River lady from the great tract of the west bank owned and exploited by the Rockefellers. She kept it just as it was: no modern suburban houses, it was still not even a village—nice old white frame houses, sometimes with black iron grillework. Stories about her, Dobbs Ferry, etc. The Murphys' house is rather like Talcottville, but built about 1700, at one time the capital of New York, the mayor of New York had lived there. Dawn told a story about a lunch with Esther, at which Esther talked all through lunch, and then finally, "But you were going to say something." "I was going to say, 'Hello, Esther.'"

I thought of Scott's story about telling Hemingway that his book [*Tender Is the Night*] was based on the Murphys. Hemingway had said, "I don't see how you could write a novel about them. I don't see how they could be anything more than subjects for a ballet."

March 23, Saturday. Dinner at the Lowells': Léonie [Adams], Morton [Zabel], the Tates. An orgy of poetic professionalism and politics, Léonie holding forth indomitably. She had told me that Stanley Kunitz had been entirely invented by Allen, who had gone around everywhere on his lectures and public readings telling people what a wonderful poet he was, and when I said, at the Lowells', that I didn't care much for his poetry, Léonie put her finger to her lips to hush me. Elena said it sounded like people talking about the stock market. I had seen the Tates, Cal and Kunitz at the Algonquin in the afternoon. I had talked about the Princeton Club and Kunitz had said that at the time when they were bulldozing the foundations of the old building, they had thrown out a lot of statues with the general debris. It was a collection of what must be Sumerian statues which someone had given to the club and which had been put away in the basement. Now they had been simply thrown out, and people were picking them up. Where were they now? I asked. The people had just carried them home. They were beautiful! How did he know? He knew some people who had carried off several.

It was the first night of Lillian Hellman's play [*My Mother, My Father and Me*], and she had invited us to a little party afterwards at a nightclub in a place called Blair House. The place itself was a horror: deafening, dark, cramped, people doing the twist in a very narrow space. I was stunned, and we didn't stay long; but Elena was enjoying herself. She insisted that in some way it was possible to talk with a din like that going on.

March 24, Sunday. We met Helen at the airport in the early afternoon, and then went out to the Thorntons'. Atmosphere somewhat strained, Daphne very much pregnant and full of apprehensions: that, on account of nuclear testing, the child might be a monster, etc. I brought up unpleasant subjects which Elena and Henry warned me off. It was evidently hard on Henry, but the baby is due in May. The little girls loved the puppets we had given them, but they made their mother nervous. A certain *gêne* [uneasiness] in the afternoon. We went for dinner to the Piping Rock Club, which was not big and smart as I had expected, but small and quiet with Audubon prints—the building old-fashioned American, with those white hand-carved fireplaces. Daphne is really quite miserable with her pregnancy, and sinus trouble, for which her gynecologist had done nothing and which she was only just getting attended to.

March 25, Monday. Henry came to dinner with us at the Algonquin and seemed much more cheerful away from home. Afterwards we went to *Lord Pengo*, for which Sam Behrman had given us tickets. The reports about it had been so dim that we were surprised to find how good it was: very funny, Charles Boyer excellent, but the part about the son who wants to be a modern painter perfunctory and unconvincing.

My unaccustomed gaiety and running around here have been putting a strain on my heart, and last night, after coming back from the theater and eating two fat peach halves in the Algonquin dining room, on top of the double Scotches I had been having before and during dinner, I had, when I went to bed, the worst attack since last November. I had done a good deal in the morning and early afternoon, getting my bridgework put back by the dentist, leaving Father's watch with the broken hand to be repaired at Cartier's, checking my balance at the bank, then having lunch with Cartier-Bresson and a quite attractive young woman who seems to be a current New York girlfriend— after which he came to the *New Yorker* office in order to photograph me. His photographing makes me nervous. He always has his little camera ready, and though I like him and like to talk to him, it does rather put me out to find the conversation disturbed by his suddenly becoming intent on my face and snapping his little camera. He even had it in evidence as we were going up in the elevator. (He says he does not like portrait photography.) As the result of the breaking down of my cardiac equilibrium, I am handling myself today as if I were a porcelain teacup that had already been cracked and mended. I had also been much annoyed by having the bridgework from my lower jaw which I had had put in that morning with what the dentist called the strongest cement come out in the late afternoon when I was merrily munching peanuts with my drinks in the Algonquin lobby. I now have almost nothing to chew with in my lower jaw. It took me a long time even to get through those peaches.

March 26, Tuesday. I went for a drink to Esther [Kimball's] to ask about Sandy and sound her out about publishing the first installment of my journals. I suppose that it was the first real conversation that I've ever had with her in my life. We exchanged a few family skeletons, talked about our trip abroad in 1908: we remembered entirely

Edmund Wilson at *The New Yorker*

different things, she remembered a dachshund but had forgotten our addiction to Karlsbader Ablaten. Her first husband, Bobby Hartshorne, had been a manic depressive, he had been usually in the euphoric phase, but his spells of depression had been awful. He and her mother had died of cancer, and she didn't really think it was such a bad way to die. You had to die sometime, and it was really not so painful. Elena arrived eventually but had trouble, as I had had, on account of not remembering her last name: Megargee. Embarrassing, but Esther took it lightly. One of her friends had said that she had married a swell guy, but then he had died and left her stuck with the name. She told me that Sandy was still back in 1919, had said that Woodrow Wilson was a fine man.

March 27, Wednesday. Elena drove me out to see *Sandy in the Middletown State Hospital.* Middletown itself is a horror of flatness and ugliness. Esther had told me that Sandy had changed so much that one would hardly recognize him but described him encouragingly as "a cheerful old gentleman." He was far from cheerful when I saw him. He had indeed changed enormously. He was terribly bowed over, and his rather wide mouth was drawn down—it struck me for the first time that he had a Baker mouth— and his brows were set in a permanent frown: a permanent morose despair. He is now an old man, and his nose has become thickly salient, as I had never seen it before, like that of his grandmother Knox. We shook hands, when he appeared from the corridor, but he did not smile or show any personal response until just before I went. When talking about the other inmates—it was hard to know exactly what he was saying—he had a gleam, though a very brief one, of his old charm and humor. It was different from the time when I had seen him last. Then he had shown some personal recognition, but his answers to my questions

now were those of a gruff old man, half-muttered and as
if brought up from someone already buried. He would
sometimes mutter to himself. He almost never spoke unless
I asked him something, and then as if with reluctance. I
said that I had seen Esther the day before. How is she?
No comment on what I said. Could I send him anything?
No. Did he read much? Yes. What? Mostly magazines.
Did he read the papers? Isn't any papers. Thursday or
Friday. (This was during the long printers' strike.) His
language—Isn't any papers—seemed a little to have deteriorated under the influence of association with more or
less illiterate inmates, and yet he had kept something of
manners that made him seem like a grumpy old clubman.
Did he read *The New Yorker*? No. Would he like me to
send it to him? Can probably get it over there. I asked him
whether, as I had seen on some notice, the men and women
got together for dances. He said, "Yes: they would do that."

We went for a little walk around the building. I talked
about Talcottville and got no response. I told him about
how the wildcats and bears had been moving in up there,
and said, I don't remember hearing much about the animals
in our young days, do you? Only animals I remember were
fish. Did I have a picture of the house? No, I didn't, but
would send him one. Did he go into town for the movies?
No: he watched TV. We returned to the reception room.
Did he often go into town? No: hadn't been there since
last November, when he had bought the clothes he was
wearing. Did he know what a cult had been going on about
Scott Fitzgerald lately? Scott Fitzgerald was a nice fellow.
(They had both been members of Cottage.) How were the
Todds and Kaisers related? —I spoke of our trip to Washington. Mrs. Kaiser was my grandmother's sister. I told
him that René Champollion's wife was selling the Newport
place and the books, and said I should like to go up there
and perhaps buy some of them. André had had an excellent

library. "Yes," he murmured. "History, biography . . ."
Did he have a room to himself? No: a dormitory—with
people that he didn't seem to like. When I had dropped
into a rather long pause, he said suddenly, "Now I must
go—have to take a bath." He shook hands with me, murmured, "Thank you for coming out," and got up and walked
away down the corridor. I said goodbye to his stooped back,
but he did not make any answer.

Entertaining the Spenders—
Short Men and Tall

I wanted to see the *Old Bull House* near Goshen, which
proved to be quite easy to find. It is a chunky little old
stone house, finished in 1722, set in mildly rolling country.
The original William Bull, I now discover, was an apparently somewhat incompetent stonemason—an Englishman
from Wolverhampton, who had gone to Ireland and built
a bridge which collapsed. I suppose he had to flee the
country. There are only a few small square windows very
far above the ground level—I suppose to avoid the Indians.
Glass was expensive then on account of a British tax on
it. Another window or two have been let in lower down.
We found Louis Brown and his wife, the caretakers for
the Bull Association, who also live in the house. She is a
Bull, and the Bulls have lived in it ever since William and
Sarah. We both noticed that Mrs. Brown looked like Carolyn Link and that one of her sons did—she showed us
his photograph. Elena said that their faces looked as if they
were carved out of wood—like Swiss peasants. They do
not farm—he has some kind of railroad job. They were
just finishing lunch in the downstairs dining room, offered
us whisky and tea. Parts of the house have only just been
excavated: big old-fashioned fireplace, big beams and wide

floor planks. They took us down to the cellar, where the
Bulls had originally had eight slaves, who slept on the floor
in a dark room. It is built on the side of a slope, and there
are doors that open out on two levels. One curious feature
of the house, in the cellar and even above, was ledges of
rock cropping out. The house is hardly a real museum: a
few bad portraits, a few old pieces of furniture, including
a Bull cradle, a certain amount of china in cupboards. The
whole place was oddly sprinkled with weak abstract paintings by one of the sons. In one of the bedrooms, a branch
was attached to the bureau mirror. Little dried bats were
dangling from the twigs on threads, and a dead bee was
fastened to one by a pin. She said that he—I suppose, the
son—liked to make that kind of mobile. Elena has learned
to pretend to be impressed by these early-American relics,
and expressed enthusiasm for the stripped broad beams of
the floor, but I think actually found it rather sordid. She
had expected something bigger and grander. It does seem
rather extraordinary that the place should have become
the object of such a cult on the part of the Bulls and yet
that they should not have done more to make it attractive
and interesting. It is around this little old chunk that the
Bull picnic rallies every August. It makes T'ville look like
Versailles. Muddy meadows and roads, a big old gray barn
which seems on the point of falling in.

Natasha Spender came to dinner. She regaled me with
London gossip. She says that Cyril Connolly steals first
editions from his friends—though Stephen later demurred
to his going so far as this. Stephen had inadvertently presented him with a first edition of his poems, that had a
pasted-in page of MS, the copy which he had given Natasha
as a honeymoon present. When Stephen's attention was
called to this, he tried to get it back and offered Cyril
something else; but Cyril refused to give it up. Natasha
put it to him at last whether he cared more for his friends

or his collection. He answered that of course he cared more for his collection, and there is now a coolness between them. He also, she said, asked Stephen to give him something in order that he might sell it and buy something more desirable. Natasha has a very fine face, with her dark hair, green eyes and high forehead. She was amusing, but would occasionally drop into a mood *distrait* and unsmiling. I think that she still adores Stephen. She is still a professional pianist, plays for the BBC.

March 28, Thursday. Elena tried to call Carol, who was still out of town. She asked for *Baron von Radowitz,* and since she was always rather ironical about him and Brat calling themselves Baron, I asked how it was that they could assume this title. As is always the case with such matters, I had great difficulty dragging it out of her. There are two kinds of people who can be called Baron: the vons and the real feudal barons who are the barons of the places where they had their property. The Mumms belonged to the first class, the Radowitzes to the second. Why hadn't her father called himself Baron? I think he thought, she answered, that he was enough in himself, he didn't need it. People didn't call themselves Baron because new barons had been created—some of them Jewish, the Rothschilds—and it was now regarded as a rather cheap title. But Carol called himself Baron because he was over here to sell champagne and Americans didn't know the difference.

I went to the Epsteins' in the late afternoon for a conference about the American Pléiade project.* There were

---

* EW had developed a plan for reprinting the American classics in an elegant, efficient format like the Pléiade. Two years before, urging Jason Epstein to take this up with the Bollingen Foundation, he called it "absurd that our most read and studied writers should not be available in their entirety in any convenient form," noting that "almost the whole of the French classics" had been included "in beautifully produced and

a couple of men from the minor foundations and the big bibliographer Bowers from Charlottesville, the husband of Nancy Hale. He has no interest in literature but runs a kind of school for scholars—is head of the English department at the university. He is presiding over a complete Hawthorne, published by Ohio State University. He made our blood run cold by saying continually, "Leave it to the technicians." He trains them to run down editions and check variants. He knows nothing about the Pléiade and nothing about Harrison's Poe, which, as Jason said, was "under his nose." I said that I had just had a notice that the English set of Melville was about to be republished over here. Oh, that was bowdlerized! How bowdlerized? They had changed the American to English spelling. — He comes from New Haven, not Virginia, and I one-upped him about Charlottesville—spoke of the plaque to Minor on the university "Lawn." I couldn't remember the name of that erudite and rather absurd Richmond friend who composed the Latin inscription [see p. 691], but Bowers thought he knew who it was, and from what he told about him I am sure he was right. This character had given the Bowerses a silver tray or something with an ambiguous Latin description: read one way it seemed complimentary, but read it another way, not.

Elena had gone to see the Thorntons.

March 29, Friday. The Spenders came to dinner and afterwards we went to the ballet. I was very tired and groggy.

---

admirably printed, thin-paper volumes, ranging from 800 to 1,500 pages." In 1965 the funds seemed to be available at the newly organized National Endowment for the Humanities, chaired initially by his friend Henry Allen Moe. The project fell victim to the competing "authorized texts" of the Modern Language Association, the subject of Wilson's pamphlet "The Fruits of the MLA" (1968). Some years after his death his scheme was carried out by the Library of America, organized with Epstein's help.

Stephen has decided to spend three months a year at North-western. He thinks that this and *Encounter* will give him enough to live on. A relief not to have to write reviews. He has just done his first spell out there and has started a play in verse—boredom will compel him to write.

March 30, Saturday. Quiet pleasant day at the office, took Renata Adler to lunch at the Princeton Club, to which I am becoming more reconciled. It has at least a large quiet dining room, with the tables far apart. I have been reading Brendan Gill's book about the Century Club, and I find there are too many restrictions. Women only admitted to the art exhibitions and to lunches for non-profitmaking organizations. You can only bring one guest at a time and the same guest twice a year.

Dinner at the Grynbergs': pleasant to see them again. Sonya's formidable cousin with the deep Russian Jewish voice like a man's. She pays visits to Russia and thinks more of it than the Grynbergs do, so they never now discuss the subject. Sonya worked very hard, but mostly unsuc-cessfully, to keep Roman and me from drinking.

March 31, Sunday. Dinner at Lillian Hellman's: Lili Dar-vas, Lowells, Epsteins. Her apartment is very pleasant, furnished with a certain New Orleans elegance, pretty and curious knickknacks, a huge wooden Chinese birdcage hanging from the ceiling. I thought that Lili Darvas was a darling woman and very intelligent. I happened to be reading Molnár's *Az üveg cipö* [*The Glass Slipper*], which she told me—what rather astonished me—was supposed to be the story of her and Molnár. The heroine is a dotty little servant girl who worships a middle-aged carpenter, breaks up his marriage with a woman who does not love him and succeeds in getting him to marry her. It reminded me of Shaw's assertion that *Pygmalion* was about him and

Mrs. Patrick Campbell. She and Molnár hadn't got on and she had left Budapest for Vienna, where she acted for years and which she liked better. She is quite natural and I should think very sensible, nothing of the prima donna. With her accent, she said, it was hard for her nowadays to get a part. She had known the Höllerings well and gave an accurate description of Franz: very agreeable and clever, always working for his own advantage. I said that he was very Viennese. She demurred a moment, then said, "Yes, he is."

We went to the *Establishment*, the English review— intended to shock, like *Beyond the Fringe*. It is really very funny. It plays at a huge nightclub where El Morocco used to be. Nightclubs nowadays stun me.

April 1, Monday. <In the morning I got an April Fool telegram concocted by Elena: "We request the honor of your presence at banquet and would like you to judge beauty contest of New England chapter of Magyar women.">

In the evening I took the *Spenders* to the Princeton Club for dinner. We saw the first act of [the musical] *Little Me*, which was awful, and then withdrew to the Algonquin lobby. Stephen gave me the true version of the story about him and Evelyn Waugh which Isaiah Berlin had told me. Stephen had not offered to fix the watch but merely to take it to be fixed. He had put it in a drawer in his house. Francis Bacon had arrived with five "toughs." The Spenders had been burglarized and talked about it, and this gave one of the toughs the idea of stealing something. When Stephen had written him, Waugh replied insisting that he should come to see him in the country in order to apologize personally, which Stephen refused to do. The watch was now in even worse shape, and they sent Waugh an enormous bill, which Stephen, however, paid.

Stephen said that in America we had more gifted people than anywhere else in the world and a better machinery for killing them. He also said that he lacked energy on account of being so tall. It was short men who had the drive and accomplished solid things: Napoleon and I forget who else.* I said that I had, in that case, an advantage which I hadn't suspected. It reminded me of Scott's saying about Eliot that he had been reminded, when he met him in Baltimore, of Gertrude Stein's having said about Hemingway that he was "one of those tall men who are always tired."

April 2, Tuesday. I went to the *Lehoviches for dinner.* Two cousins who had just arrived in this country for the first time: Vladimir Volkonsky and a Tatishcheva—he from the Argentine, she from Paris. He has spent fifteen years in Buenos Aires but describes it as being dull, just as I had imagined it. They of course knew Elena's family. Tatishcheva laughed at my idea that the Russian émigrés in Paris all lived in a closed-in world. She said that the Lehoviches were not typical.

Cambridge with Elena and Helen

April 3, Wednesday. I came back to Cambridge.

Kataev, since his visit here, has been reprimanded in Khrushchev's speech to the writers, for "not knowing how to behave himself abroad."

---

* Spender had been amused in his youth when Aldous Huxley, in a round Bloomsbury accent, observed that neither could possibly be a genius, "because when you are tall, your head is too far from your solar plexus." The idea that tall men were deficient may have come to express a self-doubt the poet felt because he was so often implicitly compared to Auden, who was shorter.

April 4, Thursday. We went to *Erich Leinsdorf*'s open rehearsal. When we saw him during the intermission, he said that in Stravinsky's violin concerto—which I had never heard before—you forgot that the sounds were being made by musicians, it was as if it were real laughter. People liked it or didn't like it. It was pure musicality. If it didn't carry over, there was nothing to do—a disaster. He is always amusing and witty and is able to talk about almost anything. He appreciates everything he plays, a variety of kinds of music. But there is perhaps something about him of Franz Höllering's type of Viennese: good salesman, piquant and critical, yet able to adapt himself to anybody, any turn in the conversation, has an answer ready for anything; but it's hard to have a serious rapport with him. He is quivering with nervous vitality, responds to everything he touches, such a high-keyed and unrelaxing worker that he makes me feel idle and lazy (though of course he is fifteen years younger). His concerts and his talk are stimulating. We again went to his house—with Elena Levin—and had another delicious Viennese repast, with jellied fish, chicken, cheese and white wine.

It was depressing to have no teeth in my lower jaw and not to be able to chew, as it was to have trouble with my heart and not to be able to make love, to have gout and not to be able to get around. But now I am getting my teeth entirely sealed. Also, my tax troubles are nearly cleared up—sources of income released.

April 5, Friday. A very pleasant quiet day. Helen spent the night at the Chases', and Elena and I made love in the evening. My three weeks in New York had broken me down a little, and I began to feel some strain on my heart at the same time as the marvellous happiness—a strange mixed sensation—but, taking two nitroglycerin pills, recovered immediately afterwards and was filled with the usual well-being. I read *Humphrey Clinker* in bed. Elena did not have to rise early in the morning to get Helen off to school, so we both had a good sleep.

April 6, Saturday. Helen had spent the night at the *Chases'*, with her most intimate friend, Martha, and we went out to get her in the afternoon. *Dr. [Louis] Chase is a highly successful analyst*, apparently an orthodox Freudian. He had told me when I met him before that Sándor Radó was always talking as if he were going to make some original contribution to the subject but never came out with anything clear. He and Radó make an interesting contrast: Radó aging and, I think, rather skeptical; Chase full of positive conviction, beamingly cheerful and full of goodwill. I told him about my visit to Sandy, and he assured me that schizophrenics could nowadays be straightened out if you got them early enough, but that somebody at Sandy's stage had made an adjustment to his life and was "more serene than you or I." It was probably not a good idea to go to see him at all: it only put pressure on him to make an effort to meet me, an effort that he could not sustain, that got him out of harmony with his life in the institution. I said that he looked so morose and despairing. That, said Chase, was merely the imprint of the time when he had struggled against his condition. I told him about Esther's not letting them give Sandy the shock treatment. He said that it depended on how the patient reacted. If he did not react appropriately, it might not be continued. I gathered that he was rather leery of it. I said that Hemingway had evidently been wrecked by getting this treatment at the Mayo Clinic in Rochester. The Mayo Clinic, he said, was the very worst psychiatric clinic anywhere. It reminded me of Radó's reaction to the Payne Whitney clinic in New York, when the Stamford doctor had put

Mary [McCarthy] there.* Sándor went to see her and said
she must be taken out at once. Chase now told me of
patients at the Mayo Clinic who had been suffering from
some familiar and easily handled neurosis but had been
treated as if they were truly insane.

I asked about hypochondriacs like my father. Freud had
said that hypochondriasis was the most difficult kind of
neurosis, it was so difficult to get into their minds. Dr.
McKinney had told me that it was made particularly difficult by the fact that they could always find medical doctors
who would take their fancied ailments seriously. They
were "rather tough," Chase admitted, "but analysis could
reach them, too." Freud had thought a good many things
impossible. He had originated the great ideas, but he had
not been much of a therapist. Neurotics who, like my
father, wanted to have all their internal organs removed
—there is a technical name for this, which Chase told me
but I have forgotten—were suffering from a castration
complex, feelings of guilt, they had probably wanted to kill
their fathers. The neurotic fear of castration was the great
problem for men in this country. What about depressives?
They were also tough but could also be handled. What had
been the results of the work with hypnosis that had been
done during the war? He used hypnosis, he said—had by
using it successfully treated three or four cases; but he did
not do it any more because it fatigued him so. They would
come out with such a torrent of stuff that he could hardly
find his way around in it. What about the problem of the
patient's remembering after he had been waked up what
he had said when hypnotized? He would select certain

* In June 1938, after a bitter quarrel with EW, McCarthy spent three
weeks in this psychiatric hospital in New York City. She later claimed
they had gone to a psychiatric hospital by accident rather than on their
Stamford doctor's advice, though when I asked about this she laughed,
admitting a certain doubt.

things that he was to remember and dismiss from his mind all the rest. What about the drugs that had been used during the war? He had no use for them. The people were doped and unclear. But he had had the job in the army of finding out whether soldiers with a functional hysteria still wanted to serve or not. A man would come in with a paralyzed leg, and after putting him under hypnosis, Chase would have him walking again. Wouldn't he then develop another neurotic symptom? Perhaps, but Chase's job at that time was only to find out whether they wanted to go on serving or not. When I talked to Radó about hypnosis at the time that I got him, reluctantly, to read *Rebel Without a Cause*, he said that he never used it, regarded it as unfair to the patient. His attitude was that of a trout fisherman who regards it as unsportsmanlike to use worms. —I could see from his optimistic enthusiasm why Chase had been successful. Like any other such doctor, he encouraged his patients, gave them confidence. He is so happy knowing all the answers. He has also a pleasant habit, as I had noticed in hearing him speak at the Cambridge School on the "psychopathology of everyday life," of including instances from his own behavior when expounding some general phenomenon.

In the morning I had made at the Pangloss Bookshop a deal that greatly pleased me. The publishers had sent me two copies of Cecil Roth's facsimile edition of the Sarajevo *Haggadah*. They sell for $25, and I got the man who runs the shop to exchange one for Dyce's edition of George Peele, which I had been wondering whether I ought to buy. These old nineteenth-century editions still give me a great deal of pleasure. This one is printed by Pickering in smallish clear type with wide margins on fine white paper. Dyce's preface—*Some Account of George Peele and His Writings*—is full of long notes, quotations from Edmond

Malone, old ballads, fragments from Henslowe's diary and ancient writers, which sometimes fill almost whole pages and have themselves to be provided with secondary notes. There is no straight linear progression such as you get in modern books. These books, pleasantly cluttered up, remind me of the illustrations to *The Old Curiosity Shop*: repositories of the literary past of England, in which someone has been poking around, trying to find out what's what. They always seem to be doing it for their own amusement, with no careers to make.

I notice the word *pleasant* recurring.

April 8, Monday. When I went up to bed, I found *Helen and Elena listening to television* in Helen's room. Helen was lying in the bed and Elena lying crosswise on the bed, with her head against the wall—their long handsome legs like jackstraws on one another and both looking very attractive. They were watching the Oscars being given out in Hollywood, and Elena was laughing at it merrily. Helen would remonstrate with her for laughing—she was taking it rather seriously—but would then begin to laugh herself. This is the way that young people get to learn their standards and attitudes.

<*Dreams about Talcottville:* Two more dreams: as always, there is something in the house that I don't expect. In the first, when I went to my east front room, I saw what looked like the profile of a person in the corner against the light, then I saw that it was not real, a dummy. Then I saw that there were other things to the right: those creatures like hellbenders or salamanders—which I sometimes see in my dreams—that have taken shapes of other objects or even people. There was one particularly unpleasant bright red worm with a head like a caterpillar

that had attached itself high up on the wall. I knocked it
down with my cane and was beating it to death when I
woke. —Two or three days later, I dreamt again that I
had come back to T'ville and found a couple of men working
on the house that I did not remember to have told to come.
They were not, however, hostile, and they showed me a
part of the house that I had not known existed. It was up
a rather hidden stair through a narrow little hallway near
the front: a living room with furnishings of an elegance
such as otherwise is not to be found in the house: a kind
of highboy made of inlaid wood, books with fine bindings,
etc., and opening out of it a bedroom with a very fine old
bed. I was, of course, delighted. It was of course what I
had wanted the place to be.>

I asked Elena whether she still loved me now that I am
getting old. She said, "Old has nothing to do with it." This
touched me, she so seldom says anything like this.

With a hangover nowadays, I feel like an old man: dizzy
and unsteady, with a backache. If I refrain from drinking
at night, I am quite brisk again the next morning, though
in the course of the day, it seems to me, I get more easily
tired than I used to do.

Today is my birthday, I am 68. Tax difficulties are more
or less solved, my lower jaw will soon be rebuilt, my gout
has nearly disappeared and my heart is very much better
—hardly being able to eat on account of not having my
lower teeth has been beneficial in making me thinner—
and we now count on getting to Europe. I am pulling myself
together to do my protest and my Canadian articles. I have
been hung up and not very productive all during the last
year. Now perhaps, as Cyril Connolly said when I last saw
him in England (though without results in his case, so far

as I could see), "the old scow is off the mud."* Elena and Helen had prepared for me this morning a wonderful birthday offering: a tray with a siphon, a shaving mirror, a little glass dish and a box of black-currant pastilles, all wrapped and arranged by Helen in a fine color combination of green, orange and lemon, with a yellow rosette, a white mouse and a single yellow rose in a tumbler.

European Intellectuals

<*July 25, '63.* I came up to T'ville on June 9, and have been writing my protest pamphlet, so did not keep up this journal, am only now bringing it up to date.>

Before leaving Cambridge. Wellfleet weekend: Suzanne Hughes brought *Dedijer* to our house. He looks like the perfect ideal of the fighting Slavic revolutionist, tall, heavy, broad-shouldered, square-chinned, meeting one's gaze with defiance; but actually he is self-conscious and sensitive. He did not fit in well with the English, the only people he got on with at Oxford were the Irish and the Jews; but he could see very shrewdly what people were up to. Dons like Taylor and Trevor-Roper had to put on an act—hence their polemics about Taylor's book—and Taylor had had to take a line that would shock people. I asked him if he knew Isaiah Berlin; he shook his head: "I don't care for it." I asked him about Djilas—why did they con-

---

* In *Night Thoughts* EW teases Connolly for not getting his work done, looking back to his friend's *Enemies of Promise* (1939) and to his loyalty to literature during World War II:

> Enemies of Promise
> Cyril Connolly
> Behaves rather fonnily:
> Whether folks are at peace or at fighting,
> He complains that it keeps him from writing.

tinue to persecute him? He gave me the same story that a previous Yugoslav professor had given me. Djilas had antagonized one of the ladies of Tito's official court—they all, he said, lived in palaces clustered together (I had a vision of a Balkan city, with pretentious pink stucco buildings)—and the ladies had all ganged up on him and brought pressure to bear on their husbands. "When you don't like a woman like that, you send her bouquets of flowers—you don't say nasty things about her in print." I said that I had been a little surprised, in reading Djilas's *Conversations with Stalin*, that he should have remained so admiring and loyal so long. "I was even more so: At the time we were fighting, Stalin was the only thing we had." Though critical of the Soviet Union, Dedijer still believed in what they were doing in Yugoslavia, would not allow his disagreements with Tito's regime to be used against Communism by the capitalist press. But Djilas was an idealist—a provincial radical of principles so pure that they could not be corrupted—and when he had seen that his fellow revolutionaries were settling down as officials and doing very well for themselves, he had to be indignant about it; and the others of course resented this. He represented their own bad conscience, so they felt they had to put him away. He had again been in solitary confinement and for months was not allowed to read.

Dedijer had been writing a book about the group that assassinated the archduke in 1914. "They assassinated the right man," he said; but then went on to talk about the archduke's culture and intelligence. The assassins themselves had been cultivated, and their political movement had had connections with literary symbolism. Dedijer's English is that of a highly literate man, and Suzanne says his French is good. His handwriting, she says, is neat and tiny. His self-consciousness, his desire for approval was shown by his issuing a challenge to each of the ladies

present. He said to Mary Meigs suddenly: "You look very
much like a general's wife who hates me." He evidently
expected to be reassured, but she didn't know how to take
it, and he went on, "Why don't you come out at me like
an English lady." But this was not understood by Mary,
who was hurt and very soon left. I went out with her as
I knew that she must be offended, and she said, "I don't
want to be taken for a bourgeois snob." A conversation
about the women in America, Russia and Yugoslavia had
followed his saying that he was disappointed in the women
of his own country. He had hoped that Communism would
liberate them to distinguish themselves in the arts and
sciences; but this had not been the case—or in Russia
either. He thought that they were much more independent
in America. Elena denied this—she thought that our
women were respected less than women were in other
countries. The conversation proceeded at cross-purposes.
He was talking on assumptions—and this was true in
general—that we had a certain difficulty in adapting ourselves to. —He had tried to stand up for Djilas, and had
been, apparently, not exactly expelled but allowed to go
abroad. Suzanne said that he was determined to go back.
In the meantime, however, having finished his book about
the 1914 assassination, he was going to work at Harvard
on a study of the distribution of income in the various
countries. He was a little bit worried about how his presence at Harvard would be taken, he had heard we were
becoming so conformist. I tried to reassure him. The people
in Widener, he said, had been very helpful and friendly
—quite different from the Bodleian at Oxford—and as for
the Bibliothèque Nationale!

Silone's visit: He and Darina are back together again,
and Darina made him come to America—though he doesn't
like to travel. He was stouter and much more genial than

he had been when I saw him in Rome, and he had evidently been anxious about taking the right line. Wasn't sure whether he was going to write about St. Francis or about Celestine V, who made *il gran rifuto*, had been a hermit in the Abruzzi and abdicated from the papacy in order to go back to his saintly life. He talked with his usual intelligence, always answering and commenting seriously on subjects he had thought about. He was revising his dialogue about dictators. When I talked about the bureaucratic developments in the U.S. and the Soviet Union, he said, "Statism—I'm writing about it in my dictator book." Darina had made him visit Ireland, and he had hated it.

Ivanka Koviloska, a young woman from the University of Skopje, who is working on Scott Fitzgerald. I had already begun hearing about the Macedonian language and wondering what it was. It seems that Tito, since 1949, has been building up Skopje as a great industrial center, and the Macedonian dialect has been lifted to the dignity of a literary language. One of the great authorities on it is a Harvard professor, who has written a Macedonian grammar. They have already short story writers—though no novelists—and a highly esteemed poet. It is a curious example of the growth of minority nationalisms within the big federations. Miss Koviloska, when I said something favorable about Tito, was rather cool about him. She spoke of the bureaucracy of Belgrade, and said that she never spent much time there, merely passed through in going north. She seemed rather proud of the fact that the language was unique among the Slavic languages in having a definite article—which seems to me—as I suppose Russian то and это are—derived from Greek *oútos* and *aútós*. I bought the grammar and found the language perfectly simple—the meaning, as in the cases of the other Yugoslav languages—usually recognizable from Russian. (As I write, July 27, Skopje has just been wrecked by an earthquake.)

The Hughes divorce: This kind of thing saddens me nowadays—perhaps mainly for the selfish reason that I don't like to see the breakup of couples whose company I enjoy, and since the Schlesingers and Lowells left, there have been very few of these. Stuart went to Europe, and now that he is back, Suzanne has gone to Reno. The little boy, when the news was broken to him, asked his mother if they would now be orphans. But the situation must have been impossible. I don't understand Stuart, whom I find so sympathetic and intelligent. They had apparently been living together and sleeping in the same bed without having any sexual relations. How can this be possible with such an attractive woman as Suzanne?

Upstate after "the Life of a Monk"

T'ville. <In my boyhood, I read *Maeterlinck*'s plays up here, having found them in some upstate bookstore. (I still have the volume here, published in 1911.) Later, I read that whenever he had finished some work, at the cástle (I think) in which he lived, he would give a rousing party. While working, he had shut himself up and lived with the utmost asceticism. This made a great impression on me and, in spite of the fact that I now take Maeterlinck as a writer much less seriously than I did then, may have influenced my own practice: first the dedicated toil, then the orgy. Maeterlinck was then associated with the actress Georgette Leblanc, and when I lived in Greenwich Village in the

twenties, I was somewhat shocked to find her an aging and rather staling woman of lesbian reputation, on the outskirts of the Provincetown Players. I had had such a vision of her, in trailing robes, as the mistress of a wide-lawned château.

The knowledge that death is not far away, that I shall soon disappear like a puff of smoke, has the effect of making earthly affairs seem unimportant and human beings more and more ignoble. It is harder to take human life seriously, including one's own passions and achievements and efforts. In my tendency toward this state of mind, I have found Pope John fortifying. When over 80 and knowing he is doomed [by cancer], he gives all the energy left him to his council which will modernize the Church, and then dies with the greatest dignity: "I am watching myself die step by step."*

During the first five weeks I was up here, *I got my [tax] pamphlet written and lived virtually the life of a monk.* I had perfect quiet and freedom: no family, no telephone conversations, no newsstands and bookstores to visit, no temptations to social life. The Sharps are not here; the Crostens had not yet come; the Gauses were still in Europe. The house is comfortable and clean. Mrs. Hutchins gets me breakfast and supper.> Mary Pcolar now has three days off a week, and so is able to do more for me than last summer. I occasionally had dinner with the Morrises. When I am concentrating on some one thing, as I have

* In the catacombs of Rome a few months later, Rosalind Wilson recalls, "when we were coming up a long flight of stairs and my father wavered, the priest told him, 'Pope John was just here. You are walking in the steps of a very good man.' Father was so heartened by this thought that he almost vaulted up the rest of the way" (*Near the Magician*).

been now and as I did on the Dead Sea scrolls, I couldn't have better conditions.

The Munns have been here only twice; the Loomises are fading out. It is sad to see them now. Gertrude is slightly dotty, and Huldah has had a bad winter—ill and had an operation. She sometimes does not make connections and has lost something of her old authority. I find that I am actually now sometimes ahead of her on the local gossip, and able to tell her things she doesn't know. I have hardly thought about the family and the past which used to be so present to me—just at moments: Father reading in bed in summer, in the back bedroom that I now sleep in, that book on Daniel Boone, which he made me read and which bored me; Dorothy Mendenhall and Merwin Hart talking about Walter Lippmann, who was then first being talked about, on the stone steps in front of the house. But I now completely fill the place, and I myself am completely filled by my pamphlet. This big room downstairs is becoming more and more a library; there are so many things on the sofa and chairs that there is hardly any place for a visitor to sit. I have had a new bookcase put up in the corner, and it makes the room look less bare—my magical apparatus on top of it—"Jumbo" rising cards, goblet with colored silks, card that appears in a balloon—give a touch of unmeaning gaiety. At the time that I was working, I gave up everything else—did not try to fish, made no trips except one to Tug Hill; saw nothing at all of the country, which I usually enjoy so much. <I am glad to have got that pamphlet off my mind and my conscience—for several years now, it has been rankling with me, poisoning me, depressing me, creating conflicts of purpose of a kind to which I am not accustomed: not to have decided something, not to know what I am going to do and be able to go about it has always demoralized me: my agonizing at Red Bank

in 1917 when I could not make up my mind what to do
about the war.* I have thoroughly enjoyed my solitude,
am not lonely and do not suffer any longer from the dreadful
depressions that I used to have when in Cambridge. It is
partly that I have settled down to growing old, which in
a way makes one notice it less; and my gout is almost cured.
I do not have bad heart attacks, and though I was miserable
on my way here and after I first came back, on account of
having had five teeth pulled and the painfulness at first of
my bridge, my mouth is quite comfortable now, and I find
that it is very reassuring to be able to chew again.

I went to the Players Guild play at Lyons Falls, and saw
there *Helen Johnson, the nurse who stayed with Father* in
Red Bank, that ghastly summer when Mother was away
and I had to spend some time with him. It gave me quite
a turn. I had seen her again before, several summers ago,
but she is now very old, over 80, and it brought back again
out of the past an experience that my memory had tried
to suppress. I had been in the later years of college, and
full of intellectual excitement and my varied social life
with my friends, and poor Father was buried there, in the
uncomfortable Red Bank house, in his hypochondriacal
gloom which prevented him from taking an interest in
anything and which blanketed the future with darkness:
no real desire to live, no hope of doing anything further.
It was strange and repugnant to me to realize that a witness
to all that was still alive.

----

* EW had opposed the entry of the United States into World War I, and
was uncertain of his own course. A summer in military training camp
taught him he "could never be an officer," nor did he want to be drafted
or enlist as a soldier. He resolved the dilemma by accompanying a friend,
David Hamilton, who joined the hospital corps (*A Prelude*).

Mariska enjoys her job in the drugstore in Rome and is on excellent terms with her boss, an Italian who is going to run for mayor. He pays for her Utica night school and has given her a 1 percent interest in the business.> I get the impression that she is beginning to repeat her situation in the drugstore in Boonville: boss falls in love with her and wife becomes jealous. <She is proud of having had all B's on her Utica exams, and has evidently got a lot out of her courses: has learned about evolution, has had to read and discuss *Lord of the Flies*. It is touching and worries me to see how anxious she is to acquire education and to promote herself to a higher milieu.> Her husband is now becoming envious and talks about going to night school. She thinks about getting a job in connection with the college itself or of teaching in the Catholic school in Rome, where she says you do not have to have academic qualifications. She wonders what would happen if she should kick over the traces, nothing could stop her then—but she can't with her husband and children and her mother. — She now gets Wednesday, Saturday and Sunday off, so she is able to do more for me than she was last summer.

<*Trip to Tug Hill with the Pcolars:* Many pheasants, a snow rabbit in its brown summer coat, which George identified by its size. We found the sphagnum bog behind the gate, rich with pitcher plant in full bloom with their leathery maroon flowers that have a sinister look. George and I felt a certain interest in finding out where the road led to, but Mariska, who was driving, having been over the rotting plank bridges and through the huge flooded holes, was reluctant. We finally got to a broken-down bridge which made it impossible to go farther. I brought home some pitcher plant and arum lily, and have been keeping them in basins near the back porch. The flowers of the

pitcher plant now seem fading, but the pitchers seem mul-
tiplying and now fill the basin.>

Fern and Otis told me that *Thad* had some blown *loon's
eggs* under a bell glass that he always kept in his bedroom.
When he died, they suddenly disappeared, and nobody ever
knew what had become of them.

I haven't yet seen a chipmunk here this summer. <I
found a nest of robins outside one of the third-floor windows. When they left, I found a baby bat—had never seen
one before. It looked like a little gray demon, wings still
too limp to fly—it was groping with its little paws, trying
to climb up the glass. The orioles have pathetically built
their nest in the old dead tree out back, where they have
had no protection from the leaves. The tree on the street
beside the stone barn was rotten in the crotch between its
two prongs, and one of them came down in a heavy wind.
I had to have the rest taken down.> I have done even less
than usual about the place. Mother's peonies and Aunt
Lin's roses bloomed very much later than usual. Clara
Crowfoot now has a job and is always starting in to cut
the lawn but never manages to finish it, so that it is grown
up again before she returns. I haven't even weeded properly
the bowls and things in front of the house, but Mariska
has given me flowers which are blooming in them: pansies
and an attractive kind of peppermint-striped petunia.

<The young people don't know what to do with them-
selves. They hang around in the evenings on the corner
next to the house or sit on the stone steps in front of the
house. Last winter some of the boys broke a lot of the
windows in Carrie Trenham's house and the Loomises'
house, and wrecked the pop machine on the front of the
Roches' store. Fern says it was the Brown boy and the

McPherson boy—both families are, I think, newcomers to the village. When Lang was here, we picked up the McPherson boy, who was hitchhiking to Boonville. I noticed his confirmed sullen look.>

Scandal of ———, the teacher of mathematics in the regional school. Mariska, who worked with him in the theater, says that he has "no roots"; Lincoln White says he is "very eccentric"; for Glyn Morris, he has obviously been a painful problem: he was for a long time very sympathetic with him, then decided at the end he was impossible. He incited the students, Glyn said, to rebel against the authorities. He was himself, though brilliant, a kind of beatnik. Others say that he drank and didn't show up for class, left it to others to correct his papers. He was unmarried and lived at the local hotel, and, I gather, took his girl students for drives. He defended himself on TV, and the students as well as many others in the community seemed to be sympathetic with him. I really can't make out what it is all about. In any case, they have now got rid of him.

<*Cecil Lang* came over for a night. We sat on the back porch and talked. He comes from North Carolina and was interesting about segregation. I said that I had a certain sympathy with the Southerners, but he said he had none at all. He added, however, that he could not feel at ease with Negroes socially. I said that the Southerners were scared of the Negroes. "I'm scared of them," he said. On his last visit home, a big Negro came to the door and asked, "Is Milly here?" He was frightened, but then it turned out that the man had simply gone to the wrong house.

The days when I was working on *bacteriological warfare* in connection with my pamphlet were also the days when, in connection with Canada, I got around to reading *Anne Hébert, Saint-Denys-Garneau and Jean Le Moyne*, and the combination got me down. Those denizens of old French-Canadian *maisons seigneuriales* who exist in a damp and murky atmosphere of Jansenist religion and incestuous relationships—they chafe at the narrowness and puritanism of their Church, but they cannot really liberate themselves from it. Saint-Denys-Garneau and Le Moyne cannot even be explicit about what worries them. If you knew nothing about French Canada, you would hardly guess what they are writing about. Clotted and clumsy prose. I fell back on my usual resource of reading books by and about Shaw, Max Beerbohm and Wilde—also a new biography of James Huneker.

Bette Mele's visit. She is a very pretty Seneca woman, connected with the Crouses and all those Beaver ladies, who comes from the Allegheny reservation and went to the Indian school—now married to an Italian psychiatrist, who went to Princeton and now practices there. She had with her her three children and a tall goodlooking German girl from Berlin who was over here to qualify in English for some degree that she needed to teach, and had a job taking care of the Meles' children. A piquant combination. Bette had had a good deal of difficulty adjusting to the non-Indian world; had two years in a white school and felt that what she had learned had not been of any use to her. She had met her husband in Rochester when she was training to be a nurse there. I suppose at his instigation, she had two years of psychoanalysis. Then coming back from New York to Princeton, she had read one of my Iroquois articles. She recognized the people I wrote about, and burst into tears. She said that my book had done more for her than the analysis. I was very much touched and pleased by this. She said that her father had been a Christian but that her

mother was a Longhouse woman, who had belonged to the
Little Water Society. In reading my book, she had been
astonished to find me describing the ceremony, which she
had never been allowed to go near. When the Dark Dance
had been set up, she and the other children had been sent
upstairs and were frightened at what they heard going on
below.

Bette had taken part in the women's peace movement
and had tried to help the cause of the Senecas. She had
just been to an Indian school reunion at Onondaga and
brought me a container of ceremonial corn soup. Her husband's family [just having come from Italy] would tell her
she should become Americanized, and this made her furious. She was visiting her brother-in-law at Barnevald.
They were on their way to Blue Mountain Lake to see
some people she had once worked for. On the way back,
she dropped in again, had found her visit disappointing. I
think that she finds it difficult—from what she told me of
her life in Princeton too—to establish close relations with
non-Indians. She brought me this time a box of imported
English candy, a bottle of Moselle wine and a bag of
peaches and cherries.*

Three peace marches converged at Rome, and I went over
to see A. J. Muste. He is aging—76—and they told me
he was having to slow down. The peace marchers were
standing with banners at the gate of the air force base,
and committing acts of "civil disobedience" by going inside
and getting themselves removed. A woman who did this
was arrested. Muste seemed rather worried. A young man
came over and asked whether they could call it a day. Muste

---

* Bette Mele later proposed to adopt EW into her hereditary Seneca clan,
but he declined, saying he had not done enough to deserve the honor.
She named her son Antonio Edmund Wilson Mele "in order to put
Edmund Wilson's name on the Seneca rolls." Mele remembers him in
Edmund Wilson: The Man and His Work, edited by John Wain.

looked at his wristwatch and said that they had announced
that they were going to stay till 6, and that he thought
that they ought to stay. It was pointed out that the marchers were somewhat losing their discipline. Some were singing folk songs and others were lying in the grass. They
ought to be standing in ranks, he said. The woman who
had driven me to the gate was one of the leaders in the
movement—I had met her and her husband at Barbara
Deming's in Wellfleet—and she didn't approve of this sloppiness. A good many of the young people, I was afterwards
told—including herself—are anarchists, and do not sub-
mit willingly to discipline. What does it mean to be an
anarchist at this time? Muste had told me, when I saw
him last summer in New York, that he regretted the beatnik beards, and I did not see any among these marchers
except a well-trimmed and decorative one worn by a young
minister.

Dinner with *Walter Edmonds* at the *Towpath.*> I am
getting to know and like him better. Kay is in Cambridge
with her daughter, whose husband is in McLean's, and
we talked in a somewhat more personal way about our
wives, dogs and children. I told him the history of the
Stone House. He said he didn't know any writers except
me, and that he regarded me as "a local character." <He
really is, as Grace Root says, very shy—seems to me a
curious person: no real interest in literature, no desire to
see the world. I was surprised at his going to Iran when
his son was there.>

The Summer in Retrospect

< *Six days in New York, July 9–14.* A very satisfactory visit. Arranged about pamphlet with Muste and Roger Straus. Elena came Tuesday and left Friday. >

We stayed at the *Princeton Club*, with which I am becoming reconciled. Rooms cheaper and more comfortable than at the Algonquin, prompt room service in the mornings. Large very quiet dining room, with really excellent food.

< I saw Muste at *The New Yorker*. His shrewd and unsanguine realism when you talk to him is a contrast to the intensity and eloquence of his speeches. I said that the peace movement did not have the same leverage as the desegregation movement. The only possibility, he said, was that unemployment caused by automation might swell the number of protesters. I don't see this unless he meant that fewer people would have jobs in the war industries. He thinks that the enemy now is the military establishment, and that to get rid of it would mean a revolution. In some Middle Western city, he had talked with a security agent who had been sent out to watch their rally. The man had said, in substance, "I agree with you; but I can't do anything about it because my whole career has consisted of this work I am doing and I couldn't bring myself to let down the other men I am working with." >

I had dinner with Lili Darvas Saturday night, after Elena had left. She is an intelligent cultivated woman, not at all a typical actress—was a friend of Hofmannsthal and Arthur Schnitzler. Pleasant apartment on East 79th St.; two toy poodles, Molnár's manuscripts in a row of boxes, a big green sofa of "Hungarian Biedermeier." Since the club and the Algonquin were closed Saturday night, we ate at a good little French restaurant just around the corner from her apartment. That is the Hungarian part of town: Second Avenue in the Seventies. She is much less patriotic than most Hungarians and does not talk so much. I told her about my Hungarian friends, and she said, "You know the cream. Many Hungarians are mean and dishonest and lazy."

<*Back in Talcottville, Mariska* met me at the airport. She had a drink with me at the house and was evidently prepared to stay out to dinner, so we ate the little supper of spaghetti that Mrs. Hutchins had left for me. I played for her the whole of Kodály's *Háry János*. With her usual deftness and capability, she got the phonograph going smoothly. She was able to translate fluently and, when she relayed to me the angry speeches of the abandoned peasant fiancée, would make appropriate gestures. Of the triumphant march of the interlude, she said that though it was meant to sound rousing, it had also a strain of melancholy. She was much interested in the whole thing.

Lincoln White now has a job in a bigger town, Marcella outside Syracuse. He dropped in to see me one morning —very cheerful and evidently enjoying himself. He said that he had found hardly any prejudice on account of his being an Indian. St. Regis had been relatively quiet.> He surprised me by a sophisticated joke: When Christine Keeler's confession came out in a book, it was going to be called *My Life under the Tories*.

<The Fentons spent a night with me, July 26. They talked about their trip to Europe. It had evidently done Olive good: the first time she had ever gone. She seems to have emerged completely from the shadow of her mental illness, was amusing, unworried, quite talkative. Bill said that he found the scientists in Prague, if you did not talk

to them about politics or get into the problems of the genesis of races, just like scientists everywhere else. He is going to an anthropological conference in Moscow and is screening the delegation from the United States. —He says that the "borscht belt" is moving up almost to Binghamton—the third generation of well-to-do Jews who spend part of the week in the country. Also, that in this part of New York, civilization is on the decline, many farms are being abandoned, and that this is perhaps the reason that the wild animals are coming back. —He made my blood run cold by his account of what was happening as a result of the Kinzua Dam. The Quakers or the Indians themselves had consulted a housing expert, who had put them in the hands of some Madison Avenue publicity man. He had advised them that the only thing for them was to create an Indian Williamsburg, a replica of an Indian village. It would be a tourist attraction, would bring trade to Salamanca. Some of the Indians were quite interested in this idea, and he thought that he might even coöperate in some advisory capacity.> Myrtle Crouse, he said, did not seem to be in very good shape—I suppose she is depressed about the dam. Her daughter Maxine is married—to a no-good, according to her mother—and already has two children.

<I have lately apparently been suffering from a mild form of *auditory hallucination*. I seem to hear the telephone ringing early in the morning just as I am waking up. At first, I would go to answer it, but would find that it was not ringing. Now I simply lie in bed. The sound is only heard once. When I first got up here this summer after Rosalind had driven me and left, I once thought I heard her calling me.

The weather this summer has been hotter than anything I remember up here. This house is cooler than anything else, short of air conditioning; but it has even here been sometimes stifling, and even at night—in the morning I have occasionally waked up sweating. One day I had to have a towel while working, and it reminded me of the days in Red Bank when I was working on *Daisy* with a towel around my head. >

I did not return to writing this till Oct. 16 in London at the Basil St. Hotel. I catch up on a few T'ville notes:

Walter Edmonds told me that when he first got to know *Grace Root*, she offered them what she said was a new cocktail called a "martini."

<I once thought that I was safely remote up here from the dangers of atomic warfare; but I realize now that I am only a few miles from one of the important targets. *The air base at Rome*, it appears, supervises the equipping and dismantling of the bases all over the country, and there is a squad of pilots on duty around the clock who fly off at intervals in the direction of Russia and then back again. This is recently being given publicity after having been kept secret before. > Someone who was lately asked to visit it says that he was told by the man who took him around that he was now going to show him something that he had never been allowed to see himself. Walter Edmonds was asked to go and speak there, and was evidently flattered and impressed. His romantic imagination was touched by the idea of this disciplined unpublicized élite who were trained in this exacting service. He told me, with evident gratification, that they were encouraged to do watercolors. He knew where the bombs were kept but wasn't allowed to tell.

Difficulties of books in Canadian French: Mistranslation of a passage of quiet description in which the light snow

was falling fast: *"la poudrière éclata"* became "The powder
plant blew up"—never mentioned before or after. —In a
Paris-published edition of Gabrielle Roy's *Bonne d'Occasion, orignal* (moose), a word unfamiliar to the printer,
appears as *original*: an original in the forest comes down
to drink in the lake.

<*Elena* came in August and spent almost two weeks.
Everything went well. I understand now that one of the
factors that had made things difficult before was her worrying about and trying to keep tabs on Helen, who was out
continually with the children in the village. The boys have
now developed gang tendencies, and I was becoming rather
apprehensive myself.

I had a party soon after she arrived of heavy intellectual
concentration: Gauses, O'Donnells from Utica, Langs from
Syracuse, Walter Edmonds and his son and his wife, Bette
Mele and her husband, the Marcelins, the Callaghans with
their boy Michael, the Bests and their unfortunate daughter (now broken up with her recent foreign husband and
become rather alcoholic), the Crostens. We were pretty
well steam-rollered by it—I think that it is a better idea
to dilute these annual affairs with some local, less intellectual people. The Callaghans and the Marcelins stayed
over—I put the latter up at the Parquet in Constableville.
The next morning there was reëstablished something of
the leisurely atmosphere of prolonged and reflective conversation of the Callaghan household in Toronto, and Morley and his son, in answer to my questions, informed me
in a systematic way about politics and education and the
judiciary in Canada. Then arrived Malcolm Montgomery
and his wife and her young son from Toronto. I introduced
Phito Marcelin as the most distinguished Haitian writer,
and we gradually came to feel that there was something
wrong. We started off in two cars for a picnic, at Inde-

pendence River, but Elena with her party overshot the
mark, and my party waited there so long that I began to
get worried and drove back to the house, then back to the
river again, and met them just leaving there. We returned,
and I and my party ate our part of the picnic. I noticed
that Mrs. Montgomery always sat at an angle to the rest
of us when I was talking to Marcelin, and that when the
Montgomerys left, she did not shake hands with him when
he did. I knew that she was some kind of British
colonial—she has one of those semi-cockney colonial
accents—but it was not till after they were gone that it
occurred to Elena and me that the trouble was that she
was South African. >

After Elena went, I continued to have more social life
than one would think would be possible up there. This
seems to be a feature of American life, in the Northeast
at least, everywhere in August; but there have been times
this summer when I did not feel that I had even the companionship of the past.

I went back to Wellfleet about the 25th of August—
Hutchinses drove me to Cummington, then Dan Aaron
the next day to Wellfleet. Helen asked for dinner a *young
Hungarian professor* [István Deák] and his wife—he intelligent and a different type from the other Hungarians I
had known—less flamboyant and patriotic. He said that
when some other Hungarian had talked to him along the
familiar lines of lamenting that their wonderful literature
was inaccessible to anyone else, he had told him that he
thought a good deal of it was really very mediocre, and that
a good deal of Ady was rubbish. He cleared up for me a
number of mysteries—explained exactly the ranks that the
honorifics indicated—*méltóságos asszonyom* [my lady], etc.;
told me of a satiric dialogue between two men who meet

Michael Callaghan

Philippe Thoby-Marcelin, Edmund Wilson, and Morley
Callaghan picnicking in August 1963

and spend all their time together discussing how they shall address one another. In their present supposedly Communist society, they can't settle on how to say *you*—hence Agatha finding that in a contemporary novel everybody called everybody else *te*, and then finding another book where everyone called each other *maga*. They cannot reconcile themselves, he says, to calling one another "comrade" at all—will not accept *elvtárs* but substitute something else.

Family Problems

I struck *Wellfleet* in what was the very worst week of a summer everyone agreed was its most frenetic and overpopulated. We made a resolution—which we kept—not to go out to parties or dinner; but people almost every day came to see us, and we were making preparations for departure. Reuel and his bride were there, and I was apprehensive and dubious about her. When I first saw her, I thought she was neurotic and had an ominous resemblance to Mary. Reuel told me that she had had three children and had put them all out for adoption.* This somewhat shook both me and Elena. She is evidently a hypochondriac and has Reuel lashed to the mast. She claimed to be suffering still from some gastric ailment which she had contracted in Mexico. Elena took her to Banks, who couldn't find anything wrong with her—so she got Reuel up at 2 in the morning to take her to another doctor. She also, on account of Helen's horse, developed an allergy to horses. Reuel explained to me that many people didn't like her, and he has, on this account—her

---

* EW subsequently heard a different story from Dr. Zetzel, who examined Marcia, and shares this with Elena in his letter of September 18 (Appendix A).

extreme self-consciousness—been dropping his old friends Doc Edmunds, Charley Jencks, Mike MacDonald. It seems to me appallingly my relations with his mother all over again.

His attitude toward her is all pity and chivalry—many people, he thinks, are against her because she has been unfortunate. She married very young in order to get away from the hell of her parents—she left her husband and went back to her mother (her father and mother had separated), who was now alcoholic and always smashing up her cars. Her father, though living in luxury, would not give them any money, and she and the children would have starved if she had not had them adopted. There seems something wrong about this story, but Reuel is not aware of it, and I cannot talk to him about it. When I suggested to him that Marcia might be a hypochondriac, he was defensively indignant at once and said that I was trying to psychoanalyze her. It is too late for us to intervene.

My little more than a week in Wellfleet worked up to the climax of our leaving.

I went up to Boston on the 4th of September—we were supposed to sail from Montreal the 6th. The general hysteria of the end of August was evident even at the Provincetown airport. A loud voice declaiming and arguing was heard from behind the partition back of the counter. I had to go in a small plane for the overflow of two passengers after the regular plane was full, and the owner of the voice got into it and continued loudly to blat, justifying himself for some mistake he had made, some failure to be on hand when he should, till I told him to pipe down. The pilot told me, when I got off the plane, that he was a bad actor and about to be fired. There was a poster for one of the newspapers telling about an end-of-season riot at Southampton, in which the young people had done a lot of smashing-up and a considerable number of them had been arrested and taken off in buses.

Rosalind, who was supposed to meet me, wasn't there, and, after waiting a while, I called her up. She made no sense whatever, and when I asked her what was wrong with her, said, "I don't know" and "I don't know what's real any more." I found her in a strangely exalted state, full of delusions—she thought someone who was going to marry her was communicating with her—by means of some special wiring arranged by Steve Fassett—through the music that was coming in over the radio. The next day she went to Mass. General. I could not sail with Elena and Helen, but settled down in the Parker House—where, except for the big restaurant and the grille, the accommodations were now wretched. I seemed to be settling back into the familiar uncertain and depressing state of mind of the days of Mary's pregnancy, when she had been in the Payne Whitney clinic. The doctors thought—and, I think, rather hoped—that Rosalind had been taking the new drug which, in the guise of some sort of morning glory seeds, was then being circulated in Boston, and which in some cases produced paranoiac effects. One of the doctors had me go to her apartment and see whether there were any bottles that would show that she had been taking drugs or drinking. I searched but there was nothing—not even a whisky bottle. The place was horribly ill kept and dirty, with the four big cats crawling around, and it reminded me so unpleasantly of the sloppiness of her mother's apartment on Lexington Ave. I was afraid she was schizophrenic, but she cleared up in about two weeks, and we drove up to Wellfleet, where she stayed with me. At first she kept taking the tranquillizers, and this made her so nervous she couldn't read or bear to stay at the table to the end of the meal. When she stopped taking them, she straightened out.

It hadn't, in a practical way, worked out so badly for me, because it gave me a chance to do the page proofs on the *Protest* and pieces for my next miscellaneous volume. I wrote two new ones: the Beerbohm conversations and a supplement to the *New Statesman* article on current clichés, etc. I left on Friday, Oct. 4, and Rosalind went to stay with the Chavchavadzes. She had had news, by way of Dawn [Powell], that the *Ladies' Home Journal* was accepting one of her stories. This had cheered her up, and I hoped she would be all right. In the hospital, she said to me, when she was clearing up, "I've just written all this." I didn't know what she meant, but she afterwards explained to me that she was writing a novel about her friends who were always going in and out of McLean's; she had become emotionally involved in it and identified herself with her characters—had not been drinking much or taking drugs.

The first week that R. was in the hospital, I had seen something of Marie-Claire Blais, who is taking advantage of her Guggenheim to live in Cambridge at 401 Broadway. She had, while I was at T'ville, spent the better part of a week at Wellfleet with Elena, had talked to her every night and quite worn her out with her worries—her emotions and confessions. Elena couldn't be sure whether everything she said was true—she thought there might be an element of fantasy. She is still a prey to Jansenist Puritanism, and seems to spend half her life trying to expiate by self-mortification what she does in the other half: "*la chair*," "*les plaisirs charnels.*" She is obsessed with suffering and death, and assumes that everyone else is, too. Elena told me that when she (Marie-Claire) had walked on the beach with the Wallings' boy Christopher, E. had asked her what they had talked about, and she had answered, "*De la mort.*" About Rosalind, she asked me, "*Elle est obsédée par la mort?—Elle veut vivre*"—as if this last idea was something unusual. She found everything *"angoissant."* She went to all the movies—some several times: *8½* and *Lawrence of Arabia*— and thought that even things that were supposed to be funny were actually *angoissant*. Mary Meigs, cancelling her flute lesson, drove me down to Boston, Cambridge and the airport. We enjoyed our day together—we so rarely see one another without somebody else. We picked up Marie-Claire and had lunch at the Window Shop. Afterwards, while I did my errands in town, Mary took M.-C. to the Fogg Museum, where, she said, M.-C. paid no attention to the pictures but talked all the time. I met them there, and we investigated the new visual-arts building—which I cannot bear: it reminds me of the big garage underneath the Common, where Rosalind keeps her car—and then went and had drinks at the Engels'. This was the only time that M.-C. saw Mary, but she wrote Elena later that she was *inquiète* about Mary, whom she couldn't help identifying with Thérèse Desqueyroux of Mauriac.

It had been pleasant in a way settling down with Rosalind and living as we used to do; but up to the last days she was so terribly uncomfortable that I was always worrying about her, and these households with her can never be permanent. She is closer to me than either of my other children.

My letters from Wellfleet at this time are a journal of these days. [These letters to Elena are found in Appendix A.]

WESTERN EUROPE IN 1963–1964

London: "Lapsing Back
into the Past"

I flew from Boston to London in five hours—very smooth
and agreeable, and they give you free drinks; but you have
hardly dozed off after dinner than you wake up to see the
dawn and hear an announcement that you are about to
land. And afterwards your time sense is so upset that it
takes you several days to get used to it. You are tired when
you first arrive, having hardly had any sleep, but the morning is well advanced, so you don't find it easy to sleep, and
I became very nervous and out of gear. I kept lapsing back
into the past—1908, when I went to Maskelyne's Temple
of Mystery on Regent St. and bought my first set of linking
rings somewhere near—how I visited Harry Stanley's
magic "studio" and purchased some of his devices; the Hyde
Park Hotel in 1945, at the end of the war, when, with a
terrible attack of gout and in uniform, I limped up and
down the front steps hardly able to get around—it seemed
chronologically wrong that I should have been so incapacitated then, but that now, thanks to Zetzel's medication,
I should be almost free from gout; Knightsbridge, Mamaine
in Cheshem St. or Place—I saw Celia, she would meet
me for tea in the big lounge at the Hyde Park Hotel, just

as Mamaine used to do, and it seems to me that since M.'s death, she has got to be more like Mamaine, with whom she says she constantly identifies herself; Half Moon St., which now seems more respectable, where I felt myself walking in uniform and being shown the way back by that good-natured whore; the Charing Cross Road, which I'd frequented since 1914; the Basil St. Hotel, now very run-down and about to be demolished, disproportionately expensive in consequence—this made my earlier stays there with Elena and Helen seem now very far in the past and its deteriorated familiar features uncomfortable. All this time, I was lazy and sleepy, and it was as if my senses were half cut off. Previous visits, even at long intervals, had seemed to join themselves together and become a consequential experience which was not long and was still going on. Later on, when we visited Canterbury, I remembered how Dave Hamilton and I had made an excursion there, but by this time I had my bearings and was simply in present-day England again. Elena had just been in Frankfurt, visiting her Grunelius and Radowitz relatives, and she had had a similar illusion of having reverted to the past—she said she didn't know what age she was.

The situation at Johannisberg had been getting worse and worse. The house was now in Madeleine's name. Brat [Mumm] had had an affair with one of his secretaries. Madeleine had made a scene and fired all his secretaries, and Brat had left home and made a round of visits to his relatives, complaining to them all about Madeleine. But now, on account of their daughter's getting married, he was back in Johannisberg. Madeleine had been uncordial and unpleasant, and had tried to prevent Elena from seeing Brat alone, because she said she asked him questions that upset him; but she stayed in Frankfurt long enough to find out what the financial situation was and to arrange to sell her stock for, she thinks, twenty or thirty thousand dollars.

Some of Olili's things, which Elena is supposed to have, have disappeared. The Italian-American ex-detective [Joe Bazata] is still there, doing gardening and other odd jobs. He tried aggressive tactics with Elena—supposed she approved of James Baldwin and what those Negroes were doing. But she had sworn that she would not lose her temper.*

The Royal Academy exhibition of curiosities dug out from its storerooms: some Constable watercolors, a large bad and strange painting of a Biblical character possessed by a demon by somebody I had never heard of, rather uncharacteristic diploma pieces by well-known artists, Turner's palette. Queen Victoria's paintbox, the leather in which Reynolds posed his models, instructions to the Academy by Gainsborough as to just where his pictures were to be hung. It seemed amusing at first, then became stifling and unpleasant. A certain "fustiness," as Elena said, that hangs about painting in England. At its most claustrophobic in the Sloane Museum—but one feels it also even in the Tate. For the English, painting and sculpture are not exactly natural activities but adjuncts to the grandeur of noblemen's houses and important public buildings.

We spent an afternoon *in Suffolk with Angus Wilson* and his boyfriend Tony Garrett. They have a snug cozy little nest in the country in a little dark flint-covered house, surrounded by a partly wild garden, where roses and other flowers are still brightly blooming—one still alive white lily, of which they are very proud. The house is full of

* An American World War II veteran, Bazata was Madeleine's long-term guest at Johannisberg and, the Wilsons believed, her lover. In 1954, EW and he had almost come to blows when he paraded his neo-Nazi views (*The Fifties*).

stuffed birds, some of them under tall glasses, of the kind
they used to have in country inns, collected for decoration
by Angus. Excellent lunch of pheasant, "overcooked" potato chips, red wine and a special "sweet" made by Tony.

I made a point of going out there because the Kimballs
came from Rattlesden and Buxhall, the little villages south
of Bury St. Edmunds, which are close to where Angus
lives. Richard Kimball sailed from Ipswich on April 10,
1634. I found plenty of Kimbles and Kemballs in the local
telephone book, and in the entrance of the church at Buxhall marble plaques with the name Kemball, from one of
which it appeared that a Kimball had been church warden.
The country seemed remote and old-fashioned, relatively
undeveloped, and the day was overcast. The effect on me
was rather spooky. There was a legend about one of the
towns that a queer boy and girl had turned up there sometime in the remote past, and lived and died there—buried
in one of the churchyards? My ancestors, before turning
Puritan, must have worshipped in those little churches,
with the carved animals on the arms of the pews and, on
the ceilings, their "hammer beams" and their ranks of
wooden angels—a peculiarity, it seems, of this part of the
world—but that was now all so far away that I couldn't
and hardly wanted to make contact with it. I had a moment
at Bury St. Edmunds of thinking I might come back later
and spend a few days there at the large and apparently
well-kept-up "Angel," where Mr. Pickwick got into the
wrong room; but I felt that, after three centuries, this
would be depressing and futile.

After leaving Karl Miller's house, where we dined with
them and the Pritchetts, we went on to a party, at a Lord
Glenconnor's, for Cyril Connolly's 60th birthday. The
usual jam of people, all talking so loudly that any real
conversation was impossible unless one went, as I did, into

a little library. John Russell and his wife, Anthony Powell and his, John Betjeman (looking thinner) and his girl-friend, Sonia Orwell, Stephen Spender and any quantity of other people. Powell, whom I had imagined tall and languid, is a lively intent little Welshman, who began by letting me know that he had seen what I had written about him and hastened to add that people in America could sometimes see things more clearly than people over here where they were all so much closer to it; and he went on to talk eagerly about the sales of his books in America. I asked whether Widmerpool's financial disquisitions were authentic or double talk, and he assured me that they were perfectly accurate—he had got up the bank rate and all the rest.

I did not meet Cyril's wife that night, but Elena did, said she was pretty and looked like a Romney [painting]. We had lunch with them at the Ritz, met them in the downstairs bar, where they were drinking champagne and orange juice. Though Cyril had suggested the lunch at the Ritz, I had had a foreboding that I should have to pay, and when the check came, Elena attracted my attention to the fact that Cyril was letting it come to me. "I paid for the drinks," he said. Elena was very much annoyed with him, on account of his rudeness to her in hardly ever addressing a word to her or paying attention to what she said, but I think that this may partly have been due to embarrassment about making me pay for the lunch. He had also neglected to thank Elena for the case of Johannisberger wine she had sent him, and when I first called him up from London, he had explained at once that he had several times set out to write her a letter about it, but on account of his relations with Barbara, had been having "a poor man's breakdown." He has a queer mixture of lordly courtesy with boorishness and infantilism.

I asked him how Ian Fleming had taken his burlesque

in the *London Magazine*. It turned out that he knew
Fleming—I suppose, from Oxford—and he had invited
him and his wife to hear the burlesque read. The wife had
laughed, but Fleming had remained impassive, and at the
end had offered Cyril £100 for the manuscript—which
Cyril had immediately accepted. Cyril was obviously chagrined that Fleming had not been chagrined, even furious.
He said that he had thought it would expose him to
himself—his "adolescent fantasies"—humiliate him, dev-
astate him. Instead, he had behaved with Cyril like a whale
being nibbled at by a little fish. It seems to me that the
feeling of frustration and his envy of other writers who
have done more work and made more money is having the
effect on Cyril of making him overtly nasty about his friends
in a way I have not noticed before. Why go to all that
trouble to try to degrade Fleming? Why put poor old Guy
Burgess* into it? Why that personal burlesque on the
Spenders—Covetousness in the Deadly Sins series—in
which he tried to make Stephen ridiculous and either vi-
olated or pretended to violate the confidences of Natasha
about Stephen? He spoke of this and said that when Stephen had got wind of it, he had behaved as if he were
threatening to sue Cyril for libel. "He doesn't appear," he
said, as if this were justification. He must live more and
more in a little self-centered world, self-indulgent and
always managing to have a woman around to indulge
him—does not want to hear other people talk, pretends
polite but absent attention.

His wife's name is Deirdre, as in *Deirdre of the Sor-
rows*—and he explained to me that the mythology of
Deirdre and Cuchulain and the rest all came from the
North of Ireland before the Scots had overrun it. He had

* A British diplomat who had given secret information to the Soviet
Union, Burgess had just died in Moscow. He had a notoriously dissolute
private life.

named their daughter Cressida—a fairly unusual name, though he mentioned two or three girls of good family called Cressida. Cressida Connolly: it made two dactyls.

Compton Mackenzie: He had been in France to get away from the Edinburgh festival; his wife was in the hospital in London, apparently dying of cancer. He is now more bulky and stoop-shouldered, but still relatively brisk and alert. We had tea with him at the Claridge. He said jokingly that his principal ambition was to outlive Somerset Maugham, whom he obviously did not like—thought he was behaving abominably in bringing suit against his daughter and declaring he was not her father. This, Mackenzie said, was a delusion—he remembered her as a little girl and had no doubt she was Maugham's child. In the autobiography, pretendedly candid, of which installments had been printed in an American magazine, Maugham said not a word about boys, and that had been the whole trouble. He himself, Mackenzie said, had "had his cake and eaten it, too"—had lived long and enjoyed his life, and his books were still reprinted and read. He knew nothing about Anthony Powell, but the news of Durrell had reached him, and I gathered that he had at least looked into *The Alexandria Quartet*. About the novels of somebody, he said that when he was reading them, he didn't believe them. Even a fantasy had to be consistent—you had to be convinced it was true. Longevity and finishing his autobiography— in which he sometimes likes to show off his phenomenal memory at the expense of boring the reader—are evidently now his great stimulus to living. His cavalier courtesy is very pleasant.*

* It was fifty years since EW first read Mackenzie's novels at Princeton. A long exchange with Mackenzie is recorded in *The Fifties*, where both are critical of Maugham, in EW's view a pretentious middlebrow. Wilson was generous to Mackenzie, an unaffected popular writer with

---

Add to Compton Mackenzie: He told us that during the war, when the old Kennedy was ambassador here, he used to sit around with him drinking champagne and talking about how they could see no future for England. It was not true at all that Kennedy had recommended the United States' taking the country over.

Wystan Auden was in England on his way to the States. He gave us lunch at the Café Royal—the only place, he said, which was still the same. In England and just coming from Austria, he seemed a little different from the way he does in New York. When he called me up on the phone, he said, "Welcome to Limey!" He looks, as Elena says, like something which ought to be growing in the middle of a forest—this reminded me of his passion for Tolkien. Conversation not particularly inspired. It threw us off our former relationship to meet for the first time in England. He is doing an anthology of minor nineteenth-century poets for an American paperback series, and we talked about that. We disagree about Francis Thompson, whom I still very much admire but whom he, having just reread him, dislikes as much as ever. I noticed that he is likely to be put off by poets who are lyrical about women—Keats as well as Thompson; and I suppose that the religious emotion of Thompson also seems to him overwrought and gushing. In getting his things from the cloakroom, he relapsed into being entirely English. On those stopovers in London, he always stays with Spender, whom he still has completely nonplussed. Stephen, somebody told me, occasionally makes little digs at him but is otherwise overcome by him.

---

the vigor of the Edwardians; he speculated that, as a combination of "the actor, the American, and the Scotsman," Mackenzie was always a bit alienated within the British literary scene.

Oct. 24–26. Visit to Oxford: We spent the two nights we were there at the Berlins': large comfortable old house with servants, many pictures and lots of books—in its humanity, international culture and social cosmopolitanism, it must be unique in Oxford. Aline presides with great tact and amiability. She has perfectly adapted herself to England, but she seems quite often to go to France to escape from that almost exclusively masculine world, and in Paris, she told Elena, is likely to see nobody but women. Very quiet, pleasing and restful after the Basil St. Hotel and London: gardens, well-kept grounds, a gazebo, a black retriever who had grown so fat that they had had to put him on a diet. I said that the disposition of dogs was determined by the character of their masters, and Isaiah, who had never thought of this and who obviously had had no acquaintance with dogs, including the household retriever, said that he must study his disposition with a view to getting light on their own.

He had come to see us in London during the week when Aline was in Paris, arriving at a little later than 10:50 in the morning and staying till half past 12, and talking almost uninterruptedly. I find this very fatiguing. On this occasion, we had to have lunch with somebody and later in the day to see somebody else, and had a hard time breaking away from him. He won't, in these situations where the competition is easily overpowered and he can get the bit in his teeth, allow anyone else to talk: you have to cut down through his continuous flow determinedly, loudly and emphatically, and he will soon snatch the ball away from you by not waiting for you to finish but seizing on some new association of ideas to go off on some new line of thought. Like all professional raconteurs, talkers, he wears you out by his constant demands on you to agree, to approve, to laugh. But at home, with Aline presiding, he does not behave like this. He manages to be witty and knowing without monopolizing the conversation. I wonder whether this restraint does not have a repressive effect, so that, when Aline is away, he relieves himself by turning on the torrent unrestrainedly as he did when he came to see us. It may be, too, that, now married and living in relative luxury, he misses the relatively monastic life of All Souls. (Though he has moved his books to Headington, he still keeps his rooms at the college.) Hence perhaps his excursions to Harvard, where—except when Aline is there and he lives at the Ritz—he occupies rooms in one of the houses.

At Oxford, among the trees and the gardens of Headington House, I was impressed even more than in London by *the difference between the European autumn and ours*. Ours is so much more dramatic: sudden frosts, holocausts of foliage, clear cold stimulating days and blissful long interludes of Indian summer. Here the little leaves simply grow faded and lie inconspicuously yellow—no bright lemon and gold as with us. The grass still remains green, the flowers go on blooming, but not vividly, not sharply, like our zinnias and dahlias. A certain dimness, compared with our air, even when the sun is shining. To live in this atmosphere would impose a different mood than ours, and I shall not be here long enough to adapt myself to it.

We went to the Ashmolean Museum to see the Guedalla collection of Beerbohm drawings—sixty of them. The originals are much more impressive than the imperfect reproductions in the albums. One feels when one sees them as he made them, with the original size and color, a quite formidable vitality and power—of "significant form" as well as of something like passion in the depiction of personalities. He has sometimes been carried away by the form-producing imagination as he never is in his prose. The figures, in being distorted, become not monsters but wonderful inspired shapes. I am sorry that I did not see these drawings before writing my article in *Encounter*.

John Wain: He has just moved to Oxford, and we lunched with him at the Mitre. He was something of a surprise. Instead of the lean and sallow, cantankerous and ailing "angry young man" just liquidating his first marriage who came to see us in T'ville, we found a rosy-cheeked healthy young married man, the father of two new children by his second wife, a Welsh girl who has interested him in Wales and filled him with enthusiasm for the Welsh—there is in Wales, he says, no question of accent. He says that he feels so much the solid householder that he thinks he ought to regale his guests with a glass of the best port—but he hasn't got the port.

At 6, we went to Max Hayward's and afterwards to dinner in hall at St. Anthony's. Max seems to be better dressed and discarding his *côté* Raskolnikov. Both he and John seem to be settling down, after seeing so much of the world, to the security of the Oxford "establishment." John Wain seems partly to have dropped his provincial accent, and Max now talks more like someone like Sylvester Gates. It was "guest night" at St. Anthony's, so ladies were admitted to "hall." The dinner was a not so bad regular English dinner; the people sat close together at table, and the conversation was deafening. Across the table from us, at the end, sat the first Oxford woman fellow of a man's college. They evidently specialize in Russian studies. Ronald Hingley, who wrote the book on Chekhov, sat next to me at table. I did not think he was terribly bright. He is now translating Chekhov. After complaining that Constance Garnett had evidently not read her translations to a Russian holding the text, I assumed that he would have his own translations checked by a Russian. Oh, no: he wouldn't let a Russian go near it! They only told you what they thought you wanted to hear. He had gone from classics to Russian; had been in Russia twice. But I thought he was going to Russia in a characteristic traditional English way—like their old principle of laying it down that modern Greece had nothing to do with ancient Greece and that it was infra dig to go there or be interested in it, and their old habit of teaching French "according to the English method" and pronouncing it as if it were English.

Paris Without Glamour

On the 26th, *we flew to Paris*— both of us with bad colds. As often happens with our indispositions, Elena came down with hers just as I was getting over mine, and hers was considerably worse. The hotel Aline had recommended and to which it turned out she had recommended us was small but very clean and comfortable and not too expensive—it seemed wonderful, after the Basil St.—and we have taken two rooms and a bath, and settled down here for the winter. It has been taken over by the Ritz and is just behind its back entrance, on the rue Cambon—Hôtel de Castille.

Paris, I find, has no longer much glamour for me. In some ways it seems quite commonplace. After the war, one felt that Europe was wrecked, and this gave it a certain tragic interest, but today a country like France seems to be becoming a part of the more and more uniform and increasingly Americanized world. I went one night to the Olympia music hall, thinking I was going to see a movie, and sat through the first half of a show that—filled in with mostly mediocre vaudeville acts—consisted of American-type entertainment of the coarsest and most raucous kind: a jazz orchestra; everybody doing the twist; women torch singers, tremendously applauded, who, never letting up on their nervous twist straps, would sing with the microphone in the right hand, like a piece of garden hose. When a guitarist accompanied the songstress, also with a micro- phone tube, it looked as if they were going to skip rope. The singers and the monologuist and the team of comics all deafened you and grated on you with their horrible voices. Helen arrived on Monday, and one afternoon we took her to Versailles: a gray day and a holiday with a flock of middle-class visitors. These French were small and dreary—you rarely nowadays see women dressed with chic—and they seemed so completely alien to the château, with its gardens and great galleries and huge portraits and gigantic historical episodes, that the latter had the ap- pearance of having become disregarded and shopworn, no longer looked upon by the people with any vital relation to them and shoved away behind museum barriers. The glo- rious past was no longer there, though remotely and un- really it hovered in the background in the anachronistic figure of de Gaulle. The excitement of my visits at the end of the First World War, when I stayed at the American University Club in the rue de Richelieu and went to the Guitry theater, or in 1922 (?) when Edna Millay was here and we had our little scene in the Bois de Boulogne, or in the autumn of 1935, on my way back from Russia, when I met Malraux and the Joyces, or even coming back with Elena and meeting her Russian relatives as well as seeing Mamaine when she had just been divorced from Koestler just before her death—I remembered all these but they had now fallen back into the map of a much flatter world, on which Boston and New York and Washington were other centers of more or less activity: France and England comparatively supine while Washington more energetic and aggressive. Prices in France are high, and there is a good deal of unemployment. A taxi driver explained to me that except in the late afternoon when people go home from work and the evening at theater time, the taxis have very little business: he showed me a line of cabs for which there was no demand, standing along the curb.

Paris seems a provincial capital, which Malraux tries to make seem more interesting by cleaning up the ancient monuments and encouraging the cultural life.

The bare tiled floor and the bare autumn light through the windows of the restaurant at Versailles reminded me of excursions to Contrexeville when we were stationed during the war at Vittel: the cold tiled floors, the red wine that warmed us at dinner, the smell of the cold tiled toilet.

On our way to the château from the restaurant, I walked around a little piece of park in order not to have to step up a high stone curbing, the kind of thing which, after eating, strains my heart. But it was shorter across this strip, and Helen took the lead by crossing it. Elena, as usual when she is with us both, couldn't make up her mind which of us to stick with, so walked halfway between us. The arrival of Helen, on this account, has somewhat upset the equilibrium of our relationships, and Helen, when we are all together, becomes rather sulky and haughty. Elena insists that, in self-defense—against what?—she has to pretend to be tough. The truth is that she does not want anybody to tell her to do anything. She lies in bed in the mornings writing endless letters to friends, which she illustrates with little drawings. When I said something about her handwriting, she explained that she had five different styles of writing, which she used for different purposes. As Marie-Claire said, "*Elle a beaucoup d'orgueil.*" But I myself am proud of her competence and self-confidence.

Canada, from here, does not seem so remote as I thought it might. French Canada in its present nationalistic phase seems to make indeed a point of intense vitality in the French-speaking world. For the first time since Louis XV let them down, the mother country is taking some interest in them. De Gaulle is making passes at them, and Malraux has been over to see them. We have seen a documentary film in which they are represented as a patriotic French colony, which ought to be regarded as an integral part of the French world. There is a short speech by ————, who aims, as it is explained, to be President of an independent French Canada, and the new big buildings of Montreal are exhibited with the apparent implication that they are the world of the French Canadians.

We took Helen to *La Reine Verte*, which sounded like an interesting novelty. It is amusing, but a huge piece of up-to-date chichi: *surréalisme*, Dürrenmatt, Cocteau, jazz, electronic music, *toute la boutique*. After the first shocks and mystifications, you learn that it purports to deal with *La Mort, l'Amour et l'Homme*. Death appears to be also Vegetation and Nature, and her role resembles those of Cocteau's Sphinx and of Dürrenmatt's Old Lady. The author or the producer evidently happened to get hold of Grandville's *Les Fleurs Animées* at the moment of planning the production, and the costumes are straight out of this, as well as insects and frogs and an elegant stylized watering pot. L'Homme seems to be also a vegetable god, who, after being killed by Nature-Death, has a resurrection at the end. Familiar sentimental music at the beginning and the end. At the close of the first act, a voice in the audience shouted something about a *"blague,"* which seemed to be a feeble attempt to make out of the occasion a first night of *Ernani* or *Le Sacre du Printemps*, but it was futile. At the present time it is impossible to be outrageous: all the dissonances and surprises have already been accepted.

Reading: After having had to read *so many mediocre books* in connection with the Civil War and Canada, it is a pleasure to get back for a while to *really well-written ones*: Smollett's *Travels through France and Italy*, Auden's excellent anthology of Walter de la Mare's poetry, Saintsbury's *Miscellaneous Essays*, a volume I had never seen which I picked up at Blackwell's in Oxford. Saintsbury at his best, in his middle period: 1892—a masterly essay on the differences between French and English literature and delightful little studies of minor French writers. Also, essays on the development of English prose, which contain the germ of his later long work on the history of English prose rhythm. If these essays were ever read by the *Partisan Review* boys and the other New York writers of the same breed, they would either not understand them or, if they did, be reduced to despair. Even Lionel Trilling cannot understand why I admire Saintsbury. * The essay on the contemporary English novel is not so satisfactory. He is stupidly supercilious about Howells and Henry James, and seems to think that the return to romantic fiction—which produced nothing lasting, unless Stevenson, whom in this department I can't accept as serious literature—[resulted in something other than] emphemeral rubbish.

I saw in Paris that Paul Claudel's *Le Soulier de Satin* [*The Satin Shoe*] was being done by the Barrault theater. Though I have always been repelled by the aspect of Clau-

* It was because of "his easy handling of biography and history, his expert analysis of the technique of writing, his unexpected and witty allusions, his warm and luminous glow and his inexhaustible curiosity," EW explains in *Classics and Commercials*, qualities characteristic of his own writing. He added that Saintsbury "was one of the best English *writers* of his time." His limitation, for Wilson, was that his "contacts were all with books instead of places and people."

del, I had a certain curiosity about him, and especially about this play, which Elena says she read at 20 and was very much influenced by. I have got about halfway through, and I don't think that I have ever disliked a book so much. There are occasional gleams of poetry, but the combination of rhetoric and religiosity, of effortfully *voulu* super-sexual or anti-sexual idealism, becomes for me absolutely insufferable. The hero and heroine are prevented from going to bed together by the fact that she is married, and they will enjoy a higher bliss through this self-denial. It turns out that what impressed Elena was that the heroine was safe from temptation because she had given her shoe to the Virgin—Elena says it had influenced her not to flinch from exposing herself to temptation.

Nelly de Vogüé, who does not like Claudel either but who stayed with him somewhere and sometime, says that he had quite a heavy accent—*"un paysan"*—was a sturdy and forceful man, and that his faith did not seem quite serious: he seemed to be amusing himself.

Yet some passages in *Le Soulier de Satin*—it does aim at a certain universal scope—made me feel again the *flimsiness of human life*. Surrounded by the void of the universe, we agitate ourselves, one sometimes feels, to very dubious purpose. Our little lives soon go out, and is it really at all surprising that in order to fulfill our immediate desires, we should put out other lives, send them off into the void? Eventually we shall go blank—what difference does it make if they do?

Le doux train-train de notre vie paisible et monotone [The sweet routine of our peaceful and monotonous life]. In Paris, at the Hôtel de Castille, we have already settled down to a life which resembles unexpectedly our life in Cambridge. I read and write and buy the English weeklies (plus *L'Express*), and in the evenings we see foreign films. Usually we dine here together, and we see very few people—mostly Elena's Russian relatives. The difference is that Elena does not have to work and that I do not drink so much. Altogether it is very pleasant.

It was some time before I was able to take account of *the things that made Paris seem so different*: abolition of animals, prostitutes driven off the streets, abandonment of the use of that strong-smelling petrol in the taxis, no pretty well-turned-out women even in the theaters (everybody seems poor—Nelly de Vogüé the only goodlooking soignée woman I have seen), disappearance of the Paris *Herald*. Pet'ka says that it has been the Germans and de Gaulle who have effected the reforms, and that the habit of dressing for official theaters was discouraged after the war by the attendance of American soldiers.

The Assassination of Kennedy

Elena much upset emotionally. We both had bad bronchial and sinus colds, and we sat dismally in the hotel rooms that weekend, surrounded by the ghastly newspapers. The whole thing is sickening: sordidness of the assassins, a schizoid boy who thought he was a Marxist rebel and a boastful crook who ran a small nightclub; ineptitude of the Dallas police; humiliating position of the American President who has to chase all over the country appealing for votes. I was surprised at the reaction in France and apparently in Europe generally—which showed how much they have been counting on us as represented by Kennedy. They don't know what the U.S. is like now, seem to have thought we were comfortable and safe. Kennedy, who has been doing his best to establish an enlightened administration and to work for tax reduction, civil rights for the Negroes and a peaceful settlement with Russia, falls a victim to what would once have been called the dregs but what now constitute large elements of American society —gangsters, delinquents, the baboons of the South. When the President was received in Dallas, according to Henry Brandon, there was a plane overhead with a streamer or something that said, "Coexistence is surrender," and pickets with signs protesting against his policy in regard to the Negroes. Somebody in the South said, "Whoever did it, I'm glad he got the nigger lover!" A little while before, the peace walkers [in Atlanta] whom Barbara Deming had joined were arrested and tortured with electric cattle prods when they refused to go with the police, who were afraid they were going to enter a Negro district. Afterwards, however, they were freed and allowed to distribute their leaflets.*

Scraping off the old crust of Paris, the cleaning of the buildings. On Sunday afternoon (December 1), we went for a walk in *Montmartre*—Place Pigalle, Place de Clichy. There were a good many people out, mostly rather small in stature, very drab and unlively—not at all unlike Moscow; the streets lined with 5-franc striptease joints, booths for *friandises*, and movies full of violence and vice. I saw two prostitutes lurking around the corner of an alley, afraid to show themselves on the pavement.

---

* A few months later, EW wrote to Dos Passos: "My first thought and that of many people was that the lunatic rightists had done it. What interest would Khrushchev or Castro have had in killing Kennedy? Stevenson and the Texan Johnson had already been attacked in Dallas, and Kennedy, I am told by Schlesinger, had been advised by Stevenson not to go." From the Paris *Express* he had learned of Oswald's poor record as a marksman, and of reports of a gunman at what would later be called the grassy knoll. Ruby's murder of Oswald in the police station made a conspiracy seem more likely, though Wilson was later less sure that it was "the lunatic rightists."

When I told Nicholas Nabokov that Paris now seemed stale and flat, he said that all Europe was like that.

Elena says that sometimes when she asks for things in shops, they say coldly, "*Ce n'est pas français.*" I haven't encountered this.

Helen writes from school in Switzerland that, since the murder of Kennedy, she has been homesick to talk to Americans. I feel sometimes—since seeing Don Stewart and Tom Matthews in London—that I need to talk to Americans, but I don't have any wish to go back. I was finding it a strain before I left, and it seems even more frightening now. Nicholas says that when he was last in New York he had a certain feeling of apprehension that he might not get away without being beaten up. A taxi driver had argued with him in a bullying way, trying to convert him to Seventh-Day Adventism.

Lee Oswald's violent acts have something in common with the recent riot in Princeton and the house-wrecking by the young people at the Long Island party. I talked to Tom Mendenhall about the Princeton riot, in which they had destroyed the president's and a lot of other property—the worst so far on record in an American college. He said, "Have you ever been in a riot?" and told me about one of the riots at Yale. Though he was master of one of the colleges, he had no authority at all. If you tried to say anything to restrain them, they would simply throw something at you.

Lorraine: World War I in Memory

Trip to the north: Nancy, etc. Dec. 9–13. We did not get off till after 2, so it was dark before we arrived, and we got into such a fog—as bad as the Cape—that it was hard for Elena to drive. There were signs all along the road RISQUE DE VERGLAS, but the *verglas* [ice] hadn't yet begun. The poplars along the road were full of dark mistletoe balls, so that they looked like Christmas trees *en grisaille* [painted in gray].

We stayed at the Grand Hôtel on the corner of the Place Stanislaus, had dinner at the Café Fog, also on the square. The Place in 1918 had not been paved and there had been attractive gardens; no vehicles but a few *carrosses* [horse-drawn carriages of the gentry]. Parking cars there, they told me, had at first been forbidden; but the need had become so great that they paved it and let them in, and now the whole square is filled with what you see, looking down from above, as a lined-up assemblage of cockroaches of green, blue and beige, with an occasional red, which considerably detracts from the harmonious effect of Héré's carefully planned buildings. The same thing where there is room in the Place de la Carrière.

Here and elsewhere, I felt quite at home with the people of Lorraine: dry and hardbitten but very amiable. I saw no pretty pink-cheeked girls such as I described in "Lieutenant Franklin." The wan, dark, lean, rather sallow faces seemed to show the effects of the war; the older women *renfrognées* [sullen]. The days were misty and dark, and the weather terribly cold; in the churches, our feet would be numb, and in the Soissons cathedral I began to shiver. But, having spent two winters in that part of the world, I was familiar with all this, too. As soon as we got into the region of darkness and poplars and mist, I began in imagination to smell the manure piles and presently we passed some real *fumiers*, and I remembered that the liquid kind was called *purin*.

The second day, Tuesday, we found that all the museums were closed, so we decided to go to Vittel. The drive was attractive, for the trees were all in *givre* [white frost] so that they looked like Christmas ornaments. The countryside was flat till one reached the foothills of the Vosges. We sometimes, on account of the mist, were unable to see anything at all, then it would partly clear, and we would get a view of the fields. The same little old villages of mortar and red tiled toofs, embedded like half-buried stones in the damp but hardening soil, abject at the foot of a meager hill or clustered in a common huddle—so different from our scattered independent farms—that is topped by a wretched neglected church. —One always feels a certain reluctance in returning to something in the distant past. I had had this feeling in Suffolk, when I returned to the towns from which the Kimballs had come, and I had it also here, as we approached Vittel, and I recognized the little towns strung along the road such as the one in which Roy Gamble painted the French soldiers in the doorway, and the "shopping center" of Mirecourt, where I bought my first *Petit Larousse*. We bicycled there several times, and I remembered how exciting it seemed when, on account of having to get back to the hospital, one had so little time there. I tried to identify the bridge and the bank of the river that I wrote about in my notes, but found there were a number of bridges. The curious names of the little towns, which I sometimes recognized: Moeurs, St. Gorgon, Charmes. Our struggles against a reluctance to be carried back into the past; one feels one ought to leave it behind. One is swimming back against the current.

I hardly recognized Vittel at first, could not even get my bearings in the layout of the hotels and the park. Which was the one where I spent most of the time: the Central? Which was the one from whose window I used every morning to see the pretty little village girl emerge from the doorway of some house in which she had apparently been cleaning? The Casino, where we had spent our first night and where I later saw Charlie Chaplin's *The Pawnbroker*, had been redone in the most horrible taste. I remembered the shops in the park, where the *librairie* was in which I bought the Lemarre Michelet, but had quite forgotten that they were part of the colonnade in which people took the waters, always bleak and empty during the war. The Hôtel de France was the only one that was open at that time of year—it has always been the town hotel and has nothing to do with the summer trade. I couldn't believe that it would still be the same but it was, and was run by the daughter of the old *propriétaire*, who had got into trouble with her husband when he unexpectedly came back from the army and found her in bed with one of our sergeants—with the result that the Hôtel de France was put off bounds. I told the present lady that I had known her mother, and she said that she had spoken English very well. There was a large well-equipped dining room at the back, but the old room at the front was very much the same—with a smaller table in the middle—as when we used to dine there in winter, usually with bad colds— I remember Roy Gamble's almost voiceless hoots of laughter—with the French family who had come out of Russia; and it opened into the same kitchen into which we used to go to get warm, with the same old but polished copper casseroles and the big old low and wide stove upon which the hot soup would be cooking. The WC seemed not to have changed in location or decoration. The floor had those ugly mosaic-type tiles that I noticed also in other places, which made it look like a slice of one of the meat-loaves with insets that you get in the local *charcuteries*. We used also to go there for hot baths and an hour or two of undisturbed sleep on the frowsy old beds with their *édre-dons*. I believe that the hot water had to be heated on the stove and brought up in long-necked *brocs*. The building is small and low—I had remembered it as being much larger. The street is at an angle from the little main street, with its shops and cafés, and I remember I was always desolated by the sight of the further extension of this main street going on into the bare winter country, and some building, blunt, forbidding and dreary, that stood like an obstacle of facelessness from which the only escape was to turn to the right to the Hôtel de France.

I asked about the château where the daughter of Eve Lavallière had lived, and the daughter of the old patronne told me that it had been sold, and, incorrectly, that the daughter was dead. It was St. Baslemont, in the direction of Darney, and she told us how to get there. We saw it easily from the road, alone and medieval on its hill, and, after taking a wrong road where it was difficult to turn around without falling into a steep orchard, we wound up the hill, coming first around a peaked medieval tower, which I thought must be the one that contained the *ou-bliette* [secret dungeon]. But when we reached the top and walked around to the front, we saw that the roof had fallen in and that the place was in complete ruin. The grilled gate was padlocked and rusted. The courtyard was full of chickens, and a huge hare looked out at us from a window in the second story. I was appalled: the place, forty-six years ago, already seemed sinister and outside the present. Today it seems even more so. I went up to the farmer who lived across the road and asked him whether it hadn't burned. *"Non: il s'est écroulé de lui-même* [It simply collapsed]." I said that it was sad to see it like that, and he agreed. No one lived there. *Oh, si, la propriétaire*, who had bought it from Mlle Lavallière. She lived in the corner tower which we had seen from the road, the only part left intact. She was still alive, Mlle Lavallière—in *la dernière maison a gauche.**

We went down the hill, trying several houses: the villages around there were the most primitive I have ever seen—they were in the Middle Ages, too—sunk in the dirt and manure. We finally found the last house on the left. It was just as low and mean as the others and partly dilapidated, but Elena noticed that the windows in the middle and the door had been painted white. I knocked on the door: *"Entrez!"* She was sitting at a largish worktable, with a paper in front of her, evidently writing. I again took her at first, as I had years ago in her Vesta Victoria phase, as perhaps a man, a little old man, with white straight hair, and a squarish face that seemed to me more wooden and longer. I asked whether she were Mlle Lavallière, and she replied that she was *"le fils* [the son] *de Mlle Lavallière."* I explained that she wouldn't remember, but that I had come to the château years before. She answered that this was possible—she had got up, and, instead of being bouncing and quick, as she had when she

---

* At Christmas in 1917, EW had paid a visit to an old château, on the edge of the dark woodland extending across the Rhine into the Black Forest. "David Hamilton and I found our way there through wastes of snow scrawled with bare bristling thickets," he recalled in *A Prelude.* "We went in through a grilled gate and saw a strange Mongoloid-looking servant who crossed the courtyard and did not notice us. We were received at the front door by a hospitable little gentleman, who was dapperly dressed in brown and who spoke English with a London accent. We had been told of a chatelaine, and I suspected that this host was a woman: she reminded me of Vesta Tilley, the impersonator of English Johnnies, once a favorite of the music halls. She presented us to a little woman, mildly pretty and very retiring. They were having a Christmas party for the children of the tiny village. There were presents. The local abbé was there. We had cakes and drank cassis, the insipid blackberry wine. The jolly host or hostess presided with her hands in her pockets." *"Elle n'est pas comme les autres,"* a local woman said to the Americans of the owner of the château.

was so much younger, she stood, as she had then, with her hands in her pockets, and shifting from one foot to the other. She was dressed in men's blue jeans and comfortable, I suppose, wool-lined slippers. I said, "*Mais vous êtes Mlle Lavallière!*" "*Je suis le fils de Mlle Lavallière, Jean Lavallière.*" I then tried to bring her back by telling her in English: "You used to speak very good English." "I have forgotten . . ." She answered in English, shrugging slightly and a little more feminine. I asked if I could ask my wife to come in a moment. "*Pour quoi faire?*" She said she was working. In the little room, in fact, there was really not much place for guests. This embarrassed me, and I said that it was sad to see the château like that. Yes: she had sold the château a number of years ago. I shook hands, and we said au revoir. As I left, she said strangely—and I didn't know what to answer: "*Je suis un pauvre type!*" [poor sod]. This experience shook me: the fact that I was intruding and—politely but firmly—had been *mis à la porte*, and the sinister and incredibly old château—the stronghold of Jeanne Hachette—abandoned at last, after the lesbian revels, when champagne bottles were thrown into the oubliette; that old being—I suppose, in her seventies—writing alone in that cell, in which I wondered whether she wasn't emulating the retirement and conversion of her mother. *

The hotel in Nancy was comfortable, but the dotty de-

---

* Her mother, Eve Lavallière, a distinguished actress, had married a director, been divorced, then had an affair with a man who was killed at the beginning of World War I. Eventually she became religious and abandoned the stage. In *A Prelude* EW explains that she was "buried in a coarse linen gown," her grave "marked by a plain wooden cross." Lavallière's one child, who inherited the château from her father, "was some sort of hermaphrodite" and, after an operation, legally married the "mildly pretty" woman whom Wilson and his friend had met in 1917.

sign of the wallpaper—long hairpin-like black lines on white that could not be identified as human figures or trees or animals—and the heavy, stiff and ugly red coverlets made it rather unpleasant to look at—especially for Elena. She says that this kind of thing, like the Casino in Vittel, represents a kind of French bad taste that was thought the latest thing in the twenties. We found very much the same thing in our room at Rheims.

The next morning we visited, in the Place Stanislaus, the Musée des Beaux Arts: mostly rather inferior examples of good end-of-the-century artists—though some fine drawings by Toulouse-Lautrec. The Callots, I learned, which in 1918 I had wanted to see so much when the musée was closed for fear of bombings, were all in the Musée Lorraine. We then drove to Lunéville. When I bicycled through here with John Andersen toward evening on one trip to Nancy, I had thought about Voltaire and Mme du Châtelet; but although there is an Avenue Marquise du Châtelet, I could not find out where she lived. *
The Château de Lunéville, originally the palace of the Duke of Lorraine, was given later to the Roi Stanislaus, the father-in-law of Louis XIV, when he had been forced to leave Poland. According to the tourist information, it had been described by Voltaire or somebody as *Le Petit Versailles*, but it had not really lasted long. There was a rift between the Duc de Lorraine and Stanislaus, and S. himself had not lasted long. The château today is desolating: so cold, with no heat, at this time of year, that only curiosity could keep us going. The curator hesitated to open the door, thinking, when Elena asked him if it was

---

* Gabrielle-Emilie du Châtelet (1706–49), the mathematician and physicist who translated Newton's *Principia* into French, had a lengthy liaison with Voltaire, living with him at her château in Lorraine under the tolerant eye of her husband, the Marquis.

cold, that we shouldn't be able to take it. It was even more depressing than Hollywood or the Confederate Museum in Richmond: bare broken thin-lathed floors that must once have been parquet, lots of pictures—portraits, landscapes, pictures of the château in its days of splendor—also somewhat battered and suffering from neglect, occasionally with holes through them—sometimes very curious. The château had for years been a garrison—there was a big photograph of the soldiers returning after the victory of the First World War—and it still had the look of a garrison. The formal garden was still kept up—the museum was a fairly new project. The wife of the curator took us to an eighteenth-century chapel, where plays had also been given: pretty and well designed, but also bare and abandoned; in the balcony the boards were giving. An odd medley of odd collections: stuffed birds, the grisly contents of Egyptian graves—the biggest and, I suppose, the most serious were the rooms of a military museum. —We had some lunch in a bistro across the road: it is still true that the food is palatable in even the cheapest restaurants. For the first time since I left Lorraine, I had two shots of *mirabelle*—how it used to pick us up after our bicycling trips and our walks! I was so cold and my feet hurt so— it was as if my arches were falling as they had at the time of the war—that I needed a warmer and stimulator, so I had black coffee and *mirabelle*, and on our further travels had coffee and brandy, reverting to the days when we had first arrived in France and had to share the French mess: in the morning the wedges of unbuttered black bread and black coffee with a good shot of brandy.

When we got back to Nancy, we went to the Musée Lorraine, a very fine little museum: George de La Tour, Bellange (one of Pet'ka's favorite minor artists), and what is, I suppose, the best collection of Callot—the reddish copper plates are wonderful, as one sees them beside the prints.* Also, a curious collection of old-fashioned pharmacy jars, surprisingly well designed and decorative.

The next morning we set out for Rheims, had lunch at Vitry-le-François and arrived when it was already getting dark. Not a very attractive journey: flat country, and mostly hidden by mist. Elena says that her mother was bored by Rheims (which in the town itself is always spelled Reims), because the country around it was so dull—also, I imagine, a lack of amusing friends. They knew some of the champagne people, such as the Polignacs, but don't seem to have been very close to them. There is nothing in Rheims except champagne and the cathedral—but the cathedral is especially remarkable and I don't think it is entirely fanciful to find that it has something in common with the champagne. It is an effervescent cathedral, cheerful and full of life: the non-diabolical animal gargoyles: ram, lion, cow, donkey, etc., all with an amiable appearance; the angels with spread wings; the smiling figures beside the front portals; the rows of kings high on the towers; the *rosaces* of rich stained glass; the memory of the crowning of kings. I wondered whether having been born at Rheims and having lived there till she was 7 years old had influenced E.'s qualities. I had always thought there was something champagne-like about her, and she is proud of her champagne background, always says that it is a nice thing to make because it is entirely gratuitous and only meant for pleasure. At dinner, she had me order the *vin de Champagne naturel* which doesn't sparkle. It can't be exported and can only be had in Rheims. Also, a *soufflé au Cointreau*. I don't much like soufflés but it was very well done. It is still true

* An old art dealer, fleeing the Germans in the winter of 1917–18, had sold EW some prints made from the original blocks of this seventeenth-century engraver, as well as a copy of his popular *La Tentation de Sainte-Antoine.* Callot's irony and objectivity helped to sustain young Wilson's morale.

that in any provincial city you can still get a very good dinner, and even at a place like that Lunéville tavern a meal that is at least palatable.

I had been telling Elena at Nancy about my experiences during the war, and on our trip to Rheims she told me about her childhood there. This expedition brought us closer together; we made love with delightful success. I was afraid the trip would bore her, but she was very much interested in everything, and not made grumpy by the difficult driving. Both their houses at Rheims had been bombed, but she tried to look up the address of the one in the city. The street numbers must have been changed because the present house at 17 was an obviously prewar house with a plaque on it that said that it had been the headquarters of Dwight D. Eisenhower. They had also had a country place, where they went in the summer, and an apartment in Paris, where they spent part of the winter. They spent September in Biarritz and the Christmas holidays in Johannisberg. E. used to walk along the canal and wish they were poor so that she could live on one of the canal boats. Her father, going back and forth between Germany and France, never thought of himself as an alien in Rheims, where he always spoke French to everybody. As Rhinelanders, his family did not care for Prussia, and his mother was so snooty about it that she refused an invitation from the Kaiser to attend some festivity in Berlin. What happened when the war came was a terrible shock. E.'s father and the other German businessmen in Rheims were arrested and made to walk through the streets on their way to be consigned to a concentration camp in Brest. His French cook, a man, insisted on walking beside him. The family at first did not know where he was. They went away to Switzerland. In the camp, he became very bitter against the French. For the first time in his life, E. thinks, he read a good deal—including Joyce—she still has his copy of *Ulysses*. Her mother moved heaven and earth to get him out and finally accomplished this through the King of Spain. He got out in July 1918 and at once enlisted in the German Army—he had some desk job behind the lines. E. believes that his relations with her mother were never the same after this long absence. She used to tease him about a woman friend who, she said, resembled a crocodile. E. adored her father and used to go with him to Baden-Baden and other smart places and dance and have the time of her life. —When they had had to leave Rheims, they got word that E.'s little Shetland pony had been wandering around the streets. The racehorses had been put in someone's care but the pony had evidently got away. They never knew what became of him. E.'s father, before his marriage, had once driven a four-in-hand from Rheims to Johannisberg.

That night in the hotel at Rheims I had two of those vivid circumstantial dreams that always mean I am not working enough. Toward morning, it was a narrative that involved a number of young people, evidently inspired by E.'s reminiscences. But before that, it was a strange play that seemed to me an inspiration. While I was still asleep, it never got further than a worldly and skeptical churchman who discovers that he has Jesus staying with him as a servant and astonishes a churchman friend by telling him about this and that he is now converted. In the dream, I became diverted into imagining that I had gone to a big secondhand bookstore to get Browning's "Bishop Blougram's Apology," to see how he had handled his bishop, and then became further diverted by asking for other books that I thought might throw some light on the subject. When I woke up from this, however, I went on elaborating the drama. The bishop has just preached a sermon in favor of nuclear weapons to use against Russia, and his friend is remonstrating with him. The friend is primarily a scholar, and the bishop asks him about the authenticity of those texts in which Jesus is made to predict his second coming and Judgment Day. He is convinced that the servant is Jesus: but then, when the friend has left, he decides that he is the Devil, then that he is a dangerous lunatic with designs on his life, and shoots him. It turns out that the young servant was simply a student of sociology doing a job of field work. The bishop has projected on him the fantasies of his own unhinged mind and bad conscience. I suppose that all this was stimulated by the Kennedy assassination, the churches and the impression made by Mlle Lavallière. When I told E. about it, she said that it was thoroughly Calvinist. It was still so animated in my mind as action that I didn't see that this was so, but I afterwards decided it was: the Devil as a substitute for God. It resembled the one-act play that I wrote in my youth about the man who is visited, as the gas jet burns low, by a friend who afterwards turns out to be dead, as well as the queer play I imagined in my fever when I was having measles at Red Bank in the twenties: the Southern woman who is visited by a Negro and finds that she cannot move. I think I must write this drama.

The next day we drove back to Paris, had lunch at Soissons and saw the cathedral, more severe, less delightful than Rheims. I found that I had a reluctance actually to be in these places that figured in the war: Soissons, Château-Thierry, etc. I thought of them as totally destroyed, the countryside all a battlefield. We saw one huge soldiers' cemetery.

Gossip of the Holiday Season

In Paris, we found Alexis Léger and his wife in the dining room of the Hôtel de Castille. The next evening they sat at the table next to ours and afterwards came up to our room. He is fleeing, he told us, from the Academy, who want to make him a member. Someone has gone to the Midi, where he lives, to interview him about it, and he has come to Paris. He sits with his back to the dining room, and his wife says that the only inconvenience of the hotel is its having only one entrance. He has evidently no respect for the Academy, says that there are now only five writers in it—all the rest are dukes, generals, etc. He told us about his experiences in receiving the Nobel Prize. It is the privilege of the literary prizeman to crown the Miss Sweden of the year. She turned out to be from Minnesota. The interpreter, having looked into Léger's work, was so dismayed by the prospect of translating him that he thought he couldn't function and disappeared. *"Je ne parle pas comme j'écris,"* said Léger.*

When I told him the story of St. Baslemont [where Jeanne-Jean Lavallière lived], he said, *"Ce n'est pas un conte de Villiers de l'Isle-Adam, mais de Barbey d'Aurevilly."*†

> Janet Flanner
> Has a crusty manner.
> She sits in a bar
> Like the St.-Lazare Gare.
> But from there she pounds out her wonderful pieces
> (And is good to all her nephews and nieces)
> In the writing of which she has no betters
> Which made us all her admiring debtors.

---

* Léger's dinner-table discourse, however, was full of quotations from his famous sea poems. Jennie Corbett, EW's mother's lifelong housekeeper, had the impression that he was "in love with the Atlantic Ocean" (Rosalind Wilson, *Near the Magician*).

† Barbey d'Aurevilly was the more somber of these two fin-de-siècle French poets and story writers. EW had taken the title of *Axel's Castle* from Villiers de l'Isle-Adam's poetic drama *Axel*.

Our visit with Janet Flanner to Noël Murphy at St.-Germain-en-Laye. She had been living in France forty years, and had the same dehydrated look as Marguerite Caetani. In her speech, only occasional American intonations and ways of expressing herself left. She was a daughter of the Havemeyer family who printed United States currency, and has a big old photograph in her bedroom of the house in what is now the West Fifties but what was then, apparently, still country estates. The Ingeborgs made the ink with which the U.S. bills were printed, and Sara Ingeborg married Gerald Murphy and Noël Havemeyer, Fred.

She picked us up in the town and drove us out. She told me we had met years ago in New York—at the Bishops' wedding party perhaps, where for the first time I met Esther Murphy. Noël looked at first disconcertingly like Gillray's caricatures of George III's queen, and Janet liked to refer to her as a witch, but then later she reminded me—as Elena said she did her, too—very much of Mary Meigs, though much older. Later, after lunch, when we were talking in the living room and she was sitting in the shadow of a corner, her face became animated, and one could see that she might once have been quite fascinating. On the way we passed Tressancourt, the Bishops' former château. It was very much what I had imagined, though not in the country but embedded in the town with a wall around it. It appalled me to think of the years when John had lived there, imprisoned, on Margaret's money. Noël told us that the boys, for some reason, were always made to wear gloves out of doors. They were not allowed to play in the yard at the side, on account of supposed snakes. Margaret had tried to play the chatelaine and established some slight solidarity with some English lady in town. She has now, Janet told me, had a stroke and is confined to a wheelchair. I thought of Allen Tate's story of sitting in a café with John on one of John's trips to Paris, and John's remarking in a musing way, after a drink or two, "I would like to be fucking a blonde."

She gave us a sumptuous luncheon: a big bottle of Lauson champagne, pâté de foie gras, venison and chestnut purée, excellent cheeses, and other things I have forgotten. Her companion, a Czech woman who had formerly been a pianist, ate with us, then presently afterwards disappeared. Janet seems to spend a good deal of time there, and says that all together they constitute "a household." We talked about Katharine and Andy White and their continual hospitalizations. Janet said they were hypochondriacs who were really sick. Once Katharine had said to Janet, "Let me show you these pictures of Andy." They turned out to be pictures of his insides. Janet had said, "They look exactly like him"—which she thought Andy did not take very well. When I talked about our visit to Gerald and Sara, there was a certain explosion of resentment. They told about the miseries of Esther's later years. Partly, they thought, on account of her being in such bad shape, Gerald would never see her during the time she was lost in New York, and he would not help her out with money when she was living in Paris and Noël and Janet were coming to her rescue. On one of her visits to New York, Janet had called up Gerald and more or less bawled him out. He said that he was sending Esther $100. Later, after Esther was dead, he sent a much larger sum to the Englishman who had written about her in *The New Statesman*. They insisted that the Murphys gave money to their regular hangers-on. "They had a court and they paid for it." Esther, with her plainness and her awkwardness, her capacity for holding the center of the floor with her partially improvised stories, could not be accommodated to the little opalescent sphere in which they maintained themselves.

Noël's place was a very old peasants' farm which she

had made extremely comfortable. She had a garden and a cow, which, as we left, was being artificially inseminated with the assistance of the Czech woman. —There were the books of an old-fashioned library which included a set of very minor Restoration dramatists and a complete translation of Taine, which no one could have looked into for decades. There was something rather ghostly and depressing about the atmosphere—both expatriate and lesbian— of the close *ménage*, with its pictures by Tchelitchew and others, in the corridor upstairs and all along the wall of the stairway, of all that set when they had been young and enjoying themselves. This visit was before the one to St. Baslemont, but it has since become associated in my mind with it, as well as with John Bishop at Tressancourt, and it has made me feel a kind of horror of one aspect of the oldness of France—people living in the country in these old châteaux. Nicholas Nabokov's place, too, when on our trip before this we went to lunch there.

Helen came back from school (Dec. 18) in very good health and spirits. (She has some red blotches on her face, which she blames on the food at Gstaad—all chocolate and mashed potatoes, she says—as we used to blame our pimples on the Pennsylvania Dutch food at Hill.) It has done her good to get away from home. She seems much more honest with us.

Two of her suitcases were lost in transit from Switzerland to Paris, and Elena has been frantic trying to retrieve them. It is like getting my cartons of books, sent by *The New Yorker*, delivered after we had been notified they were here, only a good deal more complicated and discouraging; telephonings to Switzerland, trips to the station, insolence and lies of the railroad people, demands to fill out *réclamations*. This kind of thing always makes one curse the frogs. We learn from the Swiss end that the bags, not having left on Helen's trains, were put on a later train the number of which they gave to Elena. At the French end, confusion and blankness: everybody she has talked to has told her a different story—they improvise assurances and excuses.

Helen sat near Elizabeth Taylor in a *confiserie* in Gstaad, to which she had come to arrange for selling a residence connected with her marriage to Fisher. Helen said that her conversation mostly consisted of two words: *crazy* and *balls*. Mike Nichols, who saw something of her in Rome, said that she is the most banal woman imaginable and talks about herself and her life exclusively in terms of movie magazines.

Poem by Helen, winter 1963–64

> This cold hits me below the belt
> cutting my breath and pinching my nose;
> It flows down upon me from a sun-smiling sky—
>   an icy liquid draught from some overturned
>   cup up there . . .
> It crackles to my right and left
> (stiffened branches of some ragged pines),
> and bounces back, sparkling on a pristine
>   coverlet.
>   I like it when the ground
>   Has covered its wrinkled face
>   and wears diamonds.
> This big freeze has silenced all
> its icy current deadens those without defences . . .
> But me, I've got 'em—
> and I can look out rejoicing in its melting realm,
> confident of spring.

The film *Cleopatra*, of which I saw the first half in Boston before I came over but the second half of which I couldn't stand to stay for, is so stupid, in such bad taste and so incoherent and senseless that, made at such tremendous expense, I thought at the time that it indicated some great emptiness and bankruptcy in American life.

Current French slang of the young people: *les zazous* are the *hipsters*; the *squares*, identified with the older generation, are *les croulants* [the crumbling ones], *les viocques* [barely alive], *les son et lumière* [the historical past]. The authors, in *Le Canard Enchaîné*, are *les zozoteurs*. Superlatives: *formid, sensas, bouledumé (bouleversant d'humanité)*. Little Marina Shuvalov [Schouvaloff] says that *vachement terrible* is a kind of equivalent for our *terrific*—also *bovine terrible*.

Pet'ka's discoveries of obscure artists and works: the German novelist Charles Sealsfield, who lived in the United States before the Civil War and wrote novels in German about it; Bellange, a contemporary of Callot, also from Nancy, who did curious engraving with an element of fantastic horror, less dry and precise than Callot—Pet'ka likes to say that some people like to think Callot a *petit maître*; Beckford; Hugo Wolf's one opera and Victor Hugo's drawings; Sukhovo-Kobylin perhaps more important than Chekhov; Henri Monnier; Corneille's early plays. * When he came back from his trip to England, he had just discovered Corvo and was quite

---

* EW liked such literary curiosities. He once thought of writing a book on William Beckford, eccentric dilettante, author of *History of the Caliph Vathek* (1786). He mentions the "biting" dialogues of Monnier in *The Bit Between My Teeth*. In *A Window on Russia* he recounts the career of Alexander Sukhovo-Kobylin, a turbid dramatist accused of murdering his mistress.

prickly about my lack of enthusiasm. I told him that Corvo had been all the rage. He read *Hadrian VII* and *The Quest for Corvo* and later agreed that he *was* paranoiac.

Christmas Eve party at Nicholas Nabokov's: It was, as Elena said, an obvious example of each having invited his own set of people—who sat on opposite sides of the room: Marie-Claire's friends and family all together, not at all of the artistic world; on the other side, Ustinovs, the son of Haieff, Ivan Nabokov and his mother and ourselves. Lots of champagne and vodka, fish kulabyaka and meat kulabyaka, tangerine salad with café parfait. Nicholas—an excellent and energetic host—gave me a little book about Pasternak and showed me poems of Akhmatova smuggled out of Russia and printed in Munich.

He told me about the White House dinner for Stravinsky, which he flew over in order to attend. He confirmed the rumor that it had not been a success. He said that it evidently represented a merger between two incompatible groups, the non-musical group being businessmen or financiers of some kind. Leonard Bernstein had been asked, whom Stravinsky loathes. One of the businessmen asked Stravinsky what he thought of all these other Russian composers in the Soviet Union: Shostakovich, etc. He replied that he had not been in the Soviet Union and knew so little about them that he was really unable to judge. Kennedy applauded this graceful evasion, but was apparently more interested in talking to the other non-musical guests. Stravinsky had a good deal of drink during dinner, and afterwards, in a somewhat blatant way, Arthur Schlesinger said to him, "Well, Mr. Stravinsky, how does it feel to be in the White House?" Stravinsky threw out his hands and announced, "It—feels—dronk!" Kennedy said to Arthur, "Go to your kennel."

Nicholas told Elena that he didn't belong anywhere and never had belonged anywhere, and that he was on a plane with a safety belt around him flying from one country to another.

Christmas Day. Much pleasanter than it is at home, where I usually get disagreeable at some point. The element of novelty improved it. E.'s cousin Massia and Auntie Maroussia came in the afternoon, and she polished them off before the other guests arrived. Marina and little Alexandra, the Guérards and their two daughters. Nicholas Nabokov came in for a moment before dinner. I thought the dinner went off very agreeably—though Elena was dissatisfied with the turkey, which consisted of slices of white meat served on a platter with chestnuts and fragments of dressing. Macklin had brought a jar of English cranberry jelly. I was glad not to have to struggle with carving the turkey and that we did not have to stuff ourselves with two kinds of potatoes and all the rest. The directrice had gone to the trouble of procuring an English plum pudding, which the young English waiter "brought on flaming." The five girls ate at another table, and Helen seemed to be handling the situation very well. She is making very rapid progress in getting on in colloquial French.

From time to time nowadays, in almost any connection, I tend to think that human works are futile because the people who create them must die. Why go to so much trouble, expend so much energy and thought and taste when we are so perishable ourselves and even the things we construct to outlast us may in the end be perishable, too. I have felt this particularly just now in *reading Cyril Connolly's essay on the rococo.*

Janet Flanner tells me about Jeanne Lavallière that she once met her years ago in Paris, that she was the most masculine-looking lesbian she had ever seen and not particularly attractive. She had a girlfriend named Fi-Fi, and she herself was called Jeanne-Jeanne—or Jean-Jean? She had had herself operated on to release a suppressed penis, registered herself as a man and legally married Fi-Fi.

Our trip to Switzerland, Jan. 11–14, to take Helen back to school. The fog was so heavy that I never saw a single mountain, and though the Palace Hotel at Montreux is right on the edge of the lake of Lausanne, one could hardly even see the lake. The hotel was palatial indeed: huge rooms with huge beds and armchairs and chaise longues; very Victorian, at the season, almost nobody there, a few bridge-playing elderly English ladies. We found Volodya Nabokov living, as Elena said, like a prince of the old regime.* He was more amiable and a more genial host than I had ever known him to be. The ready money had made all the difference. But they live as they have always lived, in modest enough rooms. He hunts butterflies in the summer, and in the winter they see almost nobody. Volodya, but not Vera, has a certain nostalgia for the States, he says, and is going back for a few weeks in March. I was surprised to find that what he would most like to do is get

* Vladimir Nabokov and Wilson had become friends in the forties, when Wilson was helping the novelist establish himself in the U.S. In the fifties they wrangled about Freud, Lenin, and the difference between Russian and English versification, disagreeing less amicably over *Doctor Zhivago*, which Nabokov called a penny-dreadful romance (*The Nabokov–Wilson Letters*, edited by Simon Karlinsky). When the novelist began living abroad on the income from *Lolita*, the two men were already somewhat estranged. A few months after this weekend Wilson had his first look at Nabokov's translation of Pushkin, finding it "full of flat writing, outlandish words, and awkward phrases." The next year he published the review that led to their bitter quarrel.

one of those sinecures of "writer in residence" in some American college. Their boy had come down with some trouble with his legs just when he was going to get a good part at La Scala, but he seems to have recovered now. He goes in for racing cars, which must consume a good deal of his father's income.

Volodya's German publisher, Ledig-Rowohlt, was there, with his pretty redheaded wife, very Celtic and rather French from having been educated in France, and I took the opportunity to do some business with him, selling him *Hecate County* on excellent terms. I did not know that he had been previously married to [the publisher] Feltrinelli's present wife, and said something about how awful she was—at which Volodya raised his eyebrows, I didn't then know why. I think I have told of Jason Epstein's mad admiration for Mme Ledig-Rowohlt and how, when Roger Straus and I had talked about this, he said that from the moment he saw her, she made him feel uneasy. Though Jewish, she survived in Germany, and is on this account under suspicion—perhaps unjustly—of having some-how collaborated. But it was all very merry and sparkling. Elena's cousin Bettina came to lunch—she was visiting her son in Montreux. I thought she was bored, though she said she wasn't. I noticed that she and Volodya were not getting on very swimmingly, but it turned out that she hadn't known who he was.

The weather and the drinking were getting me down, but I insisted on visiting the Château de Chillon, which gave my arthritis the *coup de grâce*. I was hardly able to get around the freezing and damp old place. I don't see how the unfortunate prisoner ever survived the winters in that dungeon, in which the windows had evidently no protection to keep out the rain and the snow. There is a memorial to Byron in the dungeon, and I found that two people I talked to thought he had been confined there. The château is a ghastly old place. There is a torture chamber only one room away from the refectory.

Volodya's sister came to dinner the last night—very handsome and with a proud face. She is a widow and worked for years in the Slovak library at Prague, which she says is the best in Europe. In her quiet and stately way, she teases Volodya from time to time.

On the way back, we spent a night in Zürich, which Elena likes. It is because it has the good German qualities—mature solidity, competence—the absence of which annoys her in Paris, without the bad qualities— arrogance, rudeness—that she so much dislikes in Germany. We went to a fine museum, where we saw an exhibition of Coptic art and a room full of Fuselis (he was born in Zürich). Excellent lighting and hanging and comfortable carpets, which you don't get in Paris, where not even the Louvre is lighted.

Parisian Winter

Hiver Parisien
Le jour blafard
Apporte le cafard.

[The gray and sullen day
Brings the blues.]

La Tomate, "Strip-Tease Permanent": Jan. 25. I went to the afternoon show. The audience consisted exclusively of rather heavy middle-aged men sitting in their overcoats. They sat there as silent and solemn as if they were attending a funeral. One man with thick lenses in the front row read the paper all the time except when the girls were on. I had not been allowed to go in at once when I arrived—I suppose because the stripper was just reaching the last stage; but in a few moments the prim thin woman who sold tickets told me: *"Allez."* The *entr'actes* between the numbers were very long. Someone behind the stage was playing the piano. The theater was small and sordid —rue Notre-Dame de Lorette. Finally, a voice on a loud-speaker: *"Je vous présente la charmante* ———.*"* A tall woman who posed to canned music. Occasionally she would smile mechanically, as if she remembered that she ought to. At the end, she gave the impression of having removed her last concealment and stood with her back to the audience, wagging her behind. Most of the strippers seemed to be thinking about something else. They might have been doing reducing exercises. They did not sing or dance as they did in New York burlesque, nor have them-selves called back to take off one more garment. The men applauded only feebly. They reminded me, by their sto-lidity, of the men I had seen on 14th St. [in 1926], who, however, had to applaud enough to get the girls back. The second performer never smiled at all. There was something rather awful about their thus displaying themselves to an audience with whom no rapport was established. The acts were all very brief. They simply struck poses like the pic-tures in the cheap magazines that show nudes. All of them stripped down to their "G-strings." During one of the in-termissions, you could hear a conversation going on behind the curtain between one of the girls and someone else. The third performer gave slight gestures of vitality. She had long black hair and toreador pants—the dashing Span-ish type. Then a darkened stage, with ominous music. A figure enters with an electric torch. Then she is seen in a black maillot that covered her from neck to feet. She lay on a couch and took from the pocket of a coat on a chair beside it—I suppose that it was meant to belong to a customer—a man's wallet and counted the bills in it. Then she stripped off the maillot. Then darkness again. The audience this time did not applaud at all. They could not be sure it was over. I left after six or seven numbers. The only one of these women who was at all attractive was a blonde, who was seen only in flashes, with darkness between, in each of which she held a pose in a further stage of undress. Finally, she was seen on the couch face down, with one foot kicked up behind; then, lying on her back, with her feet artistically pointing. Her breasts, as seen in this position, were not so gross as those of the rest. I tried, by clapping loudly, to encourage the applause for this, but did not have much success.

Sheilah Graham appeared and gave me her memoirs to read. They go on from where the other book left off. I have always been on her side, but I see now, from reading this MS, her coarse and unscrupulous side, which, I am told by Tom Curtiss, has made her unpopular with the film people. Though so anxious to improve her own status and to give her children the benefit of every advantage, she is as amoral as Moll Flanders. She tells, without the least embarrassment, of her pushing and needling in Hollywood. Her good qualities, however, also come out—in the way, for example, that both her humble first husband and her old suitor, now married, the Marquess of Donegal, have remained friendly with her. But with people who have slighted her, she is very vindictive. She has grown somewhat fatter and grosser even since I last saw her, and says that, on this account, she calls attention in her column to actresses who are getting fat. She was in pursuit, for interviews, of the Beatles and Burt Lancaster, who, I gather, declined to see her. She has any amount of brass when going after her prey.

Auntie Maroussia: On this visit, Elena has liked her better and found that she was somewhat cleverer than she had given her credit for. Though well over 80, and partly blind, she is able to walk from the Gare d'Orsay to our hotel. Elena treats her like a child and takes her to the movies, which she loves, and has long conversations with her, which bring out amusing memories. There had been a hussar who was crazy about her and who had resigned from the hussars because it was contrary to the code to make love to the wife of another hussar. But when, after three years, he finally declared himself, she knew that she could not yield, saying, "I am no Bathsheba." Massia, then a little girl, called in, *"Kto Batsheba?"* [Who's Bathsheba?] and the doctor called up to talk to her about her subnormal boy. It was in her own house, and he was taking her to some festivity, and she made a point of driving in an open sleigh. Her grandmother had once danced with Pushkin. She was wearing forget-me-nots (*vee zadydka*), and he had told her, *"C'est une précaution inutile."* She still sobs over the old regime. Elena couldn't make out why she so much disliked de Gaulle, then discovered it was because he had had some officers shot, on account of their OAS activities. She is jealous of the passionate interest that both her children take in the church, and says, *"On ne peut pas servir Dieu et Maman."* Kiril is a priest and a monk, who presides in a small Russian church—an admirable and able man, who has paid one visit to Russia; but his mother did not willingly accept this, because she wanted him to have children, and, if possible, to marry someone rich. It is a nuisance to Pet'ka and Massia to have to get their mother breakfast, and Elena asked why, since she was so sturdy, she could not get it herself. She learned that Auntie Maroussia had never in her life had to get her own breakfast, and that she did not know how to put on her stockings. Elena, after having her for a night at the hotel, when I

was away in England, says that her breasts are still surprisingly firm.

With Pet'ka and Auntie Maroussia, we went to call on
old friends of Elena's mother, *Mme Meunier*, the widow of
the chocolate magnate. It was like going back to the Proust
period. She lives in a huge old hotel, with a courtyard,
walled in from the street. She was remarkably "well preserved," still quite handsome. In her youth, she had always
spent her summers on the island of Anticosti, off the coast
of New Brunswick, which her father then owned. In Paris,
she had known all the celebrities, and went to considerable
trouble to get down her albums of Sem. She was able to
tell me who almost everybody was. They had known Sem,
who, she said, was charming. He was the son of a grocer
in Périgord—which accounts for that early Périgord album. But I don't think she has much discrimination, because she also said that Forain and James Gordon Bennett
were charming. An attractive period piece.

I tried to look up *Sem* in the Bibliothèque Nationale.
Remembering my experience of the early twenties, I went
with considerable misgivings—which turned out to be entirely justified. You have to get a pass to go in. When I
found the catalogue on a lower floor, the cards turned out
not to be typed but all written out in an antiquated hand.
There are sections of the shelves with dates—books published during certain years—and these, I am told, are filed
very inaccurately, so that books published in wrong years
get in. There was only one entry for Sem, an article on
the occasion of his death, about five pages in a volume
containing journalistic articles on other subjects. I told the
woman at the desk—these are all sour elderly parties—
that I wanted to see this book and also to look up Sem's
albums—I wanted a bibliography. *"Il faut choisir."* Can't

I see them both? "*Pas en même temps.*" In the reading room,
I had to fill out two slips, and when I presented them at
the desk, "*Comment voulez-vous que j'accepte des fiches écrites
au crayon?!*" I had to make them all out again in ink. She
gave me a card with a number, and told me—I may have
misunderstood but it may also have been due to malice,
since I had been showing dissatisfaction—to go up to the
second floor. This involved climbing a high marble staircase, and I got sidetracked in a Vigny exhibition, for which
I had to pay two francs. Then I walked through long marble
corridors till I finally found an elevator and ascended to
more marble corridors, where I found myself confronted
with the door of the print department. Here a young man
was more helpful. He examined one of my many slips and
told me I should go below. He called up the reading room
to check. I went down and found my numbered seat, to
which finally an old man with a cap and a red uniform
brought the only bit of information that the library could
supply about Sem. I then returned to the print department,
and the helpful young man informed me that there was
no bibliography of Sem. "*On le connait mais il y a très peu
sur lui.*" He looked up such albums as they had, but since
only one of these was dated, there was no way to find out
their dates. The collection is extremely inadequate. I have
all the ones they had, as well as a good many more.

Mary [McCarthy] afterwards told me that the Bibliothèque Nationale had completely put her to rout. She had
retreated in such a state of agitation that she had left her
jacket behind, and her husband had had to retrieve it. It
is ironic that the most literary country in the world should
have such an execrable library.

Tom Curtiss, an Irishman from New York, a relative of
Noel Annan's—has inherited money, does movies and

theaters for the Paris edition of the *Herald Tribune* and is planning a biography of George Jean Nathan. He lives at the Tour d'Argent and took us to dinner there. I remember how, in 1908, our parents dined at La Tour d'Argent and told us about the pressed duck next morning. It has evidently changed very much. The ground floor, Curtiss tells us, is a gastronomic museum, and the restaurant is now on the floor above. We had blini with real caviar, pressed duck and some particularly rich dessert. There was a long table with a party of what we took to be business-world young marrieds—who seemed exactly the sort of thing we had read about in *Les Stances à Sophie*, that remarkable, amusing book that describes so many features of contemporary Paris:* the bad air, for example, of which the author says that several babies would have to be asphyxiated before anything was done about it. —Elena and I have both been suffering from throat and nose infections all winter, and one wakes up in the morning half-stifled. We both had to resort to a doctor. When I told him that the air was bad in Paris, he said that it was indeed. The city was working on the problem, and as an experiment had exposed a rat to the fumes of the Place de l'Opéra: "*Il est mort au bout d'une heure* [It died after one hour]."

Leonor Fini and Lepri: Little two-floor apartment in a very old building on the top floor of one of those staircases that seem about to collapse at the inner edge—very different from their old commodious and romantic rooms in Rome. She was so changed that I shouldn't have recognized

---

* Taking its title from what EW called an "extremely dirty" guardsman's song, Christiane Rochefort's 1963 best seller—translated as *Cats Don't Care for Money*—saw the bourgeois world of Paris from the vantage point of a bohemian woman who speaks the argot of the streets and eventually rejects the role of a Deputy's wife to host a striptease show.

her: no longer opulent and handsome, but aging and somewhat shrunken. She was wearing high black boots.* Lepri
seemed changed less. There were innumerable cats, many
more than in Rome. A Pole is living with them—I thought
a likable man, who works on *Preuves* and said he knew
Reuel in Paris. They have a woman who works for them
and who served us lunch. I was glad to see them again—
the first time since I had been in Paris that I had had a
session with artists who expressed themselves and were at
ease with their art; but Elena was rather uncomfortable,
felt macabre tastes and vices in the background, the only
place we had been in Paris where she thought she wouldn't
want to take Helen—she had had a glimpse of Leonor's
bedroom, everything black, which had apparently made
her shudder. She said that Leonor, at the opposite end of
the small dining table, never took her eyes off her during
the whole of the lunch. It was one of the rare occasions
when I have seen Elena intimidated. She hardly took part
in the conversation. She admitted that Leonor always
talked with good sense and intelligently, and that they
couldn't have been *mieux élevés*.

We agreed about *8½* and *Il Gattopardo* [*The Leopard*].
The ball in the latter was *merveilleux*—it was long but
then balls *are* long. Leonor read Moravia less and less.
Chirico was no longer interesting (but already he had begun
to be boring when I was last in Rome, in '45). The walls
were covered with their pictures, including a portrait of

---

* In 1945 he had described the painter Fini (1908–   ), who exhibited
with the Surrealists in Paris in the mid-thirties, as "a handsome and
voluptuous, an extraordinarily attractive woman—with large dark
round eyes and abundant dark hair, which she arranges in a style that
is copied from the ladies in Venetian paintings." He added, "She is
quite natural and talks very well—with perfect freedom and ease—
about people and pictures" (*Europe Without Baedeker*). Fini was then
already living with the Marchese di Lepri, a diplomat who was learning
to paint under her tutelage.

Genet. I asked them what he was like, and was amused that these two almost professional creators of scandal were furious with Genet for his unscrupulous behavior with them. He had borrowed for some occasion a pair of old candelabra from Lepri and then never given them back; and he had precipitated a falling-out between Leonor and one of her richest clients. "He only does it," she said, "to make an impression on people, to make himself felt." She showed me her illustrations for Nerval's *Sylvie* and *Les Fleurs du Mal*. They both gave me booklets about their work and a leaflet by Genet about her—this last of a poetic obscurity that I was hardly able to penetrate. I was sorry not to see them again. I got used to them in Rome nineteen years ago, so they do not give me the creeps, and I feel with them more at home than with most of the people we have seen.

Folies-Pigalle. One of the nights when Elena was away to be with Helen for her birthday in Gstaad, I went to the Folies-Pigalle. It seemed to have the earliest show of any of these places—first performances at 9; but when I got there, I found it began at 10, and I went to a movie across the street, something with Fernandel, which seemed to me very funny. The woman who played Fernandel's wife, I thought, was excellent in her alternations between the two great aspects of French womanhood: the hard-boiled madame at the *caisse* and the charmer who is playing the game according to all the rules—facial expressions, intonations—of the tradition of French feminine appeal. I believe that one reason that, to a foreigner, the acting seems so good in France is that the French, in ordinary life, act so much more in conversation, so that they can simply reproduce what they actually do. —At the Folies, I was obsequiously welcomed. It was much larger and smarter than La Tomate, on an infinitely superior level.

The waiter wanted to seat me at a table along the wall right next to one of the girls of the house. There were a blonde and a brunette, neither of them badlooking, and they, too, on a relatively high level. I insisted on moving farther front, but the girl came and sat beside me. She was the brunette and said she came from Corsica. She had been in Paris only three years. Before that, she had been in Geneva, where business had apparently not been good; Geneva was *très sévère*. I talked to her as to anyone else; changes in Paris, where I came from, etc. She said that she had learned French and Italian at school, Corsican was something different. She was really, as they always say, "a dancer." She would snuggle against me and take my hand, but I paid no attention. At intervals, she would remember that she must make time with a prospective customer and put her hand on my knee, tell me her alleged first name. There were not many people there—she said that most of the crowd came for the later show; there were women as well as men, they all seemed to me perfectly decent, at least to the extent they, too, might have come out of *Les Stances à Sophie*. Some of them, I think, were Americans.

The show far surpassed La Tomate. There was not, from our point of view, any real striptease here either. The girls would appear in some enveloping garment, then discard it and appear quite naked. They went in this beyond anything I had seen before: their pubic hair had been shaved, and there was nothing but a little patch—I don't know how they kept them on—to cover the slit itself; one had a pink seal, like a rose. The first girls were slim and extremely pretty; later, there were the more ample blond kind, with prominent breasts and behinds. In one tableau, the girl was posturing in back of a large brown object that looked like a huge stuffed seal. But it turned out to be an abstract object, with vaguely phallic protuberances, which the girl put in juxtaposition to various parts of her body, finally swooning and curling on her back. In between there was a chorus of men and girls who did thumping and "twist"-like dances. I decided I had had enough, but the siren said I ought to stay to see the next tableau. If you sit at a table in these places, you have to buy a minimum of a bottle of champagne, and mine now being finished, I refused another bottle when the waiter brought it. The Corsican resumed her professional routine: "*Ça me ferait plaisir.*" But I sent the waiter away and told her that I would rather give her the money direct, and passed her a bill under the table. The next act was truly *formidable*: a nude riding pinion behind a man on a motorcycle. She was evidently representing the Spirit of the Motorcycle, because she would rise into the air and stretch out above the man, who from time to time lifted his face and kissed her on the thigh. I didn't notice how this was done. It would have amused me to see the whole show, but I didn't want to fight off the champagne and to have to keep the siren at bay. It was early enough to disentangle myself without struggling against too much resistance.

I saw a good deal of *Gilles Couture*, one of the ablest of the students in my Harvard seminar. When I had asked him what he was going to do, he told me that he was going back to Canada to write in French, adding that it might seem strange to want to contribute to such a minority literature; and I think that this was one of the indications—together with Morley Callaghan and Marie-Claire Blais—that led me to interest myself in Canada. Couture was a godsend in Paris, where I found myself somewhat dislocated in having to concentrate on Canada. He supplied me with information and books from the French Canadian library, and perhaps talked more freely than he would have at home. He was still all behind the

nationalist movement and seemed even ready to think that
the bombings had had some kind of valuable efficacy; but,
having spent some time, as a journalist, trying to explain
French Canada to the American press, he had become, as
one does in these situations, at last fatigued and disgusted
with the single-minded antagonism that is imposed by
working for this kind of cause. He came to France to get
away from it, and is now working on the Larousse encyclo-
pedia and as editor for the Algerian department of
Agence France-Presse. The French are not cordial to
French Canadians, and one Frenchman, he told me, said to
him that they'd perhaps better speak English because he
would probably not be able to understand Gilles's French. *

Later, Janet Flanner produced for me a young woman
named Mavis Gallant, who publishes stories in *The New
Yorker*. I have never known another Canadian like her.
Her father was English, she told me, and her mother from
Schleswig-Holstein. She is goodlooking—dark—and enormously clever and amusing to talk to. In speaking of the
importance of the Jews in the literary life of Canada, she
said she was not Jewish, but she looks as if she well might
be, and has that need to know all about everybody that one
finds in Isaiah Berlin and others. Though Protestant, she
was sent to school in a convent in order to learn French,
and is so completely bilingual that French Canadians take
her for French. Her parents must have separated, because
she told me that "Ringuet," the author of *Trente Arpents*
[*Thirty Acres*],† had been her mother's lover, that she had
read the book at an early age and that the author had had

---

* Couture would remember how kind Wilson was to him, introducing
  him to artists, later writing an unsolicited letter of recommendation
  for a job. It was Wilson who took him to the Beatles when they performed in Paris.
† An arpent is an old land measurement, evoking the life of the peasantry
  in Quebec. Ringuet was the pen name of Philippe Panneton (1895–
  1960).

so great a prestige for her that she perhaps couldn't judge it impartially.

She entertained me with an irreverent account of the authors of the *maisons seigneuriales*. Anne Hébert, who lives in Paris, had, she said, the emotional development of a child of nine. She had been kept at home and guarded by her father, who told her that she suffered from TB, up to the time when the doctor, who knew well that this was not true, threatened to take the matter into court. The mother had not left the manor for some incredible number of years and, as chatelaine, went around with a huge bunch of keys. One of Anne's brothers lived with the mother, and the other was homosexual and lived in a small room in town. Anne liked to intimate that there had been some sort of amorous relationship between herself and her cousin Saint-Denys-Garneau, but actually this was only dim imagining. Mavis agreed with me in feeling no enthusiasm for the writers of this group. Anne Hébert, when she was writing *Les Chambres de Bois*, had said that she was having some difficulty in finding a name for a man. "*Un mari ou un amant?*" asked Mavis. "*Un amant,*" Mlle Hébert had answered in a low and timid voice. "I suggested Bruno because I was in love at that time with an Italian called Bruno—and that's not a French Canadian name." We had been debating the curious question of where *Les Chambres de Bois* was supposed to take place. I thought French Canada, and she thought France. We decided that, like a number of French Canadian novels, it was not supposed to take place anywhere. This irritated Mavis Gallant, who writes stories which are squarely laid in Canada. She said that when you sat in on a session of French Canadian nationalists, you felt that nothing else existed in the world for them. She discovered not long ago that Jeanne Lapointe thought that Ireland was still under the head of England.

I brought her and Couture together. Elena thought he

bristled a little. She had been a reporter for the *Montreal Standard*, and when she told us that she had seen a good deal of Duplessis and rather liked him, he said, "You'll have to live that down!" She told me that she had met in Paris a French Canadian Dominican and had got along very well with him till he found she was really English, after which he would have nothing to do with her.

Gilles Couture has contributed another phrase to my collection of *derogatory names for the old: pas cotés dans* [not listed in] *L'Argus*. *L'Argus* is a paper which concerns itself exclusively with trafficking in used cars.

Elena had the theory that this invidious reference to anybody over about 45 is due to the shadow of de Gaulle; but Forgue of the Sorbonne, who edited Mencken's letters and is now doing a thesis about him, tells me that the young people in France today now feel themselves quite detached from the generation of their parents and have become insubordinate as young people have never been in France before. He says that in his own youth he would never have thought of addressing a professor; but that now the Sorbonne students do everything but *tutoyer* their instructors. The student strikes and demonstrations this winter.

In the case of Forgue and of Mme Berger, a young German Jewish woman who is working on Joyce at Bordeaux, it depressed me to see how much they were becoming like the types at home who are working for academic degrees. Forgue, when he came to the States— he was at Yale—first thought of doing O'Neill, but found that the subject was preëmpted, then Scott Fitzgerald, but this was taken care of, too. So he went on to Mencken, simply because his letters were available and hadn't been exploited yet. He was going to get up psychoanalysis in order to study Mencken's personality; had decided he was devoted to his mother, but had been contemptuous of his father, whom he had used as the model for the great American boob.

He said that *zozoteurs* for *les auteurs* involves the verb *zozoter*, which is now used for *zézayer* [to speak with a lisp], and perhaps—after Gide, Cocteau, Proust and all the rest—means that the writers are more or less all sissies. He does not approve of Étiemble, says that languages are always absorbing new elements and that you cannot censor these. I think myself that Étiemble's plan is absurd. You can't very well have a board which determines correct usage and imposes fines for violations on radio, TV and the press. It is amusing that Étiemble himself likes to address his readers as *"mes zozos."*

Erich Leinsdorf spent his short February vacation in Europe and looked us up from the Ritz. He had been worn to a frazzle by his work as conductor of the Boston Symphony—nervous and anxious and fatigued from the pressures of that part of the world. Besides the season in Boston, he has to make a coast-to-coast tour and spend most of the summer at Tanglewood. He says that in the long run he won't be able to stand these schedules, and that he wants to get out of Tanglewood, but isn't certain that he'll be able to do so. He has difficulty in dealing with the board that presides over the Boston Symphony. The state he is in is typical of the general state of things at home. He had come to Europe for release, but was still harried by the exactions he had left behind and evidently had not relaxed.

My dreams about Red Bank in Paris: I would think I had gone back to the old house, which after all had not been sold. Jenny [Corbett] was staying with her relatives and, though very old, could perhaps still be brought back. I made efforts to reach her on the telephone. There was always on a convenient corner a place where I could still buy some whisky if I could only move in and arrange with Jenny.

André Dupont-Sommer: I called him up when I cut Canada short. He came around to the hotel at once and talked for at least two hours. When I had seen him on my last trip, he seemed rather low in morale. He was under constant attack by the Church and had written me, asking me, if my book was translated, please not to mention that he was a *défroqué.* But now, as Nicholas Nabokov had told me, he had announced this fact himself, and he had been elected to the Academy—now possessed a green uniform and a sword—had been given Renan's chair in the Collège de France. "I tell you this," he said, "not to speak about myself, but it shows that the free spirit of criticism is still alive in France." He and Allegro have never met, and Dupont-Sommer would like to see him; he said that—*"ce qui n'est pas normal"*—he had been making all the advances, but that Allegro had not even acknowledged his paper on the Nahum *pesher.* He hopes to go to Jordan in the spring, is maintaining friendly relations with de Vaux—I must not repeat what he was telling me—it would be fatal to have him hostile. But why didn't he publish the manuscripts from Cave 11, so that other scholars could work on them, as Yale and the Hebrew University had the first batch of manuscripts? He is full of enthusiasm and energy, and old-fashioned dry ironic French humor. He answered all my questions at length in the most lucid and orderly fashion. When I asked him about the lunar calendar of the sect turning up in the researches on Masada, he proceeded to give me two alternate explanations—*"Deuxième explication—c'est le professeur qui parle"*—He talked slowly so that I should be sure to understand him. In speaking of the acceptance of his views on the part of the clerical scholars, he asserted, *"On a fait un progrès formidable!"*—though this progress had been gradual and relative. It reminded me of Freud's saying, on his arrival in London to take refuge from the Fascism of Vienna, that progress had been made since the Middle Ages, when they would have burnt him as well as his books, when he said—Dupont-Sommer—that even with the stranglehold that de Vaux had achieved on the scrolls, it was better than the Middle Ages, when any such manuscripts would have simply been destroyed.

A recent book on the Karaites,* about which I had asked him, was disappointing. He had had a Karaite in one of his courses—*"On ne trouve pas des Karaites partout"*—and he had cultivated his acquaintance. *"C'est mon cobaye* [guinea pig]"—by which I suppose he meant that he wanted to see what effect his Karaite researches would have on the student.

England: New Friends and Old

My trip to England, March 3–9: I flew and stayed at the Cadogan Hotel, old-fashioned like the Basil St., but a decided improvement on it. The first night I had dinner with the Gateses. Even so short a flight tires me, and it takes some time for me to get adjusted to a new place. I slept in the afternoon but even so was sleepy and muggy at the Gateses'.

I tried to call up Celia [Goodman], and learned from

---

* Founded at Baghdad in the eighth century, this heretical Jewish sect rejected the authority of the Talmud and had its own calendar and customs, much like the followers of the Teacher of Righteousness. In *Israel and the Dead Sea Scrolls* EW notes that Karaites still exist in the East.

her husband that she was in St. Mary's Hospital, Paddington. I found her in what was evidently a charity ward. She had been steadily losing weight, and she had so wasted away that it was thought she ought to be checked on—rather belatedly, it seemed to me. I felt very sorry for her. She said she had been terribly depressed. They had been X-raying her lung to see if she had TB, but she hadn't had any report yet. I thought of the letters that Mamaine had written me just before she died, and I knew that poor little Celia must be thinking about Mamaine. I felt very fond of her and sorry for her. She had been reading Sophocles in Greek. I remembered that she and Mamaine had taken some Greek lessons together and had read a little Homer. She was afraid that she might have to stay on, though they had told her she would be out on Friday, and asked me to call up when I got back from Manchester. When I did, she had been discharged. I called her at home; she had had no report.

Allegros: In the evening, I flew to Manchester and took a taxi to the Allegros' at Prestbury. It was good to get out into the country after Paris: a view of green hills from my window, a good breakfast with eggs and bacon in the morning. Mrs. Allegro extremely nice: sensible, goodlooking, no class accent or consciousness, nor any local accent I could notice. She and John seem fond of one another and have two children, a girl and boy, who, I am sure, will never, as with American professors' children, be sent to an analyst. Allegro, like John Wain, has become somewhat more like any other university character—more donnish, not quite so cockney. He told me that he had been much embittered on account of his experiences in connection with the scrolls, but that he was now able to laugh about it. Rowley had done his best to get rid of him, but he was prevented by his colleagues, who thought Rowley was so prejudiced that his judgment ought not to be trusted. But he was not given Rowley's chair, for which a Jewish scholar, an Ethiopia expert, was brought from Scotland. Allegro was relegated to the routine uninteresting work of teaching young prospective persons enough Hebrew to qualify them, and to a rudimentary course in theology. He says he tries to stimulate his students to think about the historical problems, but they are almost never interested. He says he "has no academic ambitions." He has written a play with a collaborator which deals with a situation analogous to that of the scrolls: someone finds an Aramaic version of "Thou art Peter," etc., which turns out to have nothing to do with Peter—depending on a different pun —and so to undermine the authority of the Roman Catholic Church, but is prevented from making it public on account of the harm it would do. Allegro writes also popular accounts of his Middle East expeditions, which have been carried out in the teeth of the determined opposition of de Vaux, who has tried to prevent him from obtaining a license to dig. He was extremely impatient of the fact that everybody was terrified of de Vaux, who did everything to make it impossible for anyone else to do any work on the scrolls—the attitude toward de Vaux of Dupont-Sommer bore this out. De Vaux had even made a fuss when Kuhn had published something about the copper scrolls before they had been taken apart. He was allowed to see only one side of them when they were exhibited in the museum, was not allowed to turn them around and had to photograph them from the back. He came to the correct conclusion, from reading the reverse of the outside layer, that they dealt with buried treasure. All this, of course, deplorable. The successor to Rowley has also tried to ban his dealing, in his courses, with the scrolls. He was amusing about the priests in the École Biblique in Jerusalem, who he said he rather envied, with all the time in the world and at their disposal an excellent library. "They have no families—all they have to do is read." We talked the whole evening and the whole of the next day up to the time when, late in the afternoon, they took me to the Cunliffes' at Didsbury.

Cunliffes: I found the Cunliffes living in a suburban house in a street not unlike the suburbs of Cambridge. It was a bad moment, I thought, to visit them. Mitzi was away in London to attend the opening of a building—presided over by the Duke of Edinburgh—which, as she said, was "full of her sculptures." And she had also to appear in court for having bought a £300 bracelet without paying the English tax on the ground that she was a citizen and resident of the United States. The trouble was, as I remember, that this exemption did not hold for articles above a certain value, and that Mitzi did not know this. Marc was obviously anxious, and politely said that my visit was helping by distracting his mind. When the next morning he saw the story on the back page of the *Guardian*, I felt that he was wincing at what he thought would be the reactions of his academic colleagues. "If I had read that," he said, "and knew nothing else about it, I'd think it was simply a spoiled rich girl who was trying to get away with something." She was obliged to pay a fairly large fine. He was left with the little boy, bright but rather badly brought up like an American child, who interrupted the conversations, and had developed a hacking cough, to which his father paid, I thought, strangely little attention but which instantly seemed to disappear when his mother came back. A woman came in for the dinners, but Marc had to get the breakfasts. He didn't like publicity, he said, but Mitzi got herself a good deal of it. She had done work for some of the new buildings in Manchester, and he supposed that it was the kind of thing that an artist had to do in order to get herself known. She called him up and talked at immense length—he evidently found it difficult to put an end to the conversation. She wanted him to send on for a TV program some building blocks she had designed, and packing these the next day and getting them off on a train put him to considerable trouble. But he is evidently proud of her and crazy about her. I can imagine the attitude of his colleagues. They don't see very much of them, he told me. Mitzi is fairly rich, and if you put yourself in the position of having to be invited to their houses, it was painful because they had to make such an effort and were always apologizing for things.

Marc comes from just outside Manchester and confronts it with a certain defiance. He has built up there the biggest American department and the most comprehensive American library in any British university. This in itself was of course audacious. We discussed academic behavior. He said that if one of the dons publishes a book that is well received, none of the others will comment on it. Why? "It's partly the habit of reticence and the idea that his success is his private affair—and partly malignance." He likes to wear bright and startling clothes. I saw him once at a party in Boston wearing a tie with a pattern of large strawberries. When I said that he could never wear that in Manchester, he replied that it was for that particular purpose he had bought it. During my visit, he was wearing bright red socks. In literary and historical matters, he has excellent judgment and taste, and it is as if for the first time he had been introduced by Mitzi to the glories of the sense. He has taken over her flamboyance and accepted without a qualm her extreme bad taste. The house is a riot of monstrosities, cheap knickknacks, and inappropriate combinations. A violet sofa in the entrance hall, the kind that has a seat all around it; a large stuffed leather pig in front of the grate; a collection of conch and other shells; framed autographs of Lincoln and Washington. He made a point of showing me their bedroom, which displays, on the wall back of the bed, the very bad paintings of a friend, and on the opposite wall a glass case containing "souvenirs" of all the places that they had ever visited together. On the bathroom wall there are eight large photographs showing every stage of their wedding and culminating in a picture of Mitzi in her nightgown and Marc in his pajama bottoms embracing amid grass and foliage.

We interrupted a conversation with one of his colleagues in American studies to see Mitzi perform on TV—with self-confidence and authority. The ornamental building blocks were shown—they had simple enough squiggles on them—and she was asked why these designs could not be stolen and sold by anybody. She explained with satisfaction and emphasis that she had had them copyrighted. She came back rather late the second evening—apologized for being a "non-hostess," but had to go to London again early the next morning to go out to see her daughters at school. She is likable, for all her flamboyance. He represents, it seems to me, the best kind of Englishman—the kind that comes from the provinces and does not live in London. He went to Oxford but has none of its mannerisms, speaks clear and uncorrupted English.

Manchester: When I had boarded the train in Paris, there was ahead of me a slender pale-haired blonde, simply but smartly dressed in blue, who looked at an empty seat between two others, which one of the men had encumbered with his things so that one hesitated to claim it, and shrugged in my direction. I assumed that she was not English; but when we drove into Manchester, I saw several slim blondes, also well dressed, and realized that this was a Manchester type. There were many goodlooking girls. Marc said that when summer came and they put on their summer dresses, there were many that looked perfectly beautiful. Strange that the women in Manchester should be so much more attractive than in Paris. It is a big ugly overpowering nineteenth-century city, like the industrial and commercial cities in Canada and in the United States.

I had lunch at the Midlands, the principal hotel, with a darling little Irish girl from Liverpool, who had discovered John Bishop and was doing a thesis on him. I got trapped in the French restaurant when I'm sure we should have done better in the English one—very heavy and ornate after Paris, huge menus, an *à la française* very Manchester. The little Moran had a real feeling for poetry of the Irish kind the Colums had. She made me feel that the current reviewers of verse didn't even know what poetry was.

London: The first night I was back, I went to the play made from *The Wings of the Dove*. Well adapted and well acted. Aunt Maud was brought to Italy and made an important character, who was able to hold the stage like Lady Bracknell in *The Importance of Being Earnest*. The adapter had kept, in the dialogue, as many of James's lines as he could, and it was remarkable how they went on the stage. Even the last scene between Kate and Densher, which was allowed to occupy the last act, was more effective than one could have expected.

The next day, Sunday, at midday, I went out to Gravesend to get my custom-made Punch and Judy figures. Old Tickner gave me biscuits and coffee, and charged me only "30 bob" for his beautifully made figures—Punch and Judy and the conventionalized baby such as one sees in the Cruikshank drawings.* He gave me a script which had been used when P & J was given for Queen Victoria at Sandringham and Buckingham Palace. I offered to buy it but he wouldn't let me—said he had been keeping it for

---

* George Cruikshank's drawings of the most popular London Punch show of his day were first published, with the show's dialogue, in 1828.

me. He had given me a swazzle* before. Later, in London, I got an excellent beadle from a Punch and magic dealer recommended by Tickner. It was the creation of another maker of P & J figures—a man named Wal Keat, who had died. Tickner admonished me, "Please don't tell I made these for you. I haven't made anything for him lately." The moment I mentioned Tickner, the man said, "When did you see him? He hasn't sent me anything lately." It was a very much rundown old shop in a basement beside London Bridge.

That evening, I took Natasha [Spender] to *The Servant,* a well-done but rather disgusting film about a weak young aristocrat dominated and ruined by his "man." We dined afterwards at the Café Royal. She said that she had known several such cases—English servants could make you feel so uncomfortable! Story about Raymond Chandler, who had come to London and seemed to be drinking himself to death. One night, at a dinner party, his friends had been afraid that he might commit suicide, but agreed that the prospect of seeing an attractive woman would give him a motive for living, so someone arranged to have lunch with him. Natasha and her friends took turns at this for several months, then got tired and handed him over to two other women—his California secretary and his English literary agent—who had more self-interested designs on him. He was in the habit of proposing marriage to any woman he happened to be drinking with, and eventually proposed to each of them in turn—both, unprecedentedly, accepted him. One went to Hollywood with him and then decided

---

* EW describes the swazzle as "two pieces of metal, bent out from one another in such a way as to leave a small channel between them, and fastened together by tape. It is held by the tongue to the roof of the mouth, and the performer, when he is doing Punch, speaks through it in a whistling squeal." He confesses never to have mastered this device (*Europe Without Baedeker*).

not to marry him, but he had made out a will in her favor, and when he died very soon after, she inherited, I gathered, everything.

I had evidence for the first time that Natasha is very intelligent. I had never heard her talk before but she now talked most amusingly. Stephen had made it up with Cyril, though Cyril still had the book; but Natasha, though not "furious" with him, simply felt that she did not want to see him. If you reproached him, he stopped you by the blackmailing method of telling you that you mustn't make him feel guilty. Mary [McCarthy] had already said to me that Sonia Orwell was a woman who wanted "to serve," who had now no adequate object for her service. Natasha said the same sort of thing about her. She had worked for Cyril for years, then married George Orwell to make him happy when it was evident that he would not last long. She had then married Michael Pitt-Rivers, whose homosexuality had already landed him in jail in connection with the Montagu case.* I told Natasha that Mary had said that she had married her third husband [Bowden Broadwater] in the hope of saving him from his homosexuality. Natasha said she could hardly believe this, and added that any woman who let herself in for a situation of this sort ought not to have any illusions. She said that Sonia was working at "wifemanship" in the country on a great estate, and I said the same was true with Mary, who must be bored by her social life with the Common Market. When I was leaving Mary in Paris, after one of our cocktail

---

* Before the reform of the homosexuality laws, Lord Montagu and his friends Pitt-Rivers and Peter Wildeblood had been prosecuted over an "act of indecency" with some Boy Scouts, apparently because Montagu was foolish enough to try to retrieve his camera, with which a Scout had absconded. Pitt-Rivers was sentenced to eighteen months. Sonia Orwell married him in 1958, in what a biographer of Orwell calls a gesture of solidarity, and they were divorced in 1965.

sessions, I told her that I hoped she was happier with West than she had been with me, and added laughing, "What a question to ask!" She answered, "No," but I assumed that this was also a joke. "I was too young," she said, and I answered that I had been too old.

The day I left London, Natasha invited me to lunch at the Café Royal: it was quite festive, as occasions are likely to seem when one is just taking a train or a boat. There were Richard Ellmann, the biographer of Joyce, and a Russian woman who shares an apartment with Salome Halpern—both of them interesting to talk to.*

Paris. The last afternoon and evening, before we left Paris for Rome, we entertained our favorite habitués: Gilles Couture, Sonia Orwell, Tom Curtiss and Ivan and Marina Schouvaloff.

Rome: "We All Had a Very Good Time"

Rome. I have always had a feeling of relief and liberation on coming from France to Italy. Rome is much more open and cheerful than Paris, and the weather has been most of the time delightful. But, as Lepri and Fini said, it has very much changed since the end of the war—full of cars with noisy horns and with the worst traffic tie-ups I have ever seen. They make very little effort to manage the traffic. In France, the suspension of motor vehicles when the pedestrians can cross the street is usually accomplished

---

* The woman was Anna Kallin, the highly competent director of talks for the BBC's Third Programme. Salome Halpern was a Georgian princess, who before the Revolution had been friends with Stravinsky and Mandelstam in St. Petersburg. She later married an Englishman, who was now dead.

like clockwork; but here, except occasionally on the more important streets, you just walk across in front of the cars, and they are compelled to stop for you. As in Paris, the old smell of the city, which I remember so well, is gone. It was made up, I suppose, of spaghetti, cheese, horses and refuse and poverty. There are no longer so many beggars, and I have seen no children urinating in the street.

At first, I could not seem to recognize things, and this made me rather uneasy, but I soon found my bearings again and felt at home in the Borghese Gardens, where I used to go so often—entering between the eagles—to read Silone or Moravia on a bench. I used to ride in the horse-drawn *vetture*, rattling over the stones and wishing Mamaine were with me.* Elena and I—before the children —went to museums and visited monuments together, but the memories we talked about were entirely different, and neither of us was much interested in the other's. In the Forum, I would be remembering how the prostitutes took on Negro soldiers in the grass-grown chambers of the Capitoline ruins, while E. would be remembering how bored she had been when her father had made her read aloud long passages from the German Baedeker. She would tell me about her and Olili's going to balls when they had been sightseeing all day—she didn't think much of Roman society; and I would talk about the mixture of the soldiers of different nationalities in 1945, when the Allied armies had taken over the running of Rome. There were moments

* Passing through these "stone gates with the modern eagles, in *The Forties* he evokes "an atmosphere, in the spring, of gaiety, leafage, light, bright color—a mixture of grandeur and informality—so much larger and more casual than Paris or London." He had come to Rome from London, where he had fallen in love with Mamaine Paget. He returned to England to ask her to marry him, but she declined, as she was already involved with Arthur Koestler.

which reminded me of the married couple in Mark Twain's "Life among the Microbes" fantasy.*

Visit to the museum in the Villa Borghese: The glorification of the human body that one no longer finds in art—the dazzling profusion of the Renaissance, an enchantment with all kinds of life—fowls, dolphins and wild beasts, as well as human beings, sphinxes and centaurs that are half and half, the hermaphrodite who combines the sexes. But then, when we went to see Sophia Loren in *Ieri Oggi e Domani* [Yesterday, Today, and Tomorrow], it occurred to me that the naked bodies of the films were a kind of substitute for that. Sophia Loren's opulent body is displayed to great effect—and she has become a very good actress.

Strange to hear them still singing *"Oi, Mari,"* which I had heard first in 1908, when a man had sung it in the steerage on the *König Albert.* The steerage was then at the back end of the ship, shut off by a fence from the rest of the deck, and we gathered at the barrier to look and listen. I imagine that we gave him money.

Dinner with Mario Praz: Elsa Morante was there. It seems to me that Mario has "mellowed." His face less suggests the *jettatura* [evil eye]; his expression is charming and kind—though he still can't help liking to dwell on other people's afflictions. He gave a description of Cecchi's daughter, who was suffering from some blighting disease —and Elsa Morante made a point of saying that she was

---

* In *3,000 Years Among the Microbes,* the earthling-turned-microbe named B. b. Bkshp. (evidently related to Twain's boyhood friend Tom Blankenship, and sometimes called Huck) and his wife, the microbe-woman who renames herself Catherine of Aragon, cannot communicate. In a slapstick somewhat like *Waiting for Godot,* he has her restate at various speeds a formula of her faith—resembling Christian Science—to see if he can make any sense of it.

the only interesting member of the family. He told me later, at Cecchi's—what I already knew—that he had a deformed foot, which had recently been made worse by "arthrosis," so that it was difficult for him to get around, and going to excavations and such activities were out of the question. "It's the misery of my life." I remembered how at Gull Pond, when visiting us, he had taken off his clothes, apparently without self-consciousness at displaying his clubfoot, and, like Byron, turned out to be a beautiful swimmer.

His extraordinary apartment is now completely packed with furniture, pictures, curios and objets d'art. Elena says it makes her uncomfortable. She says that Empire furniture needs big rooms and spaces between things, whereas here the sofas, chairs and tables are encrusted with other things. The walls are completely covered. He has a strange little collection of framed wax figures: Saint Sebastian, John Adams. On a later evening, he produced a little woman dancer, who moved around on a table and turned her head. The machinery was eighteenth-century, he explained, but the costume with hoopskirt was Victorian. Elena feels that it is morbid, a malady, collecting for collecting's sake. But the whole thing delights me, and I find Mario sympathetic in spite of his streak of malignity. Paolo Milano told me that when one of their friends had committed suicide, Mario had said, "One must attach oneself to objects." Darina Silone says that he does not like to entertain people because he is afraid of having things broken.

In any conventional sense, he doesn't have good taste. His taste is entirely his own, and—outside of Empire furniture—he only really likes what I call the "*Prazzesco.*"

In Doney's, I was recognized by an *American woman* from the picture of me on the paperback of *A Piece of My*

Mind. She was there with *her husband*, and they called us up the next day and invited us for a drink at the Flora. They were Americans of a familiar and depressing kind. They were evidently well-off almost to the point of being rich. They had no children, and he had no occupation. They had no settled home, but roamed dissatisfiedly from place to place, always hoping to find the place where they could perfectly enjoy themselves. Had spent a good deal of time at Palm Beach, where they stayed throughout the summer, living in the houses of friends, who were glad to have somebody living there and looking after things. They had lived near Kennedy—they hadn't known him any more than to say, "Good morning, Senator." The husband asked me whether I hadn't gone to Princeton, and said that he had nearly been sent, during the war, to the Princeton training camp, but the war had ended—"not to the college, of course." She had decided that the people at Palm Beach, where they had evidently lived for years and attended innumerable parties, were uncultivated and ignorant. She had told some women that she was reading Gibbon, and they didn't know what she meant. She was lean and middle-aged, with an affectionless unintelligent face. She had been analyzed for a time but didn't get anything out of it. They hadn't had a very good time in Europe. There was nothing much to Paris when you'd been to Maxim's and La Tour d'Argent. She was obviously a dedicated drinker and, when we saw her, was making an effort to restrain herself. Elena told me that she said to her, "Wouldn't it be fun to get plastered!" She called me up, very tight, in the evening and wanted to speak to Elena, who had gone to bed. She said, "You wouldn't let me talk to you. You're one of my gods!" They were leaving Rome the next morning, and I didn't envy her husband the job of getting her off.

————

Dinner with Arbasino, who came to see us in Wellfleet and wrote a long article about me in *L'Illustrazione*, in which he got everything wrong. He is very much on the make, and we do not particularly like him. Mario and Paolo Milano were there, and the actress France Valéry, who is fascinating, with big black eyes and tiny little hands. She does television impersonations of different kinds of women, who speak in different accents—something, I gathered, between Elaine May and Ruth Draper. I wish I could have heard her, but her television show is off. The noise in the restaurant was deafening, and the academic characters became involved in a long and passionate discussion in Italian about who ought to have some chair in, I think, the University of Padua. I told Paolo Milano about my struggles with the Bibliothèque Nationale and he asked me if I had tried to do anything with the library in Rome—"It's almost imaginary." These late Roman banquets are too much for me. You are invited for 8:30, and dinner doesn't get under way till well after 9. I get sleepy and drink to keep going, then am in bad shape the next day. I am not going to go to any more of these dinners.

Dinner at the Baldinis': I always everywhere have to meet the English professors, who are likely of late years to have gone in for American. Baldini is a good old boy, who has just translated the whole of Shakespeare into prose. Beard, spectacles, the reddest nose I have ever seen. Moravia was there, with the pretty little girlfriend, part English, for whom he had created much scandal and mirth by procuring some literary prize. The book had not yet been published, and apparently nobody but Moravia had read it. He lives in a modern apartment; it upsets him to live in palazzi, gets him out of tune with modern Rome, which is what he wants to write about. I can perfectly understand this.

The Baldinis inhabit the top floor of a palazzo: five flights of huge marble steps, rather arduous for me to climb.

Rosalind and Helen arrived, and we all had a very good time.* Rosalind has been timid about getting off, but Dr. Schwarz had encouraged her, and it did her a great deal of good. She lay in bed in the morning, and she and Helen sometimes had dinner in bed, and they read Ian Fleming with voracity. Rosalind already knew Olga Fersen from having stayed there when she was in Rome before. We were likely to have lunch, if the weather was good, sitting out of doors at one of the cafés of the Via Veneto. I bought the [Paris] *Herald Tribune* every day, to follow four of the comic strips—especially the Moon Maid (*Dick Tracy*), which enchanted me. We visited old Ostia and, with Darina Silone, Paolo Milano and a young American woman poet, a protégé of his, the Russian-Jewish cultural man at the embassy and his French wife, the Etruscan tombs at Cerveteri. Also, the catacombs—more easily navigable than they were when I last saw them in 1908—they now have electric light instead of merely candles, but still spooky and claustrophobic. We perhaps started off with too many tombs—for I also revisited the "cemetery" of the Church of the Cappuccini, with its posed skeletons and walls covered with patterns of bones. Helen and Elena went, but I did not take Rosalind.

I read *Il Gattopardo* and Orlando's *Ricordo di Lampedusa*. The novel is delightful—though a little slow reading for me, on account of the varied vocabulary and the Sicilian words and references. It really derives from the Huysmans–D'Annunzio period: brilliant descriptions with

---

* To Dos Passos EW wrote, "We are here on Helen's account, having still the old-fashioned idea that it is a part of the young person's education to have seen a little something of Italy."

exquisitely chosen words—a passage on a tremendous spaghetti dish which treats it as if it were a work of art, and another on the refreshments at the party, as if it were an account of a grand parade. Suspect traces of Proust. The fragment of the unfinished sequel, *Il Mattino di un Mezzadro* [A *Sharecropper's New Day*], carries on the social degeneration of Sicily, with a grasping climbing low-class family who sound like Faulkner's Snopeses. —How colorful and crepitant Italian literature always sounds after French.

The book became a great issue when it was a question of giving it some prize. Its opponents pointed out that the author was dead. The truth was that the professional writers, as someone said, "thought the money ought to stay in the family." Lampedusa had been just an amateur. Mondadori [the publisher] had rejected the book, explaining how it might be rewritten to turn it into an acceptable conventional novel. The attractiveness of *Il Gattopardo* is due partly to the fact that Lampedusa does none of the things that a professional novelist would do.

One morning, on just waking, when we had first arrived, I concocted the first lines of "By Dark Cocytus' Shore," and then finished it walking around and at a sidewalk café in the course of the day. I suppose that, in a much transposed and subterranean way, it was inspired by my yearning for Clelia Carroll.

It was enjoyably satisfactory to have *so many of the family together* and with no duties or tasks to tax us. It made me feel that I didn't see enough of the children. Elena was wonderful with Rosalind, made a point of being with her, taking her for walks in the Borghese Gardens and seeing her off when she left. Natalia Heseltine came down from Geneva and drove them to Assisi for a night. I didn't go with them, it was too fatiguing to make any more expeditions. Climbing up and down the steps of the Etruscan tombs, with a cane and with people being helpful, had been trying and put a crimp in my legs. I feel anyway that I have had it as far as sightseeing in Italy goes. I didn't even look in at the Sistine Chapel, which was haunted by everyone else.

I went with Darina up on the Janicolo to see a Pulcinella show that was still being performed after the one at the Villa Borghese, at the beginning of the school year, had stopped. Very inferior, almost nothing but knocking about, and it had no beginning or end: it would go back and pick itself up at some earlier point and go through the same scenes again. The Devil, as in England, got the worst of it. They had what must originally have been a crocodile disguised in what at first we took to be the skin of a wolf, which fastened its jaws on Pulcinella; but it turned out to be the movie dog-hero Lassie, the Italian version of whose name we had failed to understand.*

I had a snack and brandy at a refreshment stand and asked Darina whether she didn't want a brandy, too. At first she said no, then asked, "Would you feel less lonely if I kept you company?" She is one of these clever and handsome and fun-loving Irish women that I always get on with like a house afire, and who are likely, as I found when I saw her next, to prove in the long run demoralizing.

The Cecchis: They invited me, when the family were away in Assisi, to one of their (I think) Thursday at-homes. In order to use the elevator—another of these huge

---

* "I have been since an early age an amateur Punch-and-Judy operator, and have given the subject some study," EW writes in *Europe Without Baedeker*. He identified with Punch—with the man's outrageous integrity and sense of justice, his disreputable flirtations, his contest with the Devil.

And this pair of pavid lovers
    Swayed and beckoned like the reeds —
Gelid hands that need no glovers,
The fond glance that hardly hovers,
The faint garb that hardly covers
    The faint heart that hardly bleeds.

—Edmund Wilson

A stanza of "By Dark Cocytus' Shore" with Mary Meigs's illustration of the poem

palazzi—you have to put 20 lire in a slot. I had to borrow
it from the wife of the portière, but she was evidently used
to this. Cecchi is over seventy, also very nice, as most
Italians are, the senior English and American man, but
he can hardly speak English at all, and we did not do much
better in French. He said, "You are one of the very few
Americans who speak French." I tried to explain that this
was by no means true, but I don't think I got it across.
There was, however, a literary lawyer, who spoke excellent
English and talked to me about Lampedusa. I expressed
surprise that his wife, the baroness, should have been a
psychoanalyst, and he said that she had gone much further,
had also gone in for theosophy and was the international
head of the Theosophical Society. The Lampedusas had
had no children. They had adopted a young man of noble
family, who would be L.'s heir and who had supplied the
character of the nephew in the novel. The stimulus for
the novel itself had been the awarding of a literary prize
to a cousin and close friend of L.'s who had written a book
of poetry. The story was that L. had said to himself, If
So-and-so can get a prize for his mediocre poetry, I ought
to be able to do better!

On one of the last days before I left, I had tea with
Mario Praz. He explained to me that if you asked Romans
to tea, nobody ever came. He never asked them for drinks
because he was afraid of their breaking things or staining
the surfaces of his furniture with glasses. (He has taken
the precaution of putting a plastic cover on the table where
things are served.) So he asks people only to tea, and nobody
comes, and he doesn't have to bother. An old servant
brought in a wonderful cake, very fancy and complicated,
which I found she had made herself. He had had her for
many years—she was about his age, he said—and he was
fortunate because it would be impossible to get a younger

woman to cope with all that furniture and all those objets d'art. She spent two hours every morning dusting them. I asked him what would happen to them after his death. They would go to his daughter, he said, and he supposed she would sell them at auction. You couldn't, he said— this surprised me—get the municipality to buy them and install them in a museum.

After that, I went to *dinner at the Silones'*, where I found the family and Count Morra, whom I hadn't yet seen on this visit. We talked about Edith Wharton and Berenson, of both of whom he had seen a good deal. I made one of my tactless remarks—forgetting that he was himself supposed to be an illegitimate son of the king, I asked him whether he knew the story of Edith Wharton's being illegitimate—to which he more or less refrained from responding. Do such remarks come from unconscious malice? Elena says such gaffes are natural: you have it on your mind half-consciously that some subject must be avoided. I have always found him sympathetic. His English is extremely good, and he is intelligent and quietly witty. He has, it seems, after being a very good friend of Silone's, been made the object of one of his bans, because he voted in an election of some candidate of whom Silone disapproved (Darina says that Silone is always outlawing former friends and that he now will see very few people). When Darina had asked me whom I would like them to invite, and I had suggested Morra, I had felt a certain coldness on Silone's part.

Silone told some gruesome stories about recent developments in Italian Communism. The Vatican had established a department with a Jesuit at the head, to study the Communist movement. Presently the Communist paper had begun coming out with news about the Vatican which could only have been derived from an inside source. This source eventually proved to be the Jesuit at the head of the bureau. He had—finding no doubt in the Communist Party a dedication and discipline similar to those of the Jesuit order, devoted to an up-to-date cause—become converted to Communism and now left the Church and joined the Party. But the Party then changed its line; the Kremlin now wanted to enter into friendly relations with the Vatican, and the attacks on the Church must cease. The ex-Jesuit's new occupation was gone, and he disappeared from Rome. Some time afterwards, a Roman journalist, sitting in a café in Albania, heard a man at a neighboring table talking some other language with what was plainly an Italian accent. He spoke to him and asked him what he was doing there. The stranger replied that his name was ————, which the journalist of course recognized. He had gone—or been sent—into exile—"*Un pauvre homme! Albanie, le dernier des pays* [the least desirable of countries]"—where he made a very meager living lecturing to the Albanians and telling them how much better their lives were with the blessings of a Communist regime than the unfortunate Italians were with capitalism. Another story: Three or four Jesuits who had been sent as missionaries to China were segregated and brainwashed by the Communists and sent back to Italy as Communist missionaries. The Order had to send them to a monastery and brainwash them the other way.

It is evidently true, as Darina says—though one always suspects her of exaggerating—that Silone makes it difficult to invite people in (he won't have people who only speak English). So—because, she says, he likes us—she seizes the opportunity for hospitality and conviviality, and we had to restrain her repeatedly from asking a great many people. But the evening took a riotous turn. When I had arrived from my liquorless call on Mario, I had been in need of a drink, and on my way, after the first one, to wash my hands, I had asked Darina in the dining room to give me a substantial slug for the second. The result was that when I came back I found in the tall glass what Elena calls a "mahogany-colored" one. Darina said, "I put in a little water. Is that all right?" I ought to have drunk about a quarter of it. For dinner she had provided innumerable wines, and topped it off with some fine old port, which Elena said nobody but Helen lasted long enough to taste. More whisky after dinner. I fell down going to the toilet. They came out and picked me up. Elena said that Darina was reeling and Rosalind was crying, and that when we said goodnight, it was obvious that Silone was about to make her a terrible scene—which turned out the next day to have been the case: "Is that the way to treat your friends?!" etc. He hadn't spoken to her all day.

The next day Darina called us up, was urgent about wanting to see us. Elena had invited a Russian friend, and I said that I would meet Darina in the lobby, take her to the bar and let her pour out her emotion, then bring her to join Elena and her friend. The Russian lady, a Princess somebody, who had been married to an Italian, proved, to my surprise, quite stunning: handsome, made up as a beauty, and with admirable and well-displayed legs. She did costuming for the movies and had sometimes played small parts. English perfect and very smart. But I went to wait for Darina, who is always late and at the end of an hour had not shown up. I wanted to get my prints mailed, so went off to the Piazza Navone, arranging to meet the family at Le Toré Scaline (?). They arrived, we sat down to dinner, then Darina arrived a little later, full of apologies and protestations. She sat with us through dinner, since they have their dinner later, and wanted us to go home with them afterwards—obviously to break the ice of the strained situation with "S.," as she calls him. But I was leaving the next morning and begged off.

Elena and Helen, however, dined with them the next evening. Elena reported that Silone had told some of his excellent stories, and that Helen had been well able to take part in the conversation in French.

Milan. I had to stop there a night on my way to Budapest. Marissa Bulgaroni met me at the hotel. She had hurt her leg skiing; she had it in a cast and could hardly walk. Her use of her eyes, smiles and hands characteristic of one attractive kind of woman. At the American Express in Rome, I had seen a young girl who was being interviewed go through just the same *manière*. Marissa had to leave to give a lecture on American lit. After this, I went out for a short walk. Milano is the real Italian beehive—brisk, populated and purposive after Rome. The high spacious glassed-in galleria, with its shops and outside cafés—I wished that Elena could have seen it. The packed bookstores with their varied stock—especially Feltrinelli's, opposite the hotel—a really international place. I went as far as the cathedral, but did not go in and went back to meet the woman from Mondadori's, who turned out to be a dreadful creature, one of the most disagreeable characters I have ever encountered in the publishing business. She had grown up in England and seemed Jewish, sharper and more remorseless than an Italian. It was as if Mondadori had wanted to provide himself with an assistant as deadly as Feltrinelli's wife. She tried all sorts of bullyings and ruses to make me give them an option on the first volume of my journals. I refused and insisted on $2,000 for Italian rights to *Hecate County*, only giving an option on my next miscellaneous book.

Dinner at the Bulgaronis' at the very top, with balcony and view of a rather decrepit old building. Her husband is a quiet little man—I think an industrial chemist. Remembering her as the belle of the Salzburg seminar the winter that I lectured there, I had expected something more dashing. Another couple—the wife had been to Bryn Mawr. She had worked at Mondadori, and had written a novel about it, which Feltrinelli might publish. Nice young people—the Italians, in my experience, are the friendliest, most convivial people in Europe, the easiest to get along with. Marissa and her sister translated my Indian book and did it very well. They hope to translate *Hecate County*. Like so many others, she wants to get herself sent to America to study American lit.—mainly, I think, because she wants to go to America. No children.

The Milan municipality is Communist. I remembered the Communist demonstration that I saw in 1945.

WITHIN THE SOVIET EMPIRE:
HUNGARY IN 1964

Friendly Guides

Hungary. On April 9, I flew to Milan, the next morning flew to Budapest and arrived in the early afternoon. This flight was on the Hungarian line, Malév. On the plane, each passenger was presented with a Communist newspaper in Hungarian, which announced on the front page that "everywhere and at all times" Hungary and Russia must be friends. It was just after Khrushchev's visit. Nobody paid any attention to this paper—the only other passengers were three or four Hungarian men, who engaged in gay conversation with one of the stewardesses.

Inefficient red tape at the airport. Declaration of money brought into the country. They take away your passport and don't give it back for some time. In the waiting room, I found Charlotte Kretzoi, who helped me through the rest of the proceedings. She is a former pupil of László Országh, whose dictionaries I had been using, and is now teaching in his English department at Debrecen University. I had had some correspondence with him when he read the *New Yorker* article in which I had spoken of his dictionaries, and also with her. She had agreed to do Hungarian with me when I came to Budapest. She is a handsome woman,

though for me without sex appeal: rather tall, blue eyes
with dark discolorations under them, the result, I imagine,
of much study. Her features are sharp and positive—she
did not seem characteristically Hungarian, and she told
me that she had Baltic blood, part Germanic. She said that
she was considered "a bluestocking"—which is the same
thing in Hungarian, *kékharisnya*. She speaks English with
remarkable correctness in view of the fact that she has
learned it in Hungary and has only spent a few weeks in
England, with an entirely English pronunciation and certain formality and stiffness which I found at first a little
off-putting. When she didn't understand me—which was
fairly often—she would say, "I beg your pardon." We took
a taxi to the Hotel Gellért, and she had lunch with me
there. I asked her about Khrushchev's visit, and she said
that it was the current joke that he had come to cure his
jaundice—in Hungarian, *sárgaság*, yellowness—that is, to
consolidate his position in the West in order to effect his
break with China. Though fatigued, I was not sleepy, and
we went to the National Museum, which has an archaeological as well as other collections. Very curious to see
the Roman remains from Pannonia among the primitive
relics of the original inhabitants: they set up their civilization everywhere in such an impressive uniform way—
mosaic floors, statuettes, etc. A Jewish inscription in
Greek: "To the one God." Charlotte's husband is a paleontologist, a paleoanthropologist, and she knows quite a
lot about all this.

I went the next morning to *Háry János*, a special performance for children that began at 11 or half past in the
morning. Very amusing. The recording—which I have—
gives no idea of what a production is like. It is true, as
Leinsdorf says, that Kodály is the Hungarian Rimsky-
Korsakov. The opera is full of toys and fairy-tale tricks.

The moving of the house at the frontier barrier; the clock in which the hours are round shutters that open out, and from behind which appear little buglers and other military figures, with a parade on the balcony below of other mechanical figures; the two-headed eagle of the empire, which, when it is fed with corn, stretches down its neck. Kodály himself was there. At the end of the first intermission, he appeared for a moment in a box. At the applause, he stood up and modestly bowed: a frail distinguished-looking old gentleman (now over 80), with drooping eyelids and myopic eyes. It gratified me, as few things do, to see this respect paid an artist. He left before the lights went on at the end of the second act and did not come back again.

Someone complained to me later about *Háry János*—I think one of the semi-party men at Corvina [foreign language publishing house in Budapest]—that he found it unsatisfactory because there was no conflict. This is more or less true since Háry in his boastful fantasies has only to wave his sword to make Napoleon's army fall down helpless and conquers the heart of Marie-Louise—who divorces Napoleon when she finds he is a coward—without the slightest effort. But at the court there does come a conflict between Marie-Louise and the peasant fiancée, Örzse, who has been given the job of feeding the Napoleonic eagle.

Országh called me up, and we arranged to have lunch on Tuesday. Charlotte Kretzoi had not prepared me for him. She had said that he was "rather elephantine," and I had expected a heavy professor. But she had been thinking of his broad build and his dignified, leisurely way of walking. I waited for him in the Gellért lobby and presently found standing over me a man in a beret, well dressed in the Anglo-Saxon university fashion: light brown jacket and gray trousers with fine features and a good deal of charm, who said, "Dr. Livingston, I believe." He did not seem to me like a Hungarian, but like one of those polished and cultivated people from the German-speaking or Dutch countries. I wasn't surprised when he told me that one of his grandfathers had been German, and that he had grown up in Hungary just inside the border, where the center was Vienna not Budapest. He spoke English not merely well but with elegance and with the astonishing command that is so striking in his dictionaries of colloquial English and American—though he sometimes mixes the two in rather an incongruous way. His features are curiously feminine, though not in an effeminate way. He always lived with his mother till she recently died. His attitude toward the regime is one of calm and cool disdain, and I was surprised—as I had already been with Charlotte Kretzoi —at the freedom with which he expressed it. He said that he imagined I might be tired of having my meals at the Gellért, but his tone, referring to Ibusz, the Hungarian Intourist, indicated his instinctive distaste for any official agency. He took me to an old hotel—Victorian, as he said—which had formerly been called the Britannia but, since that had been thought too imperialistic, was called now I can't remember what. He remarked, implying, I thought, that I might have been happier there, that if I hadn't become enmeshed with Ibusz, I might have been staying in some such place. He ordered an excellent lunch with Balaton Riesling, and I noticed the good quality of his conversation with the waiter, in which he made the distinction between *Kérem* and *Kérek* [words for please— the former used when asking for something concrete, the latter for something more general], where most people seem simply to attach *Kérem* to an object.

I wanted to get a copy of Molnár's *Ördög* [*Devil*], which he was under the impression he had—though it turned out that he only had *Liliom*—and he took me to his apartment. He asked me what I thought of the people as I saw them in the streets. I said that I thought that, on the whole, they made an impression of being more or less bourgeois, and he explained that, nevertheless, they were not all "white-collar workers" but that many of them worked in factories. I said that I had come to feel lately that the people everywhere were becoming more and more alike. "When you see the place that I live in, you will see something that you won't see elsewhere. Nothing's been done to it for twenty years." It was an old house built around a court—not really much more ancient and unimproved than the one in which Fini and Lepri lived—in which even the tenants were obliged to pay an old woman in order to use the elevator, and they could only go up in it, not down—why, Országh didn't explain to me. The floor of this elevator seemed weak, and I should think they would have been afraid of its going through. The stairs, when we came down, were leaning so that you didn't see why they shouldn't collapse. His apartment was at the very top, two rooms and a little hallway; the toilet had a separate entrance, as is often true in Europe. The rooms were those of a bachelor—stuffed with books, a picture of his mother and a bottle of French brandy. All the housing is controlled by the state, and after his mother's death, it had not been easy for him to keep so many rooms. He had had to fight the authorities for months for the two rooms he now occupied and for which he told me with triumph he only paid the price of one. By getting a paper stating that his huge library had the value of a private museum (of which he was the keeper) he was let off with reduced rent.

The chief authority in Hungary on English, he was something of a privileged character. As we came in, he picked up the *Guardian* and some other foreign publications. I asked him whether it was possible to subscribe to them, and he said that it would be impossible for almost anybody else, but that he was privileged because he had to keep in touch with the language. I asked whether it was safe for me to write my diary, and he answered emphatically that it wasn't. They were likely to photograph it. And be careful about letters and telephone conversations. And be careful about where you talk. They have recorders. "It's not a person who listens, but a machine that takes down what you say." The cultural situation had been loosened up, but he was afraid that the pressure of China would have the effect of making Khrushchev "pull in the reins." It had only been a few months that it had been possible to get foreign papers in the big hotels. It was hard to get books from abroad, because the government wouldn't give them enough money for an adequate English and American library—"while they're building socialism or Communism or whatever it is." He had years ago taken a degree in a little college in Florida, and last fall had spent a couple of months in Washington and New York. When I told him that a good deal that was bad was going on in the United States, he said, "I know that what you're saying is true—there's a good deal of unemployment—but don't talk like that around here. They're told all the time in the Communist press that America is going to pieces, and they don't believe a word of it. They think that America is an earthly paradise—and if you tell them that kind of thing, they'll think that you're giving them the Party line"—and the implication was that they wouldn't want to have anything to do with me. When I asked him about getting a new arm for my glasses, he said not to take it to one of the state-run places: a privately owned one would do it more quickly and better. "I confess," he said, "that I don't know Russian"—and expressed his impatience with a language in which you had to decline the numerals. I didn't mention that Hungarian, too, has some rather peculiar features. He and one or two other people I talked to seemed to resent the Cyrillic alphabet, though, as I told him, the alphabet, now that the superfluous characters had been removed, was the only convenient feature of Russian.

I had very soon become aware that they did not want to hear *Russia or anything Russian* mentioned—even flinched at my calling attention to the Russian-derived words in Hungarian. In one case of my doing this, the young man I was speaking to said, "Slavic." They would simply ignore any reference to Russia without my having brought it up. The only time I remember any Hungarian's mentioning anything Russian was when Charlotte K. said, "When I think of the masters of the short story, I think of Maupassant, Chekhov, Katherine Mansfield—and Kosztolányi." Russian is compulsory in the schools, and the students in the universities go on with Russian studies. But English is the preferred second language. Charlotte said she had studied Russian, but dropped it. Why? Because her mother didn't like it. She had dropped it when she got as far as *bumaga* [paper]. I don't know why this word should have stopped her.*

I asked *Országh* what had been the result of Khrushchev's visit, and he replied that they had hoped they were going to remove the 840,000 Russian troops, but nothing had been done about it. "He gave Kádár a decoration for services to the Soviet Union. One could understand decorating him for services to Hungary, but why the Soviet Union?" He told me that when, as a child, he had

---

* In *Europe Without Baedeker*, EW cites Kretzoi's explanation that *bumaga* sounded "so outlandish in the coarse pronunciation of the Russian soldiers." Kretzoi elaborates: "Any word pronounced in that deep, guttural, barking way made my mother wince," reminding her of "the looting, raping, etc., which accompanied these sounds."

been somewhere when Franz Josef was passing by and everybody was going to see him, his Austrian grandfather had said, "Don't go! Don't go to look at the tyrant!" So when Khrushchev had passed through Debrecen, and the teachers loyal to the Party had urged the students not to miss it, "I found I couldn't go. Many students wouldn't go—students of 18 or 20. And they're supposed to be the children of the regime!"

Visual Arts: The Tradition

I had been in Budapest some time before I saw the more interesting part of Buda—the Vár [the royal castle] and the Matthias Church—and the Margitsziget [St. Margaret's Island]. At first I would take short walks along the Bartók Béla *utca*, on which the Gellért stands. The people seemed stunned and rather stupefied, purposelessly wandering about or going about their business—the opposite of Milan. They didn't quite know where they were or what had been happening to them. I visited a few old bookstores and bought *barack pálinka* [apricot brandy] or chocolate-covered cookies at the confectionery stores, "Édesség Boltok," that sell liquor, the bottles in the windows assimilated to the confectionery by tying little pink bows around their necks.

I was gratified to find that I could read a good many of the signs, and by the time I had left I could read them almost all as well as the inscriptions under the paintings in the galleries.

There are plenty of goods in the shops, and the people are not badly dressed; but, as Országh says, the pretty women haven't yet been able to have the advantage of "style." In general, Budapest gives the impression of a rundown Central European city. The public buildings, such as the house of parliament, appeared to me grayer than any others I had ever seen in Europe. A great sad empty city, it seemed to me—few buildings had been repainted in years. Little traffic, because few people had cars. It amused me, after Paris and Rome, when a taxi driver, briefly held up on a bridge or in a narrow street, would grin sarcastically and throw out his hands. The nights that I went to the opera—since there was no convenient taxi stand—I would have to walk all the way back, and the city was dreary at night. It was very badly lit—I was told that the lights in the streets had been gradually getting dimmer for months—and this made the people even dimmer. They did not seem to be amusing themselves—straggling old women and men. Everyone is gentle and polite. I hardly heard a disagreeable word all the time I was there.

The dogs are mainly dachshunds and police dogs, as everywhere else in Europe.

Even before I had talked to people much, I found that I was irritated by the red stars on the top of the public buildings—these had been thrown down, I learned, at the time of the '56 rebellion—by the signs in Russian at the airports and stations, by the statue of Dimitrov—a Bulgarian: why?—and the street named for Mayakovsky. In front of the Gellért stands a monument—with a red star on top—to the Russians who died fighting the Germans —inscriptions on four sides in Russian, with only a kind of Hungarian footnote on one.

Gellért Hill, beside the hotel, is named after the Christian missionary who was sent to convert the Hungarians but was put by the Magyars in a barrel lined with nails and rolled down the hill into the Danube. There is a statue of a huge female figure on top. It had originally been designed as a monument to the son of Horthy, who had, in the early part of the war, been killed in a plane fighting the Russians. The figure had had a plane in her hands pointed in the direction of Russia; but when the Russians came they made the sculptor change it to what looked like an enormous tobacco leaf. Nobody seemed to know what the significance of this was supposed to be. I talked about this with Charlotte when we were riding in a taxi, and when it was a question of Horthy, she left a blank: "I don't want to say his name." Later on, in another taxi, when she and her husband were taking me to Gundel's in the Városliget, she said, "That's where the famous statue stood—the statue of the leader, I don't want to say his name—with the mustaches." I thought she meant Horthy again, but it turned out to be Stalin. She was evidently afraid to be heard mentioning any political name. The rebels at the time of the uprising had undercut the statue with blowtorches and toppled it over. Only the boots remained fastened to the pedestal. "We call it Boots Square—not in public, of course."

Someone had told me that Budapest was the most beautiful city in Europe. It is strange and dramatic, to be sure, but there is something barbaric about it. It wants to belong to the West, but one remembers the Mongolians and the Turks—a queer mixture of Byzantine and Gothic, with a good deal that is Baroque. A spiky and bristling city—churches with high sharp spires, towers with needles like stings. An element of the goblinesque, the porcupine dome of the parliament house, the ubiquitous unendearing Cupids: the pronglike shaft in front of Matthias Church, covered with bulging Cupids that remind me of torpid bees—of the same school as the plague monument in Vienna. The frenetic and convulsive statues: rearing equestrians from their fabulous monarchic past—but they are mostly of patriots and poets, and the poets were passionate patriots: fighters with erectile hair and the long defiant mustaches that challenge like taurine horns; one of the

poets is fixed in a rapture of composition, the giant figure
of Ady is both Promethean and Byronic. A hussar with
high boots and a saber; nude youth and charioteers; Place
of the Heroes, commemorating the 1,000th anniversary of
the settlement of Hungarian tribes here. The statue of
Anonymous, the first chronicler, his head encased in a
hood so enveloping that, even when one comes quite
close—and the grass before it is worn away by the people
who have tried to see—it shows only a vague deathlike
visage.* The male caryatids on old palaces, now adapted
as offices and shops, are straining necks and muscles in
agony to keep the stone façade standing.

Matthias Church, the building of which extended from
the thirteenth to the nineteenth century, much damaged
at the end of the war. This quarter was heavily bombed,
and some of the churches are in process of reconstruction,
surrounded by metal scaffolding which carries on the bristling effect. The rampart behind the church, from which
you get a huge view of the city, was built only in the
nineteenth century, yet it has a somewhat formidable be-
lated medieval look. Villas on the hills beyond, the first
magnolia and apricot blossoms. Big old palaces and public
buildings in bad repair. Looking out over Buda, with its
domes and its old rectangular square-windowed façades,
the august gray and smudged yellow sunset behind the
abrupt Buda hills, with a square monument or two of their
tops, unidentifiable in the distance. Much yellow and orange which I found attractive but which Tezla objected to
on the ground that, favored by Maria Theresa, it reminded

---

* "The author of the first Hungarian chronicle, who is supposed to have
written at the end of the twelfth century, is referred to, since his name
is not known, as Anonymous Belaie Regis Notarius, the Anonymous
Scribe of King Bela, which is usually shortened to Anonymous" (*Europe
Without Baedeker*).

one too much of the Hapsburgs.* Flatness of Pest on the opposite shore. The buildings that look not quite like France but that one feels ought to be done in engravings.

The tall statue of Kossuth in front of the parliament house. He was originally shown as tragic in the dejection of his exile and failure; but the Russians would have none of that and he now gestures in accusation. A fabulous anachronistic past: beatific saints looking out of this world in the midst of a public square; two statues at a fountain, enduring agonies, uphold their urns; bear fountain; fountain with wreathed female figure, one leg crossed over her knee; running female figure of Electric Power, with zigzag shaft of lightning.

The Art Galleries: Szépmüvészeti Múzeum: an enormous marble palace, with a classical columned front. Though I went there at noon, the day was dark, and it was only just as I was leaving that they turned the lights on—so that I didn't see the pictures to the best advantage. But although the collection is large and there are a great many famous names, I had the impression that they had acquired a good many rather second-rate specimens. There are, however, a number of El Grecos, a few Goyas and a lot of Cranachs, which I wish I could see better illuminated. Some particularly awful Böcklins, and a good deal of inferior German stuff.

The Magyar Nemzeti Galéria, which is exclusively devoted to the native art. They certainly don't have much feeling for the visual arts. The sculpture is mostly clumsy, highly dramatized like the public statues. I thought that some of the more successful paintings were the early nineteenth-century portraits of attractive and

---

* Hapsburg yellow (or *Schönbrunn*, from the Schönbrunn Palace of Maria Theresa in Vienna) is still found on public buildings from the Swiss border to what are now Romania and the Ukraine.

typical individuals. A good many large historical pictures
from the years before the 1848 revolution, when they could
only express their determination to resist the Austrian
domination by doing canvases of their war with the Turks:
the heroic Franciscan monk, the women of Eger, etc. Many
political prisoners, many heartbreaking farewells. Scenes
of country life—influenced, Elena told me later, by the
German school. I can't think very much of Munkácsy.
Huge dark realistic pictures—interiors with many figures
that usually have some social significance. I find them very
unsatisfactory: though somber, they have many empty
spaces. Hungarian painting in general is predominantly
full of brown—even a modern painter, Derkovits, a few
of whose paintings, which I liked, were exhibited downstairs. But Hungarian painting became much worse when
they came under the influence of Impressionism and began
to copy Paris instead of the Germans.

Notes written down at the time: dark colors and coarse
textures, clumsy compositions; painful subjects: political
prisoners and tragic farewells; from the obliterating low-
ering blacks of Munkácsy to the half-Cubist brown of
Derkovits. Young Egri from Debrecen, who was showing
me around, said of one of the painters that he "liked flesh,"
and especially—the flesh of women. The title of one picture was Pogányság (Paganism or Sleeping Bacchante). They
are inept with classical mythological subjects, a murky
Hungarian Golden Age, an awkward still life of elaborate
Hungarian pastry, huge paintings of historic scenes that
masked the spirit of 1848; landscapes that derived from
Corot but a little too stiff and bristling; Augustus Eggs of
uncertain style: the honeymooners in the dark inn room
embracing on the couch, with the table spread with plates
and a pitcher of wine ready for their supper, the fashionable married couple sulking; the tragic Orphans, the man

and woman in their dark clothes, she brooding with bent head and her hands in her lap, he with head in hands bowed on the table, in the bare room with nocturnal windows, lit only by a single lamp; the somewhat messy *Picnic in May* which obviously owes something to the *Déjeuner sur l'Herbe*: the ladies in bright gowns of pink, blue and red, against a background of grass of an almost Paris-green vivid green; an extraordinary Cupid and Psyche, with the Cupid suspended over Psyche in such an awkward position that he seems to be performing an acrobatic feat.

The religious pictures, it seems—and I was told that the eighteenth-century painting was mainly of religious subjects—have been exiled and segregated at Esztergom, the seat of the highest archbishop.

Ballet and Opera, the Circus, Classics in Translation

The music of course is much better. Besides *Háry János*, I saw two evenings of ballet. The first time it was two Bartók numbers, *A fából faragott királyfi* [*The Prince Carved of Wood*] and *A csodalatos mandarin* [*The Miraculous Mandarin*], with a mixed Russian program in between: first a *pas de deux* from *The Nutcracker*, performed by an antique pair of classic dancers, then modern numbers: a wildly applauded dance in which a cute little girl, in a stunt I had never seen before, would roll herself up in a kind of ball and throw herself backwards to be caught by her partner—if she had fallen, I should think she would have broken her back. In another number, the men, holding the girls horizontally, would throw them up and the girls would make a couple of revolutions in the air. This

part of the program reached a climax with a piece by Kha-
chaturian, one of those things about a wild semi-Oriental
tribe, with much whirling and leaping and brandishing
knives, which also brought down the house. I had already
seen the *Mandarin* in Frankfurt, where it had seemed
rather pointless and unimpressive; but here it was quite
different. The little hurtling reckless dancer did the prostitute; the Mandarin was made to seem gigantic, and the
battle, where he starts to pursue the girl, was terrific,
made to seem actually dangerous, when they throw a chest
at him, put him down the trapdoor and finally hang him.
The backdrop for some reason showed New York at
night—high buildings and winking signs—and it entered
my head that the Mandarin might be either capitalism,
which didn't want to die, or Communism, which couldn't
be killed. I suspect that what had originally been behind
the conception had been the indestructibility of Hungary
at grips with a succession of enemies, eventually only
subdued—when he wins the admiration and pity of the
girl in a last spasm of self-renewal. —I had not been able
to get a cab, and had had to walk to the opera house, so
missed all but the end of the other Bartók program, in
which they also did A *kékszakállú herceg vára* [*Bluebeard's
Castle*]. I had already seen this in New York and have a
recording of it, and now having seen it in Budapest, I'm
not sure I'm not rather bored by it. Bartók has explained
that it is not really a fairy tale but a kind of subjective
poem, and it certainly lacks dramatic effectiveness. I rather
resented having the latest wife succumb to being put
away. Except for the three who come for her, the other
wives never appear: they are only lights from the wings.
Bartók is hardly dramatic except in this subjective way.
The Concerto for Orchestra is dramatic, but through the
alternation of the composer's moods: the characteristically
sudden transition from quiet melancholy to boisterous self-

assertiveness. *The Mandarin* is self-assertive and dynamic, but it needs to be danced and acted.

I took the Kretzois to the *Cirkusz a Varietében*. They played a Central European music that seemed to me really to date from just after the last war. There was a sort of Marlene Dietrich *commère*, with a jaunty top hat and a long, very tight-fitting gown which showed her admirable shape. There was a circus going on in the Liget, and they had a parody of this. First someone came out from behind and told the top-hatted lady that the black panther was loose and had eaten several members of the cast. A man came up from the audience to flirt with the Marlene Dietrich, and a snarling and roaring were heard from offstage. The man at first showed terror, but then decided to face the beast, and a horrible struggle was heard. The man returned with a limp dummy tiger. "You idiot," the lady said. "That's not a black panther. You've got the wrong animal." This was followed by a not very funny act in which the man impersonated a lion shown off by a woman trainer. —A comic organ grinder, with a long cigar, and a long Hungarian mustache, entertained us with a series of gags—would take off the mustache with the cigar attached to it; put a cap down with money in it to attract more money, which was not forthcoming; walk away from the organ, which would go on playing. Then it stopped, he began tinkering with it, and suddenly the top flew off and a rather heavy, thick-ankled woman popped out, who turned cartwheels and backflips all over the stage. Her acrobatic ballet worked up to the climax of what was apparently to be a striptease. Her garments were luminous, and they turned down the lights. When there was nothing left but a bikini, the stage became quite dark. Charlotte said, "It's not going to be true!"—and sure enough, when the bikini disappeared, nothing at all could be seen.

At the finale of the first half, when the pretty and slender chorus girls were dancing in nothing but bikinis, she said to me, "This is really what you came to see, isn't it?" When we were leaving after the show, she said in her stiff British way: "The audience were lower middle class."

I had thought she was being priggish about the girls, but I was to find that behind her English façade, there was a sensitive, non-prudish and quite humorous Hungarian.

When she took me to call on the Gábor Devecseris, at the gate she said, "I must tell you a piece of gossip!" but Devecseri came out and she couldn't go on. I had known about him and wanted to meet him. He had devoted years to translating Homer—as well as many of the plays of the Greek dramatists. They had discovered as early as the eighteenth century that since Hungarian is perhaps unique among languages spoken in Europe in having long and short vowels which are as important as the stress accents, it is peculiarly appropriate for translating the Greek and Latin poets, and Devecseri was fascinated in trying to reproduce their effects. What comes out does not follow exactly the procedure of the originals—and we do not really know what this was—but does sound very satisfactory. The "long consonants" are very curious—they are the double ones which are not pronounced like single ones, as they are with us, nor yet as in Italian as two consonants, but as a single consonant heavily dwelt upon. I had noticed, when I started with Hungarian, that Mariska would sometimes tell me that I was not giving these consonants their proper value, and I found in Budapest that if I asked to be taken to the Gellért or to have the lift stop at the *étterem* [restaurant] without sounding the double *l* or double *t*, they did not know what I meant. Devecseri explained his Homer, and the mechanism of Hungarian verse, which seems very strange to us. They talk about iambics in poems which from our point of view are not iambic. The rhymes are mostly assonances—they often rhyme *m* with *n*. "A true rhyme," he told me, "is like a pinch of salt"—but then he showed me what he called a true rhyme, which was *unalom* and *malom*—not a rhyme at all from our point of view, because both words, like all Hungarian words, are accented on the first syllable. On account of all this, their poetry, which sounds beautiful when they read it, is difficult for the foreigner to manage. Though the accent, as he tried to explain to me, is supposed to be on the first syllable, there are those other values, too, and every line has a rhythm that is based on a combination of things. He read me translations of Keats and Shelley—curious to hear their lyrical effects reproduced by such different means. Someone had said that the Hungarian translation of the "Ode to the West Wind" was the first Hungarian poem. "We are a nation of translators," he said. They showed me a volume of the complete poems of Poe translated by various hands. I was told afterwards that "The Raven" had been translated some fifteen times, and in an attempt to pull the leg of the person who told me, I said that I had heard there was one in which "Nevermore!" was translated "*Nem, nem, soha!*"* He said, "Yes, but that was a parody—after the first war."

In looking at Devecseri's own poems, I saw one in elegiacs, in which he had followed the practice of Ovid in rhyming the two halves of the pentameter. He was pleased, and said, "Yes, of course, he does!—and the scholars say it is accidental! Mimnermus does it, too!" I had mentioned Mimnermus and Ovid in my note to "The White Sands," and I told him about my experiments with elegiacs. I drew a diagram of the elegiac couplet, saying that I had invented

---

* See "*Nem, nem, soha!*" on p. 57.

a chiastic method of my own for rhyming it; but before I could further explain, he surprised me by drawing the chiastic lines. "You did this," he said.

"How did you know?" "Ovid did this"—he indicated a triple rhyme. I had never noticed a case of this. He is evidently a brilliant classicist. He read us a dialogue of his own between Perseus and the Gorgon. He evidently did not know much about classical education in England, because he had been astonished by a young Englishman who recited Homer and who told him that at school and at the university, he had spent half his time on rugby and half on the classics. "I said that at least half his time had been well employed."

They had one of the little old villas in the steep hills back of Buda. "We have the ugliest statues in Budapest!"—two rows of those bumpy Cupids—one of them without a head—on the sides of the front steps. Some friend had told them that they ought to remove them and put them in the cellar. I took pity on them and said that they ought simply to clean them up. "Nothing but a hammer!" He made a gesture of smashing.

His wife is extremely attractive—red hair and large brown eyes—though her features are not all finely cut. She is something at the opera—translates and directs. He is evidently very proud of her. There were also Péter Nagy, who translated my plays* and who works for the publishing house Corvina; and a professor of Italian and his wife.

---

* *Beppo and Beth* is translated as *Beppo és Betty* and *This Room and This Gin and These Sandwiches* as *A szoba, as ital meg a szendvicsek*, in the volume *Müvészvilág* (*Artists' World*), 1959.

They had coffee and white wine and a cake-and-whipped-cream-type dessert.

It was only on some later occasion that I asked Charlotte what her piece of gossip had been. She said that she had been at a British Embassy reception and their Hungarian librarian had asked her, "How is Laci? [diminutive for László Országh]." She didn't know what he had meant, but it turned out that he thought that she was Mrs. Devecseri, and that his question had implied something serious between Mrs. D. and a well-known actor. I said that it sounded like Molnár, and she admitted that it did.

Charlotte is 36 and her husband twenty years older, but she says she never thinks about their difference in age, and I had a definite impression of good relations. She said that for years her ivory tower was the Geological Institute, and I suppose she met him there. She had hoped to go abroad to study, but events had made that impossible. At the Geological Institute, they "went to the excavations like birds in the spring." He was very much exhilarated by the recent discovery in a quarry west of Budapest of the relics of primitive man, with tools and traces of fire. No preliminary report had as yet been published, but the paleontologists were coming to see what had turned up: a professor from Harvard and the Dutchman who had discovered the Java man and whom the Kretzois had been occupied in entertaining. The Kretzois come from the old professional class, and are snooty about what is going on around them. At Gundel's, where they took me for dinner, Kretzoi looked down from our higher ground on a banquet at a long table and remarked that the people seemed rather inferior, and he thought they must be Gypsies. When I expressed surprise at this, he explained that Gypsies in Hungary were sometimes quite well-to-do, professors and professional men. Charlotte, when I first met her, had wanted to make it clear where she stood politically: she was "progressive" but implied that she did not accept the regime. She had perhaps in the past been more radical, used to march in May Day demonstrations; but I gathered that '56 had embittered her. They could not, she intimated, forgive the treachery of the Soviet Union in inviting Imre Nagy and his government to dinner, then arresting them and kidnapping them.* He was executed in '58. She told me later that she did not hate the Russians but did not approve of their system.

Politics and Official Spokesmen

In Hungary, I came to feel an *absolute hatred of the Soviet system*: its mechanical stupidities imposed on an intelligent Western people; the simpleminded cant of Soviet Marxist terminology, the restrictions which, so far as I could see, hide nothing from this alert and recalcitrant people.† They know that they belong to the lost, regard the Russians as semi-Oriental barbarians; they have regarded them as traditional enemies ever since Austria called them in to put down the 1848 revolution; they yearn toward the United States. When I asked Charlotte what the purpose was of the *New Hungarian Quarterly* published in English, she replied that it served as a "gateway."

Henry Brandon, whom I ran into in the Gellért, had just spent two months in Russia and had also been in Romania. He said that it was a great relief to get to Budapest and

---

* In fact, Imre Nagy had been a refugee in the Yugoslav embassy and was kidnapped after being given an assurance of safe conduct by the new Hungarian government.

† The rhetoric of "socialist democracy" among Hungarian officials mocked the revolutionary idealism EW had celebrated in *To the Finland Station*. He notes the "brutal" Russian repression of the Hungarian revolution in the introduction to *Patriotic Gore*.

feel oneself in the West again. Charlotte said that she thought the Tisza was the dividing line between East and West.

From the careers of the Hungarian patriot leaders in relation to the Austrian empire, one can see that the pattern has come to be that when the cause for the moment has been lost, the leader decides to work for the dominant power, cherishing inwardly the national fire, the dumb spirit of opposition. This is perhaps the situation of [János] Kádár. Bruce Carless of the British Embassy told me that Kádár was supposed to have said that he did not want the Russian troops removed because, if they were, he would be under the necessity of raising divisions of his own, yet one couldn't really believe that he didn't want them to go. He sees almost nobody, Carless says. The only news they had had of him lately had been by way of an interview with the French ambassador.

Ambiguous: In talking English with Hungarians, I found that this word was as likely to occur as in one of our literary quarterlies. The relation to the churches, for example, was "ambiguous": the attitude of the government was supposed to be anti-religious, but no one, they gave me to understand, paid any attention to this, and both the Catholic and the Protestant churches, though their property had been taken away from them, were actually subsidized by the government. They have to give "lip service," as Országh says, to the confounded Soviet ideology when their taste and intelligence and ultimate intentions are actually contrary to it. The little history of Hungarian literature, of which I have been given copies both in Hungarian and English, is an obvious example of this. It is in three sections written by three different men, and I haven't read it enough to distinguish between them, but they have to pretend to be talking in terms of socialism and capitalism, proletariat and bourgeoisie, using these categories with sometimes rather comic effect. They will speak of some writer's associating himself with the sufferings of the people and describing their condition in his work and for a time becoming a socialist, but then, coolly and without condemnation, go on to record that later on he came to lose faith in the "masses."

Henry Brandon said that in Russia the younger generations had been cultivating ideas quite opposed to the official ones, but that they were given no chance to have anything to say—"there's no way for them to penetrate." I told him that I thought that England, in spite of the grumbling one heard, was perhaps better off than the countries on the Continent. He said that the young people there were striving—more overtly and articulately—to realize something new, but that the old forces of Toryism were still fairly effective in keeping them down. I had been very much aware in Paris of this new kind of struggle between the young and the old.

The American Embassy, or legation, is a decidedly spooky place: no ambassador and Cardinal Mindszenty hidden on the top floor; soldiers, policemen with red stars on their caps guarding the front door on either side. (It is one of the impositions that the Hungarians resent that their soldiers should be made to wear uniforms that differ from the Russian ones only in color.) On the first floor small exhibitions of photographs, one American lot and one Hungarian lot—the former of Kennedy and other officials, the latter of Hungarian sports. The whole effect is disheartening: one feels that neither set has ever been looked at with interest by anyone from the other people. No foreigner is allowed to go above this floor. Shelnutt, the cultural

man, said, "You're American, aren't you?" before he asked
me up to his office.

It is only in the last few months that they have been
allowed to go more than 20 miles outside the city. When
I found that you were not allowed to send any books out
of the country—this was even something of a problem for
the Corvina people—I assumed that the legation would be
able to help me; but they couldn't unless they took them
to Vienna, and this would have been hard to manage. They
couldn't be in the position, I gathered, of any smuggling
operation whatever. Shelnutt told me that, for their re-
ceptions, he and his wife invited Hungarians and foreigners
on different nights.

At a party at the Shelnutts', one of the women who
worked there told me that one soon got used to hearing
Mindszenty walk back and forth. One of his rooms is fitted
up as a chapel, and visiting Catholic foreigners can go to
hear Mass there on Sundays. Someone who had had the
impression that his life was one of stern asceticism had
been there when his tray was sent up with his breakfast
and was struck by its amplitude. His only exercise is taken
in a small courtyard. He does not seem terribly popular
with his countrymen. Though courageous in defending his
Church, I was told that he had got a number of Catholics
into trouble by insisting that they confess their faith at a
time when this was unnecessary, and in regard to social
reforms, he had apparently been flatly reactionary: had
opposed popular education and the breaking up of the big
estates.* "He wears—what you call it?—blinders like a
horse," one Hungarian said to me.

I was surprised to find that Shelnutt spoke Hungarian,
which he had learned, before he came, in Washington.

---

* This was the Communist position on Cardinal Mindszenty. What Mindszenty strongly opposed was the nationalization of parochial schools.

Out of the nine Americans in the legation, five spoke it, though the chargé d'affaires did not. From Reinhold in Rome and from this and from Carless at the British Embassy, I got the impression that the diplomatic service of the English-speaking countries is somewhat better equipped than it has been the past. Carless is remarkably well informed—a Cambridge man, I soon guessed, from his dry and detached way of talking and his exact factual grasp.

Visit to the New Hungarian Quarterly: Országh had told me that they wanted to know if I would like to have coffee. No, tea. That was unfortunate, he said, because coffee was what they had. But he supposed I wouldn't want their Hungarian brandy. Certainly, I said. The result was that they kept pouring it for me, and I didn't notice at first that they themselves were not drinking anything. When I commented on this, the one who had brought me explained that he was going to drive me back and that one could be arrested for driving after drinking, even if one had not had an accident. I suspected that this was a trick to make trouble for people who were disapproved of for other reasons.

I told them about my Lewis County Hungarian neighbors. "We are 90% (I think) collectivized, you know. The peasants don't have an outlet for their energies."

My session at the Corvina office with Nagy and Balabán: Balabán had gone with me when I had to get a pass to go to meet Elena in Vienna. He smiled about the bureaucracy. We were sent to the Ibusz office, then to the passport officer and there we had to wait a long time. (The woman at the reception desk, though dark, with her high cheekbones and long nose, looked enough like Mariska to have been her aunt.) The woman in whose office we finally

arrived explained that such irregular trips were usually
only permitted for business purposes, but then when she
came back from the higher-up, she said, "He says that he
is a writer, and he ought to get a good impression"—
whereat we all laughed. There is always this air of a
comedy which the Hungarians are not taking seriously.
But Balabán—who evidently had to watch his words—
referred to '56 as "the counterrevolution." He was a lively
man who had learned English in England and had a somewhat non-U accent, thickset and evidently internally
strong, with strongly gazing round brown eyes.

I was not at first aware that in the presence of these
editors of Corvina, I was up against firm Party loyalty.
Tezla had warned me that you had to be careful, that
people seemed to talk so freely that you were likely to
become forgetful that the Party might be somewhere in
the background. Nagy and Balabán rather put me off my
guard—though I might not have talked differently in any
case—by certain humorous disarming remarks. Nagy
asked what I thought was the reason for the revival of
religious interest. I gave my usual explanation that a resort
to religion—as in Russia after the failure of the 1905
revolution—was likely to follow frustration of social-
political hopes. "And Marxism," said Nagy, "was itself a
substitute for religion." I agreed, and he said something
to Balabán in Hungarian. B. then said to me, laughing but
turning red, "We could have a song to sing about that!" I
said that I myself had no tendency toward religion, and
Nagy said that he didn't either—"Yet, Stalin's death made
me not sure." "You thought that God removed him?" "I
wasn't sure there wasn't something!" I said that God had
taken a long time about it. This had been said as a joke,
but I think he wanted to be sure that I understood that
he was dissociating himself from everything that Stalin had
stood for.

I said that I had heard *Háry János*, and it was Nagy who made the objection noted above that it was lacking in conflict. I was sorry that *Székely fonó* [*A Székely Spinning Room*] was not being given. He said that it was rather slight, no real drama. I told him that I had been puzzled by the peasant husband who had been arrested on a charge that was never explained and from which he was finally exonerated, when the blame was shifted to the Long-Nosed Flea—till Agatha [Fassett] had said that the point was that somebody was always being arrested. Nagy said that he thought the whole thing was supposed to be presented from the point of view of the peasants themselves, who did not understand what was going on. The arrests are unintelligible to them—and he added, "It sometimes happens still." He said that he didn't know why *Beppo and Beth* shouldn't be a success on the stage. I said that it was out-of-date, nobody in America would be interested in that period—and went on to tell them that by the time *The American Earthquake* came out, no one who hadn't remembered it could believe that [the shake-up of society] had ever occurred. "Yes, the young people here can't believe that there was ever unemployment in Hungary. They are told about it but they don't believe it."*

They wanted to know what they could do to get their English books circulated and noticed in America. In order to get them reviewed, I told them, they would have to have

---

* EW was disposed to like his translator, who had discovered his plays, but Péter Nagy's Party loyalties were coming into focus. That he was at least a sympathizer had been clear to Wilson when the volume of plays arrived from Hungary: "They have only translated two plays that were written in the early thirties, and the translator explains in a note that I am depicting the decay of the capitalist world and indicating the correct line of escape through following the Party line," he wrote to Mary Meigs in 1960, adding, "I am sure that those Hungarians are capable of playing certain scenes ironically."

them handled by an American publisher. Foreign books were simply discarded. Nagy thought that the Cold War had something to do with it. I assured him that this was not true, that there was, in fact, considerable interest in Hungary. It did not occur to me then that he could not admit that the '56 revolt had stimulated a stronger interest in Hungary than at any time since Kossuth's visit.

In the Gellért, as in the Victoria in Rome, the waiters say *M'sieur M'dame* to either a man or a woman alone. They don't know what it means.

I told Tezla that before I left I wanted to talk to a convinced Marxist. "I've been here seven months, and I haven't found one yet, but there must be some somewhere. Things are so badly run. These things aren't accidental."

It is a tight crowded hemmed-in little language—unlike Russian, which has the looseness of a large country. A danger in writing it tastelessly is that the adjectives and nouns get piled up in front of one of their possessives. *Very tight-muscled* can thus become *muscle-bound*. Importance of the verbs *fog* (take) and *tart* (hold).

Though a regular and well-organized language, it has not been developed with much aesthetic feeling. There are too many *meg*'s and combinations like *meg még*—which, however, recall our *had had*'s—and too many *maga*'s. I wonder whether *meg* [the prefix] and *maga* [self or you] and *meg* [still, yet] may not all derive from the same root.

I read Molnár's *Ördög* [*Devil*] and went to see it at the Vígszínház, where it was first done in 1907. I must have seen it not long after, done by a road company [in Red Bank], at the time when both George Arliss and Edwin

Stevens were doing it in New York. It was then audacious
and scandalous, and it made Molnár's reputation abroad.
[At thirteen] I was slightly frightened by it, and I remember very clearly the erotic opening—though the woman
who played Jolán was rather too fleshy and elderly—and
the first appearance of the Devil, but after that almost
nothing. The Devil's immoral moral lectures made no
impression on me, and since they are sometimes rather
long, I imagine that they had been cut. The only moment
after the beginning that I remembered to have seen before
was the Devil passing by the window toward the end of
the third act with the red lining of his opera cloak or
overcoat. It was interesting to find out in Budapest what
the play had been all about.

I had been told that the official reviews had been bad,
had deplored the temptation to nostalgia for the corrupt
old bourgeois society. When later, the day before I left, I
talked to Péter Nagy about it, he said that he had reviewed
it for Élet és Irodalom [an officially supported cultural
weekly] and very much disapproved of it. He objected to
its having been done with luxurious early-twentieth-cen-
tury settings—the elegant evening party, with its staircase
and the waltzes being played offstage (including the same
waltz, I noticed, that is exploited in the second act of The
Cherry Orchard). It oughtn't to be presented [with all this
atmosphere]. Why? It was remote from people's present
lives. I said that the audience had appeared to enjoy it.
"It's a rather special audience at the Vígszínház." He implied that they were a lot of old-regime nostalgiacs.

But in spite of the discouraging reviews, the play had
been going in the repertoire for months, and the audience
was thoroughly enjoying it. The audience was large because the Vígszínház is very large. Like the opera—with
its gilt and red plush—it has a shabby old-fashioned splen-
dour. Far from being presented ironically, the elegance of

the elegant classes was exploited for all it was worth. Éva Ruttkai was enchanting as Jolán: shy in the first act, when she comes to the studio, marvellously attractive in the second with the bare arms of her *decolleté*, which she handled in a scene at the end, when she is standing half turned away from the audience, in beautiful graceful gestures. The Devil was less satisfactory: too stout—Molnár makes him slender, and, as Nagy said, a sort of Onkel Teufel who is benevolently bringing the lovers together. But I see now that it was Molnár's intention to make the audience feel that they are watching the happy ending of a love story when the once "underprivileged" boy and girl fall into one another's arms offstage, and the Devil says to the audience, *"Voilà"* (being Hungarian, he accented the first syllable, so that it did not have the right ring). The husband is made the stereotype of the stupid ostentatious rich man, so the audience has no sympathy for him. The whole performance, as I did not expect it would be, was very underplayed, well-bred. The audience were not boisterous but often laughed. When, at the end of the second act, Jolán announces that she is about to write János a letter, "very stern, very dry," then, at the Devil's dictation, produces a passionate love letter—"You must never try to see me again because if we were to see one another, we should immediately go up in flames"—the audience broke into applause.

There are two anti-Semitic jokes: one at the party when the Devil is driving away the guests one by one and says something unpleasant about converted Jews, and then in the conversation between Elza and Cinka, when the latter says that one of her former lovers was called Zrinyi—"Elza. A good name. —But Adolf.—That's too bad."* I assume that in the performance they had the second, though I

* Adolf was often assumed to be a Jewish name in Hungary.

hadn't got that far in reading the text, and I know they had the first because I watched for it. Of course, the Devil and the rich young girl are here reflecting a fashionable attitude, which Molnár, himself a Jew, is exploiting for light comedy. But the anti-Semitism current in Hungary has really been appalling. They blamed the radical movement on the Jews because Béla Kun and most of his cabinet were Jewish; then, even in '56, the rebels showed anti-Semitism because several of the Stalinists were Jews (Lengyel 294–95): "*Itzig, most nem viszünk Auschwitzig* [Isaac, this time we are not going to take you to Auschwitz]" [but finish you off here] posted up on the walls.*

Very curious, as elsewhere in Molnár, the handling of the honorifics and the various words for you. The Devil calls Jolán *ön* [you] but János *te* [thou], having known him at Monte Carlo. In the scene between Cinka, the model, and Elza, the rich young girl, they alternate between *kegyed* [your Grace] and *ön*, apparently on account of not being sure whether, never having met before, they are on a friendly or a formal basis. (Karinthy's satiric skit.) Országh's dictionary says that *kegyed* is the most formal term. They both start out with *kegyed*, then Elza uses *ön*, only a moment later to return to *kegyed*.

I had been told by Eleanor Perényi and others never to use *ön*; but Charlotte admonished me that in asking for anything in a shop, I ought always to say, "*Önnek* (not *magának*) *van* something."† Under Communism, they had tried to do away with these distinctions, and it was believed

---

* István Deák believes that the émigré historian Emil Lengyel exaggerated the incidence of anti-Semitism in the 1956 revolution. There were actually few signs of it, given the disproportionately high level of Jews among both the Stalinist leadership and the revolutionary intellectuals.
† *Ön* is more formal than *maga*.

that at Party meetings they all addressed one another as
te and used the word for comrade, *elvtárs*, very unpopular
with everyone else. But I was told that there had been a
relapse into the traditional usage for *you*. When I asked
Nagy about it, he said that you had to have grown up with
it to understand how to use the different forms, but that
kegyed was quite obsolete.

Vienna, Budapest, Debrecen

Vienna. In order to buy a ticket with forints, I had had to
have a permit from Ibusz, and at the station they took my
passport and made me wait while they did something about
it. I shared a first-class compartment with an old gentleman
who spoke German and was Jewish perhaps. He would
shrug and smile with wry irony every time—and it was
often—we were visited by the customs people or had to
produce our passports. Our baggage, however, was never
opened. The train follows the Danube awhile, and one
sees it where it is clear and pretty between green fields
and trees, instead of, as in Budapest and Vienna, muddy.

Elena came to meet me, and we stayed at the Bristol.
Olgarel [Mumm] was on hand and insisted on taking us
to the art gallery in Maria Theresa's palace. The collection
here is brilliant: Breughels, Cranachs, and a lot of Dutch,
including one famous Vermeer; but Olgarel, after long
years as a guide, couldn't restrain herself from giving us
the whole program of her lectures. She would say, "And
who do you think left the tap of the wine keg running?"
The dog. "Do you think that Cranach had some sympathy
with Protestantism? You see the monk in the boat is amusing himself in rather a strange manner." (He was fondling

a woman.) As usual, she often said, "Methinks." I was nervous and very hard taxed from climbing all the marble stairs, and I finally succumbed on a bench and let them go on without me. Elena told me afterwards that she finally said, "I don't want to answer riddles, I want to look at the pictures." She says that even in her youth Olgarel had always annoyed her in museums. The next day Olgarel said to her that she was afraid she had worn me out. *"J'ai la réputation d'extenuer mes clients."*

The part of Vienna where we stayed seemed very brisk and glittering after Budapest. We went to a musical show called *Frühjahrparade* suggested by Olgarel, who accompanied us, and which was certainly, as the English say, good value. It gave the Viennese works: waltzes, the Prater, a bakery, chic women of the early 1900s; Franz Josef, played by one of their best actors, applauded on his appearance, who is represented as very *bon enfant* and is charming to the little bakery girl who wants him to help get her fiancé's song sung—which of course turns out to be a great hit and is played by a military band with bright uniforms at a spring parade, at which the detachment of Tyrolese, now separated from Austria, were enthusiastically applauded.

We sent a wire to Wystan Auden, who turned out to have just arrived, and he came in and took us to lunch and in the later afternoon had drinks with us. I had left my traveller's checks in Budapest, and he helped me buy some more at his bank. He boasted of personal acquaintance with one of the Rothschilds connected with this bank. Like all Englishmen, he likes distinguished connections. I remember his saying once in New York that he had to leave to go to see his "father-in-law." This was Thomas Mann, with whom his relationship was merely legal. He had been doing for some publisher an anthology of minor nineteenth-century poets. He hates, evidently, the fin de siècle. He won't put in anything of Wilde's, and I couldn't persuade him that he ought to include Beardsley's "Ballad of a Barber." "Can you read Ernest Dowson?!"

Olgarel pointed out to us the stone shaft with the statue of the Russian soldier. "We tolerate him," she said. "We say that he's the only Russian soldier who never stole a watch."

The last morning, when Elena had not yet had her coffee and was in one of her early-morning worrying moods— which, not sleeping in the same room, I usually miss— she flew into a fury on account of my having tried to discuss with her how she ought to assign the money which she had succeeded in borrowing on her stock in Frankfurt. She had had a bad time in Johannisberg. Madeleine had made her dine with one of her Nazi hangers-on, and she had inevitably had to dispute with them: "My sister-in-law only likes Negroes and Jews." And she felt that the loan was "risky," because Madeleine might decide to pay it off and take the stock. She entered on such a tirade that I got up and went down to the breakfast room. When I returned, she had gone back to sleep, and seemed to have forgotten about it. We made love that afternoon and parted on perfect terms.

I always react unfavorably to the Austrians: their too sweet cuisine, their overdone desire to please. "They don't really," Elena said. Tezla, who had spent a year in Vienna, found them basically hard and cold. The Hungarians are not servile or effusive, but considerate, agreeable and quiet. I remarked upon this to Országh, and he replied, "We've said that so much about ourselves that I've decided it can't be true."

Budapest again. I flew back, which avoided such official nuisances as I had had on the train; but at the customs they asked for the declaration of the money I had brought into Hungary. They didn't seem to mind my not being able to find it till I finally left the country, when they wouldn't let me change my forints for sterling but took them all and got my address and said they would send me a check for them.

My visa only let me stay in Austria till Tuesday, and I felt like a soldier on leave. Thursday was May Day. When Országh called up, I said I wondered whether I'd be missing something if I didn't attend the *May Day demonstration.* "You'll be missing nothing," he said. They haven't done much about it since '56. Before that, they were forced to take part, and now that they are not any longer, they pay very little attention to it.

I had *Országh to dinner* at the Gellért, and he brought a very nice old gentleman, the head professor of English at Budapest University. Országh had *palacsinta* for dessert, and announced that they had been made with rancid butter. Gundel, who used to run the restaurant here, would never have permitted that! I asked him what *csirág* was, and he declared that the word shouldn't be used on the menu: it was really obsolete, asparagus was now called *spárga*, but I see that he includes it in his English-Hungarian dictionary.

The young man named Hankiss whom Charlotte sent to me one day when she was at Debrecen. Extremely well read in contemporary French, German and English. He said that they were now free to print everything—"except about the things that are interesting." He didn't care much for Móricz—he thought it was old-fashioned naturalism. He had just written an article on *Who's Afraid of Virginia Woolf?*, of which he had a very high opinion.

Gyula Illyés seems to be the ranking writer. I was told that on a visit to France he had made a public statement that the thing he regretted most was being cut off from Transylvania. When he came home, I heard that he had been severely rebuked. But somebody else told me he was sure that he had been put up to his statement by the authorities at home themselves. This is what they mean by ambiguity.

The Kretzois retailed to me some of the news that had been brought them by *their paleontologists*. The women in Holland had departed from tradition: they had a diet which made them slim. But the men were just as fat as ever. Charlotte asked me whether I didn't think the Hungarian women "had too many kilos." They often have—they eat so much greasy food.

The Dutchman who discovered the Java man had told them that the prostitutes in Java, instead of soliciting themselves, had mynah birds outside their lodgings which advertised their charms and what they would do and for how much. At a party, some mischievous person substituted one of these birds for the mynah bird belonging to the hostess, so that it seemed to be speaking of her.

Kretzoi, when I told him that, in trying to learn Hungarian, I felt the law of diminishing returns applied to acquiring languages, replied that the first foreign language was difficult, the second somewhat less difficult, the third, fourth and fifth became routine, but the sixth one never entirely got the hang of, and the seventh one dropped at the end of two months.

At first I had *Charlotte* come to my room at the Gellért, but I saw that this embarrassed her, and after a rather unsatisfactory session in the corridor opposite the elevator, she asked me to come to her house on the Semmelweis *utca*. Their apartment was more comfortable and commodious than most. Országh told me that when so many people left as a result of '56, they would leave the keys of their apartments with friends, who would move in and were allowed squatters' rights. This was how the Kretzois had acquired theirs, and they were fortunate because they had three rooms—a bedroom, a living room and a sort of hall—which made it possible for them to house their books: shelves from floor to ceiling.

After a few scenes of Molnár, in which Charlotte would explain the idioms and local jokes, she would say, "Now we must have some refreshment!" and bring out a tray of delicious fancy cakes—bought from that French confectioner Gerbeaud, of whose survival they were very proud —and a bottle of excellent white wine. One day, after she had had two glasses, she said, "Wine always either makes me sleepy or makes me want to sing." I was about to say she must be tired and that I'd leave her; but she announced, "I shall sing," and, sitting in the armchair, embarked on some little love songs by Petöfi, having previously shown me and explained the text. I commented on one of her songs that the settings written for Petöfi remarkably resembled folk songs. "That *was* a folk song. Petöfi is finished."

Another day, when I arrived, she said, "Can you listen to a lady in distress? I have been weeping." I don't know whether this was literally true, but she was certainly much distressed by the disappointment of just having been told that she could not go to America on a Ford scholarship. Országh had wanted her to go when he went—his project was a history of American literature; but they had told her that they couldn't have two people going over for work in the same field. They would let her go the following year. I got the impression that the authorities were feeling that Országh had lately been getting away with too much. He had expected to go to West Germany for a Shakespeare celebration, but I knew that he had had difficulty in getting a visa, and I gathered, when he brought the other professor to dinner, that this man had gone instead. The authorities had told Charlotte that when she went to be interviewed by the Ford people, she was to pretend that she did not know that the decision had been made not to let her go, and she very much resented this, said that she would not lie. But she knew that if she made any trouble about it, they would not let her go at all. A little later, I saw Országh and Tezla at the Gellért, and they were very much annoyed at the tampering that had been done with the list of names drawn up by the Ford Foundation.

At these sessions, I came to discover, behind Charlotte's rather formal exterior, a pleasantly girlish side.

When something was said about it being warm or cold, Charlotte asked me whether I knew how to say "I am cold" and "I am warm" in Hungarian. I assumed that they were *Hideg vagyok* and *Meleg vagyok*. She said that this was what foreigners were likely to think, but that if they used these expressions, they were laughed at. They meant "I am frigid" and "I am homosexual"—the latter especially with women. What you should say is *Fázom* and *Melegem van*.

She said that about 10% of the people were Communists, and that 50% of those had joined the Party merely in order to be able to hold down official jobs. "The rest are—are normal people." Henry Brandon says in his article in the London *Sunday Times* that Kádár himself claims that only 30% support the regime.

She explained to me and wrote down a table of the various forms of address appropriate, under the old regime, to the many gradations of rank. They had completely disappeared, she said; but then added a little later that under the old regime she would have been *méltóságos asszony* [my lady], on account of her husband's rank as a professor. When I had first come, I wanted to pay her for her lessons, but she said that she couldn't think of it, that she was honored to be able to work with me. I think she and her husband regard themselves as working in fields that are properly international and in which international interchange should be made as free as possible; she could no more take money from me for helping me with Hungarian literature than he could take money from his foreign colleagues for expounding to them the recent discoveries in Hungary.

Charlotte took me to a *new Hungarian film*, the only film I saw in Hungary. I had been told that the Hungarian films were poor, but this was extremely good, well acted and well produced. I didn't notice the name, but it must have been A *Pénzcsináló* [*The Counterfeiter*], which I find listed among the movie programs. It was made from an old short story. A vulgar lower-middle-class man discovers that he can imitate exactly the bills with the head of Franz Josef, and he passes off his counterfeits and becomes rich. He marries his daughter to a young man of good family; a Hapsburg is present at the wedding party—the actor well cast, Charlotte thought. The nobles gamble with him and he loses—I wasn't sure they weren't supposed to be cheating—and the winner demands prompt payment. He has sent his family to the country, with the counterfeiting machine, and is in desperation to meet this emergency; but he is rescued when a nouveau riche, who has heard about the counterfeiter's having forged for himself a coat of arms, comes to him to have another forged, and the counterfeiter charges him a high price. The nobles, when they find out his resources, ask him to come in with them on some project for which they need a good deal of capital, but he confesses to them where his money has come from. They sternly summon him to a meeting to which he goes with apprehension; but it turns out that his punishment is simply to be that he is to drink a huge cup of wine, which is standing on the table and from which a cover is ceremoniously removed. They all get drunk together, and they go through with their scheme, which prospers. This all involves much snobbish comedy including the daughter's wedding. An example of their "ambiguity": the film plays up to the new regime by making the nobility all rascals, and the detective who has been after the counterfeiter is finally himself sent to jail by the powers who have an interest in protecting him. At the time he was forging the bills, the face of Franz Josef would sometimes look at him dubiously, with tentative disapproval. But at the end he is rapt into a fantasy of success, which begins with the kicking legs of a line of chorus girls, goes on to a reception by Franz Josef, who greets him in bad Hungarian and to whom he offers one of the cheap cigars which have already figured in his relations with the nobles, and ends in a snowstorm of counterfeit bills. So the corruption of the monarchy triumphs. Curious to compare this with the Vienna musical. Sándor Radó had said to me that the long reign of Franz Josef had given all the Hungarians a father complex. I had mentioned this to Országh, and he had said there was something in it. I see better now what they mean. The emperor was either the great eternal father, who had to be revered, or the tyrant who had to be rejected.

Debrecen. Országh persuaded the cultural bureau to send me to Debrecen in a car, and he and Charlotte and I had a very pleasant trip. They have been going there by train, which takes four hours, and coming back by plane, which takes fifty-five minutes, every week, and they had never seen anything of the towns except what could be seen from the train.

I got a lot of information from Országh, who of course knows everything about Hungarian history. He says that the type of Hungarian who has round black eyes probably comes from Romania—I remembered the Romanians in the hospital at Odessa. The ones with short hooked noses were "Turkic." There is also a flat-faced Mongolian type —such as a woman we saw at the music hall, who might perfectly well have been an Esquimau.

He said that the Church in Austria-Hungary had always been comfortable and worldly. There was even once a Hapsburg cardinal—"to pray for them—and they needed a lot of praying for." There were few really ascetic orders—no Carthusians or Trappists. No Franciscans? Yes, but not very austere ones.

I was surprised to see how well the countryside looked, all under collective cultivation. Smooth green fields, all planted with crops in big strips and with no fencing be- tween them. The *puszta*, which had once been all a waste- land, with not even trees, only used for grazing, was now almost all under cultivation—though there were a few large pig farms, cattle and shepherds with their flocks. They have planted some poplars along the roads. My com- panions told me it was just like Russia, which they had not seen, but the steppes seem much flatter: they are more monotonous, nothing at all on the horizon. They pointed out the queer wells, which Petöfi had likened to gigantic mosquitoes sucking the moisture from the earth, and quoted his poem. I was surprised to find the countryside so well taken care of, and the peasants' houses so clean-looking and freshly painted. They explained that all this eastern part of Hungary is much less densely populated than the west on account of the Turkish occupation. The natives had gone away, and, except for Debrecen, in that part of the world there had been very little cultural life.

Debrecen itself, however, is full of cultured and historical associations: Csokonai and Fazekas came from there,* Petöfi had been poor there, Ady had gone to law school; Kossuth in the Calvinist church had announced Hungarian independence in 1848, and it was in Debrecen that the new government was formed when the Germans were on the run. This had occurred in the same meeting hall in what is now the Calvinist museum in which Kossuth and his followers had their meeting before proceeding to the church, and the old wooden steps, unpainted and rather broken down, are still kept in memory of this. Anna [Katona] of the English department took me around the museum: many manuscripts of their great writers and much primitive scientific apparatus. I was surprised to learn that 30% of Hungary is Protestant. Debrecen is called "the Calvinist Rome." The first time I met Országh, he spoke of "my Calvinists" as if he somewhat depended on them for moral support.

I stayed at the Arany Bika [Golden Bull], which was being turned upside down—to the disgust of my academic friends—for the official visit of Ulbricht [Communist

---

* "The early Calvinist lyric poet Csokonai was born here in 1773; so, also in the eighteenth century, was Fazekas, the author of a famous humorous poem, *Ludas Matyi*, of which I was given by a professor there a new beautifully illustrated edition" (*Europe Without Baedeker*).

leader of East Germany]. Repainting, moving furniture, ladders—highly messy and inefficient preparations. I got some fresh white paint on my sleeve and when, back in Budapest, I explained about it, the answer was "You are the victim of Ulbricht."

The next morning I had breakfast with Miss Katona, who took me to the Déri Museum—very interesting: relics and reconstructions of old Hungarian life, costumes, rooms, instruments, tools, pottery; many statues, inside and outside, of a bad local sculptor, Medgyessy.

We drove around the town in the car by which I had come. The old streets with their one-story houses, with their bluntly arched windows and yellow or red fronts— which stretched, she told me, very far back from the streets and had long courts behind them—were exactly like provincial towns in Russia.

The Kiserdö beside the university is not a forest, as I expected, because they talked so much about it, but simply a grove that is used as a park. We joined Charlotte Kretzói there. She had been teaching *Tom Jones*, and making her students translate it. We finished reading *Az Ördög* in Országh's office. The new university building is spacious, impressive and practical. When we passed a door marked FILOZÓFIA, she told me that the only philosophy taught there was Marxism.

In Debrecen, a man stopped to talk to Miss Katona on the street. The conversation was prolonged as he backed away gesturing. She explained to me that he was the mayor's assistant, and that he had been telling her that it was still impossible to get her and her mother a better place to live. They were living in one room in one of those old bourgeois houses that had a family in every room. The housing situation in Debrecen is very bad, as it is in Budapest. The country people swarm into the cities. They don't have several families in a room, as they used to do in Russia, but the houses and apartments are terribly crowded. Péter Nagy told me that it would take ten years for them to get adequate housing.

I had the faculty of the English department both to dinner and to lunch at the Arany Bika, and paid with my extra food coupons. They wouldn't let me do anything for myself—carried my bag, went to get something I had left in the car. When I was saying goodbye to Charlotte, whom I wasn't to see again, I said that it was sad to think of all the brilliant Hungarians they had lost by emigration. "We have hidden resources," she said.

What is so saddening about the country is its history of stubborn and energetic effort that so often results in abortion. They talk in Debrecen of the historic building where Kossuth "dethroned" the Hapsburgs. Széchenyi went mad. The 1848 revolution was crushed; the 1956 revolt was crushed. Petöfi was killed at 26, fighting the Russians; Ady died of syphilis; Attila József went mad; Bartók was half-extinguished by exile.

When I was about to leave, it was explained that someone would have to ride with me—I couldn't go alone in the car. I asked why. The answer was "Police." It was a man from the French department, who was teaching French poetry and working on Blaise Cendrars. His English was hard going, and though his vocabulary in French was better, his French was hard going, too. By official arrangement, perhaps, we stopped off at a collective farm. I went first to look at one of those wells, which turned out to be broken. A stork flew up from a field, with a wad of dry grass in its bill, and carried it to a roof to be applied to its nest. I don't think I had ever seen one before: a sympathetic bird—*gólya*. Some of the people were living in their own houses, others in a small communal building. We went into a restaurant, which was remarkably clean and attractive. On the front porch, a girl was posing to be photographed in a long overcoat of wool that reached to her feet. The wool hangs down in straight strands and completely envelops the figure. I thought it must be the *guba* [shepherd's overcoat] mentioned in Ady's *Eltévedt Lovas* [*Lost Rider*]: "*Kod-gubában jár a november* [November wears a fog cocoon]"; but my companion said it was a *suba* [peasant's overcoat]. I find that a *guba* is made of frieze. I wonder whether it is white like a *suba*. My impression of everything here was more favorable than my impressions of the collectives I saw in Russia, which were a good deal more primitive.

The Tisza had been overflowing. It was silvery, winding and quite lovely in the setting of the new green of the grass and trees, among which it was spreading its silver ponds. We had to wait to cross it on a narrow bridge where the cars had to drive on the railroad track, a very unsatisfactory arrangement. When a train had gone over, we followed it, and the car at one point stumbled over the tracks.

Approaching Budapest, we had the Gödöllö hills on our left—dark, sudden and a little threatening after the flat even green of the *alföld* [Great Plain], and coming closer, one could see through the thickening day that their sides were covered with vineyards.

When we arrived at the door of the Gellért, before I said goodbye to my companion, he had to make out some kind of slip, indicating, I suppose, that he had delivered me at my destination.

Getting "a Little the Hang of Things"

My last day was crowded and interesting. *Devecseri* called me up and invited me to a dress rehearsal at the opera

(*Erkel Színház*): three short operas, A *király és az okos lány* [*The King and the Clever Girl*] by Orff, Menotti's *Telephone* and an opera by a Hungarian composer made from Mann's *Mario the Magician*. This began at 11:30, and since I was having lunch at 2 with Nagy, I wasn't able to stay for the third of these. Devecseri's attractive wife had translated and directed *The Telephone*, and I was able to tell her truthfully that the production was much better than the one in New York. The Orff with its fairy-tale atmosphere and ballet of jesters and bums was unremittingly fidgety but rather fun. Devecseri was nervous and anxious. In the car, when we were going to the theater, he said, "I will relate the contents!"; but when we arrived, the curtain was going up. In the intermission, he said, "Now I will relate the contents!" but then excused himself to put through a phone call and handed me over to a friend, who, he said, would relate the contents. But the friend's English was even worse than his—though he was full of goodwill, as they all are, and I couldn't even have made a stab at explaining anything of the kind in Hungarian—so I never got more than a dim idea of what had been supposed to be happening.

I had an instructive talk with Nagy at lunch, as I did with Országh afterwards, and was sorry that I had to go just as I was beginning to get a little the hang of things —though if you stay on too long in these countries, you are likely to get too much involved in your personal relationships and, as happened when I was in Russia, become embarrassing to your friends. Two months would have given me a better idea of the situation in Hungary.

I hadn't realized before how much Nagy was an establishment man; but it came out when we discussed Molnár and *Doctor Zhivago*. He detested those old-fashioned sets —there ought to be some way of producing Molnár in a light ironic vein at the expense of the old bourgeoisie. Of

Zhivago, he said that he had tried the German translation and couldn't see anything in it. He asked me about my impressions of Hungary, but I didn't tell him much. I said that I thought that the Russian system was something alien that had been imposed on them; that my impressions of the countryside had been good. He replied with earnest enthusiasm that it might sound like propaganda, but that if anyone had profited by the present regime it had undoubtedly been the peasants. There were relatively few of them living in the degraded condition of the past. They did not like owning no property, but in a couple of generations they would no doubt become reconciled to the new conditions. In America, he said, after all, the farmers were not free either; they had to pay installments on all kinds of things, and so were working for capitalism. I remembered my conversation with Otis Munn and Mrs. Burnham, when they explained why, in spite of the uncertainties and the hard work of the farmer's life, they would not exchange it for any other, on account of the independence it gave them. Yet I suppose that the small dairy farmer is doomed. In any case, I cannot help thinking that some definite improvement actually has been made here. In reading Lengyel's *1,000 Years of Hungary*, I had felt that the drama and romance of old Hungary produced an uncomfortable impression when one came to know that all the time it had behind it a destitute people who often died of starvation. Agatha Fassett had told me of seeing people lying dead on the Buda bank of the Danube, with nobody doing anything about them and her family paying no attention to them.*

Nagy went on—knowing very well the kind of thing I

---

* Agatha had left Hungary in the late twenties. Charlotte Kretzoi suggests that the only time she might have seen such a sight was in 1919, when an abortive rebellion of radical World War I veterans was put down with some shooting.

had been hearing from others—to explain that the intellectuals, who were most strongly opposed to the regime, were actually very little worse off than they had been before. I said that it seemed to me that the restrictions were sometimes unnecessary. He smiled and threw out his hands and said heartily, "Of course they are!" I asked about the partial restrictions on receiving the foreign press when actually many people were able to read it. "The Hungarians are great *débrouilleurs* [very good at getting themselves out of a fix]." He reminded me of Joe Freeman in New York, when he was trying to be a cultural liberal and act as an intelligent middle man between the Party and the intellectuals, but Nagy is much cleverer than Joe. Apropos of the collective farms, he told me one of the disarming stories, invariably told in the Communist countries, that we had talked about at the Gateses' and which Pauline's son-in-law—a young man in the BBC, I think—had told us were officially concocted by a special agency of the government. Sylvester had said that his heart always sank when somebody began telling one of these stories, which were always about somebody in the other world going to hell or heaven. Nagy's story was quite close to the standard model. On a collective farm, the priest has a conversation with the Party Secretary. The Communist asks, "How do you manage to keep your church full when I can get so few people to attend my meetings?" "Well," says the priest, "we both of us are promising the people paradise, but I never show them mine."

Ország was coming to see me after lunch, but Tezla called me up from downstairs, and I went down to see him. He was very much annoyed about the authorities changing the Ford Foundation's list of candidates for scholarships, eliminating the humanities in favor of science, and at the Ford people not resisting. "The authorities here," he exclaimed in a very American way, "think that they're God Almighty!" Országh arrived and said, "The American colony." He and Tezla talked about the situation.

Then I took Országh up to my room, because I wanted to talk to him privately. I told him about my lunch with Nagy and said that I hadn't understood how much he was involved with the Communist government. Oh, yes: he couldn't be editor in chief at Corvina unless he was loyal to the Party. How had he behaved in '56? He probably said some unpleasant things about Rakosi [Stalinist Prime Minister before the Hungarian revolt] which he doesn't want to remember now. But he was always called a "blood orange." Some people were called "watermelons" because they were green outside but red inside; but others were called "blood oranges" because they were red inside and outside, too. I brought up the question of getting Charlotte and László into trouble by reporting what they had said. The authorities would certainly know whom I had been seeing. They would. If I had stayed a long time and met a great many people, they wouldn't be able to pin it on anybody; but I had given my friends as sponsors, and the consequences might be very serious.

I said that I had had the impression nobody wanted to hear about Russia. That was true. They tried to ignore the whole situation. Hungarians had always had a great capacity for deluding themselves. "My life is a sham. I travel around and try to behave as if nothing had happened. We don't like to admit to ourselves that all the important decisions are made by pressing a button in Moscow." Those who hadn't escaped abroad go into internal emigration. He was forced to use *The Daily Worker* for examples of journalism in his courses, and when he petitioned to use something else, because there were bourgeois papers that were better written—he had assured them that he would disregard the content of the articles—he had had no success. All the "people's democracies" (he always pronounced this phrase with a contemptuous reluctance) were made to pay for the printing of the *Worker*. I asked him why he didn't leave Hungary. Suppose he were offered a chair in Hungarian abroad? That might be a different matter; but if he were to leave Hungary, he would have to give up his apartment for good, and would only be allowed to take with him the contents of four suitcases.

Charlotte had been complaining that Országh wouldn't call Nagy *te*; but after these conversations I understood why he continued to call him *maga*.

Suddenness of the '56 revolt: When the secret police fired out the windows at the students who had come to present a petition, it was like putting a match to a smoking fire.

HOME FOR THE SUMMER

Literary Talk and Margaret's Family

London. I flew to London by way of Brussels, sat next to a young Nigerian, with whom I had a long conversation. He had been studying at London University, was preparing himself for the diplomatic service.

My first evening in London, I went to dinner at Natasha Spender's. Sonia Orwell greeted me on the steps: "Aren't you surprised to see me?" Wystan Auden was there—he had come to England to do broadcasts on Shakespeare—and there was a Sir William Coldstream, the head of the Slade School at London University. Geoffrey Gorer came later and another man I never identified. Gorer kissed Auden affectionately, and I found myself almost submerged in the gelatinous medium of the London homosexual-literary world. At dinner, they talked about *Radcliffe*, which they called "the homosexual *Lady Chatterley*." Coldstream, who was sitting opposite me, winked at me when this talk was becoming rather thick. I don't think that Natasha is ever quite at home in this world which Stephen has brought around her. She presides with dignity at the table, but is not really drawn into the conversation. Sonia is very much in it.

Before dinner, Coldstream told us that he had been appointed to do something about the remains of Jeremy Bentham preserved in University College, London. The figure of Bentham, as I understand it, is propped up in a cabinet. I knew about this, but did not know exactly what the figure consisted of. I am not sure that Coldstream knew either, but, on consulting the Encyclopaedia Britannica, I find that Bentham left his body for dissection in the interests of science, so it must simply be his skeleton stuffed out and dressed in his clothes. The head is made of wax, but the real head is there in a casket on the floor, I think. They had told Coldstream that they thought the head was getting a little high, and would he see what he could do about it. He took the lid off the casket: "It *was* rather nasty—the hair was all right." What had he done about it? "I took it to a taxidermist, and he put some mothballs in it or something." Why had Bentham left them these remains to be preserved in this way? "Well, he was a rationalist." I can't see what this had to do with it unless it was a question of demonstrating his contempt for superstition by making people overcome their repugnance to the dead. At an annual banquet, it seems, they bring the figure in after dessert and have it sit there till the company breaks up.

I did not see Celia [Goodman]—she was just leaving with her husband for a holiday in France. She said she was all right, but they told me that she was still very thin. The Gateses were evidently out of town.

The second night, I had Wystan and Natasha to dinner at the Hyde Park Hotel, and afterwards we talked in the Cadogan bar.

I had been to the Pritchetts' for drinks: very jolly—we talked about publishers.

The third night, instead of going to the Greek production of Aristophanes' *Birds*, about which I had some curiosity, I unfortunately went alone to Fielding's music hall, which, except for one old cockney comedian, was extremely unentertaining. A self-conscious attempt to revise the music hall and to make fun, by abridgment, of an old musical comedy. The English, as in Gilbert's time, still think there is nothing so funny as a fat elderly woman being coy.

Wellfleet. I flew to Boston the next day, May 12, and Elena met me at the airport in a bright red new car.

Dinner at the Walkers', with the Chavchavadzes. After the quietness of the Hungarians and the English, the conversation seemed to me all blatt blatt. Everybody, except Elena, was shouting, including me. A lot of talk about the Kennedy assassination, about which they all had positive opinions, though none of them except Paul and I had read Buchanan's book. This is a real case of censorship and seems to me ominous. The government has somehow imposed the ban till the Warren report is out. Roger Straus says he won't touch the report. This evening made me feel what a lot of loud nonsense is talked in the United States about important matters that people want to avoid seriously considering by gregariously shooting off their faces about them. This goes on at Wellfleet all summer.

Hemingway's Moveable Feast: Very funny and for me quite exhilarating. It took me back to that period, and Hemingway was much the better for returning to it. His younger self, in spite of his meanness to others and his always giving himself *le beau rôle*, was a more attractive

person than the awful old ham he became. The chapter
about Scott and his worrying about his penis clears up my
last conversation with H., chronicled when it occurred
above.* But I still don't understand why a penis should
appear to be larger when looked at in a mirror than from
above. In his relations with the Fitzgeralds and Gertrude
Stein, it is not clear from his account that in both situations
an important factor was that Alice B. Toklas was jealous
of H. and that Zelda was also jealous. He makes himself
odious in the final chapter by telling us he was ruined by
"the rich"—after having jeered publicly at Scott for having
cared too much for the rich—and that Pauline broke up
his marriage with Hadley. I remember Zelda's saying that
at the time that H. was struggling with this problem, she
had found him a bore because he would come around and
try to make them justify the decision he had already taken
to leave Hadley. The Hemingways' habit, in Paris, of going
out in the evening and leaving the little boy with the cat
reminded me of the first time I met him when he and
Hadley came to see Mary and me at 1 University Place.
We asked them to have dinner with us, but when they got
back to the hotel, he phoned me that they had got into a
"jam" on account of the baby, which they had left in the
room alone.

* They had last met on an evening thirty years before. "Scott, with his
head down on the table between us, like the dormouse at the Mad Tea
Party—lay down on the floor, went to can and puked—alternately
made us hold his hand and asked whether we liked him and insulted
us. Hemingway told him he oughtn't to let Zelda's psychoanalysis ball
him up about himself—he was yellow if he didn't write." Hemingway
recalled the "consultation" he was to make famous in *A Moveable Feast*.
" 'Scott thinks that his penis is too small,' " he said of that incident
from their Paris days. In *The Thirties* Wilson adds, "John Bishop had
told me this and said that Scott was in the habit of making this assertion
to anybody he met—to the lady who sat next to him at dinner and who
might be meeting him for the first time." Hemingway continued, "I
explained to him that it only seemed to him small because he looked
at it from above. You have to look at it in a mirror."

But in spite of Hemingway's malice about everybody but Ezra Pound and Sylvia Beach, he brings out people's personalities in a way that makes me hear the voices of those I knew and even catch the mannerisms of those I did not. The sketch of Ford Madox Ford is perfect: his inattentiveness, his hoarse high voice. But one cannot be sure that his persistence in explaining to H. the address of the building in which he, Hemingway, had lived was not an exploit of British Lifemanship, nor that his answers to Hemingway's questions as to who was and was not a gentleman did not have an element of humor. Ford liked to pull people's legs, and there was something of this in his romancing.

Visit of the Canbys, May 29–31: Jimmy Canby and his wife had come East for their daughter's graduation from a Middle Western college, and brought her on to New York. He wrote me, and we had them come up. We hadn't seen them for eighteen years—since the last time they had been in New York and had come to see us in Henderson Place when Rosalind and I had been living there, and Elena, whom I had not yet married, had happened to be there. Now they had the daughter with them. She was quiet and shy like Margaret and looked rather like her. Jimmy said that she was the shy one of his four children and that she did resemble his mother. He himself talks a lot, and I suppose resembles his father, who had the reputation of liking to throw his weight around. I don't like to think of Jimmy, after his mother's death, spending years alone without her with his father. But though loud-talking and something of a bore, he is amiable, decent and generous. His wife is a typical California woman, healthy, cheerful and competent. Jimmy adores her and told me how wonderful she has always been. They had to give up

their ranch because "the area" (a favorite word of his) had
been all built up and his taxes correspondingly raised. They
had had to put the children through good schools and
colleges, and this had limited their resources for such lux-
uries as coming East. He now works in a bank. They were
enchanted with the Cape Cod "area," the way we lived,
with people around us that we knew and saw. I gathered
that they did not have much to do with the old Santa
Barbara drinking, gambling and fornicating crowd. Jimmy
wanted to go somewhere that was quiet and not built up
as he said Santa Barbara now is.

I was glad to see him again, and he was glad to make
connections with us again—the only connection he had
been able to make in New York was with Daisy Waterman.
I found that he had nothing but good memories of the three
summers he spent with us in New Mexico and Provincetown. He and Rosalind reminisced about their escapades
at Peaked Hill when, after Margaret and I had gone to bed
and Stella [Rosalind's nurse] was asleep, they had climbed
out the window onto the sand dune and gone off to the
Coast Guards, who gave them cookies. But the reunion
was rather upsetting for Rosalind. They had been closer
to one another than I had realized. As Jimmy said, neither
of them had had brothers or sisters, and they half became
brother and sister. It was upsetting for me, too. That had
all been something that was torn away, and I have never
entirely recovered from it. Elena was wonderful, as she
always is with visitors. We had the Givens to dinner, and
had a picnic at Gull Pond with the Wallings. Both had
known Jimmy's mother, but he did not remember them. I
don't think he had ever seen them.

It is so chilly here even in June that, since I left at the
end of September, I cannot get over the notion that it is

autumn instead of spring—the first kind of bright autumn weather.

Marie-Claire has been staying with *Mary Meigs* ever since her eye was injured when, as they were walking through the woods, Mary let a branch snap back at her. *Barbara* was away on her peace and desegregation walk, in the course of which she spent 27 days in jail, and Marie-Claire provided a companion for Mary, who was full of guilt about the accident and also, we think, somewhat fascinated by Marie-Claire. She has done several portraits of her—or rather, excellent paintings in which Marie-Claire appears. But now that Barbara is back, they have put Marie-Claire in the yellow house, and they are perhaps, though they show no signs of it, beginning to feel that they have had enough of her. She wore out and exasperated both Elena and the Wallings when she was visiting them. She thinks everybody is full of *angoisse*—for which she has now learned the English word *anguish*—and carries this to absurd lengths. She doesn't think *Les Stances à Sophie* is funny, but that the heroine suffers acutely from *angoisse.* —"*Et elle ne peut pas se sauver*"—ignoring the fact that she does get away by going into the striptease business. And she insists that *La P'tite Poule d'Eau* [*The Little Water Streetwalker*], that almost sentimental idyll, is also full of *angoisse.* When I asked where she saw it in the jolly ending and the figure of the dear and serene old priest, she said that she didn't believe in that part. I thought, however, that she had made some improvement when she told me that, although she had at first taken Simone de Beauvoir's last two volumes of memoirs quite seriously, she now thought them rather comic. She is leaving tomorrow (June 8) for Canada and a three weeks' trip with a boyfriend to Europe, but is going to join the girls later in Maine.

Last night, when she and Barbara had dinner here, I

Rosalind Wilson on the beach at Wellfleet

tried some of my card tricks on her and found that she was very sharp and did not allow her attention to be dominated by the magician. She completely messed up my extrasensory perception trick by shuffling the cards again after I had exchanged the shuffled pack for the prepared pack. I tried it on her again, attempting to prevent this, but without much greater success. She had never heard of extrasensory perception and couldn't get it out of her head that I was performing a kind of fortune-telling, that I was trying to prove something about her character. She decided that the reds were feminine and the blacks masculine, and that I was trying to make her get all the reds on one side and all the blacks on the other, and she triumphantly pointed out that she had shown that the sexes were mixed. I said, "Yes, you resist me." "Oh, yes: I can resist you!"

<As always happens this time of year, when my departure for Talcottville approaches, *Elena and I have been quarrelling*. In spite of our preoccupations, which sometimes put us at cross purposes, we do not really like to part.

The income tax people have refused to accept as part of my settlement some $1,200 that they confiscated through their lien on the Red Bank trust fund, and I'm now going to have to mortgage the Talcottville house in order to pay this—with 6% interest some $1,500.

Bad dream last night (June 7): Elena and I were in a room in which the ceiling fell and then one by one two or three gray bricks fell down, but they did not hit Elena, because she was standing back against the wall beyond where the ceiling had come down.> Then Brenda Engel came in—we saw the Engels on our trip to Boston—and we told her what had happened, then we went out with her on the Cambridge street and ran into Monroe. I started to tell him what had happened, but didn't quite want to have to tell it all again, and thought I would let Brenda tell him.

Aging Friends; Conservative Notions

<Talcottville, early June–late August.> It is now October 7. I am at Wesleyan and <only now getting back to writing this—have been occupied with getting *Canada* and *Bit Between My Teeth* finished.

When I gave Mariska the embroidered table set that I had bought for her in Hungary, her first and immediate remark was "I can do that kind of embroidery!"

I got a good deal of writing accomplished at T'ville but otherwise my summer was rather melancholy and also annoying. I was there seven weeks alone, with only two overnight visits: Mary and Barbara and the Fentons. Gertrude Loomis is quite dotty, didn't remember Rosalind when she came; Huldah is more or less infirm: arteriosclerosis. Jessie Howland, who thought last summer that her operation had cured her, is now back on crutches. Everett Hutchins suddenly died—a cerebral hemorrhage —just after he had come back from a trip to New York and had come over and changed a tire for Rosalind. Mabel, when I went to see her after the funeral, said something like "Well, we have to go on, though we don't know why we should"—it seemed all wrong that Everett should have died when he was not yet old. It reminded me of Edna Millay's poem about the death of the father: "Life must go on; I forget just why." Everett was a highstrung wiry man: I think that that truck driving killed him. He had told Mabel, when he got back from New York, that he would never make that trip again. —Old Albert Grubel is so feeble now that he has even sold his car. —The wall of the stone barn had fallen out, just as Fred Berger warned me it would do, and I could not bear to sit outdoors near those ruins. I have had Bob Stabb rebuild it, and it is costing me a lot. Also, the roof has to be repaired and painted, and the roof of the back part of the house. —Fred Reber died during the winter—he was over 90, I think, but still able to do a little work last summer. I cannot remember a time when he was not there in Boonville—in my childhood, he was a photographer. Lately, with wonderful ingenuity and skill, he did all kinds of odd jobs for me—framed pictures, refinished the bar chairs, repaired other pieces of furniture. I bought from him for $2 the big picture of the authors of America, which he had acquired from the effects of some local judge.

The Crostens were less jolly than usual, because they had left both the children in California to work at summer jobs. Lesley was waiting on table and wrote to her parents rather homesick for Boonville. On account of their moving around so much, they had given the big police dog away. I also missed him—his great idea was to have you throw things into the pond, so that he could plunge in and retrieve them. The beavers, however, are back, and late in the afternoon you can see them swimming, with silver streaks behind them—also, something white-looking in front of their noses, which we could not identify. One day the Crostens saw rollicking otters, which climbed on the beaver lodge and made the inmates furious, slapping their tails.

Malcolm and Dorothy [Sharp] finally arrived. He has

aged but she is much better than the summer before last. She can walk, though only slowly, and she seems to be clear in her mind, though she does not talk much. I said to Malcolm that he was very patient with her. "Too much so, perhaps," he characteristically retorted. Why? Because she mustn't be too dependent. He gave me a copy of an address he had delivered called "The Conservative Fellow Traveller." He was evidently making an effort to produce a declaration of his opinions about everything; but, as I told him, what with his ambiguities, his habitual indirectness, I couldn't tell what he thought about anything. He replied, "That was why I wrote it." When I quoted this later, he said, "I didn't say that—you did."

Dorothy Mendenhall died during the summer. She hadn't really been functioning for several years, and nobody, I think, felt real grief. Dorothy Sharp expressed no sorrow, and yet I think her aunt's death affected her. One felt that something was gone from the world. She had been there in the background so long—always a "tower of strength," though domineering and difficult to cope with—to her sons, I suppose, somewhat crushing.

Dawn came up for almost a week while Rosalind was there. She is in and out of the hospital and seems, for her, emaciated—rather yellow and haggard. I would be alarmed about her when I saw her in the morning. She would collapse on her bed or the couch. But she never complained and in the later afternoon always came to life again—the Towpath restaurant, drinks, she sometimes forced her wisecracks a little.

Dos, who is now a big Goldwater man, has written for *The National Review* a preposterous, hysterical piece about the San Francisco convention which sounds, as I have

written him, like a teenager squealing about the Beatles.[*]
Dawn thinks—probably right—that this is all inspired not
only by his getting back his patrimony and the property in
Virginia but also by a belatedly developed family sense, the
result of having a daughter and a genuinely wifely wife,
and by the desire "to belong"—he now wants to be an
upstanding flourishing 100% American, the kind of character that he used to despise in his youth. He takes the
same attitude about the Russians that, at the time of the
First War, he used to ridicule when we were denouncing
the Germans. He expresses himself about the peace movement in what seems to me very much the tone of Oscar
Wilde's "Those Christs that die upon the barricades,/God
knows that I am with them in some ways," and he really
seems not unwilling to advocate war as a defense against
the menace of Russia—contemplates the possibility of our
taking refuge in shelters and somehow pulling through.

It was also depressing in Talcottville to find that the
John Birch Society and juvenile delinquency had made
their inroads there. One of the good-for-nothing Sullivans
had put up a poster on the gas station in front of Elmer's
store: "Save the Republic. Impeach Earl Warren." This
had been torn down, and he then put it up in front of the
wretched house which he has bought across the street from
Aunt Addie's. Old Krieger is also an ardent convert. He
came to see Carrie Trenham and demanded, What do you

---

[*] "What on earth has happened to you? How can you take Goldwater
seriously?" EW goes on in this letter. He had earlier asked Dos how
Goldwater could be "all out for cleaning up on Russia and at the same
time want to get rid of the income tax?" Wilson explains in *Upstate*,
published after Dos Passos's death, that his friend once liked "to shock
people by his radicalism," later by his conservatism, the latter seeming
as puerile as the former. "The person to be shocked [was], in either
case, always what he calls 'the liberal,' who [was] mainly a creation of
his own, a rejected state of mind inside himself."

think of that!—the poster, then on the gas station in front
of the house. I don't like it! Then I won't work for you
any more! She had been dependent on him to do certain
things for her. He has announced that he won't work for
anybody who doesn't go along with the John Birchers, but
he mowed my back field as usual, not knowing undoubtedly
what my opinions are. It all emanates from somebody in
Port Leyden who sends them John Birch literature and has
tried to persuade the principal of the regional school to
give each of the seniors a copy of some Birch propaganda
book. The Catholic priests in Constableville are strong
John Birchers. The movement appeals to the Catholics on
account of the Supreme Court's decision about eliminating
prayer from the schools—of course, they think that Warren, because he is chief justice, is responsible for the
decisions—and also on account of the war against Communism. The John Birchers have created in T'ville a certain amount of bad feeling.

Juvenile delinquency: there is now quite a gang that, when
the boys have motorcycles, travels from town to town. I
found them all congregated one night on the corner and
on my lawn. After the Crostens, who had been there, were
gone, they slipped in the back door and stole the remnants
of a pint of whisky. Later on, I found three boys drinking
beer and drunk on the front porch. I appeared to them
with the old gun that the Civil War collector in Boonville
had offered to buy as a relic, and they immediately took to
their heels. After that, when they gathered I bawled them
out, and finally got rid of them. One of the boys with a
motorcycle was one of the Browns who have lately moved
in on Water St. He has been going with a Robertson girl
from the family who have bought Mrs. Burnham's farm
and who are not at all well thought of. He was arrested
with two other boys for robbing garages and put on parole
at Lowville. The boy got a job, and the sheriff asked Fern

if she thought he might let him off parole. Fern advised him no, but he did. Then, not long after my difficulties with them, he ran into one of the Jacksons' cows while racing a car on his motorcycle. The cow was killed and the boy was taken to the hospital. After this, things were quieter. They have done a good deal of robbing and wrecking—have been breaking the windows in old ladies' houses—the Loomises and Carrie Trenham.> Last summer a group of men and boys were jailed for stealing gas. Of course, in a place like T'ville, there is little for the young people to do, no place for them to go and amuse themselves. But it is no different in the bigger towns and the cities. <Mrs. Clark Layng, in Boonville, says that they pull up her flowers and throw them around the lawn. Early in the summer, one of Walter Edmonds's cows was shot. They had a truck to take it away to be sold for beef, but Walter came out and they fled. The poor cow was running around the field, bleeding, and died.> Sullivan's poster was torn down, but it was done by these kids—no political significance whatever.

<When I saw John Gaus at the Crostens', I thought he behaved rather oddly—seemed to avoid speaking to me. In the middle of dinner he made some remark about not having read my tax pamphlet, and couldn't bring himself to—apparently had only read the reviews and disapproved—made some crack about supposing that I was all for Goldwater. This annoyed me, and I gave him a copy of the pamphlet, which he later made excuses for still not having read. He is so much infatuated with his conception of the soundness of the democratic American community —based on what he imagines to have been this norm up here—that he doesn't want to pay attention to the unpleasant features of our life. You couldn't get him to talk much about them. Malcolm tells me that during the

McCarthy era, John would shut him up if he tried to discuss the subject.

Mariska's mother died last winter, and it is plain that that has upset her equilibrium. She either seems worried or, as one evening when she came late straight from the store, rather unnaturally merry—so that I thought she had had a drink, but she said she hadn't. One evening I took her to the Towpath, and she did have a drink and then began telling me about herself. She first said that Fiore, her "boss," wanted to make her a partner in a new venture.> He had several brothers, one of whom ran a drugstore in Oneida. Between them, they had the two drugstores, a funeral parlor, an ambulance and the cripple-equipment department in the drugstore in Rome, over which Mariska presided. Her boss had failed to get elected mayor because, she said, the people in Rome didn't want a gang of Italian brothers to get a grip on the town. <But now he wanted to buy out his brothers' interests, combine the two drugstores and make a bigger thing of it. He would make Mariska a partner and give her a more important position. I said that this sounded fine, but she was evidently not entirely happy about it. If it weren't for her husband and the children, she could devote herself to business and education. I said that the children depended on her. "They won't do anything without me. They say that picnics and things are no fun without me."> After a pause: "And who can I depend on?" I had never heard her strike this note before. I think that she had in some way depended on her mother to keep her on "that very narrow rope" that she had spoken to me about before. She now confessed that if she allowed Fiore to do so much for her, he would expect something from her, and she didn't like him well enough. I could see that it would be a mess, with both of them married, and that she was so much her own woman that she didn't want him to have a real hold on her. He was always wanting her to have lunch or dinner with him, and she had occasionally done so, in order to talk business. But if she went any further in the way of going out with him alone, everybody knew everything about everybody there, and she would certainly create a scandal. Since he had made her such a favorite in the drugstore, the other girls, I gathered, already assumed that she was going to bed with him, and were, she said, becoming hostile to her. I remembered the obviously jealous scene that Fiore had made the summer before, when we were unpacking and putting books away and he had suddenly appeared at my house. She told me that he was very jealous of me, wanted to know what she wanted of an old man.

Before this conversation at the Towpath, she had announced first that she was going to Philadelphia, then that she was going to New York. I assumed that she had gone to New York; but one night Fiore called me up and asked if she was there with me. It was Wednesday, her day off, and he knew that then she usually came to me. I said that I had supposed she was in New York. He said that they had "left it open." I had imagined that they met on these trips out of town; but I could see now that she had always gone on his trips with his wife, and otherwise left things vague and probably stood him up. When she reappeared, she told me that she didn't want her holidays controlled by him and, in order to get away from everything, without telling him, had taken the children to the Eisenhower Dam on the St. Lawrence Seaway. They had stayed in a motel—she had not had a very good time. I was rather worried about her, but when I saw her again after the Towpath, she told me that the next day she had delivered Fiore an ultimatum: either she quit her job or she had her days off to herself. She didn't give herself her usual two weeks' vacation, but saved it for shorter holidays—took the children to the World's Fair in New York. She is obviously overriding her problems by charming her customers and devotion to her children. She says that she has never been in love. She did well in her examination at Utica College, but has still not quite finished her freshman year.

<I hardly ever now think about the past of the house. Everything is my own concern. My ties with the old life hardly exist any more, and my relations with the current commune are something of a nuisance and annoyance.>

A feeling, the older I get—which I never expected to have—that earthly matters are hardly worth the effort. I've seen the best and worst that people can do, and I no longer have my old curiosity, sympathetic or antipathetic emotions. Since I'll soon be fading out of it, why bother to read books, meet people, travel to foreign countries? I feel that I've pretty well canvassed the world, and what's the use of more experience? As for women, my powers are waning. What's the use of thinking about them? All of my delightful adventures are now in the past. I sometimes enjoy remembering them, but even that is losing its attraction.

I went to Canada for about ten days after the Fourth of July—flew to Toronto with Helen Muchnic, who has a job at the university for next winter and wanted to look for a place to live. I took her to see the Callaghans. I still enjoy them—the same long sessions over the dinner table or in the front room. The same family rallies—Barry is married, and Nina is cheerfully pregnant; Michael is not married, but still has the same girl, who has the same dachshund that sits up and begs. Friends drop in from time to time. Same leisurely conversations that—with well-spaced whisky—unroll for hours. One key to these sessions' going on so long was indicated to me by Morley. He says that he makes a point of listening to what other people say—something they do not expect. People usually talk for themselves, and are likely to be surprised when they find that other people have been paying attention to them. But Morley takes them up on what they have been talking about—hence the conversation s'enchaîne. The boys to some extent kid their father. When he begins becoming pathetic about the neglect of his work, they play an imaginary violin. But the general atmosphere is one of affection and respect. Barry comes to the house every day or so to get lunch and play Ping-Pong with his father. The dreary taste and sordid detail of the household is almost effaced by all this. Back of the house, they have a lawn with a garden and birds and a fountain. They sit on a little porch, with old and shabby chairs and a table on which has been, I suppose for years, a mousetrap with an old piece of cheese in it.

Canada: Jeanne Lapointe and Marie-Claire Blais

I went on to Montreal and stayed at the Ritz—saw Hugh MacLennan twice and Jeanne Lapointe a number of times. She had come on to Montreal for the meetings of some sort of educational committee. She is very intelligent, quick and witty. We had lunch and dinner and went to an inferior French movie together, and I took her one evening to the Buells'. The first time I took her to dinner, I was surprised, in the shaded hotel dining room, lit only by the lamps on the table, to find that she seemed very beautiful, which I hadn't remembered her as being. I thought that her eyes were green. But the next day when I took her to luncheon and saw her in broad daylight, she again seemed rather plain. Her eyes were a flat French-Canadian blue, her complexion pale and mat.

The summer before last, Marie-Claire Blais spent almost a week with Elena while I was in T'ville. M.-C. wore her out with long evening sessions in which she confessed her sin and *angoisses*. She revealed the story of having been *violée* by Père Lévesque, having lived with him four months—a period of horror. Elena ended by telling her that nothing that had happened to her hadn't happened to lots of other people, and she said to me that, after all, it took two to produce such a situation and that *on ne se laisse pas violer pendant quatre mois* [one doesn't let oneself be raped for four months]. She now refers to M.-C. as "a *petit champignon de femme fatale*" and refuses to see her alone. M.-C. makes terrific demands on people, attaches herself to women and won't let go. Elena says she felt that M.-C. would have stayed on indefinitely at Wellfleet if she hadn't been firm about making her go. Later, she visited Odette [Walling] and tried to establish a similar dependent relationship. I gather that she got on Hayden's nerves by trying to probe into his personal life. But when Barbara was away freedom-marching and in jail in the South, she got her hooks into Mary and became a permanent fixture. What clinched it was the accident that injured M.-C.'s eye. It was a long time before she was able to read or write, and Mary was full of guilt, with the result that, Barbara being absent and Mary undoubtedly lonely, she stayed on and on and now lives in their other house, an integrated member of the family. It is as if they had a daughter. When I spoke of her sexual confessions to Elena and her bad conscience about them, Barbara said with satisfaction, "We've straightened her out."

In Montreal, Jeanne Lapointe and I talked a lot about M.-C. I feel that Jeanne is lonely. She is very much a part of the literary world in Quebec, but I imagine has few close friends. She asked me how I had come to be interested in *"notre petite île déserte."* It was something I hadn't known about? That was true. M.-C., I suppose, had been an unusual phenomenon and an interesting protégée. Jeanne had been through the phase of having M.-C. fasten on to her and seems to have dealt with it with good sense and firmness. M.-C. appeals to the protective instinct, and her protectors, I observe, are likely to become a little jealous of one another. M.-C., on her side, believes that everything clusters around her and does not understand that other people are occupied with their families and their own affairs. She wrote to us when we were in France that she felt that we had "abandoned" her. She called up Odette last summer and said that she was afraid that her relations with Mary had caused a *"refroidissement"* with Odette and also with me. Odette replied she did not know or care what her relations with Mary were—*"Ça m'est égal."*

I got from Jeanne a better impression of M.-C.'s "background" than I had from her own account of it as transmitted through Elena. The family did not sound on quite so low a level. The mother, J. said, had tried to improve herself. They were all *"effrayés de* [afraid of] *M.-C."* I had somehow got the impression that J. had instructed M.-C. in correct French—though I didn't see how she could have been so illiterate after eleven years in the convent. But J. told me that all she had done for her was induce her to take some of the adjectives out of her poems. She still kept in fairly close touch with her. M.-C. kept writing her letters, and they were sometimes supplemented by bulletins from Barbara and Mary. When I mentioned anyone in Wellfleet, Jeanne would add details about them—so that I got an account of Wellfleet life in the version of M.-C., which amused me very much. M.-C. told J. or someone that Elena was so broadminded and forbearing because she did not mind my spending hours alone with her. Actually, I had taken her into my study for about a quarter of an hour to talk about the Guggenheim and her work. I said to Jeanne that it must be like a novel for her. She answered, "*Un roman fleuve, et il n'est pas encore fini* [A saga, and it's not over yet]."

She had been the confidante of both parties during the Lévesque affair. She had a certain contempt for Lévesque—he was terribly vain, and she thought that M.-C. had unconsciously been writing about him in the character of the stepfather in *La Belle Bête*—and, after all, she couldn't get over the fact that Lévesque was a monk and there was a certain amount of hypocrisy about it. I said that I was sorry for Lévesque. The affair had driven him to Africa and brought his good work at Montmorency to an end; and the next time I saw her she asked me, "*Pourquoi plaignez-vous* [Why are you concerned about] *Lévesque?*" I tried to put in a plea for him, and J. demurred; but I noticed that she referred to him twice as "*le pauvre homme.*" What sent him away to Africa was apparently not expiation but his having been found out by his secretary, who had written M.-C. a terrible letter. M.-C. had brought it to J. and J. had taken it up with Lévesque. She had also arranged a meeting at the airport between Lévesque and M.-C. Lévesque, M.-C. told Mary, had wept. J. told me that he had actually been madly in love with her, made it so obvious that people were embarrassed, had said—with other people present—things like, "*Jeanne, vous êtes la mère de M.-C., et moi, je suis son père.*" He had told J. that when he was ordained his superior had warned him that a possible danger for him was that he might fall in love with an intelligent woman. Though J. had tried to restrain her, M.-C. had told the story to a number of people, and when Rosalind came to T'ville and revealed that she knew about it, I decided that it was possibly destined to become the most celebrated clerical romance since Abélard and Héloïse's.

J. said that she found it a distinct relief to be able to talk about it all with somebody from outside whose point of view was more or less objective. M.-C. had provoked such hostility in Quebec that she didn't want to criticize her in any way. She laughed a good deal about her adventures. Jeanne called up one evening and told her she had been seeing me. *"Vous avez parlé de moi!"* *"De vous, de vos articles."* M.-C. explained that she was there alone. People now didn't necessarily ask her out when they asked Mary and Barbara. Later, Mary explained to me that they were encouraging M.-C. to accept invitations to go out alone— to make her less dependent. I told J. that I expected that the next thing would be for her to go to Wellfleet to join them, and she did not like this. She said later, as if in order to put me straight, "I like men better than women." When I talked to her about Hugh MacLennan, whose *Two Solitudes* she had not cared for, I described him to her— international, goodlooking, distinguished, spoke French— but not in any extravagant way—she blushed and said, "I don't want to meet him. I should fall in love with him!" But still later when I told her she must come to visit us: *"Je vais peut-être faire mon noviciat* [I must perhaps go and make my noviciat]."

I brought *Jeanne Lapointe* to the *Buells'* one evening after dinner at the Martinique. They had invited for my benefit a man named Valentine, who was supposed to be an authority on the history of the early French in Canada. He was very tall—he told us that he could always see the dust on top of pieces of furniture—rather goodlooking and I should say a prize example of the smugness of the well-to-do Westmounters. His admiration for *la belle France* and

his interest in early French Canada seemed to be coun-
terbalanced by scorn and suspicion of the contemporary
French Canadians. He seemed totally unsympathetic with
French Canadian nationalism, referring contemptuously
to René Lévesque as "Minister of Natural Resources or
whatever he is"* and treating J. with a certain lack of
respect. If she broke in when he was holding forth, he
would say to her: "Don't interrupt me!" When she continued to do so, he would hold her wrist—she always threw
out her hands in expostulation—as a way to stop her from
talking. When he got started on how wonderful France
was, she told him that the French could be horrid. "Oh,
no: France is your mother—" "France is not my mother.
I am not even entirely French." "Oh, yes: France is your
mother. England is my mother. We can't go against our
mothers!" At one point, he said that everybody must be
silent, he was about to say something important. I forget
now what he came out with, but it was something completely uninteresting. He drove us back to the Ritz in his
splendid expensive car. I took J. in for a drink—she was
following my example in drinking double vodka Tom
Collinses—and we laughed about the evening. Valentine
loved to show off his French, which was about on a level
with mine. The wife had given me the impression of being
a rather sour and dried-up witch; but J. said she liked her
better than the husband because she knew what an idiot
he was making of himself. She had hardly said a word.
Elena told me afterwards that she had known him when
she lived in Montreal. He had pretensions to interest in
the arts. He had become converted to Catholicism—which
can hardly be typical of Westmount. Hence, I suppose,
his relations with Buell. Buell told me that he was now
spending a good deal of time working with left Catholic

* René Lévesque was the leader of the separatist party in Quebec, later
premier.

groups. They were, he said, successfully collaborating with the English—which he preferred to throwing bombs.

J. and I ended up with a real relation of palship.

Notes made in Canada:

The reference to Wolfe in *The Maple Leaf Forever*. Acceptance by the English of *O Canada*.

The word *American* today connotes something different from what it did in the past—an overwhelming prestige.

English Canadians shaking the right fist at us and selling out with the other hand.

The "ethnics"—encouraged to continue to cultivate their own nationalities and languages, and so remain unqualified for office.

Lack of leadership and coördination of the French nationalist movement.

Blaming the English for their own handicaps.

Nationalism and anti-clericalism do not necessarily go together: Ordre de St. Jean Baptiste. Contending among themselves.

Terrorists educated boys of good family.

Amateurishness of the poetry.

Historical novels: Kirby and Gilbert Parker.

French section of Montreal—houses with their long outside stairs.

Taxi driver half-French, half-Italian, who believed that in the old country they didn't live just for money but for "love." He was the last of the family left at home, living with his parents. I had asked him whether he were married. He said no, but that he needed love.

MacLean's and the *Montrealer* have a hard time getting along. The publishing world resents the Canadian editions of *The Reader's Digest* and *Time*, which take away their advertising.

Leslie Roberts spoke of his feeling of helplessness at realizing that important decisions could be made in the U.S. that would vitally affect Canada without their being able to have anything to say about them.

Loretto Callaghan thought that they would simply merge with the U.S. But how? an American asks. How can they become part of the Union? Roberts saw that this would be an impossibility; but feared that our ownership of their industries would end in political control. Our financial and industrial powers, it seems, are strongly opposed to French separatism. The French nationalist movement has its socialistic side—electric power already nationalized.

"The only country with three conservative powers: the Conservatives, the Liberals and the Socialists."

The food at the Ritz is no good; the French restaurants are much better.

It is true that the speakers of English make a point of knowing as little French as possible. Morley, who has studied French, always mispronounces French names. Stewart and the publisher McClelland pronounce Gabrielle Roy like Rob Roy. When I call up Lapointe, the editor of the French *MacLean's*, I always have to pronounce his name as English before they know what I mean. But Leslie Roberts pronounces French in a literate way.

The flag: six beavers peeing on a frog—but it seemed only too obvious that they would look to the French like rats.

Two Dreams

Father's language:
- —I'm going to touch the harp lightly (This meant that he wasn't going to eat very much)
- —well-nigh
- —I'm going to take a course in reading (some author)
- —sit there like a bump on a log
- —Your mother has stuck to me like a pup to a root
- —He don't grasp the enormity of the thing

Wellfleet. I went back earlier than usual to Wellfleet, because Reuel and Marcia had come East and were flying to Europe the first of September.

It is amazing to find that Brownie L'Engle is still running true to form. She had made a trip to Greece and told people that she realized now she was a Greek, and this explained so much about her that she had never really understood. She had annoyed Phyllis Duganne by calling her up and telling her that she knew that they would be much happier if they would live in the Provincetown house, that they were really much attached to the house—which, actually, gives them the creeps. Phyllis told her not to ruin her, Phyllis's, life. At the girls'—whom she had bullied into asking her to dinner—she arrived before I had left and broke up my conversation with Marie-Claire by immediately producing and showing us a collection of photographs of Greece. She is so immovably convinced of her social superiority that she would never be aware of how vulgar and stupid she is. But I am sure that, as in the case of

Gladys Billings-Brooks, she must always have felt that she was willing something and resented other people's happiness. Hence her impulse to make people uncomfortable, to register her own superiority. People occasionally tell me that she is really extremely kind, but the instances of her kindness I have heard are all in the nature of making her friends feel their relative wretchedness, their inferiority to her.

Mary Hackett still comes to the Provincetown house. She sometimes sees *Betty Spencer*, who years ago, when she took up with the sick Portuguese Ernest—now dead like Betty's cats, which she would have chloroformed at the end of every summer—broke off all relations with her former friends. Last summer she told Bubs [Mary] that she was having herself cremated and wanted the ashes to be sent to the dump. The question was who could she get to do it. Mary thought about it at home and finally called Betty up and expostulated with her. This made Betty very angry—she told Mary that it was none of her business how she disposed of her ashes, that she was behaving "neurotically" about it.

My consecutive dream at Wellfleet, unusually vivid and full of action. I thought, with a small party of other men, I was scrambling over obstacles in order to arrive somewhere. The leader was an incompletely identified boy that I had known in my youth in New Jersey—Sam Compton? who was engaged to my cousin Esther, and killed in the First War. I think we were wearing khaki. We got into a great barn, and the only way to get to the other end was to climb over a heap of manure which was a towering cone with a sharp top. With my dread of high places, I shrank from it, but I did get to the top and dropped and slid down. Then at the other end of the barn were windows very high up, to reach which you had to climb on old boxes and things. When I looked down, I could see that the drop was impossible. I asked one of my companions how we could possibly make it. "They're getting ropes," he said, and I saw that they were bringing long ropes out of a shed on the left. In front was a strange kind of courtyard, enclosed by a wooden curb, and full of drifts of snow and ice. I couldn't see how the ropes could be fastened to the windows in such a way that we could be let down, and I had no idea of shinnying down one. I dropped to the floor and discovered that it was no trouble at all simply to fall along beside the manure pile—there had been no necessity to climb it. I went out by the back door and walked around the side of the barn and had no difficulty in breaking through the ice drifts. Then I turned around to see what was happening to the others. My group had apparently gone, and two latecomers were there. There was a round object on the snow, and one of them picked it up. It was a human head which evidently in some way had been jerked off by the rope. I told them to hold it up so that I could see who it was. I thought that it was Sandy but from that distance could not be sure. I wondered whether it wasn't better if Sandy had died in this way.

I climbed over another obstacle, a sort of broad wall that was easy, and as I did so thought that Elena might find it strange to find people of such different kinds—the same Compton character now seemed one of the boys from Red Bank—working together to accomplish a common purpose, but decided that she had been in America long enough to have got used to this. I was now confronted by a large blank building which might have presented another obstacle, but I opened a door at the side and found myself in a long high vaulted corridor that seemed to have been newly plastered over some kind of wooden scaffolding. I looked up and around to see whether it looked as if it might collapse, but decided to take a chance and walked to the end, where I came out into a kind of park which was more or less familiar to me. There was a large hotel, which I entered—I now had with me one or two of my original group. There was a smooth and rather oily man at a kind of information desk, and I asked him whether this was the Edinburgh Hotel. It was, he replied, an Edinburgh hotel and was trying to reassure me, but I remembered that I had made this mistake and had the same conversation when I had come to this place before—he evidently did not remember me—so I cut the conversation short. Where was the real Edinburgh Hotel? Just opposite in the park. I explained to my companions and went out the front door, and there was the larger and greater hotel, which we entered by the back door. We were out of place, in our dirty clothes, among the smartly dressed people of the lounge, who all looked as if they had just bathed, but I did not really care, I was proud of my exploit in circumventing the obstacles which our leader had been so stupid as to climb over.

In a kind of little intermediate nook that led to another room, I found my Grandmother Kimball stretched on a short narrow couch: I was a little surprised by this because I thought she had died a long time ago. I should have to go and talk to her, but I wanted to press on and rejoin Elena and tell her about what had happened. On the other side of this nook was Aunt Carrie, very clean and well washed in a white evening dress. It did not occur to me to tell her that Sandy might have been killed.* I simply put my hand on her shoulder in recognition and passed on to the room beyond. On the left was a table where the Chavchavadzes were having drinks and refreshments with what were obviously ex-royal or ex-noble relatives with

* "Aunt Carrie" is Caroline Kimball, Sandy Kimball's mother.

whom they were having a reunion in Europe. I decided to skip these too, and go over to Elena, who was among some people sitting in chairs along the wall at the end of the room. But if the leader of our expedition was there? I couldn't tell in his presence what had happened. Then I found I was feeling uneasily that I might not be well received. The others might have reported that I had been afraid and let them down. This was the end of the dream.

The night after I wrote at Wesleyan (Oct. 12–13) the dream that I had at Wellfleet, *I dreamt that I had committed suicide.* It was at Wellfleet and Rosalind was there. I seemed to be the same as ever, was walking around the house. I asked Rosalind whether I still seemed solid, whether she could see through me. She answered that, even before, I had come to seem so faded that she couldn't notice much difference. I asked whether Elena had been much upset. "I don't know. She's gone to the beach." She conveyed to me that the body was in on the ironing board, but I didn't want to see it: it seemed to me I had cut my throat. I wondered why I had done it. I had thought about it several times, but what had made me carry out the impulse? It was irrevocable, and now that I was dead, I didn't know what to do with myself. What was my future?—I couldn't go on functioning. I was soon involved with Rosalind in one of our shrill disputes. She sat down and began to read, and I decided that I might as well do the same. I picked up a handful of proofs that were lying beside my chair—I think, somebody's introduction to George Borrow. I might as well go on as I had before. But before I began reading, I woke up.*

---

* This vision of the next world as an extension of Wilson's present life accords with his wish that Ecclesiastes 12:12, the "writing of books is an endless matter," be read at his funeral.

IN AND OUT OF THE THINK TANK:
1964–1965

Middletown and Other Scenes

At Wellfleet, Elena collapsed after she had taken Helen to school: partly the separation, partly that, as usual, she had exhausted herself by trying to do too much. We had to put off going to Wesleyan till Oct. 5.

Wesleyan. I found the house quite comfortable. Elena objected to the furnishings—which, it seems, are supplied to all the Fellows by the G. Fox company of Hartford, so that everybody's interior is furnished alike. She had some of the rugs removed but could never stop complaining about the lamps and saying that the living room looked like a dentist's office. But it is quieter than either Talcottville or Wellfleet. I rather enjoy this relaxed suburban life, which reminds me of Vista Place in Red Bank. Reading at night not too near my neighbors, among the lawns and the trees. I have a splendid office in the Center, postage, packing, refreshments supplied; telephone except for long-distance personal calls, and a bland young woman secretary, who is amiable, willing and fast, but not well educated, so that she makes a good many mistakes.

Middletown is an odd little unit. It used to be a prosperous riverport, dominated by the Russell family. Russell House dominated the slope to the river—a big neoclassic affair. Paul Horgan, the director of the Center, now lives in what was once the stables. But the family, as the local ladies explain to Elena, has now dwindled to an alcoholic son and someone else in a mental institution, and the mansion is used for all social occasions, such as our Monday-night Fellows dinners. The conditions for work are ideal, even better in some ways than the *New Yorker* office; but even for me life becomes a little monotonous, since my movements are entirely limited to our house, the Center and Russell House. It is all on a fairly steep hill, on which, especially in the cold weather, it is hard for me to walk even short distances. For Elena, it is lonely and boring. There is nobody with whom she can talk—except Jean Stafford, who has been ill and is now away (Jan. 4, '65). She goes to shop on the dismal Main St., the most primitive I have ever seen in New England—it is almost like a Western town, with a sordid movie house or two, dry-goods stores, old-fashioned saloons, now "bars." The town proper has declined to nothing with the disappearance of the river traffic, and the inhabitants seem quite degenerate—many Italians and Poles, a few Greeks. (Hartford, with its excellent businesses, G. Fox department store, its new Constitution Plaza and its luxurious American Hotel, seems madly metropolitan in contrast, and we occasionally go there for a spree.) Otherwise, she sits around the house, waiting for Papa to get home from his work and read the mail and have his highball. We felt at first a little like Nichols and May.

Everything was made worse by the *death of Brat*. Elena began getting letters of condolence before she knew he was dead, and it was days before she knew what had happened—she doesn't really know yet. The only member

of the family who had been notified by Madeleine was her
Uncle Arthur, whom E. phoned and who could not tell
her much. She wired Margaret Grunelius, who simply
supplied that Brat had died in an accident. It was plain
that if it had been by a plane or car accident, that would
have been specified, and we guessed that he had committed
suicide. While Elena was still in this state of uncertainty,
she attended a rather dreary academic dinner, which put
her under a strain. It turned out that Madeleine's story
was that Brat had been going on a hunting trip, that after
a *gemütlich* dinner, he had gone up to pack his things, had
not reappeared in an hour, and when the daughter had
gone up to find out what had happened, she found her
father dead. He had shot himself accidentally, according
to Madeleine, while packing or cleaning his gun. How
could it have been, says Elena, that the shot was not heard
at the time? I suppose Madeleine was frightened to communicate with the family. When she had called Arthur
up and talked to his daughter on the phone, she had made
some appeal for sympathy, and the girl had hung up on
her. Margaret Grunelius was the only relative who had
turned up for the funeral. She knew almost nobody there.
Madeleine had had the *Eitelkeit* [vanity] to notify their
acquaintances with titles, of whom she liked to boast.

A year or so ago, Brat had fled from Johannisberg and
taken refuge with his uncle and said he couldn't stand it
any longer, but Madeleine had made him come back on
account of his daughter's coming out. There was a question
of her marrying a neighbor of a very old and good family,
whose parents, on account of Madeleine, did not want him
to marry her. Brat had told someone that Madeleine had
turned even his daughter against him. He had lately had
a mistress, and Madeleine, finding out about this, had
made him go to the mistress with herself and, I think, the
daughter and tell her that he was done with her. She

sounds like Balzac's Valérie Marneffe and the heroines of the Marquis de Sade. But Elena, brooding about her, had not only decided that she is half insane—she is obviously, with her tantrums, an hysteric—but had felt, characteristically, a kind of guilt at the family's having so humiliated her. Their father, when she had first turned up, adventuring with a croupier at Baden, had forbidden Brat to bring her into the house. She was ostracized by the family and their former circle. Their neighbors the Metternichs wouldn't go to the house unless it was absolutely necessary; Carol [Radowitz], when he ran into Madeleine, brushed off her invitations. Elena is afraid she will have to sue to get anything that is now coming to her, and predicts that, having ruined her daughter's chance of marriage, Madeleine will drag her around, using her as social bait, and never let her get away.

Before this, sometime in November, I had spent a few days in *Talcottville*, to see to repairs and get books, while Elena closed up the Wellfleet house. I had not looked forward to it and enjoyed it more than I had expected. Mariska met me at the airport, and persuaded me to sit in on, and talk to, Dick Costa's class in journalism. I was already terribly tired and had drinks at the Schuyler Club, so I did not give a very good performance.* I was struck by the suppressed indignant reaction on the part of one of the boys when I said that the Warren Report was "full of holes." An unquestioning belief in the finality of this has become an item of the national credo. I spent that night

---

* He did not respond well when Mary asked whether he was ever a Communist. According to Costa, EW replied, "Mary! . . . you must never . . . *never* ask me a question like that again!" He had resisted joining the Party and was critical of its policies and leaders, yet he had shared the Communist ideal celebrated in *To the Finland Station*. After a long day and drinks, Wilson was not prepared to make such distinctions.

in Utica and Mariska took me the next day to T'ville. Mr. Fiore, her boss, had seen her waiting for me at the airport, looking, he told her, "so spiffy." He knew that I had called her at the drugstore and called me up to check whether I was there and to find out whether I should "be around long." Mary had mischievously told him that I was going to be around all winter. She was taking a week off, which worried him—a customer needed one of her braces. It was satisfactory from my point of view, because, for the first time since she had taken that job, she was able to give me a good deal of time, helped me move in at Talcottville and did a tornado job at the telephone company making them turn on the phone. She was looking much better than last summer, very handsome in her spiffy clothes.

I had dinner with the Morrises. Glyn for the first time got rather drunk and went on, to everybody's embarrassment, repetitiously about Calvin and guilt. The Loomises and the Munns came to call on me. Fern is much embarrassed about her candidate. She had refused to go to Rome to meet Miller, whom, she said, she wouldn't cross the street to meet. Even in his own district, nobody had any use for him.* When I was going and I wished bad luck to her candidate, she pretended to claw my face. When I had called her up, I had said something of the same kind, and she had answered, "I don't think I've got anything to worry about, and you can take that any way you want." Even Otis seemed to be weakening. Glyn told me that a poll taken in the local kindergartens had been almost unanimous for Johnson, reflecting, one supposes, what they heard at home. Many people were voting for Johnson who had never voted for a Democrat before or would refrain from voting at all. I had been apprehensive about staying

* Goldwater had chosen as his running mate William L. Miller, a little-known congressman from western New York.

in the house after my terrible night in November before the new furnace had been installed; but the heating proved perfectly comfortable.

I set out, on my way back, to fly from Utica to Boston, where I was going to meet Elena, who had been in Wellfleet closing up the house. But it was announced when we got to Hartford that there was "mechanical trouble" with the plane and we should have to wait several hours till the next Boston flight. I met *Erich Leinsdorf*, also waiting, and we killed time having drinks in the restaurant. He had just had a concert at Connecticut College and was on his way to New York for a holiday—very tired and complaining, as he had in Paris, of being overworked, and obviously nagged and bored by Boston. The board of direction of the orchestra—or whatever it is called—were full of hypocrisy: they would keep talking of policy on musical grounds when it was really a question of money. They had promised him an assistant who would relieve him of some of the concerts, and then failed to provide him with one. He had attempted a showdown with them: "Why beat about the bush pretending to talk about music when you are actually talking about money?" He was evidently glad to escape to New York. He said that he had been invited to a meeting of the Fellows at Harvard. I said that, on such occasions, I found it an exhausting effort to keep up with the various scholars on their various subjects, which, out of vanity, I tried to do; that I had a kind of wire recording in fields about which I knew little—my line, for example, about Italian literature: D'Annunzio underrated; Dante and Leopardi; Silone unfairly discriminated against; excellence of *Il Gattopardo*. He said that he suffered in his Boston conversations from people's not connecting with him: they didn't understand his stories and ironic remarks. He is certainly a *lustig Wiener*, as Isaiah Berlin said of Felix Frankfurter. He had a story about somebody asking Goldwater whether the Republican exploitation of the Jenkins homosexual scandal might not create a bad impression. Goldwater is said to have answered, "Well, I concede Fire Island."*

The Lowells, Moses Hadas, Stanley Dell

The Center for Advanced Studies. Paul Horgan, the director, is an endearing and slightly ridiculous figure—half-Irish, half-German, a Catholic, who spent most of his youth in Buffalo and Rochester, with summers at Old Forge. When his father came down with TB, the family moved to the Southwest. He writes novels which oscillate between these two parts of the world and has done a long book on the Rio Grande. It may be that he is somewhat "conditioned" by having been Irish-German in upstate New York. I am told that he is somehow active in the Catholic Church and has been made by the Vatican a Knight of St. Somebody.†
On dress occasions, he wears a little ribbon and an old-fashioned gold watch chain across his vest. He has students that serve drinks and wait on table in his own house and Russell House: in his own house, they wear red jackets; in Russell House on our Monday evenings, black ones. He fancies himself a man of the world. A bachelor of the type who wants to be the beloved friend and is full of sympathetic consideration and all kinds of little services, he puts one off a little at first by his anxiety to please and to be in the know. I find myself playing a game with him—playing up to his knowing everybody and all the current events

---

* Walter Jenkins, an assistant to President Johnson, was arrested in the men's room of the Washington YMCA shortly before the 1964 presidential election. Cherry Grove, on Fire Island off the south shore of Long Island, was known as a homosexual retreat.

† Horgan was made a Knight of St. Gregory; he was nominated for this honor by the Archbishop of Santa Fe.

and gossip of the cultural world; but as I see more of him, I get to like him better. He is a great devotee of Max Beerbohm and, especially, of Maurice Baring—in Catholicism, a liberal, who follows his interest in scholarship and letters, regardless of race or creed. An element of a non-affluent Maecenas. I suspect in the family background a moderate amount of money. When [Luigi] Barzini, who wrote the best-selling *Italians*, was here, he said that he had been expecting a quiet academic group, but then found himself at the court of Louis XIV. He repeated this at a banquet given in Barzini's honor, which undoubtedly pleased Paul no end. There were parties at many tables; toasts were drunk and little speeches made. Elena and Jean Stafford complained that the food itself was very inferior and by no means in keeping with Paul's dreams of magnificence. Yet he has an Irish sense of humor.

Elena thinks that he is rather imperceptive about man-and-woman relations. He had brought on [Vera] *Zorina*, a great pal of his, to perform with the students in Cal Lowell's *Phaedra*. They had a hopeless director, who left the performance inaudible because he refused to install amplifiers. Zorina says that on previous occasions, when she has acted with a college cast, she has found the students cooperative and eager to learn, but that here they were quite frozen and she felt that a barrier had been established. In the meantime, Paul had caught the flu and collapsed and had to go to the infirmary while the play was being done. He may have been nervous about the production and also about the situation created by Cal's coming on when his former wife Jean was here. Jean had told Paul that it would seem too pointed for her to go away before Cal came—she would stay one night and then leave. There was to be a dinner before the dress rehearsal; but Paul was unable to preside, and for some stupid reason the hosting of the dinner was made to devolve upon Jean. That morning she called up Elena in consternation, and we advised that she would have to go through with it: some of Paul's friends were coming from Santa Fe. Hoping to sabotage the dinner, we had announced that we wouldn't come. Late in the afternoon, she called me up in the office here and asked me to come to see her (she has an apartment at the Center). I had Elena come, too, and we tried to give her moral support—it was too late for us to arrange to attend the dinner. We left just before she had to go, and she then adhered to Moses Hadas, who sat by her and—I think literally—held her hand.

Elizabeth Lowell called up, being courteous, and the Wilburs called to give warning that Cal was on his way and precariously high. It was like hurricane warnings on the Cape. We sat beside them all at the dress rehearsal. Cal was indeed rather high—almost uninterruptably talking, except when the performance was going on. I was told that when he was brought back from Rio, he had been given enough tranquillizers to knock out any ordinary person, but that he had talked all the way on the plane. We didn't go with them after the show, but Cal, who was staying at the Center, went to Jean's apartment and sat up, she told us, tormenting her till five o'clock in the morning. She came to Elena sobbing and told Elena that Cal had said to her that he might last another ten years, but that she probably wouldn't last more than two. She left for New York that day. She, too, had had the flu. In order to avoid trouble, she of course should have left town before Cal came; but Elena got the impression that she wanted to see him. I think she is rather masochistic. But then she seems to have been happy with Joe Liebling, who was kind and amiable, and she must have been floored by his death. She is now in the hospital in New York with a slipped disc and being tested for cancer.

Cal came to see me twice during the day at the Center,

and he came to dinner at the house, and I had with him perfectly normal and interesting conversations. I always enjoy his wide range of reading and reference, and his feeling for the important things in literature.* What he says is probing and witty, sometimes perverse, with a desire to startle. His friend from Cambridge was with him—I can't remember his name—he is extremely good at handling Cal.

I have been glad to see something of Moses Hadas, who is writing about late literature in Greek and is full of his subject, about which he knows everything—has theories about everything and answers all one's questions. The language that Lucian was writing was archaic and entirely artificial; the Greek romances are based on religious rites; Trimalchio was evidently a Syrian—the end syllable of his name must be based on the Hebrew word for *king*—and the sibyl that he thought he had seen in a cage must have been a parrot or something of the kind. The Gospels belong in form to the type of biographies of wonderworkers, like that of Apollonius of Tyre. With exquisite quiet tact, he interjected, at the Monday-night dinner, out of consideration for his Christian audience, "I don't mean they're not true, but that's the type of literature they belong to." Whether in writing or lecturing or conversation, he expresses himself with elegance and urbanity. His growing up in Atlanta has combined with his natural qualities to give him a sense of style. He thinks that it is style which

---

* In *The New Yorker* two years before, EW ranked Lowell first after Auden among living poets. "He is, I think, the only recent American poet—if you don't count Eliot—who writes successfully in the language and cadence and rhyme of the resounding English tradition." Lowell, he said, had performed the feat of "making poetry out of modern Boston," even to the sloppy icy winters and the garbage pails. "The poetry never ceases to be noble, and the imagery, which is spiky and dark, is also in its way rich and brilliant" (reprinted in *The Bit Between My Teeth*).

Robert Lowell in New York City

was perpetuated wherever the Greek tradition lasted—in Lucian, Dion Chrysostomos, the Greek romances, the pseudepygrapha, Josephus, the Fathers of the Church. Josephus had to have Greek style in order to get over with the Romans. Hadas was ordained a rabbi before he became a classical scholar, and his Hebrew gives him a dimension which most classical scholars do not have—I remembered his once saying that when Gilbert Highet first came to Columbia, he had said to Hadas one day after looking the situation over, "You're the only man here I'm afraid of" —certainly a tremendous compliment. But at the time I hadn't realized how formidable Hadas was.

I had thought it would be easy to see *friends in Connecticut* who live not very far from here; but our few exploits of this kind have been dampening: Sylvia Salmi, the Red Warrens, the Winkelhorns. They supply us with complicated directions which we're completely unable to follow. We get lost and wander around in the labyrinth of state highways and back country roads, inquire at innumerable houses, when it is impossible to see anything in the dark. We are an hour or two late, and then have to find our way back. And what we have found when we got there was that the friends were very Connecticut-suburbanized. At one house where we inquired, I approached a side door next to a small-panel light window full of knickknacks of colored glass, etc. I found a man with bare feet preparing drinks in a pantry, full of rather fancy chinaware. This seemed to me very typical.

The *Dells* came over for lunch from [the township of] Washington. I was very glad to see them. Though we see one another so rarely, I am more at home with Stanley than with any of my other old surviving friends. We both escaped, in any of its forms, any kind of conforming American life, and my decision to live in the country was really inspired by his example when I visited him years ago. Also, the intellectual freedom of European culture—the only one of my college friends who had it. John Bishop had not yet been in Europe and was only beginning to learn languages. But Stanley—always inelastic in not having his habits disarranged—insisted on leaving not long after lunch. They said that they had to feed the animals.*

The director of the College of Letters [at Wesleyan] is, curiously enough, an Egyptian named *Hassan*, married to a more or less succulent little piece of Danish pastry. They invited us to dinner at 7. I was on my feet talking for two hours fortified by two drinks. The host insisted on my having another, and in another half hour I was out, sat down beside Elena and almost went to sleep. Since nothing except hors d'oeuvres had yet appeared, I decided that we had been asked for cocktails and that there was not going to be any dinner. I conveyed this idea in Russian to Elena, and we took our departure just as the soup was being distributed. It was then about 10:30. I can't imagine a worse arrangement, but Paul Horgan says that it is now quite fashionable. He finds they do it in the Southwest, too, and says that he can't take it either.

Carnegie Hall and Café Society

I went to New York in December, to deliver my Canadian book. Mary Meigs, who had brought down my puppet theater and other things and had spent the night with us

---

* Stanley Dell had been Wilson's literary friend at Hill and Princeton. Older than EW, he seemed to Gauss liberated and cosmopolitan. During World War I, the friends corresponded about one's responsibilities as an artist and citizen. In the war Dell received the Croix de Guerre. Though he later translated some of Jung's work, he disappointed Wilson by not being a writer.

at Middletown, drove me down to town. I have so little chance to see her alone, and our relationship always renews itself. I really love her and always shall. I think that she is now to some extent getting on to Marie-Claire—says she feels that she tells about her sufferings in order to draw attention to herself. She was having dinner with Lloyd Frankenberg and another man, an old friend from art school. She invited me to join them, though, with her sensitiveness to people's reactions to one another, she evidently had misgivings about my getting on with this latter, who she warned me was something of "a gigolo type." In any case, I misunderstood the address, was unable to locate the restaurant, found the Russian Tea Room crowded and fell back on Horn & Hardart [the Automat], where the food was not actually so very much worse than anywhere else in New York. We were all going to Sylvia Marlowe's concert in the recital hall of Carnegie Hall. It was a house almost entirely of deadheads—it seems that the Harpsichord Society, in order to keep its license or something—has to give periodical recitals that have nothing necessarily to do with the public.

Almost everyone I ever knew was there and at the party that followed. This was not in Sylvia's apartment but in that of her friends, [Robert] Fizdale and [Arthur] Gold, the two men who play the piano together. They said there were at least twice as many people as had been invited, and when I mentioned this to Roger Straus, he said, "Knowing Sylvia, I imagine that she had invited the extra ones herself." There were many people I wanted to talk to, but the room was so jammed and so deafening that this became very difficult. Dwight Macdonald, very drunk, trying to tell me he had always been for me—I suppose that Joan Colebrook had repeated to him some of the things I said—and wanting to know what I thought of the Warren Report, about which he was doing a long article for *Esquire*.

Bowden Broadwater, who looked very cheerful—I didn't have any conversation with him. The Podhoretzes—Midge has filled out, and I did not recognize her at first. Barbara Epstein, but not Jason; Lillian Hellman, who had to tell me who Midge was—I am getting so dim at times that I recognize faces without remembering names. Lewis Galantière and his wife—he is quite gray, she greeted me rather aggressively with "I didn't know you wore glasses!" Alan Pryce-Jones, who is fatter and has long ago left the foundation he worked for and where I couldn't imagine him functioning. Barbara Skelton, whom I had seen at the concert. She hadn't spoken to me out of English deference, and I finally spoke to her though I wasn't quite sure it was she. She had changed: instead of being juicy and pulpy, she looked rather sharpened and shrivelled. I asked Jason later what she was doing, and he said, "I don't think she knows herself. She lives in a little apartment." Red Warren and Eleanor Clark, Lloyd Frankenberg and wife. I didn't recognize the latter, though she took my arm in an intimate way. I thought she looked like a witch, but they say that she is a very good painter. Elliott Carter and his wife. He wasn't very much excited about Wilfrid Mellers's book on American music—he didn't like the "D. H. Lawrence element."* I had myself a little reacted against his trying to find something essentially "American" in every composer he dealt with; but I said that I had been impressed by it. Yes, Elliott admitted, it was after all the first time that anybody had really devoted any thought to the subject. They had played a concerto of Elliott's that I had never heard before. The concert was all modern music—which I had never heard Sylvia do—most of the pieces commissioned by her. It began with Rieti—who was also there— and ended with de Falla. Some young Americans I had

---

* *Music in a New-Found Land: A Study of American Music* (Knopf, 1965).

never heard of. Sylvia Salmi, pathetic after Herbert's sudden death, not very many days after we had seen him. He had been chopping a tree or some wood—it was totally unexpected.

Nicholas Nabokov's son by his second wife, Connie. He is a tall blond boy, not nearly, I think, so bright or as self-confident as Ivan. He has gone in for anthropology and the Indians—I had sent him to Bill Fenton. I asked about his mother. She has married another of Nicholas's old pupils and gone with him to New Mexico, where they are active in a Western version of the Annapolis St. John's. I was beginning to talk to him about her when his father's first wife, Natasha, appeared. I had seen her last winter in Paris at Nicholas's Christmas Eve party. We had a not long enough conversation. The boy left us, and she said she had "inherited" him. He was somewhat dependent on her and would come to her when he had been disappointed in his laying siege to some girl. We laughed about Nicholas's marriages. He will tie himself into knots about a woman—"Don't I know!" she interjected—marry her, have one child and then disengage himself. She said that he was now in love with a 19-year-old girl in Berlin, but, equally characteristically, was now in Tokyo. She had been to see Volodya and Vera Nabokov at Montreux. In order to *épater* people, he wore a pince-nez with a ribbon *à la Chekhov*. She said to him, after a time, "Now you've made your effect with that pince-nez. I've seen it—you don't need to wear it any more." He laughed with a hearty ha-ha—the laugh of a fat man—now that he has grown stout—that she had never heard him give before. She said that his bad manners and arrogance were the results of insecurity. I doubt this. If the old regime had never fallen, I imagine he would have been much worse. I found a place to sit, also, with Midge Decter and gave her—she seemed genuinely interested—a part of my tape recording on the

Hungarian language. Then Mrs. Stone, Eleanor Perényi's mother, came up and sat beside us—Eleanor not there, Mrs. Stone very saddled with rouge. Mary Meigs's escort was not present, and I took her home in a taxi. It is curious that she should be the only woman who stimulates me physically without my thinking about it. I kissed her a good deal. A real lust is involved with my other feelings.

Late the next afternoon, I went with her to the Durlacher Gallery, where we saw Tchelitchew's drawings and Leonid's drawings and paintings. George Dix and Kirk Askew drive us both crazy. (George Dix had also been at the party, with another—little dark—man from Durlacher. Dix had annoyed and discouraged Mary by telling her that they "weren't interested in lady painters.") They start in playing up the pictures and trying to sell you something from the moment you come into the gallery—Dix in his smooth superior pansy way and Askew in more authoritative fashion. He seems to have had some kind of stroke and now produces an impression quite macabre, moving rigidly with a stick and glaring through his spectacles. When I asked if a certain picture was sold, he answered, "Fortunately." Mary says that she never can get out of there without being pressured into buying something. She acquired a small Leonid drawing of trees. I resisted, because the prices there are very high and I had no money to squander. Mary went on to Louise Crane's. I thought I was going to go to the Argosy Bookstore near Lexington Ave., but it was cold and I had no coat, and I always forget in that part of town that it is impossible at that time of day—and especially at that season—to get a taxi. All the dark hordes hurrying. Traffic jammed, Christmas carols emanating from Bloomingdale's. I walked all the way back to the Algonquin.

I took Mary to dinner at the Princeton Club. She was wearing a delicious pink blouse that made her look like a bonbon you wanted to eat. I ordered Moët & Chandon, and when she flushed and dropped her eyes, I felt like an old rip of the champagne and lobster period about to seduce a young woman. We went to the English comedy *The Knack*, directed by Mike Nichols, very funny. Though it was written by a woman—Mary may not have known this—she appeared to resent the attitude of the rakish young man when he talked about women. Some of the bawdy dialogue embarrassed me a little in her company, though of course she is not in the least timid about this —she had been talking to me about Genet and wondering whether she ought to read Burroughs's *Naked Lunch*. We went afterwards to the Algonquin and had dessert, which we had had to miss. She said that she felt that it increased her prestige with other people to go around with me. Yet we had hardly seen anything of one another at the concert or the party. It is simply that it bucks her up to be going around not with lesbians but with a man who much admires her. I don't think this would be true of Barbara. I wanted her to stay over another night, but she said that it wouldn't do: if she did, the confounded Poors—to whom she is more or less in bondage—would be hurt because she hadn't looked them up and had spent two evenings with me. I called her up the next morning but found that she was just packing. I think she really thought that it would be unseemly to go out so much alone with me.

Conversation in New Yorker *office with Brendan Gill:* He comes from Hartford and talked about it, has an old bird's-eye view of the city on his wall, which he lovingly expounded to me. The unaccountable onion-shaped Russian spire that we pass as we go into Hartford commemorates the fact that it was Russia that gave the Colt arms company its first big order. Charles Dudley Warner had lived opposite Mark Twain, but had had a Negro mistress up the street—a situation to which his wife was apparently reconciled—by whom he had a son who became a concert pianist. Wallace Stevens had mixed little with other people in Hartford. (Hartford is mainly insurance, and they boast that, in spite of several industries, the city is very much cleaner than most New England industrial towns.) Hartford people never really leave. They may make a trip to New York once or twice a year. Brendan is a black sheep because he has gone to live there. He has an aunt of 103, whose handwriting still stands up.

His stories about the Whites: He was told by Roger Angell, Katharine's son by her first husband, that he had met his mother for lunch and she had greeted him triumphantly with "I've just found blood in my urine!" Roger hadn't known how to reply and had simply said, "What shall we have?" —Her letter of condolence to Jean Stafford after Joe Liebling's death is probably the prize of all the White stories. After expressing her sympathy and sorrow, she went on to say that she and Andy had also been ill—"I have a rash all around my rectum."

When I was taking a nap that afternoon, *Arthur Schlesinger* called me up and invited me to a party that night: "*Mrs. Kennedy and Tennessee Williams.*" I never knew how he found out that I was in New York or why he wanted me to attend this gathering; but I went out of curiosity. I had dinner at the Algonquin with the Epsteins. Jason said that there was a colony of beatniks on the Lower East Side, with many mixed black and white couples. He knew people on the Upper West Side who gave smart parties for "interesting people." Another couple in the same apartment house wanted to compete with them and invited some of these beatniks. They came bringing many others and practically wrecked the apartment. I hadn't been entirely waked up when I talked to Arthur on the phone and I didn't remember correctly either the name or the address of the people who were giving his party. With the Epsteins, I drove to a wrong address, which turned out to be a church. I had refused to tell Jason where I was going, and he was consumed with curiosity. Now I said that it was some name like Vanderweevil. "Oh, Vanden Heuvel!" he cried. "They're the people I was telling you about." (Not the ones who invited the beatniks, the others.) "Why on earth are you going there?" He gave the driver the correct address. The driver said, "It's worth going there just to see it." It did turn out to be rather remarkable, in an antiquated and somber way: an iron gate and a large court-yard. A porter told me where to go, and I ascended by elevator to an apartment, where a maid showed me into an empty living room and asked me what I should like to drink. I told her, but she did not bring it. I could hear people laughing in the dining room and realized I had come too early. But almost immediately Arthur emerged with two handsome and rich-looking ladies. Then Saul Stein-berg and [John Kenneth] Galbraith appeared, together with a tiny little man with a high piping voice, who evidently knew me, but whom I did not till later recognize as Truman Capote. When he had come to see us with Newton Arvin at Wellfleet, he had seemed to me a not unpleasant little monster, like a fetus with a big head. But now he seemed more birdlike, as if his head had shrunk. The hostess was strapping and blond—Jason had told me that she was "like Hitler." The host, as he told me and as Edith Oliver was afterwards to tell me, seemed almost nonexistent.

Jackie Kennedy came in with Tennessee Williams, who has grown a large dark mustache. She is more attractive than her pictures. In order to make her more impressive, I suppose, they photograph her in long gowns and make her look taller than she is. She has round dark eyes that do not seem too far apart, as they do in these photographs.

When we shook hands, she gave me a long interested look. I should have liked to talk to her, but I got no chance. She curled up in the corner of a couch and talked all the time to Tennessee Williams. I thought she had a pretty little figure. I sat between Galbraith and Steinberg. I told the former I had read his book on his Scotch Canadian origins. He never smiles. I had the impression, as I have had with Leon Edel, when I have talked to him about Canada, that he was a little embarrassed about it on account of having left—an impression that was later confirmed when I read Arthur Lower's review of his book, which accused him of being a renegade. Steinberg, for some accidental reason, had spent, I think, two years in the Dominican Republic, and he and Galbraith talked about that. Then I asked Steinberg about the Perelmans. Steinberg, as Sid Perelman told me, is not at all gay and whimsical, but the type of heavy serious-minded Jew who smiles almost as reluctantly as Galbraith. He was gloomy about the Perelmans— thought that it was harrowing for Sid to be a "humorist," as if Steinberg were not one himself. Then other people came in. Truman Capote kissed all the ladies mushily with an "Mm-mm-mm, Sarah," etc., and suddenly we were all moved on. Arthur announced to me that we were going "to a better party." Jackie Kennedy took her leave and Tennessee Williams took her home. I afterwards realized that this dinner had been one of the rites. It may be that she accepts these pansies, who no doubt like to attach themselves to her, because she has not been able to go around with men: they told me at *The New Yorker* that she had been going out with Charles Addams, which seems a macabre idea. She is said to have burst into tears when Williams asked her what she thought about the Warren Report and said, "How can you ask me such a question?"

We went on across the courtyard and, by gloomy cor-ridors and turning stairs, to another large apartment, where the people were very rich. There was a mixture of the old and precious with the new and extremely chichi, with the element of chichi predominating. The first thing that confronted you on entering was one of Francis Bacon's yelling popes, with a drawing by Vertès beside it. We went into a huge living room, with dark red Victorian curtains and horrible smears of abstract paintings—people would say, "That's a (something or other), isn't it?" Everybody was in evening dress—the women, even when insipid, very well and expensively turned out—like the Vanderbilt lady, who had come on from the other party. It was evidently a kind of housewarming for "these children," a pair of little White House aides who, I suppose, had just been married.* The bride had, I gathered, been a Burden. Jock [John Hay] Whitney was there. It seemed a combination of New York society with a dash of café society and, when we arrived, a sprinkling of Kennedy intellectuals. At one moment the bride sat beside me, and I asked her about two Pop Art figures standing beside the piano: a girl and boy made of wooden boxes. She admired them—"So-and-so makes them," evidently a woman in her own set. I asked about a large china tiger standing over a supine British soldier: "That's Staffordshire. Do you collect? I haven't brought the china out."

I had some conversation with Arthur and a rather nice elderly lady, who said that she was the bride's aunt and told me that she had read some of my books. Though "these children" had only just fitted up the apartment, they seemed immediately to be going to the West Coast, "to get away from the Burdens and the Twombleys." Drinks on silver trays were passed constantly by what seemed old

---

* To Meigs he wrote that the party was "a kind of housewarming" for a young couple who "had just furnished a huge apartment in what Augustus John, speaking of Wilde, called 'impeccable bad taste.'"

retainers. I asked Arthur how he was getting on with his Kennedy.* He said he had done about a third, and when I expressed surprise at a slowness which was not characteristic of him, he explained that it was more difficult than his other books because he had to write about himself and his relations with other people. A number of people left, and I left. I said goodbye to the hostess and in the hallway asked who the host was. A little blond man with a tray of drinks said, "I'm the host," and set the drinks down so that we could shake hands. I never knew why I had been asked to the first party, still less what I was doing at the second.

The next day I found I was ill, had bronchitis and, I think, a slight fever. I suppose that coatless walk had ruined me. I spent the whole day in bed in that dismal Algonquin room—finished David Cecil's book on Max Beerbohm, which was pleasant and restful reading, and started Françoise Gilot's book about Picasso, which amused me very much.

The next day I made an effort and got myself to New Haven. Elena met me there, and we had a dreadful drive, impeded by the pre-Christmas traffic and of course getting lost, to Middletown, where I arrived half-dead. On the way, Elena must have caught the thing from me, because she immediately came down with it and was a good deal sicker than I had been. She got through Christmas, when Rosalind and Helen were with us, but told me the next day that she couldn't face the puppet show on the 27th— "and you know that I don't usually fail to go through with things"—so we had to uninvite the invited. After Christmas, Elena collapsed.

* *A Thousand Days: John F. Kennedy at the White House* (Houghton Mifflin, 1965).

New Year's in the City

But we went to New York, as we had planned—Dec. 29
to Jan. 3. I was dreading having Elena drive, but Paul
Horgan came to the rescue, since he was going down, too,
and also drove us back on Sunday. It did Elena good. She
saw Martha [James] and her Russian friends and began to
look quite smart and pretty again. Martha Chase visited
Helen, and they went out to teenage parties, mainly in
company with Jonathan Frank. We stayed at the Princeton
Club. I enjoy entertaining people in the cocktail lounge
and dining room better than at the Algonquin.

Paul Horgan had arranged for Wednesday-night dinner
at the Liebersons'. The Stravinskys were supposed to come,
but Stravinsky was also ill. The next night, we had *dinner
with the Lowells*, and I had Edith Oliver come with us. I
thought Cal was all right, but Elizabeth told Elena that
he was heavily toned down with tranquillizers, and Elena's
conversation with him made her rather uneasy. When she
asked him whether, in his translation of the *Oresteia*, he
wasn't trying to liberate "the dark urges," he said that he
was. He told her that in *Phèdre*, Phèdre herself was the
only powerful character, the only one who asserted herself.
Elena reminded him of the phrase in *Athalie*: "irreparable
outrage," and felt that Cal was haunted by the idea that
he might commit one himself. That was the furthest you
could go, he said. The idea evidently attracted him. He
has established a relation with her, as he does with everybody, and she worried about him afterwards. He scares—
especially because Elizabeth tells her how scared she herself is when he gets into his manic phases. He took me
into the dining room and showed me a replica of some
awful statue connected with Napoleon, who at present is
his great admiration. We dined at a typical New York

restaurant, where we had to wait for a table and then had to wait to be served. It was an effort to talk because you had to shout in order to surmount the din of everybody else who surrounds you at tables too close together. After that, we went to call on The Little Players. They knock off performances in January in order to work on new productions. Frank Peschka listened to me on Punch and Judy with a sort of wide-eyed earnest attention. As usual, I got tired early, and we left about half past 10.

The next night was Lillian Hellman's New Year's Eve party, which Elena thoroughly enjoyed—she said everybody was "clean and cheerful." I talked to Mike Nichols a little. He is going for four months to Hollywood to direct *Who's Afraid of Virginia Woolf?* Elaine, he says, has married her analyst: they have pooled their children, and she seems perfectly happy, has directed a revue and is writing plays. He and she still appear on TV. I spent a good deal of the time sitting on the stairs with Barbara Epstein. I have never seen her so vivid, so goodlooking and so amusing. The *Review* has done a lot for her. Jason seems discontented. He is only in the background of the *Review* and Elena has the impression, though I am not sure of this, that he is put out by Barbara's importance. He talks about starting a restaurant, and everybody tries to discourage him. It is a fantasy, like the boat, which he is now about to sell. I tried to get, first Lillian, then Sylvia, to tell about what had happened to Marc Blitzstein, but the conversation was now finished. I don't think they like to talk about it. Lillian, after his murder, apparently went down to Martinique.*

We saw the Max Beckmann exhibition at the Modern

* Marc Blitzstein, the composer who adapted Weill's *Threepenny Opera* and turned Hellman's *Little Foxes* into the opera *Regina*, was killed in Martinique in 1964. It was reported to have been an auto accident, then revealed that he was beaten to death by three sailors.

museum, and for the first time I thought he was good. Helen joined us there, and we went to the Cousteau film, which is wonderful—makes the science-fiction stuff seem so specious. It is disturbing to see real human beings doing such things, and the animals they find are uncanny—some never seen before. There is a lumbering red thing with rudimentary feet that sends out and twirls a kind of fan. This is on the bottom where they only descend in a saucer, and they did not get a specimen. They have no idea what it is. It is the kind of thing I sometimes see in dreams.

New Year's evening, we came in at the Epsteins' after dinner. More or less the same old crowd: Sylvia and Leonid; the team of piano players.

After the blind little backwater of Middletown, the parties and gossip of New York are quite intoxicating.

Hungarians: On an earlier visit to New York, I had lunch with István Deák. He had been back to Hungary in the summer and had found it was more cheerful than he had been expecting. He visited a town in the country—I think the one he had come from. The country people there respected the Party Secretary not because he was a Communist but because he had been a kulak. The collectivization had been brutal, but some families had succeeded in holding out. They were terribly embittered against the regime. The young people were leaving the land in such droves that there would be no next generation to work it. The old boastful and turbulent Hungarians were now almost nonexistent—not only because many of them had been exiled since 1956, but because the ideal of the dashing feudal lord on which people had modelled themselves was now entirely obsolete. The people had been through too much—his generation were not like that. Certainly, I noted, he himself was not—he was very much Western oriented, said that there was really "not much in Hungary."

After he had come West, he had not paid much attention to Hungarian literature, did not really think much of Ady, of whose innovations in language he did not approve. He was amusing, as they always are, when I raised my inevitable question of how to say *you* in Hungarian. The old usages had been confused by Communism. He had found, when he visited the headquarters of the official history department, that he did not know how to address them. *Kolléga* and *úr* [Mr.] were out. The woman in the office called him *elvtárs* [comrade], and when he remonstrated, "I'm not *elvtárs*, I'm American," she said, "Everybody in this office is *elvtárs*." He had to write to somebody in this department and had difficulty in finding a formula for the salutation: *Kedves* [dear]—what?"

On my last visit in the *New Yorker* office, I was greeted warmly by Edward Newhouse, who used to write short stories for *The New Yorker* and whom I hadn't seen or heard of for years. (For some reason, he came to see me once in my little house in the East Fifties, when Frances happened to be there, and I remember him because he was the only person who ever saw her—except Dos, I think, once and Ann Hunicutt, when I was buying shoes for her and Adele at Bloomingdale's.) He explained that he was a Hungarian and had been interested in my grammars and dictionaries article. We talked about the Hungarian honorifics, and he told me that his father had all that at his fingertips. He went on to explain that his father had been the head, in Budapest, of the section of the police that looked after the reception of royalties and other important persons. His father, he claimed, had been detailed to Sarajevo as a guard to the Archduke, and when Francis Ferdinand was assassinated, had returned to Budapest, no questions asked: he went on with his duties as before. "They didn't care a hoot." (Ferdinand was one of the casualties to the royal family that the Hungarians had counted as retribution for Franz Josef's execution of the "Hungarian friends" in 1849. His father had adapted himself to every subsequent regime in Hungary, including that of Béla Kun, but the Communist regime fell, his associates were all executed, and he himself escaped to America when Edward was 12. In his cups he would sometimes say that he had started the First World War by failing to protect the Archduke.) Edward had inherited from his parents the old-fashioned Hungarian patriotism. In this he is unlike Deák, the product of a later period.

In the Princeton Club, I ran into *Dr. Fritsch* with his family, whom I joined for a little while at drinks and at the end of dinner. They were all very jolly and festive, Fritsch himself in high good humor. When I ran into him in Paris last winter, he told me that he had visited and had made the expedition to the top of Masada. He told me that his course in elementary Hebrew had now been cut in half. They now required only one term, and he no longer had to teach as he used to. Everything was done by a printed scroll or chart; no more writing up on the board the complicated conjugation of קטל. It sounded extremely perfunctory; but it apparently gave him time to occupy himself in more interesting directions. When I asked what he thought of Speiser's *Genesis*, he said that he had reviewed it in the *Bulletin*: it was good but he didn't approve of the theology. Albright wanted the Anchor Bible series to be "ecumenical," but he didn't approve of having a Jew—Flusser—do one of the New Testament books.

"Avant-garde Delinquents" in a Dull Season

Back in Middletown—very monotonous—dim gray post-holiday weather—Elena still rather limp, but more cheerful, smiles and laughs now more easily in a way that at first surprised me, because she says that she is now resigned to the worst, has sunk to the lowest level, can no longer hope for happiness to come, or even that life will be what she calls "normal." Women are so full of illusions about "happiness." Having Moses Hadas is an occasion for disproportionate excitement. He milks his library, as I do mine; thinks of nothing except second-century Greek.

Paul Horgan's story about A. L. Rowse, who, it seems, is always complaining that he is slighted by the nobility and gentry. John Sparrow greeted him one morning at All Souls with "Why do you think it's only the upper classes that dislike you?" This must have represented a heavy score at Oxford: perhaps the high moment of Sparrow's life.

John Cage was a Fellow for a year, and Winslow, the head of the music department, swallowed him hook, line and sinker. He gave a performance after one of our Monday dinners. I was stupefied—it was a night when beer was served, and I had had two bottles. The last thing that I remember is being given six slips of paper and told to write numbers on them between 1 and 10. I wrote 3 on them all. After that, I went sound asleep, and the only thing I was aware of was the occasional twanging of a string, as in the last act of *The Cherry Orchard*. I woke up and left when the discussion began. The next day people told me about it, and I was sorry that I had not been awake— though John Martin, who had been there, said that it was more fun to hear about than it had been to experience. Winslow had a set of paragraphs from Emerson, Thoreau, John Cage and others, which were first shuffled up, then the slips with numbers were shuffled up, and a numeral written at the end of each paragraph. This indicated the number of seconds that Winslow was supposed to pause, which he did beating seconds with his finger. The reading was accompanied by two other phenomena: the plucking of a string on a guitar and an African zither, the timing of which was prescribed but had nothing to do with the reading; and a tape recording which was turned on from time to time for a prescribed number of seconds, giving sometimes nothing, as Paul Horgan said, but a "marvellous surly silence," sometimes a humming sound that was diminished or augmented. Winslow had become rather peevish when questioned at the end. In one case, he had said, "That question is irrelevant, and it doesn't interest me." Horgan is telling people that the whole meeting was tape-recorded, and that some of my snores were included.

Moses Hadas left yesterday. He came in at the Center to say goodbye when Elena came to get me. He said that he was "cutting a corner," because he was not supposed to leave till February 1, but his sister-in-law had just committed suicide, and some other college was "trying to raid his department" by taking away two of his best men so he would have to be at Columbia to get their salaries raised. We talked about Paul Horgan. I said that when you first met him, the dropping of names was like the rattle of rain on the roof. Hadas said that his greatest creation was Paul Horgan, and that that was all part of the act. He left today, January 23, and we are going to miss him. He said that we were bored but "bored together." He had been alone, with nothing to do but his book; he had dinner alone almost every night at a Chinese restaurant.

It is almost unbearably dull here now. It snows all the time. When I come back in the late afternoon from the Center, there is nothing for us to do unless some professor has asked us to dinner or we go to a movie in Hartford. It is much worse for Elena than for me. *She* has nothing to do but work on the income tax and shop on that dismal Main St., which she says always takes hours.

Yesterday (Jan. 24) went to Paul Horgan's for lunch. Heavy snow—a prolonged visit. The McGuires and the Reeds. Paul said that he couldn't make up his mind whether to be Ludwig of Bavaria or William Randolph Hearst. When I told Dick Wilbur this, he said Paul also wanted to be Pope. The Wilburs came to dinner in the evening. We like them, but I felt this morning that this whole Middletown thing seemed to me quite unreal—not unreal in itself, but unreal to me. Elena said she agreed but had no intention of making it become real.

Paul Horgan has been in a dither about the arrival of *Father D'Arcy*. Mrs. Burford at the Center was worrying about the teapot which had been bought for his rooms here. She thought that it would not do—a too gaudy gold and blue—and decided to send it back. Paul told us that the next morning he was going to some place in Connecticut to drive Father D'Arcy back—he was "staying with some posh Catholics." This amused Elena immensely. Father D'Arcy appeared at last Monday's dinner. He reminded me a little of Bertrand Russell: small and frail, very old, almost nonexistent chin like Russell's, but without his strong aristocratic nose.

I most enjoy the hour of the drinks before dinner. The paper, by Ihab Hassan, turned out to be a literary equivalent of the doctrine of John Cage that we got at the meeting just before. This time I didn't go to sleep, but I sat in the far corner and Hassan murmured so that I could only catch fragments of sentences. At one point he seemed to be saying that literature was finished, we shouldn't need it any more. The paper was called *Metacriticism*—reminded me of Jar-

ry's *"pataphysique."** Since we weren't going to need literature, how much less should we need criticism? Hassan
is an Egyptian who came over here to study engineering.
Paul says that the professors here are breaking their
necks not to be less avant-garde than the students. It is
utterly silly that the faculty should be feeding the
students such stuff. They will make them into cultural
delinquents.

I enjoy talking to Paul when he comes into the office
here and jokes about these avant-garde delinquents and
talks about things like operas that he loves. But, tactful
and attractive though he is in his role of official impresario,
he always introduces a false note. He is too eager to play
up to everybody. At dinner, I was talking to a Romanian
who teaches French literature here. He said something I
didn't hear but something evidently unfavorable about
Flaubert's personality, and Paul overeagerly agreed: "I
wouldn't want to be in the same room with him!" I
don't believe he knew anything about Flaubert, who, unlike his writing, was spontaneous to the point of being
tempestuous and very much liked by his friends—the
warmth of his loyalties, his indignations, after Gautier's
death, about his having been driven so hard to make a
living. The discussion might have become more interesting
if Paul wasn't there to divert it with his off-center social
interventions.

Jean Stafford is back from New York, looking very much
the worse for wear. She would like to leave, she says, but
can't afford to. She reports that Cal Lowell has now left
his apartment and is living somewhere in a basement with
a Lithuanian ballet girl from Australia whom he met in
the church where his play was performed. He said that

---

* "Pataphysics" was a philosophy of life based on the essays and plays of
  Alfred Jarry, who rebelled against the idea of reason and against literature itself. He was a forerunner of the Surrealists.

she hadn't read as many books as Jean and Elizabeth had but had something that they didn't have.

Wednesday, Jan. 27. Jean came to dinner with us. She had lunched with *Paul Horgan*, who had said of some encounter with the mild and commonplace president of Wesleyan, "Vic Butterfield was in smashing form!" Had told her that Moses Hadas had been heartbroken at having to leave so soon. Nothing but his "commitments" in New York would have taken him back before the end of the term. Paul had been to see her at the hospital when she was "in traction" and had weights attached to her legs. He had wanted her to come to a dinner which he was giving for the opening night of Richard Wilbur's *Tartuffe*; had visited her a second time and insisted. She had called his attention to the fact that she couldn't get up at all, which he apparently hadn't noticed: "You poor darling!"

The next day we went to *Boston* and stayed at the Ritz, a great refresher for Elena. Thursday evening we went to *Leinsdorf*'s concert. We called on him in the intermission and got the impression that he was terribly tired. When I asked him how he was, he answered, "I'm unemployed as you see. Three concerts this week, with rehearsals and a recording." He had made shrieks of pain emerge from the minuet of the Mozart symphony (Number 33), and the last movement of the Brahms Second Symphony became absolutely frenetic. One felt that he was actually shrieking and that the orchestra was high keyed, too.

The next evening we went to the Fassetts': a cocktail supper party. Steve, who was working hard, drowned me in huge drinks, and we did not stay for the supper. I told Agatha about Newhouse's father, who had failed to protect the Archduke. She received this with scornful mockery and declared that she had known Newhouse ever since she had come to America and that his father was a little New York grocer who had never occupied in Hungary any such post of responsibility. I don't know which to believe. It is all, I suppose, very Hungarian.

We came back to Middletown Saturday and attended that night at Russell House one of Paul's "gala" dinners. This time in celebration of the arrival of *Father D'Arcy* and *the Quines from Harvard*. Father D'Arcy told Elena that, staying in the rooms at the Center, he had no one to get his breakfasts, which had never happened before. He did not know how to work the electric gadgets—"It shows how ignorant I am." He managed to open a can for the first time, but did not know what to do with the contents. He had finally had to resort to the Catholic church across the street, where the sisters provided him with something. I was so much stimulated by the wine and by sitting at dinner beside a relatively pretty and lively woman, the half-Finnish wife of the provost—a little like Gerry Allard's wife, Irene—that I effervesced with gallant compliments. Mrs. Quine, Elena told me, said that Connecticut wasn't really a state.

Sunday we dined at the *Martins'*. They live in a made-over old mill which contained also a blacksmith shop. John never comes into the Center, but he's writing a book about his experiences as ambassador to the Dominican Republic. I am more at home with him than I am with the academics. He is an old newspaperman who has done journalism of a rather high order in the fields of psychiatry and criminology; lately in the State Department and a Democratic Party worker. In the Lincolnian Illinois tradition—like Adlai Stevenson, a friend of theirs—something I understand. He was evidently much chagrined when the military in Santo Domingo upset the democratic government which the United States was backing, and he has thought of a constitutional formula to save them from their political chaos which is very much like that of Haiti. They pay no attention whatever to constitutional rules. One faction simply shoots or otherwise violently displaces another. Martin's scheme is to have them elect a President every year, in the hope that they could wait to the end of the year before throwing the government out. He still cherishes—though somewhat dampened—the ideal of the United States as a bringer to backward peoples of the democratic process. He says that de Gaulle on his trip to Latin America made two illuminating discoveries: that there were twenty-six different nations down there and that they didn't have American democracy. Martin and his wife and the two young boys are still closely, through interest and affection, bound up with Santo Domingo. They still have a house there and went down for Christmas. As Elena said, it was "an evening"—a real evening of conversation—rather than a Russell House banquet.

March 27. I find myself more and more addicted to reading Victorian and Edwardian and later English memoirs. Since coming to Middletown, I have been through the three volumes of Shaw's *Music in London*, Cecil's biography of Max Beerbohm and Max's correspondence with Reggie Turner, the first volume of Evelyn Waugh's autobiography (a good deal of it unexpectedly dull) and the third installment of Compton Mackenzie's, Gronow's *Reminiscences*, Edward Marsh's letters to Hassall, Maurice Baring's C. and *Punch and Judy*, the three volumes of his burlesques, two of his very inferior plays, and the two books about him (unsatisfactory) by Ethel Smythe and Lady Lovat.* Have

---

* Enthralled by the Edwardian Age in college, EW returned to it throughout his later years. He had recently written of Maurice Baring and later planned to write of Compton Mackenzie.

also nibbled at Jules Renard's diary. Outside of this, almost nothing except authors I was writing about: Morley Callaghan and Mavis Gallant, Mario Praz and the Marquis de Sade. Only, I think, Angus Wilson's *Late Call*, one of his very best books, and Speiser's *Genesis*, which is splendid. There can have been no other commentary like it. Moses Hadas also praises it.

It is as if I had ended by subsiding into this comfortable and familiar atmosphere when I ought to be doing other things. I had meant to do so much with Russian, but have only read Nabokov's *Onegin* and *started on, but not finished, Oblomov.*

Boston, and Upstate in the Snow

We left Middletown on March 23. Elena went on to Wellfleet, and I spent two nights in Boston. I had dinner with Rosalind, who was nervous and depressed on account of her money's having run out and her discouraging trip to New York. She went to see Dawn and was afraid she was dying. They are giving her opium now, and she says that this makes her feel better. After dinner, we went to the Fassetts': Agatha at her most tumultuous. It seemed wonderful to be able to laugh with old friends after the evenings of Middletown. At one point, Steve said that Agatha was a dreamer but that she had one foot on the ground. She seemed to resent this and retorted that she did *not* have one foot on the ground. She knows John Cage and regards him as a phoney. He had some knowledge of music but "no deeper than that," indicating with her thumb and forefinger.

The next day, I had luncheon with Rosalind and she seemed a little more cheerful. Ed O'Connor joined us for a while and talked constantly about his play, whose failure he blames entirely on Burgess Meredith. Ed's principal deficiency as a writer is his lack of a sense of scale. The book *I Was Dancing* ought to have been a longish short story, and it might have made a one-act play. After lunch, I made the rounds of Cambridge—ran into, as usually happens, familiar characters in Harvard Square: Peretz, Pipes and the man in the Russian department who had Mirsky's book on Pushkin reprinted. It cheered me up to feel that they were glad to see me—also, the people at Schoenhof's. When I came to Cambridge once before, the policeman at the back entrance of the library asked me about Button.

I met Mary Meigs and Marie-Claire at Mary's exhibition. I was as much impressed as Elena had been. She has had a sensational *épanouissement* [blossoming]. It is as if for the first time she had succeeded in realizing herself. I think that the presence of M.-C. has had a stimulating effect. She would occasionally put Barbara in her pictures and always made her look droopy and glum. There were three portraits of M.-C., and doing these seems to have set her off to painting figures as she has never done before. Two remarkable portrait pictures, one of her family, the other a multiple portrait of her mother at various times of life. When I saw these, I knew what she meant when she said she was influenced by Beckmann—something I couldn't imagine. Brighter and more daring colors. We went first to the Ritz upstairs lounge, then to Chez Dreyfus in Cambridge, celebrating Mary's pictures and M.-C.'s new book with champagne and other drinks. I am more at ease now with the two of them. They have evidently settled down to their relationship, and I have the feeling that Barbara may have been left out in the cold—she has been rather badly run down ever since her prison experience and has now gone to Florida to recuperate. M.-C. seems to me a little proprietorial about Mary, and I feel when we three are together that Mary is a little *gênée* [embarrassed]. She and I speak so much the same language, and I always enjoy so much seeing her by herself, but with M.-C. I partly speak French, and this makes conversation difficult. After dinner, we went to 8½, which M.-C. was seeing for the fifth time. Her eternal *"angoisse"*: When I told her that I had thoroughly revised the Canadian material for my book, she asked me whether it had cost me much *"angoisse."* After the movies, she remarked that that bewildered director was *"angoissé."* Mary said, "But in a cute way."*

I flew to Utica the next day. <Mariska met me at the airport. She disappointed—in fact, she horrified—me by having peroxided her hair. I told her that this was all wrong for her, and she said that other people had told her the same thing and she was going to dye it back. She has had a kind of breakdown—went to a doctor, who told her she was anemic, gave her vitamins and said that she must stop overworking, that she would have to "cut corners," so she dropped her two courses. What had definitely made her realize that she could not go on were a professor who had talked three hours about the Romantic poets without her being able to get hold of anything and then finding that she had to get through *Pickwick Papers* and *Nostromo.* We had dinner at the Towpath, and she told me on the way home that she felt as if I were her uncle. I said that I was complimented that she hadn't said "grandfather."

I had come up here to see about getting repairs made

---

* In *O Canada* he calls Blais's novels "the most unrelievedly painful that I remember ever to have read," questioning "the inevitability of so much pain." Yet in an introduction to *A Season in the Life of Emmanuel* (1966) he acknowledges her dark insight into contemporary French Canada.

on the house and the stone barn and, since it was fairly warm in Boston, had foolishly neglected to find out what the weather here is like. I found snowdrifts around the house, and it has been snowing off and on ever since I arrived—so repairs are out of the question; I can't see what has been done. But I am glad to have a glimpse of this place under heavy winter conditions, and I enjoy seeing the people here, though there has been some very bad news. Poor Mabel Hutchins has had an operation—a tumor removed from her spine—and George and Lou Munn had a horrible accident in January. George was driving Lou to her job at 7 in the morning when it was still pitch dark. The road on the Lewis County side had been sanded to the county line, but after that, it was glazed with ice. They drove over the hill at the Jacksons' without being able to see what was on the other side. A car had slipped off the road and was caught on the protective fence. A tow truck had come to haul it out, and this had held up a lumber truck. No warning flares had been set up, and George ran into the lumber truck. Lou was nearly killed, and it was doubtful whether she would live. She had broken innumerable bones and had a concussion of the skull. She will have to spend months in a cast. George was also hurt, but is now back on his job. Otis and Fern came to see me and made me rather "squeamish," as Elena says, by telling me all the details.

Dinner with Glyn and Gladys Morris. He feels that he is making progress, quite satisfied, I thought, with himself. They have started a vocational school, and he has made improvements in the house and set up a projection room in the basement, where he is able to show films. All the schools, he says, have one now, and they can get a good many films, documentaries, scientific films and old Hollywood pictures.

Cocktail party at the Towpath. Mariska was invited,

and George came, too. She wanted to stay on for dinner, but I couldn't face any more conversation, so George drove me home. He was very touching about her, and said he hadn't either encouraged or discouraged her in regard to her courses at the college—so he couldn't be blamed for anything. He is sensitive and very likable, was perfectly behaved at the party.> I talked to some middle-aged couples: the Williamses, he is a lawyer from Boonville and half-owner of Snow Ridge; and people from Rochester, who had come for the skiing. They had known Ed Mulligan, who died not long ago; also a scientist and his wife from New Jersey—he had been studying the machinery of lightning bugs and other luminous organisms.

<When I woke up the first morning here, I found that it was delightful to find myself in my own house, instead of in a hotel or a strange house.

The silence here is punctuated by the dropping of icicles and the thudding of snow from the roof.

When Mary first drove me up, I stopped in Utica to go to Planter's high-class grocery store. I wanted to get some beluga caviar, which used to last me in Talcottville for three or four days when I made it into luncheon sandwiches. I was appalled to find that Planter's had gone out of business. I found the former proprietor in the liquor store. He said that he couldn't keep the business up. The neighborhood was run down, and there was no longer much demand for such delicacies. He told me that I shouldn't be able to find any beluga caviar in Utica.

Sunday was clear and bright, and it seemed to be thawing. I had dinner at the Morrises', and after dinner, they ran off three documentaries in the basement: *Force of Gravity, Wild Life in Canada* and *A Legend of the Micmac Indians*, which last showed nothing of these unfortunate Indians but merely Canadian scenery.

I woke the next morning to find it snowing again, and heavily. I called up Mariska to ask if she thought she could make it and was told she had already left. We found that we were plunging into a blinding blizzard, couldn't even see well where the road was, followed a car ahead or the bald spots in the middle of the road. But Mary handled it with skill, never went too fast or got stuck. She thought it was exciting, and so did I—a dramatic aspect of the country that I had not experienced. In Utica, it was absolutely vile, cold, snowing or raining, and windy; streets ankle-deep in water and snow. I went to see Mabel Hutchins in the hospital—she had lost a good deal of weight and her face looked much younger and almost youthfully pretty like Beverly's. She had been through horrible weeks, had been under morphine for days, but could walk now and felt much more comfortable and was due to leave the hospital that day unless the snow prevented.> Lunch with Penberthy. Dinner with the Costas, whom I like. Talked a good deal about Mariska. He says she has become maternal with the other students in the class, who are all so much younger than she is. He says that Tom O'Donnell is getting interested in her "as a woman."

<Cecil Lang drove me over to Syracuse at 11 the next morning.> Grandeur of the country in winter, so unlike Connecticut. <I find him sympathetic, though a little bit sharply old-maidish. I like his independence and refusal to subject himself to the academic mold. He is obviously very much set up about his well-paid job at Chicago. Costa, who does not even know him, told me that his salary was $25,000. How they all know about one another! His French wife is> not pretty, but I suspect <quite bright. She has been reading Huysmans all winter and doing the same thing that Elena is doing: helping little colored children with their reading. Unlike most transplanted Frenchwomen,

she speaks English perfectly. She gave us an excellent light lunch: some consommé-type fish soup but richer, something made of cheese, watercress salad and mixed fruit dessert.>* A man named [George P.] Elliott was there with his wife. He teaches English and writes criticism. Cecil says that the Elliotts are their only real friends at Syracuse. He has got to like the upstate country, but expects, when he goes to Chicago, to forget Syracuse completely.

What goes on in my mind: partly the kind of thing I write—language and literature, current events; the thought that I shall presently be extinguished; memories of old love affairs—Frances, Margaret, Louise, Anaïs, Elena, and expectations of making more love to Elena, which can never again now, I am afraid, live up to these expectations.

<I never leave Talcottville nowadays without an uncomfortable feeling of my relationship with Mary Pcolar> not having been consummated and never to be consummated: I can't make love to her and there is no opportunity of my doing very much to educate her. Yet, as she said to me one day when she was driving me, we have, in the course of time, to some extent "grown together."

I flew from Syracuse at 2:30, and Elena met me at the airport and drove me up to the Cape. We were almost delirious at getting back. Elena says that Button howled with joy when he saw the house.

---

* The "something made of cheese" was a simple quiche, recalled Lang, who believed that EW was not as interested in food as in the interplay of personalities and ideas at the dinner table.

Absurdities and Pleasures of the Center

On the next Monday but one that followed on the demolition of literature by Hassan, the demolition of science was performed—though this time inadvertently—by a professor of psychology called Thompson. It was a rambling and absurd talk which he announced was going to be somewhat autobiographical. He began by telling something about his past career, then went on to experiments with Scotties. By keeping the young dogs for several years in boxes and then letting them out, it had been satisfactorily established that they did not get around and know what to do as well as the ones that had been free. There was another series of experiments in making rats alcoholic. The children of alcoholic mothers turned out not to be so bright as the children of those who were not. "And then we had a baby ourselves, and it occurred to me for the first time to think about what happened to them before they were born."

They would also take the little rats away from their mothers—give them alcohol or drugs or anything, and when they were given back, they would return to normal again. But I suggested that they would die if they remained in the hands of the scientists. He answered, Yes. But otherwise, they survived anything. Triumphantly: You can dope them, make them drunk, jump on them! I said that this last would kill them—Yes: that was going a little too far. One young rat, however, had got ill, and they didn't know what to do about it, so they gave it back to the mother. She licked its belly, and this made it disgorge whatever it had eaten that was causing the trouble. One of the members of the philosophy department asked some question about what happened "when the baby mouse was given back to the mother rat"—which seemed to indicate that he thought that mice were what baby rats were called: an extreme example of academic specialization. When we saw the Walkers in New Haven and told them about this, Charley said, "Oh, we're way beyond that at Yale! We make them all kinds of drug addicts—marijuana and everything." I find in the *Scientific American* an article about making rats morphine addicts. All of this seems to me disgusting.

I wrote the following letter to John Martin, and he replied in the role of bureaucrat. ["The Rat Letters" and an account of EW's confrontation with the psychologist can be found in Appendix B.]

Father D'Arcy: I got to like him, and we had him to dinner almost every week. He is more attractive than he looks at first and is capable of exciting a certain charm. He likes to talk about literature—he knows the London literary world well, and he likes to drink wine and sherry, which makes him quite animated. He told me that when he last saw Evelyn Waugh, Waugh had asked, "Are you staying long in this country?"—a crack at his spending so much time in America. One Monday evening at dinner, he had a spasm of Oxford-type belittling. Someone was going to Italy for the first time and we were talking about the different cities. I said something enthusiastic about Rome, and he shot at me, "Rome is vulgar." He went on to say that Athens was dull. I said how about the Acropolis? "That awful thing behind it!" The only things worth seeing in Greece were a few Byzantine churches. I think this was the Oxford trick of disparaging what you are most involved with in the case of Rome; or perhaps an English Catholic's resentment that the Church should be Italian. He flashes sometimes a piercing gaze, or cuts with a vehement voice that just avoids the accent of malevolence. Yet he wants very much to please. There is something quite feminine about him. He is in some way the most stimulating man at the Center.

Paul Horganisms: "Vic Butterfield was in smashing form!"; "Father D'Arcy is staying with some very posh Catholics"; "Father D'Arcy is very much U." Paul came into the Center just as Tanya, the typist, had asked me what kind of a dog ours was. I said, "There's a beagle involved somewhere." Paul: "Some very good blood there —and a marvelous cat!" But, as Elena said, it is not enough to laugh at Paul. She began by disliking him intensely, but says that she is feeling sorry for him. I can't make out whether he is simply indifferent to what is going on at the Center, or whether he worries and wants to get away from it. He keeps going on long vacations, when he enjoys his opera club box—was seen on one occasion with Zorina, wearing his full regalia of decorations. When he called me up one night after not getting back and told me about all the music he had heard, I said, "Yes, and we were sitting up here—" He filled in "starved. Well, I want to have an opera house here and a small provincial theater." I suppose that he was half joking and must actually have nursed such a dream. The rather inept snob gets in the way of the public relations man, and I don't like him in either of these aspects. Roger Straus says that when he and Dorothea went to dinner with Paul and the Liebersons, they counted the dropping of 173 names. But Paul has an attractive side: the Irishman in him can be witty.

Father D'Arcy said he thought that Paul might well resign, that the job might prove to be too much for him.* At dinner one night Father D. said that this was the first square meal he had in days. Due to a misunderstanding

---

* "It must have been rather a relief to be able to retire from that job. I kept thinking that it must be a trying, a very exacting one," Wilson would write to Horgan on learning of his departure from the Center.

on his part and the remissness of the treasurer's office, he had never been paid since he came. I took this up with Mrs. Burford next morning. She said that she was glad I had, because it would not have done any good to ask Paul whether D. had any money. He would have said, "I don't know." She took D. at once to the treasurer's office. Actually he did have a Wesleyan check as well as some traveller's checks, but he didn't know how to cash them.

As soon as I got a chance to talk at ease with the faculty and students—that is, find ones with whom I could talk —I discovered that one of their chief subjects of conversation is, What is wrong with Wesleyan? Theories: (1) the Butterfields; (2) that it is not coed, so the students do not have any girls; (3) that it has no reason for existing.

Trip to New York (April 13–15) to raise money to pay last year's exaction by the goddamn collateral agreement. Got $5,000 from Roger Straus and $5,000 from *The New Yorker* and made a loan guaranteed by Roger from his bank. *The New Yorker* much aroused by the attacks on it in the Sunday *Herald Tribune* by a kind of pop journalist called [Tom] Wolfe, a smart-aleck jellybean recently come up from the South and hellbent on making himself a reputation.

Coming back to Middletown from elsewhere is rather like one of my recurrent dreams of Talcottville, Red Bank or Wellfleet. The same unreality, the same unexpected people: Jean Stafford discovered living in a shadowy corner of the house, Father D'Arcy—why is he there?

Written at T'ville, June 14. Mr. Beatman, the obstructive buildings-and-grounds man. There was no drive for our house [at Middletown], and since we couldn't carry heavy things either from the street in front or the garage behind, we drove through the back lawn, making deep ruts of which Mr. B. deeply disapproved. While we were away over a weekend, he had a small tree planted so as to make it impossible for us to get through. Elena had no hesitation in running over the tree. I complained to Paul and he took it up with the authorities, with the result that the tree was removed. One evening I said to [George] Creeger of the English department that I thought Beatman didn't want to be accommodating to the Fellows. He replied, "Don't be paranoid"—he was just as much a nuisance to everybody else. One evening when Elena had gone to the Thorntons', I had dinner with Paul, Jean and Fran Martin (John being still in Santo Domingo*), and we discussed Mr. B. Mrs. Martin said that the old blacksmith shop which they live in out in the country is very inadequately equipped. There was only one three-quarters bed for her and John, and they did not like sleeping together—so John, unwilling to hurt Mr. B.'s feelings, had been sleeping on a kind of trundle bed. Paul exclaimed, characteristically: "These peasants!" —When I came up from Middletown to T'ville, I found that I had no socks. The secretary, Barbara Sutton, could not find them in the house—I remembered seeing a whole drawerful, which Elena had just washed and mended. I called up the department of buildings and grounds and talked, not to Mr. B., but to someone who was much exercised about the matter and could not imagine what had happened. Then I got a letter from Barbara: Mr. B. had simply taken the socks—"A secretary in Mr. Beatman's office overheard some conversation about your socks and remembered that Mr. Beatman had asked her if she would like some socks." They were sent me

* Civil war had broken out in the Dominican Republic, and President Johnson sent John Bartlow Martin back there as U.S. representative.

together with my Princetonian academic regalia (which I
had thought I might have to wear)—I suppose he had taken
these, too. There must be something wrong with him.

I was aware that Paul disapproved of, and disliked, Fran
Martin, and I could see why when she told me that he
had been ecstasizing about Dubos, the French biologist,
and she had declared that Dubos was "a horse's ass." (I
don't know how he is as a biologist—I had found him rather
stupid about other things, but I don't know why Fran
should have felt so strongly about him.) This had evidently
scared Paul to death. She has a reckless, crackling, sparkling wit which amuses me extremely. On the evening
referred to above, Jean and I had got ourselves into the
situation of having dinner with both Fran and Paul, and
I warned her that P. would not like this. His aversion was
very clear, especially since the two Martin boys came along;
but the evening turned out quite jolly—a good deal of liquor
was drunk. We went to the Monte Green Italian, good
food, quiet and commodious, which Elena and I hadn't
discovered. John Martin was still in Santo Domingo—
where Johnson had sent him as a special envoy—and his
wife had heard nothing from him except indirect messages
through the State Department. She had been suffering
from considerable tension. She had learned that he had
been cheered by the rebels and shot at by the Marines,
then afterwards by the Dominicans on both sides. At one
time, he had to lie on the floor of the embassy on account
of shots coming through the windows. She said that the
procedure had been to go straight from the embassy cocktail
party to calling in the Marines. The advisers, including
John Martin, were only consulted later.

Father D'Arcy told me that his animus against Athens
and Rome had originally been inspired by one of those

arranged tours, on which all the other travellers had been doting on the ancient world—"I always take a strong line."

We had him and the Herbert Reads to dinner together, and a quiet kind of bristling took place. Lady Read is, I take it, half-Scottish and half-Jewish, but a Roman Catholic convert. Yet I felt that she and Father D. were not quite at home with one another. Father D. remarked at one point that so many of the fin-de-siècle writers in England had ended as Catholics: Lionel Johnson, Ernest Dowson, Aubrey Beardsley, Oscar Wilde. She said, "They were being bowled over like tenpins." Afterwards, she told me that Father D. made her uncomfortable: "I felt that the black man was there."

The Reads told me that Father D. had been Father Provincial for Britain—that is, the local head of the Jesuit Order; but that he had been demoted for "worldliness," and was apparently being made to do penance by being sent to America—Notre Dame, Fordham, etc., about which Ed O'Connor had told me that he had heard Father D. grumbling (from the point of view of accommodations). Elena, before we heard this, had already suggested something of the kind to me. When I spoke of it to Paul, he protested that the Father Provincial serves a term, at the end of which he goes out of office; but then Paul never really knows what is happening.

Elena, in the second semester, found a way of occupying her afternoons by teaching colored students to read. There is a special school for this, apparently organized by the colored head of the German department, in which students and others work. It made Elena a little happier, and she would sometimes buy the children ice cream cones or have them come to the house. When she talked enthusiastically about it to Helen on the telephone, Helen said, "Don't overindulge your fairy godmother side." She found that one little girl was acutely suffering from hunger and sent her out to buy cookies. In the public schools, they push them along from grade to grade without finding out whether they can read or not. Cecil Lang's wife has been doing the same kind of thing and discovering the same conditions. Sometimes the children are defective or deaf or need glasses, but nobody finds out about this. Elena got Mrs. Jonas to cooperate. One day when a little boy had been told by Mrs. J. to write out words he could spell, he had made a list of four-letter words. A little girl came over to Elena and said, "So-and-so's writing dirty words!" E. went over and said to him, "You're 12, and of course you'd be stupid if you didn't know those words and know how to spell them, but now write out some words that you don't know how to spell."

Mrs. Jonas was so enchanted with Elena that, at the end-of-the-season party, she made me a little speech about how the moment E. came into the school, it made everything and everybody shine, and when we left, she wrote her a letter, with a present of a gold pencil.

This final party was quite successful. The Fellows and the faculty and the staff of the Center had by this time got to know each other well enough to be on easy terms, and the president and his wife weren't there. But by the time you have reached this stage of amiability and have got people sorted out so that you know which people you like to see, the year is over and the Fellows are departing.

The head of the German department and his white German wife came for drinks one day. I thought he was likable and able—he is from Hartford, and I had already had the impression that the Hartford Negroes were on a high level. If you hadn't been able to see him, he would have sounded like any other young professor. I couldn't detect any self-consciousness, though when E. had heard him speak, she seemed to think he was a little pretentious.

I am always surprised when people, writing about my books, say, like Pritchett, that I am a "misanthrope"; but when I look back on this year's work, I see that the men I have written about—Duplessis, Mario Praz, the Marquis de Sade—have been all, to a greater or less degree, remarkable for a certain malignancy.

At this time of life, when I look into my old books, it seems to me that I am trying to reread a once favorite writer that I feel I am beginning to see through.

When I said goodbye to D'Arcy at the Center, he told me about preaching, under the new dispensation, at an Episcopal church. The rector had asked him whether he didn't want to put on his robes, and he hadn't brought them. Elena said, when I told her, "He thought it wasn't a church."

Discovery of the Showy Lady Slipper

Elena and I went to New York May 19 and attended the first night, on the 20th, of Nabokov's *Don Quixote* ballet. Balanchine danced, or rather mimed, the title role, appearing for the first time in years and probably the last time in his life. It was not a very brilliant evening. Nicholas had told us beforehand that the score was made of "Ukrainian café music," but there were also invoked, on occasion, Rimsky-Korsakov and Stravinsky. The end of the first act consisted of one of those varied vaudevilles that occur in Tchaikovsky's ballets; but then the early part of the second act was a somewhat similar sequence. This broke up the dramatic line, which was not very effective anyway. Everybody was there. Nicholas had a section reserved for his friends in the middle of the first balcony: Kirstein and his brother and Mina Curtiss, Marianne Moore and John Carter were close to us. The *New York Review*ers, Cartier-Bresson, and Marian Schlesinger; but the mob at the "reception" afterwards was so dense that it was impossible to talk to anybody.

The next day Elena drove to Wellfleet, and I came up by plane to Talcottville. George Pcolar met me—Mary had to stay at the store because the other girls were off—and he told me something about their life, to which she afterwards added, so that the two accounts have merged in my mind. As a child he had been sent to a home. He is sensitive and, as she says, "insecure," and this is undoubtedly why she married him. She had gone down to Perth Amboy, after being disappointed in not going to college, in order to get away from East Leyden, but she found that Perth Amboy was hell, especially in the hot weather, where she says that, in their apartment, she smothered. Then her father suddenly died, and she came back to West Leyden. She found that her mother was about to move out and put the place up for auction. Mary averted this—she had come to appreciate in New Jersey what 75 acres of land meant. I gathered that George was at first reluctant, never having been out of industrial towns; but when he found the space and freedom up here, he came to be very fond of it. I think that he is now resigned to letting Mary be the mastermind. She seems now, also, to have her drugstore boss tamed. When he objects to her taking time off, she says, "Well, now that I've trained those girls, you really don't need me any more." And she now has further ambitions. There is a big public relations man at Osceola and she wants to have an interview with him. She is a little more easily available for me now, and we are quite excited at seeing each other—dined once at the Towpath and once at the

Bucks. On the latter occasion, she looked very handsome in a conservative lilac dress and her hair done up close to her head. She is constantly changing her hairdo and costume.

Relief at getting out of Middletown—away from having, on the one hand, to play a social role—which with the spring became more demanding—and, on the other, to gossip with Jean—who is amusing but who becomes fatiguing with her continual complaining ridicule. I was so glad to wake up here in my own house.

But it is rather sad for me this summer. The Loomises are old and failing—I've only seen them once, when I found them doing something at Aunt Addie's house. Huldah didn't look well, and she asked me what she might to do with the house—since the Sharps are not coming back. Malcolm is retiring from Chicago and has been offered some kind of job in perpetuity at Albuquerque. They are going to New Mexico to live, are going to have John's children with them. I gather that the mother is incompetent to handle them and that John by himself cannot have them. The Crostens this summer are in Europe. The trucks still go charging by, and Fern tells me that it will still take five years to finish the other road.

<I have settled down to very quiet habits—working, reading *Middlemarch* in the evenings, playing phonograph records that I've brought up here but have never yet listened to seriously. I have been particularly impressed by Ives's Second Symphony, which seems to me one of his most successful things: semi-sacred music originally composed for the organ, alternating with the comic and the rowdy—motifs from Beethoven and Brahms mixed with snatches of hymns and Stephen Foster and ending with "Columbia the Gem of the Ocean." *Middlemarch* is tran-

quillizing—that slow and solid country life in a story that goes on and on. And I am getting Robert Stabb to go all over the house and make repairs. The place is greatly improved by the trimming Weiler gave it last autumn. It gives all the good things a better chance. The yellow lilies in the choked-up back garden have come out as never before, and the lilacs have been much more in evidence. My life is so very subdued that an evening out is wildly exciting—with bad consequences the next day—I must learn to keep this down, too. An evening of talking and drinking with the Edmondses, though I left at ten o'clock, went to my head to such an extent that I came home and had the worst heart attack since three years ago in Cambridge. It kept me more or less awake all night.> I called Dr. Smith in the morning. He took a cardiogram and told me I was a "borderline case" and wouldn't need to go to the hospital. He worried me a little by coming two mornings later without my having called him. I slept and read alternately all of the next day (Sunday) and now (Monday) am completely recovered. I have subsided into a comfortable coziness—with a feeling of my parents and family still around me—finishing my correspondence and bringing this journal up to date.

I have had two letters from Clelia, who never got my perhaps wrongly directed valentine. It always seems to me a little mysterious that her style and personality charm me; but that is how women ought to charm.

<Dream in T'ville: I thought that I was talking with Elena and saying that I didn't want Helen to get completely out of touch with this place, when somebody came to the door. It was three or four newspapermen. They said that there had been a newspaper story that said I had no right to this property. I replied that the family had been living here since the end of the eighteenth century. They said

that there was some question about the deed. I said that
I couldn't comment, not having seen the story.

Bob Stabb is doing some work on the place. He has found
that the front porch and its pillars are now partly rotten.
It is depressing to see how much ought to be done—I can't
have the whole floor rebuilt; but I enjoy having people
working around the place, and it gives me a feeling of
accomplishment.

Discovery of the showy lady slipper: Walter Edmonds told
me last year that his son had found some on the Black
River and transplanted them to his place, and he called
me up this year when they bloomed. They are on the bank
of his brook—are really amazingly beautiful: the bulbous
part is bright pink—rounder, less elongated than *Cypripe-
dium*—and the streamers above are white; the inside of
the bulbous part is striped with pink dotted lines, and there
is a thing like a small petal that folds down into the bulb,
the upper part of which is white and the lower part a pink-
speckled yolk yellow. I had just learned from the Loomises
that they had one. Huldah competitively asked me how it
compared with Walter's, and I said that it was somewhat
paler, but had three blossoms instead of two. She didn't
want to tell me where she had got it from; but Mary Pcolar,
who was driving me, extorted it from her that Mrs. Weiler
had brought it. I then found out from the Weilers that
when they had first visited the place to reconnoiter it was
plastered with No Trespass signs. I called up the name
on the mailbox and found the lady of the family reluctant
to allow me to come on the place. How had I known about
it, etc.? They had moved out there because they didn't
want people around. She would have to consult her husband and call me. But she identified me as the person who
lived "in that stone house" and told me that she had been

in Beverly's class at high school. Later, she called me up
and said that they would be glad to have me come Saturday,
so I went over with Elena and Helen. The orchids were
growing in a bog, and they let us take two plants to trans-
plant. I got a good and cheerful impression of the family
and their place. It had formerly belonged to people named
Simmons, who lived in New York and only came up for
the summer. The Gilberts had only just bought it and
moved in last September. They had 400 acres, very wild,
with a delightful little lake in front of the house. They
have also, I understand, the common pink lady slipper and
the yellow kind.

The young husband's father lives with them. He and
his son are great hunters—the former works for an electric
company and the latter for a parcel shipping company, but
their chief interest seems to be their country life. They
have kennels with three or four black-and-tan hounds,
with which they hunt the bobcats who are killing the deer.
There were two dogs inside the chicken-wire enclosure
who put up a loud baying and tried to leap out when we
went up to them. The bitch, named Molly, with a sensitive, gentle face, was outside—she could leap out of anything. There was also a bouncing bull terrier who could
jump to an incredible height if you held up a stick; he
would get it in his jaws and drag it down. The young man
took me about the place and enthusiastically told me his
plans for it. There was a house in the pond for wild ducks;
on the lawn, a picnic table in the making. Some people,
he said, only got such a place when they had retired and
had only a few years to live, but he had been lucky enough
to get this when he had time to enjoy it. The former owner
had had a Polish caretaker, who had undoubtedly taken
liberties with the property, and Gilbert had found him
hunting on the place, and finally threatened to call out the
state troopers. The next morning, the dam was broken

down, and he had had to build it again. Hence his unwillingness to have trespassers on the place. His father had taken color photographs of the showy lady slippers. I promised I wouldn't tell where mine had come from.>

I get some sort of peculiar satisfaction from the infrequent beautiful things that I find up here: these flowers, Mariska Pcolar, the Seneca Little Water ceremony, this house itself, the memory of Dorothy Mendenhall, the cascade and high rock-walled glade, dripping with jewelweed and the water of a spring, of Sugar River near the railroad bridge, the late closed gentians and cardinal flowers and the whole great stairway of cascades of Independence River. Harold Frederic's novels also belong in this category.

AT SEVENTY: 1965–1966

People and Places: A Kaleidoscope

Elena and Helen came last week, and it has mostly been very pleasant: Towpath, expedition across Tug Hill, where the broken-up road has been restored but where we did not find any pitcher plants—everything is late this year. The house looks neater and cleaner than I remember its ever doing before, now that the repairs have been made, the grounds weeded out, the roofs and the porches repainted, and the rotted columns and planks restored. We had the O'Donnells and the Costas to dinner, together with a young and bright Polish boy named Kozlovsky, who is going on a scholarship to Wesleyan and whom on that account I have made connections with. He writes poetry, and he and Helen got on extremely well. Last night we had the Wassermans. Almost the only unpleasant note was struck when Helen insisted on going back to Wellfleet the day after the 4th in order to study oil painting at Provincetown.

<Have just read Lampedusa's *Racconti*, which delighted me—especially "Lighea," the story about the Greek scholar

who had an affair with a siren,* and the memories of his childhood. I loved his description of the "mastodon" mansion at Santa Margharita. My tastes would run to this kind of magnificence—having a theater on the place, etc.; but I do very well with T'ville. I wish that this house and the Wellfleet house had grounds all around them like the Edmondses'.

I am trying to run down, at Lowville, the history of the family and the house. It would appear that Thomas Baker bought this place from the Talcotts as early as 1832 and that the Talcotts lasted only two generations. There are still two or three Talcotts in Port Leyden, and I am told that I ought to talk to them. When I asked Huldah Loomis about them, she did not seem anxious to discuss them, as I had noticed before, and she said, "You know we always thought that the Collinses were superior to the Talcotts."

We left T'ville several days after the 4th of July. All the family converged on Wellfleet, and I thought I ought to be there—also, lonely in T'ville without the Sharps and the Crostens.> In the course of the summer, we had Elena's German cousin Freya (named by a Wagner-loving father), the widow of one of the Radowitz brothers. She was a darling, and I got along with her remarkably well. Then Marina Schouvaloff with all three of her children. She is crazy about America, and E. did her best to get her to accept the job offered her in New York. (Her story of Sovka's stupid servant in Paris: "*Si vous êtes le comte ———, Madame la Princesse dit qu'elle n'est pas chez elle*

---

* Six pages of the chapter on Rome in *Europe Without Baedeker* (1966) are given to a retelling of "Lighea," which EW calls a masterpiece. He identifies with the eccentric and arrogant old humanist who in youth had a three-week affair with a creature who ate raw fish and spoke ancient Greek. It has shadowed the man's adult years and leads him back, at last, to her embrace below the sea.

[If you are the count ———, Madame the Princess is not at home].") Then Reuel and Marcia, whose visit overlapped with the Thorntons' visit. I think that Reuel and Henry were glad to see one another: they talked a lot and took to playing chess just as they used to do. I told stories in the evening to the twins: my old series about the little girl and her brother and the family of bears and the mermaid. One little girl swallowed everything and showed signs of a sense of humor; the other would say, "I don't believe in mermaids!" and "Is this story true?"—"It might be," her sister said, understanding the situation better. The other would also ask why? about incidents of which I should have thought the motivations obvious.

Rosalind was there off and on. She finally, just before Labor Day, got arrested, on her way back from an evening with Chavchavadzes, for blocking traffic, with her lights off, stalled in the middle lane and half pointed in the wrong direction. They saw that she had been drinking and put her in the Provincetown jail. She called me up in the middle of the night, boohooing like a baby. Elena and I went over and, with the aid of John Snow, the lawyer, put up bail and got her out. In the magistrate's court, she insisted that the policeman's story was not true, but she had talked so wildly the night of her arrest, telling me it had taken place at North Truro, that I am not sure she knew what happened. She wants to appeal it at Barnstable since if she fails to get acquitted, she will lose her license for a year: I am depressed and worried about her.

In the magistrate's court, one saw, in the cases that came up before Rosalind's, all the sordid side of present-day Provincetown: young bums arrested for speeding, pansies caught in the act (they are trying to discourage them now). One boy was suing another boy for $18 rent: the latter was a pansy from Virginia—a beat getup with sandals. The landlord said that if he would get out of town, he would willingly forgo the $18.

Helen spent a month at the University of Tours, and Elena says that she has eliminated her Swiss accent in French.

I made a point of not having work that would require much concentration—did a series of notes for *The New Yorker* on Paris, Rome and Budapest. Wellfleet was not so much overrun as it usually is in summer, and all our friends were so busy, like us, with visiting relatives that there was little conviviality—and we are all getting rather old for it. We made the acquaintance of Aileen Ward through Brendan Gill, who was visiting her. I liked her. I was later told that she had had the extreme misfortune of a love affair with Perry Miller. Marian Schlesinger was there for a while with the children, and Arthur came later. Marian looks very well, relieved of being incessantly a hostess.

We went to a party at the Hacketts'—Chauncey has died, but Mary and two of the children were there. I went in the hope of seeing Betty Spencer, but Mary said that it was only for non-Provincetown people, and that, besides, it was no use asking Betty: she always said she was suffering from some ailment and never went anywhere. I was feeling rather low that day, and it seemed a gathering of ghosts and I seemed a ghost myself—people I hadn't seen in years: Ed Duffy's widow, Tiny Worthington—also, Brownie l'Engle and the Chavchavadzes—Paul looks pale and old, Nina in bad health.

I went down to New York for five days—September 24–29—to see *The New Yorker* and Roger Straus. Dinner with the Lowells at the Princeton Club. I ran into the Spenders, who joined us for drinks. I gave them a gloomy account of

Middletown, which I realized afterwards was an error when I was told that Natasha had been hoping to go there, because Stephen was always going to places where it was impossible for her to go. Dinner at the Epsteins': Lillian Hellman, Truman Capote, the Dupees. Jonathan Bishop's wife [the novelist Alison Lurie] came in before dinner, and I had from her the news of the family. Margaret spends a good deal of her time in a house in Vermont or somewhere, with servants and her husband waiting on her. Christopher is dead—they say he did not commit suicide but evidently died as the result of something that happened when he had been drinking—I didn't clearly understand. *

These evenings at the Epsteins' are so strenuous that I am usually a wreck the next day. The whole day at the Algonquin was a blank—I did not get up till 3:30 and was disgusted with myself. I had had some idea of going over to Queens to see Frances's aunt, but was unable to bring myself to do anything. Monday I had the Deáks to dinner at the club. Tuesday I went to see Dawn in the hospital. She was actually more cheerful than I was. She has decided not to have an operation. The doctor has told her—whether merely out of kindness I don't know—that there is a chance of her pulling through without it. In the evening I had dinner with Betty Huling. She has been in some mental institution again, having electric shock treatment, and she has lost her job on *Atlas*. It all sounds so like the old *New Republic* crisis. A rich man's son had come on the staff, and they had fired him. He then bought the magazine and fired all of them: Betty, Quincy Howe and one other man, who seem to have been the entire staff. Betty was much keyed up. She goes to the employment agencies. I hear nothing but bad news. She tells me that Louise Bogan is

---

* Christopher Bishop, one of the twin sons of the poet John Peale Bishop, had passed out while smoking and drinking. The chair he was sitting in caught fire and he died of smoke inhalation.

back in Bloomingdale's.* Betty's friend Holly [Hollister] Noble committed suicide on the same day of the year as his father had.

<I flew up to Utica September the 29th. Mary met me, but more bad news. She had thought that she had solved her problems by getting a job training stewardesses on the Mohawk line and had written me a jubilant letter; but she had had to give it up—the first time I have ever known her to confess that something was too much for her. They had had a rapid turnover in men doing this work—three in five years—and this was apparently the first time they had tried a woman. She had been led to believe that it was merely a question of supervising the stewardesses' appearance—which was thought to be unsatisfactory—and telling them how to behave, and she had at first had a man who worked with her. But then the man went away, and she found that she was stuck with the technical side, which she had not had time to master. There are five kinds of planes used, and they are all constructed differently. You have to know how they all work and teach the girls to jump from the wings to mattresses. They made her wear slacks, which she didn't like. And in all the two months that she spent there, she was never allowed to fly, so she was supposed to teach the girls pure theory—which was especially difficult at one or two o'clock in the morning when they were tired from a day's work. Mary a good deal of the time simply sat in an office studying manuals. When she was finally left alone, she couldn't face either the work or the responsibility, so she threw up the job.> She had also a terrible toothache which had gone all through her face and her head. Her Rome dentist sent her to a better man in

* The psychiatric division of New York Hospital, north of New York City in White Plains, is informally called Bloomingdale's because it is at 21 Bloomingdale Avenue.

Utica—I went down with her, wanting to see Penberthy
—and she had a horrible extraction, which involved stitch-
ing up her mouth and incapacitated her for two days. I
have by this time become so fond of her that I feel her
troubles deeply, and I am so used to having a woman to
depend on that it nowadays leaves me quite desolate when
I cannot have her to drive me and type my letters.

Read Baring's *Daphne Adeane*: insubstantiality of the
characters, not so clearly drawn as in *C*. Each of these
novels seems to be thinner than the last. And, as in his
Cat's Cradle, there is too much telling about who went to
which country house and whom they sat next to at dinner.
Also, banality of the language: "She was walking on," "I
love you more than all the world"—this latter is what they
always say.

The Marcelins have now bought a place outside of Cazenovia, and Mary drove me over to have lunch with them.
They have an old house on a hill with a beautiful view—
very little furniture as yet, but Phito has a study well
stocked with books and his collection of Haitian paintings.
Eva's sister is living with them—a rather goodlooking little
spinster. They gave us an excellent lunch: Italian bread
and ham and lots of wine. It was altogether a pleasant day.
We left before too late in the afternoon.

A Hungarian Visitor under Pressure

The Jenckses with Charlotte Kretzói came up Monday the
11th and drove me back to Wellfleet Thursday the 14th.
The Jenckses were in ecstasies about everything—house
and landscape—and on the way back rather bored me by
urging me continually to admire the scenery. I hadn't re-

alized before—never having spent that much time with them—how goofy they could be. Ruth babbles and babbles and babbles. If I say something a little sharp to put an end to it, she relapses into such silence that I am afraid I have hurt her feelings and then say something to her that only starts her off again. She is full of absurd suggestions. When we got to the Hudson, she said, Why don't we take a boat and go down to New York? and when I talked about not having wanted to join the Century Club, she said, How about the Cosmos Club? I explained that I didn't live in Washington. Having recently seen two New Mexican Indian dances, she went into raptures about the Indians and finally so exasperated Charlotte that she began taking the line that if the Indians had been more progressive, they would have abandoned their old way of life. I don't know how much Gardner is aware of Ruth's silliness—he is capable of being so silly himself. But his talkativeness is of a more practical kind. He comments on everything he sees. At T'ville, he spent a good deal of his time writing music on the dining-room table. He said this change was just what he needed.

<Mabel Hutchins was unavailable because a brother-in-law was in the hospital at Utica having a serious operation and her aunt was in the nursing home in the opposite direction and continually called her up.> Ruth and Charlotte got us breakfast, Charlotte rather getting in Ruth's way. It was all very exhausting for me. We did the Utica museums and lunched at the club Tuesday. On Wednesday, we drove to Lowville, and <Mariska, at her own suggestion, on hearing that Mrs. Hutchins couldn't do anything for me, brought us a huge Hungarian dinner: soup with many ingredients, chopped meat in cabbage leaves, pork chops and mashed potato, and, for dessert, little pastries with a variety of fillings: prunes, chopped walnuts, etc. She had brought for the middle of the table a small wicker cornucopia with large grapes and other fruit spilling out of it. Charlotte, before dinner, had a long conversation with her in Hungarian. She told me afterwards that she had come to the conclusion that Mariska would never be able to improve her situation till the children were grown up, when she would be 45. She had committed herself to her present life when she married so early and had the three children. Charotte herself had made a point of not having any children. She had told me that she and Országh, regarding me as an honorary Hungarian, referred to me as Odön Bácsi, Uncle Edmund—*bácsi* is the equivalent of Russian *batushka* [little father]. This delighted Mariska, who, I told her, had been mistering me long enough. > In the interval between leaving Mohawk and going back to her old job, she had painted a few pictures. She brought one over, which she had copied from a photograph. I did not pay much attention to it at first; but one night I put it on a chair in front of me and, stimulated by drinks, studied it. It seemed to me quite interesting: all somber Hungarian browns and greens. I wondered whether she had been influenced by the pictures reproduced in the album I had lent her of the National Gallery. When I saw the photograph she had copied, it was apparent that she had turned its bright autumnal colors into something quite subjective. The corn stalks were a ghostly gray; the hunter in the distance had disappeared; and the fence with its gate in the foreground had become an unparallel barrier.

<Wednesday evening, after dinner, we all went to the Morrises' to see an avant-garde picture, directed by Hans Richter, which I had borrowed from Renata Adler at *The New Yorker: Dreams for Sale*, very chichi. It was followed by an admirable documentary, *The Life of the Honey Bee*.

The next day we started out about 10 and—rather to the surprise of everybody—succeeded in doing the Oneida

Community and Cooperstown and making Wellfleet by one
o'clock in the morning, Gardner driving admirably all the
way. > Connie Robertson was sick in bed at Oneida but
two of her old cousins received us, showed us around and
gave us lunch with the utmost cordiality. They are like
relics of some vanished race, with their family resemblance, their old-fashioned ladylike manners and their nasal New England upstate accents. One finds that they still
feel resentment at the way the Community was treated in
its early days in Putney.*

  Charlotte (Sarolta) Kretzói. I have come to realize since
she has been over here how little I got to know her in
Budapest and how much of a *kékharinya* [bluestocking] and
pedant she is. She can become rather irritating by her
continual correcting and contradicting. She is also extremely class-conscious, telling Elena that Agatha Fassett
"belonged but didn't." Péter Nagy is under some suspicion,
as Deák had already told me, of having informed on a friend
and got him executed. I said that I didn't quite trust him,
and she said that he was half-Jew and half-peasant, implying that this made him dubious. Her father had had
vineyards and made some kind of wine that Elena knew
about. Their property had been expropriated, and now they
were trespassers if they went on their old estate. I later,
in her presence, mentioned this to Elena, and now Charlotte hastened to assure us that her father had been "rude"
with the peasants. He had been "rude" with his family,
too—that was perhaps his right—but he shouldn't have
been rude with the peasants, and they were definitely
hostile to him. She was trying to palliate the expropriation.
  In Budapest, she had talked with the utmost freedom,

---

* John Humphrey Noyes had formed his first perfectionist society in 1839
at Putney, Vermont. When they began the practice of "complex marriage" in 1846, they were forced by their neighbors to flee.

but here she felt she had to defend the regime, and it made things difficult for her. She was horrified when she read my diary article and had to give me—to my embarrassment—a certain amount of the official line. They were not really a Communist but a socialist country. They did not speak of the Communist Party but simply called it "the Party." They and the other satellites were "people's democracies," etc. She was afraid that if I published my Hungarian article as written, it might ruin Országh and her. I have therefore redone it. She had been disturbed by the difficulty she had had in getting her visa and was worried about her husband's getting one. She had found herself under the wing of the International Institute of Education—with the FBI, I gathered, in the background —and had been told that she must report to them whenever she left Boston and could not go away for more than 24 hours. But the IIE headquarters are in New York, and I told her to pay no attention. She said that in Hungary the secret police did their own spying, and did not make use of such organizations as the IIE. Deák had told me in New York of a friend of his, a philologist, who had found himself in the same position. He had wanted to travel around and visit the various linguistics laboratories, and the IIE made this difficult.

She stayed with us here from Thursday to Sunday. Elena took her to the ocean, and she wept. Hungary was an inland country. They had had only a little corner on the Adriatic, and now that had been taken away from them. E. said that Charlotte rather "got her down at first" but then she had become sympathetic. She thought that C.'s continual criticism of everybody and everything was due to her feeling an obligation not to enjoy the U.S. too much. I am not sure about this. I found that she resented certain things in my article that were not meant to be disparaging: I had written that the people looked shabby, and she retorted that the Americans were very shabby—my badly torn rain-coat was shabby. But Elena says that C. told her that she felt she could be quite at home here. What I don't understand is her recurring complaint that people are not paying enough attention to her. I have certainly done what I could for her, but she never seems to like the people—Agatha, the Kepeses—that I arrange to have her meet. She worries because Dan Aaron has not called her up. She is for some reason temperamentally always in the opposition—like Mary [McCarthy]—and always seems to want to get the upper hand—though at the same time she is rather sensitive. She complained that Országh was sometimes sharp with her; but after spending several days in her company, I could easily understand this. She is awfully academic in her approach to literature—is engaged in an impossible project of summarizing the ideas about literature of the principal American writers without otherwise reading their works. She is, however, not without literary appreciation and genuinely admires Stephen Crane. I tried to persuade her to write about Crane instead of her unmanageable subject, but of course she insisted on pursuing it.

She said that it was awful when the Russians arrived. Her parents kept her out of sight so she wouldn't be raped. She was apparently in her early teens, was wrapped up in her serious philosophical reading and didn't know exactly what it was she had to fear, but it kept her awake at night. A Russian officer arrived at the Academy of Sciences and announced, *"Les barbares sont arrivés"*—then went on to explain that the soldiers were rather rough characters. She said that you had to go to an officer—if you could reach one—in order to get the outrages curbed.

Dawn Powell's Death

While I was away in T'ville, Elena had the *fireplace* opened
and a mantel built in the middle room. The mantel is very
pretty and made from an old door. It has made quite a
difference in our lives. We have had an old-fashioned domestic life, with the fire burning in the evening and reading
Goethe's *Faust*. I remember more German than I thought,
and it is certainly Elena's best language. I go through the
text with a dictionary, then read it aloud to E., who explains what I don't understand.

It is a great relief not to have to move, and to have all
my library at hand. Have had new shelves built in my
study, and have got all the Elizabethans down for the
purposes of my academic play.*

Button died, and we couldn't get used at first to not
having him in the chair in the front room and not having
him come for a walk with us. He was old—13, the veterinarian thought—and had been suffering from uremia.

Now that my sexual powers have waned, I think about it
less but still a good deal. When drunk, I imagine impossible
conquests. When I am away from Elena, I imagine making
love to her. When I am with her, I don't very often. At
the same time, the whole thing gets to seem to me more
primitive and incongruous; the raptures are life's device to
make us carry on the species—like the attraction that
makes a male spider service its mate, only to be eaten by
her, and makes the detachable genitalia of sea animals find
their proper objects. I cannot help feeling a certain scorn

---

* *The Duke of Palermo* is set in a country college in New England. The
Shakespeare teacher has ostensibly discovered, but in fact written, an
Elizabethan revenge tragedy that is staged by the community, with
everyone from the president to the football team unknowingly cast in
roles much like their own. Wilson satirizes academia through two
professors who have come to judge whether the play is genuine.

for the appeal of those advertisements which show young couples vacationing or having dinner together. This has all been going on for so long, over and over again, on the part of so many mediocre or brutish human beings.

Dawn Powell's death: It has rather upset me. I had continued to see her over so many years and was so used to having her there. It seems that she left her body to the Cornell Medical School and her eyes to St. Luke's Hospital. I don't like to think of this. They didn't notify *The New York Times*, because her son Jo-Jo (now 44) reads it, and —on hearing of his mother's illness—after having a job in the laundry, he had to be put in the "disturbed" section of the institution where he is. She was so courageous and never complained. When she came to T'ville two summers ago, when Rosalind and I were there, she would turn quite yellow and have to lie down, but then always come to at dinnertime to have some drinks and do her best to be amusing. She talked a good deal to Rosalind about her dead husband and her son—thought of buying a house in T'ville and having Jo-Jo there with her. I told her that she would never be able to stand it. Coming from a small town herself, she took more interest in the village than anyone else who came to see me, and when I saw her last in the hospital, she asked about Carrie Trenham. She was really an old-fashioned American woman not far from the pioneering civilization: strong-willed, stoical, plainspoken, not to be imposed upon. She was nearer the East than the West. I once talked to her about Ohio, which has produced so many talented writers and so many mediocre Presidents. "It's not a Middle Western state," she said.

She was quoted in the *Herald Tribune* obituary as having said that she did not consider herself a satirist but a realist; she simply told the truth. I think that she was quite sincere in this. Though her loyalty showed that she was affectionate, her version of people's motives was likely to be cynical and somewhat sordid. I think the disaster of Jo-Jo's birth and her peculiar relations with Jo Gonsha had crippled her emotionally—she could not allow herself to believe that other people were happy with their children or faithful to their husbands and wives.

Her death has combined in a curious way with the installation of my new bookcase and the moving down into it from the inaccessible one of my Elizabethan library, which I haven't looked into in years and which rather dismays me to have at hand because there is so much of it still unread and I find that I have no longer the same appetite for it, to make me feel dislocated and not at home in my formerly familiar world. She was really closer to me than any other of my friends of my own generation—she was 67 when she died—because she was the only one that I saw and corresponded with steadily, and I have felt that some part of my own life was gone.

Reading that Goethe wrote almost all the Second Part of *Faust* between the ages of 73 and 86 has somewhat stimulated and cheered me up.

Dec. 3. Our life has been very pleasant lately. It is wonderful to be back in our own house, with enough room to get out of each other's way and all our books around us. I am reading William James's *Pragmatism*, which I have never read before—and am also beginning to enjoy "nature" again on our afternoon walks, after having been discouraged from looking at things by Cambridge and Middletown. In the evening, we have drinks and read *Faust* —we have just finished the First Part—and the fireplace in the middle room has contributed a lot to our coziness. I don't have much craving to see people and am glad to be relieved of the obligation to. We don't even want to go to

New York for very long after New Year's. I am also glad not to have to work on the writing about books that has been boring me. I expect to do as little as possible of this next year. I have been stuck for the last two or three days in my academic play, but otherwise it has been amusing me.

I begin writing again on Jan. 4, 1966.

The Epsteins spent *Thanksgiving* with us. The first night, under the influence of whisky, I had one of my fits of bad temper—threw the ashtray at the couch where they were sitting. It was partly that continual cigarette smoking annoys me. Jason never stops smoking, leaves ashtrays piled high with butts, and it seemed to me at the moment that he had come to a kind of standstill when he did nothing but smoke cigarettes and grouse. One thing that sometimes makes me rude is discovering that some man has no ambition. I was rude to a young man in some publishing house who came to see me here. He didn't want to write, said he didn't even care about getting anywhere in publishing. I can't bear the idea of anybody so uninteresting and so uninterested just wanting to get along and exist. It was unjust to see Jason in this light, and I apologized the next morning. I had said that he was just a publisher like another, and he said that I had behaved as if he were Nelson Doubleday. He is of course energetic and full of ideas. He says that he can only start things. But now Barbara, who before was so quiet and kept herself in the background, with *The New York Review of Books*, has become quite a brilliant figure—she is animated and attractive, dresses well, and rather puts Jason in the shade.

The next day, we had people in for Thanksgiving dinner, which Elena had had the excellent idea of serving buffet. This makes everything easier and more relaxed. Jason had brought expensive champagne, which made me feel even worse about having been so offensive.

Our *Christmas* was much more cheerful than usual, because we had more people staying with us: Rosalind and Helen, Cousin Susan, Semyon, the Kretzóis. Natalia [Heseltine], her daughter Biddie and Alexander Romanov were visiting the Chavchavadzes. We went over there on Christmas Eve. I did not have my usual fit of ill-temper and depression on Christmas afternoon. The Walkers gave a party at 6, and the Givens the next day.

I like to have Susan around—she is closer to me than any of my other relations. Elena gets along extremely well with her. She told me that she had once been in Red Bank when my mother played an April Fool joke on my father. She had gone to the window and exclaimed as if she had seen an accident, and then, when Father came to the window, said, "April Fool!" Father had said, "Madame, I don't think that's funny." I corrected Susan's pronunciation of Pepys as Pepps. "We call it Pepps." "Who is 'we'?" "The Minors." I sometimes, in the long run, get a little impatient with her goofiness. She told me she understood that I was going to write a book in Hungarian.

Miklós Kretzói is more remarkable than I had realized in Budapest. He has an immense amount of information about everything: not merely paleontology, but also archaeology, ethnology, linguistics, etc., etc. Since he has some artistic skill—his parents wanted him to be an artist—he also knows a good deal about art and was interested in the pictures in our middle room and at Mary's. He explained the geology of the Cape, where he had never been before. It is true, as Paul and Elena noticed, that he is quite at ease, whereas Charlotte is rather tense and on her guard. Though his English is not very good, he manages to be quite brilliant in it, because his ideas are so interesting and he expounds them with so much enthusiasm. She sometimes helps him out with a word. His German, however, is perfect, and Elena speaks German with him. I believe that E. is right in thinking him really more interesting than she is.

A large bouquet arrived, carnations and other flowers; a glass trident and little silver ball, which we are saving for the Christmas tree next year. It had a card from Mariska and her family.

We had no New Year's Eve party. Mary and Marie-Claire came over. Dan Aaron spent two nights with us. He is a tireless reader of American books—says he is going in the future to confine himself to the nineteenth century—and must be a stimulating teacher. He has a certain kind of social insight, but no large imaginative grasp or intellectual penetration. His book on American writers on the left simply chronicled articles and meetings, took no account at all of the problems raised by Marxism or of the serious criticism of it made in this country by Max Eastman, Sidney Hook and myself. But he is always agreeable to see, always of interest for the recent discoveries he has made in the field of America, and I am gratified by the interest he takes in my personal reminiscences.

The winter has been bright, mild and wonderful—the warmest and calmest I remember here. We sometimes go out for walks at noon, and I am beginning again to notice and enjoy the woods, the ponds and the bay. Six winters of Cambridge, Paris and Middletown had discouraged me with the external world.

Susan gave me a more accurate version of the story that Isabella told us in the old people's home. It was about the Earl of Antrim (not Hamilton, as I misheard it). He invited the peasant girl to tea; then when she turned up with two friends in their best clothes, he said, "The mood is off me."

Grandmother Wilson went to Castle Garden to get an Irish girl fresh off the boat. Isabella came up to her and said, "I'm going to work for you." She insisted on it, and Grandmother took her.

We were talking with the *Chavchavadzes* about *Volodya Nabokov*'s situation of not really belonging with the upper-class Russians on account of his father's having been a liberal leader and at the same time despising the revolutionary left. Elena and Paul hastened to say that the Nabokovs didn't really belong at the top. Paul went on to say that, after all, Kropotkin had been a Rurik. The implication evidently was that it was all right for a Rurik prince to be an out-and-out anarchist but dubious for a Nabokov to be a liberal.

A Cultural Establishment; Anaïs Nin

Jan. 20, '66. Trip to New York. We stayed at the Princeton Club.

The movie about bullfighting—*The Moment of Truth*—turned out to be quite different from what I had expected. It is an Italian picture, derogatory to bullfighting and with something of a Marxist slant. The Spaniard leaves the country, because he does not want to spend his life in the same primitive way as his father. He goes to work in a primitive factory and finds the work intolerably monotonous. He decides to become a bullfighter, seeing the glory and money it brings. The picture of bullfighting is far from glamorous. Its cruelty and stupidity are emphasized. The bull is tormented and tired out, and then with not so much difficulty slaughtered. You are made to feel that the only creatures in Spain who are stupider than the Spaniards are the bulls. The matador is bemused by an American girl who is crazy about bullfighting; but he presently becomes bored with slaughtering bulls and wants to get out of the game. His managers and exploiters prevent this, and he presently is killed by a bull. The film begins with the Santa Settimano in Seville, with the celebration of death and the procession in Ku Klux Klan hoods, and it ends with a funeral procession which repeats this. The whole thing might have been inspired by Mario Praz's book on Spain.

My poetry reading passed off painlessly. They paid me $500 for it—enough to partly pay for our trip. The Strauses gave us a supper afterwards. Very pleasant: they are good at entertaining—they ask a variety of people and—with the exception, to be sure, of the Berles—the people get on well together.

Paul Horgan was there, and talked a little more freely than at Middletown. He is still a little comic about it. He said that "style must come from the top," and that at Wesleyan style was made impossible by the Butterfields. He is very much hopped up by having been made a director, under Henry Moe, of the new National Cultural Board or whatever it is.* He talks enthusiastically about putting over my American Pléiade idea as the Number One Project; but I doubt whether he'll be able to swing it.

We brought back Helen and Martha, Henry and the Kretzóis, all of whom had been at the reading.

Wystan Auden came to dinner at the Princeton Club. We talked about the incompetence of the current poetry. He agreed with me that Nabokov's treatise on prosody was

---

* It was the National Endowment for the Humanities.

"bosh." He had talked to somebody who didn't know what a bacchic was.* The poets didn't understand that a poem that wasn't properly built wouldn't last—like anything that needed good craftsmanship.

Clelia Carroll was in town and invited us to drinks at her parents'. As Clelia has always seemed to me like a girl, an ex-debutante of my own generation who somehow belongs to a younger generation, so her parents turned out to resemble the parents of my coeval friends. (When I told Elena that I had had this impression about both Clelia and Mary Meigs, she said that the reason they were like this was money—"m-o-n-e-y.") I hardly talked to the father, but Elena, who was sitting beside him, reported that he reminded her of John D. Rockefeller—though a more refined version of this. He had the old-fashioned indifferent view that the unemployed could always find work if they wanted to and was against unemployment insurance and Social Security. Why should they take their unemployment insurance and go to Florida on it? Elena explained that you were obliged to stay in the state in order to collect the insurance. The mother had the nice-lady's interest in culture and paid me flattering compliments. Brendan Gill tells me that she is partly Italian, which perhaps accounts for Clelia's charm. Clelia looks leaner and older, but she has just recovered from an illness. She always refers to Philip as "my husband," and is likely to speak impatiently of his tastes. I first heard of him when she said, at the Algonquin, that she had to go to *The Mikado* that evening because "my husband" liked Gilbert and Sullivan. Today she said that she was so glad that I didn't like Tolkien because Philip simply adored it and had it on his bedside table. He is most concerned about buying up land near his place in order to

---

* A bacchic is a metric foot of three syllables, the first unstressed or short, the other two stressed or long.

keep modern developments at bay.—Fifth Avenue apartment, into which the parents had just moved: family portraits and other rather ill-chosen paintings; not much evidence of real taste.

We went from there to dinner at the *Lowells'*: Norman Mailer, who was unexpectedly quiet—I had never met him before—not throwing his weight around; and a visiting Japanese novelist who was interested in promoting peace. Cal had just emerged from wherever he had been. He was subdued and seemed aged, going gray; had just been going through a crisis of changing his analyst. This time, when he had gone off the deep end, he had bought for, I think, $3,000 a life-size statue of Tecumseh and had it painted red. I got extremely sleepy—my eyes were closing at dinner, and, to Elena's embarrassment, I found later, insisted upon leaving while we were still at the table.

There is a whole sort of *Cultural Establishment*, I realize, now in New York. There are the Epsteins and the Lowells next door to one another on West 67th St., the headquarters of the literary department; Sylvia Marlowe and Leonid, taking care of the musical end and representing the Durlacher Gallery; Lillian Hellman, in touch with the theater and a great friend of Mike Nichols (who had just called her up from Hollywood and talked for two hours about his having been fired from supervising the cutting of his film of *Virginia Woolf*—he had tried to insist on different "background music"). We went to dinner at all these places and were likely to find the same people. And one finds that Jackie Kennedy is somehow on the fringes of all this. Cal Lowell has been turning somersaults about her, and Norman Podhoretz has lunch with her so often that his wife is said to be annoyed. The Podhoretzes are also part of the Establishment: the Jewish-intellectual department. The political side is represented by Arthur Schlesinger and Richard Goodwin. Goodwin came in at Lillian's, after attending a Vietnam symposium, with an apparently rather intelligent young senator from South Dakota [George McGovern]. Though a Democrat, he was opposed to Johnson's policy. Lili Darvas, at my request, had been invited to dinner. Lillian said to Elena that with her a little Hungarian went a long way, and I could see that Lili was likely to spoil her act. At dinner, Lili took the conversation away from her by talking about meeting Greta Garbo and being enchanted, and she continued to hold the center of the stage, going on to Marlene Dietrich. Lillian murmured to me that *she* had met Greta Garbo and thought she was "a dope." It is amazing how good Lili's English is—though, as she says, she has lived here a good many years and has had to learn to act in English. She is ready, quick and witty in conversation. She came to Hungary just after I left and stayed there for nine months. She acted in Molnár's *Olympia* and was delighted to act in Hungarian again. But when I said to Lili that I was sorry I had not been able to stay in Budapest three months, she said, Oh, no: three months is too long for Budapest.

The night of my reading, *E.* went out in the slush without boots and *caught a cold* which involved some virus that kept her ill for weeks. I know from my experience at the Algonquin last winter that it is no fun to be ill in a hotel in New York. She kept chafing at the confinement of the narrow room at the Princeton Club, and her morale ran very low. She thought she had recovered and tried to do things, then had a relapse and had to go back to bed. She drove herself back to Wellfleet a few days before I left, and had an accident, smashing her fender, on the way.

I had lunch in the Princeton Club grill with *Weekes* from the *New Yorker* office. I had never seen anything much of him, but I remembered that he had been to Hill, and when I found him in Edith Oliver's office we got into conversation about the Hill. In his day, after mine and during the war, he said that it was practically a military school. But Mrs. John was still doing her stuff. She had exhibited a special film for the "bids," the women who did the rooms, to warn them against temptations and put them on their guard against getting raped. Weekes and a friend had sneaked in behind the screen and saw a man chasing a girl across a field. But the boys' legs were visible below the screen, and the women began to laugh. Mrs. John sternly reproved them, and said that the film was a serious matter. They made haste to escape. Weekes had laughed at a YMCA meeting when the reformed bum of the evening had told them that he had "first met Jesus in a boxcar," and for this was had up before the Sixth Form committee. They punished him by banishing him from any further meetings of the Y, and he was of course delighted. He was, also, I discovered, a member of Charter at Princeton. A very nice amusing rather shy fellow.

I had surprised Edith Oliver by saying that I hadn't liked Harold Ross. She said I was the first person that she had ever heard say this. But I wondered whether anybody who had worked with him had really liked him. Yes: Ruth Flint had seemed much attached to him. And when I talked to other people, I heard stories of his acts of kindness. He had given Bill Maxwell a vacation with pay in order to finish a book; and he had apologized to Dick Rovere for some piece of irritable stupidity. But those acts of consideration were occasional in a general tenor of irritable stupidity alternated with capricious acts of cruelty. This kind of despotic alternation between the agreeable and disagreeable I find absolutely intolerable. I asked Weekes how he had got along with Ross, and he answered, "All right," but then went on to tell me that he was always being fired, and had at one point been reduced to a nervous break-down.*

New attractive and goodnatured girls in the New Yorker office. Charlayne Hunter (I am not sure of her married name, she is married to a white man) does not look so handsome as she did, but she has recently had a miscar-riage. I like to talk to her and the white girl who sits opposite her about the strips in the *Daily News*. They are able to fill me in about the sections I have missed in the weekly issues—I can only get the Sunday *News* in Well-fleet. The receptionist on the 19th floor is also a good-looking colored girl, who greets you when you arrive with a delightful smile. I asked her what she was reading one day. She looked at the paperback title: *The Art and Science of Love*. "Pretty good, eh?"

I was astonished to find in the checking department an extremely cute little girl of a kind never seen there before—I hope she lasts. She had checked the French installment of my European diary. I found out later that she was a friend of Norah Sayre's, and that her family were Russian. I had her come into my office one day, and she explained that she had lost her Russian—though she does have a slight accent—but had specialized in French and went to France whenever she could. Her family had not made much of the Russian background for the curious reason that one of her parents was Jewish and the other a Cossack, so that their families had little in common and, I gather, avoided one another—they did not want to talk

---

* When Thurber wrote *The Years with Ross*, Wilson complimented his generosity: "As Yeats said of Ernest Boyd's book on the Irish Renais-sance, you 'avoided many opportunities for malice.' " He had evidently told EW that he had been at first badly treated by his boss.

about Russia. She is, however, very Russian in her high-keyed vibrancy and darlingness—like Natasha in *War and Peace*—very small well-shaped feet. I hope that she does not demoralize, or antagonize, the checking department.

Evgenia Lehovich said to me, in a dry deadpan way: "I hope you won't mind my asking you a question. Does your controversy with Nabokov remind you of anything in Gogol? I thought at once of the quarrel between Ivan Iva-novich and Ivan Nikeforovich on account of the latter's having called the former a *"nastoyashchii gusak* [a real goose]." When I told Nina Chavchavadze this, she said that the difference was that Ivan Ivanovich never spoke to the other Ivan again.*

I had tickets for Olivier's *Othello*, but Elena did not feel well enough to go, so I had Barbara Epstein to dinner and took her instead. She regaled me during dinner with talk of personalities and gossip. Jason is talking again about starting a restaurant, and is now engaged in some edu-cational project that I can't seem to understand—Barbara says that he doesn't quite understand it either. But Random House has just been bought by RCA, and he foresees that it will be ruined and wants to have something of his own on which he can fall back.

I did not care much for the *Othello*. Edith Oliver tells me that Olivier has implied in an interview that he had

---

* Nabokov and Wilson had not met since their weekend in Switzerland in 1964. After EW attacked the Russian's translation of *Onegin*—saying that its elaborate English sometimes achieved "the perverse-pedantic-impossible"—Nabokov successfully exposed the limitations of Wilson's Russian, and they lambasted each other in the letters columns of the weeklies. Like Lehovich, Wilson may have hoped for a reconciliation; but when the men reached toward each other in a last exchange of letters, in 1971, *Upstate* had gone to press with an account of Nabokov that reignited the novelist's rage.

never before wanted to play Othello because Iago always diverted attention from him. Certainly, as director he has here downgraded Iago by making him commonplace and loutish. There has always been some mystery about Iago's motives, but one can imagine a clever man wanting to make a fool of a primitive one. Iago, in the Olivier film, does not even have the interest of wickedness. The part of Desdemona is also made flat by being played [by Maggie Smith] not as an eager young girl beglamored by Othello's adventures, but as an elderly rather passé woman who is glad to marry anyone at all. I did not, however, object to Olivier's making Othello a real African. But he and everyone else shriek too much. I don't like Olivier's films. It may have been much better on the stage.

I had lunch with *Dos* at the Princeton Club—the first time I had seen him in years. He talked very hard and fast, as if he did not want to give me the chance of bringing up Barry Goldwater or any of his other aberrations. We talked about the deaths of Cummings and Dawn. I was rather surprised to find how much he was out of things—he seemed not to know anything about what had been happening in the literary world. "I see very few writers—I never did." This has always been his pose—it was not at all true in the past, but is now.

This was a day of reunions—with Anaïs Nin, whom I also had not seen for years, and Betty Huling, whom I *had* seen, but rarely.

At New Year's, I had sent Anaïs a more or less lousy picture of myself, saying that I often thought of her and had forgotten the reason for the coldness between us. I had had dinner with her at the Algonquin about fifteen years ago, then some time later I had called her up when

I had been in New York alone and had been told that she didn't want to see me, my letters to her had been few and cool. I forgot what had intervened between these two occasions. *

A letter from her reached me in New York, very friendly, explaining that she had expected me to encourage her and, I suppose, plug her reputation and that she had been miffed with me on account of my failing to but had now become more "mature," and saying that she was sending me some photographs of herself. I called her up and went to see her. I found her living in a huge housing development called Washington Square Village, just back of NYU: all long and bleak uniform corridors. She had just come from two weeks in the hospital and, as she explained, had lost weight, but she looked as young as when I had seen her last—it is true that the room was rather dimly lit—as if she had perpetual youth. I very much enjoyed seeing her: her sense of personalities and personal relations is something I don't find now in anyone else. We talked about the difficulties of publishing our diaries. She has found some way of abridging hers and is now going to bring them out; but the publishers made her get a written release from everyone she had written about. Everybody had accepted it except—characteristically—Rebecca West. As if everybody, Anaïs said, didn't know about her love affair with H. G. Wells! Henry Miller had suppressed a few details. She had been out to see him in California. He had left Big

---

* Wilson and Nin had become friends in the forties. He had favorably reviewed her in *The New Yorker*, and tried to get to know her in 1945, when he returned from Europe full of his passion for Mamaine Paget (Koestler). In her journal of that time Nin emphasizes Wilson's interest in herself. While lengthily quoting his praise, she identifies him, in a Lawrentian passage, as the male mind and patriarchal principle from whom she must flee.

Sur, because so many people came to see him, and had gone to live in Los Angeles, where he was near his children. The author of *The Air-Conditioned Nightmare* had become more or less of a bourgeois: he rejoiced in a swimming pool and all the things that people in Los Angeles were supposed to want. He had never cared about women except for one purpose, and she was the only woman friend that he had kept through the years.

Hugo was in another room working on a documentary film, and I did not see him at all. I asked what the film was about, and she answered, "Me." I started to say that I was sorry that, when I had known her, I had talked to her so much about Mamaine. "We can't talk about that here," she said and went and closed the door into Hugo's studio. On the way back, she leaned down and put her cheek against mine. She told me that she would send me the first volume of the diary—in which, I believe, I don't appear—that she put it up to all her subjects whether they wanted to be written about in it; that she thought I wouldn't have any cause for complaint. I don't know how much her reconciliation and the favorable picture of me may have been due to an eye to publicity on the publication of the diary. But I was very glad to see her again: her fine-boned prettiness and her amusing conversation, so Latin, and hence exotic in New York.

She gave me a copy of her last book, *Collages*, and told me it was her first "funny" book. It is actually not much different from her others: stories about exquisite women told by an exquisite woman.

From there, I went to 68 and had *dinner with Betty Huling*. She has had no job since leaving *Atlas* and without office relationships and work finds her life terribly empty.

Anaïs Nin at the beginning of the last decade of her life

She takes on small jobs of editing that bore and annoy her. She gets into terrible spells of depression and has twice been in the hospital for shock treatments. She tends to begin to weep at certain points in the conversation, but then pulls herself together. I wanted to have her come to Wellfleet to go through the proofs of my two old books that Farrar, Straus are reprinting,* but she said that she was afraid that it would make her too insecure to go away from her own apartment.

The Second Part of *Faust*

When I came back to Wellfleet (Feb. 24), I found *Elena* still not recovered, and she is still not fully recovered (March 3); looks sallow and complains of feeling weak. Every afternoon we go to the post office, then to the newsstand and the liquor store, and then take a walk to Duck Pond or drive around by the harbor and invariably look at the ocean. In the evening I do a little Goethe—the first two acts of the Second Part have slowed me up; play solitaire while we listen to records of Sylvia's Bach concerti or the Goldberg Variations; and I drink a pint of Scotch and sometimes half a bottle of wine. This puts me to sleep, but then I am likely to wake up and read one of Massinger's or Shirley's confounded plays. (There are, however, very funny parodies on Elizabethan plays and books of instruction on "compliments" in an early play of Shirley's *Love Tricks*. I wish I could do as well in the play that I am writing.)

Elena has lately been resenting me. She forgets my paper napkin at breakfast and lunch, and silently and stubbornly

* *The Shores of Light* and *Classics and Commercials.*

refuses to do things that I want done: getting out poison,* having my chair fixed. It makes her a little sulky when I finally get these things done myself.

Elena and Mary Meigs went to the *town meeting and left Marie-Claire* with me. It was the first time, I think, I had seen her alone since I used to take her out in Boston. I was surprised to see how much more maturely she talks, and her English is now very good. Living with Mary and Barbara has had on her a civilizing effect. At first, I played her French records by Yvette Guilbert, Jean Sablon and Henri Salvador, but I found that she already knew all about them—though she had heard some of Yvette Guilbert's songs, she had never heard any of her records.† After that, we went into the middle room and talked about Jeanne Lapointe and French Canada. Jeanne is fighting for educational reforms, but is up against, Marie-Claire says, a lot of opposition. Though Jeanne has many friends, she is "*solitaire.*" Even allowing for Marie-Claire's habitually gloomy diagnosis, I can easily believe this. She then went on to tell me how "depraved" Montreal could be. People defied the Church by celebrating the Black Mass—she had never been to one herself; but they would afterwards become complete "squares," with no trace of their former blasphemies.

Goethe: The Second Part of *Faust*, of which I have now read the first two long acts, often irritates and bores me.

---

* He means that Elena resists removing the poison, as he insisted when they were at Wellfleet. According to Jason Epstein, Wilson's unwillingness to poison rats resulted in a house that was full of them; he had several books about rats on a shelf above the ratholes. This fondness is evidenced by "The Rats of Rutland Grange," his version of "The Night Before Christmas" (*Night Thoughts*), and by his outrage at Professor Thompson's experiments (pp. 430–31).

† EW had followed Guilbert from one café to another in Paris in 1921.

He seems to have no sense of form whatever—simply strings endless incidents and creatures together, no development, no dramatic climaxes. And Mephisto is the only interesting character, and he is not human. *Faust* is open to the same kind of criticism as Wagner—that of going on too long—but Wagner, in spite of his longueurs and repetitions, is much more dramatic. I don't dare criticize Goethe too harshly to Elena. Really he has all the characteristics of Germans—egoism, blind self-assertion, pomposity, lack of consideration for others—that E. dislikes in Nietzsche, Wagner and Thomas Mann; but she does not want to see the same thing in Goethe. Faust himself is passive in relation to Mephisto, and he is completely egoistic. He does nothing, so far as I have got, but harm. But I think that Elena, who is so family-minded and always makes excuses for her brothers, has extended to Goethe, born at Frankfurt, something of her intense family feeling. One of her Grunelius cousins was in charge of restoring the Goethe house, which was bombed by the Allies at the time of the war.

I wrote this little poem for Alexandra, to whom I'm sending a birthday present of a huge collapsible paper bee.

Cet insecte vole à toi, il vient te saluer,
   Ce jour de ta naissance,
Par ton bon vieux grand-père adoptif envoyé,
   T'apportant bonne chance.

Elle voltige à toi, pleine de miel d'amour,
   Cette superbe abeille.
On n'en a jamais vu, comme en cet heureux jour,
   D'une grosseur pareille.

   Voici aussi des timbres,
   Des morceaux de gingembre

Ma rime a l'air un peu boiteux—
Excuse, je t'en prie, du peux.

Elena doesn't approve of this, says that it sounds in-
decent and isn't appropriate for a 9-year-old girl; but I
thought it sounded all right.*

Charlotte Kretzói's touchy Hungarian nationalism: I found,
when we were going through my article, that she took
exception not merely to things that might get her and
Országh into trouble, but also to my slightly comic account
of the statues in Budapest and other things which she
mistakenly thought were uncomplimentary to Hungary.
Every time I remarked on a Slavic word, she would say
that it was a "loan word." *Medve*, which was clearly *medvea*
(bear). Did I know why they had this word? Because to
the early Hungarians, the bear was a god and could not
be named, so they had ended by adapting the Slavic word.
I thought that such fundamental words as *vezetni* (conduct), *vinni* (carry), *visz* (he carries) had obviously a close
relation to *vozit'* (to transport), *vodit'* (to lead), and *vesti*
(to lead) and that the very word *jövevényszó*, that she used
for *loan word*, must have been a product of the 1830s,
when the literary language was being created. She more
or less admitted this, explaining that it did have the ear-
marks of the words that were coined at that time, and
disclaiming the 100% Magyar nationalism, of which she
hoped she would never be guilty.

When I talked to her about the Hungarian vampires, I
found that she had never heard of the Countess Bathory,
who destroyed countless peasant girls. Miklós, of course,

---

* Elena perhaps objected to his saying, at the beginning of the second
stanza, "It [the paper bee] flies to you, full of the honey of love, this
superb bee." The rest of the poem sustains the tone of an "old adopted
grandfather."

had, however, and explained that she bathed in their blood.
Charlotte said, "She didn't drink it. She used it for cos-
metic purposes." I'm going to tease her by telling her that
two of the principal exports of Hungary are vampires and
atomic scientists.

*Elizabethan, Jacobean and other English plays
read in 1965–66*

All Fools
The Tragedy of Bussy D'Ambois
The Revenge of Bussy D'Ambois
The Conspiracy of Charles, Duke of Byron (I bogged down
in the first part of this and have read no more Chapman)
The Witch
A Chaste Maid in Cheapside
Old Fortunatus
The Honest Whore, two parts
New Way to Pay Old Debts
The City Madam
Hyde Park
The Lady of Pleasure
Love Tricks
The Traitor
Antonio and Mellida, two parts
The Comedy of Errors
Patient Grissill
The Rehearsal
The Recruiting Officer
The Beaux' Stratagem
Edward I
The Old Wives' Tale
David and Bethsabe
Society

Caste
The Man of Mode
The Provok'd Wife
A Journey to London
The Critic
The Devil's Law-Case
The Two Angry Women of Abingdon
She Would If She Could
A New Tricke to Cheat the Divell
*The Shoemakers' Holiday**

There is scarcely a single one of these plays that is worth reading for its own sake. I seem to have read all the good ones already. Vanbrugh, after Congreve, is the best of the Restoration writers of comedy. *The Rehearsal* and *The Critic* as parodies are disappointing. The best Elizabethan parodies I have read are in the School of Compliments act of Shirley's *Love Tricks*.

I also read Racine's *Britannicus*, which was also disappointing.

I borrowed *Bartók's quartets* from Mary Meigs. Some of them very beautiful—though I don't like so well the ones that are always twitching. Alternation of melancholy with assertive and somewhat febrile excitement. There is something unsatisfactory about so much of Bartók. When I spoke of this to Elena, she said that he never reached a resolution, as the Hungarians cannot do. They are always discouraged or chafing, and are always left uncomfortable and uncertain. I think that is more or less true.

* He was reading these plays, he explained in a letter to Cecil Lang, for his "farce-melodrama" of academic life. In addition to the revenge tragedies, on the list are several Restoration plays—*The Man of Mode, The Rehearsal, The Beaux' Stratagem*—and two, *Society* and *Caste*, by the little known nineteenth-century realist T. W. Robertson.

Dream about Clelia, of whom I don't remember that I've ever dreamed before. I went to see her in a New York apartment, which was large but rather sloppy—the presence of children was evident—and quite unlike her parents' real one. When I looked at her to study her intently, I found that she was less attractive than I thought—somewhat more commonplace and with something of the florid face of a housewife. This was partly a taking-refuge in the first time I had met her in the Looking Glass Library office and had not particularly noticed her—a taking-refuge because, in my dream, I wanted her not to be so attractive because I couldn't have her.

—Now entering the dark defile of age.

—And dull with the first thunderstorms of spring

—If now I play at being old
    I never played at being young.

—You fade, old presences

—Vasmegye-Ungver*

I have finished *Faust* and was rather disappointed. Goethe said that it had a beginning, middle and end, but that it was not a unit. He called the First Part a fragment, and Maurice Baring says truly that the Second Part is entirely made up of fragments. It annoys me that—though Goethe seems always to be thinking in terms of the actual theater, referring to the audience and proscenium—he

---

* These are the two Hungarian counties from which Mary Pcolar's family came. The preceding lines, unrelated to Mary, would lead to the poem facing page 330.

should show, in this Second Part, so little dramatic instinct. There is no structure, no sense of proportion, no climaxes to any of the acts. He can never bring anything to an end. When you have had what seems to be a development of some idea or episode, instead of marking a division, he makes another development grow out of it and "drag its slow length along," and out of that another. The act about Helen and Faust is usually spoken of as the most important, but even considered as allegory, it seems inconsistent and absurd. Why does Helen have to be spirited away from Menelaus' palace by such a complicated device? Where did Faust's castle and his retinue come from? Provided by Mephisto, I suppose. Then, after the immense buildup, the whole thing is brought too quickly to an end by the so brief career of Euphorion. The Emperor's masquerade and the classical Walpurgis Night both go on forever and have, even as symbolic fantasies, an uncomfortable implausibility.

Faust himself is nearly always passive, putty in Mephisto's hands. And he never does anything admirable: he seduces Gretchen, who drowns her child and is executed. He allows himself to be provoked into killing her brother, Valentine. He provides the Emperor with bogus money and, in his engineering project, is responsible for the deaths of Philemon and Baucis, who are burned alive in their house, which he is taking away from them. There is a good ironic scene here, when, now blind, he hears the sound of the *Larven* [zombies] digging his grave and, believing it to be his workmen carrying out his project, cries to the long-anticipated moment, *"Verweile doch, du bist so schön!* [Linger awhile, thou art so fair!]."* It is said that Goethe, in his old age, used to walk the floor trying to figure out how to get Faust released from his contract. The device that he finally resorted to is very far from convincing. Faust is saved on account of his *Streben* [striving] but what that was worthy has he ever striven for, except possibly recapturing the beauty of Greece? And that Gretchen, through the power of her love for him, through the intervention of the Virgin, should purchase his salvation and translation, seems to me, on Goethe's part, intellectually insincere. This conclusion is made comic and even more implausible by having Mephisto's attention so much diverted by admiration for the rear views of the angels that he allows Faust's soul to escape.

Faust is completely self-centered: he takes no real interest in anyone else—a little sentimentality for Gretchen, a greedy desire for Helen. The only interesting character is Mephisto, who, as "the spirit that denies," is always throwing cold water on human ambitions—as the mythological creatures also tend to do—and disappointing expectations. This gives Goethe an opportunity to exploit his worldly wisdom, which, rather than the *Streben* of Faust, is perhaps the poem's most satisfactory feature. Mephisto is particularly amusing when he is pretending to be Faust and discouraging the young student from going in for any of the departments—deflating their departments one after the other—of medieval education.

The weakness of my knowledge of German undoubtedly largely prevents me from appreciating Goethe as a poet. Passages I find quoted with admiration or at which Elena exclaims leave me cold. I can see that he is witty, that he writes with point and that the German language lends itself to descriptions of wind and sea—of which there are a good many; but I am always haunted by his saying that he had never written a line of poetry without knowing how it had come there. Elena finds delightful lightness in choruses of nymphs and spirits that seem to me very heavy.

I was glad to be able to read it with Elena. First I would read a scene laboriously looking up at the words, then we would read it aloud together, and the meaning would come out for me better. She was invaluable in explaining to me the German historical and social background, and she also saw the sense of allegories that had simply seemed clumsy to me—for example, that Euphorion, the product of the passion of Faust and Helen (with which it seems to me much more should have been done), betrays the hopes of his parents—he is supposed to be based on Byron—by flying so high that he perishes—as brilliant children are almost certain to displease their parents.

Ups and Downs
and an Award

Danny Walker and his wife, whom we like. His reminiscences of his experiences as a magician with a travelling Ford show.* He had to take care of the rabbits and doves, found that every individual was different. The father and mother doves would spell one another on the nest when the eggs were hatching, the male regularly from 8 to 4, the female the remaining sixteen hours. The female, a white dove, did the trick, in the course of which she was produced in a pan of flame and made to vanish into a dark pocket and turned upside down a couple of times. One day when she was sitting on the nest, they took the male instead. Thereafter, whenever Danny approached the dovecote, the male would push the female off the nest and tell her to go to work.

Danny taught me a new kind of solitaire which was just what I had been wishing for—much less mechanical and simple than the Klondike and Canfield that I had won so many times. It offers a challenge and needs calculation,

* Called "The Magic World of Ford," the show traveled throughout the country unveiling new cars.

which makes it inconvenient to play while carrying on a conversation. He says that he can win it about half the time, but I have not yet won it once.

Now that I have got my Elizabethan and Jacobean and otherwise seventeenth-century books together in my new bookcase that now makes an alcove in my study, I am brought back to the world of the old English books that I was given in my childhood or that I bought on 42nd St., when I was staying with the Kimballs: Percy's *Reliques*, the Roxburgh Ballads, the Mermaid edition of Marlowe— and Mrs. Behn, whom I did not buy but about whose works I wrote a story in the Hill School *Record*. It is pleasant in this way to revisit childhood.

<On May 11, I was given a medal together with a thousand dollars by the *American Academy of Arts & Sciences*, which has its headquarters in Boston. This is really now —founded in 1780 and once presided over by the first two Adamses and Charles Francis—a phantom organization. They subsidize the rather dreary magazine *Daedalus* and give out prizes and medals provided for by various funds: the Francis Amory prizes for "outstanding work addressed to the alleviation or cure of diseases affecting the human reproductive organs," the quaint award of twin medals in gold and in silver struck from the same die, established by Count Rumford for "the most important discovery or useful improvement which shall be made or published in writing on heat and light" during the preceding two years,> and the Emerson-Thoreau medal, which I got. There are a great many members, and they meet once a month from October to May for dinner and to listen to a "communication" by some more or less distinguished person. I gave them my translation of [Pushkin's] *The Bronze Horseman*. The dinner and drinks were skimpy, as they are likely to

be in Boston: no wine at dinner and nothing but beer and Coca-Cola afterwards. Perhaps as a result of this, I behaved, I am afraid, rather ungraciously to the man from the Harvard Law School [Paul Freund] who presided over the ceremonies. [That afternoon] I had had to listen with infinite impatience to a Bach concert by the well-known organist [E. Power] Biggs, who, on this occasion, was playing the harpsichord. He was perfectly mechanical and uninspired, and when the law professor asked me if I hadn't enjoyed the music, I said "No." "Oh, you don't like that kind of music?" "The harpsichordist wasn't good." I was relieved to be told later by Loran Crosten that Biggs was a complete "dud" and played the organ in just the same way.

We sat at dinner with the Robert Fitzgeralds and Dudley Fitts, whom I had never met before. We both got a good impression of Fitts. He shares my contempt for symposiums and had refused to contribute to one that had been held by the classical journal *Arion*. He said that he liked to read Latin and Greek, and that that was all he had to say on the subject. He told Elena that his own wife had written to Johnson about the war in Vietnam and had received the same reply as Elena, that the President's heart was bleeding. Fitts added: "It must be a hemorrhage." Fitzgerald now has a job at Harvard. They have only been there two years and are not much enjoying Cambridge. They have a villa in Perugia and spend their summers there. Mrs. F. said she felt like Persephone when they set out for their villa in the spring. These people it was pleasant to meet, but such functions now fatigue me frightfully. It is boring to receive even compliments from people you do not know, and in the case of people you do know, you have no real opportunity to talk to them. We were rescued after dinner by the Pipeses as we were after the medal-giving at Peterborough. We went to their house and had whisky and an interesting conversation on Russian and Jewish subjects. *

T'ville, May 12, 1966. <This so far (May 21) has been my most depressing visit. The weather has been mostly horrible: overcast, rainy and misty. I have finished my play and the European stuff, and, as always, when I come to the end of anything and have not started anything new, I am in a state of collapse—sit drinking and playing solitaire and listening to the phonograph.

Mariska met me and brought me up and had dinner with me at Towpath, but I have not been able to get her to do anything for me since. Susan has been rather mysteriously ill, and she has been anxious about her. She now has a very full life, and I think is happier than I have ever known her. She seems really to have gone into business with the man who runs her drugstore and to have become a kind of public character. She has a charm school and gives conversation lessons to the ladies of Rome, plugs the pharmacy on TV, and evidently shares in the profits of the store—all these activities are connected with it. I asked what her conversation lessons consisted of, and she explained that the first problem was to get them off the weather; then they would talk about their children, and the next step was to get them off that. I asked her how that was done. Why, she would say that she had just read a book on child psychology. She has also joined a literary society—but has got to know only one woman— Jewish, of course—who has any cultural interests; attends PTA meetings; and is tomorrow acting as master

---

* According to Pipes, Wilson "took one look at the crowd and said, 'Let's get out of here.' When I asked why he took part in such functions, he replied, 'For the money of course.' " As the Wilsons were leaving, Pipes discovered "the check on the sofa where it had fallen out of his pocket."

of ceremonies at some sort of tap-dancing contest.>

The Crostens have been up here since April and are going to stay till September. Loran is taking a sabbatical year and working on a book on the history of opera which, since McGraw-Hill is bidding for it, may turn out to be a success. He seems to be enjoying himself. They are delighted with the wildlife about them: beavers, otters and deer; and they are surrounded with birdhouses on the trees. Loran is much concerned to keep the cowbirds out of other birds' nests. Glyn Morris is also very happy. He has quantities of federal money to spend, and talks about making Lyons Falls a cultural center for the "area."

I have been partly crippled by something wrong in the calf of my right leg—I suppose that is due to my general gouty condition and that, as usual, the gout has rushed to a part that has in any way been hurt, but I have now had it for weeks, and it doesn't get any better. <I am also depressed by the local delinquents' having smashed up the stone bowl and one of the stone posts in front of the house. They also broke into the Loomises' house where the Sharps used to spend the summer, smashed things and stole all the light bulbs—also, the house on what is called "the island."

I have come to realize that nowadays I literally cannot live without Elena. Aside from the fact that, with the Hutchinses and Mariska so busy with their own concerns, there is no one to take care of me here, we have now been together all but twenty years and, in spite of our difficulties of communication, have become quite dependent on one another.>

I have read half of *Father D'Arcy*'s new book, *Dialogue with Myself*, but don't know whether I shall go on. He is intelligent and well informed and expresses himself with felicity; but the story of Christ is to me a myth, and I have no clue at all in my own experience to the people who talk about loving God and God's love for the human race. Catholicism is to me far more sympathetic than Calvinism: Calvin's God could only be bowed down to and feared, and I'm not sure he loved even the elect. But I can't enter into the point of view of someone who talks about this love between God and the human race.

<I cleared up yesterday (May 22) from my depression and feel quite cheerful and normal again. The weather has become warm and fine. The narcissus in the back garden have all suddenly bloomed, and the dandelions are out on the lawn. I had a very pleasant dinner with the O'Donnells last night. They are appreciative of all my old anecdotes. It has also made me feel better to read Anaïs Nin's diary. It is certainly her magnum opus, and it has made me feel that I had a companion—I had been becoming so blue and exasperated.> Mabel Hutchins had made me wait in town when she was retrieving a mop handle from a woman to whom she had lent it and with whom she stopped to gossip, and on account of having supper with her sister, Beverly's mother, she was half an hour late in coming to get me at the Towpath. I had by that time had quite a lot to drink and bawled her out on the way back. I cannot depend on the Hutchinses for transportation and meals. She came back to the house and wept, and now we have made it up. I am also infuriated with Mary, who promises to come and type for me, then calls up and makes excuses, or simply does not show up at the time when she was expected. She is so preoccupied with her children and has become such a big shot in Rome that this really takes up all her time. Yesterday she didn't come to type until six because of the tap-dancing contest. I had already gone with the O'Don-

nells and left a sharp note on the door. But it gives me
pain to be on the outs with her.

<Albert Grubel is dead,> but Carrie Trenham still
alive, though I haven't seen her out of doors.

> You fade, old presences, and leave me here,
>   In dismal weather of a drizzled May;
> I play the phonograph, deal solitaire
>   Through aimless hours of Memorial Day.

> Women I'll never love, books never read!
>   My body, stiff with ailments, stalks a cage
> Of rooms; my mind, though ranging, loses speed,
>   Now entering the dark defile of age. *

Though the *Loomises* twice called on me, I was out. I
saw Huldah only very briefly. <When I had telephoned
the house that morning, Gertrude had said, "Huldah's gone
out with a boyfriend—I don't know where!" Going into
town, I saw her in front of Aunt Addie's house. The boyfriend was a boy who was working at fixing the broken
iron fence. Two delinquents had been racing in cars, and
one of them had gone off the road and wrecked the fence.
I have never seen Huldah so gray and *abattue* [worn out].>
She said that she was beginning to think that I had been
right in advising her to give the house to the Munns. She
told me that Gertrude was in very bad shape.

---

* EW's art of revision is evident in the version of this poem in *Upstate*:

> You fade, old presences, and leave me here
>   In dismal trickle of a dimming May;
> I play old records and lay solitaire
>   Through aimless hours of Memorial Day.

> Cities I'll never visit, books that I'll never read,
>   Magic I'll never master. In a cage,
> I stalk from room to room, lose heat and speed,
>   Now entering the dark defile of age.

Fern came in to see me just before I left. <She had had still another of her awful accidents. A cow had stepped on her foot, which was badly bruised and red and purple. The blood vessels were still bursting.> She told me that George and Lou, who want desperately a house of their own, have tried to buy Aunt Addie's house from the Loomises, but that Huldah, on reflection, had decided against it. They do not want to abandon their standard of orderly house-keeping to the Munns' sloppy mode of living; but it is also true that it is now impossible for Huldah to yield any of her possessions. She cannot even bring herself to make her will; she says that she supposes that all her things will be sold at auction. These are now almost the only things from which she can desire satisfaction—especially now that Florence is dead and Gertrude losing her wits. Then she says that if one of them dies, the survivor would be better off in Talcottville than alone up there on the hill.

Mary called me up, and said she was sorry about the misunderstanding, and we arranged to go to the *Marcelins'* Sunday. The house was now comfortable and cheerful. Eva had had the furniture brightly covered, and the Haitian paintings were on the walls. Terrible wind at the top of that hill. Phito misses the city, says he is a "town boy." Pierre is coming to see them, and he hopes he will stay three months, so they'll be able to finish their novel, but he has to face it that life may be impossible for Pierre in this country. Milo is somewhere on Long Island. Doctors, lawyers and other professional people have been forced to abandon Haiti. It's all right, perhaps, about the lawyers, because there have been far too many of them. Phito wants to write poetry but can't, and the émigrés he has met do not inspire him to write about them. As usual, he and I drank too much—though Eva tried to put the brakes on us—and Phito, on his way to the kitchen, fell over the record rack. I always enjoy seeing him, but now that he has learned more English, he always insists on talking it, and is harder to understand than when he murmured French.

Driving over, I felt that Mary had entered on a new phase of her life: more mature, more self-confident, better satisfied. She hopes that someday she can break off from the pharmacy and set up her own enterprise—though I don't quite know what this will be. She says that now that Ed is graduating from school and going away to college, she feels her intimate relationship with him is more or less ended.

<*Cultural explosion* in this "area"—as, I suppose, is going on all over the country, due to federal handouts and foundation grants. Glyn Morris says he has had to fight, during the winter, an exacerbated battle with Lowville in order to establish cultural hegemony. The Boonville library has been much improved—more space between the shelves, modern lighting, etc.—and Jessie Howland says that there has never been in Boonville so much demand for books. The big square old house beside the library that belonged to the miser Pratt has been left by his heir to the library and will be used for that and other purposes. (He did not leave a will, and the next of kin turned out to be a woman undertaker in Brooklyn, who did not know what to do with the home or the money. She set up some scholarships.) Then Utica College has been a great thing for Utica—as well as the Munson-Proctor museums. Two boys came to see me from Leonardsville: one teaches English at Utica College; the other, rather feminine, paints and admires Soutine [the French Impressionist]. They have a project, which seems to me vague and impossible,

of setting up a summer school at Leonardsville, where the
painter has inherited a house and some property. They
want people in the different arts to be able to talk to one
another. Somebody to come once a week to read a paper
and speak—to be followed by a discussion. I shocked them
by saying that for a painter or a writer to talk to a musician,
unless they happened to be friends and have temperaments
or interests in common, was like a carpenter talking to a
plumber. What a person practicing one art could get from
someone practicing another must come from experiencing
his work. But shouldn't they ask why? I said that anyone
with an artistic vocation rarely asks why; he practices his
art. Loran Crosten tells me that there is a great vogue for
"art centers" now, where music, ballet and theater, for
example, are supposed to be combined. He regards this
idea as futile: each of these arts has to be learned by itself.
And there is a tendency for the projects to duplicate one
another. Evgenia Lehovich says that from the enormous
available fund that the New York ballet has got, there are
now ballet schools all over the country which are often at
a loss for either dancers or instructors. Nevertheless, I
have been thinking up a project to be carried out with Tom
O'Donnell: a series of readings of papers or perhaps merely
a book of papers, intended to inform the people of that part
of New York about their local culture: Harold Frederic,
Samantha and the Widow Bedott, Tom's recent discovery
of Philander Deming, Lewis Morgan, the Oneida Community, etc.>*

---

* The Samantha books, a series for turn-of-the-century young women,
were written by Marietta Holley (1836–1936), who had been born in
nearby Jefferson County. Philander Deming (1829–1915) was a writer
of realistic stories of the Hudson Valley and the Adirondacks. Lewis
Morgan (1815–81), early anthropologist, was author of *The League of
the Iroquois*.

Another Award and
Jeanne Lapointe's Visit

<*National Medal for Literature luncheon:* It passed off quite painlessly at the Fort Schuyler Club. They had wanted me to be the keynoter at the PEN conference, but I made them come up here, telling them that my age and ailments made it impossible for me to get farther than Utica. It turned out to be a good idea to give the lunch myself, because thus I could keep them at bay, limit the number of people I should have to deal with and not have to appear in public. They had a photographer and a TV recording, but I don't suppose the latter will be shown. Roger Straus and Rosalind came up. Rosalind acted as hostess; Roger kept things going. I put Olive Fenton on my right and Mary [Pcolar] on my left. Mary was well dressed in blue and behaved with dignity, though she insisted on taking pictures with a newly acquired Polaroid camera that produced instantaneous prints which she had bought to take pictures of her teenagers before and after their charm treatment. When they asked her what she taught them, she answered, as a joke, that she taught them to drink gracefully out of drinking fountains. She only becomes vulgar when she is repeating conversations with her husband or someone else that takes her back to her peasant status: "He said," "I said," etc. She has a special tone of voice for this which I find rather grating. Harry Gilroy, the *Times* reporter, was there, whom I had known when I was in Jerusalem. There were, I think, three men from the Book Committee.

One of these men told a good story about a gigantic and complicated computer which was designed to surpass anything previously built. They fed it a difficult question and, after waiting a long time, got no reply. They tried again, still no response. The third time, a slip came out: "It says we'll have to sacrifice a goat." We discussed the sex of computers. Charley Walker had told me about seeing some men who were consulting a computer and would say, "Let's put it to him this way"—"No: let's put it to him like this." But someone else who was at the lunch said he had always heard them referred to as "she." When I discussed this with a Mrs. Moïse at Helen's commencement, she said that when it let them down, they probably called it "she": "She's broken down again"; but when it was a question of making demands on it, "he."

My most interesting conversation that afternoon was at the airport with Brett-Smith, while we were waiting for our planes with drinks. I don't think he was at home at the luncheon. Englishmen don't understand our storytelling and loud-laughing conviviality. I had been reading his father's edition of Etherege, and we talked about it when we met, but I had difficulty drawing him out at lunch. But later, apropos of my play, we talked about the literary forgers. He said that Thomas Wise used to come to see his father at Oxford. He always wore the same kind of neat suit and little bow tie—he implied that Wise was rather "jumped up." Though Brett-Smith's father was in the habit of going upstairs himself in order to get some book to show a visitor, he was careful, when Wise was there, always to send John to get them so that Wise would not have a chance to slip anything into his pocket.>— Rosalind and I flew to Boston together, and then I flew on to Provincetown.

Helen's commencement, June 10th—just like all other commencements from as far back as I can remember. I was touched to see that Helen was moved at leaving the school and at parting from her friends.

———

Wellfleet. Jeanne Lapointe came on for a few days. She —wisely, I think—would not stay with the girls, but had them find a little house for her. She came to dinner with us alone two evenings. Very jolly and quick and amusing as ever; but when one sees her outside Quebec, one is conscious of what the French of France would consider a certain *grossièreté*, grimacing and thrusting her hands— the same sort of reaction, I suppose, that the English have had about Americans. At home, she works hard on educational committees. She said that the main problem there was education. In five or ten years, perhaps, they might be ready to separate from the rest of Canada. But in the meantime, she said, the movement was better organized than ever. Mavis Gallant, Jeanne told us, is back in Canada. Anne Hébert has been there, too, on account of her mother's death, but has now returned to France. She denied Mavis Gallant's story that Anne Hébert's father had kept her confined to her bed—à la Elizabeth Barrett—on the pretext that she was ill. She declared that this story was an invention of Mavis's—*sa mauvaise langue, elle est malveillante* [she has an acid tongue, she is malicious]—M. Hébert was *un homme charmant*; but then went on to tell us that he had probably slept with Anne; that *le frère d'Anne couchait dans la chambre de sa mere jusqu'à quarante ans*; that he or another brother, with his hands in black gloves, had put them around her neck and said, "*Je voudrais vous étrangler!*" Jeanne had advised Anne to leave home.

She and Elena at dinner became quite vehement in French about Marie-Claire—Elena catching Jeanne's vehemence. She was afraid that Marie-Claire was headed for perdition: there was nothing now to hold her to the Church except Jeanne and that Belgian abbé. Elena thinks that what the doctor calls M.-C.'s anemia—she has become very thin and pale—is due to a conviction of guilt and that Mary, too, is full of guilt. Marie-Claire has apparently expressed her *angoisse* over this to Jeanne. She said—what I was already aware of—that M.-C. was completely unreliable about anything in her own life. She lived in imagination, and didn't know herself what was true. I had always had the impression that she came from the lowest illiterate level of the life of Quebec City, and was rather surprised when Jeanne told me that actually her mother was a schoolteacher—though it might have been possible that, as she said, her father had destroyed her writings. Certainly *Une Saison dans la Vie d'Emmanuel* is not really a picture of her own home. Jeanne thinks that *Emmanuel* gives the kind of picture of French-Canadian life that M.-C. thinks we want her to write, and that her present hostility toward the clergy is due to my influence. I told Jeanne that when I had expressed to M.-C. my appreciation of *le frère* Untel's second book, she had protested that either he could not be sincere or that he ought not to try to defend the Church. I had said—and Mary had unobtrusively backed me—that this lay brother's religious vocation—though, as he says, his monastic role had been something into which he had been routed very young without really knowing what he was doing—had now been accepted as something valid to whose claims he could willingly yield.

Elena and I, I suppose, are really getting a little old *pour l'amour*. Though we try it, at rather long intervals, it is likely to turn out that one of us comes but not the other. Yet when I am staying without her at T'ville, I sometimes feel a strong passion for her—based, perhaps, on memories of the past. After all, as she said last night, when we resorted to our little upstairs room, we have had almost twenty years of one another.

This June in the last few days, since I have stopped drinking, has been comfortable, companionable, delightful. I really can't stand any more to pay for a burst of animation when someone comes in for drinks with a depressed and low-keyed next day, in which I have to go around on my hands and knees.

We met *Ed and Pat Dickinson* at Indian Neck. He had just sold a picture, but the price had been to listen to two hours of conversation by the man who bought it, which involved a long account of a hysterectomy and other things that Ed said he "couldn't mention." They had then had some beer, and Ed was unusually talkative. He is now on the crest of the wave and enjoying his reputation and prosperity. He is 75 but boasts of his continuing agility. He takes sitting-up exercises on the beach—not the usual kind, which bore him, but the semaphoring gestures that he learned in the Signal Corps. He semaphores sonnets or compliments to any goodlooking girl he may happen to see on the beach.

These awards I am getting make me rather nervous. They mean that I am an O.K. character like Thornton Wilder. When I think about how stupid old frauds like Herbert Hoover and John F. Dulles get buildings and things named after them, without people's seriously protesting or considering it inappropriate, I realize that an accepted reputation can be derived from no real merit whatever.*

The *Dickinsons* gave a party for the first time in history: a buffet supper. The house was as barren and bleak as

* Wilson enjoyed repeating Roger Straus's story about a sculptor he knew who began to get awards when he was past seventy. When Roger congratulated him, he said, "The thing is to outlive the sons-of-bitches."

ever: a death mask of Beethoven, one of Ed's smaller paintings. Now that he is making a lot of money, he yields very little in his thrifty habits. He now goes to Greece, but I understand sails on freighters. He and his cousin Stuart Hughes are having quite a rapprochement. Stuart says that Ed used to be "the poor relation."

During July and the first week of August, the house was full of Elena's family: five Thorntons and little Marina Schouvaloff. Marina, who has always seemed subdued and not particularly interesting before, has now become remarkably attractive. She is natural and self-assured, speaks English exactly like her mother. She obviously takes pride in her mother's aristocratic family. We don't know whether she knows about her father. Elena first thought that she did not know, then decided she did know because she hates her adoptive father, Ivan. French girls are not independent till 21, and Ivan won't let her come to America, which is her dream. She wants to qualify to be a bilingual secretary or an interpreter at the UN.

Of the Thornton twins, Elena seems very much like my Elena; she has her sweet face and desire to please. Sandra is more astringent. She seems skeptical about fairy tales and usually succeeds in detecting my tricks or producing some plausible theory about how they are done. Little 3-year-old Nina is a holy terror. She has to compete all the time with her older sisters and is always attracting attention to herself. If an attempt is made to curb her rough-housing, she immediately begins to bawl. Her parents let her have her way, and she is becoming the kind of spoiled American child that people from other countries deplore. She is very cute and pretty, but does not look or behave like her parents or either of her sisters. Daphne says she doesn't know where she came from.

———

Helen and I put on *our Punch and Judy show*—Helen with some reluctance, since she is old enough now to be embarrassed. At the end, when the crocodiles appeared, little Nina peed her pants—I suppose the greatest tribute that a performer can have from his audience.

István Deák came to dinner. I had considered him the perfect model of the sober and reasonable Hungarian of the younger generation, and so he usually is. But after supper, I took him into my study, and we talked about Hungary, and he became quite demonstrative and vehement—a touch of the old nationalist frenzy that seems to inhabit every Hungarian.

<Reading the newspapers, and even the world's literature, I find that I more and more feel a boredom with and scorn for the human race. We have still such a long way to go, so many terrific problems to deal with. Wars are such impediments and setbacks; sex gets to seem rather silly. When I read even a love story that might once have moved me, I think, Oh, it's just a man trying to get a woman. And the books that describe these things! no matter how well they describe them. The policies of the lying governments; the standardization of exotic and "backward" peoples; the stupidity of applied ideologies; the competition for "success" and "status"; the inferiority of the human specimens that I see all around me in America.>

Upstate Again: Arguing about Vietnam

<*T'ville, from Aug. 6, 1966.* The house looks better with new screens in the windows, the roof and the back bedroom painted.

Mabel Hutchins seems in very good shape and has more

free time to take care of me. She has dyed her hair and has a new red flowered dress. Kay is working as assistant to a Boonville dentist and seems to be delighted with her job.

Mariska has dyed her hair a paler yellow, which is more becoming to her. She has lost weight and has what is for her an almost lilylike fragility. She met me at the airport and we had dinner in Constableville. It was the day of the firemen's fair and parade. Both Mary's girls were in the parade, which went by just after we had finished dinner. Susan was playing the clarinet and Janet, I think, just marching, in the contingent from West Leyden. The whole thing was touching and cheering. Each town had sent its delegation, and they competed with one another in music, display, drum-majorette stick-twirling and other tricks. In one, there was a girl who did flips; in another, the girl would suddenly sink to the ground, then quickly start up again.

Aug. 9. A cracking thunderstorm. It blew out the bulb at my writing table here. Then I moved the table to the middle of the room, and it blew out that bulb, too. I moved to the other end, and the thunder and lightning moved off. It turned out that both the telephone and the phonograph had been put out of commission. A ball of fire had been seen in the road.

Aug. 10. Mariska drove me to Utica. It was her day off from the pharmacy. She had arranged an international week for the lunch counter. Monday they had had French onion soup; Tuesday, Mexican beans with chili. Both of these had been made by herself; but now, Wednesday, it was Polish stuffed cabbage, by a Polish girl in the store. The Polish girl said that she wished it were not Mariska's day off, so that she could give publicity to the dish of the day. Mariska suggested our stopping there on the way back in order to show me the store—she said that she wanted to see how the Polish stuffed cabbage was going over.

We went to see Henry Di Spirito. I thought he was perceptibly changed. I think it has meant a lot to him to have his appointment and studio at Utica College, so that he does not have to work at bricklaying any more. He is having two exhibitions this summer and he has won a prize at Cooperstown. He does not have to pretend to be humble. His face seems even more remarkable than his shock of snow-white hair: more expressive in its enthusiasm and humor. It is as if his stony physique had become with greater freedom more flexible. His wife says that he has lately had a great burst of work; after 60, he is prodigiously productive.

Young Hungarian from Syracuse—goodlooking, intelligent, with versatile interests. Had studied engineering and history of art at Columbia; had intended to study medicine, but now wanted to write. He gallantly brought not only a bottle of Tokay and a Beatles record for me, but boxes of chocolates for Elena and Helen. Since he came at five o'clock, I didn't think I could cope with a whole evening alone with him so phoned for the Pcolars. Mariska talked to him in Hungarian—he says that her pronunciation is good but her vocabulary rather limited—while I talked to George and Ed. But the Pcolars left and I sat up with him drinking and talking about Hungary. I suffered the next day from Hungarian fatigue, but have decided that I really invite what Elena calls my Hungarian rhapsodies by stirring them up about Hungary. What he really wanted to talk about was Scott Fitzgerald.

Mariska, with her daughter Susan, drove me over to *Blue Mountain Lake*, where the Heusers are now operating

Crane Point Lodge. This proved to be a comfortable and quiet place in the woods and on the lake. It was originally a summer residence of two rich families, one from Cleveland, one from Rochester; but had now for the last nine years been rented for them as a curious kind of summer hotel. There is a huge long living room, the kind of thing I like, the kind of thing I had in the de Silver house in the Stamford woods, but on an immensely larger scale. Mignonne first told me that life there was "very healthful," and explained that they had to observe "tradition." A clientele from Cleveland and other cities had been coming there for years, and they would not have tolerated changes. There was no bar—"Isn't it terrible!," said Klaus. They gave us a whisky and soda out of their private stock but asked us not to take it to the dining room, where we were curiously eyed by the old Cleveland squares. They have to go to meals on time, and Mignonne wakes them up with a dinner bell, I think at 8. She sits doing jigsaw puzzles at the end of the long room near the entrance.

I had a strange experience when alone in this room. I sometimes nowadays have auditory hallucinations when I'm just waking up in the morning. I hear the telephone ring quite clearly; I wait and if it doesn't ring again, I know it's a hallucination. So I sometimes think I hear Rosalind or Elena calling me. But I have never had one before by day. There is a huge bear rug in this long room—a Kodiak bear. I was in rather a dim state—was still suffering from Hungarian fatigue, was made sleepy by the higher altitude. I thought this bear growled. I waited and I seemed to hear it growl again. When Mignonne came back, I said that they had evidently put a mechanism in its head in order to make it growl. She laughed and said no. I asked her whether there was not a dog around. No. >

The museum is much improved since I saw it in its early days—a great many more things to see. The art collection is now very attractive. It mostly consists of paintings by artists from elsewhere of Adirondack lakes, many of them charming.

<Walter Edmonds had written me that a *moose* had been shot at Malone—getting the man who shot it into trouble—and that a *black panther* had been reported. I now learn that somebody believes that he has seen the footprints of a mountain lion.> More animals moving back.

Weedon of the Palmer's hardware store has finally gone out of business. Everybody is delighted. He managed, however, before he went bankrupt, to sell most of his stock—he would let people in by the back door—so that he still had plenty of money. The authorities had finally to put locks on the place.

Harold Frederic:

—Unlike Howells, he likes to create unpleasant situations, in which people say insulting things to one another.

—Passage in *The Lawton Girl* about all the able and ambitious people going away and never coming back again and the mediocre stagnating at home.

—The whole thing somewhat provisory.

—Utica cold storage gentility; run-down family of ex-canallers; moderately well-to-do farmers: the Fairchilds; families in one generation made suddenly rich by the "knitting mills"; crooked swindlers and politicians; editors venial and zealous for reform; well-intentioned schoolteachers.

—Though *Seth's Brother's Wife* and *The Lawton Girl* are much more conventional novels than *The Damnation of*

Theron Ware, he always conscientiously sticks close to real types and real conditions.

—I said to Otis that the only thing I didn't find in Frederic's novels was the kind of people like our families in Talcottville. He said—what I am sure is true—that the dairy farmers up here were then an unusually prosperous lot—I spoke of the big square houses mentioned in *Seth's Brother's Wife*, already abandoned and untended. He said that the big brick Jackson place between here and Boonville had been built by a man of such overweening ambition that he was ruined by the time it was finished.

—Maudlin raptures of Reuben in *The Copperhead* when he knows that Kate loves him. Pathetic deathbed of Jessica—little Nell, little Eva, etc.—overdone, at last everybody is weeping over her; yet it is kept less maudlin than these: Frederic cannot quite be untrue to his realistic method.

<*Elena arrived*, still ill from the flu—she couldn't even drive a hired car, though later on we got one and drove. Very gloomy days at first. She said she was afraid of the old house, always had been, had to steel herself.> I made myself disagreeable about her always arriving late and under protest.

She did have to take, on this visit, some pretty severe beatings. The first was at the *Gauses'*, where we went for dinner. <I had a talk before dinner with John in his study, explaining to him about the project that Tom O'Donnell and I are trying to arrange for celebrating the cultural achievements of the region, and he responded to it rather favorably, suggesting that he might do a more or less "personal" talk about the Samantha books, Thomas Jones, Jr. [a Boonville poet], whom he knew, and Hough, the county

historian, who, he says, was the original creator of the U.S. Forestry Bureau—also, possibly, Allen Upward—all illustrating the "variety" of America, a favorite subject of his. We had three fairly stiff drinks, which may partly account for what followed.

At dinner, I set him off by asking him whether he didn't think a law should be passed making it impossible for a Texan to be President of the U.S.* He resented this extremely. He had recently been in Texas and had had himself photographed against the background of the Johnson ranch. I had never seen the aggressive and rather oafish side of him before, though I had found him rather unpleasant about my tax book, which he hadn't read. The truth is, as I told him, that he idealizes this country in terms of upstate New York as he had known it in his youth. He will not listen to criticism of anything and seems rarely to read anything critical. I had found this in talking to him, and Malcolm Sharp says he has had the same experience. Tonight he really tore into us. He declared that we were "pathological" about Vietnam and were following "the line." He had talked with school friends of Lyndon Johnson, who had said he was a splendid fellow, and they were better men than I was! Elena's attitude, he said, was a falling-back on her European background: in Europe they were against the war because they didn't like our spending so much money on it—they wanted the money themselves. My own point of view was entirely derived from my Princeton–New York Eastern background—I didn't know the rest of the country. I told him that I thought I had seen as much of the U.S. as he had, and that I had seen

* The Vietnam War had changed EW's view of Lyndon Johnson since 1964, when he was the alternative to Goldwater. Several months before this bitter confrontation, Alfred Kazin proposed a March on Washington by the literati, but Wilson suggested that Johnson already believed that "the writers belong to the category who are not with him, so against him."

a damn sight more of the world. He said that he had reports from all over the world—from his former students, who were working along his lines—and I gathered that they were all supporting the war. All the ordinary people did. I replied that Bob Stabb, who made repairs on my house, did not seem to approve of it—he had told me that the news in the papers was all bad. "Isolated cases!" Elena reminded him that a lot of American boys were getting killed, and he retorted not many. "Two are too many." More young people were killed on the roads than were being killed in Vietnam. He greatly applauded Dean Rusk, who had told them in South America that he "understood the have-nots because he himself had been delivered by a veterinarian"—implying that we had no right to speak because we had not had that privilege. The opposition to the war was all due to the Communists and the Catholics (Bobby Kennedy). I had slapped my hand on the table when he began blaming things on the Communists, and he accused us of being "emotionally disturbed." I told him that he was emotionally disturbed himself. It got to the point that to all our arguments, he would only reply, "Forget it!" I said that I couldn't forget it. "You will!" Jane took no part in the conversation. At one point, he said, "I love my wife best, but I love my country next!" After dinner, we changed the subject, but did not stay very long. He saw us into the car, but did not shake hands or say goodbye.

I decided that it was the German coming out, that in Germany he could easily have been a Nazi. I believe that his minute accurate knowledge of everything connected with the region is also a German trait. His interests are really limited. We have sometimes talked of books that we have both read—such as his early admiration for H. G. Wells—but he usually goes on rather boringly about the excellence of American institutions as he observes them in his travels around the country. I remember his eulogizing to me lately the charms of the motels—like old-fashioned inns, where you met and conversed with all kinds of people. Elena said that the evening was a valuable revelation, because there must be a great many people in the same state of mind as John;> but I think he must be a special case.

Glyn Morris, on the other hand, is quite aware of threats and problems. Yet he had a huge chunk of federal money, with a deadline on spending it last spring. He has expanded his educational bureau in Lyons Falls and has stocked it with hundreds of documentary films and hundreds of colored prints, to be shipped, on demand, to any school in the district. He has also installed video equipment, which enables you to make instantaneously on film both visual and sound recordings, and then wipe them off afterwards. There is a "psychiatric" department, where students who seem to need attention are interviewed, and there is going to be a one-way device by which teachers can watch and hear this without being seen. Glyn is delighted with this —he says that there are only two or three centers like it in the state. He is the wizard of a wonder palace. He first showed it off to us; then later, when Elena had gone and Rosalind was here, he showed it off again to her. He pointed out that a bright green carpet had been added since I had seen it before.

<We had lunch with *Grace Root* at Clinton. She is very arthritic now and has a specially made footstool with things to keep her heels from slipping. She gets around but only with difficulty. Yet she is still going strong in her role of professional hostess and *salonière.* > Her face seems to get more mannish. I already suspected her of lesbian interests, and Elena had the same impression. During lunch, she sent Elena a little vase of flowers at the other end of the

table and talked about her with special enthusiasm, and on my way to the bathroom I noticed in the corridor a back view of a slim feminine nude. <She handles her guests well, but has a rather rude way of ending a conversation when the other person is in the middle of saying something by starting a conversation with someone else. I had been writing about Kelly Prentice and talked to her about special characteristics of the people who come from Albany, of whom she seems to me a typical representative. I have a feeling that the James family must have looked and talked rather like her. She said that the conflict between the English and the Dutch might have made the Albanians peculiar, that the Dutch resistance to the English might have set them off from other people. She herself was William Bradford (one of her ancestors) till five o'clock in the afternoon: conscientious, sober, practical; but after that the Dutch blood reasserted itself: she was lazy and rather heedless.>—They trot out for me the English faculty of Hamilton and their usually boring wives, and I am now getting so that it taxes me to cope with it. There was also the daughter of an Italian who taught Dante, and I had to put on my Italian tape recording.

We went to Rome one evening to see the film of *Who's Afraid of Virginia Woolf?*, and at our dinner at The Beeches we seemed to be anticipating its mood. The ancient Roman clowning of the costumes of the waiters and the bogus Latin of the menu nowadays get on my nerves, and the food is absolutely terrible. Elena thought what was supposed to be her hamburger was horse meat. She got to talking in a rather tart way about the differences in the way that people lived, and said that she had been horrified at Red Bank to see a row of little glass animals that my mother had bought at the five-and-ten-cent store. I did not remember these. It was unlike my mother, I thought, to buy glass animals at a five-and-ten-cent store. Somebody must have given them to her. I retorted to this ugly charge by attacking the bad taste of the Russians—the walls plastered over with pictures, all kinds of little knickknacks, etc.—e.g., the Chavchavadzes' house, the Tsar's apartment in the Winter Palace. —Mabel Hutchins gave Elena on her birthday a little yellow glass cat, which she now has on the windowsill in the corridor at Wellfleet.

Our second trying ordeal was the evening before Elena left, when we went to Utica for dinner with the Wassermans. It was one of those occasions when they talk and talk and talk and drink and drink before they get around to serving dinner. We wanted to get away early because Elena had to drive to the airport the next morning, and I finally mentioned this to Mrs. Wasserman. In the meantime, I had to talk to the superintendent of one of the Utica schools, Boston Irish, and had become inextricably entangled in an interminable conversation with a lady from Edinburgh, the wife of the head of the French department. She was tight and very repetitious and difficult to understand because, I thought, she must have tried to iron out a fairly strong Scotch accent by imposing on it something more refined. I also had to sit next to her at dinner and across from the wife of the superintendent, also Boston Irish and rather hard to take. The Jews were more satisfactory. But with a man named Simon across the table, who taught public relations at Utica College, it was almost impossible to communicate because the Edinburgh lady, now more repetitious than ever, always got in the way. I ended by talking exclusively to Mrs. Wasserman, whom I liked. Jews are rarely silly or sloppy. We had to excuse ourselves as soon as dinner was over. —Wasserman has built for himself a little modern house at the corner of a suburban street, with bright flowers and a wild little grove behind it.

The last day Mary drove Rosalind and me to Utica. I had lunch with O'Donnell and Palmer, the head of the Munson-Proctor art school, and discussed our cultural project. Mary and Rosalind sat at a different table and joined us afterwards. Then we drove out to the airport and had drinks in the dining room while waiting. When I got back to Wellfleet, I was somewhat vague and confused, and it took me all the next day to recover. It is getting to be harder for me to adapt myself to the transit from Talcottville to Wellfleet.

The Cape and Martha's Vineyard

Wellfleet. A gigantic finned whale was washed up on the beach of the Wellfleet harbor—over sixty feet long. It was still alive when we went to see it, and a ghastly and tragic sight. It was still breathing, with exhalations at intervals that sounded like a bellows. Its brown eyes looked like the eyes of a wounded horse. Its flippers twitched. Its outer skin was torn off in places and its belly had been scratched and was bleeding. Its great strainer in its mouth was exposed: the "whalebone" comb, with its hairlike accompaniment. It was beautifully "streamlined" and had almost the look of some man-made plane or boat—the white underpart with its curving gray lines. The children annoyed it and tore off the loose skin. When one saw the people around it from a distance, they looked like Lilliputians around Gulliver, and made the human race look monkeylike and petty. —The next morning when the tide came in, the poor thing was dead, and they towed it around to Peaked Hill.

Cleanthe [*Weill*]: She had written me that she was coming on from Hollywood to spend some time with her hus-

band in his camp in Maine, and I had invited her to come
to see us. I wanted to talk to her about the family and was
also curious to find out what had become of her. She arrived
September 14, and proved to be quite startling. She was
carrying a good deal of baggage—including a kind of hat
box with a blond wig, which she said had not gone over
very well with her husband's friends in Maine. She is
amusing but exhibited—especially at first, when she was
trying to make an impression—the habit, which had sometimes made her mother trying, of telling long humorous
stories, from which she could not for more than a minute
be diverted, by the necessity of going to dinner or anything
else, and felt it necessary to emphasize the point by grab-
bing or violently nudging you. Her conversation is very
Hollywood—tough and sometimes witty. I had long talks
about the family, and she depressed me not only by the
revelation of what she had been through—I had always
felt sympathetic to her and sorry for her—but also by the
vituperative vulgarity of the relations between the sisters,
Helen, Dorothy, Adeline, and Cleanthe's own vulgarity in
telling about it. She seems to me exactly like her father,
very Irish, and has certain attractive qualities—is goodlooking but totally lacking in charm. (Helen and Elena
don't agree about this.) There are moments when she reminds me of Louise Connor. These attractive Irish girls,
when they get older, still depend on beauty and impudence
when these have no longer their full effect. She has really
had a horrible time. Her father took to drink and began
to be behind on his comic strip, which had to be fourteen
weeks ahead. Her mother and she periodically left him.
(After they were definitely separated, it seems, he ceased
to drink.) She told me stories of their friends in their
bohemian days—they were never, however, anything else:
Julian Street, Bobby Edwards. George M. Cohan was a
friend of Gene's. Gene would get drunk in Chinatown and

have to be rescued by Helen. Cleanthe said that she had been a little pitcher who had big ears. She finally became so neurotic—had something called narcolepsy, she was always going to sleep, I suppose to get away from the strains and the quarrels—that the doctor said she ought to get away. They went out to California, where she has been ever since. I am not clear when they spent three years in Paris.

Helen wanted her to be a painter—which she is—and believed that she was a genius—which she knows she is not. She says that she grew up as something between "a boy and a freak." She was always asked to attend to anything that needed to be mended: "Oh, Cleanthe can do that better than anybody!" I knew—though she did not speak of it—of her mother's stranglehold on her; would not let her get away; made fun of any beaux she had. When I congratulated her on finally getting away from her mother, all she said was "Oh, that!" She had known Sam Weill for years, when he had been living as a bachelor. When she married him her mother developed all sorts of ailments and died in about six months. He is a distributor of Volkswagens in the Southwest—the first year they only sold one. She told me his life history—he had for a long time been untamably difficult and now still had terrible rages. Related to the Kirsteins; from Rochester; his sister had married John Gielgud—an actress who called herself Vali. Cleanthe did not like to read, read slowly. Her mother had always read to her while she was painting. She had read—to her surprise—my Dead Sea scrolls book as easily as Bemelmans—wanted me to recommend something equally easy to read. She remembered that she had also found Surtees easy and agreeable.* When Elena asked her

---

* Ludwig Bemelmans (1898–1972) was an Austrian-born writer of satire and children's books such as the Madeleine series, which he illustrated. Robert Smith Surtees (1803–64) wrote tales of fox-hunting and created

how she managed to look so young at 55, she answered, "Arrested development." When she asked her when she had begun painting and drawing dogs instead of human beings, she said, "When I got disgusted with people." She showed us a photograph of one of her dog portraits, and it was so literally realistic that we both at first thought it was a photograph of the dog. She knows a lot about dogs and advised me against getting a bloodhound; they drooled and "were flatulent," and their skin was loose. She has always wanted a lion. Before she left, she slipped into Elena's bag a note with $50, explaining that it was to buy Helen a dress.

Cleanthe told me about the strains and uncertainties of her and her mother's getting an allowance from Adeline. Once they had all been laughing at some joke when Adeline, pregnant, came in the door. She thought they were laughing at her and for some time cut off the allowance. She arranged for them to go to France because she was having an affair with Max Bamberger, and this gave her an excuse for telling Joe Moran, to whom she was then married, that she wanted to go to France to see her sister. She had given my cousin Helen what Cleanthe thought was a really bad piece of advice. She said that if she had done something outrageous that Joe Moran was likely to find out, she would make him a terrible scene about something, so that he would be so upset that he could only think of getting her a new diamond bracelet at Cartier's and would not worry about the other matter.

Martha's Vineyard. Sept. 16–18. Like going to a foreign country: the old white houses of Edgartown, so much more

___

the comic character of Jorrocks, the sporting grocer who was the prototype of Mr. Pickwick.

civilized and suburban than the Cape; the sunsets over the sea that reminded me of the kind of sunsets that one sees from a ship stretching without horizon above an unending expanse of waters. Then, living in a rooming house, relieved of responsibilities, lying around resting and reading. The greenery more solid than on the Cape, everything seemed more substantial.

At the Menemsha–Gay Head end of the island are a few important writers—Max Eastman, Leon Edel—who go little to the other parts. The country, cliffs and beach there are still rather wild. At another corner—Vineyard Haven—is the "cocktail belt," of which I take it Lillian Hellman is more or less the queen. In the summer, says Leon Edel, such people as William Styron and Philip Rahv are there. "Down island" is Edgartown, respectable and solidly built up.

We found Esther [Kimball] living in a little gray house adequate for her needs: a big kitchen, a bedroom and bath, the garage fitted up for a guest house, with four bunks like a ship. In the bookcases almost nothing but bound copies of stuff from *The Reader's Digest*. Esther, now 69, has got to look like her Grandmother Knox. She was admirable about my memoirs. Before she had read them, I thought she received me with a look of apprehension, and afterwards she complained a little that I had not done her mother justice. But when I talked to her alone Sunday morning—the first real conversation I suppose I had had with her in my life—she admitted that her mother had not understood Sandy and that he had rebelled against her, and that she herself had also, to a less extent, rebelled against her mother's pressure. She corrected some of my erroneous memories and told me some anecdotes which I'm incorporating in *A Prelude*. She knew as little as I did about where her father went on his sprees or who his companions were. These aberrations were something never talked about.* When she talked to Elena alone, she told her that her mother had been in society whereas my mother had not. Aunt Caroline's idea of being in society was circulating in Seabright and Rumson and having the *Social Register* on the phone table. When I opened the drawer of Esther's desk to get out the telephone book, I saw that it was full of *Social Register*s. She said to Elena that she knew I had always thought her stupid—"less than the dust" was the phrase she used over and over again in speaking of the way she was treated as a girl by Sandy and me and his friends. But after all, she said, she had brought up her three boys under rather difficult circumstances—Bobby Hartshorne's insanity, etc. There was a picture of the family on the wall, and she showed us another one which included her innumerable grandchildren. —She told me that she thought I had been unfortunate in having been an only child. She and Sandy had had fun together. You could combine against the older people if you had a brother or sister.

We called on Max Eastman, who, though his voice is now that of an old man and although he has put on weight, still makes sense and—though I didn't notice it—Elena and Helen noticed that he was still putting on the charm. He seemed very comfortable there, with his beautiful view, his old dog, and his present wife and former secretary, whom it seems he inherited from Dreiser.

I spent an afternoon with Leon Edel while Elena and

* In *The New Yorker* EW had recounted the periodic binges of Esther's father, his Uncle Reuel. In *A Prelude* (1967) he describes his life of "unrelieved application" practicing medicine in New York and suburban New Jersey. He was loved by his patients, and a wing of a New York hospital was named for him. Before "carefully premeditated escapades" he briefed an assistant about his patients' needs, then disappeared. "When he was brought back home, he would sometimes spend weeks in bed being dealcoholized."

Helen went swimming. Mostly Henry James and my projected Pléiade series. He has acquired more letters of James, has tracked down the family of the expatriate American doctor that James and Miss Woolson went to, and succeeded in getting their letters to the doctor, in which he has been gratified to find nothing that contradicts his theory about them.* I'm afraid that he has got himself into a state of mind where he can't see James's gaucheries, which were due to a constant self-consciousness and too deliberately acquired assumptions as to social rank and conventions: his warning Lady Ottoline Morell, when she expressed a wish to meet Conrad, that Conrad was a rough old seaman improper for her ladyship to meet (when they did meet, of course Conrad was the soul of courtesy, and they got along famously); his wearing a silk hat, etc., when calling on some humble lady in San Francisco and his making a scene that Stephen Crane thought ridiculous when some chorus girl poured champagne into his hat; his dropping Cora Crane, etc. —Leon has straightened me out about the Betjeman-underclothes story. The underclothes and the waistcoat which had belonged to the younger Henry James who was William James's son were sent as Bundles for Britain at the time of the war. They were monogrammed HJ, and somebody at Oxford became aware that they came from a Henry James. Eventually John Betjeman got them, and Billy James—as in a Henry James story—did not have the heart to reveal to him that they had not belonged to his uncle. —Altogether a very satisfactory and agreeable afternoon, more so than if one meets in a city or even a university town.

* EW refers to Edel's account of the novelist's relationship to Constance Fenimore Woolson, who committed suicide in Venice. James grieved over her, and appears to have projected a sense of guilt in Marcher's exploitation of May Bartram in *The Beast in the Jungle*. Four long letters from Miss Woolson to her doctor are included in an appendix to Edel's *The Middle Years*.

We had dinner with Lillian Hellman, with the Edels—young Marquand came in afterwards—and lunch the next day, at which John Hersey and his wife were present. Lillian, with the aid of a scene designer, has built herself a delightful new house, on the side of the steep bank, in such a way that, whereas there is only one floor below, there are two above—four rooms upstairs. Large living room ornamented and furnished in her usual good taste, and a terrace that looks out on the little harbor. Along the front of the house are planted some kind of long-stemmed pink roses that I have never seen before: they stand up without being propped and produce a delightful effect. I can't get over her combination of elegance and "gracious living" with her embittered radicalism and the harshness of her plays. It is, I suppose, the Jewish tradition overlaid with New Orleans good living. Her eyes are sweet and friendly and still, I think, a little innocent. She gave the usual excellent meals: bluefish for dinner, one of which she had caught herself; fried chicken on the terrace for lunch.

New York Life; "Extravagant Compliments"

New York, Nov. 13–19. Sunday night we dined with the *Berlins*. They took us to the L'Aiglon restaurant, which was very expensive and, so far as my dinner went, very bad food: a martini which was no martini and swordfish which was obviously shark. At the back, draped with red curtains, a crude colored mural of Versailles, with a small real fountain playing. Crowded and so loud with talking that conversation was almost impossible. —Isaiah as effervescent and amusing as ever, but he makes such a point of knowing about everything and everybody, what everybody has published and where everybody is—and with me he can leap around among most of his fields: English,

American, Jewish and Russian, though I don't follow him in his inroads into German thought—that an evening with him is quite fatiguing. Aline acts as a counterbalance.

Monday I dragged Elena and Barbara Deming to see John Huston's film *The Bible*, which covers only a few episodes in Genesis. I had heard that parts of it were good, but though it is not so comic as most Biblical films, it is actually not any good—pretentious, inartistic, unimaginative, and three hours long. The animals in the ark have a circus interest; but, as Brendan Gill pointed out, there is not the least suggestion that everybody but Noah and his family are being drowned in the Flood.

Just before I left Wellfleet, I had had a letter from *Clelia*, telling me that she would be in New York Monday and Tuesday. She said that Brendan Gill would be coming down to Maryland the first of the week, but that she would not be there to see him. I think that she had planned it that way. Brendan has never been to the "Manor." He is *The New Yorker*'s architectural informant and was going down to find out about the model city which is to be constructed near the Carroll place. This the Carrolls describe as "the enemy." Philip keeps buying up land in order to fend off the intruders. Brendan tells Clelia that the location of the Manor will double the value of the land, but, as she says, Philip is interested in buying not selling land. She came for drinks at the club Tuesday. She explained that her mother was part-Florentine, and now I see the Italian in her. Her effort at wifemanship and absence from New York has, I think, somewhat changed her appearance: she aims to charm less, to appear more mature and responsible. But she speaks with a spontaneous candor which does charm me. She had written me that they were expecting "uninvited guests" which Brendan must have sent them: John Sargent from Doubleday and a girl of his from the Princeton University Press. The weekend was apparently embarrassing because, as Clelia said, "the end of the affair" had occurred then, and the girl, having broken with Sargent, had ended by calling up and making a date with another man. Everybody, including Clelia, had drunk much too much. When I told Brendan about this incident, he was much excited. He said that he had never gone after the girl on account of his loyalty to Sargent, but now he had a free field. She was terribly pretty and six feet tall.

I asked Elena afterwards why Clelia—who had described her first husband as a broker and "very dull"—had married the men she had. E. said that that was the way she had been brought up—she had to marry people who were rich and gold-plated socially—which of course is true. The letters she writes me show that she is intelligent and has intellectual curiosity. She said that she had been stimulated by her children—two by her first husband, two by the second—to have intellectual interests. One of the daughters has been in Greece and is studying modern Greek. I think that Clelia is stuck with something very odd down there. She has written that, in exploring the place, they have found the most curious relics of the eighteenth century, and that the tenants on the estate are in a practically feudal condition. They live in cramped quarters and more or less squalor, and it is difficult even to convince them that their dwellings ought to be improved. She wants to do something about it, but doesn't know where the money will come from. I have a special relation to her—my side of our correspondence is almost *Lettres à une Inconnue**—which has come to mean a good deal to me, and evidently something to her.

* This is the title of Prosper Mérimée's correspondence of some forty years with Jenny Dacquin, revealing their love, friendship, and exasperation with one another. EW's correspondence with Clelia consists of fifteen letters of hers and forty-five letters and valentines of his, over the last seven years of Wilson's life.

We went to dinner at the *Epsteins'* in the evening. When
Elena was getting ready, she came out of the bathroom
naked, and I saw how beautiful she still was. It both lifted
me up and baffled me. I seem nowadays to be able to do
so little about her. —I have been usually in such bad shape
after an evening with the Epsteins that I decided to take
precautions. Erich Heller was there, and we talked about
Faust, but I became so tired at dinner that I decided I'd
better leave and dragged Elena away—she said at 9 and
before we had had dessert. This is rude. I am handling
this badly. When we got back so early we couldn't sleep
and were tired out the next day.

On Wednesday, I had lunch with *Arthur Schlesinger*.
There had been a story in the paper that while Bobby
Kennedy had been waiting to vote, he was reading *Europe
Without Baedeker*. Cecil Lang had seen this and written
me that since the Kennedys never did anything without
some objective in mind, I should undoubtedly be chosen
as Secretary of State in the new Kennedy Cabinet. Arthur
said, "I'd been thinking of you, rather, as Secretary of the
Treasury." —He then told me that *The Saturday Evening
Post* had asked him to write an article on "Love in
America." He had refused at first, but when they offered
him $4,000, he felt he owed it to his children to do it. I
expressed surprise at the smallness of the sum. "For three
days' work!" he replied. He had been looking up love in
America and asked me questions which revealed his innocence about the history of sex. When, during my life-
time, had the change in sexual mores occurred? Between
This Side of Paradise and *I Thought of Daisy*, there was
already a striking difference. He did not seem to have
understood that Scott Fitzgerald's debutantes and their
beaux represented something quite distinct from the bohemians of Greenwich Village, who had been practicing

"free love" for a decade. He also wanted to know when homosexuality had presented itself as an issue and been recognized as a subject of interest, and did not seem to know that in my college days the standing joke about Harvard at the other colleges was that most Harvard men were queer. I told the story about the head of West Point writing to President Eliot, "What do you do about your homosexuality problem at Harvard?" and Eliot writing back, "We have no homosexuality problem at Harvard. What do you do about yours at West Point?"

We had dinner with *Anita Loos* that night. She holds up well at 72—though there are big dark pouches that impair the effect of her humorous round black eyes. I had known that she had known Ted Paramore, who said that he would always be afraid to try anything with her because he knew she would make him ridiculous—a fear that is fully confirmed by what she says in *A Girl Like I*. But I didn't know they corresponded and that he had told her she was the only woman he thought he could marry. She has more or less adopted a colored girl, the daughter of a friend of the maid who has been working for her for years. The friend was turned out of her apartment, and the maid asked Anita if she would take in one of the children for a little while. Anita got so fond of the little girl that she now lives permanently with her. She showed us photographs of her. She is now at the American Ballet School. Evgenia told Elena that few Negro girls could qualify for classical ballet because they were generally flat-footed, but that this one was so well made and pretty and bright that they were glad to take her on.

On Thursday, Elena went back to Wellfleet to make preparations for Thanksgiving. I delivered *Prelude* and *Daisy* to Roger Straus and had him to lunch at the Princeton Club. I had been feeling hungover and rather morose, but as usual he made me laugh and cheered me up. <He

told me of a dinner at Fred Dupee's>—he has bought a
house near the Chapmans' on the Hudson—which seems
to have been somewhat similar to our experience with John
Gaus. Chanler has rented his big house to some sort of
businessman, and <Fred had thought it a good idea to
invite his new neighbors to dinner. He also invited Dwight
Macdonald, the Strauses> and Gore Vidal, who is renting
a smaller house of Chanler's. <In the course of the after-
dinner conversation, the war in Vietnam came up, and the
businessman took a line like John Gaus's. Dorothea Straus
said that she did not want to talk about it because she felt
too strongly about it. The businessman told her that her
attitude was due to the fact that she was Jewish. Dwight
Macdonald came out on her side with his usual pugnacity
and vehemence. He said that he was an old anarchist, and
that only an old anarchist could understand how to deal
with this problem. The businessman threatened to punch
him in the jaw; but, as Roger said, "more moderate coun-
sels prevailed."> Later Roger asked Dwight how, as a
pacifistic anarchist, he would have dealt with the situation
if the man *had* punched him in the jaw. Dwight said, "I'd
have fallen down." —The Truman Capote ball is pending.
He has invited 500 people and assigned them to dinners
at various people's houses. We were assigned, with the
Trillings, to the Epsteins'; but have declined the invitation.
Roger says that the ballroom of the Plaza will be turned
into one huge "camp," and that when the moment of un-
masking comes, the squeals will be heard all over New
York.

Dinner with *Auden* Thursday night. He presented me
with bound sheets of his new collected poems. I thought
he was in very good form, and I had a very good time with
him. I asked him why he so had it in for Yeats, and he
answered that it was because at one time he had been too
much influenced by him. His own idea of poetry was some-

thing much less rhetorical. His reaction against Rilke was also due to his having been too much influenced by him. He quoted Erich Heller as having said that Rilke was the greatest lesbian poet since Sappho. As usual, the moment came—toward the end of the first bottle of wine—when he paid me extravagant compliments, said that I was the only person he wrote for—he must have meant in America—or something of the kind, that he depended on me. I had managed, before dinner, to tell him, without greatly arousing what Stephen Potter rightly calls his masterly "lifemanship," that his anthology of minor nineteenth-century verse had been made a mess of—he says that he has straightened it out for England—and that it seemed rather like another book of light verse, with a few hymns stuck in.* He seems to accept these anthology jobs at the suggestion of publishers, and then, having compiled the material, not to pay any further attention to them. We had another bottle of wine in the lounge after dinner.

I didn't drink as much as usual with Wystan, but by Friday the cold and damp weather and seeing all these people had got me down. My legs ached horribly, and I could hardly walk across the room. I had still Cal Lowell, Esther and Helen to deal with. Cal seemed to be quite in his right mind—though perhaps a little excessively on the enthusiastic side. He, too, paid me extravagant compliments: how much I meant to him, how much he had learned from me; that we were both "conservative radicals." In his case, all this was a little embarrassing; but these compliments have really pleased me and restored my morale. Arthur Schlesinger, who had just attended a celebration in Washington of Averell Harriman's 75th birthday, had also contributed by telling me that, like Harriman and Walter Lippmann, I was one of the few who had stayed

---

* *Nineteenth Century British Minor Poets* (Delacorte Press, 1966).

W. H. Auden in the late sixties

the course. —Cal thought it was untrue—as his widow had asserted—that Randall Jarrell had not committed suicide. He had been much distressed by Jarrell's death, had known him well. Jarrell had been very kind to him. He thought that John Berryman would not last very long, was drinking heavily, beginning in the morning. But he had written a new set of Dream Songs that Cal thought were the best things he had done. Berryman and his family were in Ireland.*

In the afternoon at 5, I went to see Esther in order to get more photographs. She has really been splendid about my book [A *Prelude*]. She told me of a problem that I hadn't known about. Her son Kimmy had married an English girl who was—this expression amused me, I hadn't heard it before—"not o.c.d., not our class, dear." She is the daughter of the chief electrician of Marlborough House, and her father is so conscious of his class inferiority that he will not enter the house of the Hartshornes', where he would be on an equal social footing, and could do nothing about them in London, when Esther was in England with them, except take them to a neighboring pub. Esther says that the wife is a bitch, and that she finds that, in the summer, the only thing to do is to ask her to visit without Kimmy, when she is "perfectly all right." I suppose that, when they are together, she and Kimmy quarrel. I want to see more of Esther. We have invited her to come up here when she goes to see Harriet Kaiser at Dennis next summer. As she says, she and I and Betty Fox, the daughter of her Aunt Betty Clark, are the only people left now who remember Seabright and all that.

Helen came to dinner with me at the club. For the first time, she looked to me "stunning"—glossy hair done up

* Berryman committed suicide in 1972.

on top of her head, a white dress and pale stockings. She has obviously, on getting out of school and going to Barnard, entered a new phase. She seems more mature, and I think she finds her new life stimulating. We talked about Russian, which she is studying, and Gaster, with whom she is taking a course in the Bible, and I told her about the Samaritans and the various texts of the Bible. She said, "How do you come to know all that? You're not a scholar." I was sorry I couldn't do the occasion more justice. My explanations were rather halting. By that time, I could hardly function and took two nitroglycerin pills during dinner. But my relations with Helen, seeing her in New York, were better than they had been in the country. It was also that her mother was not there. She left right after dinner, said she had to get through a book on the Elizabethan audience, was going to Philadelphia for the weekend. When I was putting her into a cab and kissing her goodbye, she rubbed her cheek against mine. She gets more and more to look like a Miller: my Grandmother Wilson, her brother Uncle Jim, and Susan and Dundee.

I ordered three double whiskies and immediately went to bed. With nothing on my mind for the morrow except to clean up odds and ends at the *New Yorker* office, I had a long and calm sleep and woke up relaxed the next day. I got back to Wellfleet for once in good condition and very glad to be back again.

Nov. 22. Elena and I had a successful session on the blue couch in the middle room—though interrupted by Charley Walker bringing a pot of chrysanthemums for Thanksgiving. I had locked the front door, but after knocking, he came around through the side door. Elena had to shout, "You can't come!" Nevertheless, we "made out," and I felt wonderfully calm and satisfied afterwards. If we don't make love for some time, we both of us get nervous and irritable. Now we are in perfect harmony—went to bed early.

An Anniversary and a Funeral

Boston, Dec. 8–11. We went down for our 20th wedding anniversary and to do some Christmas shopping. The morning of the 10th, Elena got badly on my nerves— fussing about a program that she had conceived, without paying attention to my convenience, for getting certain things done. But we had a rapprochement in the afternoon and made love. I faded out at one point but then returned to the charge with more than my usual vigor nowadays. The O'Connors sent us a huge basket of anemones; the Berlins a bottle of the best champagne, and a long rather clumsy container to keep bottles cold for picnics. Aileen Ward brought us a bottle of *fine champagne*. She and the O'Connors and Isaiah came to dinner at the Ritz. Aline Berlin was already committed to hear Berlioz's *Enfance du Christ*, but came in after dinner. The dinner turned out to be good. We had ordered rock hen, whatever that is, which was served with mushrooms and chestnuts. I had written little rhymes for the place cards which paid high compliments to everybody.

Place cards for our anniversary dinner at the Ritz

This is the place for Isaiah Berlin,
The man who is clever and yet without sin;
Who has spent years at Oxford, and yet still has stayed straight,
And has never been taken by anyone's bait.

This is the place for Edwin O'Connor,
A man of high gifts and impeccable honor;

Who has passed his whole life in the city of Boston
And yet remains someone whom nothing is lost on.

This is the place for darling Aileen,
Who has never done anything petty or mean;
She is cordial in company, prompt in the pantry,
Yet dwells in the region where few have the entrée.

This is the place for lovely Venite,
Who inhabits a palace and yet remains sweet.
She has crowned the career of remarkable Ed
And would not be deterred if he dwelt in a shed.

This was for Elena on our 20th anniversary

That we've been twenty years together I forget;
Some married men are bored, I never yet.
Your brains and beauty, your delicious meals,
Your lovely little feet at which one kneels,
Your knowledge of the world at which one reels—
All this, my dearest love, and so much more
Makes up the woman that I still adore,
Surprised to find myself now old and slow,
The man who loved you twenty years ago.

After dinner, we all went up to our room. Isaiah and I
leaped about from one opera to another: Strauss, Wagner,
Berlioz, Boito, Britten. He says rightly that Richard
Strauss is a very curious case: a man of enormous proficiency with an essentially vulgar mind. He compared him
to Somerset Maugham, but I told him that Maugham was
nothing like so good a writer as Strauss was a musician. I
don't think Isaiah is really much interested in literature
as such. I have never heard him talk about literature with
the same sort of enthusiasm that he sometimes shows about
music. He has never read Dante or *Finnegans Wake*, and
tells me that he has never finished *Faust*. What he is

interested in is ideas. His desire to know about everybody and everything seems to become more and more compulsive. When we were talking about Gounod's *Faust*, he said, as if it were something that I probably did not know and that he wanted to show that he knew: "In Germany, they call it *Margareta*, you know"—though this was of no interest and not relevant to the conversation. (Elena says they call it *Faust und Margareta*.) He gets violent, sometimes irrational prejudices against people*—for example, Hannah Arendt, though he has never read her book about Eichmann. He told us that he was going the following evening to what he called a "Walpurgisnacht"—the Lowells, Auden, Mary McCarthy and Hannah Arendt. He says that Cal is getting into the ominous state when he begins to admire Hitler. The three stages of his manic ascension seem to be Alexander the Great, Napoleon and Hitler.

The guests stayed till nearly midnight, and the next morning I prolonged the celebration by drinking, while still in bed, the *fine champagne* that Aileen had brought us. This depressed Elena extremely because she said it was the very best brandy and had cost Aileen a lot—which I hadn't known—and because we had just been overhauled by Zetzel, who had recommended my drinking less. This habit of drinking in the morning, as I have done from time to time in recent years, is really a bad thing. I lie in bed thinking sparklingly of women and of things I have written and said, but then have to recover in the course of the day and sometimes get very depressed. Zetzel told us that we both had sound constitutions, and told me that what I had been having were not really "heart attacks," as I called them, but simply "a touch of angina." A heart attack was something that would put you in bed for weeks.

* Isaiah Berlin said exactly the same thing about Wilson in his 1987 memoir in *The Yale Review*, and elaborated upon this in a 1991 interview with the editor.

I suppose that I might as well settle down to the kind of satisfactions I can have: little worry about money, comfort in sitting around reading and playing the phonograph, having books and letters sent me, enjoying a reputation and no great pressure to produce. At the same time, I get to feeling rather stuffy and soft lying around in armchairs and in bed so much of the time. For the first time in my life, I sometimes get bored with reading, and am rather disappointed in the famous books that I now make a point of reading.

I get up in the morning and make a brief toilet. While sitting on the W.C., I read the folders of old reviews of my books, in order to support my morale—though this only makes me realize again how slipshod and incompetent most reviewing is. If one reads enough reviews of a single book, one finds that they have opposite opinions and so cancel each other out. Then I sit in the middle room and Elena brings me breakfast—no longer necessarily at 8:15: I can afford to live more luxuriously. Then, instead of getting right to work, I comfortably read for a while. A light lunch while I am working, which won't make me sluggish. About 3, we go for a walk and get the paper and the afternoon mail, and talk about the books we have been reading. Back at the house, I read the paper and the mail. (Sometimes we drive to Orleans and Hyannis and return with more or less interesting purchases. Either before or after our outing, I shave to some popular or symphonic music to which I don't have to pay close attention.) Then I sit in my new alcove, hedged in by the Elizabethans, and go through part of an opera, following the libretto by the strong light of the new lamp Elena gave me. Solitaire and whisky just before and after dinner. Whisky puts me to sleep too early, and I used to wake up at 4 and read till it began to get light; but I am now getting better regulated and read to Elena while she knits or to myself—which is difficult when I drink—German or Russian, which requires some effort—haven't yet got back to Hungarian again. Nightly petting party with Lulu, who, if I stop to play solitaire, pricks my liver with her paws. Sometimes she puts her paw on a card as if she wanted to play, too. In bed, I read Scott or some current book. All day Elena waits on me or works on the house. By evening, she is likely to be tired. Lulu at night goes out and catches mice and other small animals; when she wants to come in, she climbs up to the window of whatever room she knows someone is in.

At last, unlimited Perrier and all my reference books within reach.

Waldo Frank's funeral, January 12: In the South Truro cemetery, full of old gravestones. The day was terribly cold, and Nina [Chavchavadze] and Phyllis [Duganne] looked dreadful. I thought that the Wellfleet undertaker looked at some of us with a lecherous eye. The sky was gray, the sun a mere brighter blur. The wind froze us on that bleak hill. The ceremony was performed by a rabbi from Providence, a friend of Waldo's, a scholar who has just, he told me, translated the whole of the Midrash for the Yale Hebrew series. He read partly in Hebrew and partly in English, and the Hebrew sounded very fine. He made a little speech about Waldo, how he had come to know him through a book of Waldo's about the Jews, how he had presided at Waldo's daughter's wedding; said that Waldo's imagination would go winging away into the future. Simple and austere on the winter hill. I thought it was the most impressive funeral service at which I had ever been present. The rabbi read the Hebrew extremely well, beginning with the passage from the 90th Psalm on which Watts's fine hymn is based:

Before the hills in order stood
Or earth received its frame,
From everlasting thou art God,
To endless years the same.

—and this added its grandeur to the landscape.

I had been asked to speak, but I declined. Besides being no good at making speeches, I couldn't say what I honestly thought about Waldo and his work. The most depressing thing about his death was the unsatisfactoriness of his writing and career. He said to me lately that he had been "rejected." I am sure he never knew why. He seemed to be incapable of self-criticism. Conscious of in some ways brilliant abilities and an unusually wide intellectual range, he could not understand that his practice nowhere near came up to his pretensions. I used to think about him years ago that he had no humility before his medium, never in fact taught himself to write.

We went afterwards to the Franks' house. The rooms were never particularly attractive, and now quite dismal and flat, with Waldo no longer there. The old slogan above the mantelpiece, "Dare to Do Right"; the battered set of the Conard Balzac. The sullen Jonathan and the feeble-witted Timmy. Jean poured out her heart to Elena. She had been in her early twenties when she came to work for Waldo as his secretary, and had had the mentality of a girl of 18. I talked to the rabbi. I had noticed that he read with an Ashkenazi pronunciation and now found that he felt very strongly about what he told me was the current attempt to impose on the synagogues a Sephardic accent. This was entirely artificial and had fewer vowel sounds. There was a man there who some years ago had taken us to the Rosh Hashanah service at the Hyannis synagogue. The rabbi said something to him to the effect that he would approve of the Sephardic accent, and when I talked to this man later, I found that he was a Sephardi. I believe that there is a difference between them and the other Jews. They pride themselves on being superior—more aristocratic, more refined. He and I and two other men got to talking about the differences in Judaism: Orthodox, Conservative, Reformed. I told them the story about the father who wanted to give his son a Cadillac for his bar mitzvah and asked the advice first of an Orthodox then of a Reformed rabbi. The first didn't know what a Cadillac was, the second didn't know what a bar mitzvah was. Then one of the men told a story about some people who, in a boat after a shipwreck, arrived at a tropical isle. There they found a welcoming Jew, who told them that he lived there alone and had made everything he had himself. He showed them his clothes: "I made them myself!" Then he took them to his home, which he had built. It was surrounded by gardens and fruit trees, and he showed his guests through the delightful grounds. They came at last to a clearing, where they saw two little synagogues, neatly built and elegantly ornamented. "Why two," asked one of the visitors, "since there's nobody but you on the island?" "Oh," said the proprietor with vehement scorn, "I wouldn't go to that one!"

Jan. 14. We drove to Boston to have dinner with the Kronenbergers and Auden. I talked about *My Secret Life*, which I had been reading since 2 in the morning; a degrading book—in the first part, he seduces his mother's maids and cooks; in the second, he writes mostly about prostitutes. He is almost entirely indifferent to what happens to the women afterwards, though he sometimes makes some effort to help them. He doesn't care whether he gets them pregnant and is annoyed if they bother him about it. He is well-off, and all he proves is that it is possible to get people to do anything for money. The descriptions in the second volume, as in the pornographic books, are of more and more complicated orgies which eventually become hard to follow. He complains that after horsing around with a young interior decorator—in the Victorian not modern sense—who is out of work, the young man no longer calls him "sir." Everything is described in the coarsest language, and the more than 2,000 large pages become monotonous.* Wystan asked how he paid his women. I said that he was fairly generous. Wystan said that years ago he had gone around Berlin with André Gide, and that Gide had been mean about paying his boys.

I told Wystan that I thought it was dangerous to keep on correcting one's poems: Yeats had spoiled some of his. I asked why, in his latest collected short poems, he had left out "You don't know all, sir, you don't know all." He said that it had been sacrificed to a numerological mania: he didn't want to have more than 300.

It was a relief to take a day off from Wellfleet, staying at the comfortable and quiet Ritz, with nothing except going to the Kronenbergers' to do. Almost nobody on the roads driving to and from Boston.

Lunches, Dinners, and a Poem

New York: Feb. 1–23, 1967. I went down before Elena, because Helen was in Wellfleet for a few days after her examinations. Had dinner the first night (Wed.) at the Epsteins' and as usual drank too much, carried away by the excitement of getting away from Wellfleet.

Lillian Hellman, the next night (Thurs.), to dinner at

---

* This Victorian pornography, anonymously published in an edition of six copies in Amsterdam in 1890, was reprinted by Grove Press in 1966.

the Princeton Club. I told her that she seemed so amiable and had so much New Orleans and love of gracious living that I wondered why her plays were so bitter. —She said that she had actually grown up between New Orleans and Alabama, and had disliked the Alabama side of the family. I remembered that *The Little Foxes* and *Another Part of the Forest* take place in Alabama. She intimated also that she was subject to tantrums: "You've heard about them, haven't you?" I hadn't.

Friday, conference and lunch with *Roger Straus*. Jason Epstein had told me of the horror of Podhoretz's book, *Making It*, for which Roger had made him an advance of $25,000, and then, when he had seen it, had to recognize that he would rather lose that sum than publish it. Everyone I saw who had read it thought that it was awful. It purported to be a success story—when Mike Nichols, later, heard this, he said, "He couldn't wait." It told how Norman had now no accent, had been accepted, entertained, toasted and feted by all the élite of New York— who were Lillian, ourselves, Jackie Kennedy and everybody that everybody saw without anybody else's regarding it as a sign of having made it. Simon and Schuster had also rejected it; then he submitted it to Random House, and Jason, who disliked it more than anybody, was obliged, as an old friend of Norman's, to allow Random House to take it. He said that it would indicate its quality to say that Bennett Cerf thought it was all right. There was a good deal about Jason in it, and it was one of the most embarrassing experiences of his life. It seems that Podhoretz tells in it a story about Baldwin's not giving *The Fire Next Time* to *Commentary*, as had been expected but to *The New Yorker*, which of course paid much better. Norman was furious and called up Baldwin and delivered a tirade: "You do this because you're a Negro and know that no white man can be nasty to you!" B. said, "You must write that,

Norman." Whereupon Norman wrote his article about being bullied by Negroes in his boyhood.*

I now broached the subject of money to Roger, telling him that if he bought a goldbrick from Podhoretz for $25,000, he ought to pay me more than the $5,000 a volume that had been agreed on for the pure gold of my memoirs and journals. After some squirming, he agreed to $10,000 a volume. He explained that the competition of other publishers had been compelling him to give his authors enormous advances in order to keep them: Susan Sontag, Malamud, Podhoretz. This had reached unprecedented lengths. James Jones had had I forget whether a million or half a million dollars for a novel that was said to be no good.

I found Podhoretz's book, the Kennedy-Manchester affair† and the new Antonioni film, *Blow-Up*, were everywhere the principal subjects of conversation. I think, apropos of the first of these, that it is always a great thing for people when somebody they know does something conspicuously outrageous or ridiculous.

In the evening I went alone to *Traviata* at the City Center: a very good Violetta, young and attractive, who behaved like a real woman. She only coughed slightly once—no coughing in the last act: a good idea—you can't really have tubercular coughing in an opera. The scene with the stuffed-shirt father always annoys me: I resent his complacent "*Piangi, piangi*," and feel that Violetta ought to put up more of a struggle.**

Saturday, Anita Loos to dinner at the club.

Elena arrived on Sunday.

---

* The article was "My Negro Problem, and Ours."

† William Manchester did an authorized account of Kennedy's assassination, *The Death of a President*, that Jackie Kennedy did not like, believing he abused her confidences.

** "Weep, weep," the father tells her, as he demands that she give up his son for the young man's sake.

In the late afternoon, before she came, I went up to call on Elizabeth Lowell. Cal is still in McLean's. Elizabeth, as usual, is worried. He apparently can't get out of McLean's except, as it were, on leave, because he now has no psychiatrist to be responsible for him. His former psychiatrist in New York refuses to have him as a patient any more because, he says, he can't control him. Another psychiatrist has offered to "cure" him in three years if he will come to him every day, at $50 a session—$100 if he doesn't show up. Elizabeth says that the word "cure" is of course a great temptation, but that Cal would have to buy a car in order to go as far uptown as where this psychiatrist lives, and that he really might as well commit suicide as spend three years doing this.

Tuesday, we went to *Pikovaya Dama* [*The Queen of Spades*]: horrors of the new opera house—scallops and gilt dingle-dangles below the balconies; the "Nabisco area" around the proscenium; Chagall murals that can't be properly seen because the promenade where they have been put is too narrow to allow one to get far enough away from them; most successful feature a Christmas-tree-ornament chandelier donated by the Austrian government. Having seen Meyerhold's production in Leningrad [in 1935], I found the performance almost nonexistent. The first act, as E. said, was sung like an Italian opera; then the scene in which Hermann breaks in on the old Countess and bullies her into giving him her secret, after which she dies—which ought to be so sinister and violent—went for absolutely nothing; the old lady ought to dominate the whole action, but [Jean] Madeira was merely a gentle wraith—instead of throning at the danced bergeria, she went behind the scenes, and the audience could hardly have been aware that she repeated one of the French songs. From the last row of the balcony, the stage looked almost like something seen through the wrong end of the telescope. The City Center opera—on which so much less money is spent—is very much more satisfactory: one is much closer to and "involved in" the opera and not lost in and distracted by the theater. The stock thing to say about the new Met is that "the acoustics are very good," and the faults of architectural taste are sometimes said to have been made on account of the acoustics.

Wednesday. Edith Oliver to lunch. Dinner with Anita Loos at the Harvard Club with her "escort," a young man who works for TV and who, Anita says, is always taking courses somewhere. He is extraordinarily well informed about theater and opera, has Wagner at his fingertips. He is the son of one of the top John Birchers, and though we did not discuss politics, Elena thought that he showed suspicious enthusiasm for the documentary films about Hitler made by Leni Riefenstahl.

Thursday. Lunch with the Oxford Press people. They seemed in a kind of doldrums, which contrasted with their high spirits when they first came to the Press. When I asked them about their spring list, they seemed to feel reluctance to mention any books they were publishing—no spirit of salesmanship.

Lehoviches for dinner, Lincoln Kirstein was there. I had last seen him in some bookshop, when he had told me with enthusiasm that he had just read *Illusions Perdues*. I said that I had just read it, and we talked about Balzac. He said that Balzac and Disraeli represented a kind of thing that no longer existed in the novel: non-realistic treatment of modern world, characters larger than life. I liked him better than I had when I first used to see him, when he had just come out of Harvard. He is very much less shy, talks amusingly and with a sense of who he is. Biography of Tchelitchew by Parker Tyler—I did not say in Kirstein's presence that it was a book about a pansy written by a pansy for pansies; but I found that he objected to the kind of implication of homosexuality that anyone who knew nothing about Tchelitchew would have known about him from reading this book. Everybody is agreed that it diminishes Tchelitchew as an artist. Kirstein told us that he had brought to Russia the big picture called *Phenomenon*, on which Tchelitchew had worked for years, and that nobody knew anything about him or took any interest in the picture. The Museum of Modern Art had had it sent back for an exhibition of his works, and it was now laid away in their vaults.

Friday the 10th: We saw *The Apple Tree*, a compilation of Mark Twain's *Adam's* and *Eve's Diaries*, Frank Stockton's *The Lady or the Tiger?* and a film-star burlesque by Jules Feiffer—with Barbara Harris and directed by Mike Nichols. Barbara Harris started with Nichols and May in that same Chicago group, which has really provided a school of acting. The best show we have seen in years. The end of Adam and Eve made me weep, as I am likely to do at things about old married couples.

At some point, we managed to see *Blow-Up*, though there are usually long waiting lines. I think that this film is a big fake and found many people to agree with me—though there is a great deal of discussion about it. It is like the same director's *L'Avventura*: you never know what has happened, and that is undoubtedly Antonioni's intention. The picture doesn't make any sense—so different people can have different theories. Was a real murder ever committed or was it just the photographer's imagination? Is the whole thing meant to be a dream? etc.

Saturday I had lunch with J. A. Sanders, who has edited, in the Dead Sea scrolls series, the volume with the new scroll of the Psalms. He has also on the same subject done a popular volume, which I had just read. He is a youngish man from the South, has had two years at a Presbyterian seminary and is qualified to teach—is at Union [Theological Seminary]—but not to baptize, marry, etc. He had a year with Dupont-Sommer in Paris. I imagine that he went to the seminary merely to study Hebrew and never wanted to be a minister. He had first specialized in Romance languages, then Greek and then Hebrew. I thought he was remarkably detached toward all parties in the scrolls controversy, and I think he is a new type of scholar in this field who is much less constrained by his relation to a church. I spoke of Frank Cross's theological double-talk, and he said that that had been a feature of the period—I forget the phrase for it, but a period when they had ceased to believe much but still had to seem to go along with the Church—out of which Cross came. I said something about the difficulty of the Hebrew verbs, and he remarked that Hebrew was such a verbal language, whereas Greek was a nominal one.

In the evening, dinner at Lillian's: the Epsteins, the Goodwins, a Hungarian Jewish psychoanalyst and his Russian Jewish wife, and a man named Crane or Clark that Elena says was one of Cal Lowell's "nannies," who took care of him when he ran off the track. The Hungarian, for a Hungarian, was a strange phenomenon: he never smiled and was completely silent. The party, like all Lillian's parties, was extremely successful. We didn't get home till 12, very late for us, and Lillian said she was up till 3.

On Sunday Elena says I slept till 2. We called up the Epsteins and went to see them. Barbara was there alone. Later Jason appeared with a pretty and buxom young blonde. I thought at first she was one of his cookies— thought Barbara rather subdued in her presence—but it turned out that she was his assistant in his Negro-education project. I was so overcome by the drinks after the night before that I did not wait for dinner but went home at 8. The girl kindly drove me. She was wearing a mini-skirt, and as she drove, her large bare thighs were displayed in a way that seemed to me rather odd.

Monday. Dinner at the Strauses'. I was at Dorothea's right, and across from me was a man who talked politics with great vigor and who turned out to be Robert Silvers of *The New York Review.* Jean Stafford was on my right and at her right was a Dr. Malachi Martin, whom Roger had described to me as a "Jesuit dropout." He had worked for Cardinal Bea and when the movement for reform was frustrated at the 2nd Vatican Council, he had resigned from the Jesuit order—very much as Davis in England resigned from the priesthood. Roger said that there had been some scandal about him, and it seemed clear that he had taken up with a woman from Crete—formerly married to a Hungarian—who runs a jewelry store. Roger had met him in Paris and seems to have brought him over. Why? He has done one book for Roger about the Vatican and is suspected of being the author or part author of the books signed Xavier Rynne. Roger says he knows eleven languages and at present has the job of translating the *Encyclopaedia Britannica* into Arabic. In the middle of dinner Roger introduced the subject of the Dead Sea scrolls, and from then on Martin and I monopolized the talk with a dialogue about them. He is a brilliant and witty Irishman—I was astounded at how much he knew—the texts, the problems, the personalities. We aroused so much interest and laughter by our interchange—behind Jean's neck—that I ended by feeling we were entertaining the company by one of those old-fashioned "sidewalk" conversations such as they used to have in vaudeville. Martin said that the time had come for some detached person to stand back and see the thing "in perspective." I said that Sanders was detached. "Yes, but in a negative way." He flattered me by telling me that something in my book was an example of a kind of insight that non-scholars sometimes have when the scholars themselves have missed it. Something important I should notice in column 4, line 7 of the Manual of Discipline. When I mentioned the book by Graystone that was dated from Rome and which seemed to have been written to combat my possible influence, he said, "Oh, Graystone! Even de Vaux can't stand him"— which raised a laugh. But they could not have appreciated his crack when he added, "He dedicated it to the Virgin Mary, didn't he?"* Graystone is a Marist, and the Marists are a recent order. I think this remark was due to a Jesuit snobbery toward Marists. He said of someone—I think Dupont-Sommer—that he didn't understand certain things, because he didn't understand the Oriental point of view. I got the impression, as I had with Sanders, that Martin's point of view was different and freer than any I had encountered before.

Tuesday, Valentine's Day. I was so busy with my tons of proof that I had not sent out many Valentines. For Elena and Clelia, I pasted up two that involved hearts of various colors cut out from Christmas-present paper. Clelia's was a green picture of a marsh frog sending up heart-shaped bubbles more or less in the frog spectrum. She called me laughing about it.

We had lunch at the club with Stephen Spender and Sonia Orwell. Stephen had called me up from Middletown, where he is spending a semester at the Wesleyan Center. I asked him where he was, and I thought he said, "In Princeton," but it turned out to be "In prison." He is in Father D'Arcy's old rooms, and now the only person who lives in the Center. He has the same problem as D'Arcy

---

* "It is a simple piece of Catholic apologetics, of no scholarly value whatever, intended for a literate but not learned public, and it goes about its task, without acrimony, in a tone of patient good will," EW writes of Graystone's *The Dead Sea Scrolls and the Originality of Christ.* The author "gave somewhat the impression of having entered the controversy as an official spokesman for the Vatican" (*Scrolls*, 1969).

—no place to have meals, but unlike D'Arcy, he knows how to open cans and more or less do for himself.

Auden is to be on his 60th birthday in Eugene, Oregon, and it was thought that something ought to be done about it. A gift-wrapped bottle of gin was suggested. Then Stephen and I decided to send a sonnet writing alternate lines, so for a week we were telephoning back and forth. I don't think the result was extremely successful. There is nothing like collaborating with somebody to make one conscious of how the other person's mind works. Auden had said to me that Stephen had little sense of rhythm. His lines seemed to be so solemn and to repeat so much the same idea that I became more fanciful and nonsensical.

TO W. H. AUDEN ON HIS 60TH BIRTHDAY
alternate lines by S. S. and E. W.

What matters most is hanging around words [SS]
To watch them crystallize, coagulate, [EW]
Mean what they say, yet keep their separate state,
Though sometimes as irrational as surds.
They are the slaves of thought and yet the lords;
They skim like sloops yet load stupendous freight;
They are the mass whose meaning is its weight,
The plodding pulse that flies away like birds.
You wed cold thoughts to the hard density,
With complicated patterns featly traced,
Where logic, God and nature are all witty,
All cloudily yet elegantly laced,—
Interpreter of dreams that make a city,
Great libertine, incongruously chaste.*

---

* The "surd" of Wilson's second line is a sum containing one or more irrational roots of numbers. Spender's "Interpreter of dreams that make a city" is the Shelleyan idea of the poet as unacknowledged legislator of mankind. Spender's romanticism and high seriousness were far from EW's wit, and he too was unhappy with their collaboration when recalling it twenty-five years later.

More Occasions; "A Sinister Pressure in the Air"

Sonia told me at lunch that Celia Goodman was now much better, as I had gathered from her letters.* She had been fortified, Sonia said, by discovering some sort of cult— theosophy? Barbara Skelton had married a rich man and was already, it was thought, on her way to getting out of it with a settlement. I thought I heard Sonia say something like "That's what we all get married for."

These long English lunches, with their drinking and conversation, always incapacitate me for the rest of the day. Elena and I collapsed. I went to sleep and didn't eat any dinner. Elena remarked very justly, "We ought to be very careful about what we say when we're with Sonia." When we were talking about Celia, I had said that I wished some good man would take her over. Sonia, with the practical English point of view about matches, exclaimed, "Nobody would take the risk of marrying her in her present condition!" A chivalrous American, however, would be capable of marrying her and devoting himself to her.

Wednesday. Anita Loos for drinks. Cathleen Nesbitt was there. I told her that I had been madly in love with her when I had first seen her with the Abbey Theatre, and that when I heard that she and Rupert Brooke were in

---

Edmund and Louise Bogan had had more fun when concocting a tribute for Auden's forty-ninth birthday, also in alternating lines:

> Auden, that thou are living at this hour [EW]
>   Delights us. How much duller wert thou not! [LB]
>   And we have need of thee. A drear dry rot
> Spreads its dank mould throughout the Muses' Bower;
> Orc Tolkien usurps Aladdin's Tower:
>   The Groves of Academe are cold and bought;
>   And countless other things have gone to pot.
> Oh, Wystan, hear us! Implement our power . . .

* Her husband had been killed in a hunting accident.

love, I envied him and thought he must be the most fortunate of men. She is an old lady now, with white hair, but still very handsome—a little Jenny Corbett's Irish type, but with black eyes. —Anita's Negro protégée, who is studying ballet, was very much in evidence: talking loudly and turning unsuccessful cartwheels. Elena took her into the other room and read with her. Anita does not interest her as she does me: they have no past friends and experiences in common. Anita told her maid to give me double Scotches, and to drink them was a mistake.

We went afterwards to the Russian Tea Room across the street, where I consumed with my blini a certain amount of vodka. As a result, I fell asleep at [Pinter's] *The Homecoming* and must have slept through about two-thirds of it. From what I saw of it and from afterwards reading the text, I thought it was, as Lillian says, "empty." I couldn't see anything in *The Caretaker* either. Like Antonioni's films, I don't think they really mean anything. But Edith Oliver thinks *The Homecoming* is wonderful, and Harold Clurman cracked it up in his review.

In New York, during my first days especially, I had the feeling of a very sinister pressure in the air. Just as I was leaving Wellfleet, I had a long letter from Rolfe Humphries, with whom I hadn't communicated in years but to whom I had sent a Christmas card. He told me that Helen's illegitimate son by Raymond Holden, who, I believe, had been doing well as a physicist, had been killed in a motor accident; and that a legitimate son of Raymond's by his first wife had strangled a woman and been got off on grounds of insanity. Cal was in McLean's and Betty Huling in such a neurotic state that when I called her up and asked her to dinner with us, she said she couldn't possibly leave her apartment. Elena's friend Mia Tolstoy had been mugged in front of the Russian Embassy and had her arm

broken—she was still in the hospital—where E. went to
see her; and the agreeable neighbor of Sovka's in Cornwall
that she brought to Talcottville had been raped in her
apartment and was shattered by it—she had gone abroad.
This against the background of the Vietnam War and the
news of delinquent crime. *The Homecoming* and *Blow-Up*
do not add to one's sense of security. The latter Anita Loos
found disquieting—she said it was a revelation of what
was going on with the young people.

Thursday. Elena went out to see the little girls—Henry
and Daphne are always skiing. Roger came in during the
late afternoon, and we signed a contract for the journals.

Friday. Just before dinnertime, I got furious with Elena
for I think no very good reason and went out to the Algonquin, where I found Joe Mitchell, Brendan Gill and
the girl from the *New Yorker* book room. I very soon phoned
Elena to join us.

Saturday. For a pre-birthday treat, we took Helen to *The
Apple Tree.*

Sunday. Helen's birthday, but we did not see her. We
had lunch in the Edwardian Room of the Plaza with Lillian, Mike Nichols and Penelope Gilliatt. Since John Osborne has left the latter, she has taken up with Mike. She
is very goodlooking and likable: black eyes and red hair.
She sat next to me, and we talked about people in London.
She was flying to England that night, but is coming back
in the spring to do movies for three months at *The New
Yorker.* I congratulated Mike on inducing Elizabeth Taylor
to give some semblance of acting. "I went very slowly," he
said. When it was a question of ordering lunch, he asked
for herring with sour cream and, when Lillian was hesi-
tating, said, "Everybody knows you're Jewish, so why don't
you have that, too?" She ended by ordering it. The Edwardian Room at the Plaza seems to have become a great

resort for lunching on Sundays, when almost everything else is closed. We saw Anita Loos and Norah Sayre, with a Labour M.P.

After lunch, Mike left us to take his little girl for a walk and Lillian to first have a conference with Mike about his producing *The Little Foxes* in the fall. Elena thinks that he is repaying Lillian for her having stuck by him during the period of his loose ends, when he was demoralized by Elaine. We took Penelope to the Princeton Club with us, where we had a drink in the lounge. She stood out among the ladies there by the high orange boots she was wearing. We both liked her. After our lunch, what to do with a Sunday afternoon? We talked about the dreadful London Sunday. I said that, with all the agitation that had been going on against hanging and in favor of consenting adults, there ought to be a movement to get rid of the London Sunday—that the whole spirit ought to be changed, with freedom, however, for the old gloomy habits to be continued by consenting adults. I told her that I had been sure she was goodlooking—that you could always tell that from the way a woman wrote. She said that that was something to hear on a Sunday afternoon.

When she left, we went to call on the Lowells. I announced ourselves as elderly "swingers"—which was what we were beginning to feel like. They invited us to dinner the next night.

Monday. Dinner at the Lowells'. Irene Worth was there. She had been touring the country, doing Shakespeare with Gielgud. I did not especially take to her. She has a loud California voice and likes to hold the floor, and at the same time has deliberately acquired an artificial British accent and manner. Cal at the dinner table was always as usual going off on a conversational tangent—though he often says brilliant things, this makes him rather difficult to talk to.

Tamas Breuer

Helen Wilson as a young woman

Tuesday. Dinner with Edith Oliver downtown at an Italian restaurant; then Baird's new puppet show in his new theater especially built for it. The show was much better than I had expected: very amusing unconventional acts—advertised as a show for adults. He does what I don't believe has ever been done before: combines marionettes, glove puppets, rod puppets and the kind of thing that is done in front of a black background by actors dressed in black. After the show, he took us upstairs—they live above the theater—and he and his wife gave us drinks. I had some conversation with an actor who, according to Baird, is the foremost Punch man in America. I couldn't make him out. He is extremely quiet with an amiable but inexpressive face. I couldn't tell what nationality he was. He told me he was abroad a good deal of the time; here he does television and Hollywood. In one of Ed Wynn's shows, he put on a performance but got no credit, because Ed Wynn went behind the booth, then came out afterwards with the puppets on his fingers. He makes his Punch prop open the crocodile's jaws with the stick, then stick his head behind it. I said that I had no crocodile that would be big enough for this, and he explained that he had built his himself. —Baird has only three or four Punch and Judy figures in a Tony Sarg style; but he has a collection of Sicilian, Ceylonese and other foreign puppets that he has picked up in the course of his travels. He illustrated their working at one point in the show. There are eight operators. The cobra in the Oriental scene had six wires, and the Pavlova swan at least twenty.

Horrible weather with snow most of the time during our visit. Edith got one of those private cars at the expense of *The New Yorker* to take us to and from the theater.

We saw Sylvia [Marlowe] and Leonid [Berman] twice. Sylvia had just had a bad eye operation, removal of a malignant tumor. She had a black patch over her eye and was sorry, she said, to look like the man in the Hathaway shirt ad. We invited them to dinner later, but she had been in bed with the flu and asked us to come up there. We went to see them for drinks but would not let her do anything about dinner. It always makes me feel better to see them. They get along well together and seem always to be in good humor, and they are two first-rate artists who work and produce. In Wellfleet, we see so much of artists whose pictures are never seen, composers whose music is never heard, writers who do not write or who are not really writers. Sylvia said that, on account of her eye, she had not been able to work and that not being able to work drives her crazy. Leonid said that they lived in New York just the way we did in the country. They go to their separate studios, and in the evenings they read a good deal. I think that I have been partly deluded about the extent of the social life of these people in New York. I get the impression that when we come, they have parties on our account, we provide them with a pretext.

I had lunch one day at the Century Club with Brendan Gill, Joe Mitchell and Philip Hamburger—talk mostly about *The New Yorker*. Rather pleasant to lunch in a men's club, where a reasonably priced lunch is provided, instead of the now nondescript Princeton Club, where everything is fairly expensive upstairs and the cuisine in the men's grill is wretched.

Also, a lunch at the Princeton Club with Dick Rovere. I always enjoy seeing him, but I don't exactly trust his judgment. He was at one time a member of the Communist Party, and he is subject to a dubious kind of hero worship. As I remember, he once wrote in *The New Yorker*, before McCarthy had become such a scandal, that he might possibly be a great man, and he now tells me that Johnson is "intellectually" the greatest President we have had in a long time. It seems that he and Liebling fell out seriously over the Hiss case. Rovere has always believed—which I don't necessarily—that Chambers's story was basically true. Indignant about Zeligs's psychoanalytic book on the case.

Elena, as she says, always gets ill after more than ten days in New York. Before the end of our stay, she developed sinus trouble. But she insisted on leaving, as we had planned, the day after Washington's Birthday, though a serious snowstorm was setting in. She was too hopeful because she had read in the papers that there was no snow in Rhode Island or Mass., but the farther we went, the worse it got, so that finally you could hardly see anything. She was clever enough to take a shortcut. I thought for a time we were lost, but it turned out that she had it right. We decided to spend the night in Boston. The quiet good taste and good service of the Ritz was delightful and very restful after the Princeton Club and the arduous drive. After supper, we went to the O'Connors', where Ed's mother and sister were and where, tired though we were, it was lively enough to keep us awake.

Wagner, Balzac; Thoughts about Amour; An Ex-Jesuit on the Scrolls

Wellfleet. Barbara Deming is back, with tales of her lecture tour in the East and in California. She does not seem to have encountered any very disagreeable opposition, though occasionally someone would advance the theory that what she saw in Hanoi was all a comedy rigged by the Communists. She claims to have changed one man's mind in the course of his questioning her. I felt that all this had in some way given her new stature.

When they came a second time, a curious kind of flare-

up occurred apropos of women's rights. Barbara said that
she had been telling her audiences that the women in
Vietnam were in certain ways freer and on a more equal
footing with men than the American women were. I expressed surprise at this: surely in the U.S., the women
bully and are spoiled by the men and all the careers are
opening to them. This provoked a sharp [retort] from Mary,
who complained that when she had applied for an exhibition in one of the New York galleries, she had been told
by the presiding pansy that they did not care for "lady
painters." She had resented this and, I think, must feel
in general that her being a woman has interfered with her
being recognized as an artist. I said that when I had been
in Russia, I had disliked to see women dressed as navvies
working on the roads. Barbara at once caught me up: "Ah,
you object to their being made unattractive!" Yes: of course
I did. I went on to suggest that, after all, there was a
biological difference between men and women. Marie-
Claire gave me a sly look and put her finger to her lips. I
thought this was funny.

Wagner: I have played most of his operas through twice
or more. Though a great dramatist, he is sometimes un-
dramatically repetitious: Siegfried's recapitulations of his
life in his "Rhine Journey," which is another recapitulation
and simply a piece of padding to allow a change of scenery;
Walther's Prize Song, which he first sings to Beckmesser,
then immediately afterwards at the contest. The use of
drugs and spells is ridiculous. The love potion in *Tristan*
is acceptable as a symbol for the *coup de foudre* of infatuation; but it is rather farfetched to have the blood of the
dragon make it possible for Siegfried not only to understand
the bird but also to hear what Mime is thinking when he
is pretending to be servile but actually planning to murder
Siegfried. I did not understand this scene till I read Ernest

Newman's discussion of it. Then the remarkable pharmaceutic proficiency of the Gibichungs in *Götterdämmerung*. They first give Siegfried a drug which will make him forget everything connected with Brunhilde; then later give him another which will make him remember—simply in order that Wagner can have a pathetic scene between them at the end. I have played *Götterdämmerung* twice and decided that I can't really like it. What is the point of the jarring episode in which Siegfried impersonates Gudrun? It does not make any sense in terms of the rest of the story. When Wagner was asked about *Gött.*, he seems to have taken the line "*Ça se sent, ça ne s'explique pas* [You feel it, but you can't explain it]." I think it must be a masked reference to something in his personal life.

Balzac: I have never been "hooked on" Balzac till recently. He does cast a kind of spell, but in the long run he is likely to become preposterous. He likes to invent intrigues and villainies which come too fast and which seem to be improvised—this is true not only of what happens in Paris but, in *Illusions Perdues*, of what happens in Angoulême. *Illusions Perdues* is absorbing, and one almost swallows the improbabilities: it remains somewhat plausible till Vautrin appears at the end and saves Lucien from committing suicide, when he really takes over as a supernatural being. He is, in fact, the spirit of Evil and his harangue to Lucien is powerful in its way. But in *Splendeurs et Misères*, almost everything is incredible. Vautrin and his three attendant demons accomplish too many wonders. The use of disguise becomes ridiculous. Everybody is always turning up in disguise and completely getting away with it—not only Vautrin and his staff but also the spies and detectives. V.'s aunt can be convincing at one moment as a grande dame descending from her carriage, and the next moment in rags as a *marchande des quatre saisons*. It is only in the last section that *Splendeurs et Misères* becomes a little more interesting: Vautrin in prison and with the legal officials, his relations with the underworld.

John Jay Chapman on a Balzac novel: like a live crab in your hair. You have to keep on reading—there are no chapters or convenient breaks except between the main sections. The murkiness and squalor of it even when he is dealing with the *haut monde* gets me down. I dropped it when I went to New York, but I took *Splendeurs* with me and when I began reading again, I at first had a comfortable feeling of being back in a familiar world, but then again I got sick of the turbidity and absurdity and dropped it. Finished when back in Wellfleet.

Some things—people, places, descriptions of the epoch—are described at enormous length; others, which include violent incidents—as when Vautrin pushes the spy off the roof—are passed over with but a brief mention. I think that this last is due to his writing so much and so unintermittently: he cannot concentrate properly on everything.

His influence on both Zola and Proust is evidently immense. In the case of Zola, the tendency to pile up the malignancies till they become unintentionally funny. Proust's social scenes must partly have derived from Balzac. In *Illusions* there is a kind of buildup from the provincial party in Angoulême through certain parties in Paris to a gathering at the social summit, as there is in *À la Recherche*. And the episode of Odette and Swann seems to owe something to Nuncingen and Esther.

Nobody else certainly has ever done so thorough a job on all the bad qualities of the French: their unscrupulous women like Madeleine, social *méchanceté* [nastiness], as in Proust. The scene of the humiliation of Lucien after the reading of his poems at Angoulême may partly have inspired the scene at the Verdurins', where the latter humiliate Charlus.

Passage about improbability and reality in *Splendeurs*.

Now that I can see far behind and a little beyond, the period of my own life and in fact that of known history seems to me extremely *rétréci* [shrunken]. I used to find history exciting and shall continue to read it, but I now feel that I know more or less the kind of things that happen. The closer to life you get, the more the great events diminish; the easier transportation and communication become, the less strange other places and peoples seem. (I am writing this in Jordanian Jerusalem and am not at ease with the Arabs, but since I was here last, this part of the city has been modernized and is more like any Western city.)

Though I think still a great deal about sex, it has come to seem to shrink in dignity and intrinsic importance. Thornton Wilder says somewhere that every mating is an attempt to produce a better human being, and on the higher levels this is true; but then, on the lowest level, how about the rapist and the men who will leap upon any woman? How much aimless rutting goes on—overpopulation, misery, misbreeding? To think of all those people to whom the desire to copulate has given perhaps the only interest that carries them through life.

We drove to Boston, Elena to go to the dentist, and I to get my passport, etc. I did some drinking and felt very keyed up. I wanted to make love to Elena and greedily kissed her breasts and her lovely little rose. She came, but as now happens so often, I was unable to finish in her.

Looking at her beautiful body, which does not show any signs of aging, I told her that making love to her had been the most wonderful thing in my life. After midnight, after lying unquietly awake, I got in bed with her again—she said, "Very gently," as she used to do when I came to her after she had been asleep. This time I did finish, but rather unsatisfactorily, because my penis shrank and slipped out of her before I had completely come.

I came down from Wellfleet April 22 and went to Baird's puppet show alone, went up and talked to them afterwards. He told me that the Punch man was an Englishman who had done exactly the same show for years, apparently afraid to change. He was performing now in Nome, Alaska. Baird sent me a letter to the big Guignol man in Paris, written, rather surprisingly, in perfectly good French and ending, *"Mille coups de bâton!!"**

The next day in the afternoon I went to Charlie Chaplin's *A Countess from Hong Kong*—one of the most irritating movies ever made. He doesn't understand that the comic gags which go over when he is in the picture don't do at all for good straight actors like Brando and Sophia Loren, who are only humiliated by what he makes them do. In the evening, I took Anita Loos to the Russian Tea Room for dinner and then to The Little Players. Cathleen Nesbitt joined us there. It was a Shakespeare "Jubilee," scenes, speeches and sonnets. On the whole one of their good performances—though I think it is a little uncomfortable when he has Mlle Gorance do a tragic role. But the smothering of Desdemona was more successful than the death of Traviata. —Anita does love unpleasant scandal, and

---

* "A thousand blows of the stick" is the punishment threatened by Sganarelle in the *commedia del'arte*. He was the ancestor of Punch and became a character in Molière.

regaled me with the obscene reports—which she need not have relayed at all—of some horrible scandal sheet of the omissions from the Manchester book.

Elena joined me on Sunday, and we went to the Epsteins' for dinner. Jason out of tune and grumbling, thought I overrated the Jews, on account of the New England identification with them; they were really awful people. Their complaints about the Syrians firing on them were an instance of the Jewish habit of always being in a position in which they would have something to complain about.*

Lunch with Malachi Martin: he talked about the scrolls but also what it meant to be a Jesuit. I can see he is going through a crisis on account of leaving the order and, also, Roger thinks, because his Greek girlfriend is a "ballcrusher." He expressed himself not hysterically, but I could see that he was full of emotion. The Jesuit has to learn obedience and learn to like obedience; he must suffer, but must believe that his suffering is a sacrifice to promoting Christianity. It is obvious that he is now for the first time giving expression to the scorn and resentment that must long have been rankling with him. He ridiculed the sacred relics: the arm of St. Theresa, the bones of the Magi on the ceiling at Cologne, the foreskin of Jesus, which he says caused a war (I thought this was an invention of Peyrefitte's). He told about an operation, after which he had asked what he had said under ether. The doctor had laughed and told him that he was certainly a normal man. You couldn't keep down nature. I had learned from Roger that Martin had had an affair in Rome with the wife of

---

* In his travel writing on Israel as well as in *The Scrolls from the Dead Sea,* Wilson understands the Jews through their ancient literature, projecting onto them his own intellectual energy and idealism. Epstein reacts against EW's simplification of a people, and is reduced to asserting their limitations. The friends argued these positions more than once.

the Time-Life representative, and that he had been exiled by the Church to Jerusalem, where for two years he edited a magazine. He said that Gerard Manley Hopkins had died of a broken heart, and that D'Arcy had also suffered terribly. D'Arcy, too, had his conflicts with the discipline of the order. It was true that he was being punished by being sent to the United States. He had all kinds of high connections in Ireland. He had been master of Campion College at Oxford, and had wanted it to recruit from the élite of Catholic culture combined with aristocratic blood. But this had been opposed and resented by less distinguished Catholics—"England is largely made up of Guardsmen and grocers' assistants." D'Arcy, because he was so good at raising money, had been made Father Provincial, but he now bought not one castle, as Stephen Spender told me, but three, with the money of the order. Again, it was a question of strongholds and nurseries for a Catholic élite. He had no real practical sense. Charges were brought against him, but they were never proved, and D'Arcy was shipped off to America, though his dearest desire was to live in England.

Martin is obsessed by the scrolls. He said that it was true that the Church had the policy of minimizing their importance. He blushed now for the reviews he had written. I told him that it was he who ought to be writing a book about them, but I could see, when he said that he couldn't for, say, two years, because he was still hampered by the inhibitions imposed by his old ties, that, with his enemies, as I am told, of the faith, it would be indiscreet for him to do so. I felt, when he kept urging me to go further in my speculations, that he really wanted to feed me his own ideas, though he didn't tell me clearly what they were. But he was evidently suffering from bafflement at the lack of evidence for a transition from the Essenes to Jesus. Originally, there had only been Jews, some of whom had accepted Jesus as Messiah, then something quite new appeared: the idea that the blood of a certain man could gain salvation for anyone, Gentile or Jew; and Paul organized the movement. What had happened in between? In the case of Allegro, this bafflement has evidently given rise to his theory that all the names in the New Testament really have an esoteric meaning and are connected with the Essene sect. His article in *Harper's* and a recent letter to me sound like the ideas of someone who thinks he has discovered a cipher that proves that Shakespeare was written by Bacon.

Graystone, the Marist priest who had written a book dated Rome, with a chapter directed against me and perhaps provoked by my book, Martin said had been a pupil of his and was terribly stupid, couldn't even read Hebrew. I had at first taken Martin's compliments as Irish blarney, but he now told me that since I had met him, he had read my book through three times, and that I had stimulated him to think about the scrolls again. I believe he is the only person of any intellect that my book has ever influenced.* The scholars—in spite of Albright's generous review—haven't in general had much use for it.

Lunch with Arnon, the Israeli consul: a perfect public relations man: he has all the smoothing answers at the tip of his tongue—minimizing current unemployment, the dropouts from the Hebrew University. He had been brought to Israel at the age of 12, but had been born in Vienna—which Elena had immediately guessed—and was a typical clever Viennese Jew. Likable, however. He complained that for a diplomat constantly shifted—his last post had been Ghana—there was a problem about his children's education: Hebrew was not taught in American schools.

---

* This was his first book on the scrolls, published in 1955.

ROME, JORDAN, ISRAEL

Darina Silone and the Bomarzo Monsters

I flew from New York on April 27. I find it quite exciting to leave at 6:30 and arrive in Rome at 8:30. On the plane, they give you a terrific dinner, with a large menu in French, with any amount to drink. I had a Scotch before dinner, champagne during dinner and afterwards two Benedictine-and-brandies. The gibbous moon came up, and as it rose higher, it came to look more and more diaphanous and fragile. Then soon one saw on the other side the sky turning bright red. —But one pays the next day for the lack of sleep.

Darina [Silone] met me, across the barrier, with a great embrace and kiss. She talked non-stop on our way to the hotel in the taxi. I could see she was under a strain. She had grown very stout, though she said she had recently been "sylphlike." Paolo Milano told me later that she was constantly expanding and shrinking—one of the signs that something is wrong. The Victoria was just the same old man at the desk, same fat doorman. Without Elena and the girls, I would feel a little desolate in the lobby, waiting for Darina, who is always late. I took a bath and shaved and felt fresher, but then at lunch was half-asleep. She brought her Indian priest, the young man she had along on her visit to Wellfleet, and at one moment I was a little rude with them, when she was fussing about the wine. She fusses constantly—another sign that she is in a bad condition. She is very much preoccupied with India, talks of going to work in Delhi. —I have a feeling that in the end he must have made it plain that he didn't want her to divorce Ignazio. In the evening, I had dinner with the Silones in the good little restaurant around the corner from the Victoria, where we had gone with them before. Much bad French was thrown around.

The next morning Darina and I went out to *Bomarzo* in a car that I hired at the hotel. It was a beautiful day, and the countryside was lovely; but Darina talked the whole time, as she did later at lunch and on the way back— something like six hours in all. She told me the story of her life and of her bad relations with Silone—whom she always calls "S."—says she has never been able to call him by his Christian name. Says that they have never had "conjugal relations"; but Paolo Milano tells me that her story varies from time to time—sometimes S. is impotent, sometimes their intercourse was unsatisfactory. It is impossible to tell how much of her stories is fantasy. She makes them so circumstantial that one is inclined to believe them. Says that S. has driven her into her present state of mind—that she is afraid of "going round the bend" and wants to get away. He breaks up all her friendships and eventually turns on all his own friends. She doesn't feel that she is S.'s wife—they never go out together. Milano says that it is actually true that they are very bad with one another. Darina says that S. goes out with other women —she doesn't know what he does with them.

Long story about her Italian fiancé, a lawyer who lived

in Milan and painted. Irish puritanism had kept her from any experience of sex (this, I believe, is true, and that it has had a good deal to do with bringing her to her present neurotic state). She never went to bed with this young Italian but once, and it was not at all a success: she lay there "like a statue," and he treated her "like a saint." During the war, she worked in Rome in an American news agency or for an American paper. A man began following her and propositioned her to become a spy. She disregarded this, and he followed her on the Via Veneto, flourishing greenbacks to tempt her. She paid no attention to him, but he continued to pursue her. At last, he made her listen when he told her that one of the top agents of the Gestapo wanted to see her. She went and was received with the utmost politeness. The Gestapo man, who called himself Rossetti, apologized for the stupidity of his agent—he saw that she was a lady. He tried to appeal to the tradition of the hatred of the Irish for England, but she told him that that was all over. He complimented her on her principles. At some point, he asked her whether she wasn't an English spy. Later on, at another meeting or telephone conversation, he told her he would give her a fortnight, and if she did not come round, something serious would happen to her fiancé in Milan. The fiancé, when she saw him next, told her to pay no attention. But at the end of a fortnight, his secretary called her up and told her she must come at once. The young man had gone mountain climbing and had fallen into a crevasse and been killed. She went to where his body was and was told that the two men who had been with him could not really have been members of his alpine club, because after notifying the people at the inn of his death, they immediately disappeared. The rope that was tied around him had not broken but had been cut. Back in Rome, the Gestapo man called her up and

said, "Now will you change your mind?" She arranged to
get away to Switzerland, where she was imprisoned a few
days on charges that she never could get them to tell her;
but they very soon let her go. It was then that she met
Silone. An unpleasant man at the British Embassy, who
boasted of his invariable success with women and made
advances to her, avenged himself for being repulsed by
spreading the rumor that she was an Axis spy, and for a
long time Silone believed this.

Of course, I was interested in all this, but Darina either
had total recall or was carried away by invention,
because she would continually digress, and one digres-
sion would lead to another, and I would have to interrupt
her and make her get back to the main line of narrative. But as soon as I started to speak, she would raise her
voice to drown me out, and I would have to raise mine in
order to get her to stop. Her spate of talking was uncontrollable. She seemed to want to discourage questions. At
one point she said, "I don't believe I've ever told a lie." At
Bomarzo, I shut her up in order to pay attention to what
I saw.

Bomarzo. It was one of my tottery days, not a good time
for making this visit. The park is on a fairly steep hillside,
and I thought I could not get back up the lower paths, so
Darina explored this lower level, and I took notes while
guarding her handbag:

"*. . . al cupo carattere di Pier Francesco Orsini che, retiratosi
nelle sue terre, nel 1560, diede inizio ai lavori esprimendo la
sua angoscia . . . Vicino* (same Orsini) *era gobbo e contorto
. . . Moglia attraente, Giulia Farnese, ed uno fratello vellissimo
. . . uccise il fratello, sapendo che Giulia amava il cognato*
(. . . to the somber character of Pier Francesco Orsini,
who, retiring to his estate in 1560, had the labors begun
which expressed his anguish . . . Vicino was a hunchback
and deformed . . . His attractive wife, Giulia Farnese, and

a very handsome brother [fell in love] . . . He killed the brother, knowing that Giulia loved her kinsman)."*

Then we began on the statues.

Sculptures supposed to have been made by a Turk captured at the Battle of Lepanto.

Near gate, toothed, nostrilled, popeyed face, with globe on head and edicule† on globe.

"*Voi che pel mondo gite errando vaghi di veder maraviglie alte et stupende venite qua dove son faccie horrende elephenti leoni orse orche et draghi* (You who go wandering about the world, in the desire to see high and astounding wonders: come here where there are horrid faces, elephants, bears, whales, and dragons)."

This is on a sort of stone bench.

On one of the monstrous urns that stand pedestalled in two rows: "*Fonte non fu tra chin guardia sia delle piu strane belve* (Fountain never was which had stranger beasts as a guard)." On another: "*Notte et giorno noi siam vigili e pronte a guardar dogni ingiuia questa fonte* (Night and day we are on watch and ready to defend this fountain from any damage)."

Rows of ornaments like acorns and pineapples.

Small temple, with disproportionately high vault ornamented with stone stars.

Great mask, through the mouth of which one enters a room that has what looks like a Mithraic altar: "*Ogni pen-*

---

* EW later learned that this account for visitors derived from a historical novel by the contemporary Argentine writer Manuel Mujica-Lainez. Wilson's impressions of Bomarzo led to an essay in *The New York Review of Books*, reprinted in *The Devils and Canon Barham*. Halfway down the steep hill on which sat "the imposing Palazzo Orsini" was this "flock of monsters" that had been "for four centuries left to themselves, embedded in a jungle of shrubbery." They composed "a malignant poem created by a determinedly perverse nature, which still speaks through its threatening inscriptions and petrified but animated dreams." The Italian was translated for his article.

† An edicule is a small structure used as a shrine.

siero vol[*a?*] (Every thought flies—the last word [*a?*] now defaced)."

Winged dragon with open jaws attacked by lionlike *belve* [beast].

Water god with snub nose and disagreeable expression.

Huge moss-covered woman lying on her back with her legs apart.

Mammoth elephant with howdah and figure with drum on his head—his trunk around a man whom he is obviously about to kill.

Faceless beast: many figures are badly eroded.

Winged woman with long tail; another woman with urn on her head, out of which are now growing wild plants. They preside over stagnant pools. The latter is surrounded by a strange group whose features are now partly blurred—monkey embracing woman from behind; women with men or women upside down between them.

Worn-down scarcely climbable steps.

Inscription on the miniature palace: "*Animas qui ascendo fit prudentior* (The spirit, by climbing here, is made more cautious)."

Face peering out of dried-up pool: wide nostrils, shaggy hair; huge fishlike gaping maw and popping eyes.

Toads. The monstrous tortoise with a sphere on its back and a woman on the sphere.

Giant—more than 20 feet?—who has thrown down another giant and is rending him apart by the legs while the victim is howling. Beside it, as if part of the same formation, is a thing like a huge phallus toward which an eroded ducklike creature seems to be opening its beak. The nearer inscription is mostly defaced: one cannot read much more than "—*scempio sanglante* (bloody slaughter)." The other farther inscription reads: "*Se rodi altier gia fu de suo colosso pur di quest il mio bosco auche si gloria e per piu non poter fo quant io posso* (If Rhodes was once proud of its colossus, my wood can also boast of this one and I can do no more than I am able)." Here a little cascade falling from under big elephant-ear–like leaves full of holes.

Creeping vines; lichens on the statues; little blue, white and yellow flowers; little sapling; conifers, which D. says must have been planted. On the hill beyond a gray olive grove. The old castle far up the steep hill—now the commune, that is, the town hall—overhangs and dominates all. What is striking is that the whole place is dominated by a strange poetic personality which has been trying thus to express itself—it approaches the surrealistic.

Milano: "Baroque before the baroque"; Silone says that the Italians do not like the ugly-grotesque—that it is a kind of thing that is less Italian than German.

Dinner with Milano in the evening. It was a relief, after poor Darina, to have someone listen to me and to be able to talk to Paolo about the scrolls. He says that Darina, for all her fantasies, is "an honest and brave woman."

She wanted to come to see me off, but I would not let her. I have always liked her so much since I first knew her in Rome in 1945. She was then self-controlled, extremely capable and dignified and very handsome. Milano thinks that she now talks all the time at home and is driving S. crazy. I think that, having abandoned the Church, she still needs a priest and that it has been the priest in S. who has kept her with him. Now her priest is the Brahmin-priest S. Ouza (I am not sure I've got it right—that sounds Portuguese).

For the first time, Rome gives me the impression of a rather small provincial city.

Jordan: "72 Today, Feeling Unusually Well"

I left Rome in the early afternoon Sunday. The airport at
Jerusalem is being reconstructed for jet planes, so the Royal
Jordanian planes do not fly any farther than Amman. From
there I took a bus, which got me to Jerusalem at 9. There
was a howling wailing radio program on the bus, of which
the only words I could understand were "America" and
"CIA," repeated with emphasis and followed by laughter.
I was told at the [American] School that Beirut, with its
students, was probably an excellent place for the CIA to
work on. I was received at the school by a turbanned
apparition of enormous circumference, who took me
through the patio to the Markses' house. They call this
night watchman the Hadj, a man who has been to Mecca.
He prays or goes to sleep on the little front porch. Shakes
hands with me when he comes on in the evening and always
helps me down the steps; sometimes he kisses the inmates.
He does not seem to know a word of English, but greets
one with something about Allah. A very likable old boy.
The Markses had gone to bed. When we rang and nobody
answered at once, the Hadj leaned his head on his hands
pressed together to indicate that they were sleeping. But
Aminta Marks came to the door in her dressing gown and
little bare feet, asked me to come in and got me some supper
of cold cuts and potato salad. I like them. They have three
children but are still fairly young. She has blue eyes and
would be pretty but for her nose, which is too long and
has a tendency to turn reddish. He teaches ancient Eastern
history at Princeton—says he is a lapsed Presbyterian.
They have tea at 4 every afternoon.

I enjoy coming here in a peculiar way. It is a little bit
bleak, in spite of the flowers in the patio, but comfortable,
clean and quiet. It is not as lively as when I was here

before. The archaeologists are out on "digs," and people in the school are mostly wives and children. There are, however, a young Jesuit, evidently Irish, from California, and a young man who is dean at an Evanston divinity college and who has written a book on the Testimonia and other passages from Old Testament books that differ from those in the Masoretic text. I have bought this book and am going to read it. These two and others I have met seem to represent a new type, young men who have been ordained in the ministry or become Catholic priests, but are full of slang and wisecracks and have gone in for archaeology and Biblical scholarship.

The secretary and general utility girl, Carroll Bohn, is a 24-year-old college graduate who intends, at the end of her year here, to get a bachelor of divinity degree at the Harvard Divinity School. She comes from near Akron, Ohio, where her father is something in a tire factory. She loves the Middle East and, on account of her features, in spite of her color, could easily pass for an Arab. She formerly taught school here and got in trouble for giving her pupils a folk song to sing that was said in a note to be Jewish. One of the girls threw the book down and said that she would not sign a song that had been written by filthy Jews! Carroll tried to explain that music was music, and that its merits were independent of nationalities. But the incident was made into a scandal, a story in the paper said that an American schoolteacher had told her pupils that the Jews were better than the Arabs. Carroll had to cancel the plans she had made for visiting Israel, because this would seem suspicious.

My ideas about the absence of liquor turn out to be perfectly ludicrous. The Arabs who are Christians drink, and so do a good many of the others. There is a liquor store not far away on the other side of the street, and the young people get together for a drink—in which they invite me to join—every afternoon before dinner. Two drinks apiece.

The first day I visited the museum; the second called on *Père de Vaux*. He is a most extraordinary man—the least froglike Frenchman I have ever known. L'École Biblique, built in the 1890s, is much grander and more impressive than the American school, and de Vaux, though he has now relinquished the nominal directorship to someone else, is still the controlling power. Though his habits are most austere, he thrones in his school like a Herod. He greeted me with great amiability and answered all my questions. He insists on speaking his not wonderful English. Polite and generous about his opponents: Allegro and Dupont-Sommer; but when I spoke of G. R. Driver's book, which I had just discovered in the library here, he burst out laughing. "You must see my review of it!" he said, dashed out of the room and brought me an offprint. I had been rather appalled by the book, in which Flusser, Dupont-Sommer and I are snootily brushed aside without being named, and in which Driver tries to show that the scrolls are all *post*-Christian. This uncontrollable desire to show that the Christians could not have been influenced by the Essenes is one of the phenomena peculiar to the controversy. In his review, de Vaux demolishes Driver. He marshals his archaeological arguments. He says that Driver is no archaeologist—regrets that he has to disagree with a man with whom he has been on friendly relations and who has shown him so much kindness.

I asked him whether it were true, as I had read in *Time* and as Martin had confirmed, that he had said that in matters of doctrine the Vatican was the authority but that in matters of scholarship it had no competence. He seemed at first a little worried by this, pulled his beard and said he did not remember to have said it; then smiled and said, "I would say it. My faith has nothing to fear from my scholarship." I asked him what books I should read, and he answered, Yadin's book on the war scroll and his own book *L'Archéologie et les Manuscrits de la Mer Morte*. He made a gesture of being reluctant to remember his own book, but said, "*Really*, you must read it!" As I was going, I remarked that I was getting rather old for this kind of thing. He said that he was getting old, too—his beard is now partly gray—and was no longer as he had been in the days when "we leaped like roes"—evidently referring to the passage in my book in which I said that he climbed the ruins on goatlike legs.

The next day, I had *Sa'ad*—who is around the corner in an expensive antique shop—come to see me here. They removed him from the directorship of the museum because he has no college degree, and he is said to be depressed about it. He remembered me from meeting me at the museum when I was here before, and had read my book and recommended it in his lectures. Had been all over the U.S., under the sponsorship of the State Department, exhibiting the scrolls and lecturing about them. I thought he was a little less than candid about certain things. He implied that the lack of cordiality with which *Allegro* had been met when he returned to Jerusalem was due to his lack of success, and that his attempt to do any kind of excavating in connection with the Mosque of Omar, "the most sacred place in the world," would be likely to arouse opposition. Sa'ad is a Christian. Rather an overripe elderly Arab. He speaks very good English. All the men of his generation had a "good English education" under the British mandate.

The young American Jesuit says he saw a good deal of D'Arcy in Hollywood. They went to the movies together —because D'Arcy in the U.S. is not subject to the British restrictions. He said that D'Arcy had been persuaded to buy the notorious castles by wealthy Catholic families that wanted to get rid of them and that the order was now stuck with these "white elephants." But the opposition to D'Arcy had also been due to his liberal ideas.

The reason I couldn't describe the food to Elena was that it was so unattractive that I had forgotten about it. Arab cuisine: rice and liquid stews poured over it; shish kabobs, which I find inedible. Leathery Arab bread with no butter at luncheon. Things made of dough, with chopped meat inside. Measly bananas, good oranges and grapefruit, uninteresting little things called loquats.

I was taken one night (Tuesday) to a concert by the Georgia State College Brass Ensemble. Very rousing. A seventeenth-century piece and some modern music of the more riotous Rieti kind; folk songs, jazz. Siegfried's death, "Battle Hymn of the Republic" (rather disloyally instead of "Dixie"). They told me that the Arabs recently had behaved badly at one of the concerts. At this one, the men and boys in the gallery rustled papers and talked, but were overwhelmed by a last terrific piece of the "Turkey in the Straw" kind. —Afterwards, a reception for the band at the American Colony Hotel, where I met a young man named Ross, who is the U.S. Information man.

I had dinner with Ross on Thursday. He comes from Florida, is well-read in contemporary literature. He told me before the third guest came that if he wanted a chick, he had to go to Beirut (I have certainly seen no pretty women here). "I don't buy it—unless I have to." His apartment is on the Via Dolorosa at the Second Station of the Cross. There is a stone arch over the street between his building and the next, and according to the Arab legend, this is where Pilate stood and looked down on Jesus and said, "*Ecce homo*"; but actually this arch was built by Hadrian. For his apartment, which has several large rooms, he pays only $75 a month. He has picked up an old-fashioned phonograph on which he plays a record of Noël Coward playing "Mad Dogs and Englishmen." The man who drove me there was over here doing an article for the *National Geographic* magazine. The third guest was the editor of the *Palestine News*, a young New York Jew, who had been converted to Mohammedanism and now calls himself Sulayman Abdullah. He wore a beret and said, "*Shukron,*" thank you, in Arabic when Ross gave him a drink. He has a sister who goes constantly to Israel, and I suspect some family rivalry. He talks about the policies of the various Arabian countries exactly the way the left intellectuals used to talk about the Communist groups.

The front yard of the American School is horribly littered with candy wrappers and other papers. The government wants to buy the place for offices. They have offered a million dollars. They resent the Americans having it tax free.

I visited the Church of the Holy Sepulchre, which seems more unattractive than ever. As usual, scaffoldings within and without.* It was tiring for me to walk there, and the booths in the covered *souk* disgust me. I sat down in the church and rested and read Dick Tracy, etc., in the *Herald Tribune*. Having already seen the principal sights, I doubt whether I shall go into the Old City again.

Hustling buses and cars. Since I was here last, a sort of small rue de la Paix has been built on the street that passes the school: bookstores, money changers, a liquor

---

* In 1954 he had visited this church with its precarious scaffoldings, marking the failure of the five competing sects to agree upon repairs. It seemed a "macabre, claustrophobic place," with "more bad taste, certainly more kinds of bad taste, than any other church in the world." He had explored the corners of the building, observing discussion in various languages and acts of superstitious piety. He cited a passage from the journal of Robert Curzon in 1834 recounting the remorseless scramble, at Holy Week, of pilgrims to light the candles representative of eternal salvation. In the effort to leave, the Englishman found himself treading upon heaps of bodies "black with suffocation" (*Red, Black, Blond, and Olive*). The Church of the Holy Sepulchre elicited in Wilson a skepticism reminiscent of Gibbon.

store, a candy store, all sorts of shops selling jewelry and ornaments—quite modern, unlike the old city. In the windows of the shops for women's clothes, Westernized figures of Arab-eyed girls in mini-skirts.

Trip to Pella on Friday. We started about 8:30—I in a car with the consul (Hall) and his wife and an elderly lady from North Carolina, the widow of the Pastor of the Lutheran Church. The consul soon said that he understood what Marks had meant when he said that the road was "not very good." It was the very worst road I have ever seen except that road in Haiti which the river crosses so many times: great holes and splits, hollows full of water, goats, sheep, donkeys, camels, trucks that one has to pass or allow to pass. The population here are miserable; they live in one- or two-room adobe houses. Hall says that the refugees live better than the original inhabitants, because they have schools and clinics provided by the UN. You occasionally see a woman with a long black veil, though this custom is going out. The hills are great barren folds, such green as there is, as I described it before, "like mould on enormous loaves." The Jordan is small and muddy. There are spots that can be cultivated for wheat and vegetables. Otherwise, they herd their flocks. The Southern lady kept exclaiming in ecstasy over any sign of water or cultivation in this monotonously dreary landscape and would say that the mountains were lovely. The Arabs in their cars dash recklessly and insolently hooting their horns. The people and the children and the donkeys are quite casual about getting out of the way of the cars. (In Jerusalem, they saunter along without having any system for sharing the pavement, not keeping out of other people's way.)

Hall's Arab story: A scorpion wants to cross a stream, and he asks a frog to carry him. The frog says, "I'm afraid you'll sting me." "Oh, no," says the scorpion. "I wouldn't do that! I want to get to the other side." So the frog takes him on his back, and in the middle of the stream, the scorpion stings him. "Why did you do that?" cried the frog. "Now I'll die and you'll drown." "This is the Middle East," says the scorpion.

Hall has been posted in Iceland, Naples and South Africa. "Having solved the problems [in South Africa], they've sent me on here." He says that these problems are insoluble.

At the "dig," we found the archaeologists and some young people from Wooster College, Ohio, which is financing the expedition, living in a primitive building which has been cleaned up and equipped with plumbing. The site which is being dug up is that of a large cathedral. The Christians came out there in the early days to get away from the Romans, and it became a considerable Christian settlement. They are also digging up tombs, in which they find wine jars and other things. The findings were explained by a man named Ball. I told him that he must be a relative of mine, and he said that that summer, like me, he was invited to the Ball picnic but never went. He belongs to a Virginian branch of the family, which he says did not particularly prosper. He was born in a place, he says, with the ignominious name of Ball Beggar.

Many of the archaeologists came back from their digs for the weekend, and the common room was quite lively at drink time. One of the most interesting is a nun, Sister Marie, who teaches Latin, Greek and New Testament at a Catholic girls' college in Chicago. Spent six years at Freiburg and has a Ph.D. She is pretty and well aware of it—35. I was surprised to find her wearing her pretty brown hair; but she says that they do not have to have it shaved, that that is a myth. The Jesuit tells me that they do have to trim it. She is having a sabbatical year. When I met her first, she was wearing her robe, but the next day she was in ordinary clothes, on both occasions with blunt black unattractive shoes. With all her good looks, she has a certain dogged look of strain. On Saturday, I gave her a drink and had some conversation with her about education and young people and their problems. There was also a young, lean and sunburned Dominican who told me, when I said that I had not read Aquinas, that I had a great pleasure in store for me.

That night I took out Carroll Bohn for dinner. We went to the Intercontinental Hotel, a luxury affair built by Pan Am Airlines—in spite of much protest—on the Mount of Olives. It is the regular kind of thing: cocktail lounge, Strauss waltzes, elaborate dining room. From the windows, you look down on the lights of Jerusalem. I told Carroll I was somewhat horrified by it, and she said, "Yes, when you think what it is like down there." Whiskey sours, Orvieto. It seems that the Pan Am people thought that Jerusalem would draw the rich tourists if they were given the kind of hotel to which they were accustomed.

I took a day off the next day, Sunday. I spent almost all day in bed reading a little book about Mohammedanism. They got worried about me when I did not come to meals, and sent me Sunday dinner on a tray: French fries without salt, thin tasteless slices of what they called beefsteak, ice cream which did not seem convincing.

The Markses, on Sunday evening, had a buffet supper in their house, a most successful occasion. Père de Vaux and his administrator Père Benoît were there. I told de Vaux that I had, at his prompting, changed the color of his robe from brown to white, and he said, "You see!" and called my attention to his having shaved his beard.* I had a long talk with de Vaux—mostly about Allegro and the possibility of Jesus' having had some connection with the Essenes. He believes Jesus must have known about them

---

* In *The Dead Sea Scrolls* (1955) de Vaux is described as a bearded man in a white robe.

but didn't admit any direct connection. The doctrine of Jesus is "the contrary" to that of the Teacher of Righteousness. He believes that the Teacher of Righteousness founded the sect, brought his followers down to the Dead Sea. Says that it has been suggested, as a parody of Allegro's method with the New Testament, that Allenby's name may be interpreted as *Allah nebi*, prophet of God.* It is curious the towering and spreading effectiveness that these sturdy Dominicans make in their great white robes in a roomful of people in ordinary dress.

There were also all the people at the American School, representatives of the first families of the American colony and the Arab dealer in antiques—the only honest one, they told me, in Jerusalem—who was involved in the original handling of the scrolls and who is referred to as "Mr. X" in the literature on the subject.

John Marks had just completed the sale of this property and had received a large check. He told me afterwards of the cloak-and-dagger tactics by which the deal had been approved. He had had to meet two men at a certain place, be taken by them to Jericho, where they met another man, then taken to the villa of a sheik. Why had all this been necessary? "They've been seeing too many movies." He had been subjected to repeated attempts to make him bribe people, which he had resisted by "playing dumb." Mrs. Marks says that the present school is not satisfactory for married couples, who were apparently not contemplated when the place was built. They have only one room in which to live and in which the husband works. People get on each other's nerves.

On Sunday, in anticipation of my birthday, I had a telegram from Darina: "Remembering wonderful day with

---

* Viscount Allenby was hardly a prophet of God. He was commander of the British Expeditionary Force in 1917 and Lawrence of Arabia's superior in the campaign that drove out the Turks.

monsters send affectionate birthday greetings *ad multos annos* love."

Monday. I am 72 today. Telegram from Elena: "We all seem well and shall be thinking of you Monday and send love." Not quite reassuring. I am feeling unusually well today. Wrote during the morning and at three o'clock went over to the École Biblique and had a very satisfactory interview with Père de Vaux. In the evening, I took Dick Ross and Carroll Bohn to dinner at the American Colony Hotel. There I found the Sundbergs and Père Audet, who came to our table for coffee and cognac. He is the Quebec Dominican who has written about the *Pastor of Hermas* and the *Didaché*. We talked about French Canada.

Tuesday. In the afternoon, I had myself driven out to Bethlehem with Carroll. The driver seemed a good fellow, spoke English, had visited Europe, had served for some years in the army and been wounded in the Arab-Jewish war. Carroll had warned me that the road was "curvy." There is no guard on the open side to protect you from the rock-strewn abyss below. The drive to Bethlehem used to take about fifteen minutes, but now they have to go eleven miles out of their way in order to avoid crossing Israeli territory.

We went first to Shepherds' Field, where the shepherds are supposed to have heard the angels singing. This seems only recently to have been made a shrine. There is a grotto with a smoke-blackened ceiling, in which the shepherds are supposed to have been, but which for centuries seems to have been a shelter for anyone who cared to stay in it. (I notice that Stewart Perowne does not include it in his account of Bethlehem.) A young Franciscan from Cleveland showed us around. He lives in Bethlehem but comes out and stays there alone as guardian, with for company only a swarthy handyman. The little church was only quite recently built: a dome with small glassed aperture, in order, he explained, to express the light brought by Christ's birth in contrast to the somberness of some other sacred place commemorating his end. The Church of the Holy Nativity is much more attractive and interesting than that of the Holy Sepulchre. Originally built by Constantine, it was destroyed one does not know how, but rebuilt by Justinian. Both the Roman and the Greek Church represented. Two Armenian priests were chanting without an audience. Fine mosaics rescued from the church that was first built. Hadrian tried to make it a temple of Adonis as he built a temple of Venus on the Holy Sepulchre. I did not go down to the stable where Jesus is supposed to have been born, where they have a stone manger, or the cell in which St. Jérôme is supposed to have translated the Pentateuch, on account of the steep steps. There is a terrific Christmas service with mobs of people that Carroll tells me she attended. As at the Sacred Fire at the Holy Sepulchre, she says that it is quite frightening.

From letter to Elena*: I enjoyed my stay on the other side, but I rather dislike the Arabs. They are always waylaying you or leaping out at you and trying to sell you something for which they overcharge you. As they told me at the school, "There's no question of right or wrong. They just want to take all they can get." (I went rather *octorogno†* when I wrote you from Jordan because correspondence is censored and sometimes suppressed.) Nor do I much like old Jerusalem. When you first go there, it stimulates the imagination, but on this visit I did almost no sightseeing. I did, however, on my last day, make a trip to Bethlehem,

---

* EW taped a copy of this long letter into his journal.
† This compound literally means around eight corners; it is used by EW to mean indirectly.

where I had never been. The road there is the most fright-ening I have ever been driven on: mostly on the edge of abysmal drops and full of abrupt loopings—in going around one of these, you may suddenly be confronted with a huge bus. —The Church of the Holy Nativity at Bethlehem is much more attractive than the Holy Sepulchre: built by Constantine, rebuilt by Justinian. You enter by a small low door, intended for the double purpose of preventing the Crusaders from riding their horses and camels into the church and of promoting humility on the part of those entering in approaching the birthplace of Christ. Also vis-ited Shepherds' Field. The little church was guarded by a single Franciscan, a chinless young man from Cleveland, who complained about the scorpions.

The last night, the Markses gave a bang-up dinner, with whisky, wine and liqueur—which I have never known them to provide before. Aminta Marks is languishing after a year at the school and eager to get back to the States. The food is enough to get anybody down, and she says that she longs for a little more "spontaneity." About a quarter to 6, all the younger inmates—including the nun—get together in the upstairs common room and have about two drinks of Scotch each. They say that this has made life much easier at such close quarters.

Israel: Flusser, Yadin, Agnon, Kollek

[*Letter to Elena continued:*] I was driven over to Israel on the morning of May 10 in a car from the consulate. The city has been much cleaned up and built up since I was here before, and is now a well-developed town, which gives an impression of solidity. The King David Hotel is crammed with very bourgeois and not particularly attractive visitors from all over, who have come for the festivities of Independence Day. They have given me splendid rooms, with a basket of fruit from the manager.

I had dinner last night with Moshe Pearlman. Do you remember that he came to dinner with us once in New York? He is likable and a very lively talker: politics, literature, language. The great question they now discuss is whether their original idealism is fading—since many are leaving Israel—and how they can carry on.

I have been feeling very well. I think that this bright dry climate is good for me. Even my scrofulous condition has disappeared. There is very little drinking. Pearlman last night offered me nothing but beer, though there was a well-equipped bar. Plenty to eat of a Jewish and Middle Eastern kind. With breakfast and lunch you get two kinds of cheese.

I have had to leave the King David for a night because my rooms had been booked in advance by somebody else coming on for the Independence Day festivities. I go back tomorrow afternoon. I am staying with a very nice young couple—born here, he a lawyer—who speak English pretty well, having been for a year in London. A pretty little girl, who speaks only Hebrew, so I had to resort to my handkerchief mouse and guessing which hand the coin is in. I am going with them to the "Tattoo" tonight, a kind of drill and entertainment in the stadium. The American papers this morning had nothing but bad news—with Johnson telling his little daughter that her father might be responsible for starting World War III. I spoke of this to Mr. Cheshin, the young lawyer in whose apartment I am staying, who said that to them here Vietnam seems remote, because they are living in fear of a serious war with the Syrians. Now, after lunch, the Cheshins have gone for a rest. She has been working her head off in connection with the celebration.

I have been having, as I did before, a very active and

enjoyable time. I first called on [David] Flusser, who since his marriage and professorship at the university has become extremely stout. His English has somewhat improved, but not enough to make him entirely intelligible. When I see him again I'll revert to French, in which we're both at a disadvantage. From the moment he came into the room, he talked a torrent, pouring out his ideas, each one of which suggests another. He was funny about his visit to Harvard to take part in a symposium of Christians and Jews. He said that the professors of theology in America were mad about eschatology (the Last Judgment and all that), which affects them "like an aphrodisiac," and that the symposium finally came down to a debate as to who has the most eschatology, the Christians or the Jews. He thinks that the vogue of eschatology is bound up with existentialism. The existentialist has to decide in the present; the eschatologist expects a decision in the future. (As I gathered later from an article in *Time*, it is rather that they try to transpose into terms of the choices of the present the moral judgments which were formerly predicted as to take place on the Last Day.) He gave me a humorous description of an eschatological theory that everything in the Lord's Prayer applies to the Last Day—that "our daily bread" really refers to the manna that is promised then, the expectation of which he says would not satisfy him. He said to me, "When you were here before, I did not know that you had supernatural powers, that you could write such a book." He is married to a German Jewish woman from Hamburg, who spent the war in a concentration camp in Holland. She seems rather shy and subdued. (It turned out that she knew very little English.) They say that even at home he never stops talking. He told me a long, rather weird story about the birth of one of his sons being in some way connected with an incident about Yadin and something Biblical—I think, in connection with the date.

The next day I went to see Yadin, who couldn't be more different from Flusser. He is tall, goodlooking and cosmopolitan. He speaks English incredibly well and has a great deal of charm. He held me spellbound for two hours and a half, talking about the scrolls. He and Père de Vaux think, as I do, that Allegro is dotty in his theories about the New Testament. He tells me that the BBC had a recent symposium in London, in which he and Allegro and two other scrolls scholars performed, and that it had never been published as it was supposed to be—he believes because Allegro got rather the worst of it and has prevented its publication. He says it was the occasion for more plain-speaking than has ever occurred before on the subject, and that I ought to try to get a transcript.

On Friday Teddy Kollek, the mayor of Jerusalem, took me and an American photographer around the city, ending with a visit to Agnon. The old man has a very fine face—unlike the photographs, which make him look ugly. He speaks only German and Hebrew, so Pearlman interpreted between us, and we exchanged well-turned compliments. We drank לחיים, "L'ḥayim," "to life," in cognac. He gave me a bunch of flowers, then another bunch of flowers from a vase in the living room, and then, as I was going, another flower, which he picked in the front lawn. He gave me one of his books with an inscription in Hebrew: "To the honored Edmund Wilson, who has been graced by God with an eye to see and a heart to understand." (I am enjoying all these compliments.) Kollek had warned us that we mustn't stay long, since Sabbath begins Friday afternoon and Agnon would soon have to be taking his ritual bath. His street has been named after him, but he lives in the utmost austerity. When asked what he would do with the Nobel money, he said that he did not intend to use any more margarine. (Butter is not kosher—at the hotel, you cannot get butter in the restaurants that are kosher.) He says that he is rather frightened at the prospect of his reception by the Jews in New York. He tells about getting the prize in a way that makes it sound like one of the stories he writes. He had spent the whole day attempting to get the plumber and always being frustrated —the man was never there or never seemed to get his message. Then late in the afternoon somebody knocked at the door, and he thought, At last, the plumber! It was a man from the foreign office announcing the Nobel Prize. *

On Saturday, I went to the School of Archaeology, the counterpart of the American School on the other side, where I met much the same kind of people: American archaeologists and Biblical scholars. They had a "cook-in" at 1:00 on the terrace. I met there a jolly and learned rabbi, who teaches at Hebrew Union College in Cincinnati. He invited me to his house, and we had a good round of American highballs—with his wife and two teenage daughters. Then for dinner we went to the house of a youngish Hebrew poet—born in New York, his wife a sculptress. Lea Goldberg came in afterwards—the touching and sympathetic woman poet from Russia whom I had called on before in Tel Aviv. A good deal of local wine was drunk; but this and the highballs were due to the fact that everyone except

---

* Ten years before this meeting, EW had called Agnon a writer of genius, defining his subject as the humor and pathos of people who lived demanding intellectual and spiritual lives in a simple environment. Comparing him to Kafka, Wilson noted that Agnon's hero would never, like Joseph K., "confuse his duty to an imperfectly accessible God with his duty to established society." When Agnon got the Nobel Prize a year before this meeting in Jerusalem, Wilson noted that the old culture of the ghetto seemed to be losing its authority in his work; yet this work conveyed to readers "a world that is transcendent and timeless, that is subject to binding obligations and which may always be illumined by a divine light."

Miss Goldberg came from the U.S. Misha Cheshin offered me a glass of wine at lunch, but says that there is very little drinking here—he himself drinks wine only on the Sabbath; they have no alcoholic problem, no one is ever drunk on the streets. (But when we came back from the Tattoo, he opened a cupboard which contained every kind of liquor, and we both had a shot of Scotch.)

Earlier than all this, Moshe Pearlman took me to the new museum, which is mostly in very good taste. There is a large expanse behind it with a mixed display of sculpture—part of it is a bequest from Billy Rose—that ranges from Rodin and Maillol to those unappetizing objects and contraptions that you see in the New York museums. [Letter to Elena ends.]

Cheshin spoke with alarm of the possibility that the six Arab nations might gang up on them. I said that Nasser was occupied with Yemen. Yes: this might be the moment to strike. "We can't stand it! They mine the roads so we can't drive there with our families!" —Both Misha and [his wife] Ruth are seventh-generation Palestinians. They compared notes on their families, and it turned out that Ruth's family had been there two years longer than his. Her great-great-grandfather had founded the first Hebrew-language paper in Palestine as well as the first Jewish settlement outside old Jerusalem. —Misha, when I asked him whether they played cards much, said that they did to some extent play bridge, but that it was rather looked down on as "decadent." His driving us to the stadium was frightening. He would say, "Oi, oi, I am so nervous!" and seemed to be almost hysterical. (They are having a conference in Tel Aviv about reducing car accidents. They give medals for safe driving.)

"Tattoo" performance at night in preparation for Independence Day; 17,000 people in the stadium. A terrific

demonstration: feverish, high-keyed, a little sinister. The American consul told me that someone had said that there was a little the note of Nuremberg. Nasal fast-paced Jewish music from loudspeakers: popular songs and marches. An element of the circus—lights turned off and on to emphasize special events. Units would march in—all the branches of the service. The only weapons permitted were such light ones as rifles and antiaircraft guns. By the terms of the armistice, heavy armament was not allowed in Jerusalem, so no tanks or planes or heavy artillery was paraded. The British, who have interests in Saudi Arabia, brought pressure on the Israelis to enforce this in deference to the protests of the Arabs, who regarded the demonstration as a hostile and defiant act. Ben-Gurion, who did not approve of this deference, ostracized the occasion. But there was no mistaking its militant character. It began with the tattoo proper: the drums. *Tattoo* in this sense is British, and the evolutions that followed owed a good deal to the British: swinging of arms, long stride with the legs apart, keeping step during a halt, stamping. The first big entrance was made by the commander of the local unit, who, preceded by a guard of motorcycles, was driven around the ring in a car; then other officials; and, finally, the President, with motorcycles ahead and beautiful white horses behind. (In going back through the gate, one of these slipped and fell and broke the rider's leg.) Everyone stood, and the national anthem was sung. Then the lights were turned out, and lights were seen coming down the aisles. These were soldiers with bulb-like epaulets on their shoulders—white, bluish and pink. Everybody clapped. Illuminated choirs sang. Great cauldrons that burned gas were lighted—nineteen, one for each year of liberation— and blazed through the rest of the show. At the end, shattering gunshots were heard at intervals—one for each of the units as, one by one, they marched out. —After that, I was told, dancing in the streets till far into the night.

Also saw, the next morning, at the stadium, the rallying and start of the parade, which was more or less the same thing, though not so elaborate. —I went afterwards to Kollek's house, where I met a number of people: the Liberian ambassador and his wife, Dasya Chalyapin's brother, an English Jewish lady, who had contributed to the Masada excavation, and Pearlman's very nice sister. Kollek has a splendid library, especially dealing with this part of the world, and collections of ancient pottery and jewelry, etc., in glass-protected cupboards set in the walls. Handsome and dignified wife; pretty little girl with red hair. They took me to the house of a man named Sherover, one of the few local millionaires. He has built himself a wonderful house, with walls of specially made mosaics and a collection of modern pictures, mostly in very bad taste: The one of which he is proudest is an interesting portrait by Repin of Chukovsky in his youth: he looks ironic with his black slanted eyes. Sherover bought it for $35,000. He arranged, it seems, our first loan to Russia, and was suspected of being a Soviet agent. I suppose it was on this account that he went to live in Venezuela and became a Venezuelan citizen. Now he lives in Jerusalem, having married an Israeli wife. I sat next to him at lunch and found him most amiable; but, with his gray eyes and rather neuter face, he does look like a shifty character. We had lunch in a roofed-over gazebo—very modern: the top was a kind of pinched-in bonnet. Sitting on my other side was Harry Zinder's wife. She told me that her family were Sephardim who had come straight from Spain to Palestine in 1560. When I asked her whether she knew Grodzensky, explaining that he had worked on a Yiddish paper, she said—I thought rather snootily—that she didn't know much about the Yiddish-speaking people.

Second visit to Flusser: I had had lunch at the university and arranged to go to see him later. —I brought his wife a dozen roses—I thought the poor good woman needed them: her ankles are swollen like gateposts. When I entered with the bouquet, I explained that I had brought it for his wife. "Wife, appear!" he called. Flusser told me about his visit to Delhi, as a representative in some kind of conference. When he left, he was the only one who was treated as divine: they kissed his feet. He is such an extraordinary figure that I can well believe this. One man said to Flusser, "I understand your problems: I have read *Exodus*." F. swears that he himself has not read *Exodus*.* He is primarily, I think, a student of religions. I told him that Mohammedanism bored me. He agreed that the Koran is unreadable. Then he told me that the dynamitings and other annoyances on the part of the Syrians were the result of the belief of the Arabs that they were still fighting a holy war. The Jews, by Talmudic times, had already given up this idea (he attempted to explain away "an eye for an eye," etc.); but the Muslims believed they were defending their religion when they blew an Israeli up, whether a child or a woman, as they had when they were fighting the Christians. And it was also a feudal mentality, with its long tradition of feuding. The Israelis would attempt to retaliate, on the ground that it was the only language the Syrians could understand, but they did it without much conviction; "and they don't succeed." The difference between the Christians and the Jews is that the Christians have an ideal of forgiveness and loving your enemy, where a Jew can remain indifferent.

* They refer to Leon Uris's popular novel about the struggle of the European Jews to establish a homeland in Israel.

He is really an exceptionally brilliant man, and I am glad to see that people who write on the scrolls—Yadin and Dupont-Sommer—are now making acknowledgments to him. In his own way, he is quite religious: talked, as he had when I was here before, of the "spirit" that is the great thing in life and that informs every religion. —One of the things that make him look strange and Mephistophelian is his large batwing ears that have no lobes but grow right into his face. They tend to be pointed and glare out from his head. The only time I have seen this before was on the unattractive Pole on the train when I was coming out of Russia [in 1935], whom I described in my Russian diary.

The Light of Jerusalem

A certain bleakness and emptiness about Israeli Jerusalem; and yet it is stimulating. It is partly the light, I suppose: "I am the Truth and the Light."* It ought to be a peaceful place among its quiet and pastoral hills: one regrets that it should be so uneasy, but I suppose it has always been so more or less. —One feels that the Jews who have returned must feel themselves half in a vacuum.

The food in the hotel here is peculiarly unappetizing and lacking in flavor. Always cottage cheese and the other kind of cheese for breakfast. No toast on the Sabbath and only eggs boiled the day before because no cooking can be done. In the two kosher restaurants of the hotel, you can only get margarine if you order meat, on account of the

---

* EW was now in the modern Jerusalem that was all that belonged to Israel before the Six-Day War. In an earlier account of visiting the city, he is "waked up every morning early by the bright, firm, and even light, looking out on translucent clouds that hung in a pellucid heaven." Much of the attraction of Jerusalem, he writes, "resides in its combining luminosity with bareness."

Mosaic prescription that a kid seethed in its mother's milk cannot be eaten. Milk and milk products can be consumed only from four to six hours after meat has been eaten.

Spicehandler brought Arnold J. Brand to see me. Born in Boston, teaches in California. He is writing an exhaustive work on Agnon, has been working on it seven years. Has lately seen a lot of Agnon, has been in and out of his house and says it is deliberately desolating. Says the old man is a rascal: lives in a fantasy and misrepresents events in his life, the truth about which Brand has tracked down. I told him that it might produce a trauma to interfere with Agnon's fantasy life. "Yes," he answered: "he might not write any more." But Agnon couldn't read English. I asked him whether he had heard the story about the prize and the plumber. Oh, Agnon had made up those stories years before he got the prize, in prospect of eventually getting it! I imagine Agnon pulls Brand's leg. —They have the Jewish habit of showing up and making fun of their great men. I noticed at the Grodzenskys' a similar tone in regard to Yadin—for his showmanship and skill at publicity.

Moshe Pearlman came to dinner Thursday the 18th. We talked for hours. I have a good deal of admiration for him. He knows a lot and is able; is dedicated to Israel. He says that he does not conform with all the observances himself; but if it had not been for the narrow Orthodox, like the old-timers in Mea Shearim, the Jewish people would never have maintained their identity and they would not be here today. He tried to figure out the considerations which must have dictated the dietary rules. Pigs and a certain kind of fish were scavengers, etc. They had done the best they could with conclusions drawn from their observations. He coached me with Hebrew script, which I have about given up trying to read. He said that it had taken him a year to learn Hebrew, being tutored and devoting to it half of every day.

The morning of the 19th, Spicehandler drove me to the hospital, where the small new synagogue with the Chagall windows is. They are gorgeous with their bright blues and blazing reds. Reproductions give no real idea of them. One of my dim and unsteady days.

In the evening, dinner with the Grodzenskys and their married daughter and her husband. As they said, quite a modern apartment. Very pleasant. Grodzensky is humorous and kind, with what Dos used to call the Yiddisher charm. His wife is much more American, also agreeable and intelligent; seems younger than he. Daughter pretty; her husband teaches English at the Hebrew University; he just spent two years in English Cambridge; also goodlooking and seems to have brains; born in Palestine. They told me that there was a very large Hungarian population; much of Mea Shearim was Hungarian. (Yadin had told me that they often, in Hebrew, used a vocabulary similar to the Dead Sea sect.) Agnon's piety, they thought, was something of a pose. Gershom Scholem at the university was the only person who dared to tell him this to his face. Agnon would protest, "I'm a good Jew." We talked about Hebrew, which Mrs. Grodzensky said was "murder." How, without pointings, could you tell whether מלון meant a dictionary, a hotel or a melon?* Grodzensky said that some concessions were now being made to indicate certain vowels. One of the things that Brand found out about Agnon was that he had not been born on the day he said. Grodzensky explained that when his father had come to

---

* Hebrew does not usually use vowels in its written form. The word מלון means "dictionary," "hotel," or "melon," depending on how the letters are pointed: מִלּוֹן, "mee-lone," means "dictionary"; מָלוֹן, "mah-lone," means "hotel"; מֶלוֹן, "meh-lone," means "melon."

New York from Russia, he could not bring himself to write, as had been actually the case, that he had been born on the 4th of July. He thought that it would create the impression that he was playing up to the United States, so he put down another date.

Grodzensky says—what had already struck me—that Flusser has so little in common with academic people that he is something of an oddity at the university. He said also—what surprised me—that he was essentially a *yeshiva bocher* [student of the Talmud].

(I met Scholem when I lunched at the university on the 17th. He is an authority on the Kabbala—I notice that they accent it on the middle syllable. He evidently comes from Germany; told me about a "Third Part" of *Faust*, written by a Friedrich Fischer, who became so irritated by the Second Part that he was moved to write a burlesque of it. I must look this up.)

The women wear brightly colored waistless dresses, like bags—with green and orange or pink and blue stripes of the kind that are painted on toy tops.

The museum—built to follow the hillside—lots of space, everything admirably exhibited. "Shrine of the Book": walled approach of rough stones that are built to slant from the bottom. Inside an effect of caves is aimed at: exhibits of contents of the Bar-Kochba cave; then the shrine proper: Thanksgiving scroll very dark brown, almost black in spots; Manual of Discipline, beautifully written and preserved; Leviticus fragment from Masada, blackened and apparently unreadable, but a photograph shows that it is perfectly clear when photographed by infrared rays; the tantalizing Habakkuk *pesher*, with bottoms of the columns gone, and the equally tantalizing but perhaps not so interesting fragments of the Children of Darkness and the Children of Light; the Genesis apocryphon partly in lacy shreds. At the center of the large pale inverted bowl, crinkled (?) on the inside, is a platform with an opening in the center, from which rises a kind of pedestal on which rests a circular display of the complete Isaiah scrolls which goes all around it. From this rises a blunt clublike prong, which looks rather phallic but is thought to suggest the shape of the jars—or it might be the handle of a huge stamp. Above it is an opening in the ceiling, and it was designed originally as a fountain, which would send a stream beyond the roof so that the water would fall on the dome, but this was thought to be injurious to the scrolls. Each of the cases with the finds from the cave has boxes of crystals in the corners to keep the exhibits dry.

Jerusalem at night, jewelled with street lamps on the main streets, the quiet low hills beyond, no obliterating blaze like a modern American city; a swift rush and hum of cars but not an overwhelming noise of honking.

The fat bourgeois middle-aged or elderly people in the King David who have come on for Independence Day, contrasted with the Israelis: they are purposive, active and do not put on weight. —The Palestinians, quite unlike anybody else. —But the others are touching: they are proud of Israel, and have come on to see the best it has to offer.

Teddy Kollek came in to see me the night of the 21st, after a meeting. He said that the people I saw in the King David were all elderly and rich enough to stay here. The young people went to hostels. —The man who had taken me around the museum had explained that its segmented architecture was due to its having been designed to follow the contours of the hill, and that the new houses and other buildings had all to be made of blocks of the same pale stone. Kollek told me that everything new was controlled by a planning board. They were laying out the highways with a view to have them eventually enter the other half of the city.

He said that he had his number in the telephone book in order to make himself accessible, and that he was likely to be waked up in the middle of the night by someone complaining that her neighbor's dog was keeping her awake.

I talked to Cheshin on the differences in the sound of languages: Hebrew a verbal language, which always sounded emphatic and forceful, Russian a plaintive language, which, even in speeches that were meant to be rousing, had a pathetic and whining sound. I had watched the back of *President Shazar* when he was reading his speech at the Tattoo and noticed how it jerked when he was making some point. But Cheshin had a very low opinion of Shazar, who, he reminded me, was just a figurehead. He always sounded "pathetic," whatever he talked about. Why? "Because he is a Russian." His speech was of no interest.

On the Eve of War

Visits to Yadin: On my first visit, he talked about the influence of the Sect on early Christianity—thought John the Baptist certainly influenced by it, may have come out of it, Jesus probably not, but Paul had evidently absorbed its doctrine. Thought that the importance given Damascus in the Essene writing and the conversion of Paul on his way to Damascus ought to be looked into. There might still have been some of the Sect in Damascus and Paul might have been influenced by them. I said that it was on his way there that Paul is supposed to have been converted: "I leave that," and he passed on. The Gospels were less historical than polemical documents, and he thought that the presence of the Romans is to be felt where it isn't mentioned. People would have gone to Jesus and said, "Rabbi, what attitude should we take about the Romans?" He would say, "Lie low for the present—we'll deal with them later on." There were recurrent references to swords, inconsistent with the doctrine of forgiveness, which may have been imposed on Jesus later on: "I come not to bring peace, but a sword" (Matthew 10:34); "and he that hath no sword, let him sell his garment and buy one" (Luke 22:36); one of the followers of Jesus cuts off the ear of the servant of the high priest (Matthew 27:5)*; and Simon called the Zealot (Luke 6:15) is named as among the disciples of Jesus.

I did not mention the crisis till he had called a taxi for me. Then I asked him if it was a comedy. "It's a strange comedy, with their troops massed on our side and ours massed on the other, and 700 tanks on each side. If they block our shipping, there'll be war."

He has good easy manners, quite far from pomposity or self-consciousness.

Third visit to Flusser: He was perturbed about the crisis.

---

* EW adds the following footnote:
This incident is differently told in each of the four Gospels. In Matthew (26:51) it gives rise to Jesus' telling the man to "put up again thy sword into his place: for all they that take the sword shall perish with the sword"; in Mark (14:47), Jesus says, "Are ye come out, as against a thief, with swords and with stares to take me?"; in Luke (22:49), Jesus' followers ask, "Lord, shall we smite with the sword?" —then after the ear has been cut off, Jesus answers, "Suffer ye thus far (*Eatoe ews toutou*)" (Knox translates: "Let them have their way in this"); in John (18:10), it is Simon Peter who cuts off the ear [of the servant Malchus], and Jesus says to him, "Put up thy sword into the sheath: the cup which my Father hath given me, shall I not drink it?"

He greeted me with "The War of the Sons of Light Against the Sons of Darkness!" He made his deadpan jokes as he always does: "You remember the cloud that Moses saw over Elath!" Elath, just above what is now the Gulf of Aqaba, was then held by the Arabs, who intended to block their shipping through the Red Sea. (I can't find the Biblical reference. Moses, in Deuteronomy, tells of passing through Elath, but there is nothing about a cloud.) But he said it was very unpleasant to have something like that looming—with two young children. "Suppose this whole thing here should be wiped out." The prophets were always right. The Jews were being punished for their sins in the past by disasters that had already occurred, or they were to be punished for their sins in the present—and since the Jews were always sinful, the prophets always came out on top. What saint should we ask to intercede? Jeanne d'Arc? No: she would be working for Nasser. Aquinas, perhaps.

I told him Yadin's ideas on Jesus. "Yadin was a soldier: he thinks in terms of militancy. The weight of Jesus' teaching is different." He then proceeded to give me the most eloquent discourse on Jesus I have ever heard. He is about to write a book about him in German, which he says Rowohlt will publish. The Teacher of Righteousness and Jesus were doing entirely different things. The Teacher was trying to establish a little utopia cut off from the rest of the world. Inside it, they were forbearing toward one another. But beyond that, everyone was an enemy and they had declared war on everyone else, the Romans, the Jerusalem establishment, the priest-kings and the Pharisees and Sadducees alike. The T. of R., Flusser now believes, did not die a violent death—he draws this conclusion from one of the fragments. Jesus, on the other hand, is telling them not to resist authority—"Render to Caesar," etc.— it only makes them stronger, and they will only put you in prison. "The kingdom of God is within you." Yet Jesus was crucified.

In the course of this conversation, Mrs. Flusser, at the back of the house, was listening to the news on the radio. F. went out to find out what it was. Eshkol, the Premier, had just made an appeal to de Gaulle. When F. came back, he said, "If Jesus were alive today and heard that Eshkol had appealed to de Gaulle, he would say, 'Poor man!' " I suggested that Jesus might say, "Poor man!" about Nasser, too. F. was silent a moment, then admitted, "Yes: he would say 'Poor man' about Nasser—but he wouldn't be particularly interested."

I had had dinner at the King David, just as I had done when I was here before, with that nice man in the English department of the Hebrew University, Adam Mendilow. He surprised me by telling me that he had been in the university thirty years. He and Moshe Pearlman have completely lost their attachment to and dependence on England, have something of English manners but feel under no obligation to conform to British convention. He said that Flusser was rather "uncouth," as indeed he is, and I heard from some other source that it had been difficult to fit him into the academic life.

Moshe believes that he has found in Tennyson a conscious construction of symbols—words and lines repeated, etc.—that shows a kind of overall philosophy or vision. This is the kind of thing that they seem to be doing everywhere. He said that *The Vision of Sin* contains a wonderful rendering of an orgasm. I have looked it up. I suppose he means the first part. Perhaps.

Fourteen Jordanians—including three tourists—blown up by a bomb in a Syrian car. —In the course of this crisis,

Jordan has broken off relations with Egypt—they had, in the name of Arab unity, to swear to coöperate with it.

I had my plane reservation for Wednesday morning, and Tuesday afternoon the consul called up to say that he had just had word from Washington to tell the Americans to leave.

Last evening in Jerusalem. Moshe P. had called me to say that he would try to come by for a drink, and he arrived with Teddy Kollek and a former Israeli ambassador and his wife. I told Moshe about my last visit to Flusser, and when I mentioned Eshkol's appealing to de Gaulle, the lady corrected me by saying "reminding." We did a good deal of laughing. I asked Kollek about his garbage disposal: Did they have a dump? Yes. Moshe wisecracked: "And it's all Teddy can do to get it back on the streets."

I got up at 5 and waited downstairs for a car. We hurtled through the winding hill roads that have no fence or guard on the side above the abysses. The driver was gesticulating so with his right hand as he talked that you were afraid he would forget to steer.

The Tel Aviv airport was pandemonium. I was feeling rather faint and was further fatigued by the hubbub, the shrieking and howling. There were foreign Jews of the most varied kinds. Stout old men, with open necks and Ben-Gurion gray hair; chattering Europeans; bushy beards; young and old Orthodox figures, the young men with sprouting black earlocks and beards under their chins, with spectacles and the long black coats that reach almost to their ankles. The old ones you can read about with sympathy in Agnon, but seeing them there in the crowd and with the young ones who were starting on their Orthodox lives, one couldn't help feeling a little of the repugnance and sense of futility that Joe Liebling told me he had felt at seeing these Orthodox rabbis and members of their congregations get off a plane in New York, so shambling and pale and uncertain, so little adapted to the modern world —and that Leonard Woolf registers in the latest volume of his memoirs. —The Air France bureau, with its three or four personnel, was in a state of high-pressured excitement that combined the hysteria of French officials with the high-pitched shrieking of excited Jews. I find that at the Air France desk, there is always an enraged French family making a fuss about something. It was the same thing when I left Paris.

Paris

The plane itself was a great relief. It pays to travel first class. Good food and drinks and attention. The little hostess was the most attractive I have ever seen: black eyes and sharp nose; she must have been from the country, not Paris. She had a natural instinct for making everybody feel that she had a special personal relation with them. She announced, in her English version, when we were passing over Rhodes, that L'ile de Rhode was "Rhode Island." They had also done this on the Jordanian plane in which I flew from Italy. In this case, I set her right. She was cute about it, but I doubt whether she is capable of changing something she has learned by rote.

I was even fainter when I arrived in Paris. I was welcomed at the Castille, which has all the same personnel. This speaks well for the good relations maintained by Mlle Casado. She has somewhat aged in the last three years. The old cage elevator now, at my age, makes me even more nervous. When it didn't work at first, the chambermaid said, "*Il est capricieux.*" If the door has not been firmly shut, they have to go up and attend to it. I tried coming down the stairs, but was on the top floor and couldn't make it: they are slanted down and more and more shallow. When I used to go down in the elevator with Elena, I used to counteract my fear of falling by looking at her and talking to her.

At the Castille as at first in Rome, I realize how much she adds to my life, how much affection and glamour. The old hotel seems horribly dreary: same old shabby and uncomfortable little lounge, same old month- or year-old picture magazines, left behind by the guests. I found a large bottle of red Johnnie Walker in my room, a present from Mlle Casado.

I went out to the rue de Rivoli, more afraid of the traffic, in crossing the streets, than ever, and it seems more undisciplined than ever; and visited Galignani's, but my sight was so dim that I couldn't read the titles of the books, and I returned to the hotel.

I made connections with Janet Flanner and had drinks with her and Natalie Barney at the Continental in the old sepulchral-palatial bar. For the first time, I noticed on Janet's part a reaction of feminine silence and deference: I had the advantage of having just arrived from the scene of operations and being able to report on things they didn't know about.

It is curious to find in Paris that all the shops one knew are just the same—after three years. In New York, hardly anything stays the same from one year's end to the next. The only change I noticed was that the *librairie* in the rue Cambon was no longer functioning.

Thursday. Dinner at the Castille with Massia, Auntie Maroussia and Pet'ka: They appeared swathed in black, in mourning for Uncle George, the general. Pet'ka had a black suit and tie; Masha had a black thing over her head and looked almost as if dressed for her coffin—she also looked more shrunken and paler than ever. Pet'ka seemed in good form. He and I did most of the talking. Auntie Maroussia was uncharacteristically silent but would occasionally interject some clear and firm remark or request in English. The question of Johannisberg was broached, but Pet'ka presently suggested we drop it. Auntie M. had been visiting there, at the invitation of Madeleine, and had obviously been gratified by this, but had apparently also been aware that a struggle was going on between Madeleine and her daughter over the young man the latter had married. Though technically now the host, he was made to sit at table below Madeleine, was helped last and generally slighted. I gathered that this had set up in Auntie M. something of an internal conflict. Marina afterwards told me that she thought that the young man was innocent and didn't really know what he had got into.

Pet'ka said he would phone me the next day and arrange another meeting; but when he did, he said there was a situation. A big oak tree near the house had been blown down by the queer current *tempête*, and the house had just missed being crushed.

In seeing them, I felt again how much Elena embellished one's life, how much she meant to these relatives.

Thursday. Lunch with Bourgois and de Roux. They took me to a restaurant in the Palais-Royal—the Grand Véfour. They said it was the best restaurant in Paris, and I can well believe it. They say it has been more or less the same for two hundred years. Used to be frequented by Cocteau, who made a drawing for the menu.

Drinks in the Ritz bar with Mary [McCarthy]. Her hair is somewhat graying, and at first I thought she had lost some front teeth, but she explained that they had grown apart. Her husband came in to get her. He is quite good-looking and seemed pleasant. She must have managed to mature in these last years. Janet [Flanner] says that she now knows perfectly how to handle herself socially and has been good with West's children—which she never was with Rosalind.

Saturday. I spent the afternoon in the *Luxembourg Gardens*, where I hadn't been in years, had even forgotten that it was on the other bank. I went there to see the big Guignol man, Desarthis, to whom Bil Baird in New York had given me the letter signed "*Mille coups de bâton.*" He was not there at first, but his son admitted me to the "représentation" in the little theater of *La Révolte des Poupées*, a special performance for schoolchildren. The character Guignol has to baby-sit with two naughty little children, who torment him to desperation. The spectacle is varied with pantomime elements: ballets and appearances of fairies and devils. Not at all on a level with Baird and The Little Players: much cruder, with much less taste and imagination. By the end, Desarthis *père* was there. Another show was about to start, and he took me in. This was a conventional Guignol, all done by Desarthis's son. When I went behind afterwards and complimented them, the father said that it was full of rough edges, that it was the boy's first performance of this, that it would be better when they had done more work on it. It amused me that he had been doing Guignol so long that he habitually talked like Guignol: "*C'est mon fils—ha ha!—M Baird—ha ha!*" (I learn from Baird's puppet book that Desarthis is himself a second-generation puppet man, and that he started performing at 7.) Guignol's favorite expressions besides "Ha ha!" are "Oopla!" and "Aw-w-w," which indicates extreme disgusted astonishment. As in Punch, a policeman is killed, but as not in Punch, he is later brought to life. I asked

Desarthis why Guignol wore a pigtail, and he explained that it was due to his origin at the time of the Revolution.

I sat on the benches of the Luxembourg Gardens or sat in the shade on the benches. Very pleasant on Saturday afternoon. With its dapplings of light and shade and its young mothers wheeling their babies, it reminded me of Impressionist paintings. But the gardens are in rather shabby shape. Many statues of poets, etc.: Hérèdia, Massenet, Chopin, Verlaine, Théodore de Banville—some of them cracked or broken.

Marina had asked me to come to dinner at about 6:30; but no driver ever knows the way to the rue Henri-Pape, and the people in the neighborhood are likely not to know either, and I did not at once find the concierge to find out where their apartment was—so I did not arrive till about 7:30. It didn't matter, however, because Marina and the girls hadn't yet come back from the country. Ivan did not at first hear the bell, explained that he was rather deaf. He gave me Scotch, as he considerately always does. He had been playing solitaire with an incredibly worn and torn pack of cards. I showed him the two-pack kind that I now always play, and he was fascinated and wanted me to do it again and again. An old Russian lady arrived—the archetypal old Russian lady, and sitting behind the table and watching the game upside down, she at once began eagerly to take part and went more quickly and cleverly than we did. She had the copy of *Encounter* with my article on Mirsky, hadn't known that the Schouvaloffs knew me. She had known Mirsky since they were children—her family's estate was next to his. Her maiden name had been Popova—rather plebeian, it seemed to me, for a friend of the Schouvaloffs—and she had been married to an Englishman named Pitts. —At last, Marina and the girls arrived: young Marina very pretty but looking a little different, perhaps on account of the darkness of the room; little Alexandra no longer little, but a well-grown, quite buxom girl. When I told Ivan that he ought to come to America, he would say rather grimly and pompously, "I have work to do."

Sunday. I had thought that they were going to call me up and arrange to have lunch and go to the Soviet film *Borodino*; but I heard nothing from them and could not call them up because they had no phone. I decided that either Ivan had made a scene or that their failure was due to Russian vagueness.

I waited till 1:30 and then went to lunch with Lottman. After lunch, we went to the new Buñuel film, *Belle de Jour*, the most pornographic I have yet seen—one of the pictures like *Last Year at Marienbad* and Fellini's and Antonioni's latest, in which you are not supposed to be sure what is real and what is taking place in somebody's mind. They simply make me impatient.

In the evening, I had dinner with Dupont-Sommer. The dining room was closed at the Castille, so I took him to the Continental. We had a whisky in the old bar and a bottle of wine afterwards in the dining room. He had brought me a handful of offprints, talked even more animatedly than usual. He denied the story that I had heard from Nicholas Nabokov that, at some radio symposium on the scrolls, he had announced himself as a *défroqué*. He asked me, in the new edition of my book, to take out the reference to his having been a *défroqué*—which I promised to do. I used the word *"avoué,"* and he corrected, *"déclaré."* He was not even now sure that de Vaux might not have, among the Cave 11 manuscripts, *"quelque chose de redoutable* [something formidable]." I said that I thought that at the present time de Vaux wanted to show himself a Christian, *"bienveillant envers tout le monde* [well-

intentioned toward everyone]." He was silent and his usually smiling face fell into an uncomfortable frown. He said
that I couldn't have seen the "*féroce* [critique]" that de
Vaux had written of one of his books—I suppose the first.
We parted on almost convivial terms.

Monday. Marina called me up to ask what had happened
to me—they had expected me to luncheon. Alexandra had
been hanging out the window. If a definite appointment
had been made, it must have been blurred by the wine
and whisky. I asked her to lunch at the Castille. It was
the only time I had talked to her *tête-à-tête*, and it was
almost as if she were talking to Elena, referring to people
by their first names that I had to get her to identify, and
assuming that I knew all the family situations. The relation
between Ivan and young Marina had been getting worse
and worse—"almost as if it were love." The poor girl would
have to pay for my having turned to talk to her, when they
all came back from their outing, after having talked before
to Ivan. She was going to stick it out till March in order
to finish her schooling, and then come to the U.S. for good.
Marina said she had thought of divorcing Ivan, but didn't
want to leave him alone and thought she was too old to
come to New York and take on a new job. When Alexandra
had heard her speak of having divorced Semyon's father
—which she didn't seem to have grasped before—A. became rather panicky, as if, I suppose, she feared that her
parents might be divorced. (The girls had shown me their
rooms, plastered Russian-style with all kinds of pictures.)
Marina still remains something of a loyal old-fashioned
Russian snob. I told her that I was going to send Pet'ka
Paul Chavchavadze's book, but that it would have to be
kept from Auntie Maroussia. He had been quite objective
about the Revolution. When I said that he had shown Tsar
Nicholas as stupid, Marina cried out against this. I added

Elena's remark, apropos of the novel, that you had to have something between Trotsky and Auntie Maroussia. To my surprise, when I got back and told Elena about this conversation, she, too, protested that the Tsar was not stupid—though he was surely the stupidest monarch in any position of importance since George III.*

---

* Ancestral revolutionary prejudice distorts EW's view of George III, who was scarcely stupid, though certainly stubborn and eventually insane.

AFTERMATH OF THE MIDDLE EAST:
1967–1968

Family and Scholars

Elena met me at the Boston airport. We had dinner, at which I talked, and then we went to bed. It is better to land in Boston, on account of avoiding the New York customs. I had a long wait for my luggage, but you don't have to cope with the Manhattan madhouse.

Tuesday, Memorial Day, everything closed, but I went over to see *Frank Cross* in Lexington. I could see that it was true, as Dupont-Sommer had said, that he had made *"beaucoup de progrès."* He now pushed theological questions off into the remote future by saying that the matters revealed by the scrolls were important archaeologically and historically—"and perhaps eventually theologically." He had evidently seen a good deal of Malachi Martin. He said that he was a "tragedy" and that some way would have to be found for him to use his brilliant abilities—he had already been offered academic jobs. That if a Jesuit got into a scandal with a woman, he could never be released from his vows—which I should think would always leave him feeling guilty. He was amusing about J. T. Milik, who he seems to think is also a victim of the conflict created by his priestly role. Cross said he was an alcoholic and, having got quite drunk at Bethlehem, was something of a problem at a gathering in the director's house at the school—to the consternation of de Vaux, who said Milik was ill and saw to it that he got home. The next day another of the scholars had asked Cross if he had noticed anything odd about his own conduct. He had been with Milik and got equally drunk, but instead of becoming disorderly, he had sat rigid and glassy-eyed, holding himself down. Milik could not restrain himself from chasing the women in the corridors of the École Biblique. I said that not very many women were allowed in the École Biblique. Mrs. Cross said, "You only need one."

Allegro: Neither Sanders nor de Vaux nor Yadin, Dupont-Sommer nor Cross took seriously his present theories about the New Testament. De Vaux said that when he had first come to Jerusalem to work on the scrolls, with Rowley's recommendation, he had been a well-trained young Hebrew scholar; that he had got along badly not merely with Rowley but with the Jewish scholar who had succeeded him at Manchester. Sanders had written to *Harper's* to refute Allegro's article. Yadin had had a confrontation with him at the BBC performance—apropos of Allegro's charges that de Vaux was concealing something —at which Allegro had given them nothing but his New Testament theories. Dupont-Sommer regretted this line. Frank Cross thought that Allegro was now somewhat paranoid: aside from his *New Testament* theories, he believed that everyone else was in a conspiracy against him.

Father D'Arcy came to dinner Tuesday night. When I had asked him on the phone how he was, he replied, "Oh, middling." Elena thought he had aged. I told him that I was very glad to see him and that having served a term at Middletown was almost like having been in the army together. He said, "Yes: it leaves its mark." I told him of the interest of the Jews in Jesus, which of course gratified him. He said that the influence of no other figure had ever been so widely felt. When I told him about the Catholic Church's having refused to let Scott Fitzgerald be buried with his family in the Baltimore Catholic cemetery, his only comment was "Narrow!" He did not approve of the visit of "His Holiness" to Fatima, did not believe in the appearance of the Virgin to the three little girls. Elena, whom he obviously likes and admires, insisted on driving him back to Boston College.

News from the Middle East. Strange to think that I have just seen the people and places that are now appearing in the papers. Teddy Kollek insisted on driving through Jerusalem at the time it was being shelled, in order to encourage the people. Shells went off behind and in front of the car, and a bullet lodged in its side, which he said he would keep as a souvenir. The Markses got away from Jordan just at the moment when Mount Scopus was shelled and the dome of the Church of the Dormition was hit. The dowager Mrs. Vester of the American colony refused to move.

Visit of the Canbys, June 5–8: Jimmy and Mary and two of the children that I had not seen before: Joan and Jamie. Strange that Jimmy should have inherited so little of his mother's thoughtfulness and style; but he has not had much education. He was all ready to go to college when his father died. Jim *père* in the Depression had lost almost all his income from the Pennsylvania mines. I always have a guilty conscience about Jimmy, on account of having let Margaret go out to Santa Barbara with no money and then finding that, on account of Jim Canby's losses, she would have to stay out there and scrape along all summer. I am always glad to see them, but seeing them rather upsets me. Elena

finds Jimmy touching: he brought her some flowers to plant
from Orleans. One thing he does get from the Scotch
Presbyterian side is a very strong conscience. He declared
that he was a square, and declared and loudly reiterated
that for him it was "black or white, not gray"—by which
it turned out that he meant that he believed in marital
fidelity, no playing around with other men and women.
He says that California is so much built up that it is no
longer pleasant, he would like to have a place in Maine.
His wife says that he longs for his ranch. They are em-
barrassingly glad to visit us and say from time to time how
wonderful it is. Camilla [Austin], he says, has changed
since Perry died and she has come back to Santa Barbara,
is avid for social life in a way that she never was when
she was frowning on Margaret's love of gaiety. He has only
been able to give his girls two years of college at Stephens
College in Missouri; but Joan wants to have more, and I
am trying to get her something at Smith. He takes the
children's education very seriously because he did not have
a chance himself. On this trip East, they made a point of
showing Joan and Jamie Washington, and also the sights
of Boston. They are all very California-ized.

The last lusts gutter out.

A force that keeps driving, nagging one that one has no
memory of creating oneself.

That all this fuss should be made about getting one's
penis into a woman—filling people with rapture and despair and stimulating them to all kinds of heroisms and
excesses.

Yet homosexuals don't seem to have flowered and borne
fruit, don't seem to have fully matured: Auden with his
appetite for Tolkien.

———

Usual annual scene with Elena about my going to T'ville—but this time, though very bitter, brief. She sat on the stairs and spat out at me, "I hate you!" The next morning everything was normal and, as usual, she apologized for losing control of herself. To keep herself under control is one of her chief ideals. It was a pleasant relief after Mary [McCarthy], with her love of a good old dramatized Irish scene.

Visit of Reuel and Marcia: She is expecting a baby about next December—is much less neurotic now and has pretty well got over her shyness. She and Reuel called on the Jenckses and the Chavchavadzes, whom they would not see on previous visits, in quite a normal way. Reuel has now grown quite heavy and sometimes almost obstreperous, and makes me feel rather old and small. He has grown a beard to cover up some kind of eczema on his face, and it does not ill become him.

Visit to Lillian Hellman on Martha's Vineyard. All very pleasant and jolly. Mrs. Marshall Field was staying there. She was interesting, as an Easterner, about Chicago. She is from Albany—partly Dutch: her maiden name was Praya—and bears out my theory that Albanians are a special breed with a conviction of superiority and unshakable self-confidence. Marrying, as Ruth Field did, would mean little to them.

Lillian gave me the Modern Library volume with six of her plays. I read all that I had not seen, and I wish that I admired them more. I think that Lillian is a real case of a Jewish writer whose work suffers from the characters not being Jews. It is always the same jarring and jibing family. The old lady in *Autumn Garden* is quite an amusing character, but the sharply witty things she says sound

Jewish rather than Southern. Harry Levin agrees with me that the strength of *My Father, My Mother and Me* lies in her tackling for the first time here an actual Jewish family and writing, as Harry says, instead of the usual sentimental Jewish thing, something outrageously sour. The trouble was that it was too sour to be a laughing success. I was astonished when she told me that *Another Part of the Forest* had been originally conceived as a farce.

We had lunch and spent an afternoon with the Edels, talking constantly about Henry James, which amuses me but bores Elena—who, however, was able to go in swimming. Leon has discovered some evidence showing that *The Turn of the Screw* was closely bound up with James's buying Lamb House at Rye and a certain dread of going to live there alone. I think that Leon is usually right about these things. Much to-do about whether James ever consummated any kind of sexual relationship. This has got Leon stumped.

> Henry James
> Was no good at games:
> He just sat indoors
> With a couple of whores. *

Visit of Marina and Alexandra: Alexandra is 11 now, very bright and droll in her spontaneous remarks. I gave her a magic performance the first night they were here: rising cards, etc. She was evidently very much impressed by the red-feather pen that I use as a wand—*la plume magique*. In the end, I said, "Well, that's enough for tonight." "*Assez d'émotion,*" she assented. The second night I gave her another performance and wasn't sure that she didn't see how some things were done, and she wasn't *à la Russe*, playing up to me by pretending not to. She said this time that

---

* This quatrain is found at the end of one of the ledgers of the 1960s.

something was *"très amusant"* when she had before to Elena said, *"C'est miraculeux!"*

She said to her mother, *"Edmund nikogda ne krichit na Elenu* [Edmund never raises his voice at Elena]." Marina is very much fed up with Ivan. She spoke for the first time to Elena of Ivan's homosexual past: *"Il a des méchancetés* [the vices] *de pédéraste."* I talked to her about his writing. She said that some of his shorter things were better than the long novel, *Khleb i Moloka* [*Bread and Milk*], which, she thought, had too much of Joyce in it. He adored Joyce, and she didn't, and "That's what all the trouble is." It seemed to me strange that all the trouble should be caused by disagreement about Joyce.

Marina tells long stories about Russians that I never can understand. I asked who Mrs. Pitts that I met at her house in Paris was, and I never really found out because she went into one of her stories. Who was Mr. Pitts? "Oh, I don't know. An Englishman." Difficult for her to answer a direct question. Elena says she has always done this. It is characteristically Russian and akin to their gift for fiction (like their lying). This tendency is the explanation of the difficulty of finding out the truth in such matters as the death of Alexander I and the Grand Duchess Anastasia— also, the truth of how *Doctor Zhivago* got out of Russia: the Brussels Exposition, etc.—stories and counterstories, everyone wants to make up a story.*

Arrival of Thorntons: Elena and Sandra less shy, Nina not quite such a nuisance. The twins have pretty little

---

* EW had been correlating the Russian language with impressions of the national character since his four months in the Soviet Union in 1935. In *A Window on Russia* he notes that the Russian *Vryosh'*, for "You lie," has come to be used with the meaning "You're crazy! You're talking nonsense!" Citing Turgenev, he believes that lying is a characteristically Russian vice, "bound up with the exercise of the Russian imagination, which excels in the novel and drama."

hands. They still like to hear the story about the little girl and the bears, which I have been telling so many years and am getting rather tired of, but they apparently would rather have me tell it than read them something. I now have the little girl married—her young husband doesn't approve of the bears, friends from before their marriage, and won't learn to talk the bear language.

Elena worries because Daphne brings pressure on Henry to earn more money, and they always live beyond their income. She doesn't like his having social relations with the Jewish members of the firm. But he seems to be resisting this pressure. —I nevertheless like Daphne and get along with her very well—I think because she doesn't like Jimmy [Elena's ex-husband], who for some reason doesn't seem to approve of her.

Country Excursions; Rosalind at 43

<*T'ville*. After day in Boston, arrived by plane on July 20th. Mary drove me up and was in a very bad mood. She had just had a row with her boss, and their relations seem to have suffered a fundamental change. He has evidently made her drop her charm school and other extra-pharmaceutic activities, and she claims that he drives her so now that he will hardly give her time off for lunch. She has been working very hard this week and will be next, because it has come her turn to cook. In the spring, she took Susie and one of her girl friends to Spain and Portugal on a tour that for Mary and Susie cost $1,200 for two weeks. She says that now she has once been to Europe, it will be easy for her to go again. Susie can speak some Spanish, and Mary thinks that her health is better and that the trip has done her good.

I found Rosalind and the house in better shape than I

had expected.> Mrs. Hutchins had, as usual, put everything in order, and Rosalind has really made an effort to
pull herself together. She gets me breakfast at 9, and we
go into Boonville at 3. She is very careful about drinking
—will not drink anything if she has to drive any distance.
Otherwise, a glass of wine. But she still has two wild cats,
who run away and hide whenever they see me. The new
one is obviously in a traumatic condition, having been in
her former mistress's apartment for a week after she had
died before anyone had yet discovered it. Rosalind's old
convertible is falling to pieces. I have made her get two
new tires put on, and a new muffler and exhaust have
been ordered. The back has come down and has never been
fixed, and when it rained the other day, it became a trough
full of water. When I called her attention to this, she said,
"I bail it out." I am also making her get this attended to.
She is still rather childish with me, but when other people
are around—as at the Morrises'—she behaves in quite a
grown-up and dignified way.

The Morrises had gone to Bass River, with the idea of
spending three weeks on the Cape, but were appalled and
hampered by the summer traffic and finally driven away
by the constant rain. They came to drinks at Wellfleet one
afternoon, and I was regretting that I should not be seeing
them here. But they left the day after I did, and I was
astonished when Glyn called me up and said that they were
back in Lyons Falls. He told me that he had said to Gladys
that they could watch it rain just as easily and more comfortably at home. We have been to dinner with them twice,
and he took us up for a tour of Tug Hill.

<T'ville is rather fading out on me, but it makes it less
lonely to have Rosalind here. I have had, as I always do
when I first get here, a wonderful sense of quiet and
freedom, all my time to dispose of myself. The traffic is
not so bad, and the delinquents either working or mar-

ried.> No kids on the steps as yet. Mabel Hutchins is cheerful and well.

<I am reading the biography of Cole Porter, and I can hardly believe, at my age, that I really lived through all that period and that I did all the things that I did—Mary Blair, Frances, Margaret; *Vanity Fair, The New Republic.* Some wonderful things to look back on, but also naïve and nasty things that I hate to have to remember.

The Crostens came in for drinks. They told me about the jobs to which they had to resort in New York when they were first married. She worked as a detective for a law firm till she quit when she became too sympathetic with a client she was hired to spy on; Loran worked as a gigolo escort and was warned not to go to bed with the ladies that he escorted. At night they would tell one another about their day's adventures.>

Beverly and her husband were here, with their two very cute little girls, she looking very pretty again. She has been mowing my lawn. She hasn't seen her father since she's been married, and he didn't come to her wedding.

<*Expedition to Sodom:* I have always been curious about this place—how it came to be named that, how the inhabitants felt about it. I assumed that like other names around here, Carthage, Rome, Utica, Ithaca, Tyre, Poland, Denmark, Copenhagen, Russia, Peru, etc., it had simply been picked at random, by ignorant people who ran through atlases, classical dictionaries and Bibles. They thought that Sodom must be all right because it was found in the Bible. These names I have always found irritating.

I got the Pcolars to drive me over there one Sunday. It proved to be quite a long way—to the east of Speculator —in a wild and primitive part of the Adirondacks. I began to think it probable that the people who lived in Sodom had never read the Bible. A few scattered camps, a few inhabitants—we wondered what they did. We had lunch at a rather crude restaurant. After this, the road was no longer surfaced. Someone from whom we asked for directions said of Sodom that it was down the road: "You just wink your eye"; and actually we passed through it without noticing it. Then we asked a man who was evidently a summer visitor, and I inquired why the town had been named that: "I don't know—they missed out on Gomorrah." When we succeeded in identifying Sodom, we found a motel there: the Black Mountain Ski Lodge and Motel, run by a German Jewish couple from New York, Karl and Erma Kappler, who had come there four years ago. There were a few Jewish camps there. When I asked about the name, Mrs. K. said, "God was kept busy knockin' off the horns of the people." "Horns?" She stuck two fingers up from her head. "When he decided to wipe it out, he certainly made a good job of it. What I call Gomorrah is down the road. If it was cleared away, it would be beautiful." I thought this must be some sort of eyesore, but Mary said afterwards that she thought it was "a house of ill repute"—which I had difficulty in imagining in that hardly populated spot. Mrs. Kappler said that a man who, I gathered, had recently bought property there wanted to have the place known as Peaceful Valley. She referred me to the Methodist minister, who she said was a fine man.

But the minister explained that he had only just come to the church there and referred me to the minister of the Pentecostal church, a Mrs. Allen. He said that this was one of the "more emotional" sects. Glyn Morris tells me that they are the same as the Holy Rollers. They have religious orgies, at which they babble with strange tongues; and we found, after driving over a terrible road, that the Allens were preparing for one—a picnic and camp meeting:

a tent pitched in the yard. Mrs. Allen was a sturdy and pleasant woman. She said that she had been born in Sodom and always lived there, and taken the name for granted, and that it had only been lately that people had been asking about it and that she had given the matter any thought. She said that there had been a Mrs. Clarkson there, who had originally been a Hudnut, and that her papers, which might throw some light on the subject, had been given to the Blue Mountain Lake Museum. We exchanged addresses and promised to send one another anything we might find out. When I left, she said, "God bless you.">

Expedition to Clinton: I had called up the Briggses and Grace Root. I invited myself to call on Grace and asked her not to have any of the college people. She asked eagerly whether my "nice wife" would be with me. <She is now almost completely immobilized. She explained the account of herself that had puzzled me last summer, when she had said that she was a New Englander all day, busily writing letters, etc., but that at the end of the practical day, the Dutch side of her took over. She simply meant that she then began to drink like a Dutchman, and said that she would now illustrate it and had a bottle of wine brought in. We talked about Albany, her elaborate garden—she said that she had got to prefer plants to people—and a neighbor who was the grandson of Grant and occupied much with the American Legion. Her son and his wife came in,> he seeming rather unoutgoing and wooden, she blond, handsome and never smiling. <We talked about the Middle East, where he had gone first in the State Department but afterwards as an agent of Standard Oil.

The Briggses picked me up. I had just read his dissertation on Harold Frederic and thought it was the best thing I had seen on him. I found them more interesting than I had last summer, when I had had little chance to talk to them. She is extremely attractive and bright, went to a Radcliffe program after college and has worked in publishers' offices. I took them to dinner at the rather curious Alexander Hamilton Inn, where I was staying: TV, a small refrigerator with ice cubes, but no telephones in the rooms. Whisky in my room afterwards.

I stayed in bed all through the next morning, then went to the Briggses' for lunch. They have just adopted a baby, and their cat has just had kittens. They had invited only Charles Todd and his wife. He occupies an old-fashioned chair of rhetoric and oratory, and is the man who has just discovered and is making the big hullaballoo about the Utica universal genius, A. B. Johnson. He is celebrating an anniversary of Johnson's birth or death by two days of festivities and tributes at the Munson-Proctor Institute, upon which he has been working for a year and for which he is bringing from all over the country—and even one from Sweden—scholars who are interested in Johnson. These are to end with laying a wreath on Johnson's grave and a bang-up cocktail party. He is himself mostly interested in literature, used to know Eddie Marsh and has read a lot in all that period, says that "Dover Beach" is his favorite poem and is a most enthusiastic fisherman. He is entertaining to talk to except that the conversation always gets back to A. B. Johnson. The Briggses and his wife kid him about this, and I felt that the next step would be a theory that Johnson wrote Shakespeare. One cannot help being driven into a certain antagonism to Johnson. Tom O'Donnell and Briggs and I are really beginning to feel that we are running Harold Frederic against him. Tom has been assigned the function of speaking on Johnson's fiction, which he says is mediocre—"If he was ahead of his time in semantics, he was far behind it in fiction." He says that Johnson is about to be canonized, and he is going to play *Advocatus Diaboli*. I remarked to Todd that Grace

Root found the unpublished autobiography boring, and he was rather miffed at this: "Grace is not an intellectual. There are beautiful descriptions of an autopsy and a hanging, and Grace wouldn't like those." When mention was made of our original plan to have performances the week after his, he protested: "I don't know whether Utica could stand having two great men sprung on them, one after another." I told him that I had a suspicion that he himself had invented Johnson, and he said that Lewis Jones had accused him of this. > His wife, who says that life has not been the same since Charles discovered Johnson, is amusing and witty. She knew the Bishops, and we pursued the conversation that we were having about them last summer. She rather admires Margaret, in spite of understanding her character—says—what for me doesn't make it any better—that she hasn't the slightest idea of how destructive she is. <Altogether a very gay Sunday lunch that lasted till late in the afternoon.>

In the month I have spent with *Rosalind*, I have got a better idea of her present state. Living here has been a good thing for her; it has obviously expanded and aerated her life after her dirty and slatternly little apartment. She has got to know the people, and they seem to like her. She now knows her way around. She is trying to control her weight—goes in swimming every morning and takes walks, skips lunch and will not eat sweets. She has been most conscientious about not drinking (which has not been the case with me—I've consumed about a pint of whisky a night)—only an occasional glass of wine. When we went to the Tharrett Bests' party, she really put herself under discipline. She explained to me—quite truly—that you had to drink to get into the spirit of an affair of that kind; that she would put in a brief appearance and have one drink and leave—and she actually lived up to this. With me, she is partly still infantile, begins to squeal and shriek when I complain or ask her to do something she does not want to do. I suppose I to some extent provoke this by a sharp peremptory tone. With other people, she seems automatically to giggle and laugh; but she has a pretty good idea of returning hospitality and what to do as a hostess.

I'll just have to accept her the way she is and not expect anything different from her. I'm giving her $5,000 a year. I don't believe she'll get a job, and I've told her that she'll have to get along on this—that I'll also pay her doctors' bills. But I have been extremely depressed by what she has been reduced to—when I think of how pretty and cute she used to be and the hopes that we used to have for her, all the summers I spent with her and all her grandmother tried to do for her. She is now 43 and seems to have no ambition and no realistic plans, no one she is really close to. She gets my breakfast at 9 and does various chores during the morning but lies in bed most of the afternoon and evening, seems never to sit outside, except for a short time on the porch when she is giving her cats their outing. These cats are still quite wild, they run away when they see anybody but her. Her whole life seems to be ending in a blind alley. She reads biographies of Lytton Strachey and Sir Richard Burton, the kind of thing that entertains her. I occasionally hear her pounding her typewriter or see her writing at the table in her room, but it is probably merely letters to friends.* I believe that her relations with her friends—with whom she always seems amusing and merry—are the things that she now most enjoys. I don't think she depresses *them*. I don't know whether underneath she is really bitter and sour, or whether that is just

---

* Perhaps EW does not give Rosalind enough credit here. Though she had seemingly abandoned her literary career, the detail of the stories in *Near the Magician* (1989) suggests that she was setting down bits of her own history and of her family's.

the effect that *I* sometimes have on her when I jar on her dream world.

"Pent-up Emotions" with Mary

After all the bad food in the local restaurants and with a disinclination I have for dinners in our own dining room, I was driven into a morbid desire to dine at The Ferns in *Old Forge*. I tried the Crostens, the Edmondses and the Pcolars on the spur of the moment, but none of them would go. Rosalind was still suffering from her enteritis, for which she had been taking her combination of atropine and belladonna, and was unfit for such a trip.

The next day, I called up Mary [Pcolar] and invited them all to go to Old Forge. She said they were all tired from the night before, when she had attended to the refreshments at the firemen's annual celebration, but that she would take me over. She turned up looking very well in a dress like orange sherbet and a little crystal necklace that she had bought in Madrid. On the way, she explained that all morning she had been wheeling wheelbarrows of cement to make a curb along her garden. This had made her feel better, she said, by getting her out in the open after the social life of the night before. I felt her arm and said she was strong, and she brought up a hard lump of muscle to show me how strong she was.

The Ferns turned out to be closed, on account of its being Monday, and we took a chance on a largish hotel that was called the Moose Head Inn. This proved to be a quite festive occasion. There was only one girl taking care of the whole dining room, so the service was very slow; but we had two rounds of champagne cocktails and a bottle of white wine with a dinner better than most. There was a huge moose head with its antlers hanging over us from the wall behind. It was one of our long rare conversations when we become quite personal and gay. We talked about the changes in the Catholic Church, and the celibacy of the clergy. I told of Malachi Martin, etc. She said that she supposed that the duties of a priest stood between him and women the same way my books did with me. I think that I was slightly annoyed by this and took it as a kind of challenge. As her face flushed, she became very beautiful. I told her so, and said that her appearance changed so much at different moments. That was what her children had told her when they found her looking plain: "Ma, you don't look a bit like you do when you're talking to people at the store." She said that when she broke out against George, he would not answer back. This would irritate her: "Why don't you say something?" This is one of the things that the Hungarians have in common with the Irish: the need to express themselves in scenes. It reminded me of Mary [McCarthy], and I was glad that I was not under the necessity of taking part in these scenes any more.

I was surprised that she drank so much wine, yet drove so well on the road back. When we were on a dark part of the road, I told her to pull up, that I wanted to kiss her. She did so, and we had a real kiss: it was clear that she was no novice. I had never kissed her before except in a perfunctory way. I put my hand over her breast and encountered something stiff. When I asked her whether she was wearing "one of those things," she said, "No: that's me." I wanted her to stop again, but she said, "No, once is enough—I can't stop, there are cars behind me.—How would we explain the accident?—Have to put you in the back seat!" I looked out rather wistfully at the little hotels and the stretches of black thick woods. It had given me a spontaneous reaction to kiss her—something that has not happened to me in a long time; but I was afraid I had had too much to drink. I told her that she had a lot of pent-up emotion, and she emphatically agreed that this was true.

<*The Tharrett Bests' bang-up party*, given for their married daughter and her husband. I have never seen in Boonville such a demonstration. Tharrett had a policeman in front of the house to check on invited guests and show them where to park. A little grandson opened the door, greatly enjoying himself. The family received at the entrance. Inside was all the local buzzwuzzie of Boonville, Alder Creek, Utica, etc. A bar with a bartender.> Much boring conversation. A retired bank director from New York told me that his family came from Leyden Hill, people named Jenks and Hall, of whom I had never heard. A somewhat grisly divorcée—whom Tharrett had previously encouraged to send me some of her poems—introduced herself and followed me around, explaining that a group of these poems was to appear in the *Beloit Poetry Journal*. Another woman told me that I had been greatly admired by Somerset Maugham.* Rosalind, when she left, indicated, sitting in a chair, "an old lady who knew Grandmother." I made a point of sitting down beside her and found out that it was the hated Mrs. Seifer, who has so many of the best family things in her house. I explained that I was no longer able to identify Cousin Nelly's house, because I could no longer see the quotation on the door: "Open locks, whoever knocks." She said that she had taken it off because it invited unwelcome visitors. Her two daughters were standing behind her chair. I left her very soon on the excuse that I wanted to see Penberthy. <I took him out to the iron benches behind the house, and he

---

* Wilson's attacks on Maugham had undoubtedly made the novelist detest him.

gathered three Utica businessmen to join us. This turned out to be the most interesting conversation I had. We were all wearing party jackets of different colors from our trousers. This was commented on; and it seemed to be a "status symbol." One of the men was the head of a company that had managed to function in Utica after all the other "knitting mills" had been driven south by the New York State social legislation. It makes special clothes for arctic and antarctic expeditions—made to order for any degree of cold and any velocity of wind. They are evidently complicated and costly. Now they also make costumes for astronauts. His account of what the astronauts have to go through was rather grisly. They can't carry any water so as not to increase the weight, and have to drink their own urine, which is made potable by some process. They defecate into a capsule in their rectums, and the capsule then goes down into their pants. >

When I had told Rosalind about this party, she said that it "sounded ghastly." But when she got there, she enjoyed it more than I did. When I said that it had been a bore to hear about the bank director's Leyden family, she said that she had found it interesting. I believe that she may get along with all these Boonville people better than I do. It will be a great thing if, as I hope, she can become a local institution.

<I had to come back to Wellfleet—and was rather glad of the pretext—in order to supervise the reconstruction of my end of the house.> Mary drove me to the airport on the 17th. I told her that our trip to Old Forge had been for me a romantic evening. She said that all the next day she had been thinking about champagne cocktails. I said that we must have some more. She laughed and said— what amused me—"You don't have to be a Hungarian, but

it helps." She said she'd been as if in a dream, and this somewhat embarrassed me.

<Having been in so short a time in so many places I already knew—Rome, Paris, Jordan, Israel, Boston, Wellfleet and Talcottville—it seems almost as if I were in them simultaneously. They no longer seem remote from one another, requiring an effort to reach.> The Mohawk line now has two flights a week from Utica to Boston in forty-five minutes. <I can feel myself equally at the American School, the King David Hotel, the Hôtel de Castille, the Boston Ritz, the Hulbert House and the Blacksmith Shop; and see all the books in the bookcases in both my houses at any moment.>

Summer's End on the Cape

I found young Marina at Wellfleet. She is now very mature, and so attractive and well developed and sophisticated about sex that I am afraid of her following the example of her mother, who told Elena that when she was younger she had to go to bed with a man every day. Her hair is a rich kind of yellow. She has got rather heavy, but says that she expects to walk it off when she becomes a guide for the UN. She sometimes looks like her mother, but something else is now emerging—the traits, I suppose, of the father, who I believe is unknown. She no longer calls Ivan "my father," but says simply "Ivan." We told her that she must not be too bitter about him, and she said that she tried to hold herself "aloof." They have a curious schedule by means of which, in the Paris apartment, they manage to avoid one another. When she comes home, he shuts himself up in the living room that is also their dining room, and they never have meals together. I am beginning to understand why her mother said it was almost as if they were in love. She has wanted him for a father, and he has played this role in a peculiar way, making her read Tolstoy's *Detstvo* [*Childhood*], etc.—over which she says she suffered—breaking up her engagement to some young man, worrying for fear she would lose her virginity. On one occasion, Elena says Ivan came to her room with a threatening fist, announcing, *"Je vais te battre!"* She replied, *"Vous ne me battrez pas,"* and thrust him out by the shoulders. Her sexiness must make him both desirous and envious. In any case, he resents her. She also, I feel, assigns me to a sort of fatherly role. She is quite coquettish with me, waits on me and listens to my lectures on literature. It is pleasant to have her around, and I shall miss her after she goes. She says she is already neurotic about going back to Paris. Our jolly dinner at the Blacksmith Shop, when I said that she was 21 in order to have them serve her a cocktail. She turned on all her feminine charm. She has her mother's wonderful vitality and appetite for life.

This has been a messy, muggy summer—in Talcottville, with rain at some point every day: a sudden downpour which would not last long but for the time being made it so dark that people could not see where they were driving. Then the Wellfleet house torn up and disorganized by the reconstruction of my study. I read in the middle room, write letters on the dining-room table, and other things in the little house. The dampness puts a crimp in my joints, and the rain has kept Elena from swimming. She gets tired and exasperated.

This horrible weather still continues. The stickiness and sunkenness and sunlessness of yesterday, Sunday, I have never known equalled. It seemed to me very much worse than the humidity and heat of Red Bank, which I never minded so much. My inertia and dullness were complete. The little house, where I am now obliged to write till the work on my study is finished, makes things even damper and more muffled and moldering. The old boys' and children's books; the relics from the Thornton family's occupation, inevitable squalor of children, even when one tries to keep them in order. I found the old volumes of Conan Doyle's stories that I bought to read to the boys—this seems a long time ago now—and read a volume through. They are like the Sherlock Holmes stories, but the unravelling of the mysteries has little dramatic interest because there is no Holmes: someone makes a statement or writes a letter which quickly clears everything up. I looked into that old story that scared me so in my childhood, in which a medium at a séance materializes a unicorn. I first saw A *Study in Scarlet* and *Round the Red Lamp* in the book rack on the living-room table in my Grandmother Kimball's house. Uncle Paul had probably brought them for her and Aunt Laura to read. Conan Doyle seems rather stale, too, implausible. Otherwise, I have been reading the second volume of Anaïs Nin's diary and getting bored with the bums that she cultivated in Paris. Also, Tolstoy's *Iunost'* [*Youth*]. This is interesting and full of insight—remarkable that he wrote all this series [*Childhood, Boyhood, Youth*] in his twenties—but I now feel a certain distaste in reading about life in old Russia—the dismal provincial town of Groza, and even this superior milieu. The damp makes my knees, neck and shoulder ache.

Gilbert and Marian Seldes for drinks (Saturday), as well as all *the Schlesingers*, which included Arthur and Marian and all four of their children, with the husband of one of the girls. I asked Arthur what he thought of the state of the country: "Confusion, a madhouse." What would be the result? "Catastrophe." I enjoyed the wisecracking of Gilbert and Arthur and gave out drinks from the sofa and I think acquitted myself pretty well. But when I was seeing the Seldeses off, I had such an urgency to pee that I had to go to the back of the house and wasn't able to hold out till a spurt had partly wet my pants. In the toilet was a young mouse desperately swimming around. I picked it up by the tail and put it on the brick walk, from which it later disappeared. Then I had to go back to the company, with, Elena says, my pants still unbuttoned. The incident seemed to me typical of the general atmosphere. My sphincter and inguinal muscles and the muscles of my throat are weakening.

Sunday, drinks at *Aileen Ward's, with Bill Maxwell* of *The New Yorker* and his wife, Larry Noyes's niece. Strange that I should live to know the niece, now the mother of two girls, and that she should hardly have known Larry and should be almost entirely in the dark about her cousins the Browns. Her father, Bob Noyes, was a lumberman and she grew up in Oregon. She says that her great idea, when she was young, was to get away from, not cultivate, her family. She said that Larry's sister Julia de Forest, who died, it seems, not long ago, had been very cold and formal. Larry must have been cold, too.

Maxwell said that Shawn was a curious combination of Napoleon and Saint Francis.

Sept. 3. Party at the Chavchavadzes' for their 45th wedding anniversary. They have a rich German-American patron who provided liquor galore. Everybody seemed to have grown very old. Elena said it looked like a geriatric clinic: nobody except Joan Colebrook, Odette [Walling], and one or two others under sixty, and those not far from it. I became involved with Brownie L'Engle as soon as I came in the door. She has grown somewhat stouter and now wants people to call her Lucie, would say to Francis Biddle, "My name is Lucie," but he continued to call her Brownie. She was full of enthusiasm about the Israelis winning the war, had listened to the radio for hours, wanted to hear about the Dead Sea scrolls. (Elena has a new story about her. Brownie met her in town and inveigled her into having a cup of coffee with her. Elena also had a doughnut. They contended about who should pay, and finally Brownie said, "I'll let you pay for the doughnut.") I was rescued by Katherine Biddle, who was quite amusing and lively. Allen Tate has just had twins by his ex-novice.* Katherine's poems of rejected love which recently startled us in *The New Republic* were inspired, she told me, by the plight of Isabella Gardner after being abandoned by Allen. Conrad Aiken is back at Brewster and suffering from poison ivy. Francis is rather dim. Bessie Breuer is now so gray that I did not at first recognize her. Joan Colebrook had been back to her old home on the Great Barrier Reef. She got *The New Yorker* to send her to Australia, where she had not been for years and where she spent, I think, six months. This made her more interesting than usual, and I had a conversation with her when almost everybody else had left. I feel, as Charley [Walker] does, that if you live up here, one of one's most earnest wishes gets to be that Paul [Chavchavadze] and Joan will get something published. Ed Dickinson I met at the bar, where we both helped ourselves to Scotch. As usual nowadays, he was lively and cocky. Francis Biddle doesn't like him, but I don't know why. The party, we thought, was a great success. The people, just because they are that old, had all known one another from a long time back and got along

---

* Before taking final vows, Helen Heinz had withdrawn from the religious order to become Tate's third wife.

well together; and one did not feel any strain of the cost of hospitality to the Chavchavadzes. But Nina does not look at all well.

Penelope Gilliatt's visit: Abundant red hair—her maiden name was Conner—very pleasant and easy to get on with—she laughs heartily at all my jokes. Told Elena that she and John Osborne had apparently been happy together till Osborne became quite deranged and blamed on her everything bad in his recent life. She has now taken up with Mike Nichols and has been living in his apartment in New York while she does summer movies for *The New Yorker*. She spoke of the "genius molls" in London. I had thought of them as writers' molls. I think she felt that she was one herself: Kenneth Tynan, John Osborne, Mike Nichols.

She told me of going out to dinner in London at seventeen, and misunderstanding something said by the man sitting next to her wearing garters—a Black Rod?* She mistook the word *fellow* for *cello*, and they had a long talk about the cello, in which neither of them had the least interest. She said that it was an example of the silliness and futility of London social life.

Sept. 30. My new study and attic are all but finished. Elena has been madly cleaning and painting, it is mainly her design. But sorting out and organizing the books still confronts me as a very heavy job. I have accumulated a huge junk heap of stuff that I am going to sell or give to the Yale Library. I alternate by being depressed at the staleness of all these old volumes relating to subjects that years ago I have read up and written about and satisfied

---

* A Black Rod is an official in the House of Lords and usher to the Order of the Garter, responsible for maintaining conversation.

at getting my library really for the first time manageable
and a more comfortable desk at which to work.

I noticed one day for the first time that Elena has little
fair hairs growing out of her upper lip and cheeks. It had
never occurred to me that, even with age, this could happen
to her. Nina now has quite a black mustache.

The Pamet Road girls seem under a strain and look as
if they were wasting away. It is thought that Marie-Claire
may have TB. I haven't dared to tell them but I couldn't
get through her last book [*L'Insoumise (The Unruly)*]. It is
labelled "*roman*," but it is really a kind of prose poem—
all up in the air, does not take place anywhere and seems
to have no contact with any recognizable reality. "*Nous
n'aimons qu'une chose dans la vie, c'est notre souffrance. Je
vais souffrir; c'est une nécessité pour moi comme de sourire*
[We like only one thing in life, and it's our pain. I am
going to suffer; it's as necessary to me as smiling is]." You
don't know what the hero is suffering about, since you are
told that his family are in easy circumstances, nor why—
about the only real occurrence that I found in the first
fifty pages—he should have stolen something from a
woman in the Métro. I think that Marie-Claire has really
settled down to suffering as a way of life, and that this
involves making other people suffer—in fact, Mary and
Barbara. At the end of this paragraph, the hero says, "*La
consolation n'est pas mon métier.*"

Carolyn Link came to dinner the 28th. She has had a
serious illness and, I gather, an operation from which she
nearly died; but she said that it aroused in her a spirit of
defiance: she wouldn't give into illness. She does look very
much older—still writes poetry and is about to publish
another small volume. She has any number of grandchil-

dren. Elena likes her, and of course I am fond of her, but I have never got over her marrying Henry, and seeing her makes me depressed.

New York State Interlude

We drove to Boston Oct. 10 and spent the night at the Ritz; went on to Cummington the 11th and spent the night with Dorothy Walsh and Helen Muchnic. Seta Shuvalova [Schouvaloff] came to dinner. Her friends had brought her on, found her a place to live and a little work to do and given her a warm welcome. She talked about Ivan's fiction—thought it didn't carry the reader along. She said, of *Evgeni Onegin*, that people tended to think Tatyana's husband older than he was. I had assumed that he was considerably older than she on account of his being described as a *vazhni* [important] *general*. I noticed for the first time Seta's resemblance to Ivan and Alexandra. We went on to T'ville the next day—dined at the Parquet.

At T'ville, I began reading Holroyd's biography of Lytton Strachey, which had occupied Rosalind during the summer. I understood what she had meant when she said that it told her more about Strachey than she wanted to know. Heinemann, for some reason, had sent me paperbound pages of both volumes, though only one is yet out, and I went on reading it till after I was back in Wellfleet. It becomes a kind of "way of life." I don't believe that any such day-by-day, play-by-play biography has ever before been published in England: comic and rather repellent and in the end pathetic. To imagine those whiskered Cambridge men such as Strachey and Maynard Keynes kissing and rolling round together! Then, later on, it gets so complicated when [Dora] Carrington and Strachey set up housekeeping together: she marries Ralph Partridge, then has an affair with Gerald Brenan behind the bushes while Partridge is fishing, then Partridge finds out about it and is furious and gets another girl, then Carrington gets interested in the other girl.

The O'Donnells came up to dinner with us, and we arranged about the Harold Frederic situation.

On the 15th, we went to Ithaca and spent two nights in a Hilton hotel run by students as a school in hotelkeeping—many novel gadgets but not very comfortable. The first night, with Jonathan and Alison Bishop, we had dinner with the Morris Bishops. I didn't know why Jonathan had been ill, and now learned from them that he had had a relatively minor but extremely unpleasant operation. The next day we went out to Geneva, in order to have lunch with Mrs. Florey, who had been writing me about her days at the Hill. She had come there to be near her son, who was an Episcopal minister, but said she didn't see very much of him. She talked all the time—due, I think as Elena said, to her not having had anybody to talk to, had only been there three or four years. She would take my glass to fill it, then stand in the middle of the floor going on with some endless story. If *I* started to tell *her* anything, she immediately vanished to the kitchen to do something about the lunch. I did not get from her about Hill as much as I had hoped. She had not been there long and had not liked it. She had been married to Briggs, the mathematics master, the son of Dean Briggs of Harvard, and always spoke slightingly of her husband. When she was having a child Mrs. John [the headmaster's wife] had been very kind to her, had had her come to the Meigs' house to be taken care of, but she had paid for it by having to be prayed over. When Professor [John Meigs] had met her wheeling a baby carriage, he had said, "You're beginning to have a soul at last." She was very much frightened of him.

She lived on the elegant street of old residences in Geneva, but the town was not so chic for its period as I had expected it to be.

When we got back to Ithaca, we delivered to Jonathan the books of his father's that his mother had planted on us. —His three boys were goodlooking, rather resembled John. Elena was impressed by the attention their mother gave them, putting them, as E. said, before the guests when it was a question of being with them before they went to bed. We had stayed to an eggplant dinner.

We left the next day and had lunch in Cazenovia with the Marcelins. Phito, who had been celebrating prematurely, was quite tight when we arrived. He took me into his study and mumbled in his most indistinct way. I thought he said that Pierre, in the summer, had stayed *"pour trois semaines"*; but it turned out that Pierre had been with them all summer, and that the *trois semaines* were the length of time that Phito had managed to stop smoking.

<*Harold Frederic festival, the 19th:* Said to have been a great success, was certainly well timed: O'Donnell and Garner in the afternoon, the first on Frederic in Utica, the second on him in England; that evening, me on his works, and Briggs on Frederic and Howells—only three hours in all, and we finished promptly at 10. Party at the Schuyler Club afterwards:> I had invited the Munns, the Morrises, the Pcolars (only Mary came), the Howlands, the Marcelins, the Bests, the Penberthys, the Wassermans. Grace Root came to the lectures, but not to the party. <This, I think, was a success, too; but almost everybody stayed in the ladies' lounge, where the bar was, with the inevitable cocktail-party result that nobody could move or hear what other people were saying—though the whole ladies' dining room had been cleared. I finally went in there and had some real conversations. Mary Pcolar found a Hungarian, who had left in '56 and was teaching American

lit. at Hamilton. They talked Hungarian while his French wife talked French to Phito. —The Gauses had come to the afternoon session. They also dined at the club. When I left the table, Jane came over and talked to Elena, whom she was obviously glad to see. When I came back, I sat down with John and talked about Thomas Jones, Jr. Any awkwardness was thus got over.>*

The Marcelins drove back to T'ville with us. Terribly bad weather: snow, rain and very strong wind, but the hall had been nearly filled. I slept late, but Elena filled the morning talking to Phito about civil liberties. Phito had brought me a Haitian picture that I had admired at his house, and I gave him one of my old bar chairs.

Before that, filigree of fine twigs and branches against a sky of dry pink.

Elena drove back on Sunday. The Costas came to dinner with me, and I took them to the Parquet. Read them part of the Introduction to the Russian translation of Wells and advised Costa against the journalistic style that he had sometimes dropped into, in his book on Wells. I was relieved to find that he was aware of this and already regarded it as a problem.

<Dinner with the Howlands the next night. John had been studying card tricks out of the Al Baker books I gave him. It will be another hobby to help him through the Boonville winters.> I worked on them my extrasensory perception trick. Jessie partly messed it up by giving the cards a shuffle, but they were properly mystified. Lesley ex-Crosten was there.

---

* In *Upstate* EW is grateful their "old friendly relations seemed to be restored," since Gaus was to die shortly thereafter in May of 1969.

Among the Literati: Anaïs Again

Tuesday the 24th. Mary drove me to the airport, and I flew to New York. The club and the Algonquin being full up, I had to get a room at the Royalton, now, after its long career as a bachelor apartment house, turned into a shabby hotel. I thought about Uncle Win's [Winfield Kimball] having spent so much of his life there and finally dying in his sleep. He didn't know George Jean Nathan, who had also lived there, but had noted him in the elevator going up to his rooms with a series of girls, who were invariably, like Nathan, pint-size: Marie Doro, Lillian Gish.

Elena flew down from Wellfleet on Wednesday. The Epsteins came to the Princeton Club, but Jason, after a drink, had to go away to have dinner with Norman Podhoretz. Barbara and Elena and I had dinner together.

The 26th. Lillian's *Little Foxes*, directed by Mike Nichols and excellently acted at the Vivian Beaumont Theatre: one of the best American productions I have ever seen in New York. Afterwards, a large party given improbably at Luchow's. The explanation was, according to Jason, that the present owner of Luchow's is a "climber" and offered to give the party there at his own expense. It was a really dreadful party: rooms above the restaurant too small and constricted, place so crowded and music so loud that it was impossible to talk to anybody.

I'm not sure what we did the next night—went, I think, to *Bonnie and Clyde*, the film about the bank-robbing young couple. Not bad as a picture, but rather disgusting.

Saturday. Dinner at the Epsteins'—Cal Lowell and Lillian. Cal and Jason had been down to the big Washington demonstration against the Pentagon and were very funny about it, but Cal said that it had been one of the fine moments of his life—had marched arm and arm with Norman Mailer and Dwight Macdonald, and had apparently been rather scared when soldiers pointed guns at him.* Elizabeth [Lowell] hadn't come because she was writing a review slating Lillian's play. Cal, after dinner, began to go on to me about the Bible, which for some reason he is teaching at Harvard. His line, when he had talked about it on a previous occasion, had been Wasn't it just a lot of old Jewish folk tales?; now, he would keep reiterating: "Edmund, what do think are the best things in the Bible?" Afterwards, he wrote me a letter in which he apologized for having been "loud and rude." I guess the subject of this sacred book arouses the New Englander in him: he doesn't know what attitude to take to it—downgrading or enthusiastic.

I had had lunch that day with Arthur Schlesinger at the club and the next day—Sunday, when Elena went out to the Thorntons'—in both cases, to talk about Svetlana. Arthur, who, in the summer, had spent a week or two in Russia, said the Russians were convinced that we were building up a plot to throw cold water on the fiftieth anniversary of the October Revolution. The publication of her memoirs was to be the climax, and they had begged Arthur to get this postponed. He had talked to Chip Bohlen about it and interested him in bringing pressure to this end; but the publishers had thought that at that point too much of the book's contents had already been made public. Patricia Bohlen, who had also talked with Arthur, said that in Moscow people had been planted on him to make an appeal to the government; that she didn't think that Bohlen had taken it very seriously; and that, in any case, what business had Arthur, who makes a fuss about Soviet censorship, to try to get our government to interfere with plans of publishers? I agreed. He is naïve in so many ways.

---

* Mailer would chronicle their experience in *Armies of the Night* (1968).

I had discussed Svetlana earlier with Roger. He says that her lawyer, General Greenbaum, has been making money on her in every direction, collecting 10% on the earnings of her book; that she has also been exploited by the TV people—landed in just the kind of publicity that she had been anxious to avoid.

Monday. We took Helen and Tanya to dinner at the Princeton Club and afterwards to *Rosencrantz and Guildenstern Are Dead*, which I had already read and found rather disappointing. It was somewhat better on the stage; but seems a rather juvenile performance, in obvious imitation of *Godot*; and the attitude of R. and G. is rather like that of children to what their elders are doing: they don't understand what is going on.

A crisis has occurred at the Ledkovskys', where Helen has been living. Their boy, Helen's great beau, who has been studying at a Greek Orthodox seminary, has decided that he is not going through with it and is coming home. This means that he will want his room, so Helen can no longer stay there; and the family are thrown into consternation, because they are very pious—the father is a specialist in Russian liturgy: writes music and trains choirs. Helen will stay now at the Winkelhorns'.

Elena left on Tuesday, could not take New York for longer than a week. I stayed on at the Royalton till Saturday. —I had dinner with Penelope Gilliatt that night and took her to Marlene Dietrich. Dietrich got a tremendous ovation. There was an element of obvious lesbians in the audience, and Penelope, who knows her, says she appeals to women as much as men. The next day I took P. to Lou Tannen's magic shop, where I bought three simple tricks for her little girl and a set of linking rings for John Howland. I commiserated with Lou Tannen, because we both had arthritic thumbs—the worst possible thing for a magician. He has given up dealing with elec-

tronic devices, because, he says, when they are out of
order, he doesn't know how to fix them. Penelope was a
perfect audience for the simple enough tricks he showed
her. She is a wonderful audience for any man she likes—
she laughs at all my jokes and plays up to what she thinks
is the "image" I want to project—and one could easily
become addicted to her. She is not bitter about John Osborne and is obviously affectionate about Mike. She is going
back to England to get the divorce—dreads it: it is more
disagreeable in England than here. I remembered Mamaine getting divorced from Koestler. I imagine that the
trouble has been that she has wanted to please her men
too much. An embittered quarrelsome fellow like Osborne
probably wanted a woman who challenged him.

That night, Thursday, I had Anita Loos to dinner at
the club. We talked until about 10, when she had a car
sent for her. We have a period and acquaintances in common but not a real past, so that we cannot be on intimate
terms. Talked about Cole Porter, whose biography I had
read last summer. She thought he had collected his wife
as a beautiful expensive object—was completely homosexual and had treated her rather badly, had probably never
slept with her. But Anita is always likely to see the ugly
side of people.

The next day the same kind of evening with Anaïs—
more interesting because more intimate. I learned for the
first time why she had suddenly refused to see me. She
had felt that my review of *The Glass Bell* was a turning
point in her reputation and that I hadn't followed it up in
the years when she was publishing her books and people
had been neglecting her or making fun of her. At the time
she had known me, she had been frustrated because she
wasn't able in New York to assemble the same kind of
circle that she had been accustomed to in Paris. She
wanted to ask me a question before she published the next

volume of her diary: had there been anything personal about my dropping her at the time? I assured her that there had not been. I had written her a letter about her books which she said had profoundly depressed her. Sensitivity was her "flaw." She had not understood, and still, I think, does not understand, that I was trying to tell her that she would not attract attention or even get readily published if she continued to offer thin slices of a larger more ambitious work which ought to be more comprehensible. *

I asked what she had been living on when she was entertaining so freely in France, and she explained that she had gotten married and that her husband was often away travelling as a representative of the City Bank in New York. She had been married at 20, but had left out of this version of her diary all the "bourgeois" side of her life. This had been explained by her literary agent in the introduction, which I had not read. Hugo had not wanted to be mentioned because it would not look well at the bank for him to be known as the husband of Anaïs Nin. I had never understood, and still don't, her relationship with Hugo. She has evidently a fantasy life—of which the diary is a record—that is quite apart from him. † I pointed out that it is only in the second volume that the reader is told that she has a husband. Yes, she said, she shouldn't have mentioned it even once. She couldn't explain why she had to go back to America, because this would have involved explaining that it was because Hugo had to go back.

---

* "I enjoyed our reconciliation," Nin wrote to Wilson after this meeting. "I have missed your civilized and sharply accurate criticism in this age of inchoate, wild adolescent reviews."

† The banker Hugo Guiler took the name of Ian Hugo when he became a filmmaker and illustrator of Nin's books. There were many who did not understand their marriage. Aware as Wilson was of Nin's sensual exploration of the female psyche, he did not know that by this time she also had another man, with whom she lived in California, commuting by plane. When in New York she stayed with Hugo and maintained a close relationship.

—Even in the light of the club, she didn't seem to look any older than she had more than twenty years ago. She told me that she was 65 and Henry Miller 75. When she had been in California, she had listened to him talk about the Japanese nightclub girl he had just married, but wouldn't go to see her. She did all her writing now in California, where she had friends—found it impossible to work in New York.

I had lunch next day with Tom Matthews. He has been divorced by Martha Gellhorn and has married an English-woman, of whom he seemed very proud. He explained to me her distinguished connections, but I have forgotten what they are. He is always in the pants of some woman. He wears a hearing aid, and rather cultivates the character of a gruff old English clubman. He wonders whether he ought to come back to America. He had just been for a visit to Princeton, which, though much changed, had made him nostalgic.

"Monotony of My Life and Its Limitations"

I flew up to Boston that afternoon, but the Cape was then so foggy that the Provincetown plane didn't fly, and they drove us there in a Hertz car.

The next day I found myself in total collapse and couldn't do much of anything for several days. When I first got to New York, I was sleepy all the time. If I took a second sleeping pill because I had not drunk enough to put me to sleep, I could hardly wake up all the next day. All this coming on top of our activities up in the country. Trying to finish up some work in the *New Yorker* office, I got through what I had meant to do, but when I came to read the proofs in the country, I decided that I hadn't done it very well; seeing people and talking and drinking or going to the theater every night and sometimes having talkative lunches; getting taxis in sometimes pouring rain; and tottering out to go to the bank and make some purchases had completely put me out of commission. It is a bore to be tired so easily. Elena, having had to do all the sometimes difficult driving—bad weather, road construction—seemed to be as exhausted as I was.

Monotony of my life and its limitations: I wake up first about 4 and read for a couple of hours. I look up from time to time and gauge how near morning is by the blue of dawn outside the window. Then I go to sleep again and have an unpleasant dream, from which I wake feeling rather worse than I had at four o'clock. I sit on the edge of the bed for a while and stare at my bare feet. I look in on Elena, who is lying in bed and who may or may not have had a good night. She says that she will soon give me breakfast and I tell her there is no hurry. I then go to my bathroom and sit on the toilet, reading Jules Renard's journal or something, which helps me to face the rest: getting the yellow goo off my tongue with a washcloth or towel, hawking up blood-embrowned phlegm, perfunctorily brushing my largely artificial teeth. I then sit in the middle room, and Elena brings me breakfast, at the end of which I take a digitalis. Before breakfast, I do serious reading, which I continue for a time after; but during breakfast, I read papers and magazines, which are easier to skim through and handle. I don't get to work as a rule till eleven or twelve o'clock. Since I have been back from New York, I have done nothing but *New Yorker* articles, writing letters and catching up on this journal. About 3, we go to town for the mail, the papers and a pint of whisky. If it is fine and I feel up to it, E. takes me for a little walk like a dog, or a short drive. In the late afternoon I get a drink and shave, playing the phonograph—for which the enlarged room provides much better acoustics. Then I go into the middle room and play solitaire, slowly nursing my drink. Elena gets us a modest supper, after which I read or play more solitaire or am so muggy and sleepy that I go to bed and take a Nembutal or a whisky and go right to sleep. I now try to resist the temptation to finish my unfinished drink in the early morning or to supplement it from downstairs. If I do, I lie in bed, my mind very active with attractive ideas, which, however, when I come to rather later, I know that I am in no shape to realize and can only crawl to my bathroom and mechanically get a new day under way.

Eben Given brought Rosalind back and came in. He was rather tight and, when I asked him what was the news with them, burst out with an account of young Eben's family. His wife, whom Eben had refused to meet, was an Indian, and he turned out to have three children, not, as they had thought, one child, by her. They had finally been produced [for the grandparents] at Truro, and the wife was so well behaved and the children so cunning that Eben felt he had to accept the situation. But her first husband lived with her and young Eben, and the man seemed to be a bum. The woman also had two children by this man. Phyllis's daughter in California [by her first marriage] had also married an Indian. Maud Emma had had an Indian ancestor, and I told Eben that the Indians were creeping back. When he left, he said, "Well, I must get back to the reservation!"

During the summer, Maud Emma died at 102. It was evidently a relief for Phyllis. Her mother had seemed hardly to recognize her—would say, "It was sweet of you to come to see me," as if she were only an acquaintance. But Rosalind tells me that when Phyllis went back to Maine, she would sometimes think at night that her mother had come into the room.

November 22. I have done four *New Yorker* articles* and must now get back to the scrolls, as soon as I have brought this journal up to date.

Our Thanksgiving: At the end of the week before, we learned that Helen, now living at Sovka's, was in bed with a "virus." Elena went down to take care of her—the Winkelhorns were going out of town for the weekend. She brought *Helen* back Monday night. Helen then got rapidly better, but Elena took to bed, and the situation was made worse by her drinking, instead of her intestinal medicine, some sort of skin lotion called calamine, which contained carbolic acid. She managed to throw it up, however. We had invited the Epsteins and Penelope, but called them up and uninvited them, and spent the holiday—it was filthy sloppy weather, dark and continually raining—without seeing anyone at all. Thanksgiving is now so pointless that perhaps the best way to deal with it is simply to ignore it.

Penelope Gilliatt says that when Philip Toynbee gets drunk, he has to be put away in whatever house or apartment he happens to be, and that he complained on one occasion that the family with whom he had spent the night hadn't written their names in their books. This was the only way, if he woke up with no one around, that he was able to tell where he was.

Old songs of my childhood go through my head: Harry Lauder, "I Think I Oughtn't Auto Any More"; "Bake Dat

---

* These were three installments of *A Prelude*, expanding upon his youthful journals, and "On the Eve," derived from his notes in Israel before the Six-Day War.

Chicken Pie"; "He Goes to Church on Sunday"; cockney songs of the music halls, songs from *The Red Mill* and *Forty-five Minutes from Broadway*; "The Girl I Left Behind Me"; "Take Me Back to New York Town."

Father's language:

—to make some sort of fist of it

—weltering around in a Dead Sea of mediocrity

—cataclysm

—zounds

—*vapid* was another of his favorite words

—a different breed of cat

January 2, 1968. Went to bed after only two drinks, read Macaulay till late, then took a sleeping pill and went to sleep without difficulty, got up a little after 8 feeling quite comfortable, got to work on Dead Sea scrolls soon after breakfast. Recovering from the holidays and feeling this morning quite fit. Reading Tolstoy and Macaulay alternately. New little brown puppy given to me by Rosalind for Christmas. She got him from the SPCA. He has a short tail and black muzzle and evidently has boxer blood. Is still in the chewing and not housebroken stage, and though appealing, and I think fairly bright, he is something of a little nuisance.

Feb. 5–8, Boston. Saw Cross, worked in [the Harvard] Divinity School: the stacks are stifling and no light in the aisles. —Marian Schlesinger and the Pritchetts came to dinner with us at the Ritz. Victor, with William Plomer and Angus Wilson, has just received the C.B.E. He says that the Queen slips a medal on a ribbon over your head, and that it can be used to cure warts. —The next night, Wednesday, we had dinner at the Levins'. The Pritchetts are living next to them, and the L.'s had had them for drinks. I had heard Harry say a few years ago, "You know he's an autodidact," as if he were saying, "He used to be a Nazi," something even worse than "He's a homosexual, you know." Now he said that Pritchett was "mediocre in this rather poor period of English literature—he has no originality." I spoke of *The Living Novel*, which Harry had no use for, and *The Key to My Heart* and *London Observed*, which he had not read. I said that I did think that Pritchett had originality. "I'm sure you do," he sulkily said. I always feel with Harry that he is another dog just ready to start a dogfight. His formula that I have noted lately of saying "I'm sure you do" instead of discussing the matter, in order to cut the conversation short, is his way of exercising restraint so as not to fly at the other person. It makes things very uncomfortable. He is frustrated by not being an artist, and his style gets more pompous and pedantic and he becomes less capable of saying a good word for everybody now writing, especially in Boston and Cambridge.

It gets to be rather a bore involuntarily trying to remember the words of Harry Lauder's old songs: "The Kilty Lads," "She Is My Daisy," "I Love a Lassie," "Stop Your Ticklin', Jock!," etc. The songs from *The Arcadians*.

The Givens told me that when *Bill L'Engle* died, *Brownie* immediately said, "Now I won't have to go to St. Augustine this winter!" But this is natural and human enough—like my mother's saying, when my father died, "Now I can have a new house!"

—The low gray lake dense-hemmed by misty brown.

January–February–March: incredible monotony of life up here working on scrolls.

Ed O'Connor's unexpected death in March—will leave a terrible gap in our life here. He was 49, but seemed in his prime—still young and full of vigor, and a contrast to our writers who don't write, painters who don't paint, etc. I thought the novel he had been working on about the old cardinal who couldn't understand what—with all the new reforms—was going on in the Church had great possibilities. A truly truncated career. And no more hope of seeing him on the beach or in the Ritz grill.

Auden on Social Distinctions; Malachi Martin on the Church

Trip to New York and Charlottesville, April 3–17: I had dinner, as usual, the first night with the Epsteins, the second night with Auden, with the usual uncomfortable consequences the next day. Wystan tends nowadays to plug with me that we both belong to the professional middle class, who are the pillars of civilization. There was, he thought, no distinction here between professional people and those in trade; he remembered his mother's saying of somebody: "What can you expect of someone in trade." I said that when I was in college, there *had* been a marked distinction, and this surprised him. He asked me whether it wasn't true that I never felt myself inferior to anybody. I told him that in my youth I had rather resented the millionaires. I think that he himself had actually resented being looked down upon as a doctor's son—he had told me that one reason for his coming to America was that, passing through on his way from China, he had discovered that there were no such social distinctions. He said that he *had* regretted not having been sent to Eton. He also asked me whether it was true that I never bought anything that I couldn't pay for right away—he apparently never even had accounts at stores and thought that buying in installments was appalling. He had been told that if this kind of buying should be stopped, our whole economy would collapse. Money wasn't important to him: you had to have enough to live on, but otherwise, it didn't matter. Of course he has no family to provide for.

I asked him how it had been possible for everybody in London to know that Day Lewis would be poet laureate. He said that if you belonged to "the family," you knew. But how? "You just know. Betjeman is too funny. Graves is too old. Day Lewis is a friend of Princess Margaret."

Elena arrived on Friday. I took two separate rooms at the Princeton Club, because our habits conflict so, she waking up at 6 and agonizing till she gets her coffee and I waking up at 4, reading for an hour or two and then going to sleep again just as she is ordering her coffee.

Dinner at the Strauses': Dupee, Daphne Hellman, Vincent Sheehan and a man from South America and the *Times*. Dorothea, always attractively and expensively dressed—always in a new genre, this time Empire—is an excellent hostess, and we always enjoy these evenings.

Saturday. Ralph Hinchman to dinner at the club. Old, gray-haired, more set in his ways and more reactionary than ever. He was something of an ordeal for Elena. He didn't understand what the Negroes wanted that they hadn't got: they'd been liberated, they had the vote, etc. He thought Nixon was the man for President: he'd had experience—the recommendation that he always makes for himself. He abominated Bobby Kennedy. He thought that

FDR had been "the most evil man of our time," and he
hated to use the stamps which at present have his head
on them. His son had started in with a greeting-card business which at first had confined itself to, I think, birthday
greetings, but he had expanded it to all kinds of greetings
and was now doing very good business and Ralph is evidently pleased with him. At a fairly early hour, he had to
go back to Bronxville. He is a semi-retired broker.

Sunday. Elena went out to see the Thorntons and came
back rather dissatisfied. Henry had had to leave early to
go to a bankers' conference, and Elena had come away
more than usually out of tune with Daphne.

I had lunch with Arthur Schlesinger at the King Cole
Room of the St. Regis—the best solution, it now seems to
me, for the problem of where to eat on Sunday. We talked
about politics and the Lytton Strachey biography, which
he is going to review. He was bored and repelled by it.

We went on to see Mike Nichols and Penelope. He is
living in more or less luxury—has a large young Great
Dane bitch and a little fuzzy white dog that belongs to the
rather odd-looking small butler, perhaps a Puerto Rican.
Penelope has a nurse for her pretty little girl. I tried to
make her the jumping mouse, but it didn't come out very
well.* From their high window at 1 East 81st, we watched
the parade for Martin Luther King winding through Cen-

* "Edmund had a trick with a white handkerchief that he called the
jumping mouse," Penelope Gilliatt recalled. "He found it difficult with
arthritic hands and was abashed that he couldn't manage what he
wanted for the child he always called 'the little girl,' my daughter Nolan.
One Christmas he had both of us to stay at Wellfleet and did Christmas
stockings for each of us. They matched, in every particular, except
that my daughter's had a huge stuffed tiger at the top. Then it snowed.
My daughter and I had to go back to New York in a blizzard. From
Penn Station Nolan trudged through the snow, clutching Edmund's
huge tiger, saying repeatedly—as he would have done—'I can manage,
Mommy, I can manage.' "

© *Jerry Bauer*

Penelope Gilliatt

tral Park.* Arthur then left to play tennis. Jackie Kennedy
called up and said she was coming, but I got the impression
she was vague about it, so forgot about it and left before
she came. Mike got tickets for the new Kubrick film *2001*,
and took Elena, Helen, Penelope and me to dinner at the
Plaza Oak Room. I am now getting so deaf that I couldn't
hear what they were saying unless Penelope, who sat beside
me, talked into my ear.

Monday. Lunch with Roger at the club—business and
gossip as usual.

We had been planning to go in the evening to Mike
Nichols's production *Plaza Suite*, but Elena had been to
Dr. Hicks and the next day to a gynecologist to find out
why her insides were disturbed and she had been swelling
up lately. The gynecologist found nothing wrong and Hicks
told her that all her organs seemed quite normal. But he
had given her a shot of something which had expelled her
urine, and when I had waited some time in the lobby and
was about to call up her room, she phoned down that she
had just fainted, so we did not go to the show. I sat beside
her bed till she felt better.

Tuesday. Malachi Martin came to dinner with me while
Elena had dinner with Jean Stafford. Martin told me—
what explains a good deal—that de Vaux was not really
so narrowly orthodox as his behavior might lead one to
believe. The point was that the École Biblique was a Dominican institution that had no official position. The official school of the Vatican was the [Pontifical] Biblical
Institute in Rome; and when the École became the center
for the disturbing and newly discovered documents then
giving rise to speculation, he became afraid of being ac-

---

* King had been assassinated in Memphis a week before.

cused by the Jesuits of shaking the Catholic faith and
having his school closed. This would account for his public
line. Martin said that the first reaction of the Church was
one of foolish alarm. Instead of looking calmly at the scrolls
and absorbing them into their Catholic history, they had
been too frightened to deal with them at all. When Martin
had been writing his thesis, they had cautioned him not
to touch on the contents or to venture on interpretation,
but to confine himself rigorously to the text: his work was,
I gather, simply an examination of the writing of the various scribes. The Vatican had, at one time, made an effort
to buy the scrolls, and they had sent a spy to Israel, after
the Hebrew University had acquired the first lot, to find
out exactly what was in them. —Martin said, as had Frank
Cross, that Milik was a bad alcoholic. He had twice helped
get him into a straitjacket.

As seems inevitable, he got later on the subject of his
ordeals as a Jesuit priest. The three things that a Catholic
priest had to accept were the divinity of Jesus, the resurrection of the body, and the immortality of the soul. If
your colleagues in the priesthood began to be aware that
you were entertaining doubts, they avoided and eventually
ostracized you. They themselves might be loyal to their
faith only by observing its ritual, and keeping its creed in
a shut-off compartment rather like the doublethink of Orwell. They might interest themselves in other things, but
they had always, in their thought, this permanently paralyzed area. The Jews were in the same situation. —What
could be done about ecumenism? Concessions could be
made up to a certain point, but they could not go on indefinitely. There would always be a point at which they
would have to stop: otherwise there would be no religion.

A University Between Past and Present

Charlottesville. We left Wednesday and got there by plane in fifty minutes. I thought of my trips with Father in a slow train, which frequently stopped; at the stations, Negro mammies would sell fried chicken out of baskets.*

We stayed at a Knott chain hotel, the Thomas Jefferson Inn. Food not particularly good, more or less the same as everywhere North. I tried the griddle cakes to see if they were any better than at the Princeton Club. They turned out to be exactly the same: sourish, coarse and too thick. In Baltimore, the same thing. Elena says they are all made from the same instant batter. In the hotel one felt some tension as a result of King's assassination. There had been threats from the outside, Susan told us, of a riot in C'ville. I noticed a change from the past: the waiters and porters said "Yes, *sir,*" instead of "Yassah."

I spent a good deal of time in the hotel room, reading in a comfortable chair: outside the window, the pleasant sight of white dogwood and purplish-pink "redbud" (Judas tree). Elena spent more time with Susan and did more sightseeing than I did. She has a slightly goofy side that goes with Susan's goofiness—she likes to say "Nice!" about people and things—and I think she is on closer terms with Susan than any other member of the family has been. (Mary McC., who always classed people according to whether she thought they were for her or against, com-

---

* As a boy EW had enjoyed going to Charlottesville when his father "straightened out" the affairs of his widowed Aunt Susan. "We would range through the campus at night—the Rotunda, in which the skeletons of prehistoric animals were grinning with great fangs in the darkness—the shadowy white colonnades in which the professors lived—peeking in at low windows where our elders were dining and drinking claret or at the basement of the medical school where the stiffs were laid out in the dark" (*Night Thoughts*).

plained that she could never be sure with Susan, who always maintains an unruffled surface and whose tone with everybody is uniformly amiable and polite.)

I have decided that the best thing to travel with—New York last winter and Israel last spring—is a volume of Balzac. You sink into the familiar Balzac world with the familiar Balzac characters. In the end, you may become disgusted by his sketchy and implausible inventions—which must have been written when he had become too tired—and repelled by his inveterate habit of having the good people undone or destroyed by the bad (see the strange sort of eulogy of unscrupulous power at the end of *Le Curé de Tours*). But I was reading a particularly good one, *La Rabouilleuse*. It is true that the two good old ladies are snuffed out by Philippe Bridan; but Joseph Bridan is allowed to succeed and become a great painter. And Philippe and the other Napoleonic veteran—who have distinguished themselves under their leader but, unwilling to serve the monarchy and not very well treated under it, bring their Napoleonic characteristics into a civil life that has no place for them and become cruel and insolent scoundrels—are interesting and well described. Instead of being allowed to triumph, one is made to kill the other in a duel, then condescending to serve again, to be left by the enemy to be killed by his own soldiers, with whom he has made himself unpopular.

The first afternoon, when we had just arrived, Elena went to Susan's house without me. The cat was just having kittens, and this rather upset Susan. When four had popped out, she left the house. She said, and later repeated to everyone, that she had thought the cat was a male or a "neuter," whatever she meant by that. She evidently did not understand about a tomcat's retractive penis. When she came back, there were six kittens.

Driving around with Susan and hearing her explain

things is very much like driving around with Father and her mother, Aunt Susan, and hearing her explain; but Aunt Susan had a lighter touch and a more amusing way of telling stories, which Susan can only imitate: she goes on, never stopping, relentlessly, making no break between one subject and the next; her old-fashioned language is sometimes unintentionally funny, as when she said that some man had "had no liaison," meaning that his conduct had been chaste.

On Thursday, Susan gave us a party. I was surprised that so many people whom I had not met when I was here before recognized me, when I did not recognize them— except vaguely A. K. Davis, the perfect old Virginia fuddydud, now retiring as head of the English department. Nancy Hale Bowers was there. I had only met her once, at Peterborough [New Hampshire] and did not know who she was till she told me, on account of her acquired Southern accent. When I remarked on it, she said that she had tried to resist it but supposed that she had taken it on by osmosis. Her rather horrible husband, the bibliographer, was also there. He assured me that he was in 70% agreement with Lewis Mumford's article in *The New York Review* attacking the MLA editing of Emerson; but it turned out that his objection to that method was that there was a much simpler way of accomplishing the same thing and indicating the word that the author wanted to leave on record. I could see that he had no real interest or taste in literature. Lang says that when Bowers edited *Leaves of Grass*, it was said of him that he had done everything about it but read it. Nancy Hale enormously admires Elena, and invariably comments on her beauty and charm even in her presence and hearing. Elena says it is because they are both tall and blond.

Good Friday. Snack lunch after church with the Mayos—this light after-church entertainment seems to be a regular tradition. I hadn't wanted to go, having met Mr. Mayo at the party, where he had talked to me about writing something about duelling in American fiction—he is in the history department; but Elena wanted to see the inside of one of the houses on the Lawn, where they live, and thought his wife was not uninteresting. This turned out to have been someone else's wife, and both Mayos were as bad as I expected. Mrs. Mayo picked me up at the hotel. She immediately asked what I liked to drink after breakfast. I said that I didn't drink during the day. "Whiskey sours are nice on a hot day" (this turned out to be her favorite drink). It is hard to fight off drinks in C'ville. I settled for Bloody Marys, but Elena succeeded in refusing anything. Mrs. M. then said, "Tell me about Elena." I asked her what she wanted to know. "Where did you find her?" I explained that it was on Cape Cod. "Well, you found something pretty nice!" Mayo is a curious case: though he comes from Maine, he has completely mastered the Virginia vein and accent. His only trace of New England is his pronunciation of words like *charge* ("chairge"). His volatile adaptability is, however, probably accounted for by his mother having been Irish and his father French Canadian. His name, his wife told me, has nothing to do with Ireland, but was originally Méaux. He is also a terrible bore in the classical Virginian way—fluency that never stops of pleasantry and reminiscence, everything reminding him of something else. He and Susan together were as stultifying as the Bloody Marys, and I got away as soon as we could. We talked, without explanation, about families and local events that we knew nothing about. Also, conversations about cats and dogs seemed to be inevitable: I had one with Mr. M. while Mrs. M. was showing Elena the house.

Susan is terribly afraid that when the present tenants of her basement go, if she applies through the university, she may have to have colored ones. She also feels very strongly about the problem of non-segregated housing; on account of her disagreement on this issue, she has resigned as vice president of the League of Women Voters. The old black section of the street that runs past the university has been torn down and replaced by other buildings. I did not see the colored part of the town, but E. says that it ranges from suburban homes exactly like equivalent white ones to wretched primitive shacks.

Saturday. Dinner at the Langs': Susan, the Bowerses (he came in afterwards), the Shannons (he is president of the university) and a Jewish couple from the university (he had been working on Dos Passos). Violette's mother went upstairs before dinner with the little boy. She looked so young, with quite a pretty face, that I was surprised to learn that she was over 80 and had just had a serious operation. I sat next to Nancy Hale, and we talked about Elinor Wylie, whose biography she once wanted to write, and at which she worked. She shared my low opinion of Nast and my very mixed opinion of "Crownie."* Somebody said something about somebody's not being "out of the top drawer," and she said that there was no top drawer any more. I said that it was different in different places. Nancy Hale: "You have to stay a long time in any place before you find out what it is. If you went to Philadelphia and didn't know what a Biddle was, you wouldn't notice anything special about Biddles." —The Langs' house was so much like their house in Syracuse that I sometimes forgot for a moment that I wasn't there: same porch on the same side, Cecil's complete Pléiade at same end of the living

---

* Condé Nast, who began his publishing empire at *Vanity Fair* when young Wilson worked there, seemed to him pushy and vulgar—"the glossiest bounder I have ever known" (*The Twenties*). EW also deemed the editor, Crowinshield (Crownie), a lightweight, though he was fun when improvising games with the staff and satirizing stuffed shirts in after-dinner speeches.

room, same turtles belonging to the little boy, exactly the same dining room. I suppose that this kind of house is standard for the "better class" of families in the residential section.

Easter Sunday. I took a walk with Cecil while Elena was at church. He had never been around the Lawn; he has his classes come to his house, and has, apparently, only one hour a week—so he had never before really seen it. I took him to Poe's room and the plaque for Minor, of which I am rather proud:

IN MEMORIAM EDMUNDI MINOR WILSON MDCCCXCVII MCMXXXV LEGUM BACCALAU REI HUIUS UNIVERSI-TATIS ET EA ET MAIORIBUS FILII DIGNI HANC TABU-LAM POSVERVNT AMICI AMICVM ET DULCEM ET FACETUM FESTIVIQUE SERMONIS ET IN AMICITIA BON-ISQUE OMINIBUS FIDELEM MOERENTES*

I said, "How did you happen to come here?" He thought I meant why and made a money-getting gesture with his thumb and forefinger. *How* he had happened was through knowing Bowers, who had a course in bibliography at Chi-

---

* In memory of Edmund Minor Wilson, 1897–1935, Bachelor of Law of this university, which with her sons worthy of their ancestors placed this tablet, friends mourning a friend who was pleasant, witty, of cheerful conversation, and faithful in friendship and in all good things.

Littleton Wyckham, the Richmond lawyer who composed this plaque, described Minor Wilson to EW as a charming talker who made people laugh for hours at a time. Susan Wilson believed that drinking caused his death. In fact, Minor died of pneumonia during a swimming trip —having promised his fiancée not to drink, he refused the rum which his companions hoped would revive him. A friend who recalled this had been reluctant to see a plaque put up near the Rotunda for someone who had not been particularly distinguished. The honor of which Wilson was "rather proud" mirrored the ineffectuality he felt among these latter-day Virginians.

cago. He told me that, in the booklet that was given new students [at the University of Virginia], they were told always to speak of *Mr.* Jefferson, never to call the Lawn the campus, and never to say freshmen, sophomores, etc., but always first-year men, second-year men. I said, "You're happy here, aren't you?" He shook his head: "I like the house, I like the landscape, I like the pay," but he didn't enjoy the students, out of whom he got no response, because they only wanted to be Southern gentlemen. The hippie-type students of Syracuse and Chicago had been much more interesting. And there were no homosexuals on the faculty—though he thought there was perhaps one. I asked whether he thought they needed them, and he answered that he did: they were much more lively and stimulating than the ordinary run of professors. He said he had "rejected" the South and did not feel he had to worry about its problems; he thought that, in *Patriotic Gore*, I had been too favorable toward it. This came, I think, from being non-U in North Carolina. —Elena came to lunch at the Langs'. I was somewhat surprised to find that she liked Cecil and thought him interesting. —The dinner the night before had been a masterpiece of Violette's exquisite cooking and Cecil's choice of wine. We had had each a typed French menu in front of our plate. —Susan told us that Violette, who had been teaching Negro children, had not been able to understand why she could not use her influence to get two Negro girls admitted to a superior white school.

I remembered on Sunday that, in showing François-Michel Lang an easy card trick the night before, I had neglected to explain the whole point: announcing what the cards would be before they were pushed out, so had to repair this error. It is embarrassing now that drinks should prevent me from performing these little operations successfully. —I have found lately that I have completely forgotten things that people tell me occurred in the past. In connection with François-Michel's turtles, Elena tried to remind me that, since we have been married, I once had some turtles. Nancy Hale assures me that I sat next to her twice at dinner at Helen Simpson's. I remember going to a party there, to which I took Sid Perelman, but never a dinner. Also, Rosalind's visit to T'ville, of which Susan speaks. She also tells me that I wrote my mother during the First War that at some point I wore sabots stuffed with straw and found them very practical. It is as if these things had never happened, and I have difficulty in believing they did.

Sunday night. Drinks with Susan's boring young downstairs tenants. Like Mayo, the husband, Robert Hubert, only wants me to autograph books. In the evening, we got out old family photographs. Very pretty pictures of Susan. Elena asked her if she had ever been engaged, and she answered matter-of-factly that she never had but had once had a beau. It seemed to be a matter in which she felt no interest.

A Scholar on the Scrolls

The next day, Monday, we left about noon for Baltimore. I had had some idea of taking in Dos and John Biggs, but visits have become so depleting that we decided to skip them both. Clelia had urged us to come to see her, and I had written long before suggesting the 15th, but one of these curious unexplained blanks in our communications had occurred and I had heard nothing from her. Traffic going into Baltimore as crowded and held up as in any other American city. We stayed in Baltimore at the Belvedere, full of bulky drunken delegates to some conference. We dined in the Falstaff Room, where the poor old colored

waiters, most of them bulkily fat like so many Balti-
moreans, were rigged up in Elizabethan costumes. This
restaurant made a very bad impression. The food, as usual,
was unattractive. The people were unattractive. A huge
bar ran the whole length of the long room. I hurried away
to see Albright, but was a long time getting a cab. Mrs.
Albright told me that there were very few cabs in Baltimore
in proportion to the population; but I think that the recent
curfew had something to do with it, too. The driver said
to the doorman that there were few cabs that night because
there were so few people out. There was a young Negro
woman in the front seat, and he asked if I would mind if
he dropped her first. After she got out, he explained that
she worked in a hospital and usually took the bus, but that
he had picked her up and dropped her at the corner, not
in front of her house, because she had told him that her
husband was jealous. I spoke of the recent turbulence,
and he said that it had been "terrible," and hoped that it
wouldn't begin again. I think that he was sincere. There
must be in Baltimore many of these friendly and easygoing
Negroes who are simply embarrassed by the rioting.

My evening with *Albright* was extremely stimulating
after making conversation with those nitwits of the South;
and in fact restored something of my appetite for life. He
feels he is at the top of his profession and thoroughly enjoys
himself. He told me I was a mere boy compared to him—
I said that I was 73 (almost) and he countered that he was
77. He is extremely proud of the fact that six of his former
students are at Harvard and that most of the volumes of
the Anchor series of the Bible were assigned by him to
other students. He says that the Jesuit Dahood who is
doing the Psalms had thrown more light on the Psalter
than anybody since they were written. He told me this
with absolute glee. I don't remember ever knowing a
scholar who so wholeheartedly revelled in his subject. He

gave me candid opinions of the other scholars. Dupont-Sommer was not quite tops, but he had been the first—which I didn't know—to identify the Dead Sea sect as the Essenes at a time when he, Albright, had been groping around with the scrolls and didn't yet know what to make of them. Vermes was all right, but not particularly interesting, which was my impression. Allegro had started in promisingly, but was now quite off the track. His Jewish boss at Manchester—de Vaux had said the same thing—didn't get on with him much better than Rowley. The Shapira strips were certainly not authentic. Allegro knew absolutely nothing about Jerusalem in the eighties. Albright's opinion was evidently supported by firsthand accounts he had had from people who had known Shapira and regarded him as a pretentious charlatan.* Albright was laughing and giggling like a demon all the time that he was saying this, and a smile never left his lips. It amused me that he would break into scholarly scandal. "Allegro tried to date Frank Cross's wife, you know." I said that he had a very nice wife of his own. "He doesn't pay much attention to her." Driver had got himself a title only by campaigning for Harold Macmillan, just before Macmillan had had to resign [as Prime Minister]. Driver's new book was so expensive that he hadn't wanted to buy it, but he had borrowed it and been through it, and there was nothing that he "could use." Martin's book was nearly useless: it should have been a few pages instead of two large volumes.

---

* In the 1880s, a dealer in rare books and scrolls named Moses Wilhelm Shapira almost sold to the British Museum, for a million pounds, "fifteen fragments of a manuscript written on skins and so blackened as to be almost illegible, which included the Ten Commandments and the Shema" (*The Dead Sea Scrolls*, 1969). He had previously sold some faked Moabite stone gods, and a French archaeologist persuasively argued that the "strips" were forgeries. As a result, Shapira's family, who had counted on being rich, were ruined, and he killed himself. Wilson sympathizes with them in *The Dead Sea Scrolls*, though Albright and Frank Cross kept him from regarding this discovery as genuine.

When I told him that Martin had left the Jesuit order, he said he hadn't known this—"Did he want to get married?"

He explained that he had both glaucoma and a cataract, and the cataract wasn't yet operable; while talking, he played with an iron frame which I seemed to remember from my previous visit and which I took to be something for holding lenses. His bad eyesight made travelling difficult—so he had not been to Israel lately—but he had no reason to complain because it "gave him more time at his desk." Though he is said to be ruthless with opponents, I was struck by his generosity in acknowledging the achievements of other men. He told me with excited enthusiasm that someone had just read the Sumerian tablets that had been lying around at Pennsylvania and elsewhere and had found in them great revelations—"the oldest civilization!" He talks fast with a thoroughly international accent—an *r* that seems to me German. He was born in South America and spent years "in the field" in the Middle East. When I left, he walked several blocks with me— much more briskly than I could; he says that he likes to walk at night—to take me to a corner where I could get a taxi.

APRIL–DECEMBER: 1968

Visitors and a Trip to Chicago

April 22. Visitation of Chanler Chapman, with his son:* the latter quiet and blond. Elena thought at first that he looked almost spartic, and when I would look toward him in the course of his father's tumultuous conversation, I found that he did not smile. One doesn't know what to make of him, with his combination of Chanler, Chapman and James blood. He is in his early forties, has married a Negro girl in Puerto Rico and has several children by her—"I think that when you've had children by a woman, you ought to take the responsibility of marrying her"; he showed us pictures of the family at lunch: one of the children in a swimming pool was as black as he could be. It seems that all his wife's relatives have moved into the

---

* Chanler's father was John Jay Chapman, whom EW makes a kind of intellectual father in *The Triple Thinkers*, admiring his direct and personal criticism of the classics and integrity as a radical reformer. In 1933, not long after John Jay's death, Wilson had sketched the son against the backdrop of a Hudson River estate and a moral heritage to which he was inadequate (*The Thirties*). These two encounters, separated by thirty-five years in the journals, suggest Wilson's disappointment that such distinction as John Jay Chapman's is difficult for Americans to sustain from one generation to the next.

house with them—as Hatty's more or less did with me.*
His name is John Jay. In Puerto Rico, he is a mailman.
He told me that he liked to collect fine books. He thinks
the danger to mailmen from dogs is overrated—he had only
been bitten once. I should have liked to talk to him more,
but Chanler talked all the time.

Chanler is likable and amusing, but extremely
fatiguing—loud and full of bad language. He is 67 and
calls himself, correctly, an adolescent. He told me that the
Coffee House had asked him to resign—I don't see how
any club could stand for him. He is giving up his dairy
farm and the *Barrytown Explorer* and going to devote himself
to local radio broadcasts. Was much exercised over Saul
Bellow's having put him in *Henderson the Rain King*, which
he seemed only to have just discovered.† He is cultivated,
fairly well-read—and in his father's international way,
hitting the high spots—a very self-confident and fairly
intelligent judge of people, has all the Chanler love of
adventure—it is a pity that he also has so much of the
Chanler uncoördinated craziness. He is reading Gibbon,
which he loves. He had come to Boston on a sort of pious
pilgrimage to the Tavern Club and St. Paul's School. All
this element of the past, somewhat incongruously, means
something to him. He speaks excellent and humorous colloquial French—he had at some time some kind of a job
in France. I told him Paul Chavchavadze's story about de
Gaulle. "We know that you are marvellous, *mon général*,
but someday—we mention it with extreme reluctance—

* Hatty was an aged black woman who kept house for EW during the
thirties. When he was living at Trees at Stamford, she and her grandchildren occupied one wing of the house and he the other.
† Eugene Henderson, who in Bellow's novel becomes the Rain King in
Africa, is a spoiled, tormented man, the scion of an intellectual aristocrat like John Jay Chapman. Henderson's character, estate, marriages, and son recall Chanler.

we shall have to consider the question of where you would care to be buried. *L'Arc de Triomphe?"* *"Auprès de ce soldat inconnu* [Next to the unknown soldier]*?"* *"Les Invalides?"* *"A côté de ce caporal* [Beside the corporal]*?"* *"Jérusalem?"* At this point, Chanler put in for de Gaulle, with a gesture: *"Dans ce petit coin-là?"*—*"Je vais téléphoner. . . . On dit en Israel qu'on sera très content de permettre qu'on vous enterre là-bas* [In Israel they say they'll be happy to permit you to be buried there]. *Mais on demande deux millions de francs."* *"Deux millions de francs pour trois jours seulement!* [Two million francs for only three days!]" —It is disconcerting to see somebody so genuinely superior in so many ways— his face sometimes reminds me of his father's—so much of a mess in others. He doesn't drink nowadays, refused the suggestion of wine at lunch with a loud emphatic "Nah!," but I sneaked one in the kitchen toward the end of his visit and hit the bottle after he left. He has the boring habit of comparing me to Dr. Johnson. I feel that his present wife must manage him much better than Olivia, who, with her quiet old-fashioned ladylikeness, must have had a dreadful time with him.

April 28. Post-Russian Easter Party at the Chavcha-vadzes': Walkers, Joan Colebrook and Brownie L'Engle (she was delighted to be asked, they said, telling them that nobody invited her any more). Brownie has now grown quite stout, says she is 83, which surprised me—but for what Elena calls "limited" and I call "stupid" people, it may be easier to grow old. Always in character, when she first arrived she made no comment on Nina's magnificent daffodils—eighteen varieties, Nina says, and other flowers—but immediately commented on the collapsed old barn, which they hadn't had the money to rebuild. Joan Colebrook is much better since she has been to Australia for *The New Yorker*. She saw and played with a young echidna. They have taken three articles at $5,000 apiece. She is going back for a longer stay.

At my age, I take a certain comfortable satisfaction in easy-going negative decisions: *not* to raise certain questions in conversation, *not* to explain certain things. I am closer to the attitude recommended by Jowett: never apologize, never explain. Why bother? I used to feel an obligation to correct people, to hold up my side. Now I don't feel that it matters. —I feel that I don't have to argue or try to give people information about things that I know about but they don't—though I still sometimes find myself under compulsion to rectify mistakes I have made in conversation, later on when the people I have been talking to have undoubtedly forgotten what I said. When, in the course of college lectures, I have corrected minor errors in previous lectures, the students have sometimes laughed.

Reading Macaulay's *History* and the biography of Lytton Strachey makes me realize that I fail to mention them in listing the writers who have influenced me (at the beginning of *The Bit Between My Teeth*).

May 7–9, Boston. The Ritz was full, and we had to stay at the Parker House, which is now a Knott chain hotel and has completely gone to pieces—even the food in the new dining room is not good any more: when I ordered shad roe, what I got was, I am sure, cod roe; the rooms have what are more like cots than beds; no theater-ticket bureau, no New York papers at the newsstands; everything unclean and cheap. We went to the Bolshoi Tuesday night: very old-fashioned and sometimes clumsy; I can see why Balanchine couldn't stand to stay in Russia; Pavlova's Dying Swan, as danced by the present prima ballerina, simply flopped and raised one arm straight up in the air.

Saw Zoltán [Harasjti] in the lobby—I didn't recognize him at first: his hair is perfectly white, and he has grown a small beard.

My birthday was principally occupied in going to the aurist and the dermatologist. Dinner with the Pritchetts: very English dinner. Lillian Hellman came in after dinner; but I mostly talked to Victor. We agreed that the Soviet spy Philby was being raised to the status of a great Englishman—Burgess and Maclean were weaklings.

The next day Elena went out to Chicago, and I came up to T'ville. <Mary met me> and looked rather pale and thin, not so handsome as usual. She said she was beginning to feel middle-aged. I took her to the Parquet, and we had a bottle of domestic "champagne." She was somewhat upset by a car accident which her boy had just had. His car was badly smashed, but he wasn't hurt—somebody had run into him.

<Hearing on new road took place Monday night in the schoolhouse—a four-lane road, with two outside roads, soft shoulders for parking—man who presided says that he hates to touch stone houses, though they were threatening to cut off my front steps.> I am getting Perry Williams to defend my interests. <After the hearing, Otis came over, and we had a serious talk. He, too, is discouraged by what he calls the "riffraff" who are making T'ville look so tumbledown—to be so plagued by these poor and ignorant children, in two families fatherless. When I first came back, I asked Mabel Hutchins whether they had been up to much mischief. No: she thought they were pretty quiet since three had been arrested and fined. Otis says that he has thought of moving away, and Frances O'Donnell complained to me as she has never done before that last winter they ran over everything with their snow machines. They had ridden though my currant bushes and partially killed them.>—The old brick Collins house

where we used to spend our summers has been painted an ugly pale chocolate, which everybody here dislikes.

Sunday was Mother's Day, and as Mary wanted a fuss made over it and invited me to a celebration with all the family, I took them all to dinner at The Beeches and regaled them with California champagne; then we went to the movies at Rome: *Guess Who's Coming to Dinner*, Spencer Tracy, Katharine Hepburn, Sidney Poitier—nice white girl who gets engaged to an able and ambitious Negro doctor who is going to Africa to work for his people.

Chicago, May 18–21. Coming in on the plane, you look down on what look like rows of parked cars, which are actually little box houses. Reuel says that Elena spoke of this, too. —I stayed at the Country Club Hotel a block or so away from Reuel, where Elena had also stayed. As she said, it seemed more or less all right if you had been staying at the Parker House. I had forgotten how, in the Middle West, everybody engages you in conversation—in the elevator, in the lobby, in the hallways. Someone had just been murdered not far from there. —Reuel's apartment is quite adequate: five rooms. I found the pictures I had given him on the walls: Rowlandsons, Callots, an old Russian print of Hell; Marcia had bought prints of ikons. I could not do much about the baby: all babies look more or less alike, and aren't interesting to men till they get a good deal older.

On Saturday afternoon, Reuel took me out to the Brookfield Zoo. We saw the pack of wolves that I had read about in the Museum of Natural History magazine. The men who wrote the article have been able to study this pack, first brought to Chicago as cubs, as apparently no pack of wolves has ever been studied before. They have a rigid social organization. There was a top wolf and an upper class, who hold their heads up and their tails out straight. The inferior ones hang their heads and carry their tails down. There was a billboard with pictures of them, so that you could tell a wolf's status at a glance. It is only the upper class who put their legs up when they pee—it is marking off an area as their property. The writer of the article tells of an upper-class pair copulating when the bitch saw another pair copulating which, for class reasons, she did not approve of; she went after it and broke it up, dragging her male with her, fastened to her but headed in the other direction. It reminded me of Lucretius: the lovers pulling in different directions, but still, like dogs, stuck together.

The most interesting feature was the porpoises—I didn't know they had them out there. They give two or three shows a day in the tank, and they seem to know the routine without any cues except the appearance of the props. When it is time for the show to begin, they all stick their heads out of the water and make a squawking-quacking sound. Their heads look more like birds' than like animals', and they do not give the impression of being fish. They ring bells, jump through hoops, throw basketballs into baskets—they only made one miss—and make incredible leaps over a hurdle that is held higher and higher, at the highest, something like 25 feet above the surface of the water. After a stunt, they swim madly around, smacking the water with their anchor-shaped tails. When white caps are thrown into the water, they lift them up on their heads. One of their most remarkable feats is to raise themselves upright above the water, with only their tails submerged, and move backwards till they flop on their backs just as they reach the opposite side of the tank, but without ever hitting their heads. Their sense of distance seems to be perfect, as when they judge the height of a jump. A man feeds them small bits of fish. One porpoise rose up before him in such a way that he could shake his fin. They seem as close to human beings as any sea lion or dog.

That night Reuel and Marcia had to have dinner with a bosom friend of Mary's whom they had never met. She turned out to be the Italian writer Gaia Servadio, part Sicilian and, Roger Straus tells me, part Jewish, married to a Scotchman with a castle, who used to be Berenson's secretary. Very slim and goodlooking blonde, but with a rather ominous habit of showing her clenched teeth in a way I assume to be Sicilian. Very ambitious, Roger says, with a kind of salon in London both political and literary. My conversation with her at dinner turned into a name-dropping competition of a kind that I had hardly expected to encounter: Rome and London were covered pretty thoroughly, with brief trips to Israel and Paris. After dinner, we had drinks at the Ambassador, a man with whom Reuel had been doing Spanish having joined us. The waiters— characteristic of Chicago—were in hunting costume, with red coats. This social effort much fatigued me, and I spent the next day recovering. Roger says that a day when one does not see Gaia is like a week's rest in the country.

<Chicago, which used to have a kind of grandeur and, before I spent a summer at the university, a certain romantic quality, is extremely unattractive now.> The Congress Hotel made me think of Louise [Connor] and made all that seem very remote, though I still indulge in erotic fantasies about her, and the park at the university reminded me of Mary [McCarthy] in shorts and a bright blue and red blouse playing baseball with amused young men against a green background of vivid green grass. But <the high buildings here and there have upset the proportions of Michigan Avenue; the Art Institute, from a

distance, is now almost unidentifiable, and some very ugly new ones are going up, a black towerlike building, for example—insurance, I think—that is truncated at the top; the people seem less dynamic, pale and measly city dwellers, joyless; and the Negro slum of the South Side is squeezing against the university, and the university people are afraid of more riots: there are rumors that, at some time this summer, they are going to take random potshots at whites. The Negro streets are full of damage: broken panes and boarded-up shops, with a self-defensive SOUL BROTHER painted up. The whole effect is claustrophobic: you find yourself in the middle of the Middle West, and reading the papers, you feel that all the horrors of a hateful, convulsive and chaotic civilization are closing in on you from every side. Reuel and Marcia will be very glad to be getting out the first of June, after three years of it, in spite of facing the eight-day journey in the station wagon with the baby.>

I called twice on Napier Wilt, whom I hadn't seen for thirty years. It was pleasant to talk to him again—an old Indiana gentleman, very good taste and judgment, dry more or less deadpan humor, occupied with scholarly pursuits which involve a good deal of tracing down sources in papers and magazines, but also a dedicated teacher of the old-fashioned Chicago pre-Hutchins type. He still lives, a confirmed bachelor, with the same non-academic friend that he lived with when I knew him before, who has something to do with feeding the army. They have a cat, a cook who has worked for them for years, a big plant in the living room that looks like a rubber plant, and a garden on the edge of one of the parks where they grow both flowers and vegetables. He is an authority on American drama, and I found out from him about some old melodramas which I wanted to look up in connection with my Open Letter to

Mike Nichols.* Wilt, since his partial retirement, has taught in Turin, Hong Kong and Helsinki. He says that he has come to the conclusion that American education, bad though in many ways it is, is perhaps the best in the world. In Italy, he found out, in connection with *Daisy Miller*, that the students did not read the books about which the professor was lecturing: they took the professor's word for their contents and significance, had been doing this, I suppose, for many years. In Hong Kong, they never had the interest to read a chapter or a paragraph beyond what they were assigned, and were intimidated, as he discovered, from reading a rather erotic masterpiece, which was on the shelves of the library but from which they were warned off. One boy told Napier that his father told him he "was not married" till after he had been married. In giving them *The Catcher in the Rye*, he asked the boys whether a Chinese boy would, like Salinger's hero, pick up a prostitute and take her to a hotel. The boys failed to speak up; a girl spoke up and said, "A Chinese boy won't do anything." He thought that Helsinki was fine: the students were interested and bright, and they owned their own dormitories.

Reuel talked to me quite a lot about the present weaknesses of the educational system: competition between the colleges, getting names that don't do much teaching, widening gap between the faculty and the administration. I had noted this last at Harvard: demands from the administration supposed to be met by graduate student papers which had not yet been written: only a couple of pages and an outline, so that the students find themselves burdened

* Describing these old plays in his "Open Letter to Mike Nichols" in *The New York Review of Books* (1969), EW calls on his friend to revitalize American theater. He concludes: "If God were not thought to be dead, I should beg him to spare you, my boy, and to preserve you from the fleshpots of Hollywood."

with an accumulation of unfinished papers.* Reuel says
he is seriously interested in the problems of education but
doesn't approve of the recent riots or of the idea that the
students ought to run the college. —Reuel had also talked
to Elena about the good that he thought might come from
teaching foreign languages—the general understanding
that might be prompted by exact comprehension of what
other peoples were saying.

Upstate Round

<It was a relief to get back to T'ville, where the air was
clear and the weather cool, to escape from the stifling
Chicago heat which was beginning to set in when I left.>
—Mary drove me up from the airport and talked to me all
the way about the showdown she had just had with Alex.
It had been set off by what she said was his brutality in
his treatment of a young girl who had twice missed her
period and might be pregnant. Mary looked up the young
girl and told her to see a doctor. But I imagine that blow-
up was something that had for a long time been coming
on. She didn't like his behavior about his 12-year-old boy,
who worked in the store after school and to whom he
wouldn't give a raise. And he had made her give up her
extra-drugstore activities—the charm school and the conversation classes—because they took too much time from
her duties in the store. I had difficulty in getting her off
the subject. She is at her worst and most common when
she is indignantly recounting a conversation with someone
that she wants to put in an unfavorable light: she always
makes the other person talk in a high and hypocritical

---

* EW had the impression that the Harvard faculty had to prove to the
administration that their students were doing publishable work, leaving
them the burden of following through on ambitious outlines.

voice. I took her to the Parquet and had her drink some domestic champagne. She has got herself a job at the cosmetics counter of Goldberg's, the Rome department store, and, having had the critical scene with Alex, is starting in there Monday, June 10.

Thursday, May 23. Dinner with O'Donnells—talked about cultural demonstration for October, also about the MLA: Tom is doing Howells's poetry for them, Bowers sends him orders to check hyphens in the case of words divided from one line to another, etc., and Gertrude says that he has been talking about the MLA just the way I have. Talked with Bill Fenton about the Iroquois.

Friday, 24. Morrises.

Saturday, 25. Howlands, with Stephen and Gretchen Crosten, and a young architect and his wife—he is building new houses for both the Crostens and the Howlands. <I got John started with magic last fall, which I thought would help to carry him through the boredom of the winters, and he mastered a card routine which I didn't know and which he has learned to do very well. He now performs tricks for his customers, when they sit around the Clark Layng furniture store more or less as if it were a club. Someone had said to the Howlands that they had never known a furniture store where the furniture was so much used. This is due to old Clark Layng's genial spirit.> He is still there every morning at 7.

Sunday, 26. I took the Morrises to dinner at the Ohio Restaurant, of which I had heard so much. The man who ran it, I had heard, had been chef at the Waldorf-Astoria. You have to reserve a table in advance. But it turned out to be very depressing. Ohio is an out-of-the-way little village. I don't know where the clientele comes from—Utica, I suppose. They are elderly, and talk in extremely low voices. The whole effect is subduing. When we laughed, our neighbors looked around. The food was not especially good. I have no desire to go there again.

Monday, 27. The Heusers' day off from the country club outside Utica that they are running this summer is from Sunday night to Tuesday morning, when they come up and spend it at the Towpath. They invited me to dinner there, and set out an attractive little table with white tablecloth and clear glassware in the living room. I had never seen them completely off-duty before, and spent a very pleasant evening with them. Mignonne says she wants to write about her experiences as an innkeeper—some of which have been hilarious. <She and Klaus laugh a lot about their customers. I remember Elena's saying that somebody had said that one of the great advantages of marriage was having somebody to laugh with about things that you couldn't laugh about with anybody else.> I am glad this is true of them. It must be one thing that makes them so genial.

Tuesday, 28. The Morrises invited me to dinner again. Three documentaries in the basement and discussion of the local accent. Barbara Erwin says that *wunt* for *won't* sounds all right to her, and I had just noticed that she used it.

Wednesday, 29. Mary drove me to Utica. I had a whole list of things to do, but it rained torrents and was very windy. I wasn't even able to get my hair cut because the barbers don't work on Wednesday. We had lunch at the club, and I got across the street to Grant's, where I bought the new biography of Ellen Terry. Mary got lost on the way to the zoo. She drove nervously and was much upset by Alex's having called her in the morning and told her that on account of her bad reputation from having gone to a motel with a man, some woman wouldn't come into the store. Mary said that this wasn't true, and that even if it

had been, it was none of his business. We gave up trying
to go anywhere else, and came straight home. She was still
full of her break with Alex. She had made it definite, and
he has let her go from further work at the drugstore. She
was enjoying her vacation, had a sense of release and freedom; but she talked about Alex all through lunch and all
the way back and rather exhausted me with her demands
for sympathy and disapproval of Alex. The final outrage
seems to have been that he had accused her of putting
something in his coffee—poison or a Mickey Finn?—in a
cup that she had nothing to do with making. She also said
that he strongly wanted her back.

Thursday, 30. Memorial Day, more cheerful than that
of two years ago. I had nothing to drink last night and
woke up to a sunny morning. I have been feeling rather
guilty about frittering my time away: reading endless papers
and magazines, writing nothing but letters and drooling
along in this diary, dipping into old books I had already
read, and going out and talking every night. I got stuck
after the second act of *Osbert* before I went to Chicago,
but have now thought of a way to go on with it. I am,
however, lukewarm about it and have thought of giving it
up. Shall attack it again tomorrow, however.*

Made three trips to Utica with Mary, and only on the
last succeeded in getting my hair cut and my shoes shined.
On the third trip, we also found the zoo and afterwards
visited the museum, and felt that we had had quite a
cultural day. On that day, the 9th, we had dinner in Rome
at the Italian restaurant there, run by the same people
who run The Beeches, a family who have been there running restaurants since the 1880s. Much better than The

---

* For several decades EW had been coming back to *Osbert's Career, or
The Poet's Progress*, having in 1930 published part of what became the
first act as "Beautiful Old Things" in *The New Republic*. The play
appeared in 1969 (*The Duke of Palermo and Other Plays*).

Beeches, which is pretentious and expensive and absurd with its waiters in togas and menus on huge scrolls in Latin; a good old-fashioned Italian restaurant. Afterwards, we went to a movie: Sidney Poitier again, this time the Negro as hero-detective. I could hear hardly a word—it was like watching a movie in a foreign language. Mary, on the way home, explained it to me with perfect lucidity. —She said that her family begged her to stop talking about Alex and his pharmacy, and I hoped that she had stopped when she went on to describe her son's commencement. She was so proud of his high marks and showed me his graduating paper, of which I could make nothing at all, because it was all about the industrial chemistry of good products. But then, when I had come back from New York, she had been stirred up again by Alex's getting into her car and talking, she said, for an hour and a half trying to make her come back to the pharmacy.

I went to the Talcottville O'Donnells' for a drink and they asked us to stay for supper. On the way, I stopped in at the Browns' to tell them not to cut my corner on their motorcycle, leaving big gashes in the grass. I asked why they didn't get licenses so they could go somewhere with their cycles instead of just buzzing along the side roads and the schoolhouse lane. Didn't they have money enough? They said that the problem wasn't money for the licenses but the $140 for compulsory motor insurance. I felt rather sorry for them. Their mother, it seems, pays little attention to them and spends a good deal of her time with a boyfriend. The house seems perfectly bare—no trace of a "woman's touch"—a table, a few chairs. —The O'Donnells complained about them bitterly. In winter, they drove into the O'Donnells' drive. One of the Sullivan boys, who had been in the insane asylum, had two guns. Just before I went to New York, I heard that the sheriff had taken them away.

A Birthday Dinner and the Aspen Award

New York, June 10–16. I flew down in the morning, and Elena joined me at the Princeton Club. In the evening, we went to a dinner in celebration of Father D'Arcy's 80th birthday. It took place at "21," and what we found rather astonished us—although it must not be forgotten that Father D'Arcy is a considerable snob and that he was made Father Provincial in Britain because he was a money raiser. The hostess was a huge rather handsome Austrian, whose name was Engelhard. We learned afterwards that her husband was one of the richest men in the world, who owned all kinds of mines all over, especially in South Africa. He was not present. But a sort of co-host and hostess were, named Schrady. She had very thick dark hair down over her shoulders and told me she was partly Hungarian. Roger Straus told me afterwards that Father D'Arcy had had Schrady's first marriage annulled, so he could marry "the Viennese bombshell." Schrady is a commercial sculptor, who does pieces for people like U.S. Steel and gets tremendous prices.

The party's foundation was rich Catholics and an aging café society, including the Duke and Duchess of Windsor, who were looking rather moth-eaten. Windsor is wrinkled and sad; Elena found the Duchess "frightening"—a skeleton and covered with makeup; but when I looked over at her during dinner, she seemed a little more human than I had imagined: fairly high rounded forehead, and a pleasant kind of smile. There was also a sprinkling of *New Yorker* writers. Phyllis McGinley had been asked as a Catholic, but Ved Mehta didn't quite know why he had been asked: he knew the Schradys but had met Father D'Arcy only two or three times. We sat down, in the reception room, at a table together, and Ved and I talked about

Kipling. Phyllis, with, as Elena said, her "loose mouth," remarked that we were "all Catholics here." Elena answered that the Windsors were not Catholics and we were not Catholics. We were served copious caviar. In the middle of the floor was a youngish man, in a black jacket, a white turtleneck sweater and a pair of red pants, who pirouetted and talked animatedly with many gestures. I was told that he was a Hungarian photographer.

At dinner, before which Father D. said grace and everybody stood, I drew two dreadful companions: Anne Fremantle, a boring Englishwoman, who thinks she can write and is a professional Catholic convert, who is always plugging Catholic authors; and Diana Vreeland, the editor of *Vogue*, who is as hard-boiled as Mrs. Chase but louder and more vulgar. I couldn't understand something and explained that I was getting deaf. Vreeland said, "You're not deaf! You're not listening! You don't give a damn!" I said that I reached the stage when you don't distinguish consonants. "You're not deaf! You don't give a damn!" She reiterated this several times, and I finally said, "I really am getting deaf, but it's true that I don't give a damn." After we'd talked a little about Jeanne Ballot, Crowninshield and Condé Nast, she turned abruptly to Ved Mehta, who was next to her: "Now I'm going to talk to *him*!" When I turned around to see Elena she seemed to me a little pathetic, as I had never known her to appear before, and she seemed so at the Aspen dinner, at which, as she says, she had to work much harder. She had much better luck than I did: Senator Mansfield, on one side, the majority leader in the Senate, who said that he was afraid these assassinations would lead to a repressive reaction; Lord Somebody, the British consul, on the other. She was at Windsor's and D'Arcy's table. Windsor talked German all the time to the two Austrian ladies. Father D., as usual, tossed his head up and down, as Elena says, like a pony.

At the end of the dinner, the sculptor presented to him what E. says was a horrible little statue, a priest made a little speech of tribute and Father D. responded with a little speech, in which he said that, in his childhood, someone had asked him which he loved better, his father or his mother, and this had shocked him because he had always felt that he loved them both equally—and that he was now in the same position as between the U.S. and England.

After dinner, E. played up to the Lord—with a kind of snobbery which, though always latent, she rarely makes explicit. He had asked her whether she thought Father D. really liked this kind of thing, and she answered that he was now very old and couldn't tell a false duchess from a real one. I got us away as soon as I could, though I think that Elena would have liked to stay longer. Her slight discomposure, so rare with her, was due, I am sure, to emergence from a secluded monotonous life into something entirely different, but I am equally sure she enjoyed it. —A day or two after this, Anne Fremantle called me up. Going along with her Catholic line, I had talked about Maisie Ward's biographies and Wilfrid Sheed's reviews, about which last I had expressed some enthusiasm. She said eagerly she must have me meet him. I had forgotten about it, but she had phoned to say she couldn't find him. I said something about its not having been the kind of party I should have expected for Father D. "How delighted," she said, "he must have been to dine with his sovereign!" And as for her having sat beside me, it was something she could always tell her grandchildren! Roger says she "drives him up the wall," is always trying to get him to publish her books.

On Tuesday, we went to Mike Nichols's *Plaza Suite*.* Before the curtain went up, a woman sat down behind me,

* Nichols was directing this trilogy by Neil Simon.

with a very loud harsh American voice. I turned my head, without seeing, to suggest she might pipe down, but this had no effect. Elena said something in Russian about the wife of somebody we had seen the night before, and when I looked around, there were the Windsors again, the Duke, whom E. had not noticed, as well as the Duchess. The lady behind me wasn't what I had expected but a not-bad-looking woman with red hair. E. recognized her as a Drexel Biddle whom she had known in connection with Walther [Mumm]. She had one of those atrocious Philadelphia accents and, E. thought, was talking so loud because the Duke was deaf. I had not noticed before how very short he is. —The three plays were very funny but the actors too consistently noisy, no variety or modulation. Nicol Williamson plunged through all three plays at the top of his voice, with the same violence. Although I had thought he was British, he seemed to give every evidence of being American; but Penelope told me he was actually Scotch, and one of the few British actors who could convincingly play Americans. All the three plays sounded as if they had been written by Mike Nichols, but he hadn't contributed much to them. It must be a new kind of comedy, which he himself has helped to establish.

Aspen Award, Wednesday: Up to a few days before the dinner, I had not been informed exactly when and where it was supposed to take place, so I wrote to William Stevenson, the president of the institute, and had no reply. Friday I called up Aspen. They told me that Stevenson had sent me a wire and read it to me: black tie, Waldorf-Astoria, eight o'clock. I never received this wire and explained this to Stevenson as soon as I met him. He said, "I'm very embarrassed." The "small dinner" turned out to consist of forty-eight people—only three of whom—Paul Horgan, Roger Straus and Henry Moe—did I seem to have anything in common with. Elena sat between Stevenson and the oil millionaire who had put up the money, and I, as at the other dinner, had horrors on either side. Elena had the impression, as I did, that we had come to a foreign country. She found out what the institute did. Bell Telephone and IBM, it seems, send their employees for cultural improvement to schools which they maintain themselves. The institute does that for other corporations. In the course of their two weeks, they devote two days to Plato, two to the Gospel according to Saint Matthew—Elena added "two to Scott Fitzgerald," and Arthur Schlesinger, when I saw him, added "one to Allen Ginsberg."

They were predominantly big executives and oil millionaires. Stevenson's wife, on my right, was a stupid and aggressive bore. She began by saying, "You wrote *Finlandia*, didn't you?" I said, "No: that was written by a Finn." Roger was on her other side, and suffered as much as I did. I inquired of Mrs. Stevenson who the only goodlooking women in sight were: a Jewish woman with a great head of bronze hair and a cunning little Japanese woman. She said she didn't know them, and I felt that she resented my asking about them. Roger had the Japanese on his right, and told me that when he made a remark or asked her a question, she would only giggle: "Ee-ee-ee." Elena found out that one of the big executives had picked her up in Tokyo, brought her back, divorced his wife and married her. The lady on my left talked and talked and talked—I think they were both quite zozzled—till I finally was so rude as to ask her not to talk so much—I was feeling fatigued and nervous, and the prospect of the long dinner appalled me—to which she paid no attention. She spoke of her husband and her having been at the University of Chicago. I thought she meant that he was teaching there, and, going into my academic routine, asked what he taught. She said that he didn't teach—they had both been students there. What had he studied? "Business." What was he doing now? "Business." It turned out that he was the oil millionaire who gave the money for the awards. He winked at me from across the table, perhaps in sympathy with what I was suffering. When I spoke of her to anybody afterwards, they would say, "She's pretty, isn't she?" She may have been so once. Paul Horgan declared he was devoted to her; but he has to keep in with these people— he has a fellowship this summer at the institute, where he will give them his lecture on Maurice Baring—so they will learn about Maurice Baring as well as Plato and Matthew. I tried a conversation with Dorothea Straus, on the other side of the table, about Tolstoy, whom she had just been reading; but we had to shout so that I gave it up. Then I talked to Paul Horgan across Mrs. Anderson. When she heard that we were talking about Baring's novels, she broke this conversation up by talking about some second-rate novel she had read.

In introducing me, at least two of the speakers referred to Muhammad not going to the mountain, etc. Paul Horgan read a little *éloge*, and we exchanged some amiable kidding. In acceptance of the award, I read a little speech, borrowed partly from Gilbert Murray's *Humane Letters and Civilization*—I had been asked to say something about the humanities—partly from the first piece in *Bit* [*Between My Teeth*]. I had been drinking all the wines, and I found my pronunciation a little blurred; but they had been drinking, too, and most of them wouldn't have understood what I was talking about anyway. After dinner, Mrs. Stevenson rather disagreeably challenged me: "Why didn't you list *Hecate County* in *Who's Who?*" I said I had. "No: it isn't listed. Why did you leave it out?" I insisted that I hadn't. She then produced a *Who's Who*, which I suppose they had been passing around in order to find out who I was, and found *Hecate County* listed. She must have been too cockeyed to notice it before. There was a little man named

Whitman there, who, Roger Straus said, wrote the best obituaries in New York. He had evidently been working on mine, and asked if he could come to see me. I told him that I never gave interviews; he just wanted to come to see me for background material. He afterwards asked Elena if she wouldn't try to persuade me.*

As we were leaving, Paul Horgan said to me, "I can't think of any harder way to get $30,000." You felt about these people that they were perfectly self-confident, that they could never have any misgivings, with those mountains of money behind them, about being vulgar or boring. They lived in a world of their own and couldn't imagine, I think, how they would seem to other people. Elena said that she thought that the philanthropical oil millionaire was as much astonished that I knew nothing about him as I was to find that the people of the institute, who had come to a dinner in my honor, knew nothing about me. The whole thing was slightly humiliating.†

* The lack of an interview would not keep Whitman from justifying Straus's praise. His obituary of Wilson in *The New York Times* of June 13, 1972, spans his entire career, ranging from the criticism for which Wilson was famed to *Memoirs of Hecate County*, which made him notorious, with quotations that convey his outlook on books, politics, and manners. Beginning on the front page and filling an interior page, the obituary is accompanied by another *Times* reporter's assertion that "if there is an American civilization, Mr. Wilson has helped us to find it and was himself an important aspect of it."

Whitman's report in the next day's *Times* on the Aspen Award dinner and Wilson's talk is reproduced on the opposite page.

† Wilson was inclined to expect little education and culture from the very rich, and didn't like accepting money from people he did not respect.

In an account of this dinner at the end of "Wilson at Wesleyan," Paul Horgan shows how uncomfortable the critic was. He was half-drunk, and self-consciously interrupted Horgan's introduction. Stevenson made a flowery tribute calling Wilson "Bunny," as only old friends did. Wilson leaped for the check, crying out, "Tax-free! Tax-free!" Horgan says he humiliated "his host and benefactor," Stevenson, who asked him to autograph a copy of *The Shores of Light*, by insisting that Stevenson spell his name.

Edmund Wilson Criticizes War As He Accepts the Aspen Prize

By ALDEN WHITMAN

Accepting the $30,000 Aspen Award for his contributions to American culture, Edmund Wilson took the occasion last night to attack the war in Vietnam, donnish "hostility" toward science and provincialism in literature.

The 73-year-old author and literary critic spoke at a private dinner at the Waldorf-Astoria Hotel that was attended by 48 persons, including businessmen, foundation executives, President Johnson's adviser on the arts, a publisher and a dress designer.

In thanking the Colorado-based Aspen Institute for Humanistic Studies for its check, Mr. Wilson said that he was "particularly grateful because it is tax-free." In a reference to Vietnam, he added:

"And I am immensely gratified that not a penny of the money this institute is awarding me will have to be contributed to the $8.9-billion which are going for this disgraceful war."

In an interview before the dinner Mr. Wilson said that he planned to use the entire $30,-000 to live on for the next year and a half.

Turning to what he called the gap between letters and science, Mr. Wilson told the dinner.

"It too often seems to me that at the present time this gap is made to draw a line between what are called the liberal arts, on the one hand, and every kind of science, on the other.

"In certain academic communities, it is rather disturbing to find that a certain hostility has arisen on the part of the faculty that represents the humanities toward the departments that represent the sciences. They accuse them of narrow specialization when they are often narrowly specialized themselves."

This, he said, is a "rather stupid line."

Inveighing against parochialism and citing his own cultural aims, Mr. Wilson said that writing about literature had, for him, always included a "discussion of comparative values."

"My function [as a critic]," he explained, "has been to make an effort to concentrate synoptically, as they say of the Gospels, to bring into one system, the literature of several cultures which have not always been in close communication, which in some cases have been hardly aware of one another."

Mr. Wilson's award was given him by William E. Stevenson, president of the Aspen Institute. The prize was established in 1964 by Robert O. Anderson, chairman of the institute's board and of the Atlantic Richfield Company, an oil company.

In addition to Mr. Stevenson, who is also a former Ambassador to the Philippines, and Mr. Anderson, those on hand last night to fete Mr. Wilson included Roger L. Stevens, the White House arts adviser; Harold Altschul, the stockbroker, and Walter J. Pedicord, a vice president of International Business Machines Corporation.

Also, Alvin Eurick, president of the Academy for Educational Development; Roger Straus Jr. of Farrar, Straus & Giroux, the publishers; Paul Horgan, the writer, and Larry Aldrich, the dress designer.

Clipping from *The New York Times*, June 13, 1968, taped into the journal by Wilson

On Thursday, at the Princeton Club, we had *Henry, Lillian Hellman and Penelope to dinner*. Mike was in Mexico for his film. A very pleasant evening. But Henry's face would fall into moments of dislike or moroseness—which has not been characteristic of him. Elena says that Daphne nags him and brings pressure on him to make more money. He has to work very hard, and still takes night courses at Columbia.

We devoted Friday afternoon and evening to seeing the Soviet version of *War and Peace*. Well cast and directed by [Sergei] Bondarchuk, who plays Pierre—a two-part abridgment of the Russian four parts. The dubbing has been complained of, but otherwise I suppose that few people would have come to it. As it was, at the afternoon showing, there was only a handful of people. I was quite moved by the first of these parts, which followed the book pretty closely; but they lose track of the characters in the second and try mainly to produce a spectacle, like *Exodus* and those other Biblical pictures: Borodino, the burning of Moscow, Napoleon's retreat through the snow. They did not have the wonderful scene at the end, which shows Natasha and Pierre in their domestic phase; but, instead, the announcer declaims a piece of Soviet mush about peace.

On Saturday, Elena went out to see the Thorntons. I had lunch at the Century Club with Arthur [Schlesinger], and Lewis Galantière joined us. Lewis has shed his thick-lensed glasses, and this improves his appearance, shows a certain bright-eyed fineness; but he has been having cataract problems and has to have contact lenses. Arthur says he is out of politics, the only leaders he cared about are dead. He thinks that [Eugene] McCarthy hasn't got a chance, but I am not so sure. How explain the increasing violence—hadn't it always been characteristic of America? I said that I couldn't be helpful—told him about John Birchers and delinquent kids in T'ville, a microcosm of the country. —Elena came back with her cousin Freya's son, who had driven with her to the Thorntons'. He is a pleasant young German officer (his father was a general). He had been here two weeks and was just going back. He had evidently been sent on an educational visit, and had visited the Pentagon. His opinions were not so reactionary as Elena had feared. He told me that the National Democratic Party did include a number of old Nazis. We had dinner at the Epsteins', with Mike and Penelope and Edith Oliver. Penelope has been working at *The New Yorker* writing her movie reviews just below the office where Edith pounds out her Off-Broadway reviews, without—this is so characteristic of *The New Yorker*—their ever having met, so I thought I ought to bring them together and got Barbara to invite them.

Mike, back from Mexico, explained that they were using that country instead of Sicily for the movie of *Catch-22* because Sicily was much too populated. Penelope seemed rather apprehensive because they have had to buy up old planes for the film, and these planes are hard to get around inside, where I suppose he will have to direct it. He had picked the site of the airport for picturesqueness without realizing that it was rather impractical to have the airstrip running into the side of a mountain. He said that he was stalling off the making of the picture. I had read in the paper that Mike had already had a million-dollar advance for the film and would get a handsome percentage of the profits. It would probably take two years. "And then to have somebody tell him that they don't like the end!" I had said this about *The Graduate*. I told him about the boys in T'ville. "Don't they ever think of going to New York?" He had once been a busboy and waiter in an upstate hotel near Kingston, had lost his job as a waiter from being too snappish with the customers in order to let them know that he was something better than a waiter. There was a boy he had known in the town, that he had been very friendly with, and this boy had been unable to imagine his taking a train to New York or even getting away from that town.

I had thought I would make love to E. the Sunday morning before she left, but had drunk too much the night before, and was afraid I couldn't bring it off. It was sad for us to part like that. But I always make excuses to myself on account of my increasing impotence.

<America has changed so much that when I visit Chicago or New York, I almost feel that I am seeing a foreign city. Airplanes give travel a different aspect. Going so quickly from place to place—I got back to Utica in forty-six minutes—has the result that on arriving somewhere you can still see quite clearly the place you just left, as if they were interchangeable. The airports have a special character—they are quite unlike railroad stations: not smoky, well managed, streamlined. My impression of New York was sinister—especially along Broadway and the streets in the Forties that run across the avenues: women in skirts so high that they make them look like little girls—one of them had yellow stockings on her little unattractive legs; Negroes much more in evidence than I remember ever seeing them before; young people as to whom you couldn't tell whether they were pimps and prostitutes or simply hipsters and swingers. On one of the cross streets, an elderly woman was sitting on something and crying, "Look out for your bags and wallets! They'll frisk you here!">

Summer Living

T'ville, June 16. Mary [Pcolar] drove me up from the airport. Rosalind gave me an unpleasant welcome; she appeared in dressing gown and curlers and was very rude to Mary. I asked her to phone Mrs. Hutchins, who is on the same line as I, and you have to employ a certain technique, which I have not mastered, but Rosalind last summer had. She said she had forgotten how and went over to Mrs. H.'s barefoot. In the meantime, Mary found out how to call her and got her before Rosalind arrived. This made R. furious, and Mary sat on for a while, but did not finish her drink and presently left. R. then made me a scene. She said that everybody thought that Mary was my "mistress," though she knew this was not true, and intimated that she couldn't be cordial with her. Rosalind was ill before she came up here, with a temperature, she says, of 104, and she is only just recovering (June 21).

<*My Showy Lady Slippers* are almost all blooming: five are in flower and bud—though the one that has flowered is as yet rather measly. Bob Weiler is a good gardener. He has weeded out Mother's peonies, which are splendidly blooming now, as well as the currant and gooseberry bushes—more gooseberries now than we have ever had before.>

Bill Fenton spent Wednesday night here (June 19). He is as full of beans as ever; I was burning rather low. He says that the Salamanca Indians, who were driven out of their homes by the dam, now have $18,000 houses, with splendid bathrooms and sandalwood finishings, and a longhouse with many electric plugs, so that they can have radio or television or anything there. Young Einhorn from Lowville tells me that they also have oil furnaces, but often can't afford the fuel and have to fall back on the potbellied stove. I was surprised to find that Einhorn was working at Buffalo for an anthropological degree and knows a lot about the Iroquois. He knows Bill Fenton, and I don't understand why the latter has never told me about him. A bright Jewish boy from New York City, whose wife has Micmac blood.

June 21. Mr. *Roberts* stopped by, Otis's old friend, who came from a farm down Water Street here. He represents the next to best element of the village as I used to know it: literate, decent, intelligent. He has spent his life working for Ford in Detroit, is now retired and reads and travels—has been to Eastern Europe and is now going to Russia and the satellite countries.

The orchids in front of the house are out now, with bright deep pouches, and they look quite jewel-like.

June 22. Dinner at the Edmondses'. He has put on weight—I suppose, on account of his heart, not being able to be very active. He was worried about the little attention that his new book, *The Musket and the Cross*, had had. I don't think he understood that, a long and solid historical work, it wouldn't attract the same kind of readers or demand the same kind of reviewers as his novels. I told him this, and he said that he supposed he had been spoiled. His son Peter and his wife were there. Peter is more a man of the world and has somewhat wider interests than his father. He has been in the diplomatic service in Iran and Afghanistan, has mastered Persian and Arabic in what seems to me a thoroughgoing way, and is now in Washington in the State Department, which he calls the Fudge Factory. A great admirer of Kennan. One can talk to him

as one can't with his father. There is an old-fashioned
head-of-the-house big-landowner authoritarianism not entirely concealed behind the shyness and politeness of Walter. My visits to him for some reason seem to have a bad
effect on me. It is partly because, I suppose, they involve
a certain element of insincerity: I have to pretend to take
him seriously, and I think he is aware of this—though he
is always complimentary about my books and writes me
appreciative letters. Also, I envy him his large quiet place
in contrast to my village annoyances and the traffic speeding
past the place. After one of my previous visits, I had my
worst angina attack up here and had to call Dr. Smith.
This morning I woke up after a horrid dream: I had thought
that I was in France and needed to go somewhere. I said
that I wanted a taxi to a little man I thought might be a
taxi driver. He didn't respond at first, but then took me
somewhere—I had thought to his cab—but it proved to
be a barbershop and he evidently wanted to shave me. I
got up from the chair, but he had somehow got my shoes
and he evidently wanted to shine them. I had a hard struggle to get them back and had to beat him with the handle
of my cane. I was restrained by the thought that I mustn't
hurt him any more than was necessary. My worst dreams
are when I give way to violence or am afraid of unopposable
merciless evil.

<This summer has so far, I think, been my pleasantest
one up here. Old age has its compensations. I feel that I
can loaf in the morning, worry less about what I am going
to write, and about the gaffes and errors I have made. My
regrets are mostly about the things that I can't any longer
do; but I think about old love affairs, and this does not
impose upon me any further responsibility for them. Mabel
Hutchins has more time to devote to me, and Rosalind
keeps me company. All kinds of people write me, and I get

a lot of papers and magazines. I probably waste time, however, with the magazines, and many of the letters I get are a bore: requests to do boring things, advertisements, petitions and protests, schoolchildren asking questions, letters from lunatics and crackpots. People have asked me out a lot, and sometimes I have had to refuse in order to get a night to read. The weather has been mostly delightful. General pleasant feeling of being more involved in the community, discussing the local problems with the T'ville O'Donnells, the Munns and Chet Rice. John Howland has put up a bluebird house and a bird feeder.

June 23. The Heusers for dinner: a giddy evening. They didn't arrive till after 8, because it had been a beautiful day and people had lingered on the golf course. Then Klaus had cut his finger on a knife, just coming short of cutting a muscle. There had been a surgeon playing golf and he had taken Klaus to the hospital. They appeared, already rather tight, in a new trailer for two, Mignonne with a red bobbed wig that made her look rather disreputable. They were relaxing from a week of work and the strain of Klaus's accident. Another drink or two really had them quite chaotic. Mignonne recited a bawdy poem. I asked her where she learned it, and Klaus said, "In the convent." Klaus made a bawdy joke at dinner, which was rather improper in the presence of Rosalind, but I don't think she understood it. He suddenly announced in the middle of dinner: "I am the Baron Gasthaus-Heuser!" They left very soon after dinner, because their daughter Monique was over at the Towpath, though they obviously wanted to stay. Klaus shook hands with me several times and insisted on showing me the trailer: all kinds of electric lights and an electric toilet that flushed with some smell-killing chemical. Mignonne took their new young spaniel called Alfie for a walk on a leash but unleashed him when she got into the trailer and carelessly stood in the open door. Alfie immediately leapt out and ran around the road and the lawn. He had spent his first six months in a kennel and was neurotically shy of people. When let out now, he was intoxicated with freedom and would not allow himself to be caught. Mignonne spent a long time trying to lure him and keep him from being run over. Finally she gave it up. Rosalind and I sat on the back porch and watched him on the lawn. He barked in a dog's howling way, communicating with other dogs. We called him but could not catch him. In the morning, he was still around, and Mignonne came over and got him. The enforced decorum and discipline of their regular routine as "innkeepers" must be rather hard to keep up; but Klaus told me rather late in the evening that they really "liked people," liked to observe them, they were all different; and it is true that they genuinely like to please. Mignonne says she wants to write, that she loves to write letters—I had noticed that her letters to us were longer and more friendly than was needed for practical purposes—and now she has the idea that she would like to write about her experiences as an "innkeeper"—in which I encouraged her.

Lunch in Cazenovia at the Marcelins'. He has finished his and Pierre's new novel, *Tous les Hommes Sont Fous* [*All Men Are Fools*], but as usual is still revising. Pierre is back in Haiti. Phito said, "*Il est inexportable.*" I am surprised that they are able to get through the winters up here, but they say they are both recluses. >

Sometimes it is comfortable and familiar to have Rosalind around, but sometimes she gets on my nerves—her always high-pitched voice, due to living with her deaf grandmother, and her habitual laugh that sounds like whooping cough—then I speak sharply to her and she flares up childishly.

<We went to dinner at the Einhorns' in Lowville. He gave me a very fine False Face mask made by a Cayuga. He has a curious story about a Seneca girl who worked for them. She began developing something like fits and became quite incompetent. They sent her back to her reservation, and the False Faces and the Husk Faces both operated on her—and she completely recovered.>

The 4th of July we celebrated with the Morrises and O'Donnells at the Morrises'. Glyn and Tom seemed to get on splendidly talking about education.

<*July 7*. Picnic with the Crostens at *Independence River* to which the Howlands later came.> Rosalind didn't come because she had crippled her foot by dropping a jar of cold cream on her toe. <I stayed behind while they went up to the falls. It is strange and sad to think that only a few years ago I was able to walk up by the path or scramble up on the rocks. I drank the rest of a gallon of white wine, played with a little pale coffee-colored kitten that Stephen Crosten's friend from Canada had brought and read in a paperback of Yeats's plays the boy had also brought along. His poetry still moves me. The visitor is in our State Department—which he said he was about to leave—and in the consul's office in Montreal. He says that in Canada he has found that it is impossible to be, as he wanted to be, a foreigner. They think either you are pro-English or an American who wants to get something out of them.>

The next day, the 8th, was a bad day. <The night before I had enjoyed when we got back here. I played Loran the

first side of *Bomarzo*, and he thought it quite good, as I did. He had said that Britten was the English Meyerbeer, and I said after playing the opening that I supposed he would say Ginastera was the 12-tone Meyerbeer. "No," he said. "The 12-tone Verdi."> I thought this was excellent. But this led to whisky after they left, and awful depression the next day. The surveyors came in front to take bearings for the new house; and behind, old Rutledge sat on the back porch, drinking beer, according to Mabel Hutchins, so that he shouldn't have to share it with his wife. He finally collapsed on the ground and passed out. Mrs. H. didn't want to go to his house and ask his wife to get him home, because she was afraid of finding her in the same condition. At last, however, he came to life, sang a little, wept a little and got himself home. "Thanks, thanks," he said. "It's so nice and cool and quiet here. It's terrible at home!" It was hot, and they live in a little box of a house.

July 9. Drinks at the *Ryders'*. The Ryders have had their hardware store in Boonville for two generations. Ron is a curious type. His real interest is his collection and publication of photographs of old Boonville life. They have a pleasant new house on Post Street. Mrs. Ryder used to be a schoolteacher.

July 10. Mary drove me to Utica. Strange muggy blank-gray day, and Mary, in the depths of gloom, hadn't slept the night before, not satisfied with her new job, which she says is easy but boring; the higher-ups don't treat her with the admiration and respect that she was formerly used to at the pharmacy. She has already been giving voice to her criticism. Obviously weakening about returning to Alex. We had lunch at the club, then I shopped at the Boston store and Bremer's liquor store. Then we called on the O'Donnells and I talked to Tom about our October performance and the MLA. Mary had to get back at 6:30 for a "picnic" at The Beeches for the National Business and Professional Women's Week, so we left rather early. She stopped in Rome to get gas at the gas station next to the pharmacy. Alex appeared and came to speak to me while she was in the ladies' room. He said it had been bad, very bad, but he hoped it could be smoothed over. She had been extremely capable. After that, I had Alex and the pharmacy all the way back to T'ville. Things had been disorganized since she had left; he was taking the new girl out to lunch, which he had never done with anybody but her, trying to pretend that she was just as good! Her old customers came in at Goldberg's and told her how much they missed her at the pharmacy. I told her that Alex was in love with her and that that made things difficult. "Oh, he's crazy about me! He's mad about me!" But he didn't know how to deal with women. He was sharp with her in the pharmacy, so people wouldn't think he was in love with her; but that only called attention to it. Their relation had the same kind of friction and rows as husband and wife in business together. Why couldn't their relations be platonic like those of brother and sister? He makes her all kinds of promises, but she knows he won't keep them. I am glad I am not in Alex's position, but I never see enough of her to get the difficult side of her personality, and I am fond of her and like to be with her. I like her precision and competence. And I always feel sorry for her. She says that if she only knew what she really wanted to do, she would do it; but she feels so "boxed-in" and helpless.

<Elena came Friday the 12th.> She relieved the tension between Rosalind and me, but she and I had our inevitable summer quarrel about Talcottville.

<We had supper with the Mihalys on a horribly hot day. He insisted on taking us to see Deerlick Rock, a local landmark which I had never known and of which not even the Loomises had ever heard. It is a huge brownish boulder that covers five acres. An Indian couple are supposed to have jumped from it because they were for some reason to be separated, and at the French and Indian Wars a French company are supposed to have left a cache of money buried at its bottom. Mihaly bought it some years ago and turned it into what he calls a "park." He has planted a lot of trees, and one of his sons with his family lives there. The mosquitoes and the heat were too much for me, and I did not attempt to climb it; did not even ascend again to his museum, which we had visited at lunch and which, in that weather, was suffocating. Like most Hungarians, he is very fatiguing. He told us at supper about his life. He was middle class, he said; his grandfather had been a landowner with quite a lot of serfs. His father had, I gathered, been a radical, who had written a number of books and had had to leave Hungary on that account. In one of my books, Mihaly had been surprised to find such names as Marx and Liebknecht, authors he had once read. His father, in the United States, had first tried to import *ásvangi viz* [Hungarian mineral water], but few Hungarians here could afford it.> —Young Einhorn told me that Mihaly was not entirely popular with the other Hungarians there. They had the same kind of complaint as the Poles: that they had been sold, on false pretenses, land so rocky that it did not lend itself to farming. Mary said her father had bought their 175 acres from Mihaly, and that it was pretty rocky for farming, but they had not complained about it. A Hungarian, however, had recently told her that Mihaly had been suspected of fraudulent dealing in connection with the Hungarian Center. He had charged them too

much for the band and other features on the occasion of their get-together. This was why it had been abandoned. This is not necessarily true.

<*July 18*. We had a mopping-up party such as we haven't had for years: Perry Williamses, Crostens, Howlands, Morrises, Einhorns, O'Donnells (T'ville). Elena and Rosalind and Mabel Hutchins worked hard over it every day, and the guests seemed to enjoy it. Discussed the delinquents and the new road.

One of our last nights, the motorcycle brigade, as Elena calls them, came back from a field day, as Mabel Hutchins thought, more or less drunk, and made such a racket in the road in front of the house that they woke up Rosalind and me. They were trying to stop cars and made them swerve. When Rosalind yelled at them, they scattered. She had threatened to call the sheriff. Then I woke up and saw what was going on and called the sheriff. A young part-time deputy came over. He had a gun but was rather frightened and failed to catch anybody. One of them was hiding in our shrubbery.> R. went after him, and he ran across our lawn and away by the back of the house, R. calling after him, " 'Fraidy cat!"

We came back to Wellfleet on the 23rd. Rather an arduous trip. Elena drove to Albany in the rented Avis. From there we flew to Boston, then Provincetown.

Ailments and Satisfactions

September 5. I came down with what turned out to be the shingles, a horrid old-age disease. You get inflamed, then blisters—I thought at first it was some kind of bites— then it is a nasty big sore. Burke arrested it with injections and pills, but these medicaments dope you—I felt as if I hardly existed, and now as if I were rising from the dead.

September 10. I have had a succession of uncomfortable ailments, all the results of old age. I am losing my flexibility and my energies. I keep thinking, This is not my normal state, these incommodings will presently pass—but instead of getting better, my conditions will probably get worse. There is a comfort in resigning oneself, just sitting around and reading the papers, allowing oneself to be waited on without having a bad conscience; but there are moments of depressed impatience—no bicycling, no swimming, no lovemaking. I used to start drinking at the end of the day just before I finished my writing, then play the phonograph while I shaved, then afterwards have people in to talk to; but now, with the shingles and the drugs for it, the first drink, instead of picking me up, lets me down and the second sends me to bed, sometimes without bothering about supper. My most positive pleasure is finding that I can still write—and I accomplish something nearly every day, though with occasional complete blanks. I don't like falling asleep during the daytime so much and try to hope that my tendency to lately has been mainly due to these drugs.

<*T'ville. September 27–October 20.* Mary met me. She is reconciled with Alex and beaming over it. She is getting more money, and I think more time off. We stopped at the gas station near the pharmacy. Alex was there and came out to greet me, also beaming—quite different from their meeting at this gas station when I was here before. He talks as if he were going to proceed with the enlargement of their little empire by buying the building next door.>

When Mary and I had lunch at the club, she became engaged in conversation with the old Italian waiter and barman who is a privileged club joker, and she rather astonished me by falling into a degree of familiarity with him that I don't imagine any other lady there would have condescended to. She told him a story about three old men. One said, "Gosh, that girl is pretty—I'd like to kiss her!" Another said, "I'd like to kiss her and I'd like to hug her!" The third said, "I'd like to kiss her and hug her—and what was that other thing we used to do?"

<Rosalind said that Mrs. Hutchins had said of the Di Spirito stone animals, "I guess those monsters will be glad when Mr. Wilson gets back!"*

General letdown after nomination of candidates. Even Fern is evidently not enthusiastic about Nixon—says that she and Otis sat up late talking about elections. An interview with Humphrey in *The Saturday Evening Post* made me think he was more intelligent and better informed, with a wider perspective than I had supposed. Suppose I'll have to vote for him against Nixon.† —The Russian invasion and suppression of Czechoslovakia and the interminable New York school strike make the world look very gloomy.

Mary drove me to Palmyra on a Sunday. I have written a description of it in the last chapter of *The Dead Sea Scrolls* II. Not hard to see how, in the vistas of that country from the ridge of the high steep "Hill Cumorah," having had little reading but the Bible, Joseph Smith should have imagined himself as a Moses and fabricated his Book of

---

* These stone animals were out on the lawn when EW was there, but otherwise kept in the house.
† EW had supported Robert Kennedy, who had been assassinated in June, then Eugene McCarthy.

Mormon.* At the Mormon Bureau of Information, a Mormon woman missionary, exhaling friendliness and solicitude to inform us, supplied us with brochures and folders and ran for us a colored film in which a highly idealized Joseph Smith was shown having his revelations. We went into the town for lunch and saw that all the other churches were flourishing—though the old lady who ran the inn said that the Mormons were making progress. It was one of those "better class" inns, and the lunch was better than usual. We drank a bottle of wine and loosened up the conversation as we had at the Moose Head Inn. Thought of going on to Rochester, where Mary had had a desire to eat at a restaurant made out of old railroad cars, but, after lunch, had decided to return.

Elena arrived on Thursday.> She had been cheered by staying with Marian Schlesinger in Boston—they had gone to an evening at Galbraith's house, where someone had lectured on the commercial aspects of art. The next night, she had dined with her Uncle Arthur's widow, Truda, who, she said, seemed much improved, not so harsh, extremely amiable.

<We went to lunch with the Briggses at Clinton on Sunday. An afternoon of jolly shoptalk, which I seem to need from time to time. Edwin Barrett and his wife were also there—he does Shakespeare and Elizabethan drama. Many wisecracks and much laughter. Grace Root had asked us to come to her house after lunch—she was giving

* EW's skeptical view of Mormonism went back to his own boyhood, when his father and he, preparing for a trip to Salt Lake City, "read up" the Book of Mormon and decided it was "dreadful stuff" (A Piece of My Mind). In The Dead Sea Scrolls, where this passage is rephrased, the success of Mormonism is attributed to the organizer of the religion, Brigham Young.

a lunch for some of the students at the new girls' college [Kirkland], which was just entering upon its first year.> The ones we met were not very attractive and did not seem promising. <Nor did the curriculum seem very highly developed—no languages and all the sciences lumped under one course called Science. The girls very soon left, and we had more shop. Grace Root> seems now to be even more immobilized; but drinking quite a lot of wine from bottles which she keeps at the foot of the table, she <still is in very good form, dominates and leads the conversation and plays her expected role.

The most beautiful fall here I have ever seen. We go for little walks every afternoon—drive out into country and take some uninhabited, unfrequented road. Foliage so wonderful that, at this time of life, I hardly try to describe it: rose-orange, blood-orange, lemon, pale or deeper copper. One road ran uphill through a wood toward a tunnel completely yellow, a little falling stream below. Almost no frost, and this produced different effects from the sudden blasting blazes of red. Sometimes a gold-soaked mist. I told Elena how much I had been enjoying that week, and that the only impediment had been her not enjoying being up there as much as I did. She replied that there was something chemical about one's enjoyment of places.

It all ended in rain on Saturday, and the trees were now more denuded.

Before Elena came, Mrs. Hutchins came down with a cold, and I saw that she could hardly get around, so I decided to spend two nights at the club and had a very comfortable spree. Since I had been there, they had got a new manager—extraordinary and unaccountable:> Charles Helmsing. <I thought his accent German, but he told us that he was Swedish—then it turned out that he

was partly Russian,> descended from someone named, I think, Franz Kurakin, of whom I had never heard but of whom he spoke as someone of importance. He spoke Russian—I tried him with a Russian remark, which he at once repeated in English. He had lived most of his life in Canada, had lived next door to Morley Callaghan and had walked with him every day on his daily outings. Blond hair, blue eyes, rather finely modelled, very cultivated and sensitive and surprisingly, in some ways, well-read: knew all the French gossip of the fin de siècle and a lot about royalty. I said that I had read Philippe Jullien's book on Robert de Montesquiou. When I found that he had it, he sent a servitor to get it from his room. A new staff had been installed: a blond boy with an old-fashioned rather non-hippie goatee, who had a young wife, and a colored boy with a curious jacket that went almost to his knees—I saw him wearing it once in the street. The colored boy brought back the wrong book, then was sent again and again brought the wrong book. "My poor boy," said Helmsing, "it's a red book." This time the boy found the right book, but it turned out to be purple not red. (In the middle of this, I called up Morley, who said that he knew nothing about Helmsing. He does take a walk every day, and Helmsing probably did see him, but wanted me to think he knew him.) He said that he had spent some years in Paris, had gone back to Canada, where "it didn't work out." I wondered whether he always got into trouble on account of some bad habit or something. The Costas had the impression that he might be homosexual. I asked Jo why she thought this, and she replied that though she didn't expect to have men make a great fuss about her, she could tell if they didn't respond to her as a woman. We would run into Helmsing everywhere, inside or just outside the club, and then have conversations with him. He drank with us quite a lot, and one evening, after Jo and I had been to a film outside of which we had run into him, evidently just about to go in, we sat and drank in the ladies' lounge. He simply produced a bottle of whisky, as if it were his own house. I don't remember signing any check, and am curious to see what kind of bill I'll get.

There are now three little movie theaters in a cluster on the corner next to the club: "Cinema 1 2 3." I took Jo Costa to the Jeanne Moreau film in 2; and the next afternoon tried Cinema 1 by myself. It was something called *Campus Confidential*, which was frankly pornographic to a degree that I didn't know was possible for a publicly shown film. It begins with what is supposed to look like a clean well-ordered college. Then we get a couple of nude lesbian girls about to go into action when a third roommate appears and halts the proceedings. No voices except that of a horrible smooth lecturer. "The orgy begins Friday night and lasts till Monday. Fred's parties are always groovy. We're only young once." Almost an hour of nude bodies writhing around. Drug-taking till the boys and girls have to be put away in a padded room; girls' pubic hair only lightly veiled, men's erections barely masked; a couple of naked male homosexuals embracing and kissing; boys going down on girls—when they reach the important spot, you only see the upper part of the girl, her face twisting in ecstasy. At the end, on Monday morning, they are going to class with their books, apparently none the worst for their weekend: "We're only young once," etc.

One night, when I had had something to drink, I heard the whistles of the local gang and saw three of the teenagers under the street lamp in front of the house evidently preparing some mischief. I went out to drive them away. They said something about having the right to be on the public

road, but I advanced on them with my stick, slowly and
flatfooted and inexorably like the Teutonic knights in *Alexander Nevsky*, and they retreated before me. When I seemed
to be near enough, I took a slash at one of them with my
stick; but he either fell back in time or I hadn't been close
enough, and it was only a swipe in the air. I might have
hurt his face badly, and he might have been able to sue
me. I turned off into Chet Rice's house, and the three
went off down the road arm in arm. I had half a bad
conscience about it afterwards, but also a certain satisfaction at feeling that I had scored. They didn't congregate
there again.

<Our session on the Iroquois on October 16 was not so
well attended as the one last year: we had to compete with
a concert by the Utica Symphony Orchestra. Bill Fenton,
Tom O'Donnell and myself. The Iroquois. Arthur Einhorn
and I lent costumes, masks, etc. Party afterwards at the
club.>

I should have mentioned that, before Elena came, the
Morrises took Barbara Erwin and me to one of four subscription plays from N.Y. that are given every winter. I
hadn't known about these and was surprised to find what
a tremendous social occasion it was. At the club, almost
all the tables were taken, including those in the men's
dining room, in which ladies were now allowed. I bought
the party champagne. When I asked the old Italian waiter
what kinds they had, he looked it up and said, "Brut, very
fine!"—he thought that brut was the brand. Barbara was
in a mad state of exhilaration at getting back from Lyons
Falls, she said, and prepared to make a night of it. But we
found ourselves in the very back row of the big Stanley,
mostly used as a movie theater, and could neither see nor

hear the musical, *Man of La Mancha*, which did not seem
to me, in any case, very interesting.

Rosalind arrived on Saturday, and we left the next day
about noon. Spent the night at Cummington with Dorothy
and Helen, with the usual special pleasure in their comfort
and conversation. Seta Shuvalova [Schouvaloff] came to
lunch the next day. I can see, when her face becomes
animated, that Alexandra somewhat resembles her. She
said that she was glad to hear that, because she had always
minded so much not being a beauty. She told us that her
grandfather had been present at the digging up of the graves
of the Tsars, when the coffin of Alexander I had been
found to be empty. This had always been kept a secret till
the Bolsheviks dug it up again and also found it empty.
Discussion of the holy man in the East who was supposed
to be the Tsar in retreat. The Russian love of working up
mysteries: Anastasya and Sukhovo-Kobylin's supposed
murder of his mistress. Shuvalova's dignity, tall stature
and erect carriage—at 77—when we took her back to the
house where she lived, and she crossed the street and went
up the steps. She talks English correctly and clearly, very
carefully and deliberately, as if she had just come from
her governess and had not had much experience speaking
it. She takes all her hardships calmly, never expresses
surprise or distress, or complains of the difficulties of
adaptation.

The colors of the trees intensified on the way from Boonville to Cummington: reddening peach and lemon turning
more golden, the starker landscape of winter appearing.

Elena dropped me off in Cambridge and went on to
Wellfleet. I drank almost nothing that night, but woke up
in the morning half-alive and with an acute pain in the

base of my spine. Could hardly get around; went to Filman to see about my will and found I could only half see him. Tottered around Harvard Square afterwards and didn't know what to do with myself till five o'clock, when I was going to the Pipeses'. Luckily I ran into Pipes, who immediately took me to his house, where they revived me with some whisky and we had some gay and interesting conversation. They are, I think, the most stimulating people that I now know in Cambridge—more range of interest and freedom from submission to the academic milieu. They always travel as much as they can. Polish Jews: Dick tells me that they are not only, as Reuel says, throwing Jews out of their jobs in Poland, but actually aiming to make it *judenfrei*, just packing them into trains and sending them abroad. But he explained that to be a Pole was like belonging to some secret order: with any kind of Pole you met anywhere you had a bond of understanding.

But otherwise this was one of my worst days lately. I went back to the hotel from the Pipeses' and went to bed without any supper. The next day I felt much better, went to see Zetzel and Dr. Pollen, who both told me that all my troubles were due simply to lingering shingles. I had lost 20 pounds, which to Zetzel seemed rather puzzling. But nowadays I eat so little and don't even drink very much.

The curious thing is that since I have been back in Wellfleet, I feel so much better that it is as if I were starting life again. E. has re-covered the kitchen floor and scraped the paint off the floor in the vestibule and made everything beautifully clean.

New York: Gossip and Old Friends

New York, November 15–23. Elena came down with me on Friday and left on Monday, having, as head of her district of the League of Women Voters, to attend an important meeting. She had been urging everybody else to attend these meetings, then skipped one herself, so she felt that she had to be there. —I went straight to *The New Yorker* Friday afternoon and went through the scrolls proofs with Whitaker. *The New Yorker* is terrified of libel suits now: people think they are rich and are constantly threatening them, and Greenstein insists on my toning down some of my remarks about the Biblical scholars. —When I got back to the club, I found the Lehoviches there having dinner with Elena. Quite groggy the next day.

Clelia called me up at the club the next morning—I never recognize her voice at first—and explained that she had not written because Philip had been in the hospital having a lung operation. —Dinner at Lillian's Saturday night: Epsteins and young Marquands. When I asked Jason later what Marquand did, he said, "He has the greatest block in literary history." Talk about Jackie Kennedy and Onassis. Mrs. Marquand, who had met Onassis, said, as someone else had done, that his attraction was that he liked women and that he concentrated on one in such a way that he convinced one that he was extremely interested—could also, however, turn it off. Was Jackie actually pregnant? The Trillings had deplored the marriage: the Queen had degraded herself. It seems to me strange that people like the Trillings should take Jackie K. so seriously, idealizing her as royalty. The Askews were also there. Kurt has given up his gallery, and Constance is now an old lady. I have never liked them much, but they became so much *habitués* of the Muriel Draper world of the thirties. With Constance, I talked about Muriel, Esther Murphy, Lorna Lindsley; so few of us left, she said. Kurt seemed a little more human than when you saw him as a picture dealer, talked more or less frankly about current values.

Sunday. Went with the Epsteins in the afternoon to the Beatles film *The Yellow Submarine.* Amusing but almost two hours of animated cartoon is perhaps a little too much—Surrealism, Dali, Cocteau, Disney. Afterwards, went to their apartment and got away after only one drink. Bob Silvers, who gave me a briefing on Jamaica; Cal Lowell, who has found some drug that keeps him on an even keel but has given rise to thyroid trouble. —From there I went up to Penelope in Mike Nichols's apartment. When Mike is not there, it seems rather incongruous as a background for Penelope. Her pretty little girl, who looks like Penelope, was there. The dogs are boarded out somewhere. There are now two of the big ones. They have fired the butler who was there before, who she says was "ambiguous in every way." She had wanted to do it, but Mike had thought it would be better for him to. Elena arrived from the Thorntons' (she thought that the crisis had been weathered: Daphne had gone out, Henry had had little to say about it), and Penelope gave us dinner in a room with posters on the walls by modern Parisian artists.

Monday. I went to see Betty Huling in the afternoon. She has moved out of her nursing home into the Fifth Avenue Hotel. It was shocking to see her reduced to a little gray-haired thin old woman. She just lies there uncomfortable and unhappy, says she can't read for more than a few minutes; a refrigerator but nothing to cook on, hasn't brought any silver from her apartment, has visited it once but going up the stairs was too much for her; too expensive to have meals sent up, so she manages to go out to eat. Awful to see such a vigorous outgoing and extroverted woman reduced to such a state of helplessness: "I can't *do* anything!" Still suffers from her depression. Her sisters have never come on to see her, but she has friends in the neighborhood: Helen Good came while I was there. She went through a horrible operation with her lung. I don't think they have told her her cancer is fatal. She gave me a long description of her illness as if she still had a chance. Very hard to make conversation with somebody in this condition—though I made her laugh by telling her about the dinner at which I got my Aspen Award.

Before my visit to Betty, lunch with the Oxford people. Brett-Smith says that their business has doubled in size. I got the impression, as I did before, that they are no longer so happy in their jobs.

Tuesday. Lunch with Roger. He told me that he had been sitting in London in a hotel lobby with an Italian writer and her two children. He had noticed that the little boy's fly was open, but thought that at 6 years perhaps it didn't matter. But then the little girl put her hand in and began playing with him. The mother had said, "No, dear, not here."

I had arranged to have dinner with Wystan, who was supposed to come to the club at 6. I waited an hour before he turned up, already, I think, rather tight. Though he had been several times in the Princeton Club, he had gone by mistake to the Century Club next door, and it was only when somebody came in whom he knew that he discovered he had got into the wrong place. I thought he was relatively demoralized, like everybody and everything else in New York. He had been at his place in Austria at the time of the invasion of Czechoslovakia by Russia, and he had written, he said, for the first time in years, a purely political poem. He was getting out another book of poems. He had written a review for *The New Yorker* on the recent book on Wagner, and we discussed Wagner at some length. I asked him what he made of *Götterdammerung*, and he said that it was splendid, a grand opera; but I couldn't seem to get him interested in the very curious story, which I think must have been provoked by something in Wagner's personal life. This is consistent with Wystan's idea that, in the case of an artist, the connection between his life and his work is unimportant and doesn't deserve attention. As usual, we drank too much wine and the next day I was the worse for it.

Wednesday. Lunch with Wilfrid Sheed: very interesting. He has had polio and walks with a cane; spectacles, a face which indicates unconsciously a good deal of suffering endured; unsubdued and rather bristling black hair. It seems that Maisie Ward is his mother and his father the Sheed of [the publishing house] Sheed and Ward, an Australian. He said that, expatriated and declassed—I don't know what he meant by this last—he had taken the Catholic Church as his fatherland. When I said something about Father D'Arcy's being better educated than Father [Fulton J.] Sheen, he said that Father Sheen was better educated than he seemed to be. He had worked for him at one time as his secretary, and saw that Sheen had allowed himself more and more to cheapen himself as a popular exhorter. He had inspired the Catholic journalist of *The Hack*. I felt that it pained and embarrassed him when I told him about the Dominicans and the Jesuits in connection with the Dead Sea scrolls. He had evidently read my books attentively and those of the other writers of my generation— asked questions about Hemingway and Fitzgerald. I was surprised to learn that *Office Politics* was based partly on what he thought was the situation at *The New Republic* when Elmhirst intervened*—also, on Alan Pryce-Jones under whom he had worked in some connection. He said

* In 1941, with the war beginning, Leonard Elmhirst, the Englishman who had heretofore supported *The New Republic* without interference, sent over his son-in-law, Michael Straight, to impose an interventionist line. There had been division among the editors since Herbert Croly's death in 1930, and when Straight took over, Wilson and others on the staff resigned. The magazine's new stance was welcomed by sympathizers with Great Britain and with Stalin's Russia, but *The New Republic* lost credit among independent radicals.

that he had never been able to penetrate beneath the small talk of Pryce-Jones. I told him there was nothing there.

Had Penelope to dinner at the club and afterwards went to *The Charge of the Light Brigade*, which she was seeing for the "umpteenth" time. The house was not very full, and I think it was true that the American audiences did not really understand what it was all about: the English mixture of nostalgia for nineteenth-century England with ridicule of the British dodos who were responsible for the military disaster. Afterwards, we went back to the club and had a couple of rounds of drinks in the second-floor lounge. I started to explain my book about representational language* but, by way of the old T'ville grammar and rhetoric, got off the track onto discussing the importance of the old-fashioned study of "rhetoric," which she had been drilled in, too, and we ended more or less by toasting such figures of speech as zeugma and chiasmus. She has read Kinglake and Stanhope's conversations with Wellington. She qualified for Oxford but, on account of her age, I think—she was in her teens—they wouldn't let her in yet. It is extraordinary, her feminine quality of wanting to please men—which one finds so seldom in America carried to that degree. When I had wanted to get to the movie on time, she was ready to reduce her dinner to the same meager proportions as mine.

One night I had a dream in New York in which I thought I was going to bed in a sort of dormitory with, I think, half a dozen other couples. I had a well-built goodlooking but slightly elderly and not especially attractive woman, and my prospect was that later all the couples would change off and I should go to bed with all the other women. But I couldn't succeed with the first one. I fucked and fucked,

---

* EW never completed this project, though there are pages on the subject in the files dating from his Harvard seminar.

as I thought, lustily, but I found that I couldn't come. Very frustrating. I woke up.

Lunch with Arthur Schlesinger. When I talked to him about the Kennedy–Onassis marriage, he said that he was at first incredulous, then horrified. I said that she had evidently always had a café society side. He said that somebody who knew her well had told him that before she married Jack, she had cared about nothing but international society, and that Jack had got her away from this. But until she married Onassis, Arthur had never realized how important this element in her nature was. He had thought she was very bright. This event had profoundly shaken his faith in his ability to judge character. He said that he enjoyed swinging, too, had once met Onassis at El Morocco. He had been surrounded by a retinue of yesmen, had held forth to Arthur with his fascist views. Arthur had suddenly said to himself, "What am I doing in El Morocco listening to this fascist?" He got up and left.

Thursday. I went up to see Roman Grynberg, who had a stroke last June. Difficulty of getting taxis one of the features of New York that make life so disagreeable. The taxi that I finally took broke down—the batteries for the lights were exhausted—and a second one took me to West 75th St., and I had to walk about to the river, along which a cold wind was blowing. Roman was on his feet when I came, but he could hardly move or talk—smiled with effort from time to time, answered questions with effort, but I could not understand him, and Sonya had to interpret. It was even harder to make conversation with him than it had been with Betty Huling. Depressing and baffling to find these old friends like ghosts in another world. Sonya told me an amusing story of how Roman had written to Chukovsky about something and—I suppose so as not to get him into trouble—signed the letter with the name and

under the address of a woman friend of theirs. This started
a correspondence which went on for two years. Roman
discussed Russian literature in such a recondite and erudite way that Chukovsky was quite astonished and addressed him as *"udivitel'naya Sasha"* [remarkable Sasha].
His letters—Chukovsky is 80—were verging, said Sonya,
on the passionate. Then Roman had his stroke, and the
correspondence suddenly ceased. Chukovsky still doesn't
know about the hoax, and Sonya pledged me not to tell
about it. This seems to me very Russian. —Sonya came
out to the elevator with me and insisted that he would
never get well—I had been trying to give him hope. His
stroke on top of his angina made the situation hopeless.
She said that for three months she had not been out of the
house. But she has always been a great complainer and
worrier. I am awfully sorry for them, though.

After the Grynbergs', dinner across the park at the Lehoviches'. I went to the ballet with Evgenia. I supposed
that she always had the entrée, but she told me when we
got to the theater that she had called up the agent and told
him that she wanted two tickets for Mr. Wilson of *The
New Yorker*. She had in this way saved $12. She asked me
whether I minded. —Her son, who had been in Vietnam,
had never expressed any protest. He had spent seven
months in Russia, where he had gone with an unprejudiced
mind, but from which he had come back with no use for
the Soviets. He has now got a year off to study in Washington on one of those scholarships. —I was struck by the
fact that even people like the Lehoviches who have been
living in New York more or less contentedly for years now
say that life there is intolerable. The Lehoviches' great
idea is to get out to their Long Island retreat.

Friday. Went to the opening of the *Rheingold* at the Met
with the Strauses, Bob Giroux and Susan Sontag. I mistook
Bob Giroux for Bob Silvers and talked to him about Jamaica

and *The N.Y. Review*, and only at the end of the dinner discovered who he was. Does this mean that I am getting *gâteux* [senile]? I never have much conversation with Susan Sontag. Roger can't quite forgive me because I am not impressed by her. When I talked to her about the movies in the car, she discussed them in her usual pretentious and esoteric way: *Yellow Submarine* should have stuck to one style, it was a mixture of too many, an "anthology." When I spoke of *The Charge of the Light Brigade*, she said she had liked the interpolated animated cartoons summarizing English history, which I had thought insignificant and had entirely forgotten about.

A new conductor and director from Salzburg has been producing the series of the *Ring* over here. Auden said of the first one, the *Rheingold*, that the stage was kept so dark that it seemed to have been designed for an audience of owls. The same thing was true of the *Walküre*. Sitting in the first balcony, I couldn't see a single face or clearly what anyone was doing. The first scene's being under the Rhine seemed to give a plausible excuse for the dimness, but the next out-of-doors scene with Wotan, Fricka, etc., was equally dim. Loge, as Giroux said, looked like a bald-headed eunuch and hardly flickered; the giants were a kind of cavemen of not commanding height; Erda was a dim moon of light simply cast on the backdrop while the rest of the stage was in utter darkness. The Nibelungen in Nibelheim crawled on their bellies like lizards: one couldn't imagine them active at an anvil. When, at the end, the gods were supposed to enter Valhalla, I thought that at last we should get some light; but the thunder clouds never cleared up, they only had a dim rainbow across them, which never became a ramp for the gods to cross. I couldn't see Valhalla at all, though I am told that it was perceptible, and there was no way for the gods to get there, so they simply remained on the stage. I was surprised that this production got some very good reviews. It seemed to me to represent the general eclipse of the period. There was no trace of the fairy-tale element that ought to make the opera so brilliant.

"A Definite Point Has Now Been Passed in My Life"

The Pipeses came to Wellfleet for a night. I enjoy them but was feeling lousy with something like an incipient cold that affected my right eye. Pipes has a wide range of interests that makes him unusual at Harvard: literature, music, painting as well as his political activities and his specialization on Russia, which he says he sometimes thinks of dropping. He is amusing and likes to laugh.

He says that a sure social resource at Harvard, when other topics fail momentarily, is stories about Arthur Nock. I couldn't remember having heard any of these. His maid is supposed to have entered his rooms and found him stark naked standing on his head. She exclaimed, "Oh, my God," and he said, "No, Arthur Darby Nock." Someone came and put a couch in his corridor: "What's that for?" "It's for people to decline on." "All right, if they don't conjugate." He must have told these stories himself. They are in line with the professional eccentricities of the English universities. It is supposed to have been known that Nock was in the habit of pinching the girls who worked in Widener. A student tried pinching one and was slapped in the face. "But you let Mr. Nock do it." "Mr. Nock is a great scholar."

Our life is so quiet and monotonous that a visit like that of the Pipeses seems to me wildly exciting and probably puts a strain on my nerves. I invariably drink too much.

—Irene Pipes had told me in Cambridge that when she

had gone to Israel, she had been shocked to see on a toilet roll the characters of the sacred language.

December 17, 1968. A definite point has now been passed in my life, which up to now I have felt to be a more or less straight and organic development. I no more take much interest in my old books—they tend to seem to me more ephemeral—and when I pick one up, even such a recent one as *Bit Between My Teeth*, I seem to have broken off from it, I read it almost as if it had been written by somebody else. Is the texture as well as the content really mine? —Am I still the same person that I was in my boyhood in Red Bank?

Wilfrid Sheed and his girlfriend came up on December 26 and stayed till the next Sunday. Elena didn't like Miss Ungerer—with reason or not, I don't know. She says she is used to having people like her, and she felt that Miss U. didn't. Miss U. had worked for Eugene McCarthy, and they argued rather hotly about him and Kennedy. Elena is so infatuated with the Kennedys that she became emotional and rather venomous. —Wilfrid made on me the impression of being embarrassed by the Church and really wanting to get out of it, but being prevented by fear of the hell that his parents would raise. Miss U. accused him of having tried to know as little about the Church as he could. —He told me that his mother read quantities of detective stories, but refrained during Lent, at which time they accumulated in piles.

A young couple from the Job Corps came in for drinks on the 16th. I had been working all day on my proofs for the *Scrolls* book, and would far rather have relaxed with a drink and the phonograph. These two young people depressed me profoundly. He is Jewish and has a black beard that makes him look like a Hebrew prophet. She is pale blond and has pale blue eyes, with glasses, and two long wisps of hair hanging down on either side of her face. She gives piano lessons; he has been teaching two and a half years at the Job Corps. They have a boy 5 years old. She was very quiet; but he is a pseudo-serious-minded blah-blah young révolté. He is resigning from the Corps with much indignation, wanted to read us the letter he had written them, but I didn't give him any encouragement. Full of rage against discrimination in the hiring of Negroes; but it turned out that in the Job Corps here they had actually six or seven. He studied government at Boston University and is now going back to get a Ph.D. in education "—just for practical reasons": it made it easier to get a job. He talked continually about his "ideas" about education, about which he had nothing concrete to say—all "problems," "methods," "decisions." He wanted to teach people how to make decisions. When I pressed him, "Well, how to vote." Nothing but abstract words. I told him that education—aside from reading and writing and the multiplication table—was intended to teach you to do something, to master some art or craft or some technique. He had no interest in this. Elena said you had to learn some discipline. Why? Why did you need discipline? All this in a very loud voice and mispronouncing, as I was tempted to point out to him, *impotent* as *impótent* and *salient* as *sallient*. "Of course, education is emotional—I admit it's emotional!" He was bitter about all the bureaucrats—the bureaucrats who work for the National Park and have little or nothing to do. He doesn't realize that what he is aiming at is to become a bureaucrat himself in the educational field—in which, furthermore, many of the teachers are very badly educated. He had called up twice asking to see me; said he had looked forward to meeting me for ten years. It had taken him ten years to read *The American Earth-*

quake, which had been given him by his wife and which he had only just finished. Did I consider that the Depression had resulted in a revolution, that the present demonstrations amounted to a revolution? He agreed with me that they hadn't. What did I think was going to happen? I told him that I had no more idea than he did. His 5-year-old was going in for art, and he didn't approve of what they were making the boy do. He thought that this was outrageous. They would kill his "creativity." He was a disturbing example of what I hadn't seen in person: the idiotic desire of the young people to blame everything wrong on somebody else, and to manufacture grievances. I became more and more snubbing, though I tried to keep things goodhumored. —He had had no Jewish education and couldn't read the שלום [Shalom] on the mantelpiece.

The Stacy Mays: We had dinner with them a second time, in order to see Venite [O'Connor]. May is a good old boy and intelligent, but bores me. The things we talk about—having lived through the same period and known some of the same people; he is 75—seem terribly stale: *The New Republic*, Meiklejohn at Amherst. And we have the same conversations, tell the same anecdotes. —Venite is extremely lively, seems partly to have got over Ed's death. When I first knew her, she never talked, and after her marriage, never talked much: Ed did all the talking. But now she is full of opinions and ideas, many of them so amusingly malicious that she feels afterwards that she ought to apologize for them. She looked very pretty in her thin blond way and was wearing a pretty dress. She lent some flavor to the Stacy May flavorlessness. She talks about herself and her life in a way I had not heard her do before. She had been very poor, became a radical—Max Eastman became her hero, but now she thought him "hollow," rather underrating him—she was no longer a practicing

Catholic, and would not allow the Church to declare her first marriage to a Jew nonexistent, since it would make her boy illegitimate. Some of this she told Elena.

Balzac: I have been reading more Balzac and have been somewhat surprised by two stories—"Le Cabinet des Antiques" and "Les Secrets de la Princesse Cadignan"—in which the fashionable belle turns out not to be made so much of a bitch as the reader expects. She puts herself to a good deal of trouble to go to the rescue of young D'Esgrigons, who has ruined himself for her; she goes away and apparently lives happily with the great writer D'Arthez, whose innocence has formerly been contrasted with her pretended innocence, in which he believes. Balzac, before this, has so deliberately played up the hypocrisy she practices in her scenes with the writer that we wonder whether he had been preparing this surprise all along or had changed his conception of her character from the part he had first written. Was there a much earlier first draught? —"La Maison du Chat qui Pelote," however, has all Balzac's demonic tendency to torture his good characters. Is it plausible that the painter in this story should so completely have lost feeling for the wife whom he had married for her beauty as to destroy his portrait of her in her presence?

EARLY 1969

Stalin's Daughter

Svetlana (January 19 & 20)*: Elena and Nina both much
worked up about her visit. At the last minute, Nina called
up to say that she had never in her life been so nervous
about meeting anybody. Elena seemed to be dreading her
because she had always had a prejudice against her; but
made a rich chicken dish for Sunday dinner, for which
the Chavchavadzes brought her to our house. Helen came
from Boston for the occasion. —Svetlana made a hit with
everybody. She is over 40 but does not look her age. She
is very pretty and with her character and brains must have
had men after her all her life. Her appearances on TV and
in photographs give a misleading impression of her because
they make her look much bigger and more substantial than

---

* Over a year before, EW had sympathetically reviewed Svetlana Alliluyeva's *Twenty Letters to a Friend*, parts of which had appeared, with
great fanfare, in *Life* and *The New York Times*. Objecting to the assumption that she had fled the Soviet Union to make money, he recounted her life after her mother's suicide—which her father's bullying
had helped to bring on—and her defection when taking her Indian
husband's ashes to the Ganges. Wilson's admiration for Svetlana's character would be justified by *Only One Year*, which he called "a unique
historical document" that would take its place "among the great Russian
autobiographical works: Herzen, Kropotkin, Tolstoy's *Confession*."

she is. She is small, with nice soft brown hair, rather large round eyes of a peculiar pale color of green, a somewhat elongated and pointed bird-like nose and a small mouth. She has small hands and feet. Elena says that the way she uses her hands shows that she has been frightened all her life: she flicks her thin little fingers as if she were accustomed to warding something off. She is simple and well-bred—rather shy but with very firm opinions. Before dinner, she argued with Elena about Solzhenitsyn. She had just read *Rakovyj Korpus* [*The Cancer Ward*], and she said it had horribly depressed her—much inferior to Pasternak, about whom she is enthusiastic. Elena insisted that it had cheered her, but Svetlana, who had after all come from Russia, denied that there was anything cheerful about it.

She is completely pessimistic about the Soviet Union. I said there was some opposition now, wasn't there? Five or six people protesting over a literary trial in a country of 200 million?! In Russia, no student protests such as we are having here are possible. The students who protested would be simply thrown out, and so never get an education. She talked strangely about the Revolution, as if it were not something of crucial importance. In Russia, there had always been rebellions, and they had not accomplished anything.

Nina is not well and was already quite tight, sticking assertively to her flat statements, which were not necessarily true, in such a way that it was impossible to argue with her and one simply had to disregard them. Paul had a bad cold and was full of pills. At dinner, things became at first a little bit embarrassed and awkward. For some reason, the Russian alphabet became a kind of issue. Nina asserted emphatically that she still wrote all the old eliminated characters, that the language didn't look right—she once told me it looked "naked"—without them. She had had to learn all the hard signs, and seemed to imply that she wasn't going to give them up. Paul, too, said that he couldn't write any other way. Neither Paul nor Svetlana could seem to see that the Russian *e* was different from ours (for a foreigner, it is the most difficult sound to master—I don't know why they thought that they had to have an *f* for foreign words); why was Alliluyeva transliterated with a *y* before the *e*—why was Dostoevsky? S. blushed during this conversation, but firmly held up her end.

Svetlana asked us whether it was true that, in America, you bought the dishes all prepared and had little to do beyond heating them up. Elena refrained from expressing her scorn for this kind of cookery (Nina evidently does this to some extent). When we talked about Nina and Elena making excellent Russian dishes, she said with a certain sharpness that she knew nothing about Russian dishes, could only make Indian dishes such as curry. When we were sitting around after dinner, S., at one point, got up and joined E. and Helen in the kitchen. E. had already discovered she liked her, because she was quite "straight," and was now very much touched by her interest in Helen, whose age she asked. She explained that her own daughter was 18, and showed them a picture of her. E. said that one of the things she had held against S. was abandoning her children. Her 20-year-old has married and she does not even know whether she has a grandchild. She has had only twelve letters from her son, and has not heard from him in a year. Then I took her alone into my study and talked to her without any awkwardness till E. came in and said that Nina would have to be taken home. S. knew none of my literary friends in Moscow. Of course they are or were older than she, but she must always have led a very restricted life.

The next night, Monday, we had dinner at the Chavchavadzes'. It was rather a strange evening and left me

feeling rather uncomfortable. It becomes a little difficult
to know how to talk to Svetlana. She is so bitterly opposed
to Soviet Russia that she won't hear a word in its favor;
but then if you make fun of things that happen there, you
only get a wry little smile, and you realize that, after all,
her papa was the man who was most responsible. You don't
know what approach to take; but she has developed a very
ready but also very firm attitude for dealing with all sorts
of approaches. When I remarked on what good fellows
Leonov and Kataev were, she would say, "We have a different idea of them." They had both been against Pasternak, had voted against him in the Writers' Union. I said
that I hadn't known that. "They all did." Paul had been
getting publicity, which he undoubtedly enjoys, on account
of translating her book; a man from Reuters had called
him up from London at four o'clock in the morning. He
said with pride that the two leading families of Georgia—
that of Chavchavadze and that of Stalin—were now united
in this enterprise. (It turned out that this remark had been
based on some note of the kind in the press.)

We tended to talk across Svetlana, while she sat very
restrained and silent. I would then turn to her and talk
to her and she would readily respond with the charming
smile of one who knows how to charm men. When talking
of people of the old regime, she remained perfectly blank.
Nina told her that she ought to know Evgenia Lehovich;
but she did not say she would like to, and there was nothing
that she could say when, for example, Nina mentioned
that she was the daughter of a grand duke. One felt a little
that Nina was challenging her. They talked about the
Kremlin, and Nina told her about visiting it "as a tourist"
in her girlhood. Svetlana said, "Your Kremlin and my
Kremlin are different." She had to live there at one time,
and it had been a most unpleasant experience. But she and
Nina seemed to have been touched by one another. When

she was out of the room Nina told me that the night before, when going to bed, Svetlana had put her arm around her and kissed her.

She is contemptuous of American "liberals." It is the old story of people who have never been in Russia and know very little about it telling her the Revolution was all for the best, and things can't be so bad as she thinks. "They don't understand. They think 'father-daughter.' They can't understand why I feel as I do." The alphabet came up again, and we began having the same conversation, but quickly changed the subject. I had felt the evening before that her hatred of Russia was even to be seen in her disavowal of knowing anything about Russian cooking. When she travels, she gives herself an assumed name. It was suggested that she should travel down to New York with me, but then she said she had to get to Princeton late in the afternoon and would go early in the morning by bus. Elena afterwards told me that she was afraid to travel alone, so I called up after we left and offered to have her go with me. It hadn't occurred to me that it was possible that, with her bitter outspokenness about the Soviet Union, she might be afraid of assassination, as her father had had Trotsky murdered. She has bought a house in Princeton and says she is happy with it—has also bought a Dodge. —In certain lights, she looks older than she does when you first see her. —She says she does not speak much Georgian, has been to Georgia only once.

Penelope's Stories; A Boyhood Memory

January 21 (Tuesday). I flew to New York late in the afternoon and got to the Strauses' for dinner a little after 8. It was a dinner for Peggy Guggenheim, who Roger says has somewhat "mellowed" and is a good deal preoccupied with her children. I sat beside her at dinner, and we talked about art. I don't believe that she really knows much about it except from the point of view of the dealers. Lillian [Hellman] was on my right. She is going to live in Boston, can't stand N.Y. any more. Eileen Simpson and her husband (she was John Berryman's former wife). She says that John has cut off his Ancient Mariner beard and is working at a new "image." She doesn't see him when he comes to N.Y., but his presence as a nuisance is always felt in poltergeist manifestations: tables collapse and candelabra fall. Paul Horgan: he has himself well dug-in, as a permanent Fellow, at Wesleyan, with his little house, on which he has made improvements—though the Center has now been taken over by the university and is much debased, he says, in quality.

January 22 (Wednesday). Lunch with Roger—we talked business and gossip. Saw *Penelope* at the [*New Yorker*] office in the afternoon. She said she was half-dead from her attempted flight from Mexico, where Mike is making *Catch-22.* Two engines on the plane broke down, and they were flapping around in the air at a tilt. At first, the Mexicans told her not to worry, implying that the English were timid; then they realized that the situation was dangerous, and a man who was "green with fear" said, "The Englishwoman is right!" and seemed to think that since she was English, she would know what to do. They asked her to come to the cockpit, which, terrified herself, she did. They asked her, "What shall we do now?" but she hadn't the least idea. They said they would know what to do if it was only one engine but not what to do about two. They finally got back to Mexico City with an emergency landing; but she found that since, on leaving, she had turned in her departure card, the authorities said that they couldn't let her go without her getting another one. This was discussed in a metaphysical way, she said, like "the meaning of meaning." She tried to impress them with the situation and how shaken up she was, but none of this worked. Then she thought of bribery, something she had never tried but which they had undoubtedly been waiting for all along. The minute they got the money, they let her go. She seems to have a proneness to comic adventures, but it is, I suppose, rather that she has a genius for making things comic. She shares my distaste for Spain—its cult of death and its bullfights. I told her about Praz's book, and she gave me an account of a bullfight she had seen which was very much like his. One bull sat down and wouldn't fight, and the bullfighter did something objectionable, which provoked the virulent anger of the crowd. She was English, she said, and didn't like to see the horses staggering around after they had been gored by the bull. She had gone with Kenneth Tynan and Hemingway, who both fancied themselves as connoisseurs and quarrelled violently about a certain point. The issue was whether or not the banderillo had been correctly placed. Tynan said it was four inches off. When they parted that evening still arguing—the fistfight took place the next morning—Tynan's final fling to some nasty remark of Hemingway's was: "You wouldn't know about four inches!"

Wystan Auden for dinner. We didn't do so much drinking or stay up so late as usual. He says that he never reads or writes at night—has a drink or two and goes to bed at half past 9. That evening he left at 10: "We're elderly squares now." He and Sylvester Gates had been to the same "private school." Gates had told me that his principal memory of the war was not getting enough to eat. Wystan said that when he had had the bad sportsmanship to take an extra slice of bread and margarine, the presiding master had said, "I see that Auden wants the Huns to win," and this had given him the idea that Germany was associated with forbidden pleasures. We had our usual conversation about the current ignorance of the technique of verse. He complained that the reviewers of his books never spoke of his prosodic virtuosity. For example, nobody had mentioned, in writing about his last book, that it contained a poem in stanzas. I said that I thought William Carlos Williams had ruined American poetry by leading most of the poets to give up verse altogether and lapse into "shredded prose." He said that he didn't care about the early Williams, but that he had learned something from the later Williams. I said I couldn't see any influence. "It's there." "What do you mean?" "Technically." "How?" "Length of lines." I still don't know what he meant.

He thought Eliot's line "Why should the aged eagle stretch his wings?" extremely funny, and raised one arm for a wing, then shook his head and dropped it. He had been reading Pope with enthusiasm—didn't like the excremental book of the *Dunciad* but admired the last book. Resorted much to Pope and Horace these days. Was much impressed by Wycherley's asking Pope to correct his verses, when Pope was a boy of 15. We were in agreement, however, that Wycherley was not much of a writer. He told me for the second time lately that he had been furious that I had exploited backward rhymes before he had thought of it. But it has taken him years to come out with this.* During a pause in the conversation, he makes a sound, "Um—ah," which is his equivalent for the usual English "Hm."

January 23 (Thursday). At 10:30, Esther and Bobby Hartshorne picked me up at the club and drove me to Red Bank. Bobby so much resembles John Amen, face, build, loud

---

* EW called his backward rhymes "amphisbaenics," from the mythological serpent with a head at either end. They consist of rhyming syllables where the vowel sound recurs but the consonant sounds are reversed: gulls/slug and reed/deer in the opening stanzas of his 1948 poem "The Pickerel Pond" (*Night Thoughts*).

positive voice, self-assertive nose, humorous remarks, law practice, that I kept feeling I had simply slipped from one form of John to another. Esther had had Sandy cremated —he had died of pneumonia—and the ashes buried in the family plot and a little service held there. I found cousins that I hadn't seen for years: all three of Esther's boys and Nat's very pretty wife. Margaret [Rullman] and Charlotte were there, a Betty Clark, now Fox. Esther, again, on the way down, gave me her priceless expression "not o.c.d." about Harriet Kizer's daughter's husband, a riding master. Betty Fox said that she had been afraid that I would call her Bibi (actually I think it was Chérie). I had tried to remember her childhood nickname but couldn't. *It came back to me*, in connection with her, that hers, when she was a little girl, were the first female genitals I had ever seen. It was in a bathhouse at Seabright. She was so young that her nurse thought it didn't matter for me to see her naked when she dressed her. But I was older than she, and for me it had been a revelation. I thought about it in connection with the strapping and box-bosomed elderly woman she had become. She said I hadn't seen her for fifty years. She gave us drinks and a very good lunch. She lives next to the Rumson Day School, where Rosalind and Bobby went. It now has a large annex. They talked about a crisis it was going through. The headmaster had retired or been retired on some issue of desegregation. I gathered that he had been in favor of it—there were two Negro pupils at the school.

It became quite jolly at Betty's, though we talked a little about Sandy. Esther said that her father had always told him that he didn't have to be a doctor. It was his mother who insisted on it. He had flunked anatomy in his third year when he still lived with his mother and Esther at the top floor of the N.Y. house, and the situation was terribly tense. He was always walking the floor, and Aunt Carrie and he had dreadful quarrels, in which Esther had to act as intermediary. —It is appalling to me now to think of his fifty years in that institution—a total blank for that personality that had so much humor and charm.

When I got back to N.Y., I went for relief to the *New Yorker* office, dropped in on Sid Perelman and wanted to get him to go out for a drink, but he had to do something else—so took Brendan Gill to the club. He hadn't heard about Philip Carroll's having had an operation for cancer of the lung. I told him that Clelia had asked me to be sure to let her know whether we were really going to Jamaica, and then had written me that Philip, without her, might be going "island-hopping" and might look us up. This made Brendan laugh: "You were hoping to see Clelia and are going to get Philip."

Elena arrived after Brendan left. She told me that Svetlana had kissed Nina goodbye.

January 24 (Friday). Sheldon Meyer for drinks to talk about scrolls book, followed by Penelope for dinner.

January 25 (Saturday). Arthur Schlesinger for lunch. Talk about movies that pretend to be serious actually going too far in pornography. —*We called on Betty Huling* at the Fifth Avenue Hotel about 3. She was more responsive in conversation than she had been when I saw her last, and I told her she seemed better, but she said she wasn't. That Englishman at *The New Yorker* who seems to me phoney though she says he "hasn't a phoney bone in his body" had been to see her and, when she asked whether the doctors thought her illness was permanent, inexcusably said that they did. Dreadful to see her strong personality, all that heartiness and goodwill, reduced to such a diminished body. She couldn't eat, food was repulsive. She seemed to be reading a little more, but not much. —Barbara [Epstein] for dinner. She said that she had never really been able to believe in anti-Negro and anti-Semitic behavior but had lately in the former case come to realize that it was real. I was so sleepy I went to bed immediately after dinner. Elena stayed talking to Barbara and telling her about Svetlana. We had already told so many people that we had made an agreement before dinner not to bring the subject up.

February in Jamaica—Ackee Poisoning

Jamaica. We flew there on the 26th. The vague Mrs. Fenn did not meet us as she had led us to believe she would, but we managed to call her up and took a taxi to the house, which was much more attractive and livable than Adelaide [Walker], in her overwrought anxiety that everything she did should please, had given us the expectation it was. In fact, having suggested it in the first place, she ended by almost discouraging us from coming here at all. Two large bedrooms, each with a bath, and a living room in between. Violet, the built-in cook, is so deaf it is hard to communicate with her. She has a little dog, Fifi, who kills the chickens on the place, and two children, a niece and son (?) Mrs. Fenn doesn't know; 70% of the population are illegitimate. They live in a little house outside the main house.

—The palms flap their big foolish fronds. As Elena says, the colors in Jamaica do not lend themselves to being painted because they are too coarse. The green of the palms and the blue of the sea do not go well together. A coconut palm in the back yard has a rather ugly cluster of yellow coconuts. Almonds are constantly dropping from the almond trees. The most conspicuous birds are what we call turkey buzzards but what they call John-crows. The first night we came, the chirp of some kind of little cricket sounded very sweet and well tuned. It seems to say *piréet, kyuur* or *pire-eet*. Like the words I hear in my incipient deafness, it doesn't have clear vowels. The fireflies are huge. There are all sorts of red and pink flowers, more or less flamboyant, poinsettia, bougainvillea, begonia, hibiscus, etc. Our back lawn is on the sea, but there is a little wall of rocks that prevents me from climbing down. Farther to the right, one reaches a little cove, but both it and the water along here are studded with tufa rocks, which makes it impractical to bathe in except on a very clear day when one can see the rocks and avoid them.

The wide and calm unquiet sea.* Elena rashly asked Violet to give us a native dish. She produced what is called "salt fish and ackee—" which I afterwards found described as a dish highly esteemed by the natives but less by other people. Ackee is a pendant to a kind of fruit and is poisonous until it is ripe, when it opens by itself. The fish—cod, probably imported—did smell rather rank, and E. didn't attempt to eat it. I, however, did eat some of both the ingredients. I couldn't sleep and took two sleeping pills, a glass of whisky and a glass of vodka. Suddenly I began vomiting violently. I felt horrible and began bellowing; but E., at the other end of the house, couldn't hear me. I felt poisoned through and through, and my mind was in a condition of agony and chaos. I don't remember ever having

---

* EW used these first impressions in verse that he incorporated in *Holiday Greetings and Desolating Lyrics*, sent to his friends the following year:

TRISTES TROPIQUES
The palms that stand flapping their foolish fronds;
The phantom of Fleming diffusing James Bonds;
The almond trees dropping inedible nuts
On lawns that are littered with cigarette butts;
   White beaches, coconut debris.
   The wide and calm unquiet sea.

Wilson borrows the title of Claude Lévi-Strauss's anthropological memoir.

suffered in such a peculiar way as this. I was knocked out all the next day—it was as if I had been disintegrated. The doctor from across the way came in the afternoon, and eventually I recovered. A few days later we read in the paper that two small boys had died of ackee. —The fruit here is mostly too sweet and the vegetables are completely insipid.

The Fenns seemed almost nonexistent as actual people in my communications with them, and when they came to see us at the cottage they seemed hardly less so. He comes from Vermont, but is completely deaf, so, as she explained, one can hardly talk with him. His only communication was to tell us several times that sometimes the sea was so high that the water came into the living room. (Otherwise, there is only a variation on the beaches of about a yard in the tides.) She is the daughter of a "non-conformist"—in her case, a Baptist minister—whose father had first come to Jamaica. The non-conformists had helped the slaves, and her grandfather here had hidden them; the Anglicans had wanted to keep them enslaved. She does not respond readily to smiles, and this impedes conversation: low-voiced, impassive, remote, dignified, perfect decorum and a certain maintained formality. Perhaps all this results from being a non-conformist at odds with the old English upper class. She has, however, been very kind, and she loosened up to some degree when we went up to see her on her hill at Brown's Town, and she gave us an excellent tea. Her husband from time to time glided in and out of the room like a phantom. This is like living in a vacuum. One realizes how much difference it makes to deprive oneself of one's environment. The difficulty here is to keep awake and to force oneself to accomplish anything. One's mind becomes *tabula rasa*, and if, for the moment, I lie awake and have any mental activity, unconnected images from the past simply drift through my head without apparent selection and with no directive purpose. It gets on my nerves and annoys me to go to sleep so much.

Yet this vacation has in a way brought E. and me closer together. I like to be able to see her sitting with her beautiful bare legs and feet. She always wiggles her pretty little toes in response to what she is reading—an expressiveness which perhaps makes up for her habitual self-control in maintaining the reserve of the rest of her demeanor. When she is telling me something, if her hands are not working, she even gesticulates with her toes. She has been going to swim alone the last two weeks; but yesterday I went in at the public beach for the first time since we arrived. Water is quite warm—too warm for E.—but it bucked me up and made me feel better. We have been reading Russian fiction—E. a volume of Tolstoy's short stories, a translation of *Besy* (*The Devils*) and Bulgakov's *The Master and Margarita*; I, a volume of Tolstoy's posthumous writings. We have also read books on Jamaica and *The White Witch of Rose Hall*. This latter relates itself to a kind of tradition in Jamaica of the uncanny and the fantastic: *The Monk*, William Beckford, even Ian Fleming (you can't fit Noël Coward into it!).

Jamaica, so far as the people go, seems to me a dismal place. Bottom layer of black peasants, mostly illiterate, who don't even go to school. Middle class of mulattoes, who regard themselves as an élite, and are trying to breed out the black strain and are even embarrassed by their negroid relations. Diluted English like Elsie Fenn who carry on an etiolated British tradition. A few whites who keep to themselves and make a point of not interbreeding. The country is very poor, and there is a new tourist trade which is intended to make them money. This is imposed, artificial and slightly unpleasant, has no organic relation to the native life. There is a flagrant example of the tourist hotel almost next door to us here. As Elena says, as soon as you go in the door, you feel a "hostile and sullen" atmosphere. No one of the service people smiles at you. The waiters are more amiable than most, but in the bar someone stops you at once at night if you try, as I did, to go in with a sport shirt. The color line is severely drawn, and the black employees obviously resent it. We stayed for dinner one day—the dining room isn't open till 8—and the black head-waiter lectured me on coming in without a reservation. I interrupted him and asked for a table, whereupon he gave me a dark look and insolently went on insisting on the necessity of asking for a reservation. The dinner was none too good and, without the tip, cost $16. Will never go there again. The people are dreary to the last degree: mostly washed-out couples, Canadian, American or English. They are rich enough to afford it and evidently trying to think that they are having a good time. On a dance floor in the middle of the dining room, they would revolve very slowly to slow music. Later on, an old couple—she in a red mini-skirt—who must have been taking lessons at Arthur Murray's, spun around and did their separate and passing steps with sobriety but pleased with themselves; they were applauded when they finished, with moderation. They were accompanied by a kind of calypso team—guitars, drums and rattles—monotonous and with no spirit. All these people are horribly depressing. They are apparently the same kind of people who used to go to Miami—now they are moving on to Jamaica.

February 10, Sunday. The hotel has a beach segregated for whites. We go to the public beach next to it, where today there were plenty of blacks swimming. They are physically quite handsome, when not wearing their dingy clothes, and look fine against the blue sea. I am enjoying the water again after not, I think, having gone in at Well-fleet at all last summer. The life here has come to seem quite delightful. But I am already making plans to go back the 1st of March. This kind of Southern climate really does not agree with me: beach house at Santa Barbara—sudden sunset, placid sea that never reaches a climax, monotonous pouring rains, no sense of divisions of time, people languidly amusing themselves.*

We decided in the late afternoon to go along the coast to Duncan's to try the Silver Sands restaurant, which Mrs. Fenn had recommended. It proved to be farther away than we had thought, and when we got there we had the very worst dinner I ever remember to have tried to eat. First we went into a dark funereal bar, where nobody else was sitting, and after a long delay were served drinks that had almost no content. Then in the dining room—as Elena said, the place was a *pension de famille*—we were served first a very thin soup made out of some otherwise used-up fowl; then salt fish and ackee, which we skipped; then a plate of what they called ham and a plate of what they called turkey—this latter evidently frozen and completely inedible—with various vegetable odds and ends; and finally, a little slab of what they called fruitcake. Price: $12 something. By that time, it was dark, and E. had a difficult drive back. She had to go very slowly, and the trucks never turned down their lights, but blinded her with their glare. She said it was the most trying piece of driving she had done since our winter trip to Nancy, when the roads were all sheeted with ice. —When we got back to the house, we had a real drink, and I devoured two bananas. I went on to drink too much in bed and got up and wrote the following note: Peculiar footlessness of ideas that pass

---

* EW remembers the autumn of 1928 in a cottage on the Pacific near Margaret Canby, whom he married a year and a half later. To Maxwell Perkins in New York he had written: "All the days exactly alike," adding, "If you stayed out here very long, you would probably cease to write anything, because you would cease to think—it isn't necessary out here and the natives regard it as morbid."

through my head here—importance of being somewhere where people are doing something. Otherwise, just nature, nothing.

Kingston and Tolstoy

Read *Tolstoy's Otets Sergei* [*Father Sergei*]. It makes the same kind of unsatisfactory impression as *Smert' Ivana Il-icha* [*The Death of Ivan Ilyich*]. I don't believe in these late stories of Tolstoy's, always intended to prove something and incompletely invented. He would never have presented such implausible characters in the days of *Voina i Mir* [*War and Peace*]. It begins, perhaps, in *Anna Karenina*. Would she really have thrown herself under that train? I have never quite believed it. And would it really have been possible for Father Sergei, a former dashing officer and man of the world, to have lived for years in that cave? He has wanted to excel in everything and when he discovers that the girl he is going to marry, and whom he idealizes, has been the mistress of the Tsar, he throws her over and, unable to challenge the Tsar, whom he has formerly idealized, to a duel, he decides to top him by piety, by self-humiliation, and goes into a monastery. From there, he goes on to the cave. A life devoted simply to hard living and prayer seems to me incomprehensible for such a man. In consequence of apparently healing a sick boy at a nagging insistence of his mother, he gets a great reputation as a healer, a *starets* (holy man), and crowds of people come to him for cures and advice in their various difficulties. This is beginning to alienate him from God: he is doing this not for God but for people. (I can't understand this. What would he be doing for God and to make himself holy simply by performing his devotions?) He begins to take pride in his position, almost to believe in his powers as a healer.

The climax of this phase is that he rapes, or has intercourse with, a sick girl who has been brought him. He then becomes a vagabond and achieves his final victory over himself when he accepts 20 kopeks from some upper-class people in a coach and on horseback, who speak French. He had been known for his outbursts and bad temper which had made him, in the army, insubordinate, and he has now got the better of these. But would Tolstoy, with his pride of rank and his opinionatedness, ever have been able to subdue himself to this degree? The temptations of spiritual pride, of ungovernable sensuality, of determination that no one should top him—as Gorky said, he and God were like two bears in the same cave—were perfectly comprehensible to Tolstoy, but he obviously cannot imagine, because he does not describe, the life of Father Sergei in the cave. He made in this direction his more or less silly gestures, but he never submitted himself to such a discipline.

I happened to have picked what is apparently the first edition of Tolstoy's posthumous writings brought out by Chertkov in Germany. Chertkov indicates by notes and brackets the passages censored in Russia. All the interesting part about the Tsar in *Hadji Murat* has had to be cut; and in *Otets Sergei*, all references to Nicholas have also had to disappear, so that the point of the breakdown of Sergei's engagement and his wanting to top the Tsar is lost.

Kingston, February 11–14. We flew down—found Hilda Hodgson on the plane. She has aged and is not quite recovered from a serious operation—Elena thinks, cancer. Curious to think of that group of rich Canadians wintering at Port Antonio.

Kingston we found almost as unattractive as it had been reported to be. Mostly rather improvised-looking shops strewn about with large new square white buildings—official or business—here and there among them. Mrs. Fenn had recommended the Melrose Hotel, which we were told by Morris Cargill had been considered good forty years ago but which is now extremely low-grade—most of the people are sojourning Canadians who seem to be at loose ends. Elena suffered more than I did because, in the course of my reporting career, I have had to stay in so many unattractive places. Everything needed repair, and very few things worked. The air conditioner made a terrible noise, and the lighting was inadequate; no telephones in the rooms; a rather off-putting smell. The terrace where they had drinks was sometimes made unattractive by a native drinking with low-class Canadians and bursting into loud Negro laughter. The lunch was so inedible that, except for breakfast, we never ate there again—tried to get a room elsewhere on the hills but everything was full up. February is a busy season. We were continually being warned about going out at night.

I went to the American Embassy and was sent to the "Information" man, whom I saw the next day. He had no idea who I was, but it turned out that he had formerly been posted in the Embassy in Haiti and knew the Marcelins, Eva having at one time worked there. He succeeded very promptly in getting Morris Cargill on the telephone, who invited us to lunch at the Mill, one of the good restaurants. He was very agreeable, a mixture, he told us, of Jewish, English and Negro, somehow descended from the Beckfords, his family still living on and working the banana plantation at Highgate, which they had had since the seventeenth century. The Cargills had been Scotch Covenanters and they had been intermarried with Huguenots. His wife was Jewish, he said, and their adopted daughter Negro. Like Figueroa, whom we afterwards met, he had been to Oxford and, with his fluent Oxford patter, reminded us of Isaiah Berlin. He was a conservative, he said, thought it was a great mistake to try to have everybody educated. Jamaica was probably the country that had the most mixed population in the world, and now the tendency of the tourist hotels to exclude the Negroes was working against the direction they had been aiming toward; but they had to have this tourist exploitation for economic reasons. There was a genuine Negro and mulatto aristocracy—not a middle class, an *aristocracy*. Their adopted daughter had been educated abroad and had recently inverted the traditional situation by failing to approve of an American Negro who had been paying her attention because he was too coarse.

About their literature—they suffered from their social ambivalence: who were they writing for? There was very little audience in Jamaica, and if they aimed at England and America, they couldn't help distorting their point of view. He felt in some ways that he had more in common with the people on his plantation than with anybody else. —He had with him Wycliffe Bennett, one of the black aristocrats he had mentioned, and with him he talked a kind of "shorthand" that could hardly be used in a book. Bennett ran the JBC [Jamaican Broadcasting Corporation]. He and Cargill were trying to give it some substance and some cultural quality. General atmosphere of pioneering that one found in Russia and finds in Israel. Bennett is very agreeable and the most self-assured and well-bred Negro I have ever met—does not look as if he had any admixture.

Bennett said that I had a distinguished name: Edmund Wilson. I said that I *was* Edmund Wilson. He evidently misunderstood this, said, "Your first name." I repeated that I *was* Edmund Wilson. "*The* Edmund Wilson?" "Yes." Cargill laughed and, apologizing, explained that he had had no idea of this. Gayne had simply called him up and said that there was an American writer named Wilson there who would like to speak to him. He thought this was a great joke on Gayne, but it had not surprised me: I can't remember that anybody, including the cultural liaison men, at any American embassy, has ever known anything about me—except in Rome, where the ambassador had to transmit to me the Kennedy medal. But the red carpet was at once rolled out for us. Bennett went to the phone and arranged to have us invited to the reception at the university that evening.

This was given for an English Princess Alice, who has become a sort of patron for Jamaica. From a long time back, she has been spending her winters here and has been raising money for them and helping this new University of the West Indies. The Governor General of Canada, which is doing business with Jamaica, is on a visit here and having a great fuss made about him. He was also present on this occasion. All the cream of the officials and the intellectuals were there. We sat at the back of the open court, and they brought to us the librarian, who had read my *Scrolls* and hoped I had changed my views; an Englishman named Waterlow, a former Communist, who had read at least part of *To the Finland Station*—he has been there advising the government about tropical medicine, and is now, as I afterwards read in the paper, going back to England to teach at the London School of Economics; a man named Figueroa, with a huge white beard, almost very Oxford, who puzzled me at the time; the novelist John Hearne, quite white and, as I guessed rightly, Irish, but with a broad rather negroid nose; a lady who said that she stood in awe of me: she had been aware of me as a mighty presence somewhere in the intellectual world, and it seemed incredible to hear that I was there in person among them. This kind of thing rather embarrasses me: I wonder whether it isn't a mistake for me to

appear in person at all—I must be a disappointment. —
Two black youths from the States walked through and said
loudly, "This is all a lot of shit!" Otherwise, the party—
at which drinks and hors d'oeuvres were sold—was remarkable, in contrast to our parties, in the quietness and
decorum of the voices—quieter even than an English
party, which can, on occasion, be pretty noisy.

The next day we went to the Figueroas'—pleasant tropical house open to the light and air, with rooms without
real doors, that open into one another. Pictures in very
bad taste, mostly by native artists. I feel that Figueroa with
his Karl Marx beard is a sort of pretentious blowhard, who
is vain of doing a variety of things none too well. I have
looked into a volume of poems that he gave me. He talks
all the time, showing off. Besides lecturing on literature
and writing these poor poems and some fiction, he is the
head of the education department. It is true that they all
have to do several things in order to make a living. He is
evidently one of those university men who have enlisted
in the cause of Jamaica. He was going to Santo Domingo
to lecture. (He is, it seems, a Sephardic Jew.) They were
having a council meeting at the university to discuss a
federation between the various islands—common under-
takings like this university. I gather that the federal idea
was defeated. I suppose it's a problem for them to assimilate
Castro. —Mrs. Figueroa, who seems to be an Indian
(ancestors from India), was quite unpretentious and more
interesting. She had a long talk with Elena and took her
the next morning to the straw market, where she bought
hats with loose straw fringes for our girls and the little
Thorntons. Rather lousy lunch at the college cafeteria.
John Hearne later brought his daughter, who had been in
England since she was something like 4 and had only just
come back to Jamaica.

In the evening, we went to the "Pantomime," the script

for which was evidently quite sophisticated, having been written by the brother-in-law of a professor who drove us home from the university. The college arranged tickets for us, and we sat in the first row of the balcony; but most of it was in the Jamaican dialect, and we couldn't understand it except when the speech-making preacher and the officials talked more or less straight English. It was called *Anancy and Doumbay*. Anancy is a Jamaican folk hero, a spider, who wears a top hat. At the beginning of the second part, he is let down from the top in a web. Doumbay is the spirit of evil, whose presence is indicated by thunder and horrible shrieks from a loudspeaker and who appears at one point in a long dark red cloak and semi-Mephistophelian costume, and apparently has everybody subjugated. The common people are represented by a woman of the people and her followers, who come to make demands on the officials, in the center of whom sits the white king. The woman leader of the forces of rebellion was evidently a popular *vedette*, all of whose cracks were received with laughter. (I learned later that she was Louise Bennett, a very well-known figure and a poet in the local dialect.) She had small feet and skinny legs (I think that all their legs are too thin) but above them a huge broad-bosomed body, which flounced in and out. An occasional rousing song. A young couple of lovers, who sang a song that seemed to owe something to that of the young lovers in *South Pacific* and was blended at the end with the menace of Doumbay motif. In the second part, Anancy appeared and announced that he had vanquished Doumbay, but was followed by another character who declared that he had killed Doumbay. How had he done it? By "POWEH!" (evidently a reference to American Black Power). But then it turned out that neither of them had put down Doumbay, who was presumably still at large. A room at the back of the stage was opened and revealed the white king, who now took his place on one of the thrones, the other of which had been claimed and occupied by a snooty high-heeled black regime. The old kingship seemed to have resumed.

More Tolstoy: "What Is to Be Done?"

February 20–21. Visit to Hilda Hodgson near Port Antonio, at Fairy Hill. A whole colony of rich Canadians. At the house of a Hartland Molson with a Hungarian wife, I was reminded of Santa Barbara, and thus assumed wrongly that he was a rich and idle fellow with no serious interests. I talked about the inferiority of American beer to Canadian, and we discussed the difficulty in Jamaica of getting any work done: from doing anything that requires serious effort you lapse into writing letters, and from letters into post-cards; then postcards become too much of an effort, and one feels that one can't get oneself from the couch to the writing desk. Actually, he is a hardworking senator in Ottawa, and interested in some reform bill, and is called in to the councils in Jamaica.

This part of the island, intensely cultivated, is a kind of earthly paradise, contrasting with ours, which is rather scruffy. Royal palms, variety of hibiscus. Hilda has a very well-organized garden—in one case, she has contrived a clever effect of having red hibiscus sprinkle with its wide-scattered flowers a plainer bush of green and white leaves. Handsome hedges, a swimming pool, perfectly rolled and tended lawns. House with blue views of water from the windows of both sides. Spanish jars which Molson and Hilda's husband have busily been collecting. Feeders for hummingbirds—glass containers of red syrup. Humming-birds, it seems, are attracted by red. In Hilda's perfectly appointed house, with its beautiful *mise-en-scène*, in that corner of this miserable island, I kept thinking of the song from *One Touch of Venus*, "The only way to be very happy is to be very very very rich." Elena is perfectly vague about where the Hodgson money comes from—"mines or something." —Hilda has aged and looks haggard. She discovered that she had a cancer and has had one breast and part of an arm removed. She is very serious-minded, reads, subscribes to *The New Yorker, The Listener* and *The Observer*, has contributed to building up the Toronto and Montreal orchestras; but I have never heard her express an unconventional taste or an interesting opinion. She is unusual among the English Canadians, however, in that she speaks very good French, and says that she tries to see as much of the French as possible. Her Aunt Connie lives not far away. She is a formidable old lady who has hard *r*'s and has travelled everywhere—rather like an American woman. Her house is full of Haitian pictures—most of them very good. These painters seem to have passed, since I was in Haiti in 1949, out of the most primitive phase into something more sophisticated—just enough so that the effect is still happy. She showed that her taste was really good by criticizing in no uncertain terms some very bad paintings in a house to which we went when the owners were away.

At dinner, a retired Italian ambassador, Direge (?), and his half-American wife and the Molsons. The Italian had been at Port-au-Prince before he came to Jamaica, and seemed infatuated with it. He defended *le roi Christophe*, insisted that the stories of his cruelty were not true, and seemed even to have a tender spot for Duvalier, who, he said, could be charming; it was not true that corpses had lain in the streets. For conversation with the Hungarian lady, I had only to mention Hungary, and she was off. —We had lunch next day with people named Mather whom Elena had known in Canada and of one of whose daughters she was godmother. They pronounce the name Mayther and say they have no connection with our Mathers. A professor from Toronto named Bells came in who is a nephew—I think it is—of Katherine Mansfield and a cousin of Elizabeth of the German Garden. I was surprised to learn that the latter was a tireless nymphomaniac.* He stayed only briefly, explaining that he had to go to lunch with an English colonel who, if you were on time, thought you were late.

February 22. John Hearne for lunch. The combination of Irish and Negro is singular—his face is quite square and heavy, but his blue eyes have something of the charm of both. We talked about Jamaica, his daughter who has lived in England and is so far left that she doesn't believe in the kind of writing he does—"a gentleman's occupation," indulged in by an individual—thinks one ought to be engaged in some communal activity. He had recently seen Anaïs Nin in California; confirmed her report that Henry Miller was now something of a Los Angeles square. He and I agreed that we had never been able to read a book of Miller's through.† He believes that Jamaica is destined to end as a Canadian province, as Phito once told me in strict confidence that the best that could be hoped for Haiti was to be taken over by the UN.

They don't like to hear much about *Haiti*. It somewhat degrades them to realize how the mixture of blood has

---

* *Elizabeth and Her German Garden* (1900), by Countess Mary Annette Beauchamp Russell, was a popular feminist satire about a German woman whose husband (called the Man of Wrath) alternately oppresses and abandons her, leaving her to pay passionate attention to her garden. The Wilsons' Wellfleet neighbor Phyllis Duganne (who did not much like Elena) had suggested that it described her relationship to EW. He was amused to learn that Elizabeth's original had interests other than flowers.

† However, EW echoes Miller's title, *The Air-Conditioned Nightmare*, later in Naples, Florida.

worked out there. They look down on it. But foreigners who know both countries feel, as I do, that it is far more interesting than Jamaica.

Mrs. Fenn came to see us to discuss our departure and the rent. I pointed out that our leaving March 1 would involve an extra day. She answered with gracious dignity, "I hope you will accept a day." When I saw her off in her car, she asked me when we were leaving—which we had just been discussing at length.

When we were driving back from Ocho Rios, a black man apparently tried to hold us up. He tried to block us and got out of his car, and yelled, I thought, "Avis!" Elena thought, "Hey, Miss!" She was going slow enough so she could swerve quickly and pass him. He followed at first, then we lost him. —Elena mastered quickly and competently driving on the left side.

Tolstoy: I Svet vo t'me Svetit [*And the Light Shines in the Darkness*] and "Molodoi Tsar" ["The Young Tsar"]. In the first of these, the brackets show that censors had removed most of the vital discussions of orthodox religion and of serving in the army, thus leaving very little; the second was not printed at all. In most of these posthumous pieces I have read, Tolstoy is wrestling with the problems of contemporary Russian church and government. He comes rather naïvely to the disparity between Christian teaching and the policies of the Church, having apparently just discovered them in middle life, like Nikolai Ivanovich in his play. As for the state of the Russian economy, the poverty of the peasants and the luxury of the landowners, it was a question to faze anybody. From Chernyshevsky to Lenin, they had been writing pamphlets on *Chto delat'* [*What Is to Be Done?*]. (Nina Chavchavadze sometimes still interpolates in a conversation, "What to do? What to do?")

Tolstoy usually falls back, as in these pieces and *Otets Sergei*, on the idea that since one cannot change society, one must focus, as an individual, on achieving one's own salvation. In "Molodoi Tsar" the young Tsar looks forward to a rest on Christmas Eve after wearying weeks in office and signing that day a number of *ukazes*; but as soon as he falls asleep, he enters a hideous dream in which a spirit takes him around and shows him the horrors of contemporary Russia, sometimes the result of his own commands—a family, for example, completely drunk, as the result of his licensing the sale of liquor, with a sick child in the house. When he wakes—or thinks that he wakes: he is apparently still dreaming—he addresses to himself an agonized soliloquy: "But what shall I do? . . . Shall I kill myself? Shall I abdicate?" In the next room are his wife and an aged courtier, a friend and adviser of his father's. The old courtier tells him, of course, that it is only the incomparable loftiness of his soul that makes him sensitive to the sufferings of others, that Russia is all right, the people are not poor but prospering; whoever is poor deserves it; only the guilty are punished—although there are mistakes, of course. The Tsar is not responsible for everything. Trust God to forgive you and to guide things aright. The wife, however, does not agree with this. She has suffered a good deal, she says, thinking of his frightful responsibility. And she has concluded that his only course is to delegate most of his power to the representatives of the people. But he ceases to listen to either. The voice of the guide in his dream speaks to him in his heart. "You are immensely more than the Tsar," it says. "You are a man—that is, a being who has at present arrived in the world and tomorrow may disappear. You have a greater responsibility than those of your office, than responsibility to your subjects: the eternal responsibility of man to God,

to his own soul, to his salvation and service to God, established in the world of His kingdom. You cannot act in
relation to that which has been and will be, but only in
relation to that which you must do." What exactly does
this mean? It is, in any case, very far from the Marxist
idea, inherited by Lenin, of changing the world. *

When I am tired of reading about Jamaica, with its heavy
and horrible past, its tentative beginnings in literature, its
dubious, precarious future, I go back to reading Renard's
journal, and it soothes me with its long past, its established
tradition of literature, the cultural atmosphere of Paris,
which so much is taken for granted. Yet what vanity and
competition among writers whose names have just barely
lasted and whose works are hardly played or read. Even
Renard is proud of his decoration, and confesses that he
likes to wear his red rosette.

Elena goes in the morning to swim in our little cove,
threading her way among the tufa blocks; I have my breakfast of kipper or oatmeal, orange juice, toast and English
gooseberry jam, Blue Mountain coffee that you put in your
cup by the spoonful. Then I read *The Gleaner*, then do a
little writing. About 12, we go to the public beach. We
sit around reading Russian fiction and eating crystallized
ginger, of which Elena has always been fond. She has got
through *The Possessed, The Brothers Karamazov* and *The
Master and Margarita*, and a volume of Tolstoy's short stories. We are likely to go to sleep in the afternoon, wake
up after an hour; then look up some disappointing restaurant. We are permanently disappointed now and, though
Violet's cuisine is monotonous, have decided to dine at

* EW had been impelled by this idea in *To the Finland Station*. Though
long disillusioned with Soviet Russia, he still respected the dream of
change through reason and will.

home. Bed early; I sit up and read. The rats get into anything left within reach, and we hear them wrestling in the kitchen with cans of nuts and "Poppycock." Violet has trapped two.

It is gratifying to see Elena not breaking her neck about cooking and everything. It even annoys her slightly if Violet isn't always on hand. It is partly that the kitchen seems to her messy and makes her *brezglivyi* (squeamish)—she doesn't want to know too much about what goes on there.

Goats with little kids; a donkey nearby that brays; humped Indian cattle with their cattle egrets, white with long flexible necks; cling-cling birds—a kind of grackle that haunts the outdoor restaurants and lives on the crumbs of the customers: black, with pale eyes and a harsh whistling cry.

A Loss, and "A Kind of Regeneration"

March 1. We came back to N.Y.* Three days had Elena down with sinus again, and the Thornton situation was no better than ever. Henry had not yet had the courage to tell Daphne about the amount of his debt or that her mother had made it possible to settle it. I stayed a week. Usual routine. Epsteins, Roger Straus, Wystan, Penelope, *New Yorker* office, Berlins, Arthur Schlesinger (who told me that Marian was "finally going to give him a divorce" so that he could marry the Emmet woman), Lis Shabecoff (Mrs. H——) for drinks, immediately followed by the Per-

---

* They might have liked to stay longer on the island, he wrote to Celia Goodman, but "a few Greek and Hebrew words [in his *New Yorker* articles] threw the printers and the office into such confusion that I had to come back from Jamaica in order to straighten it out." He added, "I feel from this and other signs that the magazine is rather demoralized, as I believe the whole of the East is since Nixon was elected."

elmans for dinner. The night we saw *The Prime of Miss [Jean] Brodie*, before I met Elena and Penelope at the Russian Tea Room, Henry, bringing his mother's scarf, had a drink with me at the club. He looked to me very pathetic. He said that E. only upset Daphne by talking to her on the phone. I communicated this to E., who turned out to be deeply hurt by it and didn't call her up any more. I think she thought she had been accomplishing something. Daphne had taken to her bed and, from what I heard about her, seemed to be in a neurotic state. I suggested an intelligent psychiatrist, which Henry, of course, didn't want. I asked what Daphne's accusations against Henry were. I was thinking that her charges that he was deserting her and no longer cared about her might have been transferred from her father, as had been the occasion with Mary in transferring her complaints against her uncle to me. But Henry said that she made no accusations to him directly, but only to his mother.

After Elena left I took Penelope to *Hadrian VII*. It didn't have the nasty sharpness of the book. The Berlins had come one afternoon for drinks; then, after E. left, I went with him to a celebration for Cecil Roth's 70th birthday. Some of the people were interesting; I got stuck with one man who was a bore. They were a very varied collection. I seemed to be the only goy. Many professors; one woman who taught Russian literature at Queens. One tall blond Bryn Mawr graduate who, though married, seemed got up like a lesbian, in a black semi-riding costume, with white silk scarf around her neck. Isaiah and I left early and went to the Blackstone. Aline had skipped the party and gone to a movie. I don't think she would have been at home in Roth's milieu. I had a good conversation with Isaiah. We talked about Israel and the Jews. He is much better when other people are not around and you can pursue one subject consecutively. Before, at the Princeton Club, any name

would start him off when he had just been started off by
the previous name, and I always had to set the conversation
back.

At some moment, Wystan had said that the only thing
to do about the poor was to burn them up.

Betty Huling died March 2. She was cremated, and her
ashes sent to Bennington, where she was born, and buried,
with no service. So abounding in good nature and affection
and energy and humor, to be extinguished as a suffering
withered wisp like this. She was very unlucky in her parents, her weak father, who disapproved of her and refused
to see her, her tyrannic, reactionary disapproving mother.
She fought a battle all her life against her lot. Nothing
but tough and vigorous New England heritage. She never
could have been married: too bossy, too independent and,
though not sexually, too masculine. The conventional had
always been alienated from her. Her friends in New York
say that her sisters on the Coast made no sign. Frances,
with whom she had been preoccupied, was obsessed as
usual with her horses, and Betty had not seen her for
years. I suppose they knew no one to write or phone—but
they must have made some communication. Her N.Y.
friends wanted to have a larger announcement of her death,
but this is all the *Times* published:

Elizabeth Huling, an Editor
With New Republic 1934–50

Elizabeth Huling, for many years a member of The
New Republic's editorial staff, died Sunday at Poly-
clinic Hospital after a long illness. She was 68 years
old.

Miss Huling, who was graduated from Vassar College, joined the magazine in 1934 and was copy editor
until 1950, when the periodical moved to Washing-

ton. Miss Huling was a friend of Edmund Wilson, Malcolm Cowley and Otis Ferguson, among other regular contributors to the magazine.

In 1961 Miss Huling became head of the copy department of Atlas magazine, then edited by Quincy Howe, and remained there until 1965.

In Wellfleet, on March 12, I had a sudden seizure, curiously not unlike my ackee attack in Jamaica. I had had two days of exacting work on the page proofs of my scrolls book, and the change from my easygoing life turned out, at my age, to be too taxing: first, a chill which made me shake all over, then vomiting and fever. When I recovered, I was weak for a day, then perfectly all right. It was as if I had been taken down a peg, was older and yet more comfortable; enjoyed sitting around with my books and mail and the very pleasant weather. I now find not only that I'm not attracted by food, but that drink no longer attracts me. I thought at first that red Johnnie Walker was no longer the same as it had been and I might like Dewar's better, which I had followed Lis Shabecoff's example by trying; but again stopped drinking without finishing my first or second glass. Before that, I had tried pale dry sherry, but found that you can't drink more than a small glass of that. Since I've been back, the only three- or four-glass evening I've spent was set off by a call on the Chavchavadzes. I feel much better now in the mornings, clearheaded and not under a nervous strain. I think that the feeling of relief at getting out from under the pressure of the Dead Sea scrolls has something to do with my well-being.

In the meantime, before my seizure, Elena had had a collapse, couldn't eat and stayed all day in bed, so very unusual for her. Banks said that this sometimes happened on readjusting oneself from the tropics—said he had never

seen her so run-down. I think that the Thorntons have
got her down, as her family had after her first trip to
Germany after the war. She had also left Wellfleet on bad
terms with Rosalind, and I had found that Rosalind was
still idiotically resenting her on account of her attempt to
intervene to get R. a job with Little, Brown. Elena says
she cannot bear to have people dislike her, as Daphne, too,
now neurotically does. The situation with Rosalind, however, is now much better since she has had her little apartment in Wellfleet. —Our illnesses, Elena's and mine, have
in some way brought us closer together. Even when she
was feeling so low, she still had her sweet humorous smile
for me, the Aunt Elinka side of her. She now says she is
almost normal, but wants nothing but not to see people
and a chance to do things around the house.

Isaiah told E. that Svetlana, whom he had seen in
Princeton, had said that Nina talked so much that she
couldn't get a word in edgewise. Nina was struck, as I
was, by the gaps in her knowledge of history, of what had
happened before the Revolution. She now longs for such
judicial guarantees as had been established under the Tsar.

These murders here that rival the English moor murders
are also not cheerful to come back to. Rosalind thinks there
is a murder cult, and the number of women's bodies found
and the fact that they were dismembered and apparently
bitten, and that one of them was beheaded, do suggest that
more than one person was involved and that there was
something very queer about what was going on.* There

---

* During the winter of 1969, the mutilated bodies of nine young women
were found at the Truro cemetery, where they were said to have been
lured to buy drugs. As a young Portuguese suspect was sent off for
psychiatric tests, he encouraged the police to "keep digging" (*Near the
Magician*).

was evidently some imitation of a primitive cult in that murder of the anthropology female student in Cambridge. And then it seems possible now that it is taken by hippies as a sign of virility to have had the daring to murder a girl.

Eben Given on the murders: he's (the supposed murderer) 20 years old. "He's right up there at the top!" This was half joking, of course, but not without a note of "local boy makes good."

Visits from Penelope and the Spenders. Stephen said that Wystan had written a poem for his birthday, but somehow it never reached him—though W. read it aloud to him later. He said that this failure to make connections was typical of his relations with Wystan. I hadn't known before that he was aware of his lifelong inability to keep up with Wystan: he has always been left behind by W.'s audacities and eccentricities, and thus astonished and abashed.

Now that the scrolls are off my mind, I have felt a kind of regeneration—inspiration for writing on Svetlana, new introduction to *Finland Station*, Barham review, T'ville memoir and memoirs of the twenties, all more or less bound up with one another. —But the old bridge came out of my lower jaw, and Donovan has had made a completely new plastic one, which is supposed to be hung on one of two teeth still left in my lower jaw but which doesn't work, comes out right away. So, having to live on Wheatena and Cream of Wheat, it has become a nuisance to eat. More dreary and fatiguing dental trips to Boston—more disabilities of old age interfering with plans for work.

Svetlana, May 5–8, 1969: She was tired when she arrived, and looked older and less pretty than she had seemed

when she was here before. The next day she crushed her
finger in the front door, and after, Elena told me, a moment
of hysteria because the finger was very painful, she became
very pale and sallow. Her pretty brown hair, small hands
and feet—which last I saw at the Duck Pond beach. When
the Walkers came in, she perked up and turned on her
charm, pretending to listen with interest to what they said,
etc. She told me that both Brezhnev and Kosygin were
complete mediocrities, quite incapable of governing Russia.
They had got where they were by accident and would be
"pushed out by the [Red Army] marshals," and that would
be a great deal worse. I told her about the Walkers' having
thrown over Communism for the Church, and she said
that when one embraced religion, one forgot all about Communism. Elena thinks that under her dignified surface she
is really very tense. She says that when Svetlana's finger
was crushed by the wind blowing the door shut, she sat
down in the kitchen and Elena was afraid she was going
to faint. She kept saying that she couldn't stand pain—
"perhaps it's imagination"—but she couldn't stand the idea
of people's suffering physical pain! —I invited the Pamet
Road girls in after dinner May 7. They were as unhappy
as she was, and didn't stay long. She said that they made
her feel pity. It is true that they don't look happy, and
Barbara looks terribly run-down.

May 8, 1969, my 74th birthday. I spent the day in sloth
and the doldrums. Champagne at lunch—Svetlana insisted
on making the cork pop to the ceiling. My not being able
to make love, not being able to swim or take much exercise
and now, with my lower teeth gone, not being able to eat
anything but the softest food is getting me down and making me feel frustrated. Had some drinks and went to sleep
very early, but had bad dreams and woke up feeling
horrible—partly from worrying about Svetlana and how to

write about her. But read Macaulay and somewhat re-
gained my equanimity and my inspiration to live.

"A Thin, Subdued Spring"

<*T'ville, May 11, 1969*. We first spent a night in Cambridge
at the old Continental Hotel. Dr. Donovan at last gave up
on the bridge he had made for my teeth and suggested my
trying another dentist. The night of May 10, we were both
under a nervous strain: Elena woke up for her usual worrying spell and woke me up to worry, too; when I went to
sleep, my sleep was horribly tense. Worry about teeth,
Rosalind, Svetlana. Mary P. met me at the airport. To my
surprise, she didn't go on about Alex. Dr. Smith had told
her to take six weeks off, and she looked quite pretty and
rested, was wearing a becoming brown dress that went
with her coloring, her hair now more or less natural. Had
really resigned from the pharmacy and had been offered a
job as study superintendent at the West Leyden school.
As a result of the lack of teachers, they have adopted a
policy of "para-professionalism" (*para* is the fashionable
prefix) to make it possible for people without degrees to
qualify as teachers. The job won't begin till fall, but in
the meantime she may go back to the pharmacy for one or
two days a week. I took her to the Parquet for dinner and,
in spite of my weariness, in order to be able to talk, drank
a cocktail and a bottle of Piesporter. It was a relief to talk
to her about Svetlana and explain Tolstoy and the Russian
Revolution—she had imagined that Tolstoy had had some
connection with the Revolution. When I said that on account of her Soviet education, we had discovered there
were great gaps in Svetlana's knowledge both of the tsardom
and the Revolution, she said regretfully, "And mine, too."

When I went back to the house afterwards, I unwisely

drank quite a lot of a bottle of Old Bushmill's Irish whisky that I had bought on my way through Boonville. I did not feel very lively the next day and, sitting here in the room where I work, in the afternoon—it was getting cold—I had one of my horrible chills—till my teeth were chattering and I could hardly use my hands. I got to the living room and lay down on the red couch, but then vomited all over everything, and could hardly get to the phone to call Dr. Smith—couldn't see to use the telephone book, fell off the chair in the hall, couldn't get Mrs. Hutchins. Smith had to finish with his patients in the office. Mrs. H. came before he did, but I was on the couch from 6 to 8 hours, feeling terrible and almost incapable of turning over. Smith found fever of 103. Gave injections and pills. I finally got myself to bed, and Mrs. H. spent the night in the house with me. Still wobbly Thursday and Friday.> The doctor found my liver enlarged and advised me not to drink, which I haven't been doing. He said, "Life is no fun if you don't cheat a little, but you oughtn't to cheat all the time."

<Only today, Saturday, do I begin to feel pleasantly normal. Yet I find it enjoyable to be here: quiet, a thin, subdued spring. Rather than attack Mrs. Ginzburg's chronicle of her Soviet horrors [*Journey into the Whirlwind*], I went on reading in the biography of Firbank—not as bad as the one of Barham but not a "critical biography," full of more or less uninteresting facts about where Firbank was at different dates, exactly how he arrived at Oxford, no real evocation of the atmosphere of the period.> I was glad that I had taken the precaution of bringing all my Firbank duplicates up here: I was able to look up passages and dip into stories. I found reading him and about him reassuring as Firbank himself said about *Under the Hill*.

I was tottering for several days. <On Sunday, Mary Pco-lar drove me over to see the Marcelins. It turned out that she and Di Spirito had been having quite a rapprochement.

She had been out with him on an expedition and had in the car a little landscape she had made—very Hungarian palette, brown with a note of purplish blue—and a clay bust which did not resemble her and which I did not like at all. Both Phito and I thought immediately that, with its masculine head and sly one-sided smile, it looked like "Voltaire *jeune*." I had some apprehensions about Eva's translation of the novel, but was relieved to find that she had a good sense of literary English. She had sometimes taken over French expressions where they didn't belong, but was aware of the dangers of this and was revising it from this point of view. Phito didn't quite understand the objection to the beginning—protested that it summarized the situation, that certain people did really talk and write like that, of which he showed me an example. I had for the first time an almost entirely intelligible talk with him—his English seemed to have got somewhat better—about Haiti, Marx, his brothers, etc. I told Eva as I came in from the kitchen that we had had an unusually satisfactory conversation. She said that she could suggest an explanation: that we were not full of whisky as we had always been before.

I talked, in connection with Jamaica, about the mulatto élite in both places. But "No more!" he said about Haiti. He said about certain people that they were of good or fairly good family; then, throwing out his hands and staring, he declared that there was not really so very much difference: they had all been originally slaves!> Pierre, he says, when he gets drunk, is likely to inveigh against Duvalier, and has been once beaten up and once put in jail. *La Bête* has, it seems, sold 80,000 in the English *Time* magazine edition, which they used for a kind of book club. <I told Phito that I was getting old—(terrible thundercrack in the middle of writing this—I thought the house had been hit—all the lights have gone off)—he said that he

was, too. I said I was ten years older, that he had the advantage of me—"*Mais je suis en exile.*"> He is very anxious to go back to Haiti for two months—Eva does not want to go with him. He has evidently been thinking a lot about the situation. Duvalier might be fading out, but his son might come in and would be no better. We sat out on the lawn among the apple and pear blossoms and looked out at the wonderful view. The winter up there was terrible, and they think they can't stand another; but Phito doesn't want to go back to Washington.

Going back, it was 5 when we arrived in Rome, and the two films were the two Sidney Poitier pictures that we had seen last summer. I was extremely annoyed because I had left my glasses at the Marcelins'. <We didn't want to have dinner yet, and bought a paper to find out what was going on in Utica.> The most promising prospects were *Mayerling* and *Ghosts Italian Style*—so we set out for there. Mary told me about her recent troubles with Alex. She said he had been overworking her—she had to attend to her surgical devices, keep the accounts and do other things. She had complained about this to Alex, and he had brought in a new little girl and given her first the accounting, then other things. He had "just wanted to stick a finger in my eye." He had told her that she was jealous. Finally, she had gone to Dr. Smith, who had said that she oughtn't to have gone back to the pharmacy and that nobody had to stand persecution by his employer. When she told this to Alex, he had said that she seemed to be very thick with Smith. She said that it was just that he was a wise man, and quiet. Alex's wife, Barbara, had social ambitions, wanted status symbols. I asked what status symbols they longed for. "A swimming pool . . . wants the pharmacy to be successful . . . You can't talk about Stan Kramer to Alex because Stan was elected mayor and Alex was defeated."

In Utica, all the doors of the club were locked, on account of its being Sunday night. I rang the bell and Helmsing, the mysterious international and cultivated manager, appeared in his blue dressing gown and bare feet, for which he apologized, and I apologized for getting him out. <We proceeded then to the movie and caught most of *Mayerling*, which was a terrible load of Hollywood grandeur and elegance, with no human appeal. Catherine Deneuve showed no sign of emotion; Omar Sharif was Arabian and wooden. But it did not bore Mary so much as me. I asked Mary whether she could fall for a grand duke like Sharif, and after a moment of puzzling about how to reply, she smiled and said yes.> We went then to the Italian Savoy restaurant in Rome, where I have come to feel very comfortable, and the food of its kind is good. We had a bottle of Piesporter, and I was able to eat a plate of well-seasoned spaghetti. I explained to Mary such historical events as the French and Russian Revolutions. I rather enjoy this, but she sometimes asks probing questions to which I haven't answers ready. (The storm has quieted down, and the lights have been put on again.)

<Glyn [Morris] ties up the general disquietude with the much talked-of "identity" problem. I got something out of this conversation: the idea, my formulation, that the big power units such as the U.S. and the U.S.S.R. don't give people any identity except the bureaucratic one of bureaucrats, and that this stimulates the small fanatic nationalisms: Scotch, Welsh, French Canadian, Czech, Polish, Swiss French, German and Romansh, etc.—which provides them with a national identity.

Velli, when I went to see him, implied that Donovan and Cutler had made a botch of their lower-jaw bridge, and said that it ought to be possible to fasten the bridge further, as I had suggested, by putting pegs in the roots

of the lower teeth. He has sent me to a Lowville dentist
—which makes me feel more cheerful.

It sometimes seems to me strange that I am still alive
and writing this diary.

At moments, especially when reading in bed, I have a
brief comfortable feeling of renewal of something in the
past—through a book, a passing contact with some old
phase of life, something I recognize, a reassurance cropping
up in my now infirm self.

May 20. Dentist in Lowville in morning: some hope,
clean well-equipped and staffed; he had had a case of a
woman with only one tooth in her lower jaw and given her
something she could chew with. > In the afternoon, Glyn
took me over to visit the Mennonite community at Croghan,
which I hadn't known existed. We visited the bishop, very
German—all the names are German—a tall and dark
farmer, with pale blond wife and daughters, who did not
look flourishing and who I thought could have profited from
some of the gayer clothes that the Mennonite girls are
supposed to do without. He took us to the church—white,
no steeple, bare and ample, only a pulpit at one end; cemetery neat and trim, the little stones in rows all exactly
alike. Mennonism is almost five centuries old. They have
not kept up the old costume, with special hat and coat and
no buttons but hooks.

<Since the two or three days of pouring rain, the coun-
try was flooded as I have never seen it: the pastures turned
into lakes, the Black River all over its bordering fields,
Sugar River a turbulent muddy torrent, a pond in our back
lot. >

Humiliation of Old Age

June 2–10, New York. Monday. Arrival. Penelope had broken her little toe, so I went up to her house to dinner instead of her coming to the club.

Tuesday. Lunch with Whittle about Trumbull Stickney.* Nice but not brilliant young academic type. —Clelia for drinks at club. She had invited Ted Gorey, as she used to invite Brendan Gill at the Algonquin; but I had a few minutes with her before he came—told her about my dream, etc. I hadn't noticed before what sturdy legs she has. When Ted arrived, she became very talkative: I had the impression that she was hungry for gossip and New York conversation. She and Ted prattled like children. I asked whether she and Philip never came to town for sprees: they used to but didn't any more: she hated New York so—claimed that she had three times come to N.Y. because I had written her I was going to be there. If this was true, she can't have gotten much out of it: we still hardly know one another. When I told her that I was going to tell the Epsteins all that she and Ted had said about them, she was actually worried for fear I would do this and threatened to repeat what I had said about Margaret Bishop. I wrote her afterwards that I had told the Epsteins how she had deteriorated, and it appeared from her reply that she had believed this, too. —She adores her 17-year-old girl, who seems rather bright—studied modern Greek, has been in Norway and wants to go back. Clelia attracts as does a woman one admires and hardly knows. I was struck by her rather cold-looking forehead and eyes, with the sharp and almost cutting nose that suggest her father's

---

* EW's 1940 piece about this cultivated New England poet, who "never arrived artistically at the expression of his full personality," had just been republished in *The Bit Between My Teeth*.

financial acumen (he is now over 90). —I think she has a very hardheaded side—which contrasts with her animated excited interest, derived, I assume, from her Italian side, that makes her face flush and her eyes become more responsive. —Ted Gorey parried my suggestion that he publish a large album of a number of his books on the ground that he didn't want his very limited editions to be reprinted. I was surprised when he told me that they had sold about 5,000 each. —Dinner with the Epsteins: Jason has gained weight again—is still preoccupied with Canada.

Wednesday. Lunch with Roger. Elena arrived late in the afternoon, and we went downtown to dinner at 68, which is now no good—service and food terrible. We missed the first half of *Lola Montes*, for which we didn't much care anyway—though Peter Ustinov was good, as the ringmaster, with his flat declamatory French.

Thursday. We went to *If*, a British film about a bad public school, where the boys are kept down and unmercifully flogged, etc., but then they revolt, build a fire under the hall where a general is making a patriotic speech, then machine-gun the escaping crowd from the roofs. I was somewhat shocked, as I had been by *The Charge of the Light Brigade*, at the English turning against themselves, and the picture, from the point of view of encouraging bad conduct on the part of the youth, seemed to me much worse than anything I had seen that had been made over here. Penelope says that the last reel was not shown in England.

Friday. Went to the Oxford Press, to arrange to have them send out copies of the *Dead Sea Scrolls*, which, although they told me they would be, are not available yet. It seems to me that the Oxford Press is the worst-organized and most irritating publishing house that I have ever done business with. I became very disagreeable with the girl who was sent out to see me but had no idea what to do. Sheldon Meyer was at first not visible but did presently appear, and the best he could produce was red-bordered Dennison labels to be pasted in. When I had asked Meyer about Isaiah Berlin's book, which had been published and was being reviewed in England, he said that they were still waiting for the manuscript. The financial and the manufacturing ends are out somewhere in New Jersey, and this makes things delayed and difficult. You have the feeling that the editors don't really know what is going on. Brett-Smith and Meyer are away a good deal of the time, the former usually in some remote place. It seems that Brett-Smith does a good deal of business in buying and selling rare seventeenth-century books in connection with his father's library. You feel a curious lack of interest in the Press—perhaps because they are not entirely free, always a branch of England.

Was also rude to the headwaiter at the Algonquin on account of the expensive and unsatisfactory food. I should apologize to him later for this—as I asked Meyer to apologize to the girl in the office for me. I imagine he neglected to do this. My lunches with Brett-Smith and him are quite jolly, but they never take notes, as Roger does, about what I want done, so nothing is ever done. I told them I wanted a *full* index, but what I got was the usual sketchy kind—which occasioned corrections, holding up publication.

Saturday. Roger sent a limousine to take us out to lunch to Purchase, where he lives in his grandfather Oscar Straus's house. Attractive place, lots of lawn, flower bed in back and a fountain—house built, I think, in the eighties, with all the rooms opening into one another, like our old house at Red Bank. His son has a new house on the place. Very pleasant. Leonid [Berman] and Sylvia [Marlowe] came over. They live in a strange kind of small dwelling with two studios, on the estate of rich people named Milliken. Evidently something of a rich Jewish colony: Lehmans, Knopfs, etc.

Back in New York in the evening, I took Elena to see *Succubus* [sic].* It was terrible, bad Hollywood surrealism, sex, general mess, with lurid coloring and lighting. We did not last long. This corner of 42nd St. and Sixth is full of stores that seem to sell nothing but pornographic books and pornographic movies called "flesh flicks" (patronized and admired by Brendan Gill). Bad-looking crowd of people: pansies dressing the part, etc. General effect disgusting and, to Elena, rather frightening.

Sunday. At 6:15, Anita Loos's party at the Museum of Modern Art. Showing of her Hollywood movie scripts, made when she was in her teens: Mary Pickford, Lionel Barrymore, the Gish girls. Rather dull, except one called *Meal Ticket*, where the non-working father and brother take the money the girl earns as a chorus girl, and are finally made to go to work. I seemed to recognize it from her memoirs, and she confirmed that it was her own life. We went afterwards to the Russian Tea Room, then to Penelope's, which, for me, was too much. Penelope was to join us at the show, but was held up by the Latin Country parade, and came to sit beside us after the pictures had started. She kissed me, seized and stroked my arm, and, as it were, jumped all over us, licking our noses, like a red-haired collie dog with a long nose and brown affectionate eyes.

The next night (Monday), Lillian Hellman's dinner given by Little, Brown to celebrate the publication of her autobiography. It was in a very grand, somber, expensive, high-ceilinged restaurant of the kind that Malachi Martin

---

* A succubus is a female demon who seduces men. Since there were several such creatures in the film, EW notes that the plural *succubi* was more appropriate.

had taken me to for lunch a few days before. Both with several floors, many steps and no elevators; both more or less labyrinthine; both incredibly expensive. When Martin had learned about my teeth, he suggested an *omelette aux fines herbes*, which turned out to cost $6; (he was evidently an habitué, talked familiar French and Italian to the waiters—Roger tells me that his present lady thus keeps him in style—he seemed now less a defrocked fish out of water than a maturing man of the world); and Jason told me that Lillian's party must have cost $2,000. It was too much for me—I wanted to go home after the long preliminaries of drinks; but then the dinner began to appear and I sat talking and eating the rice from the chicken with the Strauses and Laura Perelman. Lots of people I should have liked to talk to, but I can't take it any more. Never even saw Sid Perelman and Mrs. Field, who were there. Couldn't keep up with Lionel Trilling on the Yahoos and Houyhnhnms in *Gulliver*, about which he was expounding a theory, and at this point broke away. Most embarrassing feature of old age is that your sphincter and urinary muscles grow weak like the others: disgusting mishap at the Royalton before Elena came, when the former gave way before I got to the suite, and I had to give my underclothes and shirt to be burned. At the party, my bladder did not quite hold till I got to the remote and obstacle-obstructed men's room. I came back with my trouser leg wet, but was pigeonholed by Arthur Kober, who, as Lillian's ex-husband, had made a little speech at the dinner and who now, on the way up and on a bench in the hall, told me something of the story of his life. He said I was a Renaissance man.

Lunch the next day (Tuesday) with Evgenia [Lehovich]: Svetlana, Paul Chavchavadze, etc. Svetlana is so very intelligent, conscientious, interested in so many things, amusing; general good humor.

Highmarket: "Huge Carcasses of Prostrate Bones"

<*T'ville, Friday 13th.* Dentist, almost 2-hour session. I am impressed with his expertness,> certainly in a class above Donovan. <I had had little sleep the night before and was very much fatigued. The next morning horrible chills, temperature about 104, blank vomiting with nothing to vomit; knocked out for three days. Dr. Smith attended to me; Mrs. Hutchins nursed me, spending the night here. Unconsciously asleep most of the time—at the times when I was awake enough, reading snatches of the Hemingway biography. A certain monotony caused by his invariably turning nasty and picking a quarrel with anyone who has done anything for him, and his repeated self-injuries through clumsiness—really self-inflicted wounds. He had a high sense of honor, which he was always violating; he evidently had a permanent bad conscience, which I suppose kept him drunk more and more. It is altogether a depressing story, because his work was deteriorating. Then his competitiveness that could become so disagreeable. It seems that Archie MacLeish decided not to go with him to Africa because he could foresee what he would have to endure if he shot a bigger lion than Ernest.* —My book† arrived in the first stages of my attack, and I at first didn't even have the energy to look at it. When I did I found a horrible *and which* sentence on p. 130—not only *and which*, but the sentence did not make sense.

---

* This is the only sympathetic reference in Wilson's writing to Archibald MacLeish, whom he considered an imitator of modernist fashions without the artist's understanding of suffering. MacLeish's literary career, which led from the world of the ex-patriates to the State Department under Franklin Roosevelt, is subjected to devastating satire in Wilson's poem "The Omelet of A. MacLeish."

† *The Dead Sea Scrolls* (1969).

Glyn faithfully came in to see me and helped keep me going by talking, as he had after my first attack. I may have bored him with my old stuffy anecdotes. —They left for Maryland on the 18th, taking Barbara Erwin with them to help them get settled, I suppose—they said they were "weaning" her gradually. >

It has occurred to us, in talking to other people, that what I have been having are malarial attacks. Have had a blood smear made in Utica for Smith to diagnose.

The yellow lilies are out in the back garden, and the Showy Lady Slippers in front of the house. I go out to look at them from time to time: the roundish streakish bright pink lip, speckled inside, with its three white streamers, and the pink-dotted yellow patch hooded away above it. They are thriving and have multiplied here, but the plant in the back garden seems to have died. They give me much pleasure.

<Mabel Hutchins, at dinnertime, wanted to know if I minded if she asked a question. She had heard that there was a group in Lowville who gave parties at which all the wives threw the keys to their houses in a pile. The men wore loops—a single loop—in their ears and the women a single blue earring, which contained a contraception pill. Each of the men would pick up a key and go to the house of the lady to whom the key belonged. "Suppose the man didn't like the woman." "Well, I guess he'd have to lose the key." "Did I know whether this was true?"> She thought my dentist, who wore a goatee, was one of the members of the group. Dr. Miller has sideburns but no goatee and doesn't strike me as quite the man for that kind of game. <I asked Fern about it, and she said, Oh, that was at the Elks Hall, and they didn't do it any more.

————

I went to Clinton and took the Briggses to lunch.> Margaret is still very pretty, though now rather shapelessly expanded. With their little adopted son, she seems the kind of woman who should have had children; but she told Mary that internal complications had prevented it.

<Ezra Pound, as I had heard in New York, had been visiting here without publicity. They had dressed him in a gown at the Hamilton commencement, and he had received a tremendous ovation. His policy now is not to speak but to maintain a polite silence—quite different from his behavior, according to Grace Root, when he had come to Hamilton before. That he was to come to lunch at the Briggses' that day was sprung on Margaret Briggs only that morning, and she broke her neck producing the lunch. But the great man never spoke except to say, when asked whether he would have light meat or dark meat, "Just as it comes," and, as he was leaving, to make some apology to Margaret for giving her so much trouble. One exception: when she asked him how he found New York, he answered, "Too many people.">

Mary and I called on Charles Mihály. I showed him the Civil War bills that I had found in a drawer in the house here. He gave us little glasses of his very bad sweet homemade wine, produced, Mary says, from grape juice.

When I came home, Rosalind was there. <A fit of coughing after dinner turned into another attack—perhaps my worst. No chills and fever this time: I was sweating all the time (hot weather), but the vomiting and diarrhea turned me inside out and left me very faint. Knocked me out for nearly a week.

Artist from Thailand that I met at the Morrises'. We were talking about the present boom in sex, and I asked him whether it had much publicity in Thailand: "We live in a different culture. We think that it is something private between two people." —I explained that I was somewhat deaf and didn't always hear what he said. He explained that they thought in Thailand that it was bad manners to talk too loudly.

The departure of the Morrises has left a gap, a blank. I feel that I am now so much more out of touch with what is going on in the local community.

4th of July. Hardly a firecracker, no celebration. Tamest, blankest 4th I've ever known. Rosalind and I tried to find some excitement by driving to Cape Vincent. No traffic to speak of, the town itself dull. The old summer hotel has been torn down, and I didn't see the quasi-museum.> Dull evenings with the Pcolars, also in pursuit of entertainment. <Movies: *Funny Girl, Love Bug*—both pretty terrible, but I had the interest of watching their reactions, which are exactly what the Hollywood people count on. I tried to tell them that *Funny Girl* was no good, but Mary loves Omar Sharif, and George laughed at all the jokes. They did, however, admit that they had thought *Star!* very bad, and said that *Funny Girl* seemed good if you had previously seen *Star!*

I went into *the old Collins house*, where we spent so many summers—could hardly recognize anything, the rooms completely gutted, with only a minimum of necessary furniture. The lady of the house an unattractive tough farmer's wife. The married son lived on the second floor, so I couldn't go up to see it because the baby was asleep. I bought two hooked rugs made by the daughter-in-law for $25.

———

Highmarket [an abandoned crossroads village]: a well-patterned old white door on a background of peeling asbestos shingles that imitated pale brownish bricks. —The vast gray capsizing barns, and the smaller ones settling askew. Huge carcasses of prostrate barns, mixed bones sticking out of the heavy hide; squalor of asbestos-shingled small house, with the front porches fallen through.>

Elena came to meet me July 12, at *Cooperstown*, where they were celebrating the opening of the new library. I saw Henry Moe there, and he told me the Aspen humanities award had been discontinued by the trustees. I told him that I hadn't been much impressed by the cultural qualifications of the Aspen people and he said, "Oh, God, no!" He says that he is going to try to persuade the man who put up the money to confer it through some other agency. —The Otsego Lake looked quite romantic and beautiful. We stayed in a motel on its edge, but were kept awake by stamping and loud talking on the part of the people above.

The next day we went back to Talcottville. The Briggses and the Marcelins came over to lunch one day. We left for Boston the 22nd and stopped off that night at Cummington.

I went into the *Beth Israel Hospital* on the 24th. Had a horrible time there. The constant damp weather brought on a bad attack of gout, made worse by the three hours every morning that I spent in the X-ray department in the basement, dressed in nothing but a loose gown. It was torture to get off and on the X-ray tables, and the place was so cold that my bronchitis got worse, and by the time I got back to Wellfleet, it had become, with the gout, my most serious ailment. I struggled to get off one of the X-ray tables, in order to void a painful enema, and an oaf

of a boy held me down. He kept saying, "Lay down," and
I finally made him correct it. A Yiddische mama in charge
called me "dear," and was very comforting. They didn't
find out anything except that I had slight diabetes, and
Zetzel said that there was "indirect evidence" that I was
carrying some kind of parasite. It is evident that in this
part of the world they don't know much about tropical
diseases, and they always seemed to change the subject
when I brought up malaria, and scouted the theory of ackee
poisoning because this is not supposed to involve fever—
though they found a paper about it in some medical periodical. I couldn't stick it out more than five days, and,
in spite of Zetzel's protest, left on the 29th, when Elena
drove me back to Wellfleet.

I felt only half alive and told Elena Levin one day that
I felt as if my life was finished, but I hadn't recognized
the fact. I didn't know then that my temperature was 101.
I had two attacks after that—high fever and convulsive
vomiting, but they were milder than at T'ville.

Weather here terribly hot. Mrs. Hutchins came back
with us and has been a great help. When she has nothing
else to do, she polishes up the silver, which she says she
enjoys. I have done nothing since I got back—I am writing
on Labor Day, September 1—but will do an article on
Richard Barham and correct proofs on Svetlana and Ed
O'Connor. It has taken me weeks to get over the hospital.
I would even get a sore back from working an hour at my
desk here.

Penelope came up for a weekend, looking rather lean and
haggard. She had a private conference with Lillian, and
L. told Elena afterwards that she and Mike have now
broken up. He has telephoned her from Hollywood that he
has been living with another woman a month, and that he
is coming back to New York and wants her to vacate his

apartment. Her movie notices have been sounding rather labored. I wish she would find some man who is intelligent and with whom she could live.

<Helen Augur wired me to call her in California, "dying of cancer." When I spoke to her, she told me about her tumors, and I could see that she was relishing it as she had always done all her ailments. I asked her whether the doctors had told her she was dying. She said no, but she knew she was. I said I had been in T'ville, and she at once began to tell about some illness she had contracted when she was living there—hadn't found out what it was till afterwards, something you got from living in caves; gave me the scientific name, as she has always loved doing. There is a niece out there who looks after her. She is in a sanitarium.>

My life here now has its comfortable side. Sitting in armchairs with my feet up, reading books and magazines, brought breakfast and mail in the morning. But it makes me impatient to be sleeping so much and not to be able to get across the room or to put a book back without difficulty.

Svetlana at the Chavchavadzes', September 8–12: Old difficulty of talking to her—so many delicate subjects: *Ivan Groznyi* [Ivan the Terrible], for example, conversation about exactly what *groznyi* meant. It only occurred to me afterwards that Paul had been playing down the frightening aspect and emphasizing the "harsh" and "severe" in order to spare her feelings—or perhaps it was in his usual attempt to play down the bad sides of the tsars. When I first came into the narrow dark hallway, she came up to me and kissed me on the cheek. I couldn't see her very well, and she said, "Look at me! Look at me!" I remembered then that Stalin, in his late apprehensive years, used to demand of visitors of whom he was suspicious, "Why don't you look me in the eye?" —I suggested that, for the Soviet Union, her book might be such a bombshell that they simply might decide to ignore it. She said that they were not bright enough for that, that they would say, as they had done of her first book, that it had been written by the CIA and circulate scandals about her personal life. —No one could give a gloomier view than she has in her book of what has been happening in Russia, but if you speak of the outrageous things, you feel that you are being rude. She can only smile slightly and wryly, if you tell her of something comic. —She says that she now feels quite at home with the Chavchavadzes. She prefers to come up here by bus because she does not have to give a name, and she has people all around her. —She is irked a little by the conventionality of Princeton. The ladies put on stockings to walk a block or two on the streets.

Bert Wolfe and Ella turned up in Provincetown, trying "to recover his youth," he said. He has aged so I shouldn't have known him; Ella more recognizable, but her hair is white. He has evidently no Marxism left and is strongly opposed to Communism, but he still retains the Communist habit of talking the other person down. When I saw him years ago in Brooklyn, he had already lost most of his faith, but when the Labor Theory of Value was mentioned, his former combativeness revived, and he at once produced the old untenable Marxist proof. I doubt whether he would do so today. —Aggressive Communist glibness in having the answers to all the questions: don't let the other person have a moment to argue or doubt.

New York: "Something Solid and Real in My Mind"

New York, September 17–24. Elena went down with me but, as usual, succumbed to a bad cold and went back on Saturday. Thursday she went out to the Thorntons'. Daphne had gone for a week to her mother's. It turns out that she fractured her skull from a fall when she was skating last winter, and she still has bad fits of dizziness. Henry had wanted Elena to come out, but Daphne had made arrangements so that there wouldn't be room for her to sleep there: a woman to look after the children, with a retired policeman husband and a little girl of her own. E. thought she would make trouble if she pressed Henry to have her somehow sleep there, or if she spent the night in an inn or hotel. I had dinner with Penelope, and we didn't go anywhere. Elena came to us in the second-floor lounge, where we were drinking, pleased to see us and smiling and looking so pretty, her long flowery dress swirling around her.

<Saturday night, after she went back, I explored West 42nd St. again; saw a dreadful double feature: *The Magus* and *The Libertine*. Walking home, even that short distance, I found extremely difficult. I bought a Sunday *Times*, which was terribly heavy, and scrapped half of it in a trash can, then went into the next movie I passed, to go to the men's room, without noticing what it was; but when I was coming out I saw on the screen a huge close-up of a woman's cunt. It was horrible,> like one of things described in *My Secret Life*, which the author says almost prevented him from having intercourse with the owner<—like something raw and unappetizing in a butcher's shop. The woman was rhythmically wriggling and caressing herself and opening her cunt with her fingers. This was followed by another similar spectacle. Then there was another more elaborate film, with dialogue and a rudimentary plot, which I couldn't understand because I couldn't understand what they were saying. Among scenes of lesbianism and cocksucking, with the lower party out of the picture, there was a rapist who committed three successful rapes; in the case of the last woman who was sitting in her bath, he drowned her by lifting up her legs so that her head was under the water, then carried her nude to a garbage dump and dumped her. He was made an unattractive character and finally shot; but this kind of thing ought really to be censored: it shows the young delinquents how easy it would be to slug a girl and rape her and get away with it.>

The next night I took Penelope to a big preview at the City Center Opera of Boito's *Mefistofele*. Tremendous success, ovation. It hadn't impressed me much when I played it on records, but it seemed on the stage quite magnificent. Huge choruses of angels in the prologue and in the love scenes, wonderful duets with a melodious volume of sound. Mephisto, in the modern fashion, was naked except for a jockstrap and seemed rather a tragic figure as he was dwarfed by the presence of God, overpowering on a half-lowered backdrop, or cavorted hysterically about the stage, sometimes on all fours—not fiery but pale and grizzled. —*Penelope* is getting to be a little of a problem. She kissed me on the cheek during the admirable duet of Faust and Helen, and she kisses me at every opportunity, even when I go into her office on some perfectly prosaic matter. She also caresses me with her hands in a way that I find rather embarrassing. But Helen [Wilson] did this, too, at a movie, when I said something that she wanted me to think was especially amusing. It may be a kind of fashion.

Penelope told me the story of her visit with Mike to his Jewish mother, who she said was more embarrassing and dreadful than anything he had been able to concoct with

Elaine for their telephone sketch. —Dinner on Monday with the Epsteins. Jason was going to Chicago to attend the trial of the seven demonstrators during the Democratic convention, which he thought would last three months. He contemplates writing a book about it. He had given up his paper for schoolchildren, which no longer exists. He once confessed to me that he could only start things. Barbara is flourishing with *The New York Review of Books*. Her legs in her short skirt and white stockings looked plumper than I had remembered them. —Film of *Justine* with Helen and Christopher Walling. He has got a job as a research man with *Time* and has grown a great head of black hair that rises in a lump and does not hang down. He seems to have given up on his mother—who he thinks is now too dim, too much out of touch with the world, ever to hold down a job in France.

In New York, working on proofs, I found myself quite comfortable and competent again and began to put together in my mind a new volume of literary essays. This gave me satisfaction—something solid and real in my mind that I shall gradually bring into being. In this case seven of them already written.

Novelists, Poets and Monsters: A Dozen Essays*

> [The Original *Waste Land* MS.]
> Edwin O'Connor: A Memoir and a Collaboration
> The Fruits of the MLA
> The Aftermath of Mencken
> [How Not to Be Bored by Maurice Baring]

---

* Ten of these would be posthumously published as *The Devils and Canon Barham*. In his list EW brackets those unwritten. He never wrote either the article on Mackenzie or the account of Imre Madách's *Az ember tragediája*, a famous Hungarian drama of the mid-nineteenth century, partly derived from *Faust*.

[Compton Mackenzie]
The Devils and Canon Barham
Two Neglected American Novelists
    I. Henry Fuller
    II. Harold Frederic
[Az *Ember Tragediája*] ?A Hungarian Classic
[The Monsters of Bomarzo]

*Russian Group**

    Pushkin
    Tyutchev
    Gogol
    Turgenev
    Chekhov
    [Notes on Tolstoy]

The Strange Case of Pushkin and Nabokov
Chukovskaya and Svetlana
Svetlana's Whole Story, and Some Other Stories
Bulgakov, Solzhenitsyn, etc. ?

[Notes on Russian Language]

---

* These are some of the pieces that would be assembled in A *Window on Russia* (1972), along with further notes on Pushkin and an essay on Sukhovo-Kobylin subtitled "Who Killed the French Woman?"

LIFE AGAINST DEATH:
FALL 1969 TO WINTER 1970

With Mary and the Millers

<*T'ville, September 24*. Mary met me, and on the way to T'ville told me about her experiences (four weeks) of presiding over the study hall at the West Leyden school. She says she is still a little uncertain about how she likes it; it is something of a strain to keep order all day among children of a variety of ages; but it is evident that she has also been enjoying it. She has, I suppose, a technique of charming or fascinating them and at the same time preserving discipline. Told me about one boy punching another thus causing trouble. She reprimanded him, and this aroused his sister to come to his defense and threaten her: "You'll be sorry for this!" She sent them both to the principal, and when the girl came back, she apologized, and Mary talked to her sympathetically. She made a point of being reasonable, allowing for their points of view. She could read when she sat at the desk, then would walk down the aisle and check on what was going on. I imagine that she is going to be a success at this; and she is hoping, when the new regional school opens, to be promoted to be a librarian.

Helen Augur's sister called me up to tell me Helen had died. Her doctor, on account of her hypochondria, had been inclined to treat her illness lightly, but it turned out that she actually had cancer of the lung. She was cremated, and her sister Dorothy—named, she tells me, after Dorothy Mendenhall—brought the ashes on to have them buried in the Adams family plot in Lowville (their grandfather, William Adams, had been the head of the Lowville Academy). > Dorothy showed signs of the same tendencies that used to irritate me in Helen: annoying oversolicitude: during the service at the grave, she whispered to me to put on my hat for fear I should catch cold. <I used to discount Helen's statements about how dull her brothers and sister were, but so far as I could see, she was right. The brother told me anecdotes of Helen's misfortunes when she was young—such as riding down a hill on her bicycle and riding right into a lake. "She was always rather different from the rest of us, you know." I took them all to lunch at the Hulbert House, and we all had a drink. > There was an Adams cousin from Lowville who was the daughter of the former proprietor of the Lowville *Something-Republican*, on which she had worked for years. She had been around more than the others.

Lunch with the Marcelins at Cazenovia (September 21). They have been much upset about Pierre. He had been staying with them, and seemed to have become quite schizophrenic—had always been somewhat queer. He had come with the idea that they would start another book; but they had to ship him back to Haiti, where he would be more cheaply taken care of than would be possible in an American sanitarium. He got married not long ago, and they report that he said to them that there must be something wrong with the woman or she wouldn't be unmarried at 40. —Later Phito told me, with some concern, that he

thought the whole question of "race" was more or less
nonsense. He never knew what to call himself in appli-
cations that asked about race. What race could he be said
to belong to? The assumption seemed to be that he was
Negro because he had some Negro blood, although he was
mainly white.

When *Mary and I* got back in the late afternoon, we
went to the Parquet for dinner. The conversation got rather
sexy—she admitted to having read *Fanny Hill*. On the way
back, I made her stop the car on the dark road across to
12A before you get to T'ville, and we did some enthusiastic
kissing. "I don't know when you'll find me in this mood
again." She came into the house with me here. I did not
turn on the living-room light, and we did some more kissing
on the sofa. I found out what her personality was like
when she was excited and being made love to: "U-n-n-
no!—It would make me feel guilty . . ." (when I told her
that I wanted to see the rest of her body, she said with
conscious humor) "I'm perfectly beautiful, but no." I took
out my cock, and she felt it. It was gratifying to be conscious that it was capable now of an erection. I kissed her
as long as it seemed rewarding, and in my pauses she
sometimes gave me little kisses on the cheek. She would
murmur little remarks so softly that, in my deafness, I
could not understand and would have to put my ear to her
mouth and ask her to repeat it. It was faintly comic and
out of key. "I want to, but I won't." I never knew a woman
so armored with heavy bra and "foundation garment": I
couldn't even find a crevice. She couldn't have expected
passes: she must have done it for warmth. "I don't get
dressed to be undressed." "I'm afraid you'd have a heart
attack." She did not seem eager to go, but finally left. As
she got into the car, she said, "Thanks for trying." This
passage, though indecisive, cheered and bucked me up. I'd
hardly known I could have a spontaneous erection, and I

was glad to feel that my relation to her had progressed to something hot and physical.

<*On Saturday night, September 27,* the Browns were having a birthday celebration, and the boys were racing up and down Water Street and on the main road. The racket was so annoying that people thought of calling up the state troopers. One of the Young boys and Timmy Munn, Otis Jr.'s black-sheep son, who had run away once or twice, were racing two other boys on 12A. They didn't arrive at the T'ville church, where the other boys were waiting. Somebody went back to find out what had become of them and came back and said to the boys who were waiting, "If you can pray, you'd better start now." The Young boy and Timmy had run off the road and smack into a tree. The Young boy was dead and his neck was broken. Timmy was badly injured and taken to a hospital. When I asked Fern about him the next Thursday, she said he was still unconscious from concussion. They don't know who was driving. —I talked to Barbara Erwin about Timmy. She had had him at one time as a pupil, and said that he was not a bad boy, she found him sympathetic; but, like his mother, he didn't fit into farm life. He would come to school in the morning after attending to the cows, and drop his head on the desk and go to sleep.

October 1. Lunch with Dr. Edgar Miller, the dentist, and his pretty brunette wife. I was surprised to find myself there in the heart of old Lowville. He has built a comfortable modern but old-looking house, now covered with ivy. They have four children, and he does sculptural figures out of old railroad nails and such materials. I was surprised to find them Democrats and liberals—they thought Nixon's utterances "ludicrous"—he had failed, in the last election, to vote for either of the presidential candidates. His

family came originally from "Leyden." We went to his brother's really fine old house—brick, with handsome white doorway and windows. It had belonged to Hough, the county historian and called the Father of American Forestry, and there is a plaque in his honor beside the door. They both know quite a lot about local history, and lent me two books with sections on John Brown and Thomas Baker. The bathroom has old-fashioned washstands in mahogany (?) wooden boxes; handsome old turning staircase. Mrs. Miller a fine-looking elderly woman with graying hair. Afterwards we came over here and continued drinking wine and talking.> They left around 6.

After so much drinking, <I went to bed early; then woke up between 2 and 3 and finished Macaulay's history. Though he was dying, he more or less rounded it out by writing the deaths of James and William detached from where he dropped the main narrative. Quite fortifying to find him sustaining it, with the same high morality and thoroughness, through the parliamentary developments of the bills connected with the Irish forfeitures—same patience and eager interest.>

Sunday, October 5. John Hearne spent the night of the 4th here: very intelligent and pleasant, understands everything immediately, talks well, wide range of interests. He talked about the Jamaican writers who insist on the "Jamaican" approach, a Jamaican kind of fiction, a Jamaican kind of poetry, etc; where there is so much varied and interesting life to stimulate one to imaginative writing without bothering about the Jamaican approach. Sunday morning we drove, following Mary, through the gorge to Hamilton, where John is writer-in-residence at Colgate. We met the Marcelins and had a drink at the Hearnes' house. His English wife, though somewhat solid in figure, is handsome. Two-and-a-half-year-old daughter, blond with big round blue eyes. The meeting between Hearne and Phito went off very easily—they talked about West Indian writers. Lunch at the Hamilton Inn in Clinton—all very agreeable.

Mary drove me back. I asked whether she had all her armor on. She explained that she had to wear a special bra to keep one of her breasts up. She had a "mastoid," a lump from her lactic gland when one of her children was born—had to go to the doctor every six months to make sure it wasn't cancer. —On the way home, she stopped at her house. The trees beyond the front fence presented a kind of wall of golden fire, like the fire that surrounds Brunhilde. On the lawn was the skeleton of an old buggy, just the seat, the two wheels and the two shafts, quite paintless—she said it was "just for ornament"; some member of the family had made a flight of steps to the house, wide and crude and painted a discordant dark red. Inside, she had done much work, had built a number of cupboards, driving all the nails and putting on the hinges herself. Small rooms, with low ceilings, that followed no familiar pattern, still rather peasanty. The girls were sitting comfortably in front of a fire—one studying at a table, the other reclining in a blanket and listening to and watching television. —She has got George to occupy himself with civic enterprises like her own. He is at present town assessor and is active in the Veterans of Foreign Wars.

October 7. Dinner with the Edmondses: I always find myself talking directly to Kay, while Walter and I are at an angle to one another. He says that he is now going to see the world—go to Europe and visit other countries, says that he is going to mature at last. I had never heard him admit his immaturity before. He has just published one children's book and is about to write another.

October 8. Went at 3 with the Millers to their camp at Crystal Lake, a small and pleasant little body of water, which resembled the "ponds" on the Cape more than most of these Adirondack lakes do. The land belonged to their grandfather from the end of the eighteenth-century; Ned's brother now has the old camp. Ned's new one is a fine modern little house on the hillside, surrounded with glass and views of the lake. Ned Miller's statues and wall designs made of horseshoe nails, railroad nails, etc., a kind of transparency of silhouettes made from the top of an old car. On the lakeshore, which is sandy, a beach house in the form of an African hut—a kind of totem pole made of cement poured into a mold in the sand, with, as Miller pointed out, both women's breasts and a penis. He is very proud of everything, showed me drums and masks from Haiti, some wooden dishes from Korea. He had spent a year in Korea in the infantry, wasn't against war as he now is, they had to burn some of the villages in order to avert the danger of our boys' getting venereal disease. A table with butterflies caught by the children and covered with a coat of plastic—this not very much of a success. His wife, Anne, does ceramics, of which she showed me some pretty blue specimens. They are both very intelligent and well informed about what is going on in the world. She writes a kind of free poetry, which shows she has had no literary training—on the rare occasions when she does rhyme, she is likely to rhyme *m* with *n*. I am going to convey to her that these writings will be of no interest to anyone but her children. They show her constant longings for something beyond and better, though with a certain enjoyment of her current life and love for her husband. She is 41,—is a small and pretty brunette, with vivacious black eyes. Their friends the Wolfes came to dinner. They constantly see one another and travel together. Mrs. Wolfe seems to be Jewish, and her husband, once district attorney and now a lawyer in Lowville, who specializes in divorce, also looks rather Jewish but is Catholic and did three years in a seminary in Montreal. I seemed to please them by telling them I had heard they were the only liberals in Lowville. Ned replied that their neighbors thought them much too liberal. (Anne Miller's poetry is full of rebellion against convention.) They are anxious to be "with it" in, however, a somewhat bourgeois way. Ned had immediately shown me several issues of one of those pornographic magazines called *Avant-Garde*, bolstered for respectability with a serious article or two, and the Wolfes brought in an album of Picasso's erotic drawings which they were either lending or bringing back.

Thursday, October 16. The Morrises, Barbara Erwin, and the Krakowskys in the evening. Glyn has been getting homesick in Maryland, hasn't got to know people yet—two nights a week teaching education. He has been putting on weight. —The Krakowskys very German-Jewish—he rather aggressive, smoking big cigar—he said that Mrs. Ginzburg talked so much about literature when she was in prison, and thought so much about royal historical characters having been in prison there, that he would have given her another eighteen years.* His wife is fat, has enormous ankles and legs, but rather a cute face. She took what I thought rather a curious line of declaring that the survivors of the Nazi camps were distinguished by disagreeable and "predatory" traits, as if they had been at fault to survive. When I told Elena of this, she said that it was caused by their guilt at having escaped themselves.

I left T'ville on the 21st, spent the night at the Utica Club, and Helen Muchnic came at 1 the next day to drive

---

* EW had now reviewed Evgenia Ginzburg's memoir of jail and exile (*The Devils and Canon Barham*).

me to Cummington. Elena met me there and we spent two nights instead of one: the Pritchetts to dinner the first night; the second, Seta Schouvaloff, Dan Aaron, the nice little Czech girl who is Helen's successor as head of the Russian department and her husband, an intelligent Oxford-educated Bengalese. Dorothy [Walsh] and I argued about science and art, the difference between humans and animals, free will and determinism. She thinks in definitions, and makes clear distinctions, which I don't, between these pairs—I think it goes back, by way of Catholicism, to the medieval way of thinking: St. Thomas?

We came back to Wellfleet the 27th.

Visit of Daphne's mother with Russian lady from Newport. Mrs. Seller looks rather like a dog. Elena had invited the Chavchavadzes for dinner in order to make the banalities of the visitors bearable. I talked to Paul about Peter the Great, disregarding the fact that even the Russian lady very likely also knew about him. She talked Russian to the Chavchavadzes, who thought she was even more middle class and deadly than Rita. She asked them what I did. Elena took them for a ride and showed them Arthur Schlesinger's house, and one of them said, "He's a banker, isn't he?" I have never seen Elena dread a guest so much or be so little prepared to deal with her.

T'ville, Saturday–Friday, November 8–14. Three of my teeth in my upper jaw came out, and I went up to get Miller to fix them and to see how Rosalind was getting on. After a two-hour session at the dentist's Monday morning, I was completely immobilized by gout and couldn't cross the room without help—if nobody was in the house, had to let the telephone ring. Sat in my big chair with the footrest, my legs wrapped in a blanket. Mabel Hutchins took attentive care of me. Rosalind at last is quite energetically looking for a job. Dr. Miller and his wife came in to see me at the time when I couldn't move—so did Barbara Erwin.

I had arrived on Sunday in very bad shape. I was exhausted with drinking the night before and very faint at the Boston airport—long trip in rather a rattletrap plane that stopped off in Providence and Albany with a kind of loose crash. To my surprise, I landed at the airport in a dense fog, denser than anything I remember on the Cape. You couldn't see anything between Boonville and Talcottville on either side of the road. Mary could only guide herself by the two white lines in front of her. We actually passed my house—though the light on the porch was on —without being able to see it, and were beyond Locust Grove before we knew we had gone too far. We had had dinner at the Savoy. Alex Fiore and his wife had been there and joined us after dinner—so I had to bring them a drink and make conversation. At the house, sat up and talked to Rosalind, drinking: result, after the dentist, collapse. The foggy damp weather continued almost the whole week I was there—horrible for my gout—only a few hours of sun one morning. I have never known anything like this up here. I had wanted, on Tuesday, Armistice Day, to go to Colgate with Mary in order to see John Hearne, but I wasn't able to make it. I could only see her for a drink at the Hulbert House for about an hour and a half, because she had to drive the girls places. It always gives me a pang to part from her. —She had told me that at her party for sixty young people, one of the girls had come to the house and asked for ten aspirin tablets and Coke, out of which she was supposed to get a kick. The Pcolar girl was horrified. They refused to give it to her.

Intellectual Conversations;
Louise Bogan's Death

Thanksgiving, '69. John Hearne and his wife and little girl, and Penelope and Johnny Colebrook, Mary and Marie-Claire to dinner—all very jolly due to our effort to redeem Thanksgiving, that meaningless holiday.

Christmas, Penelope and her little girl—all more or less painless. For dinner, Chavchavadzes, Joan [Colebrook] and Johnny, Christopher Walling and his mother, Jane Brown and perhaps some of her children. Argument about John Kennedy assassination. On both occasions I went to bed early. Guests, I think, enjoyed it rather more than I did.

Trip to Boston and Northampton, January 8–13, 1970. Lunch with Tom Mendenhall about his mother's autobiography passed off very amiably. I was relieved to find he could laugh about her. He told us about travelling with her in his youth. She insisted on carrying the letter of credit rather than his father and had it in a "marsupial pouch" under her skirt. Instead of going to the ladies' room to bring it out when they were going to the Morgan Bank, she got it out in the Place Vendôme and had Charles and the two boys stand around her. The boys were much embarrassed and pretended they didn't know her. They were further embarrassed when Gertrude Stein appeared, with clipped hair and masculine clothes, and she and his mother threw their arms around one another.

When Tom's father died and they were about to bury his ashes, she told Tom to "go get Grandfather." She had had his ashes on a shelf for years without doing anything about getting rid of them, and now she was going to bury them and her husband's together.

————

Dinner with the Levins: Harry has at last resorted to wearing a hearing aid—a new kind. It seems to have made him much much more amiable. Elena said that it relieved for her the strain of being on edge all the time to be sure that he understood what was being said. I may be getting one presently: my inability to hear the consonants is getting to be rather serious.

Couldn't keep awake when I got back—if I sat down to read, I went to sleep. Had to struggle against it—a nuisance. May be paying for all my activity on the trip. Awful cold snap, with snow, which made one uncomfortable. According to the *Globe*, the cold had a demoralizing effect on Boston.

New York, February 4–8. Wednesday, Epsteins for dinner; Thursday, lunch with Roger. He mentioned two writers he thought were "losers"—then added that Susan Sontag was not. Arthur Schlesinger said that Penelope Gilliatt was masochistic. Dinner with Sylvia and Leonid. Sylvia agrees with me about Marie-Claire—says she is a *"porte-malheur* [bringer of evil]"—she talked incessantly to Sylvia about her eye's having been injured by Mary, gloating over her sufferings, though Mary, in her troubles with her own eye, on which she had had two operations, had had a much tougher time. Friday in the afternoon, concert with Elliott Carter's new piece, for which Sylvia, recovering from flu, had given me her ticket. The Carter piece impressed me more than anything else of his I had heard: more ferocity and violence than I knew he had in him.* I ran into Gardner Jencks in the intermission. He was very much hopped up about the concerto: he had heard it four

---

* Evidently the Concerto for Orchestra; this piece would gain the reputation of Carter's most synoptic and exhilarating achievement.

times and said it had "opened up" all kinds of things for
him. He hadn't much liked Carter's music before. They
had been doing almost but not quite the same thing, and
that had produced his prejudice against him. Elliott wanted
things to fit; Gardner wanted them not quite to fit. He
came down with me to the club, and there Ruth joined
us. I was surprised to see her looking much more handsome
than she usually does in the country. She said that she
always had so much to do in the country that she could
not keep up her appearance. Philharmonic Hall is as unattractive as all these Lincoln Center buildings are. Leonard Bernstein has perfected the technique of his conscious
theatricality to a point where his performance distracts
from the music: bounces up and down, keeps time with
his foot in what is really a dancing step, waves his arm in
graceful undulation, turns from side to side, makes as if
collapsing with his arms and knees at the end of some
movement where the music collapses.

In the evening, took Helen to Molière's *Don Juan*, done
by the *Comédie Française*. I had always been curious to see
this, but I wish I could have seen [Louis] Jouvet. The man
we saw was stiff and unsmiling—you couldn't imagine his
charming all those women. Instead of having Don Juan
vanish, being carried off to Hell in the end, he simply
flopped on the stage. Sganarelle, instead of shouting his
horror at his master's career of crime and complaining at
not getting his wages, is represented as torn between these
feelings and an admiring grief at losing him. He tries to
make the corpse sit up, then lets it flop on the ground
again. Helen said afterwards, "They want to make it homosexual." She is better, more mature with me in New York
than at home in Wellfleet. I was glad to see she understood
the French so well, explained to me the scene with M
Dimanche, which I had forgotten though I'd just read it

and Helen hadn't. Children at that age are probably always better without their parents.

Saturday. Lunch with Arthur, who said that he had always felt that there was something solid in the U.S. that had endured in spite of everything and that could still be relied on—did I still feel this? I tried to explain that it was the old educated middle class that was going to pieces everywhere, but I don't think he is accustomed to thinking about things from this kind of social point of view.

Dinner with *Wystan Auden*. He is getting, like everybody else, to find New York too unpleasant to live in. He told me how much his friends meant to him: I had remained his friend, he could count on me. I believe that these unmarried men are likely to be dependent on their friends in a way that married men never are: Alec Woollcott, Frank MacDonald, Henry Fuller.* Wystan had only lost one friend, Benjamin Britten. I said that I didn't care much for Britten's *Midsummer Night's Dream*. He said that it was quite impossible to write music for the *Dream*. Shakespeare had already written it. We discussed the question of juxtaposing two words one of which ends with the same consonant with which the next begins. He says he has written "Italian nation" but agrees with Tennyson that you ought to avoid conjoining two s's. He said that he never read his reviews, but then complained that nobody ever gave him credit for his metrical mastery. —Wystan, as usual, celebrated his deep respect for the professional middle class and its consecration to work. Said that his whole point of view derived from his having been born before the war in

---

* The critic Alexander Woollcott (1887–1943) and Frank MacDonald (1874–1952), a Princeton dilettante, appear in Wilson's early diaries. His essay on Henry Blake Fuller, the Chicago novelist (1857–1929), was published in *The New Yorker* in 1970 and reprinted in *The Devils and Canon Barham*.

1907. I was able to boast that I was born in the nineteenth century.

Louise Bogan's death: Someone had been coming to see her and found the door locked. There was to be a little funeral at Campbell's, but I went to the concert instead. There is supposed to be a memorial service later on. *

March 5–15. Trip to New York. Regular old routine: dinner at Lillian's on the 5th: she has sold her old New York house, thinking she could no longer stand N.Y. and intending to live in Boston, but I suppose she has found out, in her Cambridge *pied-à-terre*, how deadly that part of the world is and has returned to the New York house, where she has to live now on the top floor and be mercilessly socked for rent by the landlord. Cocktail party for Malachi Martin's book at the Strauses' the 6th. A mob, the kind of party I have managed to avoid for years and that I did not expect: I supposed it would be simply for a few learned men. Got Wilfrid Sheed sitting in a corner and had a conversation with him, spoke of religion for the first time. I said that I couldn't even understand the idea about Christ: sent down by the Father to suffer and redeem the human race. If you believe this, you will be forgiven. What sense does this make? Wilfrid modestly replied that this doctrine had the advantage of providing a Christian intercessor.

I said to Malachi that, after his admirable exposition of the history of Judaism, Christianity and Islam and their obsolescence, their impossibility at the present time, he had left the impression of a vacuum, had barely mentioned Marxism, the substitute religion that had come to fill it.

---

* He had known Louise Bogan since the early twenties, and she had been the most important woman in his life between his marriages to Margaret Canby and Mary McCarthy. They shared a love of poetry, liquor, and literary games, and supported one another's artistic ambition.

He said that he had never thought of this, that he wished I had spoken of it to him. Later, when I had lunch with him at the club and I described to him St. Basil's in Moscow, with all the little cells of its honeycomb made to appear all the more sinister from containing, instead of the images of saints or other holy figures, only pictures of and quotations from Marx and Engels and Lenin; St. Isaac's cathedral in Leningrad, at the time I saw it [in 1935] turned into an anti-religious museum, with nothing but horror pictures of the monstrosities perpetrated by fanatics, including at that time the Nazis, and a sinister old woman in black demonstrating Foucault's experiment—of which she superciliously pretended to be astonished that one had never heard—by explaining the long pendulum suspended from the center of the high dome, as it was shown, by the movement of the earth, to be swinging obliquely from its first direction—at all this Malachi professed an astonishment which was plainly sincere: "You don't mean it!" Strange that, so immensely versed as he was in everything about the religious, he should have failed to be aware of the importance to men's minds of Marxism, of which the vision and mythology are now as absurd, almost as much irrelevant to modern conditions, as any of the religions he has studied.

I took Penelope and her little girl to a Saturday matinee of Bil Baird's puppets. I became aware that my heart was in bad shape. I had difficulty standing up and had to lean against the wall during the intermission. We went afterwards to the Algonquin for something to eat. I talked to Penelope about the lack of gallantry of men in England to women. They seem never to take the women, unless they are married to them, home. Penelope agreed and said that the women dreaded hearing, "And now I'll put you into a cab." I told her that when Mamaine and John Strachey had gone to see Koestler off to Israel, John in the cab coming back had made passes at Mamaine. Penelope gave me a protracted twinkle, which meant I don't know exactly what—perhaps that the same kind of thing had sometimes happened to her. I was all right when sitting there, but when I got out, it was almost impossible for me to get to the Princeton Club, could hardly walk a block and stopped to lean against the Hippodrome Garage. Penelope tried in vain to get a taxi, and I finally made it to the club and was able to sit down in the lobby. Recovering from one of these strains is like the surcease from an aching tooth.

Elena later joined us. She has been terribly distressed about Daphne's trying to keep her from seeing the little girls. All kinds of carefully planned pretexts. Had to take them to see her sister's baby that Saturday afternoon; next Saturday the christening of the baby, so there would be no point in Elena's staying over. When I called up Henry, I told him that Elena had burst into tears after her telephone conversation with Daphne, who had been blocking her every attempt. "Oh, dear. I don't know what to say. Everything is very complicated." They are still living beyond their means, Henry is in debt again, and he can't speak of these matters to Daphne. I am afraid that by the time she gets over her fractured skull, she will have him and Elena so terrorized that her tyranny will be permanent. One of her manias is keeping after Henry for not earning enough.

Sunday. Lunch with the Pritchetts at the King Cole Room of the St. Regis: it cost about $50; two martinis completely put me under. My heart was going under in general but I didn't know it yet. Epsteins in the evening. Jason has worked himself up into one of his states of hate against Judge Hoffman of the Chicago Seven trials, increased by Hoffman's anti-Semitism. He says that he has tried to find some way of looking at Hoffman so that he does not hate him, but has been unable to find any such way. Those hates are a bad thing for Jason. He made a mistake at Doubleday by getting one against Douglas Black, and he suspects that he did the same thing when he interviewed the government man about our Pléiade project.

Monday. Lunch with Roger at the restaurant downtown where I used to have breakfast with Magda [Johann, in 1926]. As Roger says, it has all the appearance now of having been turned into a brothel: the inside has been done over in a luxurious mahogany style, and there are pictures of nude women about to be fucked. In the evening, we went to *Child's Play*, an effective horror play about a Catholic boys' school. It was well acted and directed, but doesn't really make sense. We sat at the end of the first row, and a cold draught blew through all the time, which made my cold worse. I set out the next day to go to the memorial service for Louise Bogan at 3 at the National Institute [of Arts and Letters]; but I stopped to see Hicks on the way and he told me I ought not to go, because I would give people my infection. So I went back to the club and went to bed. I remained there till Elena left on Friday. I was trying to read Conrad's *Secret Agent*—very boring, full of the old-fashioned psychologizing of the Henry James era. I succeeded in finishing it, though. Some of these novels of Conrad's present a challenge to the reader to get through them. I had a similar experience with *Nostromo*, which I read part of in the hospital at Wellfleet. I was well enough on Saturday to go with Penelope to Fellini's *Satyricon*—long and elaborate, a rather unpleasant effect, a piling up of horrors and monstrosities.

Defying the Doctors; Henderson House

I went back to Wellfleet on Sunday. Thought I'd better
take Dr. O'Konoki's advice and get a cardiogram at the
Hyannis hospital. Great difficulty getting in and out of the
car. They took me up in a wheeled chair. When the woman
who took the cardiograms sent mine to the doctor and got
his report, she said I shouldn't leave the hospital without
seeing him. He was a Greek with the strange name of
Grammaticus, who told me I had an infarct, stopping up
of one of the cells that feed the heart its oxygen, that I
had had a heart attack and that it would be dangerous for
me to leave the hospital. So I went home and got my things
and came back. I lasted in the hospital only till Saturday,
then left against the doctor's advice, after signing a paper
in which I absolved them from any responsibility as to
what might happen to me. They take your temperature
and your blood pressure and samples of your blood and give
you pills every five minutes. The food without salt is inedible. Everybody says "O.K.?" after every remark in a
way to drive you crazy. The hospital has a new wing, only
open a year—financed, I imagine, by Kennedy money—
which they seem to be crazy about. They have all the latest
gadgets. You are wired to what they call a monitor that
projects at a distance like television the action of your heart:
a black background against which travels a parade of little
insect-like *l*'s—in amber or in green light—that hop down-
ward to show your heartbeats. There is one in the patient's
room and another outside where it can be watched by the
nurses. As somebody said, the next step would be interpolated commercials. It is a terrible nuisance being wired
to this, having an oxygen tube hung on your nostrils and
having your artery fed through another tube connected
with a high-hung jar of glucose and water so that you can't

go to the bathroom and can't move much without getting tangled in them. I came out as weak as I did from Beth Israel.

Elena had had the bed from above the study brought down into the small study, so that I would not have to go up the stairs, which had become more and more of an ordeal. This proved to be delightful. With its four windows, the little study is the lightest room in the house and lined with my pictures and books. *Nostromo* had gotten me down. They gave me medication in the hospital which made me go to sleep all the time. I would go to sleep in the middle of a paragraph and when I waked up would have lost the place in the static and too complicated narrative and begin again several pages back and keep on reading for some time before I realized I had already read them. So I investigated Petronius intensively for the first time since I had read him at college in Bob Scoon's Silver Latin course. The film [*Satyricon*] does follow the original more closely than I had remembered, but, as Penelope says, the tone is quite different. The original, though sometimes satirically coarse and macabre in a comic way, is less menacing and more cheerful. This week of convalescence constituted, I suppose, some of the happiest days of my life. Everything was done for me by Elena, and it did not cost me discomfort to get from place to place. I did not worry about my obligations except writing my T'ville book, which was easy—my writing table is just at the foot of my bed. I have decided to give up boring novels, not to feel that I have to finish them: *Mademoiselle de Maupin, Peregrine Pickle*, Conrad—with such limited time left me, what is the use of reading anything that does not instruct or amuse me? Petronius and his problems seem more enjoyable. —After a while, however—this is Sunday, I have now been laid up a week—one does become a little restless.

It disillusions me now with life, to become aware of how long everything takes. We have not yet completely sloughed off the absurdities of those old theologies—see Malachi Martin's *Encounter* piece—that have been hanging around our lives for thousands of years. Our clumsy and partly unsuccessful efforts to breed a better race. And actually setting foot on the uninteresting moon makes the earth accidental and smaller and the universe somewhat more knowable but less interesting. Heaven and God are not up there. The moon has no more personality.

Nina says that Svetlana calls Paul *ty* [thou] and *Dyadya* Paul [Uncle Paul] but insists on calling Nina *vy* [formal you] and Nina Georgevna. She calls Svetlana *ty* and Svetlana. Svetlana won't allow herself to be given her *otchestvo* Iosevna [patronymic of Joseph]. Nina, who has almost no hair left, has taken to wearing a dark high wig, which looks quite natural and grand, and is becoming.

<*T'ville, May 11, '70.* The trip turned out to be painless: Elena drove me to the airport, and a porter with a wheeled chair got me to the plane. Mary met me at the other end. Her job disappears with the reorganization due to the new regional school, and she seems discouraged, says that the kids are impossible to control—though, talking about it later, she spoke of cases in which she had become interested in her relations with particular children. In one case, she had walked down the aisle weeping, and she thought this had made some impression. Thinks of going back to Alex. She has decided to go spend the $2,000 she has saved on a two-week trip to Hungary that will also take in a few days in Paris and London. Had promised her younger daughter a graduation present and has decided that this will be it.

I have had one of the beds moved downstairs, and I find

Edmund and Elena Wilson in the blue room at Wellfleet in 1970

it pleasant enough to live in my study just as I did in Wellfleet. The first week I had Mabel Hutchins stay at night, but now I don't need her any more. I am now very much better (May 26), can get around with little discomfort—go upstairs only once a day every day or so, and space my guests and excursions.>

On the 16th, Mary drove me over to Mohawk to see *Henderson House*, where Teddy Roosevelt's sister Corinne, married to a man named Robinson, lived in a "castle" built by his Scotch ancestor. We were misdirected first by a man in a garage to something called "the Manor," a strange old replica of an Irish castle, very ugly and uncouth, rough uneven stone, unornamental fountain painted blue, built in the 1860s—thick dark stone walls, the upper story burned. It is now a restaurant, where we had our lunch. Luckily, the people at the table next to us, of whom I made inquiries, lived very near Henderson House and told us exactly how to get there. They had known Mrs. Robinson, who died only five years ago, and had bought a set of Chippendale chairs when the furniture from the house was sold. The place proved to be well worth visiting. It is on a high hill and the view is the most tremendous that I have ever seen up here: a great expanse of the Mohawk Valley, with the enormous billowing hills, now green under a gray-clouded sky, mildly rainy, but the tempered spring effect is attractive. The house itself, which took seven years to build—limestone dragged up from below—is in good taste, unlike the bogus Irish castle. Steps rather like ours here of slabs of stone, two rounded half-towerlike protuberances on either side of the front door, for the broken windows of which the present owners had to get curved glass made, a stone wing also rounded to one side, chimneys with crenellated tops, high French windows on the bottom floor, a flag run up on a long pole on the peak of the roof above the front door, a fancy trimming of white ironwork on the ground, along the windows and on top of the house. It is now called Gelston Castle after some similar place in Scotland. All the furniture and ornaments were sold by the family except things that were difficult to move: barrel organ made sometime before 1820, which the present occupants haven't been able to find out how to work, a carved marble fireplace from Italy, which they haven't got around to washing, and a solitary chandelier.

The place was put on the market after Mrs. Robinson's death and bought by a couple named Blair—she a straight clear-eyed Scottish woman (by way of New Jersey)—I didn't see her husband. They have turned it into what they call a "home for the handicapped," which seems to mean a home for dimwitted old ladies. Mrs. Blair seemed to have been hurt by the Alsops' having deplored this, and she had written one of them a bitter letter.* But it is true that it is rather melancholy to see the old ladies sitting around. It was Sunday, and a few of them were holding a service, one playing the piano while the others sang hymns in one of the once splendid rooms. There are miscellaneous and horrible objects which the Blairs have evidently been gatherers of in the Third Avenue type of antique shops and have installed in the big central chamber. The old ladies are encouraged to make ceramics in a kiln with which the Blairs are equipped. I bought an elongated pussycat with slanting aquamarine glass eyes and ruby glass gems on its collar, and Mary bought three beer steins, one with the inscription "My answer is, Maybe. And that's final," and two that say "If business interferes

* Joseph (1910–89) and Stewart (1914–74) Alsop, syndicated Washington columnists, were grandsons of Corinne Roosevelt, Theodore Roosevelt's sister, and as boys spent their summers at Henderson House. In *The Saturday Evening Post* they had lamented the transformation of the house into a retirement home.

with your pleasure, give up business." These objects showed the same lack of taste as the miscellaneous objets d'art. The Blairs found in the toilet, slipped down behind the sink, the following quatrain by Mrs. Robinson, who, in my boyhood, as Corinne Roosevelt, published some volumes of poetry:

> While the 'pump' is all undone,
> Do not let the water run.
> Spare the John whene'er you may
> And pray the wind will blow all day.[*]

The Desire to Transcend Human Limitations

<Rosalind—now living in Aunt Addie's old house—had heard about a restaurant called the *Buffalo Head*, which has become very popular. When I spoke of it to Mabel Hutchins, she said that she thought it was so much in demand that I might have to reserve a table. It turned out (May 19) to be the very worst of the bad restaurants around here. It is at Forestport and is one of those Adirondack places where the bears come to eat the garbage. It seemed to me irresistible to conclude that the bears had had the idea of running a restaurant. The cuisine seemed very bearish: almost nothing but big chunks of meat—beef and pork; no soup and poor wine, not chilled. The customers also looked like bears: the big barrel-shaped men and women that live on the farms up here. I drank a whole bottle of the wretched white wine in order to forget my surroundings.>

---

[*] In *Upstate*, EW removed this account of Henderson House from the record of 1970, expanding on it in the background chapter, "Hardships and Dream Pockets."

May 24. Mary drove me to Clinton, where I took the Briggses and the Todds to lunch. "Lafe" (for Lafayette) Todd had told me that he was born in Chautauqua County, just outside *Lily Dale*, the spiritualist village, to which the house of the Fox sisters has been moved. <He told me the story of a séance at which John Mulholland, the magician, had been present. He had broken the circle of holding hands by joining his two neighbors' hands and leaving himself free, and when some kind of glowing mass appeared above their heads, he stepped out and turned on the light, which revealed the medium walking around with a stick at the top of which was a wad of phosphorus-saturated cotton. For having been found out, this medium was had on the carpet by the ruling committee and expelled from the association. This seems to me very unjust.> He has offered to take me over to Lily Dale later in the summer. He said it has somewhat declined.

May 26. John Hearne came for the night. Very interesting to talk to, as always. When I first saw him up here, he had thought that some of his students were bright and was rather pro-American. But in view of "the events of the last two months," he has become rather "pessimistic." Abbie Hoffman and Jerry Rubin have been to the college, and he thinks they are rather bad news. It is all a performance with Hoffman, and John feels that he really wants to burn and kill, that his mentality is totalitarian. But he has talked to serious students and been struck by their bitterness and sense of frustration. He said when I asked him about "Black Power" in Jamaica that this doctrine rather lost its trenchant edge in a county which was 95% Negro. There had been nothing like the kind of rebellion they are having in Tobago and Trinidad. But he also said that he was taking a "share" in his mother-in-law's house in Sussex, is building an annex to it in case he has to do a "bolt." The big Negro agitators are not allowed to come to Jamaica. Very satisfactory to talk to: when you ask him a question, about a political situation or what the president of Colgate is like, he thinks about it a moment, then gives you a serious answer. He doesn't entirely agree with my theory of the literary "slobs." He agrees that James Jones has nothing to do with literature, but thinks Norman Mailer important, likes *Why We Are in Vietnam* and his book on the Washington demonstration. He finds Susan Sontag stimulating as a critic, but thinks her last novel is awful.

Rosalind says that when John was here, the local boys put broken glass on the floor of the garage. She says that a new car always "brings out the worst in them."

Going to the *Savoy* for a long dinner with Mary is beginning to get me down a little, because eventually people she knows—and she seems to know almost everybody—come over to our table, and I have to talk to them. The head salesman for Utica Beer, a big red-faced balloon of a man—she is hoping that her graduating son, who has qualified himself as a chemist of food products, will get a job with this company. Also, Alex, her boss, and his son—and others—were there.

<*June 3.* Trip to Hyde Hall. Alternating sun and soaking rain. The skies up here, which I find rather hard to describe, seem to correspond to the country in covering more space than seems appropriate to our dwellings, cars and people—more appropriate to the lives and imaginings of the Indians. A white bank of cloud above a long green hill,

darker green forested on top; the gray rain clouds that seem the emanations in vapor of remote invisible beings that move them slowly and, as it were, waveringly. Shreds of mist dripping here and there on the hills around Cooperstown.

Hyde Hall: Big dominating domineering Georgian façade 190 x 90. Four stone pillars almost Egyptian, composed of round segments of stone, upholding an ironwork balcony, somewhat fancy but in an august way, and an entablature with a classical pediment, oval window in the middle below the roof and below it four square ones. Two kinds of stonework—one closer than ours, one smoother and tighter joined. Built 1813 to 1830–33; stone brought up from Albany. Old wooden barn collapsed. Little stone outbuilding with narrow cells as if for slaves. Looks out on Lake Otsego, hill behind it where banal Bouncing Bet now blooms. Big old trees. Courtyard in middle of house, full of weedlike vines. Inside, signs UNSAFE. All dark—how did they light it? Plaster fallen off ceiling showing slats. Marble fireplaces in every room dappled black or white, modern bathroom seats. A few photographs lying around—a Tauchnitz, *Lord Ormont and His Aminta*. Wallpaper peeling off wall. Big kitchen, library, chapel. In outside repository, completely disintegrated piano still in crate—said to have been sent from England and supposed to have been in time for some big party—when it didn't arrive in time, according to the story I was told, the lady of the house simply scrapped it. The white woodwork is like ours here—also, the banisters and the brown curlicued fringe along the stairs. Old mattresses lying in a pile in the upstairs hall. Desolation of even those rooms in which the family used to live when they came up there for the summers. Too dim to see ceilings. Furniture stored away, to be brought out when the place is restored—which is going to be terribly expensive and take a long time, and Lewis Jones says they haven't raised the money. >

I took Mabel Hutchins to see the Cardiff Giant at Cooperstown. It has suffered a good deal of damage during the winters from being exposed without shelter in a pit. They have a cover over it now, but its genitals and toes are badly eaten away. *

Pratt House: very square and up and down. Brick with white wedding-cake woodwork at the entrance and high narrow windows; along the flat roof a curious fitted trimming of what must have once been red, white and blue scales of slate; a square-topped tower on top. —White elaborate hoods over windows—mosaic effect of ornamental shingles—three stories—tower with peaked cap ⌒ and iron balcony—behind it, on the flat roof, little white-railed porch like a playpen. Pratt's collection of antique cars sold at auction after his death.

Anne Miller: "The Situation Has Comic Possibilities"

<*June 12.* In the morning, went with Anne Miller to the chasm on Sugar River under the railroad bridge, which I don't seem to have described in this journal before and

---

* The Cardiff Giant was a stone statue 10 feet 4 inches tall, purportedly a petrified man, a hoax that had fooled Emerson among others, and evoked EW's sense of his disintegrating body. "Eventually it was acquired by the New York Historical Association, and was exhibited in a pit, where it lies as if stiffened by death, with its immense square skull and imposing penis, the product, it seems to me, of an overwhelming compulsion to create some superhuman being to walk those New York State hills, where the Word of God had not been spoken." This passage in *Upstate* concludes, "Poor old giant! One can't help pitying him. Like all statues, he represents the desire of human beings to transcend their human limitations."

which I wanted to see again.* Anne helped me through the stones—I could never have managed without her—she wore tennis shoes and a tennis dress; and when we got to the swimming hole and cataract, she went off from me and with her back to me took off her dress near the falls and went in swimming naked—I saw her slim brownish figure from behind, and she looked very pretty. Two tragedies occurred here: a boy was found drowned—it's not known whether or not he committed suicide—and two girls walking on the trestle were overtaken by the train: one lay down on the ties and let the train pass over; the other, the Erwin girl, I think, tried to hang on with her hands and fell off.

When you get beyond the broken stones, among which grow blue bugloss, buttercups and wood anemone—with a sprinkling of forget-me-nots and violets and occasionally the inevitable beer can, spearmint wrapper, black marks of picnic fires—you find yourself in a high-walled chasm of stratified limestone rock which is feathered with green fern and lined in the cracks with green moss. Birds flit back and forth between the walls. The river runs shallow here with moderate rapids. The cliffs where they overhang are dripping with springs, and across the river, the farther one goes, the more densely they are plumed, grown with trees: ash, feathery hemlock, elm—bushes of sumac. A dead tree droops down over the stream. The cascade is white, rather crooked and ragged. Below it, a brownish froth floats on the swimming hole, and this, and what she

---

* As a boy Wilson kept an enlarged photograph of the river in his room in Red Bank, and in old age he liked to recall how his cousins and he enjoyed playing around "its Big and Little Falls, and its flower-and-fern-hung high stratified sides; or among the fields of long grass, with their concealed and untroubled ponds" (*Upstate*). In "The Old Stone House" (1933) he recalls having idealized "the farther and less frequented and more adventurous bank of Sugar River, which had to be reached by wading."

thought was a stagnancy of the water in a kind of inlet, made Anne think that it might be polluted and made her dubious about taking the children here. A stretch of primitive landscape invisible and little frequented just off the traffic of Route 12. Above the chasm, against the blue, the coverlet of small dappling clouds crawls slowly below the sky.

Young hell-divers of several summers ago—skim along the surface like aquaplanes, then dive and swim under water for quite a long distance before they suddenly reappear. >

When Loran Crosten was driving me that afternoon, a cloud of brown dust was rising from somewhere among the green hills. It was Delio's operations quarrying Dry Sugar River. <—The Crostens have bought the place across the way from them, where the children used to annoy them. They found behind the house a horrible dump of garbage, old cars and junk. The inside of the house was more horrible still: an upstairs room where the children apparently simply peed and shat on the floor. The man worked in the furniture factory in Boonville. Loran is going to have the house razed, and they think of having a biological laboratory established there, where the hormones of insects will be studied. —Life at Stanford had, they told me, been quite nerve-racking: bombing of the music school threatened, the windows of their house broken, sleepless nights, calls from the police to look out. >

Anne Miller: When she came to see me with Ned, after very slight acquaintance, she gave me a big kiss on the mouth. When she came to see me later by herself, we did a great deal of kissing and I proceeded to further intimacies. "I am a very warm person," she said, as if to explain. Anecdote about firemen waving to her and saying "Peace,

peace!"—she was evidently making a play on "Piece." I
could hardly believe this and made her repeat it on a later
occasion. I gave her a good deal of Moselle wine; criticized
her poetry: she has no idea of rhyme or meter. We agreed
that writing poems is therapeutic—I told her Edna Millay's
saying, parodying an ad for apples: "A sonnet a day/Keeps
the doctor away." She seems to have been carrying on some
kind of affair with someone for two years, trusted me to
be discreet, showed me one of his poems, which was just
as undistinguished as hers and sounded very much like
them. I explained the various kinds of metrical feet and
suggested her trying a sonnet. When she did, it didn't
come out right—she said that she didn't know why, but
when she got to the last lines, they always come out too
long. I don't understand her yen for me at my age, and I
don't believe it was inspired by her finding that, according
to that list in *Esquire*, I was supposed to be one of the
hundred most important people in the world; she had already begun to show her interest in me. She is very pretty,
brisk, bright—flirtatious but also realistic and direct. I
told her that all the men in town must be in love with
her—after a moment's silence, "A few," as I had answered
when Mary told me that I must have had many beautiful
women.

She had had a date with me another afternoon to explore
the part of Sugar River beyond the railroad bridge, but
called me up and explained that something had gone wrong
with her car and she had to have it repaired. Much later,
she called me up—it was too late for our walk—and I
invited her over for a drink; but she had to get the children's
supper. But to my surprise, she very soon called me to say
that Ned knew she wanted to see me and had offered to
attend to things himself. I found that I was excited in the
same way I used to be when I had a rendezvous with a
woman—something that hadn't happened to me in years

—stopped writing, stopped playing solitaire. But nothing happened except a little kissing—it was then that I gave her most of my instruction in writing verse—rather sloppy, we were drinking more of the Moselle. She is very quick in her replies and in picking things up. The second time I read her poetry, I found that she had already understood how to criticize it herself. She proved to be extremely knowledgeable about flowers, plants, trees and rock formations. Returning from our walk, she had guided me back to the road with her quick attentive observation of what was going to be difficult for me and what I ought to do— after which she produced a bottle of a cheap kind of wine called Ripple, to which the Millers seem to be addicted. We went into the roadside snack restaurant. I followed her example and had what was known as a "sausage sandwich"—which turned out to be terrible, but her merry and friendly companionship could make me enjoy anything. —I had asked her whether her husband didn't object to her seeing other men. "You asked me a strange question," she said on another occasion. "Nothing illicit. I know where I belong." When she came to say goodbye to me the day before I was leaving, I saw the dark top of her head just above the wooden bar across my front windows, as she came past them along the porch with her brisk unselfconscious step.

One day when I had been calling on them, coming out of the house, I found the children playing happily on the lawn—it reminded me of my boyhood at the Collinses'. They turned cartwheels and flip-flops for my benefit. There were dogs, a basset hound who belonged to Ned's brother across the street, their black mongrel and a greyhound that belonged to a neighbor, which she said was an idiot. My impression of a very happy household. I thought that Ned, when I first saw him this summer, seemed a little embarrassed, as if he knew about, or suspected, my necking with Anne; but Rosalind afterwards told me that he had been calling on her, bringing her bottles of Ripple and, she said, making passes at her, and it may have been on this account. Anne has long phalanges in her fingers and toes. I held her feet when she had pulled up her knees on my couch, which did not in the least embarrass her. It seemed natural and pleasantly sensuous. This all seems rather odd for me at 75. The situation has comic possibilities. Three of my old upper row of false teeth came out, and Ned had to put them back. I don't want to spoil, by my attentions to his wife, my relations with the best dentist I have ever had. And he says that I may have to have the same kind of arduous operation on my upper jaw as on my lower.

<*Wellfleet, June 23–August 16, 1970*. Back in Wellfleet June 23rd.> The wet sticky stiflingly hot messy American summer.

<I don't remember ever having suffered from the heat to such an extent anywhere—even in New Jersey. I was just crawling around, and it was all I could do to accomplish a little work every day. Tania Ledkovsky helped me with my Russian chapters; she had brought up her father's Russian typewriter. She was born in Germany and has never been in Russia, but she studied Russian intensively with a teacher. She corrects my Russian and always understands the grammar.> Admirers consumed a certain amount of her time. Mike Macdonald wants to marry her. Her grandmother is Nicholas Nabokov's sister, but she doesn't seem to like either Nicholas or Volodya very much: she says that Nicholas is a snob, and that they don't approve of Volodya's bitchiness about all the other writers. —Elena Levin says that she looks like a *boyaryshnya* [a boyar wife], very tall and handsome. <What with children, grandchildren and friends of everybody, all in the hot weather, the summer

was crowded and confused—too much for me—and Elena was exhausted. Reuel and Marcia went to France, where they stayed in Mary's apartment (she is in Maine), and left the little boy Jay, two and a half, with us. Tania, when she was done with my typing, acted as nursemaid for him, sleeping in the little house with him, and getting rather worn out dressing him and giving him baths.>

Penelope with her little girl came to see us. I played my double-pack solitaire almost every day, and it never came out right. I had a hemorrhage in my right eye, as well as one other uncomfortable pain in my heart, and the three teeth in my upper jaw came out again. Usual prostration, when I got out, from more than one strong drink. I went to Grammaticus in Hyannis, and he told me to leave off taking diuretic pills—since when I have been returning to normal. Taking one every day had reduced me to helplessness. At one point, I found myself getting so weak that I couldn't sign my name properly. Diuretic pills are the current medical fad and, I believe, really deleterious. It was taking them that made Elena faint on our last visit to New York, and Mabel Hutchins, who had also been taking them, almost fainted at Wellfleet. I brought her on to be a help; but Elena as usual insisted on trying to do everything for everybody herself, and Mabel was turned into more or less of a guest. The mosquitoes were a constant nuisance. I had to get up every night to kill them. They are no longer using the same methods of mosquito control. Elena says they are now "castrating" the males, but actually they were trying to sterilize them. Also, fleas from the animals, and many earwigs in my part of the house.

<T'ville, August 16. I was glad to get back to T'ville. The weather had cleared up and it was cool. Mary met me and told me about her trip to Europe. I felt that she was rather let down now that she was back again. She had evidently been having trouble with George, whom she had

left to get his own meals (Susie has a job at Old Forge) and who is sore at her for having spent $2,000 on her trip and to some extent run into debt. She has returned to her job with Alex and seems rather apprehensive about it, though she is pleased that people in Rome greet her on the street and tell her how glad they are to have her back. >

August 24. I have dined out every night except one. It is good to have the Morrises back in their own house. Only difference that their old cat is dead, and that they now have a new one, to which they have given the Welsh name of Megan.

Anne Miller came to see me one afternoon. I had told her to come at 4 but she arrived a little after 3, when I had just shaved and was not yet dressed, and stayed until 7, telling me about her family problems. She did not bore me, however—so lively, bright and quick—and so tempting with her bare little legs, arms, and her pretty slim figure. She must be starved for people to talk to. She says Ned is not really happy, has been practicing so many years in Lowville. —He has put back very firmly two of my teeth and is going to work on the third.

<Bob Weiler has had two bad accidents. He first caught his hand and got it mutilated in a machine at the mill; then had a motor accident and, I believe, broke a rib or two.

Three boys from Boonville have been arrested for "drag racing"—who can drag farthest after putting on the brakes. One of these is said to have put up quite a struggle with the police. >

Mediums, Clairvoyants, and Healers

<*Trip to Chautauqua County, August 28–29–30**: Lafe
Todd of Hamilton drove Austin Briggs and me over. He
comes from Dunkirk, near Fredonia, and knows all that
county well. I wanted to visit the spiritualistic town of
Lily Dale. Beyond Syracuse the landscape is perfectly
flat—the fields of corn give way to miles of vineyards drap-
ing their supports of posts and wire. We stayed at a peculiarly dreary Vineyard Motel. Immediately drove over to
Lily Dale, named after the waterlilies in the little Cas-
sadaga Lake which Todd says he used to sell as a boy,
charging more for the rare pink ones than for the white
ones. He and his family, who owned property there—his
grandfather's large, elaborate and somewhat fantastic
house, red brick with white trimmings and a turret—never
went to Lily Dale—except to sell waterlilies there—and
regarded it as a "sore" on the countryside. Austin and I
had the impression that it was a much queerer place than
we could have imagined, quite cut off from the outside
world. Austin felt we were surrounded by a conspiracy; I
was reminded of the beginnings of Algernon Blackwood's
stories—like the one about the city of sinister cats. It is
protected from invasion by the lake on one side and by a
very ancient forest on the other: tall maples with naked
trunks that only put forth branches with leaves toward the
distant tops. Yellow jewelweed below; the Inspiration
Stump on a pavement made of stone blocks, each cut with
the name of a distinguished medium. A barbed-wire fence

---

* It was a long drive from Talcottville to the western end of New York
State near Lake Erie. In *Upstate* EW describes the spiritualist community of Lily Dale. Lafayette Todd recounts the expedition, Wilson's
last foray as a working journalist, in the Spring 1973 issue of *New York
History*.

shutting the community off from the outside world. The religion is a corporation, run by a rigorous committee, which can expel an exposed medium like the one exploiting ectoplasm exposed by John Mulholland, and can sue a visitor who breaks up a séance and thus endangers the life of the medium. But Todd was told that trances and trumpets were now forbidden—perhaps because they are easy to expose and demand a higher degree of competence than their mediums are capable of today. There is nothing now but what is really fortune-telling and "healing," announced on the white sign board as "Mediums," "Clairvoyants" and "Healers." Population, Todd says, used to be 5,000; now, his lawyer friend thought, not more than 1,000. In winter, most of them move to another Lily Dale in Florida. One of the factors which had given them a bad reputation was their having open sewers which drained into the lake, but these had been got rid of.

The place has a strange appearance. A gateway where you pay 75¢ admission, over which a large sign advertises it as "The World's Largest Center for the Religion of Spiritualism." An imitation-bronze fountain, a woman with a gushing urn. Huddled houses, with steep sharply peaked roofs, as if the town had never been at all planned, and a few with the white fringes of wooden lace and spindle-ribbed porch railings characteristic of this part of the world; a few desultory flowers: geraniums, gladioli, begonias. A small white office building, with a sign behind the counter: "Phenomenon. Reincarnation. This may be observed at many offices after 5 p.m. when all the dead people come to life." The woman who was presiding explained that this was a "jest." Fat elderly women with glasses, the usual type. No children; I saw only one dog near the gate—he may have strayed in—a collie. The young squint-eyed girls looked as if they were in training as witches. People are allowed to rent houses there, but can't buy property unless they accept the faith. The library is very old-fashioned, with its lean and white-haired librarian and its torn and black-covered books, all about spiritualism. The cottage of the Fox sisters, a small and plain frame building, has been burned down. Its site had never since been built on and was commemorated with a plaque. Ugly and clumsy pagodas. A city of sleazy fakers, all working together—uncomfortable and unreal.

We attended two so-called séances—the first in the large assembly room, where a chinless man in round glasses gave reassuring predictions to people in the audience, which he pretended to get from the spirits at his side: the sick relative would get well, the questioner would take the desired journey. He had the most nasal and piercing old-fashioned preacher's voice that I have ever heard anywhere. They had been singing hymns of which the printed words were supplied, and the meeting was closed by a blast from the organ. We saw this man again on the second day outside. He had changed from a blue suit to a brown—we had the feeling that he was keeping us under observation. He continually rubbed his hands, even off the platform. Todd had asked him after the meeting where something was, and the man had seized his arm hard and, Todd said, "massaged" it. As a boy selling waterlilies he had had some unpleasant experiences, and believed that the 20% of mediums who were male were mostly homosexual. —The second séance took place out-of-doors, the medium speaking from a little open-faced "temple," with a sign that said, "In Memory of Mother." The first woman we heard was the same elderly type; her interview Todd thought was a plant—her answers perfectly fell in with the medium's suggestions. For the rest, it was a question of the medium's "feeling her way." She would look down from time to time, as if she were listening to the spirits. "Is there an Ed here?—He's fond of fishing, I can see him reeling in his fish" (pantomime). "Is there anybody here who dropped something on his toe?" She would say, "Thank you," with satisfaction when the answers corresponded, and on one occasion she said that a little spirit girl by her side was clapping her hands with joy. Same reassuring answers. Then she turned over the platform to a man, a very dubious-looking character, with a slight accent which I thought was Germanic but which Lafe thought was Irish. He identified a truck driver, and told him that he was going to drive a "box car" (a vehicle with wheels that can be hitched to a truck or carried onto the cars of a train). —Mediums, Todd told us, were often consulted about the stock market, scored heavily if investments went up. Austin and I made an appointment with a medium, a Mrs. Wilenski, who said, "I'll try to squeeze you in," but she wasn't there the next morning. We went away and came back again, but saw there were several women waiting and finally gave it up.*

I was reading Kingsley Amis's *Green Man* in that dreary hotel, which suited the spirit of Lily Dale—an erotic ghost story, evidently influenced by the ghost stories of M. R. James, antiquarian documents. God comes in at the end, in the guise of a friendly and disarming young man. The pornographic part is funny but the whole book is unsuccessful. Sad to see Amis, who was already reactionary, apparently going religious.

Some of the worst food and wine that I have ever had anywhere. On the way, we had a sandwich at one of the chain restaurants of Holiday Inn which is even worse than the Savarin restaurants: cafeteria with no trays and paper

---

* According to Austin Briggs, they were going to try to materialize Scott Fitzgerald. Wilson, who had been going around with his usual yellow legal pad making notes, believed that the séance was canceled because the people of Lily Dale suspected he was a writer who could expose them.

plates. The people look fairly primitive and very unattractive: usual thick loutish farm types and pale gray-eyed ill-built Poles—no pretty girls. Menu at the motel the same as all over: rubber turkey with dressing, lobster tail and various kinds of steak. Todd took us to a better place: the White Inn. Better food, but dreadful white wine called Emerald Dry, horribly harsh and sour. Todd called my attention to the fact that in these places there is always a Hammond organ playing, but at the White Inn there was an organ played by a real man.

Todd said that his great-grandmother had been present at a reception for Lafayette and had named her son Marquis de Lafayette, not knowing that Marquis was a title. When she found out, she changed it to Marcus. Hence Todd's first name, which has given him his nickname, pronounced Lafe.>—He kept repeating, "You can't go home again," and said suddenly, the day we were leaving, "*Je n'aime pas les Dunquerquois* [I don't like the people of Dunkirk]" and later that he was glad to get the hell out of there. <—He tried to get me Saturday night to go to a birthday party for a woman his father had known who was 102 years old. I firmly refused and spent the evening getting up on current events reading *Newsweek, Time* and *Life.* I was kept awake by a thunderstorm, but even this was rather flat. The next morning they told me that the party had been dreadful. The centenarian was indisposed and didn't come, but before he was aware of this, Austin had been trying to figure out which of the ladies was a hundred years old. They were all very aged schoolteachers. He and Todd said they drank too much bourbon, and that I had been wise not to go.*

On the way back, I was half asleep in the back seat

---

* Briggs and Todd had actually enjoyed the party. They agreed to exaggerate the decrepitude of the ladies so that Wilson wouldn't feel he had missed anything.

when the car in front of us, with East Indians—husband, wife, woman in a sari and young boy—rose in the air and landed upside down. I did not know what was happening. When they said it was a blowout, for a moment I thought we had had a blowout.

Saturday we went to Chautauqua—surprised to find it so well kept up and respectable, had imagined something more vulgar and sloppy. Good music, Todd tells me—a small core of intellectuals who enjoy the cultural advantages and pay no attention to the religion. Otherwise, strict ban on alcohol—the big old-fashioned hotel has none of the splendor of the one at San Diego—no bar; the high rooms seem empty and insufficiently ornamented. >

"You Can't Erase the Past"

< Trips to Cherry Valley, September 2. >

Took another look at Hyde Hall without going in. That old boarded-up slab of masonry, with a ragged screen of trees behind it. —A man was checking the bats in the part of the house on the upper balcony with a view to having them exterminated.

< Lunch with A. P. Whitehead in the old Campbell house—New York lawyer, Princeton '31, hunting and drinking type, unmarried, strange potato-in-mouth way of speaking which almost amounts to an impediment and which would be impossible in a courtroom. Old part of house from 1796, later part added between '53 and '63, frame house painted yellow, good portraits of women in dining room and big engraving of banquet after Waterloo with Wellington standing in the center, guns from the Revolution and after, framed letter to some ancestor from Fenimore Cooper. He does a great deal of entertaining,

but the house, where he comes only in the summer, is now a white elephant, which he wants to get rid of. Too expensive to keep up, no more family reunions. Nothing to do in winter but hunt. All those people—Campbells, Robertsons, Clark—knew each other and would visit back and forth—visits would sometimes last two months. Not worthwhile to have house insulated for winter; upstairs, like mine, quite cold. Carved mantelpiece in old part; in the newer part, plaster moldings that are rather out of keeping. He asked us whether we would have "still wine" or champagne. I said still wine but he insisted that we might as well have champagne. Mary was driving and drank only a sip. When I was drinking, he said, "It's just like water." Must have thought we weren't drinking enough. —Evidently thinks about things very much in terms of money, plays a role in the management of the Historical Association. Has two farms.>

Otis and Fern came in after dinner. Timmy was to appear in court on Friday. It is true that the Youngs are suing the Munns. <Timmy, after the accident, went out to California and investigated Haight-Ashbury, which horrified him: filth, every kind of degradation, boys so drugged they could only mumble, promiscuous girls getting pregnant. He came back so disgusted that the family hoped it would sober him up. Yet he and another boy have been arrested for breaking the windows in the Town of Leyden building, which also involved breaking the windshield of a car. Fern denies that he can be taking drugs, but Frances O'Donnell says that he looks and acts as if he were: only half there.>

<The old set of Charles Reade is here that my grandfather gave my mother, and a two-volume edition of *The Cloister and the Hearth* that belonged to Uncle Paul. It was

one of my grandfather's favorite books, and I decided to read it, which I have been doing off and on all summer. I finished the day before yesterday (September 4). It is hard to understand the raptures of Swinburne even on the part of one so given to raptures. John Hearne smiled about it, said there are "good bits," though it was rather long—he had read it when he was 12, and he implied that it was only good for 12-year-olds, as to which I find I agree with him. A kind of improvised adventure melodrama, which one is always conscious that the writer does not take quite seriously himself: "Gerald caught Margaret, but was carried down by her weight and impetus; and behold, the soil was strewed with dramatis personae." The picaresque first half is more or less amusing with its element of historical background; but the second part *does* drag with its continual invention of obstacles to prevent the lovers from getting together. Then the very tedious pathos of the inevitable Victorian deaths, with the union still unreconsummated. It is even more implausible than some of Scott. Readers must have been very naïve.

I have started *The Bible in Spain*, in the hope of a better long nineteenth-century book for reading in bed that will console me and on which I can rely. I need something I can go to sleep on like a Nembutal capsule.

Tug Hill: a great shaggy beast lying as if with its head between its paws.

Mary on the Women's Liberation Movement: women have their place and men have their place—the women protesting are too masculine for their own good—a woman has to be "dumb like a fox" sometimes. >
She is back with Alex, somewhat let down and depressed. <Susie has married a three-quarters Cherokee Indian boy, who does logging. > No such "production," as

she calls it, as about Eddie's wedding—but she says Susie wanted it that way. The newly married pair are living in the little outbuilding formerly occupied by Mary's mother. They can't spend the winter there. Mary wants them to get a $6,000 "mobile home," which they can have on the Pcolar place.

<Dinner with the Edmondses>: Walter looks thin and old. <He says they have seen black panthers and something he took for a wolf.

Dr. Smith always refers to old age as "up there." "Clark Layng is way up there, too.">

Mary reads the astrological column in the paper every day, though she does not take it very seriously. She is Aquarius, and, I think, rather pleased by the fact. I am Taurus.

The Acme market has burned down—all its stock is destroyed. Thought to have been due to wiring of electric refrigerator.

<*Roads:* Mania of road-making. Glyn took me up on Tug Hill along a road, lately being improved and widened, that seemed to have no purpose or point. The few old gray farms are abandoned or ruined, and the only thing of interest one could think of was that the road branched off to the fire tower; but the fire tower sends out signals, and why widen the road in this connection? —When I was driving out with Mabel and her grandchildren one day, we entered a road in a forest that seemed to go on for miles without leading to anything except a few camps, yet was also being worked on and widened.>

———

Visit to the Marcelins: Mary went this time on the Thruway and missed the exit to Canastota so we had to go on to Syracuse. Then we repeatedly took wrong turnings at Cazenovia. When we finally found Bingley Road, Mary said, "We'll take an eraser and erase all that." I said, "You can't erase the past." "What shall we do then, spill ink on it?"

Phito is very pro-Arab, talked about their contribution to civilization, etc. When we were leaving, I said, "À bas les Arabes!" "À bas les hommes!" he replied.

The water at the Pcolar house had sprung a leak and Mary got from Chet Rice some fixture which proved not to be right. I hadn't really grasped before that even taking a short road it was 45 minutes into Rome, which she had to drive every morning. But she said she didn't mind it: in the interval between leaving the family and going to work at the store, she could live in her real self, be independent of other people. Spoke of this with a certain eloquence.

"At Home in the Twenties"

Anne Miller: I had been to see Ned in the morning. He had made the "partial denture" too high, and it was painfully cutting into my cheek. Anne came to see me at 3, and as usual we polished off two bottles of Moselle wine. She told me that she liked to touch people and allowed me to feel her all over, but refused the "final favor." I gathered that when, as she told me, Ned went out and she didn't know where he was, he must have another woman, or women. Inveighed against the pettiness and meanness of the people of C——. She had to go to some sort of occasion given by a woman who hated her, but felt that she had to invite her. The wives of dentists were horribly dull, all they wanted from life was mink coats. She complained of acquaintances who were so ignorant and unsophisticated that they didn't know what fellatio was—if you talked about it, they wouldn't know what you meant. She says she is "on the pill" and takes one every day. She does a good deal of talking to justify her behavior, positively declares her "principles," one of which is not to "put the horns on" Ned. Doesn't like to be in cars and on lonely roads. What she means, I gather, by "games," which she says she doesn't indulge in, are forms of lovemaking. I said I loved to caress her: "You may." She was afraid I'd think that she was a teaser. We did a good deal of talking about love and marriage. She had no use for weak men. She made the familiar complaint that Ned was "selfish," preoccupied with his profession, but he would do anything for her. She had, however, known a man who loved her devotedly enough to satisfy her emotionally. She was 40 now. It didn't seem wrong for men to see her in nothing but a bikini, but it was a little bit shocking to have a man lift up your skirt. Unusual good nature and frankness. She had some Indian blood. Black eyes which she would make very round when announcing her principles or registering amazement at the behavior of the community. She told me that she had induced Ned to compromise with the Lowvillians to the extent of leaving off the single long earring by which I found he was generally known.

The next evening, Tuesday, she came in here after dinner at her house. Talked at length about her love affair with the clergyman—no hope for it—it was partly on her account that he had gone to Fayetteville. She had been very close friends with his wife. Had one lover and didn't want another—until now he had been the only real great love of her life. She liked the way I "touched" her but wasn't in love with me—sex may not be real love. I invited her to do fellatio, but she said, "I'm a lady." She began writing poetry only three years ago, when she first got to know her clergyman. She feels that she has always been expecting something that she has never had. —"Two empty bottles of white wine"—might work for the end of a sonnet. I always provide two bottles of Prinzessen Moselle, and we always drink them up.

> Black head that hardly topped the window bar
>   little brisk brown legs
> That ran to the long phalanges of toes.
> Two emptied bottles of pellucid wine

<Trip with John Howland to what's left of Dry Sugar River. You thread your way among the skeletons of stone crushers and mountain range of blacktop, which generates an unhealthy mist, and find what's left of Sugar River: a great rectangular hole of a quarry, gutted to gray walls of striated rock, with feeble streams trickling down its walls. It has been bought by the man named Delio—Glyn thinks to supply the materials for some road that he knew was going to be built nearby. We drove around but I couldn't identify the strange woodland, with its creviced blocks like the bed of the old river, that one had to go through to find the water gushing out of the hill and heading for the Black River, with the old mill and its huge millstone lying flat in the grass.

The dear old maple in front of the house is beginning to turn with autumn, the reddish orange appearing in the middle—the last time, I suppose, that I shall ever see it. It is going to be cut down for the new road, when a large strip of my property will be taken probably beginning next May.

Gertrude Loomis walked down in the middle of the road in her nightgown and dressing gown, and called on the

Mooneys, whom she didn't know. Huldah had to round her up. When I stopped to get some photographs from Huldah, one of them of herself, and the Talcott genealogy, she said that "that minx" had probably stolen them. This set off on Gertrude's part a tirade of denial and denunciation. Rosalind says that Gertrude is dangerous now. She once put a belt around Huldah's neck, as if she were going to choke her, and Huldah found a knife under her pillow. But Rosalind says that when Gertrude had to go to the hospital with a broken leg, Huldah missed her and was glad to have her back.>

When Anne had told the new Episcopal clergyman that she was Z [as her departed lover had referred to her], he had exclaimed, "Z?"—and this had much embarrassed her, she had felt that she had the Scarlet Letter emblazoned on her gown. Her husband had said to her, "Now don't unfrock any more Anglican friars!" I said I hadn't known there was more than one. She answered, "One and a quarter." I think that she really suffers nowadays from having her lover removed.

Second Return to T'ville: Z undressed almost completely and sat cross-legged on the bed. I stroked her brown body delightfully and kissed her all the time. She said she was underkissed. I told her that if she would forgive my saying so, I thought she was not fucked enough. She said she would forgive my saying so, but implied that it was not that she was underfucked—she thought she was mainly "oral." When I kissed her on the eyelids, I told her they were salty. She said, "I cry a lot." This rather surprised me. We discussed pubic hair. What was it for? I suggested protection. But she thought that this couldn't be true, because men's beards weren't needed for protection.

She said that I was extremely gentlemanly, but that I

didn't take off my socks in bed—it is true that I was wearing uncomfortably bristling double garters.* I apologized and started to take them off, but she politely prevented me. I told her that there were men who didn't even take off their shoes.

The second and last time I saw her we finished three bottles of Moselle, a pint of Johnnie Walker (partly by me after she left), and by her the beginning of a bottle of gin. I told her that she would have been quite at home in the twenties.

I asked her about the open-mouth kissing that always occurs in the movies. I had never done anything like that. What could it consist of? She thought at first I was "pulling her leg." Then she showed me with open mouth and playing her tongue around inside mine. "When you do that, you've got it made."

—wonderful to feel a wet, gluey, reeking cunt.

A Surprising Conquest and Six Weeks of Misery

Anaïs Nin came to the Princeton Club to show me the passages about me from her diary. She had come on from California to take care of Hugo, who had had some eye operations. They were otherwise separated, she said. She had written in the diary that she found me aggressive, arrogant, authoritative, like a Dutch burgher in a Dutch painting, and with shoes that were too big. She had become frightened of me and had had to escape. I had made her more feminine and elusive. I seemed to represent the kind of solid respectability that her whole life was pitted against. I made her correct a few details about Mary [McCarthy]

---

* Born at the beginning of the century, Wilson never gave up the habit of wearing garters. There is a scene in *The Twenties* where he falls asleep after a party without taking them off.

and a few characteristic inaccuracies. She said that I had given her a set of Emily Brontë—as if there could be such a thing, actually it was Jane Austen—and she had been offended and sent it back—which was not true, she had kept it. Of course, she said, it was impossible to print the best things about our relations. She had warned me that I shouldn't recognize myself. I spent two hours with her —I had forgotten what good company she could be. We talked about current French and English books and agreed about many things—notably Lawrence Durrell: that the only good thing in *The Alexandria Quartet* was his lavish and colorful word-painting. She thought that he had gone over so well in America because this kind of rather lush writing was a relief from the plainness and bleakness of the Hemingway kind of thing.

O. drove me to the club and came in for a drink; but since it was election day, the bar was still not open. I went in but all the bottles were locked up. We went up to the second-floor lounge and were soon kissing on one of the couches. I turned off the lights. The club was deserted. "I want to go down on you"; but I couldn't feel much. She said, "We'll soon be fucking. We'd better stop." The big open doorway worried her—she didn't like open doors on such occasions. I took her up to my room, and got her to take off her clothes. Her body was prettier than I had expected. Firm but not large breasts; cunt small and charming and pink, but rather far back, with a little fringe of hair. Beautiful sheer ivory white skin, the kind that goes with her hair. She disillusioned me about my conquest by saying that she had two other "fucking friends." When she got up to go and was putting mascara on her eyes, she said, "People will know that I've just been fucked. I look like a woman who's been fucked." "Not enough," I said.

It's strange that now that I'm 75 and can only get an

erection at half-mast, two such attractive women as she and Z should offer themselves to me. O. said, "It's your brain," but couldn't help giggling, as I did.

End of October beginning of November, '70. Horror of New York: worse than ever, traffic, telephone, mail. Henry says that they are building downtown more enormous office buildings, one without even a cafeteria to give the employees somewhere to eat. I wanted to order the car service to go to the opera and get away afterwards, but found that the club cars were on strike. —I doubt whether I shall ever go to New York again.

We spent almost six weeks of misery in the city, first in Lillian Hellman's apartment, where I was suffering from an accumulation of phlegm in my throat, which kept me awake at night to cough and bring it up; then a week in Doctors' Hospital. Hicks prescribed an antihistamine, which dries up your throat and urine, at the same time as diuretic pills, which make you piss. Saltless diet with the dull hospital fare. Only normal moments reading Mandelstam's widow in bed, a book in itself depressing. Only agreeable feature, the river, with its tugs and other boats, out the window. Elena came and brought me things every day. Personnel always changing and variety of nationalities, some could hardly talk English. Technician who tried to take blood specimens when I was sitting on can or talking to the doctor on phone—I had to fight him off. Very weak when I came out. Hicks told me that they had tried to fire somebody and found they had a strike on their hands for violating the Unfair Labor Practices regulations: the whole staff had quit, nobody to run the elevators. After that the Princeton Club, where Elena collapsed, ran up a high fever. A young Negro doctor came, who evidently did the right things. We then went on by plane to Boston, spent two nights at the Ritz to give her time to partly recover. She made it driving to Wellfleet, but it took us several days to function again.

By getting our references for doctors from Martha James, we found ourselves going to nearly superannuated old colleagues of Dr. James's. Elena at first sent Penelope for her ear abscesses to a very deaf old ear doctor, who could not understand that she intended to go not to Cuba but to California and went on talking on that assumption. He got much interested in her red hair and examined the roots to see that it was not dyed. She afterwards went to a clinic. A younger man then laughed when she told them he had explored her ear by means of, it seemed, an antiquated technique which involved a copper wire.

We saw a number of people: Arthur Schlesinger and his *lyubovnitsa* [new love], the Berlins, Auden, Penelope, John Biggs, Marion Amen and the Dells, but I couldn't do them justice. If they stayed to dinner, I'd eat separately in the bedroom. I had invited Wystan with Penelope, to see what he'd do when confronted with an attractive woman. What he did was sit with his back to her when he sat beside her at the dinner table. They told me that out of a clear sky he said that at the age of 6, he had come into a room and found his parents transvested in one another's clothes. This had shocked him, and I wondered whether it had had the effect of making him confuse the sexes. I asked Penelope to tell about the dead mouse which had frightened her when she was alone in the apartment. This stimulated Wystan—still with his back squarely to Penelope—to tell about having been obliged to kill some mice at his Austrian place. Why? "Because they were eating food that didn't belong to them." (The severe and censorious moralist.) They put out some crumbs for them, but the mice had invaded the cookie jar.

In the hospital, I was dreaming one night that I was with Frances again at Talcottville. Since I hadn't seen her for so long, it was as if I had to seduce her again, to get her into bed—the bed was at the front of the big sitting room, in which my bed now is. When, with joy, I was just about to possess her, the nurse tapped my shoulder to wake me up and take the medicine. After she left, I lay thinking sadly about the enjoyment that had been interrupted.

Boston, December 10–13. I told Zetzel that I was becoming impotent, and he laughed and said that a 90-year-old patient had just made him the same complaint.

Elena, sleeping in the Ritz beside me, half waking said something about "Poor Brown." He had struggled against the cage at the kennel, and she had been worrying about him.

A relief to get back to *Wellfleet* and see the tops of trees and birds out the window, as I lie in bed, instead of the office buildings.

Brown had the mange, all skin and bones, his ribs showing. Before long my whole skin erupted, and the itch was driving me crazy. Dr. Locke in Provincetown decided it was probably the Benemid. I stopped it, and the eruption subsided. This and my throat condition had made me so uncomfortable, kept me from sleeping, that it didn't seem worthwhile to go on living like that. I doubted whether I'd ever make 80.

Nina Chavchavadze spent four days with us in Wellfleet while Paul was away in New York. She is now in pretty bad shape: hair, teeth, stomach, itching skin. It was a great thing for her, she said, to have somebody else's cooking than her own. It has given her something new to talk about that the theory has been propounded that Jack the Ripper was the Duke of Clarence. He was the brother of George V and her cousin, and she tells everybody that her mother did not like him. She sits every night and drinks bourbon but goes on talking in her definite way—her old anecdotes of royalties, who bored her. When she was young, she was in full reaction against her royal background; but Xenia, her sister, went along with it. Her mother was scandalized when they decided not to dress alike. She met the Kaiser only once and thought him pompous. Her mother had a story about having been present when he was watching an archaeological excavation and leaned over and fell into the hole.

I tapped a rich vein of *vran'yo* [Russian lying] when I asked Paul Chavchavadze about that subject. His grandfather in Petersburg had gratuitously invented a story that a lady who kept a successful salon had suddenly hanged herself. This spread all over the city, and the grandfather, a little worried, at last called up the lady's house. Her maid or companion said, "The countess is resting. She's rather tired from hanging so long."

FINAL NOTES: 1971–1972

"An Empty Arena"

T'ville, May 11, '71. They say I bring bad weather, and
the beautiful Tuesday on which I arrived has been followed
by two vile days—last night (Thursday) it froze, and Rosalind says that today is one of the coldest they have had.
I arrived just in time to see my favorite old tree taken down
and the limbs sawed up. They want to take the strip of
land, with the steps, in front of the house, and Penberthy
is coming up today to investigate. Many barns have collapsed under the snow. Continual roaring of bulldozers.
Patches of snow still left. Gladys Morris is apparently
dying—Glyn says she rambles and doesn't make sense. His
sister is staying with him, and he has somebody to cook.
Mabel Hutchins is incapacitated—Kay and Mildred made
my bed and made the bottom floor habitable. Fern has had
one of her innumerable accidents or illnesses—I haven't
seen her. Gertrude Loomis in a home. Everything rather
desolate. Stone bowl and finial have been toppled—the
latter perhaps somehow by the snow, the former must have
been by the kids. —Still burning and smoking ruins of
houses on other side of road. —Weather just like October.

————

When I went to New York in May, I took Penelope, Nolan and her nanny, Christine, to the circus, moving in the wheeled chair—two cops lifted me down the steps. Afterwards, back at the Princeton Club, Penelope, knowing I needed support, helped me up to my room. The night before, at the O'Neill play, my left leg had buckled under me and I, at the time of the intermission, had fallen down in the aisle. In my room at the Princeton Club, Penelope and I had three drinks each. I, having had nothing since morning, merely took a few chews of a sandwich, then swallowed the three martinis in rapid succession. The result was that, after Penelope had left, I tried to sit on the edge of the bed, came down very hard on the floor and fractured a vertebra—though I didn't know what was the matter till much later when I had an X-ray at Hyannis. I was in pain the next morning, and Martha James, warned by Elena, came in like a good angel, got me through breakfast, called a Sunday doctor and brought me a "walker." I called Elena and she came down. We spent some dreary days at the Princeton Club, where those top-hatted *Spy* caricatures depressed me. I insisted on going back to T'ville, where I could not get out of bed without agony, and finally got Mrs. Stabb, a trained nurse, solid German, to look after me. Bob Stabb boasts that she can pick him up and carry him: huge piano legs. I went back, after a few days, to Wellfleet. Rosalind did not want to have to take me to the airport, and I got John Howland to do it. The Millers and Glyn Morris had come to see me, but I couldn't much enjoy anybody.

Wellfleet. I spent monotonous days, which, however, at first I half enjoyed. I would sit in my big red chair looking out into the depths of greenery: bees feasting on the white flowers, and little white butterflies. These were calm and restful hours, but at night sterile fantasies of O. and Anne

Miller, as before I had gone away, when even then I wasn't able to satisfy them. A long period of almost complete eclipse. When I finally went back to T'ville for a week, I was still in no condition to enjoy things—saw Penberthy and people about selling the house, got Ned Miller to fix my teeth. Anne, the Howlands and Glyn Morris had all come to see us at Wellfleet. I usually received our guests in my dressing gown, pajamas and slippers. I had written Bomarzo and Teenage Caveman, and had begun on the early drafts of *The Waste Land*, but at T'ville time sped and I didn't write a word, read nothing except Borrow's *Zincali* and began Knapp's biography of Borrow—I find Borrow very comforting. *Le Cousin Pons* disgusts me and gets me down.

Spent two nights with Helen Muchnic and Dorothy Walsh on way back from T'ville. Rosalind drove me to Cummington without making any mistakes, and Elena came to get me. Going up to my bedroom, I stumbled over and down the step and fell—my back has been difficult since, and I hope I did not make it worse. Much groaning on my part, which embarrassed me with my hostesses. The Pritchetts came to see us. I like him and like his work, but in some ways he makes rather heavy demands: laughs too much, and you have to laugh with him.

Back in Wellfleet again. My sleepless nights get me down—I do a good deal of reading at night: Ibsen, *Le Cousin Pons*, and falling back as usual on Sherlock Holmes, which I have now pretty well exhausted. *Emperor and Galilean* is incredibly dull for so good a craftsman as Ibsen; *Pillars of Society* is much better than *The League of Youth*. If I don't get out for a ride, I can't sleep, and suffer from what Elena calls *angoisse*. I look forward to going to Tucson, but Elena doesn't want to miss Christmas here, as I feel I must.

Paul Chavchavadze died during the summer, leaving

Nina alone and miserable. Peggy Day came to look after her, but always had to get away to go somewhere else— "*Kakaya sueta!* [What a bother!]." She likes to have dinner at 9, as the rest of us know to our cost, and Nina likes to eat at 7. Nina was, however, much improved by some days in the Hyannis hospital. She now goes so far as to drink cranberry juice instead of whisky, and gets around much better.

Pathetic-sounding letters from Mary Meigs, though she writes she is very happy getting settled in the country in Brittany. Her two companions at first were away in North Africa, but, having had Mary make all the arrangements, are now, it seems, again with her. I told her, before she left, that I was afraid she would wake up someday and find herself in the middle of a Balzac novel and asked her whether she had a fine grip on her money. She assured me that she did and that the girlfriends cared nothing about money. This is natural, since they are spending hers.

When Barbara [Deming] came to see us, I talked to her for the first time openly about Mary and Marie-Claire, to whom I referred as "that little bitch." Barbara demurred: M.-C. was more complicated: "a little *witch*." I said that, in writing her from Paris, when M.-C., on account of the injury to her eye, was first getting her hold on Mary, I tried to warn her against M.-C. Barbara answered very truly: "You can't warn somebody in love."

Mrs. Boss, the practical nurse, who always calls me "dear"—I suppose that this is professional—and Geraldine, who takes my letters from dictation and types those of my articles which are not intended for *The New Yorker*. I am getting myself to say "O.K." and "There we are!"

Second printing of *Upstate*. *The New Yorker* has sent back Bomarzo and Teenage Caveman. Other articles they have kept for about a year. I think that I am petering out with them.

Songs from the whole of my past life that irrelevantly go through my head, as it were recapitulating the years: "Hill, dear old Hill," "We'll give a cheer for Princeton, for Princeton win today," "Here's to you, ———, here's to you, my jovial friend" (Princeton faculty song). "More work for the undertaker" (Yale), "A wee doch-an-doris," "Stop your ticklin', Jock," "I'm on mah way home from a weddin'," "*Bonjour, belle Rosine,*" "*Ton syrop est doux, Madeleine,*" "K-K-K-Katy, beautiful Katy," "Keep your head down, Allemann," "Take me out to the ballgame," "Her name is Louisville Lou," "Yankee Doodle," "Shake That Thing," "Blue Tango."

At the Boston hospital, too, they ended every statement with "O.K.?" This got on my nerves, and they wouldn't know how to take it when I said, "No, it's not O.K." or "I don't know whether it's O.K. or not."

They wanted me to have a "pacemaker" for my heart, gave me a regular concerted sales campaign on the subject invoking Justice Douglas, who is supposed to be climbing mountains on the strength of it; but I resolutely refused. I don't want electrodes attached to my heart, and I suspect that this is simply the latest medical fad. As usual, I got out as quickly as I could.*

We have seen a good deal of the Levins. Harry, who has a new hearing aid, is, as Elena says, "more friendly," but I am also more struck by his aridity. He seems to read

---

* The pacemaker would surely have prolonged his life; but it was characteristic of Wilson to insist upon carrying on this battle against death without what he considered artificial help.

nothing now except books by other professors and knows
what they have all written on their literary subjects. I
want to talk to Elena [Levin] on Russia, but he has his
ways of making this impossible. I wish he knew some
Russian himself. Also, he runs down everybody else: André
Malraux, Isaiah Berlin, etc. He has become the perfect
type of the envious literary man *manqué*, but is not so nasty
with me any more (that is, to my face at least). He surprised
me by sounding me out as to whether I would accept an
honorary degree from Harvard. The faculty, it seems, now
have something to say about who gets them.*

I suppose I still partly enjoy this life—I have made for
myself the conditions I wanted: surrounded by my well-
chosen books, which allow me to check on anything I want
to know. But it is horrible not to be able to get around—
not to take out a book or put it back without disproportionate effort. To get to the bathroom is a chore.

Klute, the film with Jane Fonda. I couldn't understand
a word and didn't know what was happening. Katherine
[Biddle], whom the Jenckses had brought and who was
sitting next to Elena, had brought her hearing aid, but
would say from time to time, "I am confused." I don't
think she had ever thought much, perhaps did not even
know, about that world of call girls and dope addicts. Elena
said Katherine winced at the bad language used by Jane
Fonda. It seems that she worried all through about how

---

* While sometimes making Harry Levin a scapegoat for literary academics, EW continued to enjoy his wit. A limerick in Levin's hand is taped
into the journal, titled "On the Occasion of Being Attacked by the
Soviet Delegation at an International Congress":

> A polemical lady from Russia
> Said, "If I don't dig ya, I'll crush ya.
>   You can't get eclectic
>   With my dialectic.
> At least you can't do so in Russia."

to talk about the picture, on her way home, to the French couple who worked for her as chauffeur and cook.

In Provincetown, we had gone to see a play by Arturo Vivante. Since I hadn't been able to hear, I had an entirely false idea of what it was all about. Actually, it was about an anthropologist and his wife who were paying a professional field visit to the Esquimaux. They decide to go in seriously for the Esquimau code of hospitality, and when a young American drops in, the husband lets the wife seduce him. But I didn't know they were reading all their lines and, seeing the husband with a fairly thick ms., I thought he was writing a novel and had come to a "block," that he gave it to the wife, who encouraged him. I thought that the young caller was an Esquimau and that the novel was submitted to him. I learned in the intermission that they were all reading their lines, and then couldn't account for the fact that the husband was sitting in plain sight of the lovers, apparently studying his part. The seduction turned out to be a regular striptease that went on for a long time: she undressed both herself and the boy, and then got on top of him. At one point, when his torso was bare, I thought she was going to take out his cock and go down on him. The actress was the only one who acted, and she was altogether too smug and arch. She exasperated and antagonized me.

Escape from the Planet of the Apes—which I made a point of seeing because Penelope had said it was funny. We thought that it could hardly have been worse: forced, unpleasant and suffering, as Elena said, from the director's not being able to make up his mind what direction the film was to take. You are first made to sympathize with the chimpanzee couple and their baby, then you have to see them shot down in order to save the future human race from being dominated by chimpanzees. We laughed afterwards over our waste of time at spending two hours or more at it. I was glad to have Elena to laugh with—covered over discontent at having watched the picture and had an *"angoisse"* of my heart in coming out of the theater by talking with her and going to bed with a couple of drinks.

Penelope's visit in October: Worried about John Osborne. He showed signs of persecution delusions, wrote letters to the papers, of which he sent her a copy, accusing them of having prevented the production of one of his plays. Called her up at night and talked for two hours, made difficulties about seeing Nolan. Had torn the wig off one of Nolan's dolls to show what Mike Nichols's head was like. Seemed to want her back, felt that he needed her. I advised her to let it alone, leave his wife to handle him. —Lillian Hellman, though she never met him, said that he was evidently a cad—but that women liked cads. Penelope still seems to love him, to be in doubt as to whether she shouldn't still go to help him. She thought, as the Pritchetts did, that his last play was very bad.

Seta [Schouvaloff] said that, with Russians who were rude with her, perhaps especially on account of her former high rank, she could simply rise above it, feel that from her vantage point of moral superiority she could afford to look down on them and ignore it. She announced this quietly, with perfect tranquillity.

December 12, 1971, Wellfleet. When I look back, I feel quite definitely divided from my earlier self, who cared about things in a way I no longer do. All that comedy and conflict of human activity—one gets to feel cut off from all that. One cannot even imagine any more the time when one had once participated. One ought perhaps to have died before reaching this point, when one still had the illusion of participating. All that energy expanded to peter out!

One looks down on an empty arena. What were we all doing there?—running about, jostling and shouting, exchanging vital gossip—involved in great world wars now as trivial and futile as we used to think the Balkan wars were.

Naples, Florida: "A Sunlit Hell of Dullness"

Naples, Florida, January 9. At Wellfleet, before I left, I found myself surrounded by my books and other belongings, but was now alienated from them, couldn't really connect with them. Uncomfortable.

Svetlana, it seems, has been sending Nina, since Paul's death, $300 a month. Now, February, it turns out that there is trouble between her and her husband. Though Svetlana does not say so, it is undoubtedly the Montenegrin mother-in-law who is the irritant. The Frank Lloyd Wright foundation is a commune, and Svetlana complains that she has been made to do community work, scrubbing floors, etc.—just the kind of thing she was trying to get away from when she escaped from the Soviet Union. Her husband says he was not responsible for this, and it was no doubt an attempt of the Montenegrin woman to humiliate her. Svetlana left the commune for California, where she had her baby; then took a house not far from her husband. He has talked about divorce; she not. He has confessed that he may have been in too much of a hurry about marrying Svetlana and asserted that, having devoted his life to the Wright foundation, he cannot abandon it now. In the newspaper photographs, she looks very hurt and unhappy.

Naples, Florida: January, February, March 1972. When I was here on my way to Haiti and had to spend a night in Miami, I thought I had never seen anything like it. This makes, for different reasons, a similar impression. It is the paradise of the retiring middle class, and of an emptiness I should hardly have thought possible. One end of the town, the wealthy end, is made up of imitation French châteaux in confectionery colors like Necco wafers: pale strawberry, lemon and lime. Except when they are driving in fast cars one never sees the inhabitants; occasionally a maid with a white toy poodle on a leash. The roads are mostly blind alleys that end in loops. This end of town is full of "condominiums" and more are constantly being built. The Beach Club Hotel, according to one old inhabitant—built eighteen years ago—was once the last building here. It is now hardly more than the beginning of the new real estate "development," which is supposed to extend miles farther along Alligator Alley, a flat and desolate region, where only a few ragged palms grow and some uninviting canals have been dug. When we asked a man working on the road where the alligators were to be found, he replied, "Over there somewhere." We finally turned back: it was all exactly alike. Lots of building operations that make a lot of noise in the mornings.

The people here are almost incredible, and yet they represent the American Dream. I said that it was like living in prison, and Elena said, "A sanitarium—not so much different." Monotony: I cannot now, as Elena can, even go swimming or walk on the beach. Retired executives with potbellies, their dumpy rather dowdy wives. Otherwise, white heads and wheeled chairs. Everybody seems contented. They cluster around the pool in the afternoons and mornings. They think it is cold, but E. says it is tepid. A variation was introduced when a few small children and grandchildren came. One little girl who loved jumping

in—she did this about fifty times. Sally Palmer and her
3-year-old little girl. She was quite pretty. She was married
to an English "civil servant" but came from Columbus,
Ohio—had learned a British restraint. Much preoccupied
with her father, whom she often mentioned. She was having a kind of trial separation from her husband and was
staying with her family in Columbus. She seemed to feel
that her husband had lost interest in her—the old Anglo-
American story; these marriages seem always to break up:
Adelaide and Bosanquet, Bettina and her husband. (This
was a case of a German woman and an Englishman, but
it involved, after she married, a social demotion for Bettina,
because her husband was not upper class—Esther Murphy
and John Strachey, Kay Edmonds and Walter.) The trouble
is that the American girls can't accept the roles that the
Englishmen expect of them. Sally had liked Paris but had
spoken as if she had had to see, and too exclusively, too
many Englishmen. Her husband had been to Oxford,
which he remembered with a slight effort, but was apparently somewhat worried by having gone to a minor public school. He wrote pamphlets and books on subjects which
she didn't understand—paid visits to the U.S. She had the
absence of sex consciousness which may have been due to
two brothers, but which I attributed also to her having
been the wife of an Englishman. She is the only woman
here who has anything like style. —How do these people
fill their time? Elena thinks that Mr. Collins, who has just
retired, is bored, doesn't know what to do with himself,
so picks up cigarette butts and tries to police the place.
He was the president of a bank in Duluth and likes to
think how much colder it must be in Duluth. His elderly
wife went to Smith and has Eastern pronunciations,
though she, like him, came from Duluth.

Yellow and red hibiscus flowers—no suckers dropping
from the palms—no traces of wild life whatever except

pelicans and other birds—lakes full of ducks and other water fowl, which Audubon must have studied, now built up, surrounded by houses. Sunday as empty as any other day. —No: because by afternoon, the loud sounds of music arose from the courtyard: old songs and dance music from the twenties and drinks were circulating; Mr. Collins, slightly drunk, was presiding—Mrs. Collins told me twice that her husband was an extrovert, and said that she was supposed to be an introvert and had had a breakdown at college. Mr. Collins wanted another drink, but she wouldn't let him have it. I invited her to sit down, but she said she had to go to attend to dinner. The owner of the building was there, and I thought I identified him as the corpulent exhibitionist who flopped into the pool so loudly that he splashed the water around, did a crawl stroke with a maximum of upheaval and, when he raised his head above the surface, flushed himself with a violent snort. —The music went on till late. One old lady, in a sprightly manner, was twitching her feet in time. Loud lawnmower like a plane overhead. On the big estates, no tennis courts. Very seldom a dog barking. Palms planted in rows. Names of roads that suggest pirates' exploits and naval operations.

No corner drugstores or convenient grocery stores. No community existence of even the Middle Western kind. Traffic and crowding of shoppers like Wellfleet in August. You can't get anywhere without a car and distances too far to walk. Elena was afraid to ask what people's politics were—our enthusiasm for McGovern was coldly received by Collins. She was sure they were all Republicans. Elena had her car smashed up at a crossing by being run into by an old Lithuanian woman, and we had to buy a new one for over $2,000, a blue station wagon. The magistrate and the cops took a brutal tone, and the whole episode made her so apprehensive that she didn't want to drive for days—avoided Route 41, full of traffic and lights that held you up. Elena doesn't understand that a magistrate is the lowest form of judge and rude almost by profession—as she doesn't understand that the deal between the ITT and the Republican Party is more or less a matter of course and would not discourage any Republican. She thinks people ought to be shocked.[*]

Desolate Marco Island: they are also extending in this direction, want obviously to make it another Naples. A sunlit hell of dullness (air-conditioned nightmare).

I found that Mrs. Collins was quite scared of a man she called "the owner"—not the man I saw in the pool—and looked around to make sure he was not listening. She had complained about the music Sunday and was always, she said, complaining—rather humped.

Happily sunk in Balzac again.

Easy to get to bathroom.

Elena follows the primary elections and has become somewhat addicted to TV.

Young Collins son-in-law who is working for McGovern in Wisconsin (?).

June 11, 1972: The Stone House

T'ville. May 31–June 5. Rather a desolate stay: Mrs. Stabb, Mrs. Seelman nursing me. Mrs. Hutchins had to go to Syracuse to be with her son George in the hospital, in consequence of a bad accident—he was pinned under his truck, ribs broken. Rosalind in bed with a stomach ailment.

Millers and Glyn Morris madly working for McGovern. Democrats up here in hiding, people in big places Repub-

---

[*] An antitrust suit against the International Telephone and Telegraph company was settled by the government when ITT pledged to underwrite the forthcoming Republican national convention in San Diego, a secret at first known only to Nixon and his inner circle.

licans. —Two movies: *Godfather* and *French Connection*, bang bang. —Painful getting in and out of theaters. —Ned Miller harangued me about diet as if he had had a religious conversion.

Pushkin Note.
Tennyson and Musset.
Tennyson's *Elaine*: And white sails flying on the yellow sea. "One of the greatest painters now living pointed out to me, with a brief word of rapturous admiration, the wonderful breadth of beauty and the perfect force of truth in a single verse of *Elaine*—"

Father's language: "besotted with egoism"

For E:

Is that a bird or a leaf?
Good grief!
My eyes are old and dim,
And I am getting deaf, my
    dear,
Your words are no more clear
And I can hardly swim.
I find this rather grim.

Edmund Wilson three days before his death

APPENDIX A

Letters to Elena in Europe, 1963*

Sept. 11, 1963
Wellfleet

Dear Elena: Rosalind is still in Mass. General . . . She has confidence in Dr. Schwarz, and if she has to continue to stay in a hospital, will go to Mass. Memorial, to which he is attached. He turns out to be a former student of Dr. Zetzel's, and he will keep in touch about Rosalind.

I had lunch on Tuesday with the Zetzels, and we discussed Rosalind's case. On Monday I had lunch at the Park House with Reuel and Marcia. Zetzel had seen Marcia that morning and, I gather, could not find much the matter with her, but he put her on a diet. She and Reuel are headed west—he finally made connections with the university.

Rosalind is beginning to remember a little what happened to her and she is losing some of her misconceptions. She told me she thought at first that the doctors were all

* Ellipses indicate details which have been omitted.

actors made up as doctors, and now she says as a joke that the young doctor in charge of her case gives the impression of Ed O'Connor impersonating a psychiatrist—and I find him a little boring myself. This breakdown has evidently been coming for quite a while. Paul Brooks says that her work was deteriorating, that she was behaving rather irresponsibly . . . If she really clears up completely, I should like her to come up here while I am here.

I am going to start in on my Canadian piece. I saw Marie-Claire several times and took her to the movies twice. She explains things to me that I don't understand. I haven't heard a thing about her personal affairs; she always has talked to me very intelligently about literature and Canada. (Of course she is very much impressed by you and hopes she can consider you "mon amie.")

I am surprised at the voracity with which she reads— knows all about Emily Dickinson & Virginia Woolf. We went to two movies together. I also saw part of *Cleopatra*, which was badly acted, badly directed, badly written, stupid and vulgar throughout.

I had dinner last night with the Chavchavadzes. They have acquired a cute and lively little pug dog, to which they are much attached. Nina has had a rather alarming nosebleed, after she found that alcohol was repulsive to her, and now she doesn't drink at all!

Barbara drove me up here from Boston. She had just come up from Washington, when she had been given the for her rather taxing job of screening the recruits for the peace march. She was confronted by such problems as whether one should make it a principle to exclude marijuana smokers and drunks—but sometimes one found that they were serious . . .

It is beautiful up here now and would be pleasant now that the [?] are mostly gone. I miss you terribly. If I have to stay a long time, you might come back, and then we could go to Europe later, before Christmas. Tell Helen how sorry I am that I see her so little lately.

Mary is going to take me to town. Before then, I'll call up the hospital and let you know what they say. I've got a woman—Caroline Tibbetts, who says she once did some cleaning here—to get me breakfast, etc. She's coming in this afternoon. (She has been here, and this is all settled. She is getting me supper tonight.)

Where did you put the George Grosz catalogs? Where is the thing you put over Button's chair? He is here with me, and Betsy has brought me his food. How do you turn on the furnace? It's beginning to get colder.

Please call up Simmons at W. H. Allen and explain the situation and thank him for making the hotel reservations. If you have time, why don't you call up the Spenders?

All my love,
Edmund

I have just talked to the doctor at the hospital. He says that Rosalind shows some slight improvement—is "nibbling at the edges of her delusions." I'll go down to see her next week. He says that Dr. Schwarz has told him that she has three times before had the delusion that somebody is going to marry her.

Page proofs of *Protest* have just arrived.

Sept. 15
Wellfleet

Dearest Elena:

Rosalind is evidently much better. She called me up to say, "I'm not crazy any more." They're moving her out of the locked ward. I'm driving down with Suzanne [Hughes] this afternoon, and am hoping before long to be able to bring her up here.

It is a good thing I have had to stay here from the point of view of correcting my page proofs, which had to have some serious revisions. Lulu has run away again and has been living with me here. Button comes back every day to see if you are here, then goes back to the Smiths. I have been out to dinner almost every night. Thursday I dined with the girls and the Peoples, an artist and his wife, who rented their other house; Wednesday I took Barbara to the Governor Prince; Friday I dined with the Jenckses, Arthur Berger and a naturalized British playwright and his wife who have been spending a week at the Hatches'; last night with the Walkers and Mary Hackett and Adelaide's mother, who is celebrating her 91st birthday. She was sleepy but still makes sense and had flown on from California alone. Bubs drove me home and came in and we had a talk. She had seen Rosalind the day Reuel got back and says that she talked rather queerly. She told me the whole story about Chauncey and herself and the children, which is a very depressing one. She said she couldn't have talked about it at all before she was analyzed. I understood for the first time why she had insisted on getting a separation from Chauncey. Before dinner on Wednesday, I went with Barbara to a party given by the Wallings to celebrate Christopher's going to Putney—a curious idea, I thought, since the party was entirely adult and just one of those end-of-season Cape drinking parties.

Tuesday afternoon I read the MS of a novel by Marie-Claire—something like *Le Jour Est Noir*, but not so good —monotonous and rather phantasmal.

—Have just called up Dr. Schwarz. He says that Rosalind is much better and will soon be out. He has broken the news to her that she will not get her job back, but it is a problem of what she is going to do, how she is going to live, after I leave. I am going to try to persuade Paul

Brooks to still give her a little work. Schwarz says that he thinks it is true she is writing a novel.

Sept. 18. I brought Rosalind back here yesterday. She has completely cleared up now. She had not been taking any drugs and the doctors here dismissed that idea. It seems that since the first of the year she has been working on a novel based on the people of Boston who are in and out of McLean's all the time. At one point in the hospital she said to me, "I'd just written all this!"—and I didn't know what she meant. She says that she had identified herself with the characters in her novel. The young man named Jacques she kept talking about who works in the H.M. office she actually hardly knows, she says; but he looks like your Uncle Walther, and since she is using in her novel the sojourn of Walther at McLean's, he got into her fantasy in that way. She's somewhat fatigued after her hospital experience, but already busy attending to things here. She is installed with her cats in the little house, and we have settled down for the time being to a quiet and rather agreeable life. Rosalind is touchingly apologetic about having caused so much trouble.

Zetzel is not reassuring about Marcia. He said she's "a peculiar girl." She told him a different story about the children than the one that Reuel told me: she said that she has left them with her family and that she "wanted to blot out the whole episode." She "almost had hysterics" when he wanted to examine her bowels, and Reuel was waiting outside "like a husband during a delivery." Afterwards, on our way to the hospital, Reuel stopped off at a tobacco store to buy Rosalind some special kind of cigarettes, and Marcia would not stay in the cab with me for the three minutes it took to buy them, but had to get out and go in with him.

I drove down with Suzanne and Arthur Berger and a goodlooking young Jewish businessman from Boston, who drove and who I thought might be the present incumbent. Suzanne was in such a state of uninhibited exhilaration as I have ever seen on her part before—full of conversation and girlish laughter.

In the late afternoon of Monday, I took Marie-Claire to Widener and arranged for her the privileges, and had dinner with her at the Continental, where I stayed. Conversation about literature. She has had a telephone put in.

Rosalind stopped in on Nina last night. A new Anastasya pretender has turned up from Chicago, and Nina has been offered a fee to go to New York and see her, which she is going to do tomorrow. The woman has said that she will only see Nina if nobody else is present, and Nina thinks that she will probably try to bribe her.

It is doing Rosalind good to be back up here. She says that her work had been going to pieces for many weeks before her breakdown. She couldn't concentrate on reading manuscripts, and her hand trembled all the time.

Rosalind has been cheered up by hearing from Dawn that *The Saturday Evening Post* is interested in one of her stories.

Sept. 19. Your letter just came and your birthday telegram, but no telegram about your address.

Rosalind is all right mentally but is going off her tranquillizing drug and has not readjusted herself. She says she is beginning to be able to concentrate so she is able to read again. She has gone to take a rest on the beach. I was going to invite people in for champagne this afternoon, but the Walkers are giving a party, and we are going to that. Getting meals is still a little too much for Rosalind, and we dined last night at the Holiday House.

The cartons of my Canadian books are at the *New Yorker*

office, so I am working at a new volume of literary chronicle. Am quite comfortable. When I went to Boston, I sent Lulu back to Higgins's, but now she is with us again.

The hospital expenses were over $400, and the hotel bills over $200; bills for Rosalind's garage and telephone over $60. I gave her $100 for her birthday, and Dr. Schwarz's bills still to come and she has other bills I'll have to pay. I have about $100 in the bank. I'm going to try to get Roger Straus to let me have $2,000.

I'll be staying here with Rosalind till I know how she is going to live. When I go to England, I'll fly. If you are with Bettina, that will be convenient. I suppose that you put Helen in school yesterday.

I have had oil put in, and the furnace is running, but we haven't needed it much. Mrs. Daley is doing the laundry and Mrs. Tibbetts will come in to clean.

You don't enclose the letter to Hart-Davis which Cecil Lang says he is sending. (I see you say you have sent [?] this.) Where are the George Grosz catalogs? (I have found them.)

Mrs. Guilbert is coming to work with me on the book. Getting together these old articles and living in the house at this time of year reminded me of our earlier days together. It was foggy for two days, but the weather is now splendid again.

Rosalind has just come back from the beach. She says she met Clare Leighton, who told her she was on the verge of a nervous breakdown.

Sept. 22. I had your wire back but not as yet the letter.

Rosalind is still nervous and is only just beginning to read again. She found that she wasn't able to do without the tranquillizer they gave her. Paul [Chavchavadze] is driving her down to Boston tomorrow for an interview with Paul Brooks. She is beginning to talk now about going back to her apartment, but I want her to stay here at least another week. I don't know yet when I can leave. Mrs. Guilbert comes every day to type and paste up my book. I am going to do a couple of light literary articles.

We have dined out every day except Tuesday night: twice at the Holiday House, once at the Governor Prince, once at Peggy Day's. Tonight we are going to Mary and Barbara's; now that the summer people are gone, all of the more intimate circle are giving each other parties. They are the kind of thing I had hoped never to do again, but Rosalind wanted to go, so I went. First, the Walkers on Thursday: the usual cocktail party, with everybody eager to be there—Chavchavadzes, Jenckses, Matsons, Wallings, Sheila Goodman and her husband, Mary Hackett, Joan Colebrook, Farnsworths, Brownie L'Engle, Mary Meigs, etc. Peggy Day, who was there, invited us to dinner the next night. I hoped that it would be a quiet evening, but not at all: we found Brownie, the George Biddles, that Balfour woman and her husband—I don't understand who they are—the Chavchavadzes, with Sasha—I've forgotten his last name—who looks and sounds somewhat like a shrunken version of Boris Karloff as the Frankenstein monster—and Paul's cousin, his fish-faced Georgian wife. It depressed me to find myself back again among all these old ruins, *ratés* [failures] and second-raters, getting together to keep themselves warm. We were invited to two other parties: the Carrs and Joan Colebrook, but skipped them.

Rosalind gets tired easily and has to get home immediately after dinner. I took the Chavchavadzes to the Governor Prince after the Walkers' party, but Rosalind collapsed after a champagne cocktail and had to go and sit in the car, so I cut the dinner short. After supper at Peggy's, she tried to drive home but got the car somehow snagged on what she says was a "railroad spike" along

Peggy's drive, and George Biddle had to drive us home. At the Holiday House last night, she was so nervous that she couldn't wait for dessert. But she says that every day she feels a little better.

Roger Straus is putting $3,000 in the bank.

Erich Leinsdorf called me up, wanting me to do a program note comparing Mahler and Kafka. He thinks that their ears are similar, but I can't see it. He sends his regards to you. I asked him to do something about Marie-Claire, and he cordially said he would.

Jason Epstein wanted to come up, but I have kept him off. Rosalind says she is not up to it.

Barbara has been ill. I went over there one night and found her all alone. They were to have had a musical evening with Brownie, but Bessie Breuer, who was to have gone with them, was also ill, so Mary was condemned to dinner alone with Brownie. When I saw her next day at the Walkers', I said that I had been sorry not to see her the evening before. She said, "Yes. Let me see; where was I?" Brownie, who was standing by, exclaimed, "Don't you remember me?" I had had a talk with Barbara about peace movements, etc. She has a more practical grasp of it all than I had realized.

Today it is pouring rain.

Sept. 23. Your letter from Montreux came this morning, and I am sending this off to Frankfurt. Why don't you go to England from Germany? I may be able to fly over next week. Rosalind has gone to Boston to see Paul Brooks, and we may be able to plan better after the talks with him. I miss you frantically.

Edmund

APPENDIX B

The Rat Letters

The Rat Letters, written at the Wesleyan Center, are one of those *jeux d'esprit* by which, since his college years, Wilson had amused himself and literary friends. They emerged from the "demolition of science" by the psychology professor who gave a talk on his experiments with rats. Wilson had had a good deal to drink Monday evening and missed the ostensible point of the experiments. John Clendenning, then a graduate student and a Fellow at the Wesleyan Center, recalled that Professor Thompson "was doing some research on the relationship between intelligence and stimulation in infancy." His hypothesis was "that the more you stimulated an infant the more likely you were to produce an intelligent adult. There had been scientists who believed that if you cuddled the rats and petted them they became more intelligent . . . Thompson thought that was all too sentimental and offered an alternative hypothesis that anything that you did to them made them intelligent in a maze situation compared to rats who were never touched, who weren't stimulated in any way, were simply fed and allowed to grow up. He had tried different kinds of things, slapping them around and throwing them on the floor, stepping on them."

When he said that "he also gave them measured amounts of alcohol, which also produced intelligent rats," Wilson, from his chair in the corner, "roared with laughter and applause." He then said, "You know, if you mistreat those rats too much, they'll die." Seeming "really kind of frightened in his presence," Thompson answered, "Yes, Mr. Wilson, they might die." Wilson replied, "Especially if you step on them." He got up and walked out of the room.

Achieving a more humorous view of Professor Thompson's research with rats, he wrote a protest as "A Worried Rat" whose mother had been turned into an alcoholic by these experiments. Paul Horgan—who had been embarrassed by Wilson's outburst at the talk—acknowledged this on a letterhead of "Mauser, Rattkin, Trapp, Katz, & Mauser, Attorneys-at-Law." The efforts of John Martin and Jean Stafford followed. Making fun of academic bureaucracy and Pentagonese as well as the professor's talk, Martin locates this exchange in the larger world of Malcolm X and Bobby Baker, Lyndon Johnson's corrupt assistant, as well as the cultural scene at the Center. Jean Stafford, Edmund's afternoon hostess and drinking partner, writes in the voice of the outraged mother rat.

March 3, 1965

Dear Mister Martin:

I saw you at Professor Thompsons lecture the other evening. I was hiding behind Mister Horgan's books. I want to protest against his cruelty to us Rats. My Mother was one of the ones that he gave overdoses of alcohol to and the results have been tragic. Mother is now a confirmed alcoholic. She lies around sodden with licker and we children have to keep her supplied. This is not easy.

It is one thing to whisk a box of Corn Flakes off a shelf and another to get a bottle of gin down without breaking it and to push it along the floor. It sometimes takes half a dozen of us. We have to look after Mother instead of raising families of our own. It is not true the way the Professor says that a drunken Mother has infearior offspring. My eyequeue is very high in fact I am told on a level with the girls in the middletown high school. But this cant go on indefinitely without the breed deteariorating. You know Rats have four or five litters a year and in Mothers case we dont always know who the Father was. We think that one of the Fathers may have been a common black Rat (Rattus rattus). We of course are Gnawegians. I hear that you have had some experience in supervising the Rat Race in Washington and other scenters and I thought I might appeal to you to restrain these experiments from debauching our noble Race. We rats have to keep in training. We have to be quick and resourceful. I know that we commit debreadations on your larders but do you want drunken rats in the house stumbling around and getting in peoples way and maybe biting people? One of our neighbors has deeteez and thinks she sees red and black Professors because those are the wesleyan colors. I would not want such a fate for myself and how do I know it may not overtake me if Professor Thompson gets me into his hands. I hope you will be able to influence him.

> Yours respectfully
> A Worried Rat.

> In reply please refer to:
> File #00P392FINK33@

Dear Worried Rat,

Your communication of March 3 has been brought to my attention by the Provost (and coincidentally by the Head of the Department of Buildings and Grounds, who has of late observed some rather peculiar phenomenological manifestations of an inexplicable nature—inexplicable, that is, in the light of our present state of knowledge, or rather in the light of our state of present knowledge—in the buildings which are his responsibility, especially in the cellars. I say coincidentally, although obviously true randomicity cannot be ruled out as what we are really dealing with, or not dealing with, here. Or there).

As you say, I have indeed spent some time in Washington, where it was my privilege to serve in the capacity of Consultant to the Secretary at the very time we were making a determination as to whether it might no longer be considered counterproductive to review carefully the considerations that had led us to adopt our policy vis-à-vis the Rat Race, since certain aspects of that policy while still viable did not, it appeared, work. However, before any policy decision was finalized with respect to the desirability of reviewing the considerations which had led to our initial adoption of the line of input that had in turn produced our output policy on the Rat Race, the Democrats won.

It is for this and other cogent, if I may use the word, reasons that I have somewhat reluctantly concluded that my experience in Washington is not relevant to the questions which you and the Head of Buildings and Grounds raise and indeed may safely be considered quite beyond the ambit of our present discussion. Let's skip it.

Addressing ourselves now to the question, or rather to the questions, at hand, and limiting ourselves severely to their own self-imposed parameter, it would appear to me, I would venture to say, if indeed I may speak at all in such august company, that, taking account of the interesting experiments of Professor Pygmy on the Watutsis' kneecaps, and on the other hand the exciting work of Professor

Malcolm X with the principle of randomicity as observed in the "policy racket" or "numbers game," as well as the teleological constructs of Professor Bobby Baker, we are really hardly justified in concluding that gin is harder to push than corn flakes.

I hasten to add that the case for this proposition is by no means proved conclusively—please feel free to interrupt at any time—forgive me, how *does* this light turn off? I mean on? Don't you think it seems terribly dark in here? I can hardly see the charts and graphs myself. By the way, I should have said that the little squiggle at the end of Line A on Chart B is where my wife started running the vacuum cleaner. It was dark that day, too.

In the light—I did not intend a pun here but it *is* rather a good one, don't you think? ha ha!—in the *light* of the foregoing, taken together with what we are taught by careful study of the biochemical changes, or life changes, in the science of man, as well as the recent research into other minus-6 phenomenological observations in what some call the non-science of man, not to mention the many cancer grafts on rats that have been little short of apocalyptic, and of course the well-known musicological demonstrations of Cage, Greenbaum, Wolff, and Ernst, it would appear to me safe to advance, in, I confess, the most tentative manner—and I am fully aware of all the questions and doubts that must surely be harbored in your mind, as I am also aware of the budgetary restrictions imposed upon my laboratory work, though of course I recognize the need for such budgetary restrictions; it is merely a value judgment, either the gym teacher, I mean Professor of Physical Education, would have new lacrosse rackets or I would have more rats,—tentative manner the proposition that (a) for rats, gin beats cancer and (b) Professor Thompson should drink more of it himself.

I should like to test this hypothesis on Buildings and Grounds. They could use more gin too.

Yours very truly,

Dean Squiggle

P.S. Upon re-reading your letter I fear I may not have answered quite all your questions. I'm sorry about your mother.

To Whomb It may Concerne.

Now dont think I do not know to Whomb I am writting this letter I knoe perfectly well but some People thinke they are saf behind There mask well they just have annother Thinke coming thats all. So anyways I happen to knoe that a Certain party wrote a downrite wrotten letter to another Party who shall be Nameless but not becauss anyon feels sorry for them but becuss there are some levels whicke to which a Person does not halve to stoup.

Now that certaine Party said in blacke and wite that Her Mother her own Mother was a confirmed Alcoholic and then she says I am a Drunken Mother and that they halve to drag bottles of gin down of the shealfs and push it along the floor to get it to me without braking it and she says they half to have half a dozen of them to bring the Gin down to me so I can be a confirmed Drunken Mother. A person has theire self-respect and I chouse to Resent these slirs on my dignity. Certainly I halve a drinke with my friends and callers and when you recieve a number of calers in one night you must offer Them something and out of common Decencie I have one Now and then with them but I wish to have It understood that I am simpley a Social Drinker like anybody Elsse and whatte is More I halff to take a Drinke reely quite Offen in my Line of Work for quiete Often a Gentleman Caller does not think they are halving a Good Time with us unless we agreE to drinke with Them so everything will Get free and Easy as time goes on and after all they are Paying for it. It.

So I chouse to resent the slir that I am a confirmed AlCoholic when I am just strugglinge to make a livving for my childriene and Fambily even at the cost of my liver the Dr says mine is in pretty bad shaipe from all the drinkinge I am obligued to do during my working hours and there oh schitte that Fucking ribbon is gone againe But anyways there is another Thinge I chouse to Resente and that is the Statemennt made by an unnatural Daughter that in my Case they dont always Knoe Who the Father is. Just Because THEY do not Always knowe does not Meane that *I* do not Always know Because I will have them knoe that even iff I do not Feel it Necesecary to tell them who the Father is *I* myself *Always* knoe who he is. Who do they Thinke I am anyways. After all my slavinge and work for whomb, for themb thats who, is this any Waye for a Daughter to talk about Theire *Mother*

So iff an Ungreatful Daughter falls into the Profesors' Lands Then she ought To Because she is Ungreetfull and That Is what I say.

I don't Knowe what Dean Squiggle is talking about thouhg, so I cannot Answer Him. But I hope a Certain party sees the above and I hope she knowes I am not FOOLED. (Mrs. Rodenta G. Mus, Respectfully

BIOGRAPHICAL NOTES

Information about individuals not listed here is generally available within the index and footnotes. Readers are also directed to the indexes of Wilson's earlier journals and his *Letters on Literature and Politics*.

Daniel Aaron (1912–): Critic and historian; professor of English and American studies at Smith College, then Harvard. A friend of EW's later years, he helped Elena select Wilson's correspondence for *Letters on Literature and Politics* and wrote the introduction.

Léonie Adams (1899–1988): Lyric poet admired by EW in the twenties. Married to the critic William Troy.

Renata Adler (1938–): Novelist and writer for *The New Yorker*.

Endre Ady (1877–1919): Hungarian poet who wrote about his country with techniques influenced by the French Symbolists.

Conrad Aiken (1889–1973): Poet and essayist who shared EW's skepticism of T. S. Eliot's public personality.

William F. Albright (1891–1971): Professor at Johns Hopkins; expert in Semitic archaeology, paleography, and scrolls interpretation. He read *The Dead Sea Scrolls* for Wilson, who deferred to his opinion on various scholarly issues.

Gerry and Irene Allard: Radicals with whom EW had been allied many years before, when Gerry Allard edited the newspaper of the independent miners rebelling against John L. Lewis's UMWA. Wilson appreciates Irene's Finnish beauty in *The Thirties*.

John Allegro (1923–88): British scholar of Hebrew, a member of the original team in charge of publishing the Dead Sea scrolls. He later offered "fantastic conjectures" identifying the Teacher of Righteousness of the Essene sect with Jesus (*The Dead Sea Scrolls: 1949–1969*).

Sergei Alymov (1892–1948): Russian Futurist poet and writer of lyrics for songs. He and his wife, Maria Fedorovna, befriended EW in Moscow in 1935. "Around the big table in the crowded room, some of the jolliest evenings I have ever spent," Wilson wrote in *Red, Black, Blond and Olive*.

John H. Amen (1899–1960) and Marion: Friends from the twenties. Marion had first been married to Wilson's school and college friend Stanley Dell. John was the companion to whom he dedicated the early poem "Highballs." An assistant attorney general, a prosecutor in New York and later at the Nuremberg trials, he is said to have been drinking too much during the years when he handled EW's legal business.

John Andersen: Danish-born friend of EW during World War I, self-educated in several languages. He became a farmer in Alberta and wrote novels on the side (*A Prelude*).

Roger Angell (1920–): Writer on baseball and fiction editor at *The New Yorker*. Son of Katharine S. White.

Noel Annan (1916–): British writer; later an interpreter of Isaiah Berlin, Stephen Spender, and their literary generation.

Newton Arvin (1900–63): Professor of English at Smith College and a critic in the tradition of Van Wyck Brooks. He had been encouraged to resign because of his role in a homosexual scandal.

W. H. Auden (Wystan Hugh) (1907–73): EW's friend since the late forties, when he became an American citizen. Wilson celebrates Auden's development in the United States in *The Bit Between My Teeth*.

Helen Vinton Augur (?–1969): EW's second cousin on his mother's side; a writer of popular history and biography. He describes his ambivalent relationship with her in *The Fifties*.

Camilla and Perry Austin: Margaret Canby's sister and brother-in-law. EW had appreciated their companionship in Santa Barbara after her death.

Oliver Austin (1903–88): Well-known ornithologist; author of the Golden Books series.

George Backer (1903–74): A former journalist from New York who was active in real estate, interested in the arts and Israel. His wife, Dorothy Schiff, owned the *New York Post*.

Rosalind Baker (Aunt Lin): One of EW's formidable great-aunts on his mother's side. "She had a certain high and formal coquetry and was the only person I ever knew who really talked like the characters in old novels," he writes in "The Old Stone House" (*The American Earthquake*).

Thomas Baker (1779–1883): EW's great-grandfather on his mother's side; an entrepreneur whose second marriage to the spinster Sophronia Talcott brought the stone house into the family. In the occasional verse of *Wilson's Night Thoughts* he is called "a rude Jacksonian Democrat." Aunt Lin was one of his eight daughters, as was Wilson's grandmother, Helen Baker Kimball.

Pyotr Balacheff (Pet'ka): See Pet'ka.

Jeanne Ballot: Frank Crowninshield's secretary when EW was at *Vanity Fair* during the early twenties. She had admired Wilson and was infatuated with John Peale Bishop.

Maurice Baring (1874–1945): Historical novelist and popularizer of Russian literature (*The Devils and Canon Barham*).

Natalie Barney (1878–1972): Writer and lesbian who kept a salon in Paris in the twenties.

Max Beerbohm (1872–1956): Edwardian caricaturist, essayist, and parodist whom EW had admired in college and was still writing of in the sixties.

S. N. Behrman (Sam) (1893–1973): Dramatist of manners; writer of profiles for *The New Yorker*. He interviewed Beerbohm in Italy with EW in 1954 and published a biography of the caricaturist in 1960.

Alfred R. Bellinger (1893–1978): EW's prep-school friend, who became a classical scholar and professor of numismatics at Yale. Wilson's many letters to Bellinger from college record his early literary tastes.

Sir Isaiah Berlin (1909–): British political philosopher, interpreter of Russian history and literature; married to Aline. In the decades after they met in 1945, EW and he saw each other in New York, London, Talcottville, Oxford, and Cambridge, Massachusetts. His memoir of Wilson appeared in *The Yale Review* in March 1987.

Leonid Berman (1896–1976): Neo-Romantic Russian painter, well known in New York in the sixties.

Tharrett Best: Mayor of Boonville.

Sir John Betjeman (1906–84): British poet, later poet laureate.

Francis Biddle (1886–1968) and Katherine (1891–1978): EW's old acquaintances at the Cape. He served as U.S. Attorney General from 1941 to 1945; she wrote poetry under the name of Chapin and had a lengthy affair with Alexis Saint-Léger, the poet Saint-John Perse.

George Biddle (1885–1973): Sculptor and graphic artist; Francis's brother. In 1956 he drew EW's portrait, now in the Sonnenberg Collection at Harvard.

John Biggs, Jr. (1895–1979): Federal judge in Wilmington who had been a literary friend of EW's and F. Scott Fitzgerald's in college.

Gladys Billings-Brooks: Widow of the critic Van Wyck Brooks (1886–1963), who was a major influence on the young Wilson.

Jonathan Bishop (1927–): English professor at Cornell, then married to the novelist Alison Lurie. He was the son of the poet John Peale Bishop (1892–1944), EW's close friend at Princeton and in New York after World War I. Margaret Bishop was John's widow.

Mary Blair (1897–1947): EW's first wife, mother of his daughter Rosalind. She was an actress noted for her roles in O'Neill's early plays. When her career in the theater failed, she remarried and returned home to Pittsburgh, where she eventually died of tuberculosis.

Marie-Claire Blais (1939–): French-Canadian novelist whose first novel, *La Belle Bête* (1959), was a sensation in Quebec. Wilson's interest in her work led her to Wellfleet, and she and Mary Meigs eventually established themselves in Canada.

Louise Bogan (1897–1970): Poet; for many years poetry critic at *The New Yorker*. "I always think of you as fundamentally such a strong and wise individual that I discount your anxieties and things," EW wrote in 1931 when she was in a sanitarium (*Letters on Literature and Politics*). She dedicated *The Sleeping Fury* (1937) to Wilson.

George Borrow (1803–81): British novelist and travel writer whom EW had first read as a college freshman.

Christian Bourgois: Paris publisher.

C. M. Bowra (1898–1971): British classical scholar; warden of Wadham College when EW visited Oxford in 1954.

Henry Brandon (1916–): Washington correspondent for the London *Sunday Times*.

John R. B. Brett-Smith (1917–): Editor at Oxford University Press in New York with whom EW discussed the expanded edition of *The Dead Sea Scrolls*.

Bessie Breuer (1893–1975): Writer; married to Henry Poor. She had a home on Cape Cod.

Austin Briggs, Jr., and Margaret: Young literary couple at Hamilton College, where Austin taught in the English department. John Buell (1927–): Canadian novelist who taught at Loyola College in Montreal.

Lillian Burnham: Elderly Talcottville neighbor of whom EW was fond.

Benjamin Franklin Butler (1818–93): Union general in the Civil War and military governor of New Orleans.

Marguerite Caetani, Duchess of Sermoneta (1880–1963): Katherine Biddle's half sister. She published Valéry, Camus, Silone, Graves, and others in her multilingual review, *Botteghe Oscure* (*Europe Without Baedeker*).

Morley Callaghan (1903–90): Canadian fiction writer; a friend of Hemingway and other American expatriates. In *That Sum-*

mer in Paris he describes his celebrated boxing match with Hemingway, when Fitzgerald, the timekeeper, forgot to end the round on time. Loretto was his wife. Their son Barry (1937–) would become a fiction writer, poet, and editor.

Margaret Canby (1898?–1932): A Californian of Eastern background—her father from the Philadelphia Main Line, her mother from Toronto—she was first married to James Canby, then became Wilson's second wife. Their brief marriage was complicated by her commitment to spend half the year in Santa Barbara with her son Jimmy.

Clelia Delafield Carroll (1928–): Co-editor with Edward Gorey of the Looking Glass Library, inexpensive children's classics published by Doubleday and later Random House. EW served as a consultant. She later married G. Chester Carey, Jr.

Henri Cartier-Bresson (1908–): French photographer and journalist, whom Elena had first known in Paris, when they had had painting lessons from the same man.

Bennett Cerf (1898–1971): President of Random House when Jason Epstein became an editor there.

Dasya Chalyapin: Youngest daughter of the great Russian bass Fyodor Chalyapin.

René Champollion: Brother of André Cheronnet-Champollion, the painter and socialite whom EW's cousin Adelaide Knox had married before World War I.

Paul Chavchavadze (1899–1971) and Nina (Romanov): Russian expatriates. Paul, of an aristocratic Georgian family, was a writer and translator. Nina, a Grand Duchess of Russia and the daughter of the Queen of Greece, taught EW Russian in the forties.

Misha and Ruth Cheshin: Young lawyer and his wife who were EW's hosts in Jerusalem. Ruth Cheshin corresponded with Wilson until the end of his life. She became president of the Jerusalem Foundation, and Misha was eventually appointed a Supreme Court judge.

Kornei Chukovsky (1882–1969): Russian children's author, politically independent, whose vast popularity enabled him to survive Stalin's rule.

Joan Colebrook (?–1991): Travel journalist who was a Wellfleet friend of the Wilsons'. Johnny was her son.

Padraic Colum (1881–1972) and Mary (1887–1957): The Irish poet and critic whom EW knew in New York in the twenties.

Cyril Connolly (1903–74): British critic and essayist who edited *Horizon* during World War II and remained a vital figure in his literary generation (*Classics and Commercials*).

Louise Connor: One of the Fort twins who charmed EW in the jazz age and the Depression. EW and she are often together in *The Thirties*.

George Cram Cook (Jig) (1873–1924): Cape Cod bohemian and a one-time Greek professor who established the Provincetown Players with his wife, Susan Glaspell. EW had met him when courting Edna St. Vincent Millay in 1920.

Jenny Corbett (?–1959): EW's mother's housekeeper for fifty years.

Richard Costa (Dick) (1921–): Reporter who became an English professor at Syracuse University at Utica; author of the memoir *Edmund Wilson: Our Neighbor from Talcottville* (1980). Married to Jo.

Gilles Couture (1933–): French Canadian who took his M.A. at Harvard; later a radio and television producer for the Canadian Broadcasting Company.

Frank Moore Cross (1921–): Professor at the McCormick Theological Seminary in Chicago; one of the team responsible for publishing the Dead Sea scrolls when EW met him in 1955. Later, at Harvard, he became a noted Old Testament scholar.

William Loran Crosten (1909–) and Mary: Upstate friends of EW and Elena. A professor of music at Stanford, he also composed. Stephen (married to Gretchen) and Lesley were their children.

Marcus Cunliffe (1922–90): Literary historian of America at the University of Manchester in England; a visiting professor at Harvard in 1959–60. His wife, Mitzi Solomon, was an avant-garde designer.

Thomas Quinn Curtiss: American writer in Paris; drama and film critic for the international edition of the *Herald Tribune* from 1950 on.

Mitchell J. Dahood (1922–82): Scholar of the Old Testament and the Psalms.

Martin Cyril D'Arcy (1888–1976): Prolific philosophical writer; Father Provincial of the Jesuit Order in England from 1945 to 1950.

Peggy Day: Formidable widow of Clarence Day (1874–1935), the author of *Life with Father*.

István Deák (1926–): European historian. He was teaching at Smith College when EW and he met, then became director of the Institute on East Central Europe at Columbia.

Vladimir Dedijer (1914–90): Yugoslavian economist and intellectual who had been vice premier under Tito. His account of the assassination of Archduke Francis Ferdinand *(Sarajevo: 1914)* appeared in 1966.

J. W. De Forest (1826–1906): Connecticut-born author of *Miss Ravenel's Conversion from Secession to Loyalty* (1967), the first realistic Civil War novel *(Patriotic Gore)*.

Barbara Deming (1917–84): Writer whose political ideals would lead her from marching for peace and desegregation to radical feminism. She lent EW money to settle with the IRS, and contributed to his interpretation of the symbolism of *Doctor Zhivago (The Bit Between My Teeth)*.

Gyula Derkovits (1894–1934): Self-taught artist who started, like Munkácsy before him, as an apprentice to a carpenter.

Edwin Dickinson (1891–1978): A painter known for his landscapes and figures. He and his wife, Patricia, were EW's old friends on the Cape.

Milovan Djilas (1911–): Dissident Yugoslavian political intellectual who had described the privileged bureaucracy that had emerged under Communism in *The New Class* (1957).

John Dos Passos (Dos) (1896–1970): Novelist; EW's comrade-in-arms from the 1920s on. Having made the journey to the left before EW, he had been disillusioned with Communism earlier and had since gone to the right. In 1948 Dos Passos left the Cape for an inherited estate in Westmoreland, Virginia, but Wilson kept on cheerfully lambasting his "excesses" in their correspondence.

Muriel Draper: Communist and feminist who lived next door to EW on East Fifty-third Street in the early thirties.

Ruth Draper (1884–1956): Broadway comedian, monologuist.

Ed Duffy (1899–1962): Cartoonist who won a Pulitzer Prize.

Phyllis Duganne: Writer of short stories for *Collier's* and other magazines. She and her artist husband, Eben Given, lived in Truro on the Cape.

F. W. Dupee (1904–79): Critic and professor of English at Columbia; an early member of the *Partisan Review* circle and an admirer of EW.

Maurice Duplessis (1890–1959): Prime Minister and Attorney General of Quebec from 1936 to 1940, then again from 1944 to 1959.

André Dupont-Sommer (1900–84): Professor of Semitic languages and cultures at the Sorbonne. He was the first to suggest that the Essene sect anticipated Christianity, a view EW absorbed while writing of the Dead Sea scrolls.

Max Eastman (1883–1969): Journalist and critic. A spokesman for the Greenwich Village avant-garde, he influenced EW's first appreciative account of Marxism; later he reacted against the doctrinaire and mystical elements in Marx much as Wilson did.

Walter D. Edmonds (1903–): Boonville neighbor of EW's who lived on an inherited estate and wrote popular historical novels about northern New York. Katherine Howe Baker-Carr (Kay) was his second wife.

Peter Egri (1932–): Professor of English at Eotvos Lorand University in Hungary; in 1964 also teaching at Debrecen University.

Auntie Ellinka (Orloff): Sister of Elena's mother, Olga.

Richard Ellmann (1918–87): Biographer of Joyce.

Monroe Engel (1921–): Writer and English professor at Harvard, whose memoir of EW appeared in *The Yale Review* in June 1987. He and his wife, Brenda, lived across from the Wilsons on Hilliard Street in Cambridge.

Barbara Epstein (1929–): A founding editor of *The New York Review of Books*; then married to Jason Epstein.

Jason Epstein (1928–): Editor and publisher who at Doubleday established the Looking Glass Library and introduced quality paperbacks, including the Anchor Books series, which featured EW's work. After moving to Random House he helped to found *The New York Review of Books* and later the Library of America. He and Barbara Epstein are first seen as the Wilsons' New York hosts in *The Fifties*.

Barbara Erwin: Local schoolteacher in upstate New York whom EW met with the Morrises.

Steve and Agatha Fassett: Friends of the Wilsons on Beacon Hill in Boston. The grandson of one of the robber barons, Steve, originally a music critic, recorded poets as well as the Boston Symphony Orchestra, and collected early recordings. Agatha, a Hungarian émigré and friend of Bartók, wrote a book about the composer's American years. She corrected EW's Hungarian as he learned it from Mary Pcolar.

Giangiacomo Feltrinelli (1927–72): Italian publisher who first brought out *Doctor Zhivago*.

William N. Fenton (1908–): Assistant Commissioner for the New York State Museum and Science Service. He had written of the Indian tribes of New York, and helped Wilson to get to know them during the writing of *Apologies to the Iroquois*. Olive was his wife.

John H. Finley (1904–): Professor of Greek at Harvard.

Dudley Fitts (1903–68): Poet and critic, translator of Greek drama.

Robert Fitzgerald (1910–85): Poet, translator of Greek epic and, in collaboration with Fitts, Greek drama.

Janet Flanner (1892–1978): Writer. Her "Letter from Paris" appeared in *The New Yorker* from 1925 to 1939, and from 1944 to 1975.

David Flusser (1917–): Professor of comparative religion at Hebrew University. "Mr. Flusser is a short stocky man, with sharp little cold green eyes that glint behind round-rimmed glasses, under modestly Mephistophelian eyebrows, and red hair that stands straight up from his forehead. I have rarely known a scholar who expressed himself—with all his material at his fingertips—so brilliantly and so much to the point" (*The Dead Sea Scrolls: 1947–1969*).

Jean-Louis Forain (1852–1931): French caricaturist and painter of whom EW writes, "He is certainly a second-rate artist and was apparently a detestable person" (*The Bit Between My Teeth*).

Waldo Frank (1889–1967): Novelist who often wrote about Latin America. He and his third wife, Jean, were EW's neighbors on the Cape. Jonathan and Tim were their sons.

Lloyd Frankenberg (1907–75): Poet, translator.

Joseph Freeman (1897–1965): Journalist and novelist; one of the founders of *Partisan Review*.

Charles T. Fritsch (1912–89): EW's teacher of Hebrew at the Princeton Theological Seminary in 1952; he wrote a book about the Qumran community and its scrolls.

Lewis Galantière (1895–1977): Banker who translated Saint-Exupéry and the journals of the Goncourt brothers. EW had known him since the thirties.

Roy Gamble (1887–1972): One of EW's friends in the hospital corps in 1918–19. "He was a painter who began as a follower of Whistler but had later had a certain success doing portraits of the Detroit rich" (*A Prelude*).

Isabella Gardner (1915–81): Daughter of the founders of the Gardner Museum in Boston; married to Allen Tate from 1959 to 1966.

Sylvester Gates (1901–72): Literary British banker and official; EW's friend from the twenties, when both were pursuing Magda Johann in Greenwich Village. Married to Pauline.

John M. Gaus (1894–1969) and Jane: Summer neighbors at Prospect, New York, near Talcottville. He taught government at Amherst, the University of Wisconsin, and Harvard. John was their son.

Christian Gauss (1878–1951): EW's mentor, who taught him French literature and Dante at Princeton and was a sounding board in the writing of *Axel's Castle* and *To the Finland Station*. It was characteristic of Wilson to liken someone he admired to Gauss.

Martha Gellhorn (1908–): Journalist and novelist; married to Hemingway before her marriage to T. S. Matthews. EW had known her as an apprentice at *The New Republic*.

Alexander G. Gershenkron (1904–78): Economic historian at Harvard. A polymath who ranged from statistics to Greek poetry, he published (in *Modern Philology*) a devastating review of Nabokov's translation of *Eugene Onegin*, recognized by EW as better than his own review.

Brendan Gill (1914–): Novelist and journalist; later author of *Here at the New Yorker*.

Penelope Gilliatt (1932–): British fiction writer, film reviewer for *The New Yorker*. Nolan Kate was the daughter of Penelope and John Osborne, her husband during the midsixties.

Robert Giroux (1914–): Editor in chief and partner at Farrar, Straus and Giroux. Before that, he was editor at Harcourt Brace, where one of his first books was *To the Finland Station*.

Celia Paget Goodman (1916–): Mamaine Koestler's twin. EW, who had met the sisters in postwar London, corresponded with Celia throughout the sixties, sending her copies of his books. She would edit Mamaine's letters in *Living with Koestler* (1985).

Geoffrey Gorer (1905–85): British anthropologist. In *The Bit Between My Teeth* EW had ridiculed his advocacy of the Marquis de Sade, charging that he reduced the Frenchman's felonies to practical jokes.

Edward Gorey (Ted) (1925–): Illustrator and writer known for his macabre fables, who collaborated with Clelia Carroll on the Looking Glass Library.

Sheilah Graham (1904–88): Hollywood columnist, companion of F. Scott Fitzgerald during his last years. EW esteemed *Beloved Infidel* (1958), the memoir she wrote in collaboration with Gerald Frank (*The Bit Between My Teeth*).

Shlomo Grodzensky: A Labor-Zionist publicist and writer in Hebrew, Yiddish, and English, who had come from New York to Israel after World War II.

Albert Grubel: During the fifties EW's driver in Talcottville, who regularly regaled him with gruesome local stories.

Margaret Grunelius: Cousin of Elena in Frankfurt. Elena likened the German-Jewish Grunelius family to the Buddenbrooks in Thomas Mann.

Roman Grynberg (1897–1969): Russian businessman who edited literary journals and whose New York apartment was a kind of salon for Russian writers. His mother and sister had been kind to Wilson in Moscow in 1935. Married to Sonya.

Albert J. Guerard (1914–): Professor of comparative literature at Harvard, later Stanford. In 1960–61 he and his family were neighbors of the Wilsons on Hilliard Street in Cambridge.

Mary Hackett (Bubs): Widow of Chauncey Hackett, once a law clerk to Justice Holmes, who in the early thirties abandoned his practice and moved to the Cape in order to write. Since then the Hacketts had been friends of the Wilson family.

Gordon S. Haight (1901–85): Professor of English at Yale, with whom EW had first discussed J. W. De Forest in 1958.

David Hamilton: Friend during EW's college years, one of the Yale students with whom he bicycled in England in the summer of 1914 and later roomed in New York City. David and he enlisted in the hospital corps together during World War I.

Elemér Hankiss (1928–): Historian and theorist, then in the Hungarian Institute for Literary Research, later president of Hungarian television.

Zoltán Harasjti: Rare-books librarian at the Boston Public Library; friend of Louise Bogan.

Merwin Hart (1881–1962): EW's second cousin, who in his youth ran for mayor of Utica and in the Depression became a neo-Fascist. "I came to realize, as I grew older, that Merwin was extremely stupid and that he believed in his reactionary ideas" (*The Thirties*).

Robert Hartshorne (Bobby): First husband of EW's cousin Esther Kimball. They had three sons, including Bob Hartshorne.

Max Hayward (1925–79): British translator of *Doctor Zhivago* and other Russian classics reviewed by EW.

John Hearne (1926–): West Indian novelist who portrayed everyday life in Jamaica. Under the pseudonym John Morris he wrote thrillers with Morris Cargill.

Anne Hébert (1916–): French-Canadian poet and novelist.

Lillian Hellman (1907–84): Playwright. EW and she had not known each other in the thirties and forties, when he would have thought her naïvely Stalinist, but she admired his criticism, and in the sixties they became good friends. Elena and he stayed in her New York apartment for five weeks in the fall of 1970.

Natalia Galitzin Heseltine: Russian aristocrat, a cousin of Nina Chavchavadze's, whom EW and Elena had met at the Cape.

Gilbert Highet (1906–78): British classicist who had moved from Oxford to Columbia. Admiring Highet's *The Classical Tradition* (1949), EW wrote to him an extraordinary letter qualifying and filling gaps in his 2,000-year account (*Letters on Literature and Politics*).

Ralph Hinchman: Princeton classmate of EW, a businessman.

Richard Hofstadter (1916–70): Scholar of American political and intellectual history; professor at Columbia.

Raymond Holden (1894–1972): Minor poet and second husband of Louise Bogan, who was his second wife. EW thought of Holden, a fellow Princetonian who had been on the board of the literary magazine with him, as an "amiable mediocrity."

Franz Höllering (1896–1968): Austrian-born novelist whose company EW and Elena had enjoyed at Stamford, Connecticut, in 1949 and again in Salzburg in 1954.

Paul Horgan (1903–): Novelist and essayist. In his memoir "Wilson at Wesleyan," EW appears as brilliant, shy, and very difficult.

Irving Howe (1920–): Literary critic and historian who admired and learned from EW. Thalia was then his wife.

Mark de Wolfe Howe (1906–67): Professor of law at Harvard. EW and he shared an interest in John Jay Chapman.

Quincy Howe (1900–77): Journalist; a radio broadcaster in World War II. He had been with EW in the group of intellectuals delivering food to striking miners in Kentucky in 1932.

John and Jessie Howland: Upstate neighbors. John, supposedly a millionaire, kept a store in Boonville.

H. Stuart Hughes (1916–): Historian and activist who was a professor at Harvard, then at Stanford. Married to Suzanne from 1949 to 1963.

Elizabeth Huling (Betty) (1901–69): Friend from EW's *New Republic* days, when she was copy editor of the magazine.

Rolfe Humphries (1894–1969): Poet and classicist, to whom EW had once assigned reviews at *The New Republic*. Married to Helen.

James Gibbons Huneker (1860–1921): Impressionistic critic of European music, painting, and literature who had influenced EW in college.

Charlayne Hunter-Gault (1942–): The first African-American woman admitted to the University of Georgia, who later worked on the *MacNeil-Lehrer Report*.

Mabel Hutchins: Housekeeper for EW at Talcottville. Her husband, Everett, was sometimes his driver; her niece Beverly Yelton (Wheelock) worked for the Wilsons and once helped them out at Wellfleet.

Martha James: Elena's friend in New York, the stepmother of her ex-husband, Jimmy Thornton.

William James (Billy) (1881–1961): Painter and art teacher; second son of the philosopher William James. Wilson had seen in this shy man with liquid and sensitive dark eyes "the lineaments of his illustrious family" *(The Fifties)*. Not many months after his marriage to Mrs. Pierce he died.

Gardner Jencks (1907–89): Composer. He and his wife, Ruth, had been Wellfleet acquaintances of EW since his years with Mary McCarthy.

Magda Johann: The neurotic cosmopolitan "Katze" of *The Twenties* who was the object of EW's unfulfilled infatuation in 1926–27.

Benjamin Jowett (1817–93): Oxford don and who was the translator of Plato.

János Kádár (1912–89): Communist premier of Hungary, brought to power when the Russians crushed the revolution in 1956.

Alfred Kazin (1915–): Critic and literary historian who dedicated

a collection of essays to EW and portrays him in the memoir
New York Jew. Ann Birstein was Kazin's second wife.

George F. Kennan (1904–): Diplomat and historian, author of
Russia and the West under Lenin and Stalin (1961). Kennan's
skepticism of political crusades parallels Wilson's in *Patriotic
Gore*.

Gyorgy Kepes (1906–): Hungarian-born Bauhaus artist and designer; a professor at Harvard.

Velemir Khlebnikov (1885–1922): Poet who helped to create Russian Futurism.

Esther Kimball (Megargee): EW's cousin, the sister of Reuel
Kimball.

Reuel B. Kimball, Jr. (Sandy): EW's cousin and boyhood companion, diagnosed as schizophrenic in 1919 and institution-
alized until his death in 1969.

Winfield Kimball (Win): The youngest of EW's uncles. He went
into business instead of the professions, and left his sister
Helen Wilson money that EW eventually inherited.

Lincoln Kirstein (1907–): Co-founder of the School of American
Ballet and the New York City Ballet, whom EW had known
since the thirties, when Kirstein was editing *Hound and
Horn*. His sister, Mina Curtiss (1896–1985), a professor at
Smith College, wrote about Bizet and edited Proust's letters.

Mamaine Paget Koestler (1916–54): Englishwoman to whom EW
proposed in 1945. She was already involved with Arthur
Koestler (1905–83), with whom she lived five years before
they were married in 1950. They were separated in 1951,
and Mamaine died three years later.

Charlotte Kretzoi (1928–): Professor of American literature in
Debrecen, later in Szeged, and finally in Budapest. Her
husband, Miklós (1907–), a paleontologist, was director of
the State Geological Institute and professor at Kossuth University (Debrecen).

Louis Kronenberger (1904–80): Drama critic and editor. Emmy
was his wife.

Karl Georg Kuhn (1906–): Biblical scholar, professor at Göttin-
gen, then Heidelberg, who suggested that the Eucharist of
the early Christians had more in common with the all-male

ceremonial banquets of the Essenes than with the Jewish Passover ceremony.

Cecil Y. Lang (1920–): Editor of Swinburne's letters; professor of English at Syracuse University, then the University of Virginia. Violette was his wife, François-Michel their son.

Jeanne Lapointe (1915–): Professor of French literature and French Canadian literature at Laval University in Quebec.

John Lardner (1912–60): Sportswriter; son of Ring Lardner.

Evgenia Lehovich (1908–75): Director of the School of American Ballet, she was born the Russian Princess Ouroussow. She made suggestions for EW's interpretation of *Doctor Zhivago* (*The Bit Between My Teeth*). Dmitri was her husband.

Roger Lemelin (1919–92): Novelist who wrote of the life of Quebec City.

Jean Lemoyne (1913–): French-Canadian essayist.

William and Lucy (Brownie) L'Engle: Longtime acquaintances on the Cape. From *The Thirties* on, EW notes Brownie's backbiting criticisms of her friends and neighbors in his journals.

Leonid Leonov (1899–): Soviet Russian novelist and playwright. In 1944 EW had called his *Road to the Ocean* "the sophistication of a formula" (*Classics and Commercials*).

Harry Levin (1912–): Scholar of Shakespeare, Joyce, and comparative literature. He and his wife, Elena, were friends of the Wilsons at Harvard and on the Cape.

H. G. Liddell (1811–98): British co-author with Robert Scott of the standard lexicon of ancient Greek, which had been used by Browning, Arnold, Swinburne, Pater, and Wilde, and by EW at Princeton (*The Bit Between My Teeth*).

A. J. Liebling (Joe) (1904–63): Journalist and humorist who wrote for *The New Yorker* from 1935 on.

Lorna Lindsley (1889–1967): Freelance writer, world traveler, and champion of radical causes. Her last expedition was to study the Mau Mau rebels in Kenya.

Carolyn Wilson Link: Second cousin of EW on his father's side. In her youth a published poet, she had married Henry Link, a psychologist who wrote a best-seller called *The Return to Religion* (1936).

Robert Linscott (1886–1964): Retired editor who worked for many years at Houghton Mifflin, then at Random House. He had known EW since the twenties, and in an unpublished reminiscence contrasts the critic's comprehensive intelligence with his difficulty in negotiating "the knubbly facts of life."

Florence, Huldah, and Gertrude Loomis: Aging sisters from Talcottville whom EW had known since boyhood. He enjoyed arguing with them about who had the best lady-slipper orchid or recipe for chocolate icing.

Anita Loos (1893–1981): Screenwriter and satirical novelist; author of *Gentlemen Prefer Blondes*.

Robert Lowell (Doc or Cal) (1917–77): Poet; married to the novelist Jean Stafford from 1940 to 1948; to Elizabeth Hardwick, writer and critic, from 1949 to 1972; and subsequently to Lady Caroline Blackwood.

Mary McCarthy (1912–89): Novelist and critic; the third of EW's four wives, married to him from 1938 to 1946. "I'm not sure she isn't the woman Stendhal," he had written to Christian Gauss in 1941.

Dwight Macdonald (1906–82): Critic of culture and society who lived on the Cape. Mike was his son.

J. B. McGeachie: Well-known Canadian broadcaster; in politics a pro-British imperialist.

Compton Mackenzie (1883–1972): British novelist. As a college sophomore EW had loved his work, and F. Scott Fitzgerald emulated it in his early fiction.

Dr. John M. McKinney: Freudian psychiatrist whom EW consulted during his nervous breakdown in 1929. McKinney helped him to endure his "panics and depressions" and sent him to a sanitarium where he began to recover.

Hugh MacLennan (1907–90): Canadian novelist. Enthusiastically characterized by EW as a Highlander, a patriotic Nova Scotian, and a man of the world.

Carey McWilliams (1905–80): Editor of *The Nation* from 1955 to 1975. He had been active in radical causes since the thirties.

André Malraux (1901–76): French novelist and man of letters, Minister of Culture under de Gaulle. Wilson had written the first criticism of Malraux in the United States, praising *The Conquerors* and particularly *Man's Fate*. He reviewed Malraux's later books, especially admiring *The Psychology of Art*.

Nadezhda Mandelstam: Widow of the Russian poet Osip Mandelstam (1892–1940); in *Hope Against Hope* she chronicled their experience in prison camps and internal exile.

Philippe (Thoby-) Marcelin (Phito) (1904–75): Haitian poet who collaborated with his brother Pierre on novels about the mythology of the peasants. A third brother, Milo, was memorizing the language of voodoo ceremonies when EW met the three on the trip reported in *The Forties* and *Red, Black, Blond and Olive*. Phito moved to Washington. His wife, Eva, came from upstate New York, and Wilson and he became cronies after the Thoby-Marcelins bought a house in Cazenovia.

Sylvia Marlowe (1908–81): Concert harpsichordist. Her husband was Leonid Berman.

Auntie Maroussia (Schevitch): The youngest sister of Elena's mother, Olga Mumm. Massia was her daughter.

John P. Marquand, Jr. (1924–): Son of the novelist of Boston society. John Jr. wrote under his middle name of Phillips.

Malachi Martin (1921–): Pen name of Michael Serafian. Formerly a Jesuit priest and professor at the Pontifical Biblical Institute at the Vatican, at one time on the staffs of Cardinal Bea and Pope John. He later worked as a waiter, taxi driver, painter, and longshoreman while writing exposés of the Church.

Norman and Anna Matson: Acquaintances of EW's on the Cape. He was fond of Anna and pleased when, after Norman's death, she became the wife of Philip Hamburger, a colleague at *The New Yorker*.

T. S. Matthews (Tom) (1901–91): Journalist and autobiographer who started out at *The New Republic*—where Wilson, he says, improved his sentences and paragraphs—and eventually became editor of *Time*. Wilson disapproved of the corporate journalism of *Time* and was disappointed by Matthews's career.

Elaine May (1932–): Comedian and screenwriter. Her satirical cabaret act with Mike Nichols ran from 1957 to 1961.

Stacy May (1896–1980): Economist and adviser on economic affairs.

Mary Meigs (1917–): Writer and painter. EW recounts his first dream about running away with her in *The Fifties*, and in the sixties he wrote to her often (*Letters on Literature and Politics*). Meigs remembers their relationship in *Lily Briscoe: A Self-Portrait* (1981).

Dorothy Reed Mendenhall (1874–1964): EW's formidable older cousin, whom he admired in youth and portrays in *Upstate*. She had taken her M.D. at Johns Hopkins, at the time when her friend Gertrude Stein failed to graduate. While raising a family she practiced medicine, lectured, and wrote on gynecology and child welfare. Her son Thomas Corwin Mendenhall II (1910–) was a historian at Yale and president of Smith College.

Sheldon Meyer (1926–): Editor at Oxford University Press in New York.

Charles Mihályi: Real-estate dealer and coin collector; a leader of the Hungarian community in northern New York.

Paolo Milano (1904–88): Italian writer and critic who had taught at Queens College and visited EW at Talcottville in 1953.

J. T. Milik (1922–): Polish Roman Catholic priest and scholar; a member of the original team in charge of the Dead Sea scrolls, whose work with the fragmentary manuscripts his colleagues admired (*The Dead Sea Scrolls: 1947–1969*).

Edna St. Vincent Millay (1892–1950): Poet for whom EW had a hopeless passion in 1920–21. She is the poet Rita in *I Thought of Daisy*. The memoir in *The Shores of Light* sets off their youthful relationship against the missed connections of the later years.

Anne Miller (1928–   ): Friend of EW's last years; the wife of Dr. Edgar (Ned) Miller, his dentist in Lowville. Wilson corresponded with Anne and Ned from 1969 on.

Jonathan Miller (1934–): British physician who became an actor and director.

Perry Miller (1905–63): Interpreter of the Puritan mind and New England theology; professor of English at Harvard.

Joseph Mitchell (1908–): Writer for *The New Yorker*. His "The Mohawks in High Steel" was reprinted at the beginning of *Apologies to the Iroquois*.

Henry Allen Moe (1894–1975): Long-term director of the Guggenheim Foundation who had often sought EW's advice about fellowship applicants and reviewers.

Ferenc Molnár (1878–1952): Hungarian dramatist who spent his later years in America. His play *Liliom*, from which EW was learning Hungarian, was made into the musical comedy *Carousel*.

Malcolm Montgomery: Literary Canadian lawyer who introduced EW to people in Toronto.

Elsa Morante (1918–85): Italian author known for her short novels. She had been married to Alberto Moravia (1907–90), pen name of Alberto Pincherle, Italian novelist whom EW had talked with in 1945 (*Europe Without Baedeker*).

Zsigmond Móricz (1879–1942): Hungarian writer of realistic fiction. "Seven Pennies," from which EW was learning the language, is the story of a poor family's struggle to meet their barest needs.

Count Umberto Morra (19?–1981): Writer and translator whom EW had met in 1945, seeing him as "a thorough patriot of the old-fashioned disinterested kind" (*Europe Without Baedeker*).

Glyn Morris: Former Presbyterian minister and schoolteacher who lived in Glens Falls near Talcottville. Gladys was his wife.

Robert Moses (1888–1981): Head of the New York State Power Authority, whose expropriation of much of the Tuscarora reservation for a dam EW attacked in *Apologies to the Iroquois*.

Helen Muchnic (1902–): EW's friend since the early 1940s; professor at Smith College and a critic of Russian literature.

Arthur and Walther Mumm: Elena's uncles.

Brat Mumm: Elena's brother, who continued the family wine-making business at Johannisberg on the Rhine. Married to Madeleine.

Olga Mumm (Olili): Elena's older sister.

Olgarel Mumm: An older cousin of Elena.

Otis Munn: EW's Talcottville cousin; their grandmothers were sisters. Fern was Otis's wife, Thad his father, George and Lou his son and daughter-in-law. George had driven EW on a three-day visit to Vladimir Nabokov in Ithaca during the fifties.

Kenneth Murdock (1895–1975): Scholar in early-American literature at Harvard.

Esther Murphy: Sister of Gerald Murphy and old friend of EW. In the twenties she had married John Strachey, the Labour Party politician and writer; she later married Chester Arthur, grandson of the President.

Gerald and Sara Murphy: Wealthy expatriates; the Fitzgeralds' friends in the twenties and the first models for Dick and Nicole Diver in *Tender Is the Night*.

A. J. Muste (1885–1967): Congregational minister and peace activist. Like EW he had been a social reformer in the thirties.

Nicholas Nabokov (1903–78): Russian composer and memoirist; cousin of Vladimir and a friend of Auden, Spender, and Isaiah Berlin. Ivan was one of his sons; Peter Nabokov, who was to become a serious scholar of Native Americans, was the other.

Péter Nagy (1920–): Hungarian professor, editor, and linguist.

Sir Lewis Bernstein Namier (1888–1960): British political historian.

George Jean Nathan (1882–1958): Writer. EW had once met him in the *Smart Set* offices, interjecting bits of badinage while his partner H. L. Mencken held forth, a bottle of gin between them on the desk.

Edward Newhouse (1911–): Writer who published many stories in *The New Yorker*.

Mike Nichols (1931–): Stage and film director. After the satirical cabaret act "Nichols and May," he went first to Broadway and later to Hollywood.

Arthur Darby Nock (1902–63): Classicist and professor of the history of religion at Harvard.

Laurence Noyes: EW's Hill School roommate, later one of his apartment mates in New York. Of a moneyed Chicago family, he came to seem to Wilson "the most complete case I have ever known of Eastern-oriented Western snobbery" (*The Twenties*).

Victoria Ocampo (1891–1979): Writer who published the literary magazine *El Sur* in Argentina. She translated several major writers into Spanish, and was the first to publish Borges's fiction.

Edwin O'Connor (1918–68): Author of popular novels of the Boston Irish-Americans, including *The Last Hurrah*. Like EW he was an amateur magician, and they began a novel about a magician named Baldini, in alternating chapters, published in *The Devils and Canon Barham*. Venite was his wife.

Thomas F. O'Donnell (1915–): English professor at Utica College, interested in local history. Wilson wrote an introduction for O'Donnell's edition of Harold Frederic's short stories. Gertrude was his wife.

Edith Oliver (1913–): Drama critic and editor at *The New Yorker*. She remembers her friendship with EW in John Wain's collection of essays about him (1978).

Sonia Orwell (1918–80): A literary woman who married George Orwell shortly before he died of tuberculosis; she inherited the fortune made by *Animal Farm* and *1984*, and was known for her generosity to writers.

John Osborne (1929–): British novelist and playwright; spokesman for "the angry young men." Once married to Penelope Gilliatt, and the father of her daughter Nolan Kate.

Roi Ottley (1906–60): African-American journalist who also wrote poetry and novels.

Dorothy Paget: English heiress and benefactress of Russian exiles, with whom Olga Mumm lived in London, managing Paget's racing stable.

E. E. Paramore, Jr. (Ted) (1896–1956): Playboy graduate of Hill and Yale who shared an apartment with EW in 1921–22, when Paramore was contributing to *Vanity Fair* and other journals. Afterward a screenwriter in Hollywood, he uneasily collaborated with Fitzgerald on *Three Comrades*.

Dorothy Parker (1893–1967): Short-story writer, wit, and critic of the twenties who had helped EW break into print at *Vanity Fair*.

Francis Parkman (1823–93): Historian, author of *France and England in North America*.

Mary Pcolar (Mariska, Marushka) (1928–82): Boonville companion and protégé of EW during the 1960s. "She is a very handsome girl in whom the Mongolian stock is evident: high cheekbones, slightly slanting gray eyes, set wide apart, a figure erect and well built," he writes, introducing her in *Upstate*. Married to George, mother of two daughters and a son.

Moshe Pearlman (1911–86): English-born Israeli writer who published books on Israel and its history, including illustrated accounts of Jerusalem co-authored with Teddy Kollek. He was spokesman for the Israeli Army in the first war between the Arabs and Israel, and again in the 1967 war.

Norman Holmes Pearson (1909–75): Literary historian at Yale, where he taught American studies and collected manuscript materials.

Francis Penberthy: EW's tax lawyer in Utica.

S. J. Perelman (Sid) (1904–79): Playwright, humorist at *The New Yorker*. His wife, Laura, was the sister of the novelist Nathanael West. In the thirties the Perelmans gave EW reports on the Hollywood scene.

Eleanor Perényi (1918–): Writer and magazine editor. Married to Baron Zsigmond Perényi, whose family had a castle in the Carpathian Mountains.

Martin Peretz (1939–): Then a professor at Harvard, later editor in chief of *The New Republic*.

Stewart Perowne (1901–89): Retired member of the British colonial service who wrote a series of guidebooks and arranged EW's expedition to the Dead Sea in 1954.

Pet'ka (Pyotr Balacheff): Grandson of Auntie Maroussia, Elena's aunt.

Sándor Petöfi (1822–49): Hungarian lyric and epic poet killed during the Hungarian revolt against Austria in 1849.

Jack Phillips: An often-married Wellfleet character whose family once owned much of the beach and the land behind it.

Richard Pipes (1923–): Historian specializing in Russia; a Harvard professor who would become an adviser to the Reagan Administration on Soviet affairs. Married to Irene.

Norman Podhoretz (1930–): Since 1960 editor of *Commentary*. The journalist Midge Decter (1927–) is his wife.

Henry Varnum Poor (1888–1970): Painter and ceramicist. Bessie Breuer, his wife, and he lived in the artists' community of New City, N.Y.

Richard Porson (1759–1808): British classical scholar and textual editor.

Anthony Powell (1905–): British novelist. In 1962, EW described Powell as heavily influenced by Proust (*The Bit Between My Teeth*).

Dawn Powell (1897–1965): Novelist of New York and Greenwich Village; EW's friend from the thirties on. Linking her with "the high social comedy" of Anthony Powell, Evelyn Waugh, and Muriel Spark rather than "any accepted brand of American humor," he regretted that she had not been popular with women readers, because "the women who appear in her stories are likely to be as sordid and absurd as the men" (*The Bit Between My Teeth*). Powell was married to Joseph Gonsha.

Mario Praz (1896–1982): Critic who wrote *The Romantic Agony* (1933); later professor of English literature at the University of Rome. In *The Fifties* he visits the Wilsons at the Cape, and in *The Bit Between My Teeth* EW portrays him in his Roman setting.

V. S. Pritchett (1900–): British critical journalist who was also a writer of short stories. To Wilson he represented a tradition more attractive than academic criticism.

Alan Pryce-Jones (1908–): Writer who edited the London *Times Literary Supplement* through the fifties.

Phelps Putnam (1894–1948): Poet and Yale graduate, a "clever but dissipated" romantic personality for whom EW maintained high hopes, nagging him to work. *The Collected Poems of Phelps Putnam* was published with Wilson's foreword in 1971.

Willard Van Orman Quine (1908–): Philosopher of linguistics and of science at Harvard; he had little to do with the other Fellows at the Wesleyan Center.

Sándor Radó (1900–81): Psychologist. Mary McCarthy's analyst in 1939–40; her friend later at the Cape. He had been a pupil of Freud and was interested in psychosomatic medicine.

Carol von Radowitz: Elena's first cousin on her father's side.

Philip Rahv (1908–73): Critic; editor at *Partisan Review* from 1935 to his death. McCarthy was living with him when she met and married EW.

S. K. Ratcliffe (1868–1958): British journalist and editor who lectured in the United States on India and other subjects.

Herbert Read (1893–1968): British writer on literature and aesthetics; at the Wesleyan Center in 1964–65.

Ernest Renan (1823–92): French historian and critic, author of the *Vie de Jésus*, which prepared the way for EW's account of the Dead Sea scrolls, as well as for Dupont-Sommer's. Wilson invoked his example when interpreting the scrolls in 1955.

Grace Root: Widow of Edward Root and daughter-in-law of Elihu Root, Teddy Roosevelt's Secretary of State. She was from Albany, and in *Upstate* her "clever intellectual conversation, rather old-fashioned formality," remind EW of the Albany of the Jameses as well as of the snobbish Princeton classicist Kelly Prentice.

Paul Rosenfeld (1890–1946): Critic of music and literature; EW's friend in the twenties. He is remembered in "Paul Rosenfeld: Three Phases" in *Classics and Commercials*.

Cecil Roth (1899–1970): Historian; first reader in Jewish studies at Oxford.

Dominique de Roux: Critic and head of the French publishing house Gallimard.

Richard Rovere (1915–79): Writer who reported on Washington politics for *The New Yorker*.

Gabrielle Roy (1903–83): Canadian writer.

Viktor Sergeevich Rozov (1913–): Well-known Soviet playwright.

Margaret Edwards Rullman: EW's acquaintance since boyhood. She had presented the thirteen-year-old with his first diary when his family went abroad in 1908.

John Russell (1885–1956): British art critic and biographer.

Hector Saint-Denys-Garneau (1912–43): French-Canadian poet.

Sylvia Salmi: Photographer who took a number of pictures of EW in his later years.

Norah Sayre (1932–): Writer; daughter of Joel Sayre, who also wrote for *The New Yorker*.

Arthur M. Schlesinger, Jr. (1917–): American historian who after serving in the Kennedy Administration became Schweitzer Professor at the City University of New York. Marian Cannon was his first wife; he was married to Alexandra Emmet in 1971.

Elisaveta (Seta) Schouvaloff (Shuvalova): Sister of Count Ivan Schouvaloff. For several years she taught Russian at Smith College.

Marina Schouvaloff (Shuvalova): Elena's cousin, the daughter of her mother's sister Vera. First married to Michael Vorontsow-Dashkoff, then to Count Ivan Schouvaloff, she was the mother of Marina, Alexandra, and Semyon. She headed the fur department at Christian Dior in Paris.

Gilbert Seldes (1893–1970): Editor, critic of popular culture. He and his daughter Marian were old friends of EW.

Sem (1863–1934): Pseudonym of Georges Goursat, French caricaturist. EW discusses his work in *The Bit Between My Teeth*, noting his ability to be "astringent but rarely brutal."

Gaia Servadio (1938–): Italian novelist and journalist.

Lis Shabecoff: *New Yorker* staff journalist.

Malcolm Sharp (1897–1980) and Dorothy (Furbish): Friends whom EW persuaded to spend several summers in Talcottville. She was Dorothy Mendenhall's niece, the "pretty dark cousin" whom, as a boy on summer family reunions, he had wanted to kiss. A law professor at the University of Chicago, Malcolm supported the case of Julius and Ethel Rosenberg, who were convicted and executed for espionage; he published a book about it in 1956.

Irwin Shaw (1913–84): *New Yorker* short-story writer and a popular novelist.

William Shawn (1907–92): Editor of *The New Yorker* from 1952 to 1987.

Edie Shay: Widow of Frank Shay. They had lived next to the Dos Passos in Provincetown, and she had co-authored books with Katy Dos Passos.

Vincent Sheehan (1899–1975): Journalist and biographer.

Wilfrid Sheed (1930–): Writer and book reviewer.

Ignazio Silone (1900–78): Pen name of Secondo Tranquille, the Italian novelist. In youth a leader of the Communist Party, he became an independent radical in the period of *Bread and Wine* (1937). EW first met him and his wife, Darina, in Rome in 1945.

Margaret de Silver: Widow of the liberal lawyer Harry de Silver. From 1937 to 1939 she had loaned Wilson "Trees," her country house near Stamford, Connecticut, where he wrote much of *The Triple Thinkers* and *To the Finland Station*.

Robert Silvers (1929–): A founding editor of *The New York Review of Books*.

Isaac Bashevis Singer (1904–91): Novelist and story writer who would win the Nobel Prize for Literature in 1976. His brother I. J. Singer (1893–1943), a novelist, was known for his book *The Brothers Ashkenazy*. Both wrote in Yiddish.

Barbara Skelton: British actress; at the time married to Cyril Connolly, subsequently to George Weidenfeld, the publisher.

Benjamin Smith (1850–1934): Mathematical philosopher at the University of Missouri and Tulane. A forceful man and prolific writer, he had been known for his absorption in his work.

C. P. Snow (1905–80): British novelist who wrote "The Two Cultures," a much discussed essay on the gulf between literature and science.

Muriel Spark (1918–): Satiric Scottish novelist.

Betty Spencer: Widow of the painter and architect Niles Spencer (1882–1952). In 1934 EW had dedicated to her a humorous poem about Thoreau, "The Extravert of Walden Pond."

Stephen Spender (1909–): British poet and Wilson's friend since the fifties. On an early visit to Talcottville he engraved the poem "I Think Continually of Those Who Were Truly Great" in a window of the stone house, where it caught the afternoon sun. Married to Natasha since 1941.

Ezra Spicehandler (1921–): Professor of Hebrew literature at the branch of Hebrew Union College in Jerusalem, afterward at Hebrew Union College in Cincinnati.

Jean Stafford (1915–79): Novelist and poet; married to Robert Lowell from 1940 to 1948 and to A. J. (Joe) Liebling from 1959 to 1963.

Donald Ogden Stewart (1894–1980): Humorist of the twenties whose *Parody Outline of History* (1921) EW liked to quote. Later a scriptwriter, he was one of the "Hollywood Ten" investigated in the fifties for radical activities.

Lytton Strachey (1880–1932): British essayist whose biographical portraits in *Eminent Victorians* influenced the young Wilson.

Roger W. Straus (1917–): Founder of Farrar, Straus and Company, later Farrar, Straus and Giroux, Wilson's primary publishers from 1950 until the end of his life. Dorothea Straus, Roger's wife, records visiting the Wilsons and Elena Wilson again after EW's death in her *Prisons and Palaces* (1984).

Sheba Strunsky: One of the founders of the International Rescue Committee, who was well regarded by artists and intellectuals in the refugee world.

Pyotr Struve (1870–1944): An old socialist and Elena's cousin. "Struve fell out with Lenin and has always been denounced by the Bolsheviks," EW wrote to a friend after discussing him with the novelist Leonov.

Albert C. Sundberg, Jr. (1921–): Biblical scholar.

Aleksei Surkov (1899–1983): Soviet author and a Stalinist bureaucrat.

James Johnson Sweeney (1900–86): Interpreter of avant-garde

art; later director of the Museum of Modern Art and the Guggenheim Museum.

Frances Nevada Swisher: Radcliffe undergraduate who met Wilson in a Harvard seminar and became one of his secretaries when he was finishing *Patriotic Gore*.

Allen Tate (1899–1979): Southern Agrarian poet and critic, a literary friend of EW from the twenties. In a 1940 letter Wilson notes that "Old Massa Tate has just been here with his wife, daughter, and dachshund." Married to Caroline Gordon (1905–85), the novelist, from 1924 to 1959; to Isabella Gardner from 1959 to 1966; and subsequently to Helen Heinz.

Pierre Teilhard de Chardin (1881–1955): French Jesuit and scientist who tried to reconcile evolutionary thought with a Christian mysticism.

Albert Tezla (1915–): English professor doing research in Hungary in 1964; later a teacher and translator of Hungarian.

Henry Thornton: Elena's son from her first marriage to James Thornton. Daphne was his wife.

Philip Toynbee (1916–81): Experimental novelist and book reviewer, son of Arnold Toynbee, the historian.

Carrie Trenham: Farmer who lived across the road in Talcottville.

Lionel Trilling (1905–75): Critic and professor of English at Columbia; in the early sixties still the leader of the New York intellectuals. He acknowledges his debt to Wilson in *A Gathering of Fugitives*.

Gilbert Troxell: One of EW's New York apartment mates in 1916–17 and again in 1919–20. They corresponded during World War I.

Kenneth Tynan (1927–1980): English writer and drama critic, contributor to *The New Yorker*.

William Vanden Heuvel (1930–): Democrat active in New York City reform politics, then married to Jean Stein, Faulkner's friend and interviewer.

Père Roland de Vaux (1903–71): Dominican scholar at the École Biblique in East Jerusalem who led the archaeological dig at Khirbat Qumran. The dominant member of the original

Dead Sea scrolls team, he presided over the manuscripts until his death.

Gèza Vermès (1924–): Reader in Jewish studies at Oxford; later professor.

John Wain (1925–): British poet, novelist, and biographical critic who edited the collection of essays *Edmund Wilson: The Man and His Work* (1978).

Charles Rumford Walker (1893–1974): Labor activist who translated Greek plays; EW's literary friend since their summer at the Plattsburgh training camp in 1916. In 1940 he and his wife, Adelaide, helped persuade Wilson to move to the Cape and become their neighbor. EW practiced magic tricks with the Walkers' son, Danny, later an actor and teacher of drama.

Odette Walling: Cape Cod friend of EW who had been in the French Resistance during World War II. Hayden Walling, an architect and builder, was her husband, Christopher their son.

Dorothy Walsh (1901–82): Professor of philosophy at Smith College who shared a house in Cummington with Helen Muchnic. EW considered her brilliant, saying that "if she had been a man she would have had much more recognition" (Rosalind Wilson, *Near the Magician*).

Aileen Ward (1919–): English professor at Brandeis, later at New York University. As Wilson put it to Louise Bogan, "she wrote the life of Keats."

Charles Dudley Warner (1829–1900): Muckraking journalist; co-author with Mark Twain of *The Gilded Age*.

Robert Penn Warren (Red) (1905–89): Poet, novelist, and critic. EW had praised his early work and believed his review of *Patriotic Gore* "got deeper in the book" than others (*Letters on Literature and Politics*). Married to the novelist Eleanor Clark (1913–).

Arthur Wasserman: Director of the New York State tax department in Utica, who admired Wilson's writing and made technical corrections to *The Cold War and the Income Tax*. Married to Mary.

Daisy Waterman: The mistress of Margaret Canby's father, afterward Margaret's stepmother. She had been a member of the Floradora Septet, singers and dancers of the 1890s.

Hobart G. Weekes (Hobey): An editor at *The New Yorker*.

Edward Weeks (Ted) (1898–): Editor of *The Atlantic Monthly* from 1938 to 1966. EW was known to dislike him.

Simone Weil (1909–43): French philosopher and mystic; a convert to Catholicism who became influential through her posthumous books.

Cleanthe Weill: Daughter of EW's cousin Helen and granddaughter of one of his mother's sisters, his Aunt Adeline.

Anthony West (1914–89): Anglo-American essayist who sometimes wrote for *The New Yorker*; the illegitimate son of Rebecca West and H. G. Wells.

Rogers E. M. Whitaker (1900–81): *New Yorker* writer and editor.

E. B. White (Andy) (1899–1985): Essayist and editor for *The New Yorker*; married to Katharine White (1906–85), longtime *New Yorker* fiction editor.

Lincoln White: "The Mohawk Iroquois who was superintendent at the school at West Leyden" (*Upstate*).

Morton White (1917–): Philosopher who taught at Harvard and the Institute for Advanced Study.

Evelyn Whitehead: Widow of the British philosopher Alfred North Whitehead (1861–1947), whose *Science and the Modern World* (1925) had influenced EW's thinking about literature and science in 1925–27, when he was beginning *Axel's Castle*.

John Hay Whitney (Jock): Millionaire owner of everything from race horses to the New York *Herald Tribune*.

Richard Wilbur (1921–): Poet and playwright; English professor at Wesleyan when EW was a Fellow at the Center.

Thornton Wilder (1897–1975): Playwright and novelist. EW and he seldom met, but when they did, they enjoyed talking of Joyce and Proust.

Angus Wilson (1913–): British novelist praised by EW for his realism. "No nostalgia for the twenties or the old institutions. He concentrates on the present, on the new social types that have appeared since the war, and the changed situations of the old ones," Wilson wrote (*The Bit Between*

My Teeth). The men had become friends in London in 1954.

Susan Wilson: Cousin who lived in Charlottesville, Virginia. EW was fond of her, and she was known in the family for an intellectual abstraction like his own.

Napier Wilt (1896–1975): Professor of English at the University of Chicago when EW gave a summer course on Dickens there in 1939.

Sovka Winkelhorn (Sophia Kutuzov): A Russian émigré who was a close friend of Elena's; married to Kai Winkelhorn.

Bertram D. Wolfe (1896–1977): Biographer-historian of revolutionary and radical figures.

Elinor Wylie (1885–1928): Poet and novelist; EW's pal in the early twenties when they were colleagues at *Vanity Fair*.

Yigael Yadin (1917–84): Archaeologist and leader of the dig at Masada. He had been a chief of staff of the Israeli Defense Forces in 1949–52, and would establish the Democratic Party for Change. He noted that the significance of the Dead Sea scrolls had been understood by a "very scholarly amateur, Edmund Wilson."

Morton Dauwen Zabel (1901–64): Professor of English at the University of Chicago; a critic of Henry James among others. He was EW's literary friend from the thirties, when Wilson gave him books to review for *The New Republic*.

Harry Zinder (1909–): Israeli official in press and communications. His wife was the charming Hamda Feigenbaum.

Vera Zorina (1917–): Ballerina and actress; at one time the wife of George Balanchine.

INDEX